Revenue Statistics in Africa 2021

Statistiques des recettes publiques en Afrique 2021

1990-2019

This document was produced with the financial assistance of the European Union. The views expressed herein can in no way be taken to reflect the official opinion of the European Union.

Ce document a été produit avec le soutien financier de l'Union européenne. Les opinions exprimées ici ne peuvent en aucun cas être considérées comme reflétant les opinions officielles de l'Union européenne.

Please cite this publication as:
OECD/AUC/ATAF (2021), *Revenue Statistics in Africa 2021*, OECD Publishing, Paris, *https://doi.org/10.1787/c511aa1e-en-fr*.

Merci de citer cet ouvrage comme suit :
OCDE/CUA/ATAF (2021), *Statistiques des recettes publiques en Afrique 2021*, Éditions OCDE, Paris, *https://doi.org/10.1787/c511aa1e-en-fr*.

ISBN 978-92-64-96479-2 (print/imprimé)
ISBN 978-92-64-86653-9 (pdf)

Revenue Statistics in Africa/*Statistiques des recettes publiques en Afrique*
ISSN 2617-6521 (print/imprimé)
ISSN 2617-653X (online/en ligne)

Photo credits/Crédits photo: Cover © some of the graphic elements in the main cover illustration were adapted from Freepik.com.
Couverture © certains des éléments graphiques de l'illustration de la couverture principale ont été adaptés de Freepik.com.

Corrigenda to publications may be found on line at: *www.oecd.org/about/publishing/corrigenda.htm.*
Les corrigenda des publications sont disponibles sur : www.oecd.org/about/publishing/corrigenda.htm.

Foreword

Revenue Statistics in Africa is a joint publication by the OECD Centre for Tax Policy and Administration, the OECD Development Centre, the African Tax Administration Forum and the African Union Commission, with the technical support of the African Development Bank and the Cercle de réflexion et d'échange des dirigeants des administrations fiscales and with the financial support of the European Union.

The report presents detailed, internationally comparable data on both tax and non-tax revenues for 30 African countries. Its approach is based on the well-established methodology of the OECD *Revenue Statistics* database, which has become an essential reference source for OECD member countries and many more. Comparisons are also made with the average for OECD economies and for the economies featured in *Revenue Statistics in Latin America and the Caribbean* and *Revenue Statistics in Asia and the Pacific*.

The term "taxes" in this publication is confined to "compulsory, unrequited payments to general government". As outlined in the Interpretative Guide to the Revenue Statistics, taxes are "unrequited" in the sense that benefits provided by government to taxpayers are not normally in proportion to their payments. The OECD methodology classifies a tax according to its base: income, profits and capital gains (classified under heading 1000), payroll (heading 3000), property (heading 4000), goods and services (heading 5000) and other taxes (heading 6000). Compulsory social security contributions paid to general government are treated as taxes and classified under heading 2000. The tax concept and the classification of taxes are set out in much greater detail in the OECD Interpretative Guide in Annex A.

The term "non-tax revenues" includes all general government revenues that do not meet the OECD definition of taxation. Revenues that do not constitute taxation include grants (e.g. foreign aid), returns on government market investments, rents on the extraction of resources from public lands, sales of government-produced goods and services, and the collection of fines and forfeits. More details on these types of revenues are given in Annex B.

Chapter 1 and Chapter 2 of this report provide an overview of the main trends in tax and non-tax revenues respectively in the 30 participating countries from 2010 to 2019. A special feature on the impact of the COVID-19 pandemic on public debt in Africa is provided in Chapter 3. Chapter 4 explores the level of tax revenues by main tax category and how the respective tax structures of the 30 countries have evolved since 1990. Chapters 5 and 6 contain detailed information on tax and non-tax revenues on a country-by-country basis as well as a comparison of the non-tax revenue mix over time in the 30 countries.

Avant-propos

Les *Statistiques des recettes publiques en Afrique* est une publication conjointe du Centre de politique et d'administration fiscales de l'OCDE, du Centre de développement de l'OCDE, du Forum sur l'administration fiscale africaine et de la Commission de l'Union africaine, avec l'assistance technique de la Banque africaine de développement et du Cercle de réflexion et d'échange des dirigeants des administrations fiscales et le soutien financier de l'Union européenne.

Le rapport fournit des données détaillées et comparables à l'échelle internationale, sur les recettes fiscales et non fiscales de 30 pays africains. Son approche repose sur la méthodologie bien établie des *Statistiques des recettes publiques de l'OCDE*, devenue une source de référence essentielle pour les pays membres de l'Organisation et au-delà. Des comparaisons sont également effectuées avec la moyenne des économies de l'OCDE et avec celle des économies couvertes par les *Statistiques des recettes publiques en Amérique latine et dans les Caraïbes* et les *Statistiques des recettes publiques en Asie et Pacifique*.

Dans cette publication, le terme « impôts » fait référence uniquement aux « versements obligatoires sans contrepartie aux administrations publiques ». Comme indiqué dans le Guide d'interprétation pour les Statistiques des recettes publiques, les impôts sont « sans contrepartie » en ce sens que les prestations fournies par les administrations aux contribuables ne sont pas normalement proportionnelles à leurs paiements. La méthodologie de l'OCDE consiste à classer les impôts en fonction de l'assiette : le revenu, les bénéfices et les gains en capital (rubrique 1000), les salaires et la main-d'œuvre (rubrique 3000), le patrimoine (rubrique 4000), les biens et les services (rubrique 5000) et autres impôts (rubrique 6000). Les cotisations obligatoires de sécurité sociale versées aux administrations publiques sont aussi traitées comme des impôts et classées dans la rubrique 2000. Des informations plus détaillées sur la notion d'impôt et sur la classification des impôts sont présentées dans le Guide d'interprétation de l'OCDE figurant à l'annexe A.

Le terme « recettes non fiscales » recouvre toutes les recettes des administrations publiques qui ne sont pas considérées comme des « impôts » selon la définition de l'OCDE. Les recettes non fiscales incluent les dons (comme l'aide extérieure), les rendements d'investissements publics, les rentes tirées de l'extraction de ressources du domaine public, la vente de biens et de services produits par le secteur public, et les amendes et confiscations. On trouvera, à l'annexe B, des informations plus détaillées sur ces catégories de recettes.

Le chapitre 1 et le chapitre 2 du rapport offrent une vue d'ensemble des grandes tendances de 2010 à 2019, dans les 30 pays participants, des recettes fiscales et non fiscales respectivement. Une étude spéciale sur l'impact de la pandémie de COVID-19 sur la dette publique en Afrique est présenté au chapitre 3. Le chapitre 4 examine le niveau des recettes fiscales par principaux types d'impôts et l'évolution des structures fiscales des 30 pays depuis 1990. Les chapitres 5 et 6 fournissent respectivement des données détaillées sur les recettes fiscales et non fiscales par pays ainsi qu'une comparaison des structures des recettes non fiscales dans le temps dans les 30 pays.

Acknowledgements

Revenue Statistics in Africa has been jointly produced by the Organisation for Economic Co-operation and Development (OECD) Centre for Tax Policy and Administration (CTP), the OECD Development Centre (DEV), the African Tax Administration Forum (ATAF) and the African Union Commission (AUC), with the technical support of the African Development Bank (AfDB) and the Cercle de réflexion et d'échange des dirigeants des administrations fiscales (CREDAF) and with the financial support of the European Union. The staff from these organisations with responsibility for producing the publication were: Emmanuelle Modica, Leonie Cedano, Talita Yamashiro Fordelone, Michael Sharratt and Michelle Harding of CTP under the supervision of the Director Pascal Saint-Amans, the Deputy Director Grace Perez-Navarro and the Head of the Tax Policy and Tax Statistics Division David Bradbury; Sébastien Markley, Arthur Minsat and Alexander Pick of DEV under the supervision of the Director of the Development Centre Ragnheiður Elín Árnadóttir, the Deputy Director Federico Bonaglia and the Senior Communications Manager Henri-Bernard Solignac-Lecomte; Nara Monkam, Director of Research at ATAF, Frankie Mbuyamba, African Tax Outlook & Tax Statistics Programme Specialist at ATAF, Ezera Madzivanyika, Research Manager at ATAF; Ndinaye Sekwi Charumbira, Rumbidzai Treddah Manhando, Edwin Kofi Owusu-Ansah and Mary Menta under the supervision of Dossina Yeo, Head of Division of Economic Policy and Sustainable Development, Leila Ben Ali, Acting Director of the African Migration Observatory and Head of the African Union Institute for Statistics (STATAFRIC), Jean Bertrand Azapmo, Regional Trade Adviser and Jose Awong Alene, Senior Statistician at the AUC; Chaouch Anouar, Statistician at AfDB under the Director of Statistics Department Charles Leyeka Lufumpa, and Koua Louis Kouakou at AfDB, Manager of Economic and Social Statistics Division; Secretary General Jean-Marc Niel of CREDAF; Policy Officer Gaëlle Doléans, Team Leader Economic Integration, Transport, Digital and STI Fabio Di Stefano, and Team Leader Fiscal Policies Benedikt Madl at the European Commission (DG International Partnerships). The authors would like to thank officials from the Ministry of Finance of Tunisia who prepared the box on tax reforms in Tunisia in Chapter 1. The special feature (Chapter 3) was written by Ndinaye Sekwi Charumbira and Yeo Dossina (AUC) and Sébastien Markley and Alexander Pick (DEV). Anne Thomas and Delphine Grandrieux (DEV) and Alexandra Le Cam and Marie-Aurélie Elkurd (CTP) assisted with the production and publication of this report and Stephanie Coic produced the cover.

The authors would like to thank the officials at the finance ministries, national tax agencies and national statistical institutes of the countries participating in this project who gathered and compiled the national data and provided their invaluable knowledge and expertise on their country's revenue collection systems and data. In particular, the authors would like to thank the focal points appointed for each country and their colleagues who facilitated the technical work: Seitebaleng Fologang and Winstern Kabo for Botswana; Mariame Dabo and Michel Yaméogo for Burkina Faso; Carlos José Oliveira Bentub and Hamilton Cabral Fortes for Cabo Verde; Rogangoum Kodindouma Hervé and Hassan Adoum Mbodou Mbami for Chad; Edouard Kalawa and Stéphane Nepetsoun for Cameroon; Yacouba Fofana and Alex Koula Pouhe for Côte d'Ivoire; Christophe Bitasimwa Bahii, Liliane Bilonda, Elisabeth Dikisha Dietu, Dieudonné Bukasa Kabongo, Floribert Masuku Mambambu, Yvette Barhashishwa Shabani Mwangu, Richard Kabila Mutshi and Popol Mukoko Akabuele for the Democratic Republic of the Congo; Aya Abdel-Aziz, Alaa Abdel-Rahman and Yasmine Kamel for Egypt; Teodoro Mbá, Bindang Ndong Okiri and Santiago Obama Benga for Equatorial Guinea; Eric Thembinkosi Dlamini, Nokuthula Dlamini, Mvuselelo B. Mdluli, Khulekani Innocent Mncina and Yvonne Ntfombiyenkhosi Mthombo for Eswatini; Asuo Afram and Francis Bright Mensah for Ghana; Alex Mwangi and Leonard Omondi for Kenya; Donah for Madagascar; Mofolo Makhele, T'sele Mokhathali, Tsietsi Nkoebele and Makhale Makhalanyane for Lesotho; Laurent Kalonga and Alick Wella for Malawi; Siaka Samaké and Boubacar Diakité for Mali; Mohamed Falilou Gueye for Mauritania; Meeshrani Balgobin, Dharmarajen Changeya and Roshan Oree for Mauritius; El Moustapha Bennani and Abderrahim Mezroui for Morocco; Idi Itope and Nelago Ekandjo for Namibia; Mahamadou Djibrilla for Niger; Sunusi Gwaram Shuaibu for Nigeria; Frédéric Ngolele for the Republic of the Congo; Roy Valence Gasangwa and Denis Mukama for Rwanda; Ndèye Louise Mbissine Camara Tine and Pape Malick Diallo for Senegal; Rudy Sinon, Roseline Lepathy, Ayda Noel and Yannick Vel for Seychelles; Mampho Baholo, Paul Dreyer, Lawrence Gqesha, Mamiky Leolo, Tshepo Makgoro, Denis Marais, Nontokozo Mnqayi, Vivienne Smithdorf and Darlington Zhou for South Africa; Ouro-Adoï Abdelganiou and Imrane Moussa for Togo; Saoussen Boumaiza, Raja Hadj Khalifa and Rihab Ben Challadia for Tunisia; and Ronald Nyenje Makumbi and Milly Isongoma Nalukwago for Uganda. *Revenue Statistics in Africa* is part of the Global Revenue Statistics Initiative and the authors would also like to thank the governments of Ireland, Japan, Luxembourg, Norway, Sweden, Switzerland, the United Kingdom and the European Union for their support to the broader Global Revenue Statistics Initiative.

This document was produced with the financial assistance of the European Union. The views expressed herein can in no way be taken to reflect the official opinion of the European Union.

Remerciements

La publication des *Statistiques des recettes publiques en Afrique* a été produite conjointement par le Centre de politique et d'administration fiscales (CPAF) de l'Organisation de coopération et de développement économiques (OCDE), le Centre de développement de l'OCDE (DEV), le Forum sur l'administration fiscale africaine (ATAF) et la Commission de l'Union africaine (CUA), avec l'assistance technique de la Banque africaine de développement (BAfD), du Cercle de réflexion et d'échange des dirigeants des administrations fiscales (CREDAF), et avec le soutien financier de l'Union européenne. Les agents de ces organisations auxquels la responsabilité de la publication a été confiée sont : Emmanuelle Modica, Leonie Cedano, Talita Yamashiro Fordelone, Michael Sharratt et Michelle Harding du CPAF sous la supervision du Directeur du CPAF Pascal Saint-Amans, de Grace Perez-Navarro, Directrice adjointe du CPAF et de David Bradbury, Chef de la Division des politiques fiscales et statistiques ; Sébastien Markley, Arthur Minsat et Alexander Pick de DEV sous la supervision du Directeur du Centre de développement Ragnheiður Elín Árnadóttir, du Directeur adjoint Federico Bonaglia et de Henri-Bernard Solignac-Lecomte, Chef de la communication ; Nara Monkam, Directrice de recherche à l'ATAF, Frankie Mbuyamba, Spécialiste du programme Perspectives fiscales en Afrique et statistiques fiscales à l'ATAF, Ezera Madzivanyika, Responsable de recherche à l'ATAF ; Ndinaye Sekwi Charumbira, Rumbidzai Treddah Manhando, Edwin Kofi Owusu-Ansah, et Mary Menta sous la supervision de Dossina Yeo, Directeur de la Division de la politique économique et du développement durable, Leila Ben Ali, Directrice par intérim de l'Observatoire africain des migrations et chef de l'Institut de statistiques de l'Union africaine (STATAFRIC), Jean Bertrand Azapmo, Conseiller pour le commerce régional et Jose Awong Alene, Principal statisticien de la CUA ; Chaouch Anouar, statisticien à la BAfD, sous la supervision de Charles Leyeka Lufumpa, Directeur du département des statistiques et Koua Louis Kouakou, de la BAfD, Chef de la Division des statistiques économiques et sociales ; Jean-Marc Niel, Secrétaire général du CREDAF; Chargée de mission Gaëlle Doléans, Chef d'équipe Intégration économique, Transport, Numérique et STI Fabio Di Stefano et Chef d'équipe Politiques fiscales Benedikt Madl à la Commission européenne (DG Partenariats internationaux). Les auteurs souhaitent remercier les fonctionnaires du ministère des Finances de la Tunisie qui ont préparé l'encadré sur les réformes fiscales en Tunisie au chapitre 1. L'étude spéciale (chapitre 3) a été rédigée par Ndinaye Sekwi Charumbira et Yeo Dossina (CUA), Sébastien Markley et Alexander Pick (DEV). Anne Thomas et Delphine Grandrieux de DEV et Alexandra Le Cam et Marie-Aurélie Elkurd du CPAF ont aidé à la production de la publication et Stephanie Coic a produit la couverture.

Les auteurs souhaitent remercier les responsables des ministères des finances, des administrations fiscales nationales et des instituts nationaux de statistiques des pays participant au projet qui ont collecté et rassemblé les données nationales et ont partagé leur connaissance et expertise inestimable sur les systèmes de collecte de recettes et les données de leur pays. Les auteurs souhaitent en particulier remercier les points focaux désignés pour chaque pays et leurs collègues qui ont facilité le travail technique : Seitebaleng Fologang et

Winstern Kabo pour le Botswana ; Mariame Dabo et Michel Yaméogo pour le Burkina Faso ; Carlos José Oliveira Bentub et Hamilton Cabral Fortes pour le Cabo Verde ; Edouard Kalawa et Stéphane Nepetsoun pour le Cameroun ; Yacouba Fofana et Alex Koula Pouhe pour la Côte d'Ivoire ; Christophe Bitasimwa Bahii, Liliane Bilonda, Elisabeth Dikisha Dietu, Dieudonné Bukasa Kabongo, Floribert Masuku Mambambu, Yvette Barhashishwa Shabani Mwangu, Richard Kabila Mutshi et Popol Mukoko Akabuele pour la République démocratique du Congo ; Aya Abdel-Aziz, Alaa Abdel-Rahman et Yasmine Kamel pour l'Égypte ; Teodoro Mbá, Bindang Ndong Okiri et Santiago Obama Benga pour la Guinée équatoriale ; Eric Thembinkosi Dlamini, Nokuthula Dlamini, Mvuselelo B. Mdluli, Khulekani Innocent Mncina et Yvonne Ntfombiyenkhosi Mthombo pour l'Eswatini ; Asuo Afram et Francis Bright Mensah pour le Ghana ; Alex Mwangi et Leonard Omondi pour le Kenya ; Mofolo Makhele, T'sele Mokhathali, Tsietsi Nkoebele et Makhale Makhalanyanepour le Lesotho ; Donah pour Madagascar ; Laurent Kalonga et Alick Wella pour le Malawi ; Siaka Samaké et Boubacar Diakité pour le Mali ; Mohamed Falilou Gueye, pour la Mauritanie ; Meeshrani Balgobin, Dharmarajen Changeya et Roshan Oree pour Maurice ; El Moustapha Bennani et Abderrahim Mezroui pour le Maroc ; Idi Itope et Nelago Ekandjo pour la Namibie ; Mahamadou Djibrilla pour le Niger ; Sunusi Gwaram Shuaibu pour le Nigéria ; Frédéric Ngolele pour la République du Congo ; Roy Valence Gasangwa et Denis Mukama pour le Rwanda ; Ndèye Louise Mbissine Camara Tine et Pape Malick Diallo, pour le Sénégal ; Rudy Sinon, Roseline Lepathy, Ayda Noel et Yannick Vel pour les Seychelles ; Mampho Baholo, Paul Dreyer, Lawrence Gqesha, Mamiky Leolo, Tshepo Makgoro, Denis Marais, Nontokozo Mnqayi, Vivienne Smithdorf et Darlington Zhou pour l'Afrique du Sud ; Rogangoum Kodindouma Hervé et Hassan Adoum Mbodou Mbami pour le Tchad, Ouro-Adoï Abdelganiou et Imrane Moussa pour le Togo ; Saoussen Boumaiza, Raja Hadj Khalifa et Rihab Ben Challadia pour la Tunisie ; et Ronald Nyenje Makumbi et Milly Isongoma Nalukwago pour l'Ouganda. *Les statistiques des recettes publiques en Afrique* font partie de l'initiative des statistiques mondiales des recettes publiques. Les auteurs tiennent également à remercier les gouvernements de l'Irlande, du Japon, du Luxembourg, de la Norvège, de la Suède, de la Suisse et du Royaume-Uni ainsi que l'Union européenne pour leur soutien à l'initiative des statistiques mondiales des recettes publiques.

Ce document a été produit avec le soutien financier de l'Union européenne. Les opinions exprimées ici ne peuvent en aucun cas être considérées comme reflétant les opinions officielles de l'Union européenne.

Table of contents

Table des matières

LIST OF TABLES/LISTE DE TABLEAUX

Chapter 4/Chapitre 4

Tax levels and tax structures, 1990-2019/ Niveaux et structures des impôts, 1990-2019

Chapter 5/Chapitre 5

Country tables, tax revenues, 1999-2019/ Tableaux pays, recettes fiscales, 1999-2019

Chapter 6/Chapitre 6

Non-tax revenue levels and structures, 1998-2018/ Tableaux des recettes non fiscales, 1999-2019

LIST OF FIGURES/LISTE DE GRAPHIQUES

Chapter 1/Chapitre 1
Tax revenue trends, 2010-2019/ Tendances des recettes fiscales, 2010-2019

Chapter 2/Chapitre 2

Non tax revenue trends, 1990-2019/ Tendances des recettes non fiscales, 1990-2019

Chapter 3/Chapitre 3
Public debt in Africa and the impact of the COVID-19 pandemic/ La dette publique en Afrique et l'impact de la pandémie de COVID-19

Executive summary

Achieving the United Nations' Sustainable Development Goals (SDGs) and implementing the Addis Ababa Action Agenda and the African Union's Agenda 2063 require mobilising additional finance, in particular domestic resources, to fund public goods and services. The COVID-19 pandemic has significantly and negatively impacted government revenues, increasing the financing gap to achieving the SDGs. As a consequence, the need for additional revenues has become even more critical.

Revenue Statistics in Africa 2021 presents internationally comparable indicators on tax and non-tax revenues that can help track progress on domestic resource mobilisation, and inform tax policy analysis and reforms. It also contributes to the implementation of the second phase of the Pan-African Statistics Programme – a joint initiative between the European Union and the African Union that aims to improve measurement of progress in the process of African Integration by promoting the use of statistical data of quality in the decision-making process and policy monitoring. This report provides data on 30 countries and includes a special feature highlighting the impact of COVID-19 on African debt levels and recommendations to improve debt management.

Tax revenues

In 2019, the unweighted average tax-to-GDP ratio for the 30 countries in this publication [the "Africa (30) average"] was 16.6%. The tax-to-GDP ratio refers to total tax revenues, including compulsory social security contributions, as a percentage of gross domestic product (GDP). The Africa (30) average in 2019 was below the averages of 24 Asian and Pacific economies (21.0%), Latin America and the Caribbean (LAC) (22.9%), and the OECD (33.8%).

Tax-to-GDP ratios in Africa in 2019 ranged from 6.0% in Nigeria to 34.3% in the Seychelles and Tunisia, exceeding 28% in four countries (Morocco, the Seychelles, South Africa and Tunisia). All nine resource-rich countries in this publication had tax-to-GDP levels below 15% in 2019, whereas most non resource-rich countries had ratios above this level. Resource revenues are mainly generated through rents and royalties, which are not classified as taxes in the report.

The average tax-to-GDP ratio for African countries increased by 0.3% of GDP between 2018 and 2019, driven primarily by increases in income tax revenues, which rose by 0.2 percentage points (p.p.). Tax-to-GDP ratios increased in 16 countries and decreased in 14 countries. The largest increases occurred in Equatorial Guinea (3.6 p.p.), Mali (3.5 p.p.), Tunisia (2.5 p.p.) and Burkina Faso (1.1 p.p.), with all other increases below one percentage point of GDP. By contrast, the decreases were smaller: Mauritania registered the largest decrease (2.1 p.p.), followed by Lesotho (1.3 p.p.), with all other decreases lower than one percentage point.

The Africa (30) average tax-to-GDP ratio increased by 1.8 p.p. between 2010 and 2019. This increase was lower than the increases in the LAC and the OECD averages over the same period (1.9 p.p. and 2.0 p.p., respectively). The main increases in the Africa (30) average tax-to-GDP ratio between 2010 and 2019 were generated by value-added taxes (VAT) and personal income taxes (PIT), which rose by 1.0 p.p. and 0.8 p.p., respectively.

In 2019, taxes on goods and services were the main source of tax revenues in Africa, accounting for an average of 51.9% of total tax revenue, with VAT accounting for 29.3%. Taxes on income and profits accounted for 38.4% of tax revenues. Labour taxes and property taxes remain low compared to the OECD average: PIT and social security contributions amounted to 24.8% of total tax revenues for the Africa (30) average in 2019, compared to 49.2% on average in the OECD (2018 figure) whereas property taxes represented 1.9% of total tax revenues for the Africa (30) average, about one-third the OECD level.

Taxes on goods and services were the principal source of tax revenues for 22 African countries included in this report in 2019. For the eight other countries, taxes on income and profits accounted for the principal share of total tax revenues. Five of these countries are in the Southern African Customs Union (SACU) (Botswana, Eswatini, Lesotho, Namibia and South Africa) and three are oil-rich (Chad, Equatorial Guinea and Nigeria). The SACU provides a revenue-sharing agreement whereby net customs and excise revenues received from the SACU Common Revenue Pool are included in non-tax revenues in this report.

Environmentally-related taxes are a key tool for countries wanting to decarbonise their economies and raise revenues. In Africa, revenues from these taxes amounted to 1.1% of GDP in 2019, on average, the same level as the averages for LAC and the Asian and Pacific economies and lower than the OECD average of 2.2% of GDP. In 2019, energy taxes generated 70% of these revenues in Africa on average, followed by motor vehicle and transport taxes.

Non-tax revenues

In 2019, average non-tax revenues were equivalent to 6.3% of GDP in Africa, ranging from 0.5% of GDP in South Africa to 26.7% of GDP in Lesotho. Non-tax revenues were below 5% of GDP in 18 of the 30 African countries and above 10% in five. Four of these countries (Botswana, Eswatini, Lesotho and Namibia) were net recipients of funds from the SACU Common Revenue Pool. Non-tax revenues were lower than tax revenues in all countries except Botswana, the Republic of the Congo and Lesotho.

In contrast with tax revenues, average non-tax revenues fell from 8.1% of GDP in 2010 to 6.3% in 2019, with a sharp drop of 2.7 p.p. between 2012 and 2016 that was driven by declines in rents and royalties and in grant revenues.

Sources of non-tax revenues vary by country. For nine countries, grants were a majority of non-tax revenues in 2019. Six countries (Cameroon, Chad, the Republic of the Congo, Equatorial Guinea, Mauritania and Nigeria) received most of their non-tax revenues from rents and royalties, in particular oil royalties. The eleven remaining countries, excluding the four net recipient SACU countries, relied more on other sources of non-tax revenues, such as interest and dividends and fees for goods and services.

Public debt in Africa and the impact of the COVID-19 pandemic

This year's special feature examines the public debt burden in Africa over the last decade, including the impact of the COVID-19 pandemic. Since 2010, African annual debt service payments – the sum of principal repayments and interest payments, expressed as a percentage of GDP – have increased by 1.1 p.p. which has offset two-thirds of the increase in tax revenues (1.8 p.p.) over the same period. This increase has been driven in part by a shift from concessional lending to commercial lending on international capital markets (often at higher interest rates). Increasing private financing at market rates has allowed African governments to borrow more funds at the cost of increasing exposure to foreign-exchange risk and debt service payments. Between 2010 and 2019, the ratio of debt service payments to debt stock increased for 24 out of the 26 countries for which these data are available.

The COVID-19 pandemic has severely affected public revenues and further exacerbated debt levels in Africa, increasing the likelihood of debt distress for some countries. Debt service payments are expected to increase further in the coming years as a consequence of the ongoing pandemic. At the onset of the COVID-19 pandemic, the African Union appointed a group of Special Envoys that consulted African governments, bilateral and multilateral partners, and international financial institutions, to mobilise the necessary resources to finance the African response to the pandemic. Consultations of the African Union Special Envoys concluded that fiscal reforms were an important way to ensure the debt sustainability of African countries and informed several recommendations by the African Union to minimise the debt burden in African countries, to avoid future debt distress and to support a sustainable debt recovery.

Résumé

Pour atteindre les Objectifs de développement durable (ODD) des Nations Unies et mettre en œuvre le Programme d'action d'Addis-Abeba et l'Agenda 2063 de l'Union africaine, il est nécessaire de mobiliser des moyens financiers supplémentaires, et notamment des ressources intérieures, afin de financer l'offre de biens et de services publics. La pandémie de COVID-19 a un impact négatif significatif sur les recettes publiques, creusant le déficit de financement pour atteindre les ODD. Aussi, la nécessité de mobiliser des recettes supplémentaires est devenue encore plus impérieuse.

L'édition 2021 des *Statistiques des recettes publiques en Afrique* contient un ensemble d'indicateurs internationalement comparables sur les recettes fiscales et non fiscales qui peuvent aider à mesurer les progrès en matière de mobilisation des ressources intérieures et à éclairer les politiques et les réformes fiscales. Ce rapport contribue aussi à la mise en œuvre de la seconde phase du Programme statistique panafricain, une initiative conjointe de l'Union européenne et de l'Union africaine qui vise à améliorer la mesure des progrès dans l'intégration africaine, en encourageant l'utilisation de données statistiques de qualité dans le processus d'élaboration des politiques et leur suivi. Ce rapport livre des données sur 30 pays d'Afrique et contient une étude spéciale qui décrit l'impact du COVID-19 sur les niveaux de la dette en Afrique et formule des recommandations en vue d'améliorer la gestion de la dette.

Recettes fiscales

En 2019, le ratio moyen non pondéré impôts/PIB dans les 30 pays d'Afrique couverts par cette publication [désigné ci-après « moyenne des pays d'Afrique (30) »] s'est établi à 16.6 %. Le ratio impôts/PIB correspond aux recettes fiscales totales, y compris les cotisations obligatoires de sécurité sociale, exprimées en pourcentage du produit intérieur brut (PIB). En 2019, la moyenne des pays d'Afrique (30) était inférieure à celle des 24 économies de la région Asie-Pacifique, de 21.0 %, à celle de la région Amérique latine et Caraïbes (ALC), de 22.9 % et de la zone OCDE (33.8 %).

En 2019, les ratios impôts/PIB en Afrique s'échelonnaient entre 6.0 % au Nigéria et 34.3 % aux Seychelles et en Tunisie, et quatre pays affichaient des ratios supérieurs à 28 % (Afrique du Sud, Maroc, Seychelles et Tunisie). La même année, les neuf pays riches en ressources naturelles couverts par cette publication enregistraient des ratios impôts/PIB inférieurs à 15 %, tandis que la plupart des pays pauvres en ressources naturelles affichaient des ratios supérieurs à ce niveau. Les recettes provenant des ressources naturelles sont principalement obtenues des rentes et redevances, qui ne sont pas considérées comme des recettes fiscales dans le rapport.

Le ratio moyen impôts/PIB pour les pays d'Afrique a augmenté de 0.3 point de pourcentage entre 2018 et 2019, sous l'effet essentiellement d'une hausse des recettes tirées de l'impôt sur le revenu et les benéfices, qui ont progressé de 0.2 point de pourcentage. Les ratios impôts/PIB ont augmenté dans 16 pays et diminué dans 14 autres pays. C'est en Guinée équatoriale (3.6 points de pourcentage), au Mali (3.5 points de pourcentage), en Tunisie (2.5 points de pourcentage) et au Burkina Faso (1.1 point de pourcentage) que les augmentations les plus marquées se sont produites. Tous les autres pays ont enregistré des hausses inférieures à un point de pourcentage du PIB. Par comparaison, les baisses ont été plus faibles : la baisse la plus marquée a été observée en Mauritanie (2.1 points de pourcentage) et au Lesotho (1.3 point de pourcentage). Aucune autre baisse supérieure à 1 point de pourcentage n'a été enregistrée.

Entre 2010 et 2019, le ratio impôts/PIB moyen de l'Afrique (30) a augmenté de 1.8 point de pourcentage. Cette progression est inférieure à la hausse des moyennes de la région ALC et de la zone OCDE au cours de la même période (respectivement 1.9 et 2.0 points de pourcentage). Les principales variations du ratio impôts/PIB moyen de l'Afrique (30) entre 2010 et 2019 concernaient l'augmentation des recettes de la taxe sur la valeur ajoutée (TVA) (1.0 point de pourcentage) et des impôts sur le revenu des personnes physiques (0.8 point de pourcentage).

En 2019, les impôts sur les biens et services constituaient la principale source de recettes fiscales en Afrique, puisqu'ils ont généré 51.9 % du total des recettes fiscales en moyenne, la TVA à elle seule contribuant à 29.3 % du total. Les impôts sur le revenu et sur les bénéfices ont procuré 38.4 % des recettes fiscales. Les impôts sur le travail et sur le patrimoine restent faibles par rapport à la moyenne OCDE : l'impôt sur le revenu des personnes physiques et les cotisations de sécurité sociale représentaient 24.8 % du total des recettes fiscales pour la moyenne de l'Afrique (30) en 2019, contre 49.2 % en moyenne dans la zone OCDE (chiffre de 2018), tandis que les impôts sur le patrimoine généraient 1.9 % du total des recettes fiscales pour la moyenne de l'Afrique (30), soit environ un tiers du niveau de la zone OCDE.

En 2019, les impôts sur les biens et services constituaient la principale source de recettes fiscales pour 22 pays africains couverts par ce rapport. Dans les huit pays restants, la plus grande partie des recettes fiscales provenait des impôts sur le revenu et les bénéfices. Cinq de ces pays font partie de l'Union douanière d'Afrique australe (SACU) (à savoir l'Afrique du Sud, le Botswana, l'Eswatini, le Lesotho et la Namibie), et trois sont riches en pétrole (Guinée équatoriale, Nigéria et Tchad). La SACU a mis en place un accord de partage des recettes et les recettes nettes des droits de douane et d'accise reçues du fonds commun des recettes de la SACU sont classées parmi les recettes non fiscales dans ce rapport.

Les taxes liées à l'environnement représentent un outil essentiel pour les pays qui souhaitent décarboner leur économie et accroître leurs recettes. En Afrique, les recettes tirées de ces taxes s'élevaient en moyenne à 1.1 % du PIB en 2019, soit le même niveau que dans la région ALC et dans les économies de l'Asie et du Pacifique, mais moins que la moyenne de l'OCDE de 2.2 % du PIB. En 2019, les taxes sur l'énergie ont généré 70 % de ces recettes en moyenne, suivies des taxes sur les transports et sur les véhicules à moteur.

Recettes non fiscales

En 2019, les recettes non fiscales moyennes équivalaient à 6.3 % du PIB en Afrique. Elles s'échelonnaient entre 0.5 % du PIB en Afrique du Sud et 26.7 % du PIB au Lesotho. Les recettes non fiscales étaient inférieures à 5 % du PIB dans 18 des 30 pays africains et supérieures à 10 % dans 5 pays. Quatre de ces pays (Botswana, Eswatini, Lesotho et Namibie) étaient les bénéficiaires nets des recettes du fonds commun de la SACU. Le total des recettes non fiscales était inférieur à celui des recettes fiscales dans l'ensemble des pays à l'exception du Botswana, du Lesotho et de la République du Congo.

Contrairement aux recettes fiscales, les recettes non fiscales moyennes de ces pays ont fléchi de 8.1 % du PIB en 2010 à 6.3 % en 2019, avec une forte contraction de 2.7 points entre 2012 et 2016, principalement due à une érosion des loyers et des redevances ainsi que des recettes provenant des dons.

L'origine des recettes non fiscales diffère selon les pays. Pour neuf pays, les dons constituaient la majorité des recettes non fiscales en 2019. Six autres pays (Cameroun, République du Congo, Guinée équatoriale, Mauritanie, Nigéria et Tchad) tiraient quant à eux la majeure partie de ces recettes de loyers et de redevances, et notamment de redevances pétrolières. Les onze pays restants, à l'exception des quatre pays bénéficiaires nets de la SACU, s'appuyaient davantage sur d'autres sources de recettes non fiscales telles que les intérêts et dividendes, les frais administratifs ou les frais au titre de la vente de biens et services.

La dette publique en Afrique et l'impact de la pandémie de COVID-19

L'étude spéciale de cette année examine l'évolution de la charge de la dette publique en Afrique au cours de la dernière décennie, en tenant compte de l'impact de la pandémie de COVID-19. Depuis 2010, les paiements annuels de l'Afrique au titre du service de la dette – la somme des remboursements du principal et des paiements d'intérêts, en pourcentage du PIB – ont augmenté de 1.1 point de pourcentage, une hausse qui a absorbé les deux tiers de l'augmentation des recettes fiscales (1.8 point de pourcentage) sur la même période. Cette inflation s'explique en grande partie par le recul des emprunts concessionnels au profit des prêts commerciaux contractés sur les marchés internationaux de capitaux (souvent à des taux d'intérêt plus élevés). Grâce à l'essor du financement privé aux taux du marché, les pays africains ont pu emprunter davantage, mais en augmentant leur exposition au risque de change et leurs paiements au titre du service de la dette. Entre 2010 et 2019, le ratio des paiements du service de la dette rapportés à l'encours de la dette s'est accru pour 24 des 26 pays pour lesquels ces données sont disponibles.

La pandémie de COVID-19 a pesé lourdement sur les recettes publiques et creusé davantage encore la dette africaine, augmentant le risque de surendettement pour certains pays. Les paiements au titre du service de la dette devraient continuer de croître dans les années à venir sous l'effet de la pandémie. Au début de la pandémie de COVID-19, l'Union africaine a constitué un groupe d'envoyés spéciaux chargés de consulter les gouvernements des pays africains, les partenaires bilatéraux et multilatéraux et les institutions financières internationales en vue de mobiliser les ressources nécessaires pour financer la réponse africaine à la pandémie. Ces consultations ont conclu que la viabilité de la dette des pays africains passait par des réformes budgétaires, et ont conduit l'Union africaine à formuler plusieurs recommandations en vue d'alléger la charge de la dette des pays africains, d'éviter les situations de surendettement à l'avenir et d'accompagner une évolution viable de la dette.

Chapter 1

Tax revenue trends, 2010-2019

Chapitre 1

Tendances des recettes fiscales, 2010-2019

Chapter 1

Tax revenue trends, 2010-2019

Achieving the United Nations' Sustainable Development Goals (SDGs) and implementing the Addis Ababa Action Agenda and the African Union's Agenda 2063 require mobilising additional finance, in particular domestic resources, to fund public goods and services. Taxation provides a predictable and sustainable source of government revenue, in contrast with the volatility of other important sources of public revenues, such as official development assistance and mineral royalties.

This report presents an internationally comparable set of indicators on tax and non-tax revenues which can be used to track progress on domestic resource mobilisation (as envisaged in Agenda 2063, the SDGs, the Addis Ababa Action Agenda as well as related initiatives such as the Addis Tax Initiative) and to inform tax policy and reform. The report and its data also contribute to the Pan-African Statistics Programme, a joint effort between the European Union and the African Union to support statistical capacity in Africa by providing quality revenue statistics data that can inform decision-making processes and policy monitoring towards African integration. The report provides critical information on tax systems in the region and their revenue performance in recent years as well as demonstrating the fiscal capacity of the region to respond to the COVID-19 crisis.

This chapter discusses trends in the tax-to-GDP ratio, tax structure and share of tax revenue by level of government in 30 African countries from 1990 (where available) until 2019: Botswana, Burkina Faso, Cabo Verde, Cameroon, Chad, the Republic of the Congo, the Democratic Republic of the Congo, Côte d'Ivoire, Equatorial Guinea, Egypt, Eswatini, Ghana, Lesotho, Kenya, Madagascar, Malawi, Mali, Mauritania, Mauritius, Morocco, Namibia, Niger, Nigeria, Rwanda, Senegal, the Seychelles, South Africa, Togo, Tunisia and Uganda. It also compares the averages of the 30 African countries with the averages of 24 Asian and Pacific economies (OECD, 2021[1]), of 26 Latin American and Caribbean (LAC) countries (OECD et al., 2021[2]), and the average of 37 OECD countries (OECD, 2020[3]).The discussion supplements the detailed country information on tax revenue in Chapter 5.

Tax-to-GDP ratios

Tax-to-GDP ratios in 2019

The average tax-to-GDP ratio of the 30 African countries in this publication (referred to as the "Africa (30) average") was 16.6% in 2019 (Figure 1.1). The tax-to-GDP ratio is measured as tax revenues (including compulsory social security contributions paid to general government) as a proportion of gross domestic product (GDP).[1] In comparison, the average tax-to-GDP ratios in 24 Asian and Pacific economies, Latin America and the Caribbean (LAC), and the OECD were 21.0%, 22.9% and 33.8% respectively in 2019.

In 2019, tax-to-GDP ratios varied widely across the countries included in this publication, ranging from 6.0% in Nigeria to 34.3% in the Seychelles and Tunisia. The countries in this publication with the highest income per capita (Morocco, the Seychelles, South Africa and Tunisia) had tax-to-GDP ratios above 28%. Twenty-two countries recorded tax-to-GDP ratios between 10.0% and 25.0% while Chad, the Republic of the Congo, the Democratic Republic of the Congo and Nigeria had tax-to-GDP ratios below 10%.

Figure 1.1. **Tax-to-GDP ratios and total tax revenue (excluding social security contributions) as a percentage of GDP, 2019**

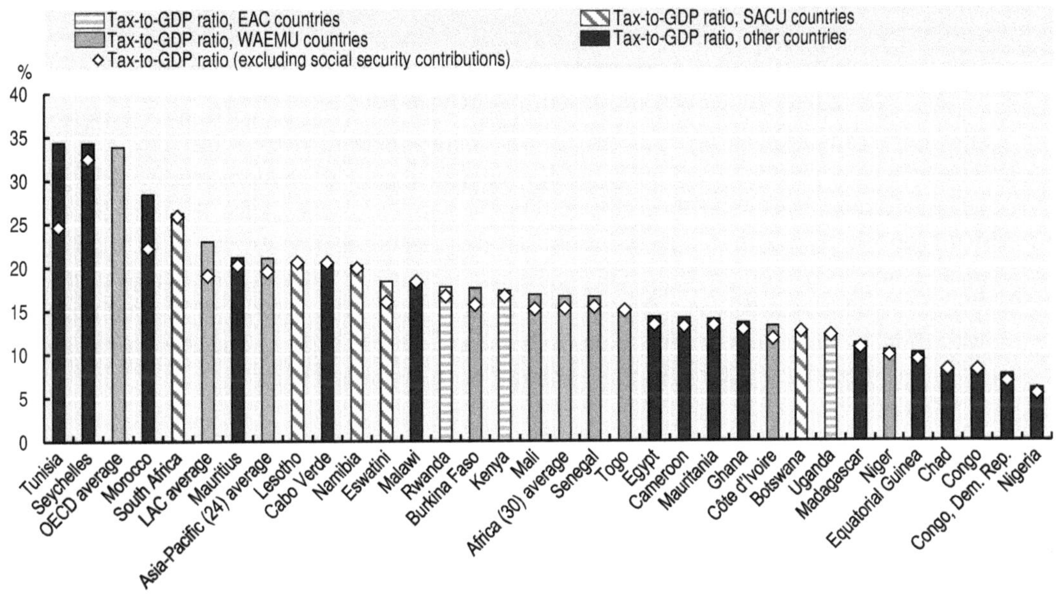

Note: Data include sub-national government tax revenues for Eswatini, Mauritania, Mauritius, Morocco, Nigeria (state revenues only) and South Africa for 2019.

The Africa (30) average, the averages for Asia-Pacific (24 economies), LAC (26 countries) and the OECD (37 countries) are unweighted.

The Africa (30) average should be interpreted with caution as data on social security contributions are not available for Chad, the Republic of the Congo, the Democratic Republic of the Congo (prior to 2012), Madagascar (prior to 2011), Togo and Uganda and are only partially available for Cameroon and Senegal. Social security contributions for Botswana, Lesotho and Malawi are deemed to be null as they do not meet the criteria to be classified as social security contributions set out in the OECD classification of taxes in the Interpretative Guide. See the country tables in Chapter 5 for further information.

The tax-to-GDP ratio for South Africa includes payments made by South Africa to the Southern African Customs Union (SACU) pool.

Source: Tables 4.1 and 4.2 in Chapter 4 and (OECD/AUC/ATAF, 2021[4]), "Revenue Statistics in Africa: Comparative tables", OECD Tax Statistics (database), *http://dx.doi.org/10.1787/be755711-en.*

StatLink *https://doi.org/10.1787/888934281790*

Box 1.1. **Methodology: the tax-to-GDP ratio**

The tax ratios shown in this publication express aggregate tax revenues as a percentage of GDP. The value of this ratio depends on its denominator (GDP) as well as its numerator (tax revenue). Both the numerator and the denominator, GDP, may be subject to historical revision.

The numerator (tax revenues)

This publication uses revenue figures that are submitted annually by focal points from national ministries of finance, tax administrations or statistics offices. Historical tax revenue data are subject to revisions each year, with more important revisions in latest years. Past figures may also change from one edition to the next when new data are obtained by focal points to improve the publication. For example, this is the case with the Seychelles, which provided revenues collected by the Seychelles Pensions Fund for the first time in this edition.

Box 1.1. **Methodology: the tax-to-GDP ratio** *(cont.)*

The denominator (GDP)

The GDP figures used in this publication are sourced from the *World Economic Outlook* (WEO) published by the IMF. Using these GDP figures ensures a maximum of consistency across countries, as well as international comparability. GDP figures are also revised and updated to reflect better data sources and improved estimation procedures, or to move towards new internationally-agreed guidelines for measuring the value of GDP.

The most recent available figures from the WEO were published in April 2021 (IMF, 2021$_{[5]}$) and include GDP revisions made by some countries to align with the most recent System of National Accounts (SNA 2008). In this edition, the Republic of the Congo, Rwanda, South Africa, Togo and Uganda have rebased their GDP data, resulting in lower tax-to-GDP ratios in these countries, and on average, than those shown in the 2020 edition of *Revenue Statistics in Africa*. The difference between the 2018 tax-to-GDP ratios in the 2020 and 2021 editions ranged from 0.1 percentage points (p.p.) in Uganda to 4.8 p.p. in Togo; and the Africa (30) average for 2018 is 0.2 p.p. lower in this edition than in last year's edition.

Many of the countries in this publication belong to regional organisations whose members adopt common tax and external tariff rules and form a customs union.

- The average tax-to-GDP ratio of the three East Africa Community (EAC)[2] countries included in this publication was 15.7% in 2019, which was below the Africa (30) average. Tax-to-GDP ratios in Kenya and Rwanda exceeded 17.0% in 2019 and amounted to 12.1% in Uganda.
- The tax-to-GDP ratio for the six West African Economic and Monetary Union (WAEMU)[3] countries included in this publication averaged 14.9% in 2019. Ratios varied across member countries from 10.4% in Niger to 17.6% in Burkina Faso. In 2015, the WAEMU set a goal for member countries to achieve tax-to-GDP ratios of at least 20% by the end of 2019 (Diallo, 2018$_{[6]}$). As the goal was not attained by any of the member countries, the WAEMU adopted an action plan in June 2019 to help them to reach this target. The actions range from the improvement and standardisation of the collection of VAT, excise duties and direct taxes to the reduction of tax competition among member countries. However, in light of the COVID-19 pandemic, the WAEMU took the decision to suspend the goal of reaching a tax-to-GDP ratio of 20% as well as other convergence, stability and growth objectives to allow member states greater financial flexibility to contain the negative effects of the crisis (IMF, 2021$_{[7]}$).
- The average tax-to-GDP ratio for the Southern African Customs Union (SACU) countries (see Box 2.3 in Chapter 2) was 19.6% in 2019. Tax-to-GDP ratios[4] in SACU countries ranged from 12.6% of GDP in Botswana to 26.2% of GDP in South Africa. The evolution of the tax-to-GDP ratios of SACU countries since 2010 is discussed in Box 1.4.

Changes in tax-to-GDP ratios between 2018 and 2019

The average tax-to-GDP ratio for African countries increased by 0.3% of GDP between 2018 and 2019, driven primarily by increases in income tax revenues (0.2 p.p.). Tax-to-GDP ratios increased in 16 countries and decreased in 14 countries. The largest increases between 2018 and 2019 occurred in Equatorial Guinea (3.6 p.p.), Mali (3.5 p.p.), Tunisia (2.5 p.p.) and Burkina Faso (1.1 p.p.), with all other increases below one percentage point of GDP. By contrast, the decreases were comparatively smaller: Mauritania had the largest decrease in the tax-to-GDP ratio of 2.1 p.p. in 2019, followed by Lesotho (1.3 p.p.), with no other decreases of more than one percentage point.

Figure 1.2. **Change in tax-to-GDP ratios between 2018 and 2019 (percentage points)**

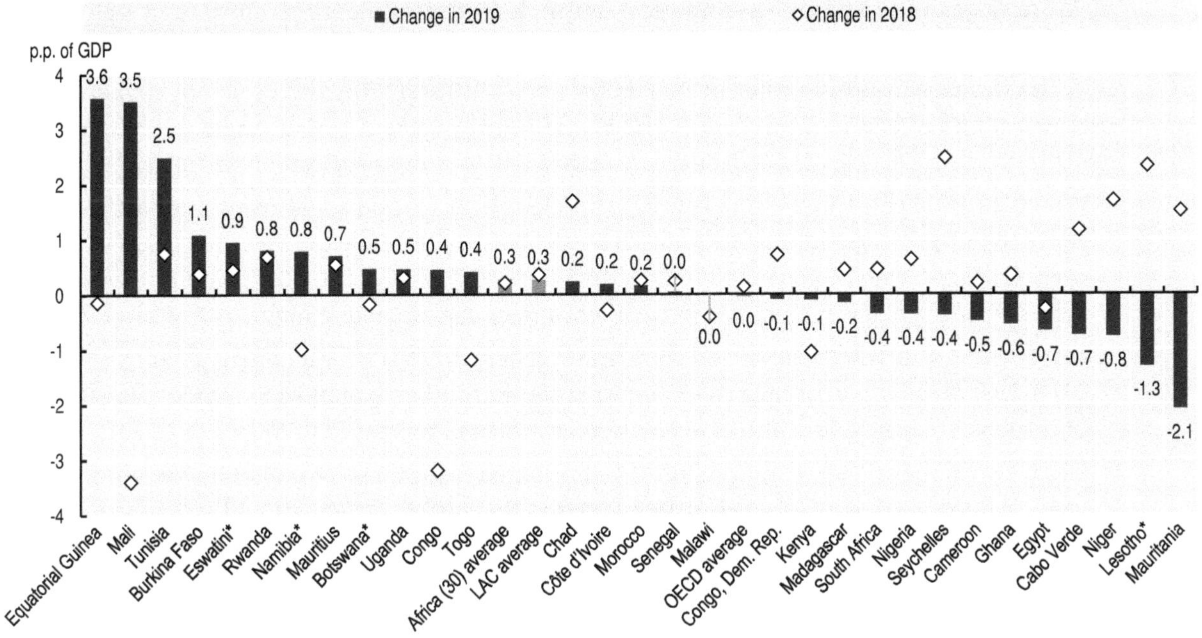

Note: The figures include sub-national government tax revenues for Eswatini, Mauritania, Mauritius, Morocco, Nigeria (state revenues only) and South Africa for 2019.

*Eswatini, Lesotho, Namibia, and Botswana report their figures using an April-March fiscal year. This means 2019 figures for these countries include revenues up to 31 March 2020, during the beginning of the COVID-19 pandemic. See the notes to the country tables in Chapter 5 for further information.

The Africa (30) average, the averages for LAC (26 countries) and the OECD (37 countries) are unweighted.

The change in the Africa (30) average should be interpreted with caution as data for social security contributions are not available or are partial in a few countries. See the country tables in Chapter 5 for further information.

Source: Authors' calculations based on data in Table 4.1 in Chapter 4 and (OECD/AUC/ATAF, 2021[4]), "Revenue Statistics in Africa: Comparative tables", *OECD Tax Statistics* (database), *http://dx.doi.org/10.1787/be755711-en.*

StatLink *https://doi.org/10.1787/888934281809*

The strong rise in Equatorial Guinea's tax-to-GDP ratio between 2018 and 2019 was driven by an increase in income tax revenues of 3.3 p.p., almost all of which was principally due to higher corporate income tax (CIT) from oil companies (3.2 p.p.). The increase was driven by a strong increase in nominal tax revenues (39%) against a decrease in nominal GDP (12%) (Figure 1.4). This difference is driven by a lag of one year in the impact of oil prices on tax revenues: the strong increase in CIT revenues from oil companies between 2018 and 2019 was driven by an increase in oil prices of 17 USD a barrel between 2017 and 2018, resulting in the higher profitability of oil companies in 2018. The oil sector represents the predominant sector in Equatorial Guinea and generated about 69% of tax revenues and 97% of exports in 2019.[5] In 2019, Equatorial Guinea continued to experience recession for the seventh consecutive year, with the predominant impact in 2019 being felt by the oil sector (AfDB, 2021[8]), suggesting a possible decline in these revenues in 2020.

In Mali, the tax-to-GDP ratio increased by 3.5 p.p. between 2018 and 2019, following a decrease between 2017 and 2018 of a similar magnitude (3.4 p.p.). As a response to the decline in tax revenues in 2018, Mali introduced measures to shore up tax revenues, which included the rationalisation of tax exemptions, the reinforcement of controls and audits, the digitalisation of tax and customs administrations procedures, and the deployment of online filing and payments (World Bank Group, 2020[9]). Revenues from all major tax categories increased between 2018 and 2019, with VAT revenues contributing the most to the overall increase (VAT revenues increased by 1.4 p.p. without increasing the standard VAT rate). In addition, the government gradually collected VAT arrears and strengthened the monitoring of VAT taxpayers. Coupled with a robust economy in 2019, the tax measures adopted by Mali led to a strong performance in tax revenues in 2019 (IMF, 2020[10]), (World Bank Group, 2020[9]).

The increase in tax revenues in Tunisia between 2018 and 2019 was driven by higher revenues from personal income taxes (PIT) (1.6% of GDP), CIT (0.6% of GDP) and social security contributions (SSCs) (0.5% of GDP). These increases followed the adoption of tax measures:

- PIT: PIT rates were increased (Tax Law 2018 articles 41; 46; 47) and a new contribution, the social contribution of solidarity (CSS), which is calculated as an additional 1% tax on income), was introduced. The CSS generated TND 330 million in 2019 (0.3% of GDP). In addition, a wage increase for the public sector after two general strikes contributed to higher PIT receipts.
- CIT: The CSS, which is also levied on companies, generated TND 101 million in CIT (0.1% of GDP). Base broadening through the 35% corporate tax rate being applied to a wider range of companies (Article 29 of the 2018 Finance Law) further increased CIT receipts in 2019.
- SSCs: A public pension fund reform in 2019 contributed to the increase of SSCs in the same year. Law No. 2019-37 of 30 April 2019, increased the age of retirement and employers' contribution by two percentage points. An additional increase of the employee contribution of one percentage point took effect in January 2020.[6]

Figure 1.3. **Change in tax-to-GDP ratios by main tax heading between 2018 and 2019 and by country (percentage points)**

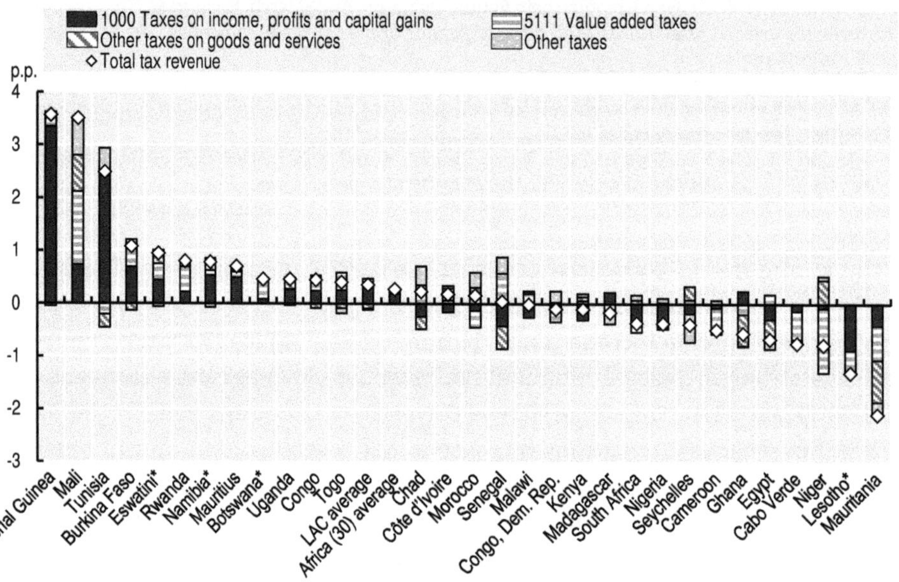

Note: The figures include sub-national government tax revenues for Eswatini, Mauritania, Mauritius, Morocco, Nigeria (state revenues only) and South Africa for 2019.

*Eswatini, Lesotho, Namibia, and Botswana report their figures using an April-March fiscal year. This means 2019 figures for these countries include revenues up to 31 March 2020, during the beginning of the COVID-19 pandemic. See the notes to the country tables in Chapter 5 for further information.

The Africa (30) average, the averages for LAC (26 countries) and the OECD (37 countries) are unweighted.

The Africa (30) average should be interpreted with caution as data for social security contributions are not available or are partial in a few countries. See the country tables in Chapter 5 for further information.

Source: Authors' calculations based on data in (OECD/AUC/ATAF, 2021[4]), "Revenue Statistics in Africa: Comparative tables", *OECD Tax Statistics* (database), *http://dx.doi.org/10.1787/be755711-en.*

StatLink *https://doi.org/10.1787/888934281828*

The two largest decreases in tax-to-GDP ratios between 2018 and 2019 were observed in Mauritania and Lesotho. Mauritania's tax-to-GDP ratio decreased by 2.1 p.p. in 2019 and Lesotho's, by 1.3 p.p.

- Mauritania's decrease was due to a large increase in nominal GDP (16%) against a more limited increase in tax revenues (0.6%) between 2018 and 2019 (Figure 1.4). The increase in nominal GDP was driven by the recovery in 2019 in the extractive industries predominantly in the mining sector (iron ore and gold). This recovery did not result in strong tax revenue growth, as Mauritania collects revenues from the mining sector principally through non-tax instruments (royalties, dividends from state participation) (EITI, 2021[11]), and to a far lesser extent through taxation (mainly taxes from its National Industrial and Mining Company (SNIM), which represented 3% of tax revenues in 2019). In addition, revenues from taxes on goods and services performed less well in 2019 than in 2018, notably VAT on imports, revenues from the tax on petroleum products, and revenues from consumption duties on tea, tobacco, sugar and cement) (Banque centrale de Mauritanie, 2019[12]). This led to decreases of VAT revenues of 0.7 p.p. and from other taxes on goods and services of 0.8 p.p.
- Lesotho's decrease was mainly due to a decline in revenues from income taxes (0.9 p.p.) and a decline in VAT revenues (0.4 p.p.). These decreases were a function of the economic slowdown in 2019/20, poor mining sector performance due to lower external demand, low employment growth and the increase of a PIT tax credit (Lesotho Times, 2020[13]).

Figure 1.4 shows the increase of tax revenues and growth of GDP in nominal terms between 2018 and 2019. As noted, 16 African countries increased their tax-to-GDP ratio in 2019 relative to 2018. In thirteen of these countries, GDP growth was positive, although to a lesser degree than tax revenue growth. The Republic of the Congo, Equatorial Guinea and Namibia experienced declines in nominal GDP and increases in tax revenues. Of the 14 African countries that experienced a decline in their tax-to-GDP ratio in 2019, 12 had higher levels of tax revenues in nominal terms than in the preceding year but the increase in nominal tax revenues was less than the increase in nominal GDP levels. Two countries (Niger and Lesotho) experienced positive nominal GDP growth and negative tax revenue growth.

Figure 1.4. **Change in tax revenue and GDP in nominal currency, 2018-19**

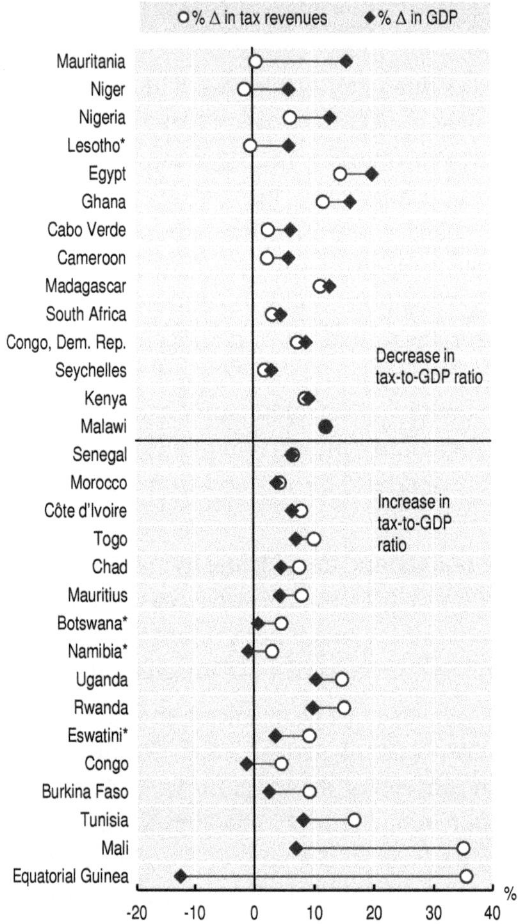

Note: The figures include sub-national government tax revenues for Eswatini, Mauritania, Mauritius, Morocco, Nigeria (state revenues only) and South Africa for 2019.

*Eswatini, Lesotho, Namibia, and Botswana report their figures using an April-March fiscal year. This means 2019 figures for these countries include revenues up to 31 March 2020, during the beginning of the COVID-19 pandemic. See the notes to the country tables in Chapter 5 for further information.

Source: Authors' calculations based on data in (OECD/AUC/ATAF, 2021[4]), "Revenue Statistics in Africa: Comparative tables", *OECD Tax Statistics* (database), *http://dx.doi.org/10.1787/be755711-en.*

StatLink https://doi.org/10.1787/888934281847

Evolution of tax-to-GDP ratios since 2010

In 2019, the tax-to-GDP ratio for the Africa (30) average was 1.8 p.p. higher than in 2010. In comparison, the LAC and OECD averages increased by 1.9 p.p. and 2.0 p.p. respectively between 2010 and 2019. The average tax-to-GDP ratio for the 30 African countries increased steadily between 2010 and 2014 with a strong increase of 0.7 p.p. in 2011, marking the recovery from the global financial crisis. Between 2014 and 2017, the average remained relatively flat at between 16.0% and 16.1% of GDP (Figure 1.5), before increasing by 0.5 p.p. between 2017 and 2019.

The Africa (30) average VAT receipts contributed most to this increase, rising by 1.0 p.p. to reach 4.9% of GDP in 2019. The highest annual increase in the average VAT revenues as a percentage of GDP was registered between 2012 and 2013 (0.4% of GDP) following the introduction of VAT in 2012 in the Democratic Republic of the Congo and in Eswatini. The slight increase in the average standard VAT rate between 2010 and 2019 from 15.9% in 2010 to 16.1% in 2019 may have also contributed to the increase of VAT receipts as a percentage of GDP over the same period.

Figure 1.5. **Average tax-to-GDP ratios for Africa (30), LAC and OECD, 2000-19**

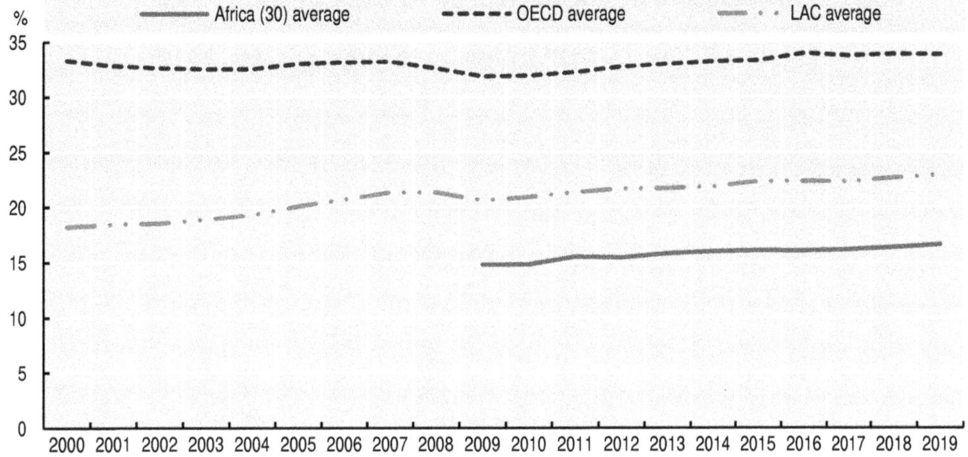

Note: The Africa (30) should be interpreted with caution as data for social security contributions are not available or are partial in a few countries. See the country tables in Chapter 5 for further information.

The figures include sub-national government tax revenues for Eswatini, Mauritius, Mauritania, Morocco, Nigeria (state revenues only) and South Africa for 2002-2019.

The Africa (30) average is estimated for 2009 as the data are not available for Chad and Nigeria. No estimation was made prior to 2009 because of the unavailability of data for a few countries.

The Africa (30), the average for LAC (26 countries) and the OECD average (37 countries) are unweighted.

Source: Table 4.1 in Chapter 4 and (OECD/AUC/ATAF, 2021[4]), "Revenue Statistics in Africa: Comparative tables", *OECD Tax Statistics* (database), *http://dx.doi.org/10.1787/be755711-en.*

StatLink *https://doi.org/10.1787/888934281866*

Box 1.2. **Distribution of tax-to-GDP ratios by country income levels**

Countries' financing needs depend in part on their levels of income, which is an important consideration in understanding tax levels in different countries. For example low-income countries face the greatest financing challenges and revenue mobilisation is particularly critical for them to obtain the necessary resources to improve the living conditions of their populations (Gaspar et al., 2019[14]). Grouping the 30 countries in this publication using the World Bank's global classification of countries by income (World Bank, 2021[15]), we can obtain comparisons of tax systems in countries at similar income levels. Figure 1.6 shows the distribution of tax-to-GDP ratios for countries within three income levels groups in 2019: low income countries, lower middle-income countries, and upper-middle income and high income countries grouped together.

In 2019, 24 of the 30 African countries in this publication were classified as low-income or lower-middle income countries, with 10 in the low income group. This group of countries showed the smallest dispersion compared to countries at higher income levels; and all low-income countries registered a tax-to-GDP ratio below 20%. In this group, tax-to-GDP ratios ranged between 7.5% of GDP in the Democratic Republic of the Congo to 18.3% in Malawi, with an average of 13.5% in 2019. In six of the 10 countries, tax-to-GDP ratios were below 16% in 2019, a level that the IMF considers too low for low income countries to finance the additional spending required for the SDGs (Gaspar et al., 2019[14]).

For the 14 lower-middle income, the average tax-to-GDP ratio amounted to 17.1% of GDP in 2019. While this group demonstrates the widest range of tax-to-GDP ratios, including the highest (Tunisia) and the lowest (Nigeria) tax-to-GDP ratios, 12 countries had tax-to-GDP ratios near or below 20%. Within this group, Tunisia and Morocco stand apart, with tax-to-GDP ratios above 28%. In high and upper-middle-income countries, tax revenues as a percentage of GDP vary greatly, from 10.1% in Equatorial Guinea to 34.3% for the Seychelles, with an average of 20.7% of GDP.

Box 1.2. **Distribution of tax-to-GDP by country income levels** *(cont.)*

Figure 1.6. **Tax-to-GDP ratios by income groups, 2019**

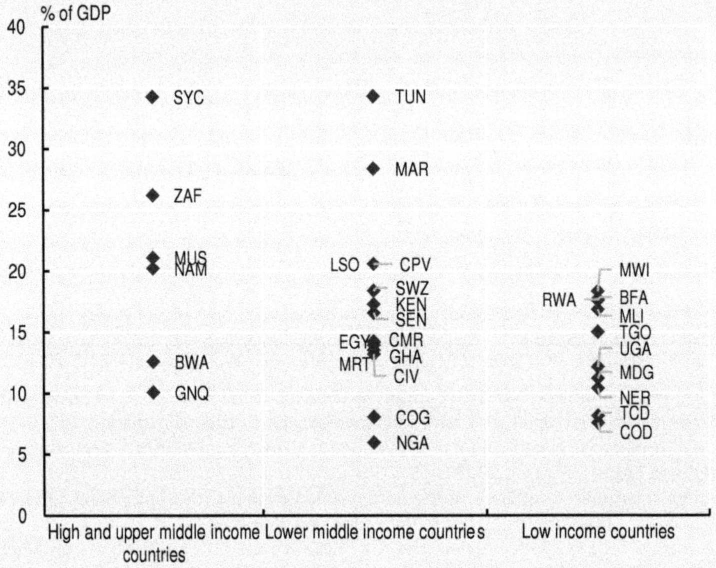

Note: The figures include sub-national government tax revenues for Eswatini, Mauritania, Mauritius, Morocco, Nigeria (state revenues only) and South Africa for 2019.

Source: Authors' calculations based on data in (OECD/AUC/ATAF, 2021[4]), "Revenue Statistics in Africa: Comparative tables", *OECD Tax Statistics* (database), *http://dx.doi.org/10.1787/be755711-en*. Country income classification according to the World Bank classification (World Bank, 2021[15])

StatLink *https://doi.org/10.1787/888934281885*

The Africa (30) average increased by 1.8 p.p. over the last decade and all the three groups mobilised higher tax revenues in 2019 relative to 2010. The increases between 2010 and 2019 were of a similar magnitude. Lower-middle income countries in *Revenue Statistics in Africa* registered on average the highest increase (1.9 p.p.) between 2010 and 2019, followed by low-income countries (1.7 p.p. on average), while the upper middle income and high income group experienced an increase of 1.6 p.p. on average over the same period. In all three income groups, the increases of tax-to-GDP ratios over the last decade was on average below 5 p.p., a level that the IMF estimated – before the COVID-19 pandemic occurred – as an "ambitious and appropriate" target for many countries to meet the SDGs (Gaspar et al., 2019[14]). This represents a challenging goal for the African countries in light of the previous decade and the impact of the COVID-19 pandemic.

Income taxes were the second largest driver of the increase in the Africa (30) average tax-to-GDP ratio between 2010 and 2019, increasing by 0.6 p.p. to 6.3% of GDP in 2019. However, income tax revenues after peaking in 2013 (6.4% of GDP), declined until 2017. The decline was entirely driven by CIT revenues, which decreased by 0.5 p.p. over the period. The fall in oil and mineral prices between 2013 and 2016 may have contributed to this decrease. Income taxes (including CIT revenues) rose again in 2018 and 2019. By contrast, within this category PIT increased steadily between 2010 and 2019, rising by 0.8 p.p. from 2.4% of GDP in 2010 to 3.2 p.p.% in 2019, influenced by higher incomes and thanks to improvements in taxation of high-net-worth individuals in Sub-Sahara Africa (Moore, Prichard and Fjeldstad, 2018[16]). As a result, the average composition of income tax has moved towards a greater share of

PIT over the period. In 2019, PIT revenues represented 51% of total income tax revenues compared to 42% in 2010.

Average revenues from other taxes on goods and services, equivalent to 3.6% of GDP in 2019, have decreased slightly as a percentage of GDP since 2010, in part due to declines in revenues from trade taxes. This decline is associated with trade liberalisation across the continent that resulted in the reduction of import tariffs, the narrowing of the base of products and services subject to excises and the elimination of taxes on exports. Tariffs will be further reduced under the African Continental Free Trade Area (AfCFTA) (OECD/AUC/ATAF, 2020[17]).

The drivers of change in the Latin America and Caribbean region were similar to those in Africa, across the same period. As with the Africa (30) average, VAT contributed most strongly to the increase in LAC's average tax-to-GDP ratio between 2010 and 2019, rising by 0.8 p.p. Higher revenues from social security contributions and income taxes (0.6 p.p. for both) also contributed to the overall increase in the average tax-to-GDP ratio of the LAC region. There is a broad gap between the level of SSCs as a percentage of GDP between the regions: in 2019, SSC stood at 3.9% of GDP in the LAC region compared to the Africa (30) average of 1.4%.

Figure 1.7. **Revenue from taxes on income and profits, VAT and other tax headings as a percentage of GDP, 2010-19**

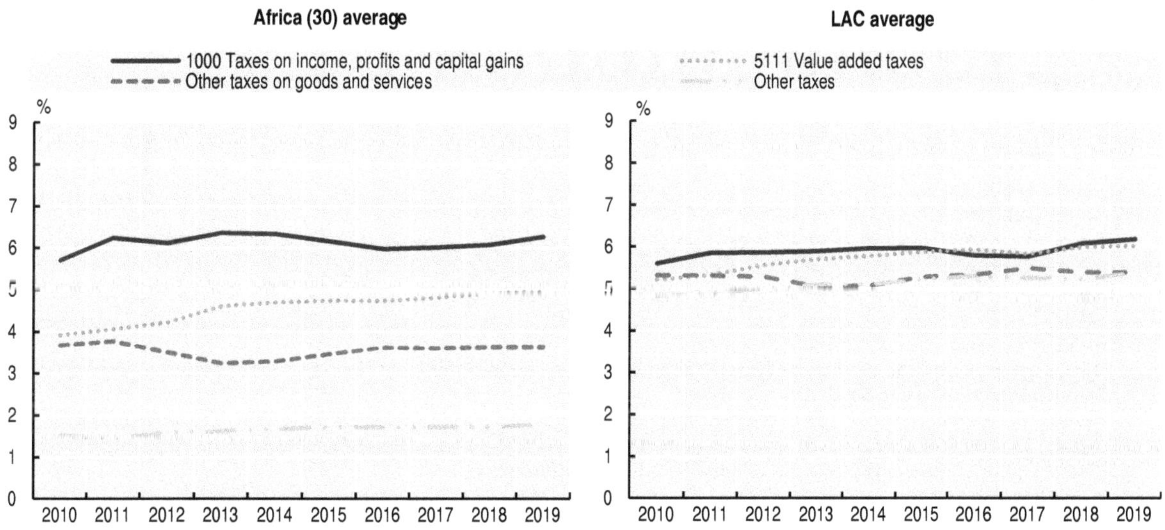

Note: The figures for the Africa (30) average include sub-national government tax revenues for Eswatini, Mauritania, Mauritius, Morocco, Nigeria (state revenues only) and South Africa for 2002-2019.

Source: Authors' calculations based on (OECD/AUC/ATAF, 2021[4]), "Revenue Statistics in Africa: Comparative tables", *OECD Tax Statistics* (database), *http://dx.doi.org/10.1787/be755711-en.*

StatLink https://doi.org/10.1787/888934281904

Tax-to-GDP ratios rose in 24 African countries between 2010 and 2019 and declined in six. Rwanda and Tunisia recorded the highest increases, of 5.4 p.p. and 7.1 p.p. respectively, while the largest decline occurred in Chad (6.5 p.p.) (Figure 1.8).

The increase in Tunisia's tax-to-GDP ratio between 2010 and 2019 was mainly attributable to higher revenues from PIT (3.4 p.p.) and SSC (2.4 p.p.). During this period, Tunisia undertook extensive tax and tax administration reforms to mobilise tax revenues (See box 1.3).

The increase in Rwanda's tax-to-GDP ratio between 2010 and 2019 was driven principally by revenues from income taxes (2.5 p.p.) and VAT revenues (1.9 p.p.). Since 2010, tax collections in Rwanda have risen steadily by an average of 0.6 p.p. per year as a result of significant tax policy and tax administration reforms aiming to offset the decline in foreign aid and trade tax revenues.[7] Administrative changes included the digitalisation of tools for taxpayers, the modernisation of collection and audits processes and increased collection of VAT arrears. With respect to tax policy, Rwanda expanded the PIT base, introduced withholding taxes (VAT and income taxes), removed tax exemptions and increased tax rates for several excises and import duties over the period. These reforms resulted in increased tax compliance, notably for VAT, and a significant increase in tax revenues across the main tax categories (Akitoby et al., 2019[18]). (PwC, 2019[19]) (IMF, 2020[20]). More recently, Rwanda enacted a new income tax law in 2018 that removed ambiguities and expanded the income tax base (Economist Intelligence, 2018[21]), contributing to the increase of income tax revenues of 0.7 p.p. between 2017 and 2019.

Figure 1.8. **Change in tax-to-GDP ratios between 2010 and 2019 (percentage points)**

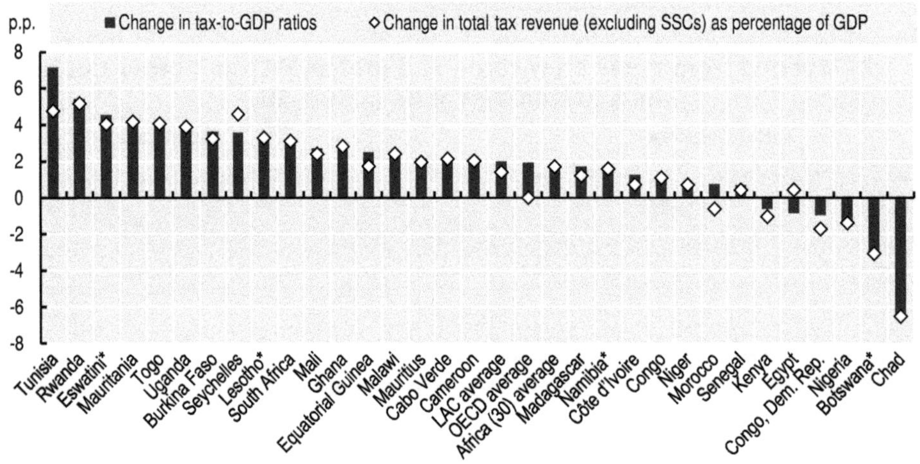

Note: The figures include sub-national government tax revenues for Eswatini, Mauritius, Mauritania, Morocco, Nigeria (state revenues only) and South Africa for 2019.

*Eswatini, Lesotho, Namibia, and Botswana report their figures using an April-March fiscal year. This means 2019 figures for these countries include revenues up to 31 March 2020, during the beginning of the COVID-19 pandemic. See the notes to the country tables in Chapter 5 for further information.

The Africa (30) average, the averages for LAC (26 countries) and the OECD (37 countries) are unweighted.

Source: Tables 4.1 and 4.2 in Chapter 4 and (OECD/AUC/ATAF, 2021[4]), "Revenue Statistics in Africa: Comparative tables", *OECD Tax Statistics* (database), *http://dx.doi.org/10.1787/be755711-en*

StatLink https://doi.org/10.1787/888934281923

Box 1.3. **Tax reforms in Tunisia**

Since 2010, Tunisia has experienced the highest growth in tax-to-GDP ratios of all African countries included in the *Revenue Statistics in Africa* publication. The tax-to-GDP ratio increased by 7.1 p.p. between 2010 and 2019, from 27.2% in 2010 to 34.3% in 2019. This increase is mainly due to higher revenues from PIT (3.4 p.p.), SSCs (2.4 p.p.) and VAT (0.8 p.p.) over this period. Increases in PIT and SSC revenues came partly from the 147% increase in payroll brought about by successive wage gains under post-revolutionary trade

Box 1.3. **Tax reforms in Tunisia** *(cont.)*

union pressure. Extensive reforms of the tax system and tax administration since 2010 have also increased these revenues, along with increasing VAT revenues. Reforms over the past decade have been undertaken along the following main axes:

Broadening the tax base:

- Taxation of distributed income and collected income from betting, gambling and lottery games by means of a flat-rate withholding tax (Finance Acts 2016 et 2018).
- Widening the applicability of the 35% tax (to include mutual insurance companies, contributors' funds, large commercial spaces, car dealerships, franchisees of foreign brands or trademarks) (Finance Acts 2018, 2019 and 2020).
- Broadening of the VAT base by removing exemptions for many products, services and public enterprises (Finance Acts 2016 and 2017).

Revision of tax rates:

- Revision of the personal income tax scale by widening the first exempt bracket from TND 1 500 to TND 5 000 and revision of the other brackets of the scale (Finance Act 2017).
- Abolition of special corporate tax rates (20%, 25%) and introduction of a single general rate of 15% (Finance Act 2021).
- Increase of VAT rates in 2018 by one percentage point from 18% to 19% for the standard rate, from 6% to 7% for the reduced rate and from 12% to 13% for the intermediate rate (Finance Act 2018).

Rationalisation of tax benefits

- Abolition of some tax benefits and re-orienting of others towards national priorities, namely regional development, agriculture, new promoters, higher education graduates (Finance Act 2017).
- Abolition of the preferential tax regime for exports and non-resident financial service providers, to ensure the convergence between tax regimes for on-shore and off-shore companies (Finance Act 2017).

Other

- Enactment of a legal framework to combat base erosion and profit shifting through transfer pricing in accordance with international standards in this area (BEPS programme) (Finance Act 2019).
- Creation of the Brigade of Investigation and Fight against Tax Evasion (BILEF) (Finance Act 2017).
- Ending bank secrecy.

The tax administration continues to focus on transforming itself into an organisation that will have a greater capacity to mobilise taxes in the future. This has meant pursuing various actions to promote digitalisation, broaden the tax base and combat fraud and tax evasion. Examples of these actions include the expansion of the exchange of electronic data between tax administrators and citizens, the implementation of electronic invoicing and remote registration, the improvement of the management of the flat-rate system, the expansion of the VAT tax base and the gradual abolition of the suspensive VAT system.

Source: Ministry of Finance of Tunisia.

Chad experienced a significant decrease in tax revenues as a percentage of GDP between 2010 and 2019 (6.5 p.p.) due to a decrease in CIT revenues of 8 p.p. over the same period. As an oil-based economy, fluctuations in oil prices directly impact Chad's revenues, which fall and rise in direct relationship with oil prices (World Bank, 2018[22]). Given the challenges Chad has encountered in mobilising revenues from other sources, the World Bank granted in 2018 financial support to help Chad improve its revenue mobilisation by strengthening tax administration and developing monitoring tools. For example, the Ministry of Oil will reinforce its capacity to audit oil operators and will develop an oil cadastre along with a contract-management system (World Bank, 2018[22]).

Figure 1.9. **Change in tax-to-GDP ratios by main tax headings between 2010 and 2019 and by country (percentage points)**

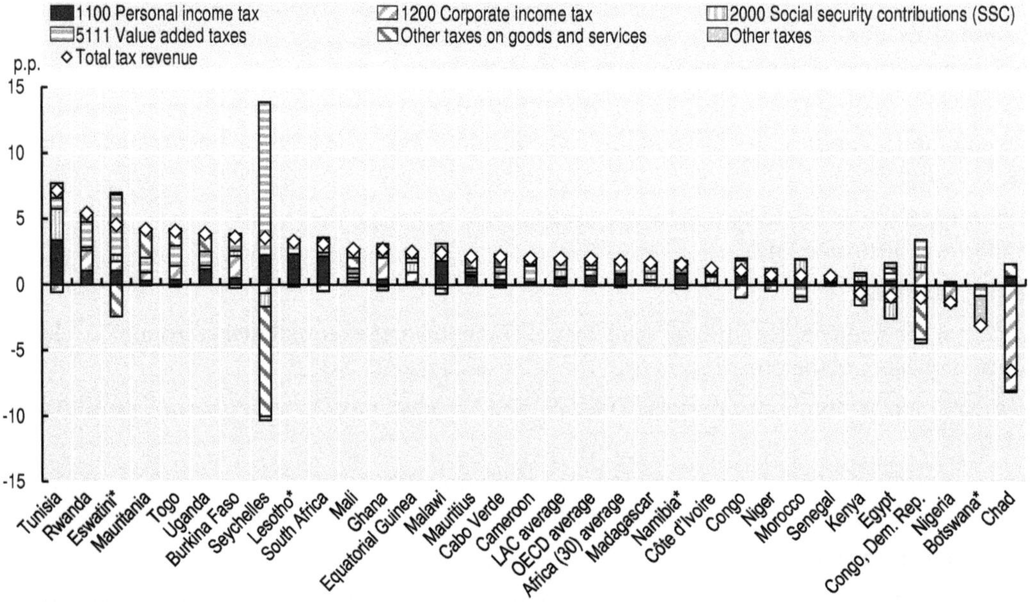

Note: The figures include sub-national government tax revenues for Eswatini, Mauritania, Mauritius, Morocco, Nigeria (state revenues only) and South Africa for 2019.

*Eswatini, Lesotho, Namibia, and Botswana report their figures using an April-March fiscal year. This means 2019 figures for these countries include revenues up to March 31, 2020, during the beginning of the COVID-19 pandemic. See the notes to the country tables in Chapter 5 for further information.

The Africa (30) average, the averages for LAC (26 countries) and the OECD (37 countries) are unweighted.

Source: Authors' calculations based on (OECD/AUC/ATAF, 2021[4]), "Revenue Statistics in Africa: Comparative tables", *OECD Tax Statistics* (database), *http://dx.doi.org/10.1787/be755711-en.*

StatLink https://doi.org/10.1787/888934281942

Box 1.4. **Changes in tax-to-GDP ratios in SACU countries**

Five of the 30 countries included in this publication belong to the Southern African Customs Union (SACU): Botswana, Eswatini, Lesotho, Namibia and South Africa. SACU was founded in 1910, making it the oldest customs union in the world (SACU, 2020[23]). The five SACU members have a revenue-sharing agreement that provides for common external tariffs and for the payment of customs and excise duties a common pool to be shared between the SACU countries. In this publication, revenue from excises, tariffs and customs duties are included as tax revenues in the SACU country that collected the revenue (South Africa) and revenues received from the SACU Common Revenue Pool are included as miscellaneous revenue in non-tax revenues (Botswana, Eswatini, Lesotho and Namibia) (see box 2.3 in Chapter 2).

In 2019, the average of the SACU countries (the SACU average) was around 3 p.p. higher than the Africa (30) average and amounted to 19.6%. The evolution of the tax-to-GDP ratio between 2010 and 2019 in SACU countries was, on average, similar to the evolution of the Africa (30) average over the same period. While the average tax-to-GDP ratio of the Africa (30) rose from 14.8% of GDP in 2010 to 16.6% in 2019, the SACU average rose from 17.7% of GDP in 2010 to 19.6% in 2019.

Box 1.4. **Changes in tax-to-GDP ratios in SACU countries** *(cont.)*

VAT revenue was the main driver of changes in both averages during this period, increasing by 1.0 p.p. for the Africa (30) average and 1.1 p.p. for the SACU countries on average. Eswatini, Lesotho, Namibia and South Africa increased their tax-to-GDP ratios by between 1.6 p.p. (Namibia) and 4.5 p.p. (Eswatini), while Botswana's tax-to-GDP ratio declined by 3.1 p.p. over the period due to decreases in revenues from income tax (2.3 p.p.) and VAT (0.9 p.p.).

Figure 1.10. **Change in tax-to-GDP ratios and by tax category in SACU countries, 2010 to 2019**

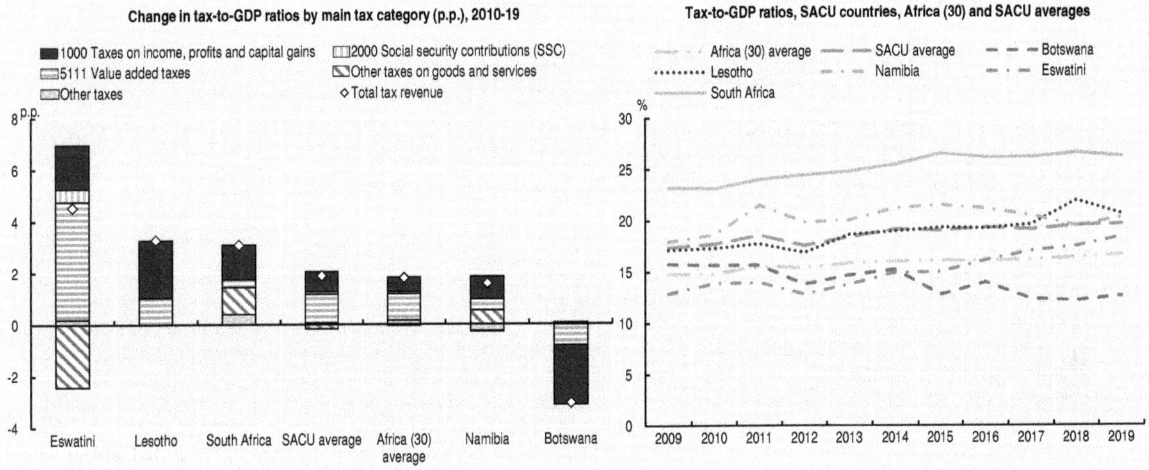

Source: Authors' calculations based on (OECD/AUC/ATAF, 2021[4]), "Revenue Statistics in Africa: Comparative tables", *OECD Tax Statistics* (database), *http://dx.doi.org/10.1787/be755711-en*

StatLink https://doi.org/10.1787/888934281961

Factors influencing tax-to-GDP ratios

Tax-to-GDP ratios are influenced by a variety of domestic and international factors. Domestically, these include macroeconomic characteristics such as the diversification of an economy, the importance of agriculture in the economy, resource endowments, openness to trade, debt and the size of the informal economy. Changes in the political situation in countries, such as social unrest and corruption can also influence tax-to-GDP ratios. The capacity of tax administrations and tax morale (or willingness of people to pay taxes) are also strongly linked to the level of tax revenues (OECD, 2014[24]) (OECD, 2019[25]). Location is relevant: landlocked countries are less able to impose taxes on goods and services entering the country than island countries. In addition, international factors, including the tax policies of other countries, can impact tax-to-GDP ratios.

Tax-to-GDP ratios tend to be higher in high-income countries: in general, OECD countries collect a higher amount of tax revenues than non-OECD countries, measured as a percentage of GDP. Most of the countries included in this publication have lower income per capita and lower tax-to-GDP ratios than OECD and LAC countries. Levels of GDP per capita vary more between African countries than between LAC and OECD countries.

Figure 1.11. **Tax-to-GDP ratios and GDP per capita (in PPP) in African, LAC, OECD and selected Asian and Pacific economies, 2019**

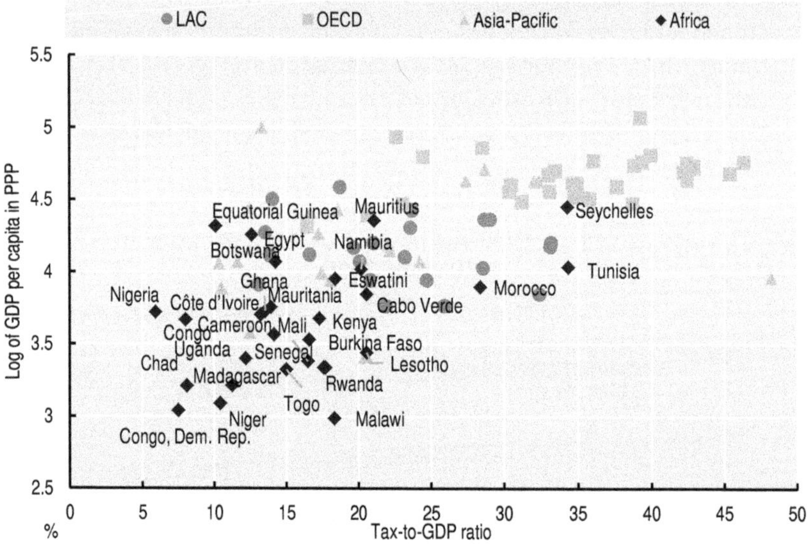

Note: The y-axis is on a logarithmic scale. The purchasing-power-parity (PPP) between two countries is the rate at which the currency of one country needs to be converted into that of a second country to ensure that a given amount of the first country's currency will purchase the same volume of goods and services in the second country as it does in the first. The implied PPP conversion rate is expressed as national currency per current international dollar. An international dollar has the same purchasing power as the US dollar has in the United States. An international dollar is a hypothetical currency that is used as a means of translating and comparing costs from one country to the other using a common reference point, the US dollar (definitions derived from (IMF, 2019[26]) and (WHO, 2015[27]).

Source: (IMF, 2021[5]) for figures of GDP per capita. Tax-to-GDP ratios are sourced from the regional *Revenue Statistics* publications.

StatLink https://doi.org/10.1787/888934281980

Countries that receive substantial revenues from natural resources often exhibit low tax ratios. They are able to resort to less politically-demanding forms of taxation (AfDB/OECD/ECA, 2010[28]), (Mawejje, 2019[29]) and often have relatively narrow tax bases. Figure 1.12 shows the distribution of tax-to-GDP ratios of resource-rich countries compared to non-resource rich countries. Nearly a third of countries in this publication are resource-rich:[8] Chad, the Republic of the Congo, Equatorial Guinea and Nigeria are oil-rich[9] countries and other five countries benefit from substantial mineral resources (e.g. diamonds in Botswana; diamonds, gold, coltan, cobalt and copper in the Democratic Republic of the Congo; diamonds, gold and cacao in Ghana; copper, iron and gold in Mauritania; iron and phosphates in Togo).

Figure 1.12 confirms that resource-rich countries included in this publication registered lower tax-to-GDP ratios than the non-resource-rich countries. In 2019, all resource-rich countries had tax-to-GDP levels below 15%, whereas all but five non resource-rich countries had ratios above this level. Further, while several resource-rich countries had tax-to-GDP ratios below 10%, tax-to-GDP ratios were all over 10% for the non-resource rich countries. In particular, the four oil-rich countries (Chad, the Republic of the Congo, Equatorial Guinea, and Nigeria) had tax-to-GDP ratios below or close to 10%. Oil revenues are mainly generated through rents and royalties, which are not classified as taxes (See Chapter 2). Developing countries encounter significant challenges to taxing extractive sectors because of longstanding tax exemptions or contracts between the country and the extractive industries benefiting local elites (Gwaindepi, 2021[31]), (Brautigam, Fjeldstad and Moore, 2008[32]).

Figure 1.12. **Tax-to-GDP ratios in resource-rich and non-resource rich countries, 2019**

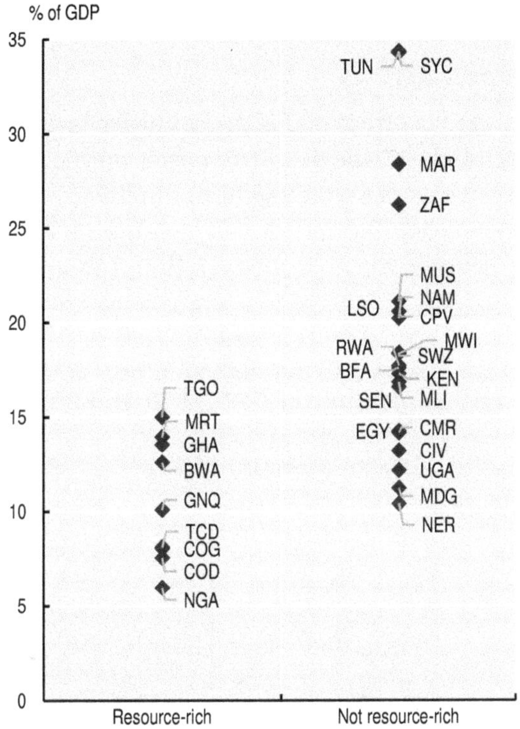

Note: The figures include sub-national government tax revenues for Eswatini, Mauritania, Mauritius, Morocco, Nigeria (state revenues only) and South Africa.
Source: Authors' calculations based on (OECD/AUC/ATAF, 2021[4]), "Revenue Statistics in Africa: Comparative tables", *OECD Tax Statistics* (database), *http://dx.doi.org/10.1787/be755711-en.*
Country classification by resource level is based on (AUC/OECD, 2021[30]).
StatLink https://doi.org/10.1787/888934281999

As mentioned previously, tax morale – taxpayer perceptions and attitudes towards paying and evading taxes – may play a role in tax levels. The OECD has analysed tax morale across different regions and examined its drivers (OECD, 2019[25]). With respect to individuals, support for democracy, faith, educational attainment and trust in government were all identified as factors influencing tax morale. Other possible drivers include perceived improvement in the quality of tax administration, making taxes simpler to pay and providing quality public services. Gender can also play a role; while in most regions men have lower tax morale than women, the opposite is the case in Africa. With respect to businesses, the study conducted by the OECD uses data on tax certainty among multinational enterprises (MNEs).[10] In developing countries, including Africa, tax certainty seems to have an impact on business, resulting in modified business structures, increased costs and changes to investment decisions. With some regional variations, both international taxation and the relationship between the authorities and businesses are consistent concerns across developing countries. In Africa, clarity of legislation and tax certainty were the highest concerns (OECD, 2019[25]).

Tax structures

The composition of a country's tax revenues across different tax types is known as its tax structure. This is an important indicator, since different taxes have different economic and social effects. The tax structures in the 30 countries in this publication reflect different policy choices, economic structures and conditions, tax administration capabilities and historical factors. Countries can be divided into three broad groups according to their principal source of revenue: VAT, other taxes on goods and services and income taxes.

Evolution of tax structures, 2010-19

Since 2010, the average tax structure for the countries in the publication has shifted toward revenues from PIT and VAT and away from taxes on goods and services other than VAT. Increases in both tax categories were significant in driving the overall increase in the tax-to-GDP ratio on average across the period. Revenues from PIT increased by 0.8 p.p. while VAT increased by 1.0 p.p. between 2010 and 2019, reaching 3.9% and 4.9% of GDP respectively in 2019 (Figure 1.13).

Figure 1.13. **Tax structure, Africa (30) average as a percentage of total tax revenue and percentage of GDP, 2010 and 2019**

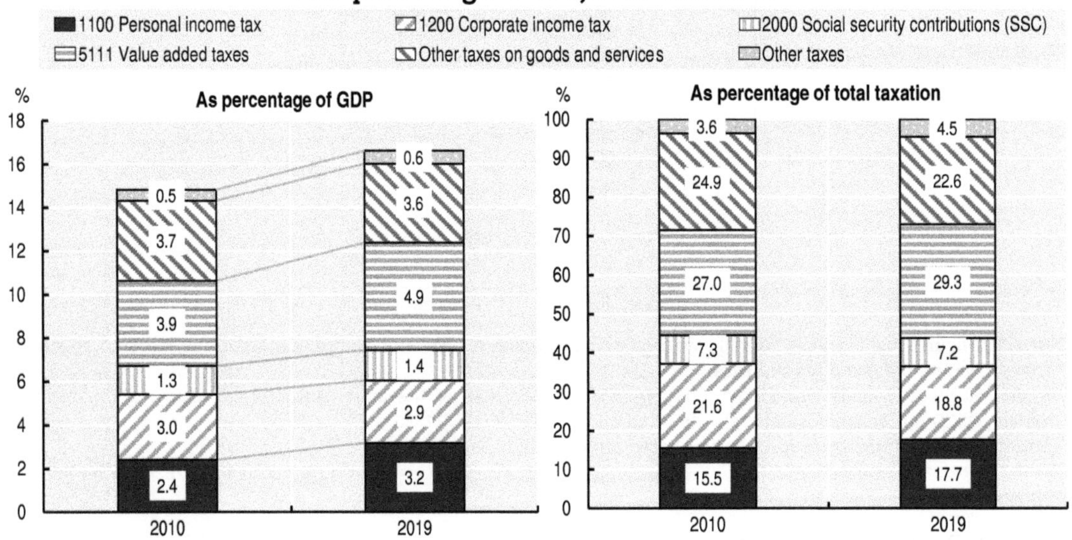

Note: The Africa (30) average is unweighted. The Africa (30) average should be interpreted with caution as data for social security contributions are not available or are partial in a few countries. See the country tables in Chapter 5 for further information.

Source: Authors' calculations based on data on (OECD/AUC/ATAF, 2021[4]), "Revenue Statistics in Africa: Comparative tables", *OECD Tax Statistics* (database), *http://dx.doi.org/10.1787/be755711-en*.

StatLink *https://doi.org/10.1787/888934282018*

The increase in VAT and PIT as a share of GDP has also expanded the share of both taxes in total tax revenues. The share of tax revenues from VAT increased by 2.2 p.p. to 29.3% of total taxation in 2019, continuing the longer-term shift toward VAT from other taxes on goods and services (including sales tax, excises and taxes on specific taxes). Similarly, the share of tax revenues from PIT increased by 2.1 p.p. over this period to 17.7% of total tax revenues in 2019, whereas the share of CIT revenues decreased (2.8 p.p.) over the same period. The average share of PIT revenues remains lower than the share of CIT revenues (18.8% of total taxation in 2019).

Tax structures in 2019

In 2019, VAT generated the largest share of tax revenues in the countries included in this publication (Figure 1.14). Revenues from VAT contributed 29.3% of total tax revenues on average, a share similar to the LAC average (27.7%), approximately 9 p.p. higher than the OECD average (20.4%, 2018 figure) and 7.0 p.p. higher than the Asia-Pacific (24) average (22.8%). However, VAT revenues for the Africa (30) average are lower than the LAC and OECD averages when measured as a share of GDP [4.9% of GDP in Africa, compared to 6.0% in LAC and 6.8% in the OECD (2018 figure)] and similar to the Asia-Pacific (24) average of 4.7 % of GDP.

The average share of CIT revenues in total tax revenue in Africa was 18.8% in 2019, above both the LAC and OECD average shares (15.8% and 10.0% (2018 figure), respectively) but below the Asia-Pacific (24) average of 20.1%. Reported as a percentage of GDP, the average shares of CIT revenues for the 30 African countries and for the OECD were similar [2.9% and 3.1% of GDP (2018 figure) respectively]; both lower than the LAC average and the Asia-Pacific (24) average (3.6% of GDP in 2019) (Figure 1.14).

In contrast, the Africa (30) average share of PIT revenues (17.7% of total tax revenues) was similar to the Asia-Pacific (24) average (17.0%), lower than the OECD average of 23.5% (2018 figure) and higher than the LAC average (9.2 %). As a percentage of GDP, the average level of PIT revenues across the OECD was more than double the Africa (30) average.

Figure 1.14. **Tax structure for the Africa (30), LAC and OECD averages as a percentage of total tax revenues and as a percentage of GDP, 2019**

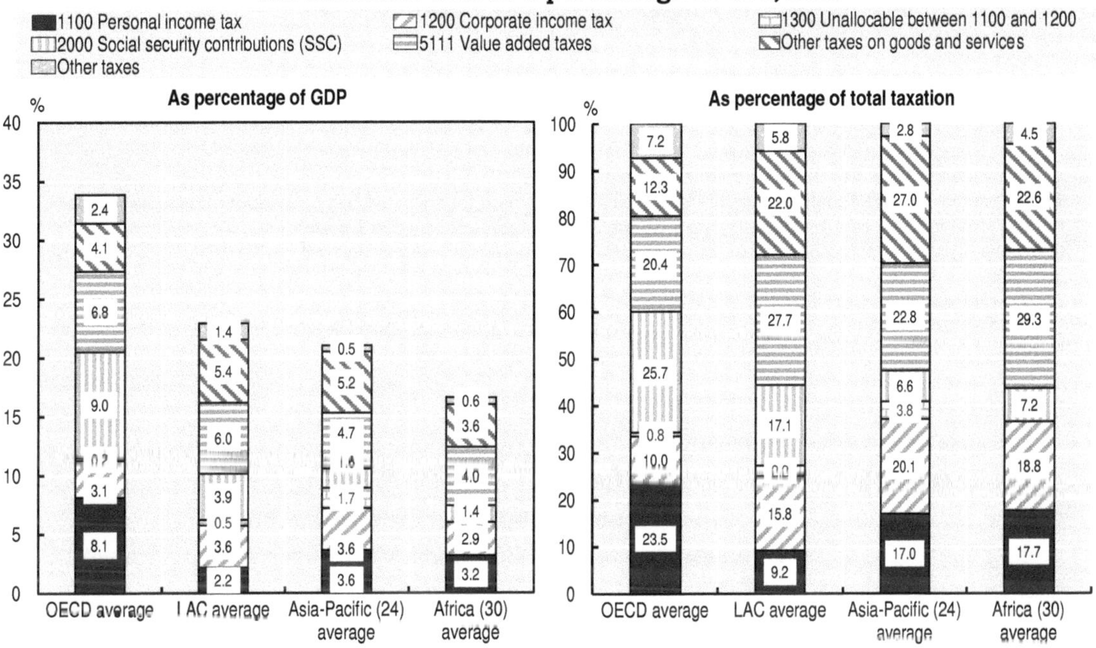

Note: The Africa (30) average, the averages for Asia-Pacific (24 economies), LAC (26 countries) and the OECD (37 countries) are unweighted. The Africa (30) average should be interpreted with caution as data for social security contributions are not available or are partial in a few countries. See the country tables in Chapter 5 for further information. The data for the OECD are for 2018 as data for 2019 are not available.
Source: Authors' calculations based on data on (OECD/AUC/ATAF, 2021[4]), "Revenue Statistics in Africa: Comparative tables", *OECD Tax Statistics* (database), *http://dx.doi.org/10.1787/be755711-en*.

StatLink *https://doi.org/10.1787/888934282037*

Figure 1.15 shows the decomposition of tax revenues across all countries included in this publication, differentiating between income taxes (both personal and corporate), social security contributions, and taxes on goods and services (including VAT and other goods and services taxes).

Taxes on goods and services were the principal source of tax revenues for 22 of the 30 countries included in this publication (the first two groups of countries in Figure 1.15). Among these countries, taxes on goods and services generated between 35.6% of tax revenues in Tunisia and 75.9% of tax revenues in Togo. VAT accounted for the largest share of revenues from taxes on goods and services in this group of countries, except in the Republic of the Congo, Côte d'Ivoire, Kenya and Uganda.

Figure 1.15. **Tax structure by country, 2019**

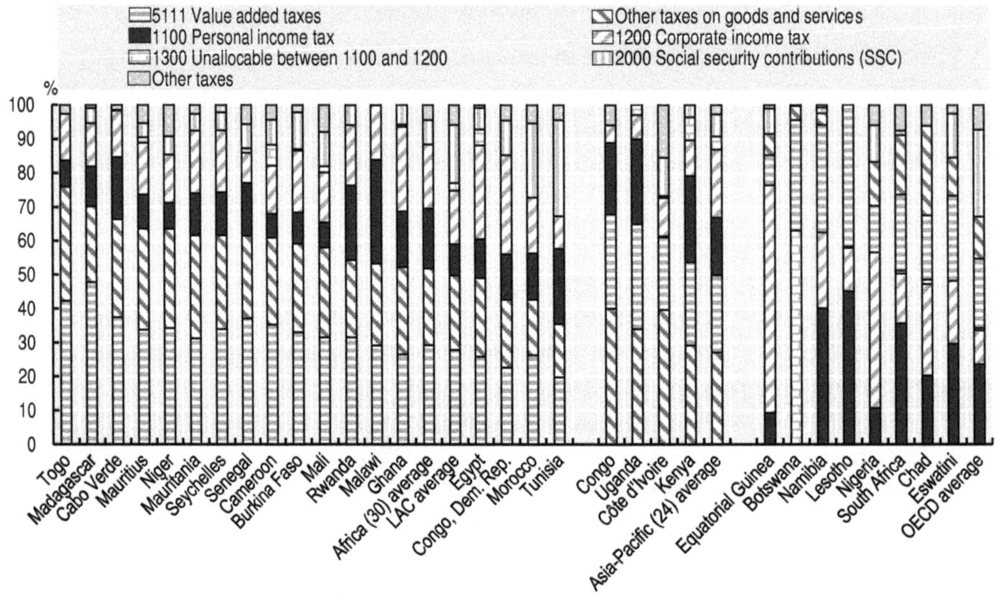

Note: Figures include sub-national government tax revenues for Eswatini, Mauritania, Mauritius, Morocco, Nigeria (state revenues only) and South Africa for 2019. The Africa (30) average, the averages for Asia-Pacific (24 countries), LAC (26 countries) and the OECD (37 countries) are unweighted.

The Africa (30) average should be interpreted with caution as data for social security contributions are not available or are partial in a few countries. See the country tables in Chapter 5 for further information.

Botswana: The breakdown of revenue from income tax by personal income tax and corporate income tax is not available.

OECD average: The data are for 2018 as data for 2019 are not available.

Source: Authors' calculations based on data from (OECD/AUC/ATAF, 2021[4]), "Revenue Statistics in Africa: Comparative tables", *OECD Tax Statistics* (database), *http://dx.doi.org/10.1787/be755711-en.*

StatLink *https://doi.org/10.1787/888934282056*

For eight countries (Botswana, Chad, Equatorial Guinea, Eswatini, Lesotho, Namibia, Nigeria and South Africa), taxes on income and profits accounted for the principal share of total tax revenues. In all of these countries, taxes on income and profits represented a greater share of total tax revenues than for the OECD and LAC averages, ranging from 48.2% of total tax revenues in the Eswatini to 76.4% in Equatorial Guinea.

Eighteen of the 30 countries covered in this publication received a higher share of tax revenues from CIT than from PIT. The share of CIT revenue is particularly large in Nigeria and Equatorial Guinea, where CIT revenues accounts for 45.9% and 67.1% of total taxes, respectively, while Lesotho and Namibia received more than 40% of total revenue from PIT in 2019. In 25 countries, revenues from VAT accounted for a larger share of total taxation than revenue from other taxes on goods and services. Only five countries received a higher share of revenues from other taxes on goods and services: Chad, Côte d'Ivoire, Republic of the Congo, Kenya and Uganda. By contrast, Botswana, Lesotho and Namibia, which are all members of SACU[11] (see Box 2.3) receive less than 5.0% of total tax revenues from other taxes on goods and services. The revenue sharing agreement between SACU countries explains their relatively low share of other taxes on goods and services in comparison to the other countries.

The importance of social security contributions[12] in total tax revenues varies greatly across the 30 countries in this publication. The share was highest in Morocco and Tunisia, at 21.9% of total tax revenues in Morocco and 28.3% in Tunisia; in the remaining countries; social security contributions ranged from less than 0.2% of total tax revenues in Cabo Verde to around 13.0% in Eswatini. This variation reflects a diversity of social security programmes and contribution rates as many countries make use of a variety of systems to fund social security benefits. For example, social security contributions in South Africa finance the Unemployment Insurance Fund while other benefits, such as social assistance programmes covering old age, sickness and maternity, are financed by general revenues. In contrast, social security schemes in Morocco and Tunisia are modelled on the French system and cover a wide range of social security benefits including old age, disability, sickness and maternity, work injury (Tunisia), unemployment (Morocco) and family benefits (SSA, 2015[33]).

Figure 1.16. **Revenues from VAT and other taxes on goods and services and revenues from PIT and CIT**

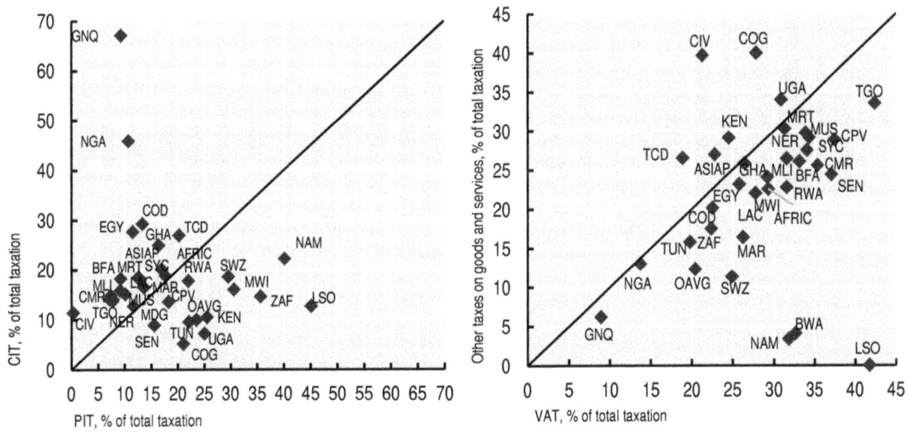

Note: Figures include sub-national government tax revenues for Eswatini, Mauritania, Mauritius, Morocco, Nigeria (state revenues only) and South Africa for 2019.

Botswana: The breakdown of revenue from income tax by personal income tax and corporate income tax is not available.

Source: Authors' calculations based on data from (OECD/AUC/ATAF, 2021[4]), "Revenue Statistics in Africa: Comparative tables", *OECD Tax Statistics* (database), *http://dx.doi.org/10.1787/be755711-en*.

StatLink https://doi.org/10.1787/888934282075

VAT revenue ratio

This section discusses the VAT revenue ratio (VRR) for the countries included in this publication.[13] The VRR "measures the difference between the VAT revenue actually collected and what would theoretically be raised if VAT was applied at the standard rate to the entire potential tax base in a "pure" VAT regime and all revenue was collected" (OECD, 2021[35]). The VRR is the ratio of actual VAT revenues to the product of final consumption (net of VAT revenues) and the standard VAT rate. The calculation is shown below.

$$\frac{\text{VAT revenues}}{(\text{final consumption expenditure} - \text{VAT revenues}) \times \text{standard VAT rate}}$$

This indicator provides an insight into VAT revenue loss related to exemptions and reduced rates, fraud, evasion and tax planning as well as weaknesses in tax administrations. However, this indicator needs to be interpreted with caution and with reference to the underlying characteristics of the VAT system in each country, as a high VRR could result from cascading effects (for example when an exemption occurs early in the supply chain) or a failure to refund VAT input credits. Other factors may also increase the ratio, for example when the place of taxation rules for international trade diverge from the destination principle or when there is a high level of informality. For example, in Africa, many workers operate in the informal sector. Not being registered for tax purposes, they do not benefit from VAT refunds on their inputs, unlike workers and companies in the formal sector (AfDB/OECD/UNDP, 2016[36]).

Figure 1.17. **VAT revenue ratio by country, 2019**

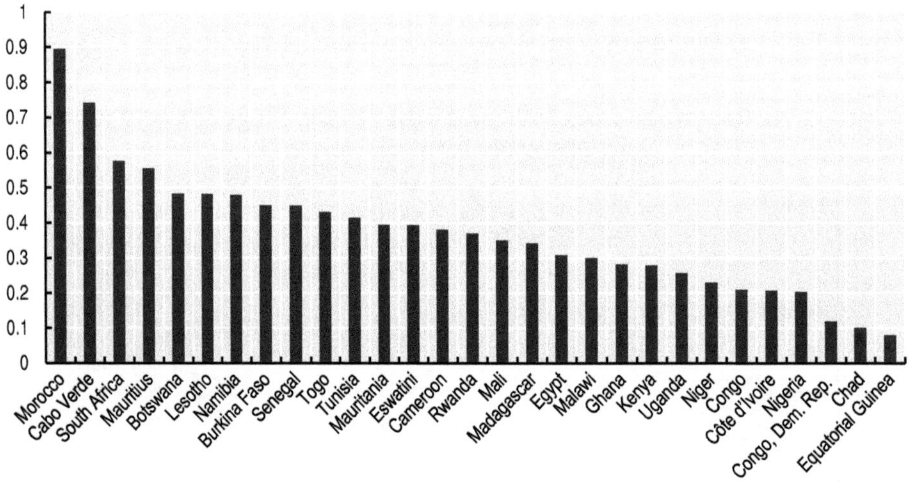

Note: The Seychelles are excluded due to unavailability of some data.
Source: VAT rates are sourced from Consumption Tax Trends (OECD, 2021[35]). Trading Economics and Deloitte websites, the final expenditure consumption figures from IMF WEO (IMF, 2020[37]) and VAT revenues from the country tables in Chapter 5.

StatLink https://doi.org/10.1787/888934282094

Figure 1.17 shows the VRRs for the 30 countries in this publication. In 2019, Cabo Verde, South Africa and Mauritius had the highest VRRs (0.74, 0.58 and 0.56 respectively) while the Democratic Republic of the Congo, Chad and Equatorial Guinea had the lowest (0.12, 0.10 and 0.08 respectively).

- The high VRR in South Africa may be explained by some features of its VAT system. South Africa has limited VAT exemptions and zero-rated products and services compared to many other African countries. In addition, the threshold for VAT registration is high in South Africa, enabling the South African tax administration to focus on larger companies (Cnossen, 2015[38]).
- Cabo Verde has a VAT rate of 15% and passed several reforms between 2013 and 2015 to increase VAT receipts (and corporate taxes). It also automated VAT revenue collection in December 2017 (UNCTAD, 2018[39]).
- By contrast, the Democratic Republic of the Congo showed a VRR of 0.12. VAT revenues have declined sharply since the introduction of VAT in 2012, from 4.2% of GDP to 1.7% of GDP in 2019. This decline and the low VRR reflect the challenges that authorities confront in administering VAT; for example, VAT on imports of mining companies is no longer collected due to difficulties in reimbursing VAT credits. The IMF has recommended a strengthening of the institutional arrangements to resume collecting these revenues (IMF, 2019[40]).

Environmentally related tax revenues

Through the Paris Agreement of 2016, countries have committed to decarbonising their economies by the middle of this century, implying a shift away from fossil fuels as a source of energy. Environmentally related taxes, and price-based policy instruments more generally, play an increasingly significant role in many countries. By incorporating a price signal into consumer decisions, these taxes give effect to the polluter-pays principle and encourage businesses and households to consider the environmental costs of their behaviour.

An environmentally related tax is a tax whose base is a physical unit (or a proxy of a physical unit) of something that has a proven, specific harmful impact on the environment regardless of whether the tax is intended to change behaviours or is levied for another purpose (OECD, 2005[41]). Revenues from taxes on energy can increase in the medium term if countries increase effective tax rates on the carbon content of fuels (Marten and Van Dender, 2019[42]). A joint ITF and OECD study (OECD/ITF, 2019[43]) shows how revenues from road transport can be stabilised in the long term through a mix of taxing distance driven, vehicles and fuel.

Although environmentally related tax revenues cannot be identified in the standard OECD classification of tax revenues, they can be identified through the detailed list of specific taxes included for most countries within this overarching classification. It is on this basis that they are included in the OECD Policy Instruments for the Environment (PINE) database (OECD, 2020[44]).[14]

A detailed examination of country-specific taxes for the 30 African countries in this report demonstrates that, on average, revenue from environmentally related taxes amounted to 1.1% of GDP in 2019, a similar level to the Asia Pacific (16 economies)[15] and LAC averages (1.1% and 1.2% of GDP, respectively) but lower than the OECD unweighted average of 2.2% of GDP. Across countries, environmentally related tax revenue ranged from less than 0.1% of GDP in the Republic of the Congo and Nigeria to 4.7% in the Seychelles (Figure 1.18). These figures need to be treated with caution as it is not possible to identify the precise level of environmentally related tax revenue for each country; the level of revenues shown in Figure 1.18 depends on the granularity of tax revenue data available.

In 2019, tax revenues from energy products generated the highest level of total environmentally related tax revenue for the countries in this publication (0.7% of GDP on average). Revenues from energy products, most commonly from taxes on diesel and gasoline, amounted to approximately two-thirds of environmentally related tax revenue on average. Revenues from motor vehicle and transport taxes represented most of the remainder and revenues from other environmentally related bases were negligible, at 0.02% of environmentally related tax revenues on average. This is very similar to the breakdown of these revenues for OECD and LAC countries. In contrast, Asia-Pacific economies relied more on resource and transport taxes than energy taxes in 2019.

Taxes on energy products accounted for the largest share of environmentally related tax revenues in all but eight countries. Taxes on motor vehicles and transport were the main source of environmentally related revenues for Botswana, Côte d'Ivoire, Kenya, Mauritius, Morocco, Nigeria and Tunisia. Cabo Verde, Equatorial Guinea and Mali levied the main part of their environmentally related tax revenues either from revenues from resource taxes or pollution taxes.

Figure 1.18. **Environmentally related tax revenue by countries and main tax base, as a percentage of GDP, 2019**

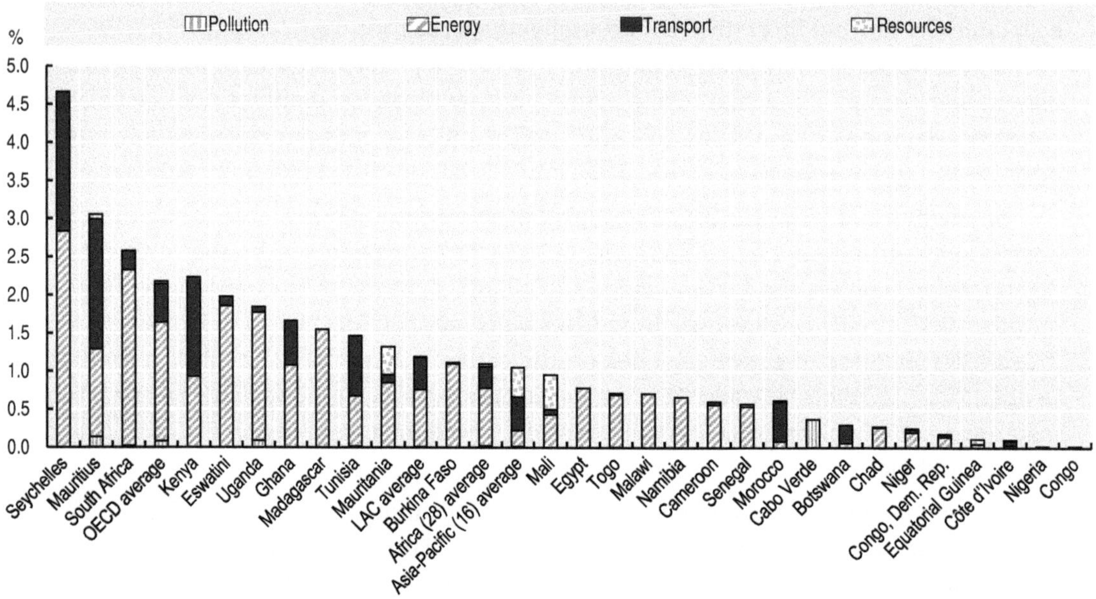

Note: Rwanda and Lesotho are excluded as it has not been possible to identify environmentally-related tax revenue.
Source: Authors' calculations based on data on (OECD/AUC/ATAF, 2021[4]), (OECD, 2020[44])PINE database for the OECD average and (OECD et al., 2021[2]) for the LAC average.

StatLink https://doi.org/10.1787/888934282113

South Africa has one of the highest levels of revenue from environmentally related taxes, amounting to 2.8% of GDP in 2019, with the fuel levy providing the largest share (1.4% of GDP). Over the past decade, South Africa has introduced the incandescent light bulb levy (2009/10); the electricity levy (2009/10); the CO_2 tax on vehicle emissions (2010/11) and the tyre levy (2016/17). More recently, South Africa introduced a carbon tax in 2019 with a tax rate of 120 rand (USD 8.34) per ton of carbon dioxide equivalent (SARS, 2020[45]) (Reuters, 2019[46]; OECD, 2020[47]).

In general, the use of taxation to address environmental issues is low in the region and there is a significant scope to strengthen this type of taxation. The underutilisation of environmental taxes in the Africa region also needs to be understood in the context of the extensive use of fossil fuel subsidies. For example, fossil fuels subsidies in Sub Sahara Africa were estimated to amount to 5% of GDP in 2013 (Coady et al., 2015[48]). Among the countries in this publication, Côte d'Ivoire, Nigeria and South Africa provided fossil fuel subsidies in excess of USD 1 billion in 2015 (Worrall, Whitley and Scott, 2018[49]). Reforming energy subsidies while at the same time implementing environmental taxation has the potential to mobilise significant government revenues and help to meet Agenda 2063 and the Sustainable Development Goals (SDGs).

As governments continue to implement packages to support businesses and taxpayers through the ongoing COVID-19 crisis, some governments are granting tax relief or waiving certain taxes. ATAF encourages African governments to "refrain from suspending environmental taxes during this period as (...) short-term tax relief should not compromise longer-term environmental goals" (ATAF, 2020[50]).

Taxes by level of government

Analysis of taxation by level of government for the countries participating in this publication is limited by the fact that data on sub-national tax revenues are only available for six countries: Eswatini, Mauritania, Mauritius[16], Morocco, Nigeria[17] and South Africa. In 2019, sub-national government revenues accounted for less than 1% of total tax revenues in Mauritius, 2.0% in Eswatini, 2.6% in Mauritania, 3.1% in Morocco and 5.2% in South Africa. In contrast, sub-national government tax revenues amounted to 15.4% of total tax revenues in Nigeria. Revenues collected at sub-national level are generally considered to be low in the region as a whole. (AfDB/OECD/UNDP, 2015[51]) states that "in Africa, on average, the weight of local government revenue is 7% of the total revenue of local, regional and national governments combined".

In general, sub-national governments in Africa tend to have limited tax collection responsibilities. The 2015 *African Economic Outlook* (AfDB/OECD/UNDP, 2015[51]) observed that "Many local governments receive a significant share of their total revenues from central government transfers". Local governments across Africa have limited resources and many local tax administrations are not adequately equipped to collect taxes or to account for them. This results in high collection costs and a large number of low-yield taxes. Moreover, processing of data on revenue collections and the exchange of information with other public institutions is poor and there is usually little co-operation with the central government. This can lead to a duplication of taxes or a levying of taxes that are contrary to national objectives (such as local taxes on export crops).

Revenues from property taxes are the most important source of reported tax revenue for sub-national governments in Eswatini, Mauritania, Mauritius, Morocco and South Africa. They accounted for all the reported tax revenue collected locally in Eswatini, Mauritania, Mauritius and South Africa and for more than 80% in Morocco. Most of the remainder derives from taxes on goods and services. In contrast, sub-national government tax revenues in Nigeria are mostly sourced from income taxes.

There are wide differences in local taxation among African countries and many countries do not levy any local taxes on buildings and landholdings, or on economic activities (AfDB/OECD/UNDP, 2015[51]). Apart from South Africa, property registers are lacking or incomplete, which is a major challenge for the collection of property taxes (Fjeldstad, Chambas and Brun, 2014[52]). In Mauritius, for instance, property tax provides a low yield partly due to outdated cadastres and valuations of property (IMF, 2014[53]).

Some countries have been working on improving their property taxes, which has led to improved land registries and better administrative tools. Morocco has been reforming local government tax systems and administrations since 2007 to strengthen local tax revenue (Boisard, de Freitas and Hidouci, 2014[54]). Côte d'Ivoire has introduced GIS software in their land registries. South Africa has successfully decentralised urban property tax collection and has developed a modern system to collect property tax revenue including use of statistical techniques to conduct computer-assisted mass-appraisals (Monkam and Moore, 2015[55]).

Although many countries have undertaken major reforms of their central tax legislation and administrations over the last decades, less focus has been put on the local government level. Central government taxation has been prioritised because of the need to reduce national fiscal deficits.

Notes

1 The Africa (30) average should be interpreted with caution as data on social security contributions are not available for Chad, the Republic of the Congo, the Democratic Republic of the Congo (prior to 2012), Madagascar (prior to 2011), Namibia, Togo and Uganda and are only partially available for Cameroon and Senegal. Social security contributions for Botswana, Lesotho and Malawi are deemed to be null as they do not meet the criteria to be classified as social security contributions set out in the OECD classification of taxes in the Interpretative Guide. See the country tables in Chapter 5 for further information.

2 Burundi, South Sudan, Tanzania, Kenya, Rwanda and Uganda belong to the East Africa Community (EAC).

3 Burkina Faso, Benin, Côte d'Ivoire, Guinea Bissau, Mali, Niger, Senegal and Togo belong to the West African Economic and Monetary Union (WAEMU, also known by its French acronym, UEMOA).

4 The five SACU members have a revenue-sharing agreement that provides for common external tariffs and for the payment of customs and excise duties into a common pool to be shared between the SACU countries. In this publication, revenue from excises, tariffs and customs duties are included as tax revenues in the SACU country that collected the revenue (South Africa) and revenues received from the SACU Common Revenue Pool are included as miscellaneous revenue in non-tax revenues (Botswana, Eswatini, Lesotho and Namibia).

5 Author's calculation based on (IMF, $2021_{[5]}$).

6 This information was provided by the Ministry of Finance of Tunisia during exchanges with the OECD Secretariat in preparation of this publication.

7 After the East African Community (EAC) Common Market was established in 2010, Rwanda adopted the EAC Common External Tariff Framework leading to a decline of revenues from trade taxes in 2010 by 0.3 p.p..

8 Countries for whom over 10% of GDP came from oil, gas, coal and mineral production for at least 5 years between 2010 and 2019 were classified as "resource-rich" (AUC/OECD, $2021_{[30]}$).

9 Countries for whom over 10% of GDP came from oil and natural gas production for at least 5 years between 2010 and 2019 were classified as "oil-rich" (AUC/OECD, $2021_{[30]}$).

10 The analysis is based on a unique data source, the 2016 OECD business survey that gathered views from senior staff from over 500 companies, almost all MNEs, providing views on tax certainty in 82 developing countries.

11 The five SACU members have a revenue sharing agreement that provides for common external tariffs and for the payment of customs and excise duties into a common pool to be shared between the SACU countries. In this publication, revenue from excises, tariffs and customs duties are included as tax revenues in the SACU country that collected the revenue (South Africa) and revenues received from the SACU Common Revenue Pool are included as miscellaneous revenue in non-tax revenues (Botswana, Eswatini, Lesotho and Namibia).

12 Data on social security contributions are not available for Chad, the Republic of the Congo, the Democratic Republic of the Congo (prior to 2012), Madagascar (prior to 2011), Namibia, Togo and Uganda and are only partially available for Cameroon and Senegal. See the country tables in Chapter 5 for further information.

13 The Seychelles is excluded due to unavailability of some data.

14 The PINE database classifies environmentally-related taxes under four bases:

- Energy: This covers taxation of energy products such as fossil fuels and electricity also including fuels for transportation such as petrol and diesel. All CO_2-related taxes are in this category.
- Motor vehicles and transport services: This category includes imports or sales taxes on transport equipment, recurrent taxes on ownership, registration or road use of motor vehicles, and other transport-related taxes.
- Resources: This category includes taxes on mining and quarrying, forestry, wildlife and fisheries.
- Pollution: This category includes taxes on ozone-depleting substances, water and wastewater, waste management.

15 This represents an average of 16 countries and not 24 as it has not been possible to identify environmentally-related tax revenue for eight countries due to data availability issues.

16 Data from Mauritius were derived from financial statements produced by Statistics Mauritius.

17 Sub-national tax revenues figures include state revenues but exclude local government revenues.

References

AfDB (2021), *Equatorial Guinea Economic Outlook | African Development Bank - Building today, a better Africa tomorrow*, *www.afdb.org/en/countries/central-africa/equatorial-guinea/equatorial-guinea-economic-outlook* (accessed on 20 September 2021). [8]

AfDB/OECD/UNDP (2016), *African Economic Outlook: Sustainable Cities and Structural Transformation*, *https://dx.doi.org/10.1787/aeo-2016-en*. [36]

AfDB/OECD/ECA (2010), *African Economic Outlook 2010: Domestic Resource Mobilisation and Aid*, OECD Publishing, Paris, *http://dx.doi.org/10.1787/aeo-2010-en*. [28]

AfDB/OECD/UNDP (2015), *African Economic Outlook 2015: Regional Development and Spatial Inclusion*, OECD Publishing, Paris, *http://dx.doi.org/10.1787/aeo-2015-en*. [51]

Akitoby, B. et al. (2019), *Case Studies in Tax Revenue Mobilization in Low-Income Countries*, *www.imf.org/en/Publications/WP/Issues/2019/05/14/Case-Studies-in-Tax-Revenue-Mobilization-in-Low-Income-Countries-46719* (accessed on 20 September 2021). [18]

ATAF (2020), *Mining Tax Policy Responses to COVID-19: Webinar Q&A*, *www.ataftax.org/mining-tax-policy-responses-to-covid-19-webinar-q-a*. [50]

AUC/OECD (2021), *Africa's Development Dynamics 2021: Digital Transformation for Quality Jobs*, AUC, Addis Ababa/OECD, Paris, *https://doi.org/10.1787/0a5c9314-en*. [30]

Banque centrale de Mauritanie (2019), *Rapport Annuel*, *www.bcm.mr/IMG/pdf/rapport_anuel_2019.fr.pdf* (accessed on 20 September 2021). [12]

Boisard, S., C. de Freitas and G. Hidouci (2014), *Renforcer les recettes fiscales locales pour financer le développement urbain en Afrique*, Fonds Mondial pour le Développement des Villes (FMDV), Paris, *http://delog.org/web/wp-content/uploads/2016/03/Etude-FMDV-Fiscalite%CC%81-locale-Villes-Afrique-8-Cas.pdf*. [54]

Brautigam, D., O. Fjeldstad and M. Moore (2008), *Taxation and State-Building in Developing Countries: Capacity and Consent – ICTD*, CMI, *www.ictd.ac/publication/taxation-and-state-building-in-developing-countries-capacity-and-consent/* (accessed on 20 September 2021). [32]

Cnossen, S. (2015), *Mobilizing VAT revenues in African countries*, *www.researchgate.net/publication/276344974 Mobilizing_VAT_revenues_in_African_countries*. [38]

Coady, D. et al. (2015), "How Large Are Global Energy Subsidies?", *IMF Working Paper*, *www.imf.org/external/pubs/ft/wp/2015/wp15105.pdf*. [48]

Diallo, M. (2018), "UEMOA : L'optimisation de la mobilisation des recettes fiscales propres, au centre d'un séminaire", *LeFaso.net*, *https://lefaso.net/spip.php?article84079*. [6]

Economist Intelligence (2018), *New income tax law comes into force*, *http://country.eiu.com/article.aspx?articleid=1636776147&Country=Rwanda&topic=Economy&subtopic=Fo_2* (accessed on 20 September 2021). [21]

EITI (2021), *Mauritania | Extractive Industries Transparency Initiative*, https://eiti.org/mauritania (accessed on 21 September 2021). [11]

Fjeldstad, O., G. Chambas and J. Brun (2014), *Local government taxation in Sub-Saharan Africa: a review and an agenda for research*, 2, Chr. Michelsen Institute, Bergen, *www.cmi.no/publications/file/5098-local-government-taxation-in-sub-saharan-africa.pdf*. [52]

Gaspar, V. et al. (2019), *Fiscal Policy and Development : Human, Social, and Physical Investments for the SDGs*, *www.imf.org/en/Publications/Staff-Discussion-Notes/Issues/2019/01/18/Fiscal-Policy-and-Development-Human-Social-and-Physical-Investments-for-the-SDGs-46444* (accessed on 20 September 2021). [14]

Gwaindepi, A. (2021), "Domestic revenue mobilisation in developing countries: An exploratory analysis of sub-Saharan Africa and Latin America", *Journal of International Development*, Vol. 33/2, pp. 396-421, *http://dx.doi.org/10.1002/JID.3528*. [31]

IMF (2021), *West African Economic and Monetary Union : Staff Report on Common Policies for Member Countries-Press Release; Staff Report; and Statement by the Executive Director for the West African Economic and Monetary Union*, *www.imf.org/en/Publications/CR/Issues/2021/03/02/West-African-Economic-and-Monetary-Union-Staff-Report-on-Common-Policies-for-Member-50139* (accessed on 20 September 2021). [7]

IMF (2021), *World Economic Outlook Database, April 2021*, *www.imf.org/en/Publications/WEO/weo-database/2021/April* (accessed on 20 September 2021). [5]

IMF (2020), Mali : *Requests for Disbursement Under the Rapid Credit Facility and Rephasing of Access Under the Extended Credit Facility Arrangement-Press Release; Staff Report; and Statement by the Executive Director for Mali*, *www.imf.org/en/Publications/CR/Issues/2020/05/07/Mali-Requests-for-Disbursement-Under-the-Rapid-Credit-Facility-and-Rephasing-of-Access-Under-49399* (accessed on 20 September 2021). [10]

IMF (2020), *The Development Path Less Travelled-The Experience of Rwanda*, *www.imf.org/en/Publications/Departmental-Papers-Policy-Papers/Issues/2020/08/17/The-Development-Path-Less-Travelled-The-Experience-of-Rwanda-49609.* [20]

IMF (2020), *World Economic Outlook, April 2020 : The Great Lockdown.* [37]

IMF (2019), *Democratic Republic of the Congo : 2019 Article IV Consultation-Press Release; Staff Report; and Statement by the Executive Director for the Democratic Republic of the Congo*, *www.imf.org/en/Publications/CR/Issues/2019/09/04/Democratic-Republic-of-the-Congo-2019-Article-IV-Consultation-Press-Release-Staff-Report-and-48648* (accessed on 8 September 2020). [40]

IMF (2019), *World Economic Outlook - Frequently Asked Questions*, *www.imf.org/external/pubs/ft/weo/faq.htm#q4d* (accessed on 6 September 2019). [26]

IMF (2014), *Mauritius: 2014 article IV consultation-staff report (2014b)*, IMF, *www.imf.org/external/pubs/ft/scr/2014/cr14107.pdf.* [53]

Lesotho Times (2020), "LRA misses revenue target amid COVID-19 economic impact - Lesotho Times", *https://lestimes.com/lra-misses-revenue-target-amid-covid-19-economic-impact/* (accessed on 20 September 2021). [13]

Marten, M. and K. Van Dender (2019), *The use of revenues from carbon pricing. OECD Taxation Working Papers*, OECD, *https://doi.org/10.1787/3cb265e4-en.* [42]

Mawejje, J. (2019), "Natural resources governance and tax revenue mobilization in sub saharan Africa: The role of EITI", *Resources Policy*, Vol. 62, pp. 176-183, *http://dx.doi.org/10.1016/J.RESOURPOL.2019.04.001.* [29]

Monkam, N. and M. Moore (2015), *How Property Tax Would Benefit Africa*, Africa Research Institute, *http://www.africaresearchinstitute.org/publications/property-tax-benefit-africa.* [55]

Moore, M., W. Prichard and O. Fjeldstad (2018), *Taxing Africa: Coercion, Reform and Development – ICTD*, Zed Books, *www.ictd.ac/publication/taxing-africa-coercion-reform-and-development/* (accessed on 20 September 2021). [16]

OECD (2021), *Revenue Statistics in Asia and the Pacific 2021: Emerging Challenges for the Asia-Pacific Region in the COVID-19*, OECD Publishing, Paris, *https://doi.org/10.1787/ed374457-en.* [1]

OECD (2020), *Consumption Tax Trends 2020: VAT/GST and Excise Rates, Trends and Policy Issues*, *https://doi.org/10.1787/152def2d-en.* [35]

OECD (2020), "OECD analysis of budgetary support and tax expenditures. 2020 country notes", *Inventory of Support Measures for Fossil Fuels databas*, *www.oecd.org/fossil-fuels/data/.* [47]

OECD (2020), *PINE database*, *www.oecd.org/environment/tools-evaluation/environmentaltaxation.htm.* [44]

OECD (2020), *Revenue Statistics 2020*, OECD Publishing, Paris, *https://dx.doi.org/10.1787/8625f8e5-en.* [3]

OECD (2019), *Tax Morale: What Drives People and Businesses to Pay Tax?*, OECD Publishing, *https://doi.org/10.1787/f3d8ea10-en.* [25]

OECD (2018), *Consumption Tax Trends 2018: VAT/GST and Excise Rates, Trends and Policy Issues*, OECD publishing, *https://doi.org/10.1787/ctt-2018-en.* [34]

OECD (2014), *Development Co-operation Report 2014: Mobilising Resources for Sustainable Development*, OECD Publishing, Paris, *https://doi.org/10.1787/dcr-2014-en.* [24]

OECD (2005), *Glossary of statistical terms*, *https://stats.oecd.org/glossary/detail.asp?ID=6437.* [41]

OECD/AUC/ATAF (2021), *Revenue Statistics in Africa: Comparative tables*, OECD Publishing, Paris, *http://dx.doi.org/10.1787/be755711-en.* [4]

OECD/AUC/ATAF (2020), *Revenue Statistics in Africa 2020: 1990-2018*, OECD Publishing, Paris, *https://doi.org/10.1787/14e1edb1-en-fr.* [17]

OECD et al. (2021), *Revenue Statistics in Latin America and the Caribbean*, OECD Publishing, Paris, *https://doi.org/10.1787/96ce5287-en-es.* [2]

OECD/ITF (2019), *Tax revenue implications from the decarbonisation of road transport: scenarios for Slovenia*, OECD, *https://doi.org/10.1787/87b39a2f-en.* [43]

PwC (2019), *Sustaining the momemtum. Rwanda's 2019/20 National Budget Bulletin*, *www.pwc.com/rw/en/pdf/rwanda-budget-analysis-2019-20.pdf*. [19]

Reuters (2019), *South African carbon tax finally becomes law*, *www.reuters.com/article/us-safrica-carbontax/south-african-carbon-tax-finally-becomes-law-idUSKCN1SW0K6* (accessed on 6 September 2019). [46]

SACU (2020), *What is SACU?*, *www.sacu.int/about/what_is.html* (accessed on 10 September 2020). [23]

SARS (2020), *Tax statistics 2020*, *www.sars.gov.za/wp-content/uploads/Docs/TaxStats/2020/Tax-Statistics-2020.pdf*. [45]

SSA (2015), *Social Security Through the World: Africa*, SSA Publication Social Security Administration, Washington, DC, *www.ssa.gov/policy/docs/progdesc/ssptw/2014-2015/africa/ssptw15africa.pdf*. [33]

UNCTAD (2018), *Investment Policy Review of Cabo Verde*, *http://unctad.org/ipr* (accessed on 7 September 2020). [39]

WHO (2015), *Purchasing Power Parity 2005*, World Health Organization, *www.who.int/choice/costs/ppp/en/*. [27]

World Bank (2021), *World Bank Country and Lending Groups*, *https://datahelpdesk.worldbank.org/knowledgebase/articles/906519* (accessed on 20 September 2021). [15]

World Bank (2018), *La Banque mondiale aide le Tchad à mobiliser et à améliorer la gestion des ressources intérieures*, *www.banquemondiale.org/fr/news/press-release/2018/07/06/chad-world-bank-helps-strengthen-domestic-resource-mobilization-and-management*. [22]

World Bank Group (2020), *Mali Economic Update*, *https://documents1.worldbank.org/curated/en/781261603955655796/pdf/Mali-Economic-and-Poverty-Update-during-COVID-19.pdf* (accessed on 20 September 2021). [9]

Worrall, L., S. Whitley and A. Scott (2018), "Reforming Africa's Fossil Fuel Subsidies", *sun-connect-news.org*, *www.sun-connect-news.org/de/articles/business/details/reforming-africas-fossil-fuel-subsidies/*. [49]

Revenue Statistics in Africa 1990-2019/Statistiques des recettes publiques en Afrique 1990-2019

Chapitre 1

Tendances des recettes fiscales, 2010-2019

Pour atteindre les Objectifs de développement durable (ODD) des Nations Unies et mettre en œuvre le Programme d'action d'Addis-Abeba et l'Agenda 2063 de l'Union africaine, il est nécessaire de mobiliser des moyens financiers supplémentaires, et notamment des ressources intérieures, afin de financer l'offre de biens et de services publics. L'impôt représente une source de recettes publiques prévisible et stable, qui contraste avec la volatilité d'autres sources importantes de recettes publiques, comme l'aide publique au développement et les redevances minières.

Ce rapport contient un ensemble d'indicateurs internationalement comparables sur les recettes fiscales et non fiscales qui peuvent servir à mesurer les progrès en matière de mobilisation des ressources intérieures (comme le prévoient l'Agenda 2063, les ODD, le Programme d'action d'Addis-Abeba, ainsi que des initiatives connexes telles que l'initiative fiscale d'Addis-Abeba), et à éclairer les politiques et les réformes fiscales. Ce rapport et les données qu'il contient contribuent aussi au Programme statistique panafricain, une initiative conjointe de l'Union européenne et de l'Union africaine visant à renforcer les capacités statistiques en Afrique, en fournissant des données statistiques de qualité sur les recettes publiques. Ces données faciliteront le processus d'élaboration des politiques et leur suivi, de manière à soutenir l'intégration africaine. Ce rapport contient aussi des informations essentielles sur les systèmes fiscaux dans la région et sur leur efficacité en termes de recettes mobilisées au cours des dernières années ; il apporte une contribution importante à la compréhension de la capacité budgétaire des pays de la région à surmonter la crise du COVID-19.

Ce chapitre examine l'évolution du ratio impôts/PIB, de la structure fiscale et de la part des recettes fiscales par niveau d'administration dans 30 pays d'Afrique, de 1990 (si disponible) jusqu'en 2019 : Afrique du Sud, Botswana, Burkina Faso, Cabo Verde, Cameroun, Côte d'Ivoire, Guinée équatoriale, Égypte, Eswatini, Ghana, Kenya, Lesotho, Madagascar, Malawi, Mali, Maroc, Maurice, Mauritanie, Namibie, Niger, Nigéria, Ouganda, République démocratique du Congo, République du Congo, Rwanda, Sénégal, Seychelles, Tchad, Togo et Tunisie. Il compare également les moyennes de ces 30 pays d'Afrique avec celles de 24 pays d'Asie et du Pacifique (OCDE, 2021[1]), de 26 pays d'Amérique latine et des Caraïbes (ALC) (OCDE et al., 2021[2]), et celle des 37 pays de l'OCDE (OCDE, 2020[3]). L'analyse proposée vient compléter les informations détaillées par pays consacrées aux recettes fiscales figurant au chapitre 5.

Ratios impôts/PIB

Ratios impôts/PIB en 2019

Le ratio moyen impôts/PIB dans les 30 pays d'Afrique couverts par la publication [désigné ci-après « moyenne des pays d'Afrique (30) »] s'est établi à 16.6 % en 2019 (graphique 1.1). Le ratio impôts/PIB correspond aux recettes fiscales (y compris les cotisations de sécurité sociale versées à l'administration générale) exprimées en pourcentage du produit intérieur brut (PIB)[1]. À titre de comparaison, les ratios impôts/PIB moyens pour la région Asie-Pacifique,

Amérique latine et Caraïbes (ALC), et pour la zone OCDE étaient respectivement de 21.0 %, 22.9 % et 33.8 % en 2019.

Graphique 1.1. **Ratios impôts/PIB et total des recettes fiscales (hors cotisations de sécurité sociale) en pourcentage du PIB, 2019**

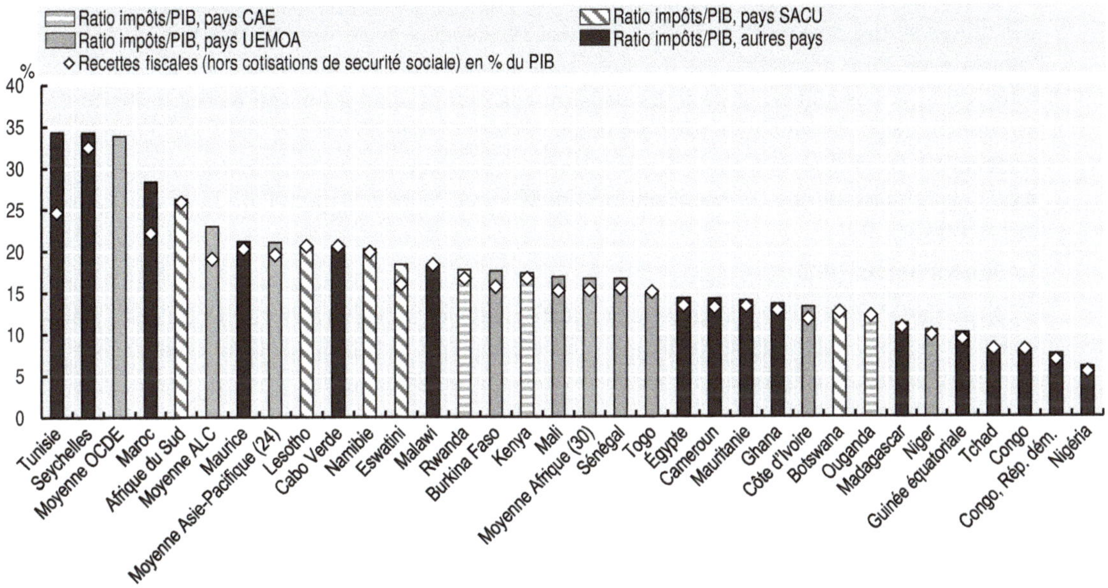

Notes : Les chiffres prennent en compte les recettes fiscales des administrations infranationales pour l'Afrique du Sud, l'Eswatini, le Maroc, Maurice, la Mauritanie et le Nigéria (recettes des États uniquement) pour l'année 2019.

La moyenne Afrique (30) et les moyennes Asie-Pacific (24 économies), ALC (26 pays) et OCDE (37 pays) sont des moyennes non pondérées. Il convient d'interpréter la moyenne Afrique (30) avec précaution, car des données relatives aux cotisations de sécurité sociale sont indisponibles pour la République du Congo, la République démocratique du Congo (avant 2012), Madagascar (avant 2011), l'Ouganda, le Tchad et le Togo, et elles sont incomplètes pour le Cameroun et le Sénégal. Les cotisations de sécurité sociale pour le Botswana, le Lesotho et le Malawi sont égales à zéro dans la mesure où elles ne remplissent pas les critères retenus pour être considérées comme des cotisations de sécurité sociale, selon la classification des impôts de l'OCDE figurant dans le Guide d'interprétation. Pour plus de précisions, se reporter aux tableaux par pays présentés dans le chapitre 5.

Le ratio impôts/PIB de l'Afrique du Sud prend en compte les sommes recouvrées par l'Afrique du Sud au profit de l'Union douanière de l'Afrique australe (SACU).

Source : Tableaux 4.1 et 4.2 figurant au chapitre 4 et (OCDE/CUA/ATAF, 2021[4]), « Statistiques des recettes publiques en Afrique : Tableaux comparatifs », *Statistiques fiscales de l'OCDE* (base de données), *https://doi.org/10.1787/7f54581d-fr*.

StatLink https://doi.org/10.1787/888934282132

En 2019, les ratios impôts/PIB ont affiché de grandes variations entre les pays couverts par la publication, allant de 6.0 % au Nigéria à 34.3 % aux Seychelles et en Tunisie. Les pays étudiés dans cette publication comptant les revenus par habitant les plus élevés, l'Afrique du Sud, le Maroc, les Seychelles et la Tunisie, affichaient chacun un ratio impôts/PIB supérieur à 28 %. Dans vingt deux pays, les ratios impôts/PIB étaient compris entre 10.0 % et 25.0 %, tandis que la République du Congo, la République démocratique du Congo, le Nigéria et le Tchad avaient un ratio inférieur à 10.0 %.

Encadré 1.1. **Méthodologie : le ratio impôts/PIB**

Les ratios fiscaux utilisés dans cette publication expriment les recettes fiscales totales en pourcentage du PIB. La valeur de ce ratio varie suivant son dénominateur (PIB) et son numérateur (recettes fiscales). Le numérateur et le dénominateur sont susceptibles de faire l'objet de révisions rétrospectives.

Encadré 1.1. **Méthodologie : le ratio impôts/PIB** *(suite)*

Le numérateur (recettes fiscales)

Cette publication utilise les chiffres des recettes qui sont transmis chaque année par les points de contact au sein des ministères des Finances, des administrations fiscales ou des offices statistiques nationaux. Les données rétrospectives sur les recettes fiscales font l'objet de révisions annuelles, des révisions plus importantes ayant lieu pour les années les plus récentes. Les chiffres antérieurs peuvent également changer d'une édition à l'autre lorsque de nouvelles données sont obtenues par des points de contact pour améliorer la publication. C'est par exemple le cas des Seychelles qui a pour la première fois dans cette édition communiqué des données relatives aux recettes collectées par les fonds de pensions des Seychelles.

Le dénominateur (PIB)

Les chiffres du PIB utilisés dans cette publication proviennent des *Perspectives de l'économie mondiale* publiées par le FMI. L'utilisation de ces chiffres du PIB garantit une cohérence maximale entre les pays, ainsi qu'une comparabilité internationale des ratios impôts/PIB. Les chiffres du PIB sont également révisés et actualisés pour tenir compte de l'amélioration des sources de données et des procédures d'estimation, ou pour appliquer de nouvelles lignes directrices convenues à l'échelle internationale pour mesurer la valeur du PIB.

Les chiffres les plus récents provenant des *Perspectives de l'économie mondiale* ont été publiés en avril 2021 (FMI, 2021[5]), et incluent les révisions du PIB effectuées par certains pays pour s'aligner sur l'édition la plus récente du Système de comptabilité nationale (SCN 2008). Dans cette édition, l'Afrique du Sud, la République du Congo, l'Ouganda, le Rwanda et le Togo ont redéfini la base de leurs données sur le PIB, ce qui a entraîné une baisse des ratios impôts/PIB dans ces pays et du ratio moyen des pays d'Afrique, par rapport à l'édition précédente des *Statistiques des recettes publiques en Afrique*. La différence entre les éditions 2020 et 2021 des ratios impôts/PIB de l'année 2018 variait de 0.1 p.p. en Ouganda à 4.8 p.p. au Togo ; la moyenne Afrique (30) pour 2018 est inférieure de 0.2 p.p. par rapport à celle de l'édition précédente.

La plupart des pays couverts par cette publication appartiennent à des organisations régionales dont les membres adoptent des règles communes en matière fiscale et douanière et forment une union douanière.

- Le ratio impôts/PIB moyen des trois pays de la Communauté d'Afrique de l'Est (CAE)[2] inclus dans cette publication s'élevait à 15.7 % en 2019, soit un niveau inférieur à la moyenne Afrique (30). En 2019, le ratio impôts/PIB dépassait 17.0 % au Kenya et au Rwanda, et atteignait 12.1 % en Ouganda.
- Le ratio impôts/PIB des six pays de l'Union économique et monétaire ouest-africaine (UEMOA)[3] inclus dans cette publication s'établissait en moyenne à 14.9 % en 2019. Les ratios variaient d'un pays membre à l'autre, de 10.4 % au Niger à 17.6 % au Burkina Faso. En 2015, l'UEMOA a fixé pour objectif à ses membres d'atteindre des ratios impôts/PIB d'au moins 20 % d'ici à la fin de l'année 2019 (Diallo, 2018[6]). Comme aucun des pays membres n'a atteint cet objectif, l'UEMOA a adopté un plan d'action en juin 2019 pour les aider à y parvenir. Les mesures prévoient, entre autres, l'amélioration et l'harmonisation des procédures de recouvrement de la TVA, des droits d'accises et des impôts directs, et une réduction de la concurrence fiscale entre les pays membres. Toutefois, compte tenu de la pandémie de COVID-19, l'UEMOA a pris la décision de suspendre l'objectif d'atteindre un ratio impôts/PIB de 20 %, ainsi que d'autres objectifs de convergence, de stabilité et de

croissance afin de donner aux États membres une plus grande flexibilité financière pour limiter les effets négatifs de la crise (FMI, 2021[7]).

- La moyenne des pays de l'Union douanière d'Afrique australe (SACU) était supérieure à la moyenne Afrique (30) et s'élevait à 19.6 % en 2019 (voir encadré 2.3 au chapitre 2). Les ratios impôts/PIB[4] dans les pays de la SACU variaient entre 12.6 % du PIB au Botswana et 26.2 % du PIB en Afrique du Sud. L'encadré 1.4 examine l'évolution des ratios impôts/PIB des pays de la SACU depuis 2010.

Variation des ratios impôts/PIB entre 2018 et 2019

Le ratio moyen impôts/PIB pour les pays d'Afrique a augmenté de 0.3 % du PIB entre 2018 et 2019, sous l'effet essentiellement d'une hausse des recettes tirées de l'impôt sur le revenu et les bénéfices (0.2 p.p.). Les ratios impôts/PIB ont augmenté dans 16 pays et diminué dans 14 autres pays. C'est en Guinée équatoriale (3.6 p.p.), au Mali (3.5 p.p.), en Tunisie (2.5 p.p.) et au Burkina Faso (1.1 p.p.) que les augmentations les plus marquées se sont produites entre 2018 et 2019. Tous les autres pays ont enregistré des hausses inférieures à 1 p.p. du PIB. Par comparaison, les baisses ont été relativement plus faibles : en 2019, la baisse la plus marquée a été observée en Mauritanie (-2.1 p.p.), et au Lesotho (-1.3 p.p.). Aucune autre baisse supérieure à 1 p.p. n'a été enregistrée.

Graphique 1.2. **Variation des ratios impôts/PIB entre 2018 et 2019 (points de pourcentage)**

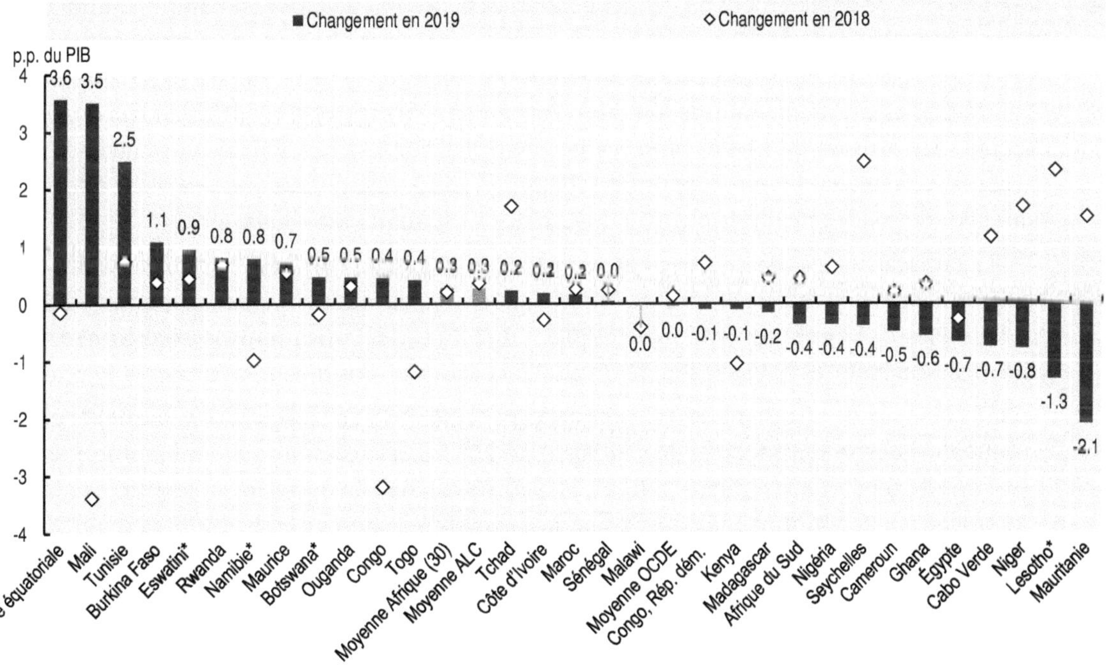

Notes : Les chiffres prennent en compte les recettes fiscales des administrations infranationales pour l'Afrique du Sud, l'Eswatini, le Maroc, Maurice, la Mauritanie et le Nigéria (recettes des États uniquement) pour l'année 2019.

*Au Botswana, en Eswatini, au Lesotho et en Namibie, l'année fiscale court du mois d'avril au mois de mars. Les chiffres de 2019 pour ces pays incluent donc les recettes perçues jusqu'au 31 mars 2020, au moment où la pandémie de COVID-19 s'est déclarée. Veuillez vous reporter aux notes des tableaux par pays au chapitre 5 pour plus d'informations.

La moyenne Afrique (30) et les moyennes ALC (26 pays) et OCDE (37 pays) sont des moyennes non pondérées.

Il convient d'interpréter l'évolution de la moyenne des pays d'Afrique (30) avec précaution, car des données relatives aux cotisations de sécurité sociale sont indisponibles ou incomplètes pour quelques pays. Pour plus de précisions, se reporter aux tableaux par pays présentés dans le chapitre 5.

Source : Calculs des auteurs basés sur des données figurant dans le tableau 4.1 du chapitre 4 et (OCDE/CUA/ATAF, 2021[4]), « Statistiques des recettes publiques en Afrique : Tableaux comparatifs », *Statistiques fiscales de l'OCDE* (base de données), *https://doi.org/10.1787/7f54581d-fr*.

StatLink https://doi.org/10.1787/888934282151

La forte hausse du ratio impôts/PIB observée en Guinée équatoriale entre 2018 et 2019 résulte essentiellement d'une augmentation de 3.3 p.p. des recettes fiscales tirées de l'impôt sur le revenu, dont la quasi-totalité provient d'une hausse des recettes fiscales provenant de l'impôt sur les bénéfices des sociétés pétrolières (3.2 p.p.). Cette augmentation est due à une forte hausse des recettes fiscales nominales (39 %) dans un contexte de baisse du PIB nominal (12 %) (graphique 1.4). Cette différence s'explique par le fait que les prix du pétrole se répercutent sur les recettes fiscales avec un décalage d'une année : la forte augmentation des recettes fiscales tirées de l'impôt sur les sociétés (IS) des compagnies pétrolières entre 2018 et 2019 est la conséquence d'une hausse de 17 USD des cours du baril de pétrole entre 2017 et 2018, ce qui a entraîné une rentabilité plus élevée des compagnies pétrolières en 2018. Le secteur pétrolier est le secteur d'activité le plus important en Guinée équatoriale. En 2019, il a généré environ 69 % des recettes fiscales du pays, et représenté 97 % de ses exportations[5]. En 2019, la Guinée équatoriale a connu une récession pour la 7e année consécutive, dont les effets ont surtout été ressentis par le secteur pétrolier (BAfD, 2021[8]), ce qui laisse présager une baisse possible de ces recettes en 2020.

Au Mali, le ratio impôt/PIB a augmenté de 3.5 p.p. entre 2018 et 2019, après avoir enregistré un recul d'une ampleur similaire (3.4 p.p.) entre 2017 et 2018. Face à la baisse intervenue en 2018, le Mali a pris des mesures destinées à consolider les recettes fiscales, notamment par une rationalisation des exonérations fiscales, le renforcement des contrôles et des vérifications, la dématérialisation des procédures des administrations fiscales et douanières, et le déploiement de la télédéclaration et des télépaiements (Banque mondiale, 2020[9]). Les recettes tirées de toutes les principales catégories d'impôts ont augmenté entre 2018 et 2019. Les recettes de TVA ont contribué à l'essentiel de cette hausse (à taux de TVA constant, elles ont augmenté de 1.4 p.p.). En parallèle, les autorités ont progressivement recouvré les arriérés de TVA et renforcé les contrôles sur les contribuables assujettis. Ces mesures, conjuguées à une économie robuste en 2019, ont permis aux recettes fiscales d'afficher de solides résultats en 2019 (FMI, 2020[10]), (Banque mondiale, 2020[9]).

La croissance des recettes fiscales enregistrée en Tunisie entre 2018 et 2019 résulte de l'augmentation des recettes tirées de l'impôt sur le revenu des personnes physiques (IRPP, 1.6 % du PIB), de l'impôt sur les bénéfices (0.6 % du PIB) et des cotisations de sécurité sociale (CSS, 0.5 % du PIB). Ces hausses sont le résultat de l'adoption des mesures fiscales suivantes :

- IRPP : les taux de l'IRPP ont été relevés (articles 41, 46 et 47 de la législation fiscale) et une nouvelle contribution sociale de solidarité de 1 % sur les revenus, a été instaurée. Elle a permis de générer 330 millions TND en 2019 (0.3 % du PIB). En outre, la hausse des salaires octroyée aux fonctionnaires après deux mouvements de grève a contribué à accroître les recettes tirées de l'IRPP.
- IS : la contribution sociale de solidarité perçue également sur les entreprises a rapporté 101 millions TND d'IS (0.1 % du PIB). L'élargissement de l'assiette par l'application du taux d'impôt sur les sociétés de 35 % à un éventail plus large d'entreprises (article 29 de la loi de finances 2018) a encore augmenté les recettes de l'IS en 2019.
- CSS : la réforme des fonds de pension intervenue en 2019 a débouché sur une augmentation des CSS au cours de cette année. La loi nº 2019-37 du 30 avril 2019 a relevé l'âge de la retraite ainsi que la part patronale de la cotisation de 2.0 p.p. Une hausse supplémentaire de la part salariale d'un p.p. est entrée en vigueur en janvier 2020[6].

Graphique 1.3. **Variations des ratios impôts/PIB (en points de pourcentage du PIB) observées entre 2018 et 2019 par principales rubriques d'impôts et par pays**

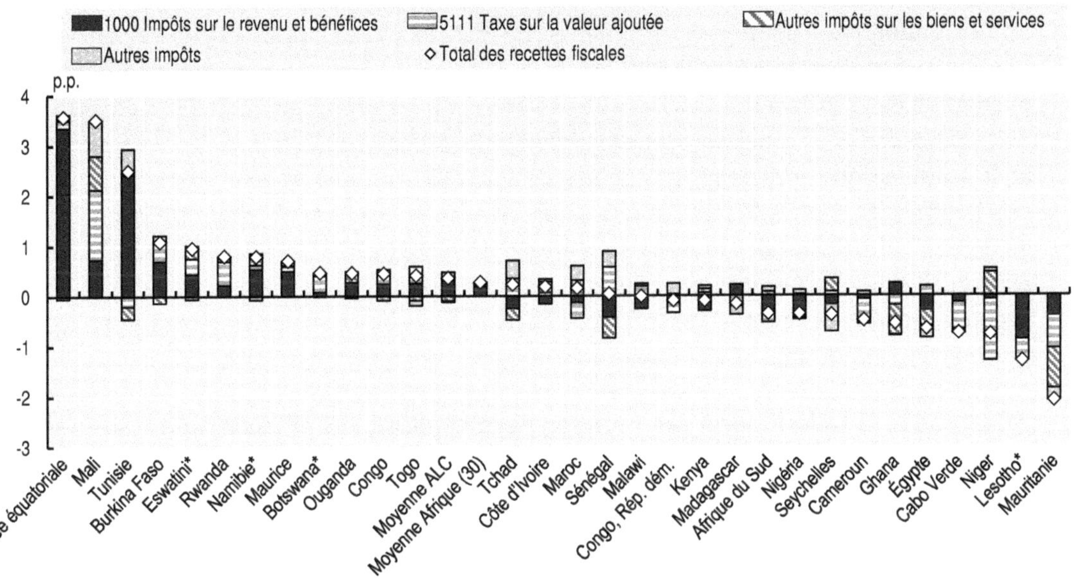

Notes : Les chiffres prennent en compte les recettes fiscales des administrations infranationales pour l'Afrique du Sud, l'Eswatini, le Maroc, Maurice, la Mauritanie et le Nigéria (recettes des États uniquement) pour l'année 2019.

*Au Botswana, en Eswatini, au Lesotho et en Namibie, l'année fiscale court du mois d'avril au mois de mars. Les chiffres de 2019 pour ces pays incluent donc les recettes perçues jusqu'au 31 mars 2020, au moment où la pandémie de COVID-19 s'est déclarée. Veuillez vous reporter aux notes des tableaux par pays au chapitre 5 pour plus d'informations.

La moyenne Afrique (30) et les moyennes ALC (26 pays) et OCDE (37 pays) sont des moyennes non pondérées.

Il convient d'interpréter la moyenne des pays d'Afrique (30) avec prudence, car les données relatives aux cotisations de sécurité sociale ne sont pas disponibles ou ne sont que partielles pour quelques pays. Pour plus de précisions, se reporter aux tableaux par pays présentés dans le chapitre 5.

Source : Calculs des auteurs basés sur des données figurant dans (OCDE/CUA/ATAF, 2021[4]), « Statistiques des recettes publiques en Afrique : Tableaux comparatifs », *Statistiques fiscales de l'OCDE* (base de données), *https://doi.org/10.1787/7f54581d-fr*.

StatLink *https://doi.org/10.1787/888934282170*

La Mauritanie et le Lesotho sont les deux pays d'Afrique qui ont accusé les plus fortes baisses de leur ratio impôts/PIB entre 2018 et 2019. Le ratio impôts/PIB a baissé de 2.1 p.p. en 2019 en Mauritanie et de 1.3 point au Lesotho.

- En Mauritanie, la baisse s'explique par une augmentation sensible du PIB nominal (16 %), tandis que la hausse des recettes fiscales a été plus faible (0.6 %) entre 2018 et 2019 (graphique 1.4). L'augmentation du PIB nominal est due au redémarrage de l'activité des industries extractives en 2019, principalement dans le secteur minier (minerai de fer et or). Cette reprise ne s'est pas accompagnée d'une forte croissance des recettes fiscales, car en Mauritanie, la perception des recettes auprès du secteur minier se fait principalement par l'intermédiaire d'instruments non fiscaux (redevances, dividendes issus de la participation de l'État) (EITI, 2021[11]), et dans une bien moindre mesure par la fiscalité (principalement les impôts de la Société nationale industrielle et minière (SNIM) qui représentaient 3 % des recettes fiscales en 2019). En outre, en 2019, les taxes sur les biens et services ont généré moins de recettes qu'en 2018, notamment la TVA sur les importations, les recettes tirées de la taxe sur les produits pétroliers et les recettes tirées des taxes sur la consommation de thé, de tabac, de sucre et de ciment) (Banque centrale de Mauritanie, 2019[12]). Cela a entraîné une baisse des recettes de TVA de 0.7 p.p. et d'autres taxes sur les biens et services de 0.8 p.p.
- La baisse enregistrée par le Lesotho s'explique principalement par une diminution des recettes tirées des impôts sur le revenu (0.9 p.p.) et des recettes de TVA (0.4 p.p.). Ces baisses sont dues au ralentissement économique de 2019/2020, aux mauvaises performances du

secteur minier en raison de la contraction de la demande extérieure, à la faible croissance de l'emploi et à l'augmentation d'un crédit d'impôt au titre de l'IRPP (Lesotho Times, 2020[13]).

Le graphique 1.4 montre l'augmentation des recettes fiscales et du PIB en valeur nominale entre 2018 et 2019. Comme on l'a vu, 16 pays africains ont vu leur ratio impôts/PIB augmenter en 2019 par rapport à 2018. Dans 13 de ces pays, la croissance du PIB a été positive, mais moins forte que celle des recettes fiscales. La République du Congo, la Guinée équatoriale et la Namibie ont enregistré une baisse de leur PIB nominal et une augmentation des recettes fiscales. Sur les 14 pays africains qui ont enregistré un recul de leur ratio impôts/PIB en 2019, 12 affichaient des niveaux plus élevés de recettes fiscales en valeur nominale par rapport à l'année précédente, mais la hausse des recettes fiscales nominales était inférieure à la croissance du PIB nominal. Deux pays (le Niger et le Lesotho) ont enregistré une croissance positive du PIB nominal et une croissance négative des recettes fiscales.

Graphique 1.4. **Variations des recettes fiscales et du PIB en monnaie nominale, 2018-19**

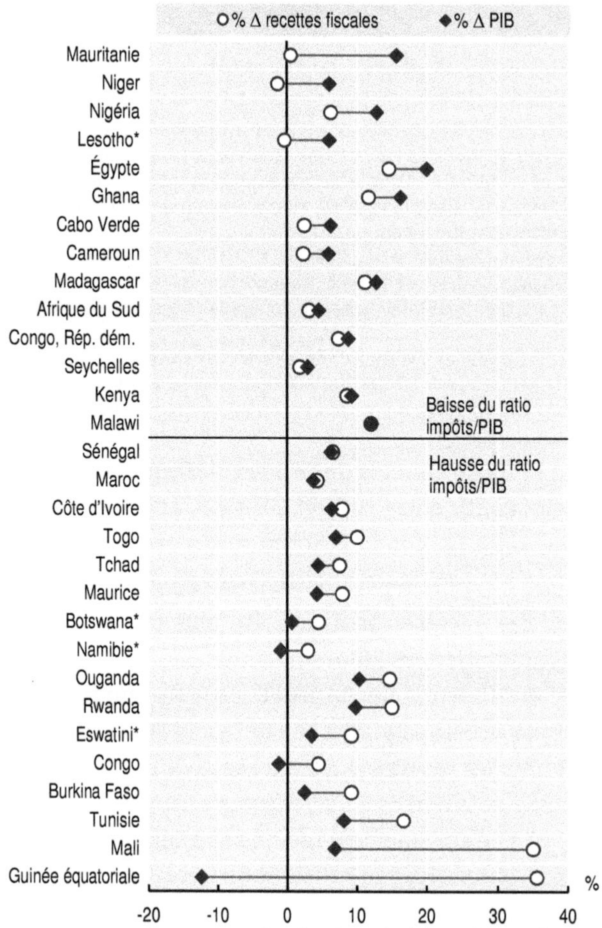

Notes : Les chiffres prennent en compte les recettes fiscales des administrations infranationales pour l'Afrique du Sud, l'Eswatini, le Maroc, Maurice, la Mauritanie et le Nigéria (recettes des États uniquement) pour l'année 2019.

*Au Botswana, en Eswatini, au Lesotho et en Namibie, l'année fiscale court du mois d'avril au mois de mars. Les chiffres de 2019 pour ces pays incluent donc les recettes perçues jusqu'au 31 mars 2020, au moment où la pandémie de COVID-19 s'est déclarée. Veuillez vous reporter aux notes des tableaux par pays au chapitre 5 pour plus d'informations.

Source : Calculs des auteurs basés sur des données figurant dans (OCDE/CUA/ATAF, 2021[4]), « Statistiques des recettes publiques en Afrique : Tableaux comparatifs », *Statistiques fiscales de l'OCDE* (base de données), *https://doi.org/10.1787/7f54581d-fr*.

StatLink https://doi.org/10.1787/888934282189

Évolution des ratios impôts/PIB depuis 2010

En 2019, le ratio impôts/PIB dans les 30 pays d'Afrique était supérieur de 1.8 point à son niveau de 2010. Par comparaison, les moyennes de la région ALC et de l'OCDE ont augmenté de respectivement 1.9 et 2.0 points entre 2010 et 2019. Le ratio moyen impôts/PIB des 30 pays africains a progressé régulièrement entre 2010 et 2014, avec une forte hausse de 0.7 point en 2011, traduisant une reprise après la crise financière mondiale. Entre 2014 et 2017, la moyenne est restée relativement stable, se situant entre 16.0 % et 16.1 % du PIB (graphique 1.5), et a augmenté de 0.5 p.p. entre 2017 et 2019.

Graphique 1.5. **Ratios moyens impôts/PIB pour l'Afrique (30), l'ALC et l'OCDE, 2000-19**

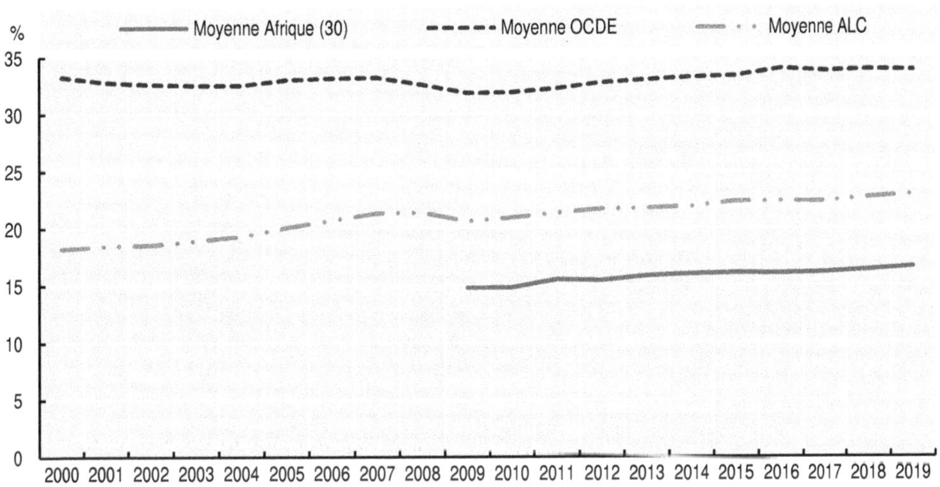

Note : Il convient d'interpréter la moyenne Afrique (30) avec prudence, car les données relatives aux cotisations de sécurité sociale ne sont pas disponibles ou ne sont que partielles pour quelques pays. Pour plus de précisions, se reporter aux tableaux par pays présentés dans le chapitre 5.
Les chiffres prennent en compte les recettes fiscales des administrations infranationales pour l'Afrique du Sud, l'Eswatini, le Maroc, Maurice, la Mauritanie et le Nigéria (recettes des États uniquement) pour la période 2002-2019.
La moyenne Afrique (30) est une estimation pour 2009, car les données ne sont pas disponibles pour le Nigéria et le Tchad. On ne dispose pas d'estimation antérieure à 2009 faute de données relatives à certains pays.
La moyenne Afrique (30) et les moyennes ALC (26 pays) et OCDE (37 pays) sont des moyennes non pondérées.
Source : Tableau 4.1 du chapitre 4 et (OCDE/CUA/ATAF, 2021[4]), « Statistiques des recettes publiques en Afrique : Tableaux comparatifs », *Statistiques fiscales de l'OCDE* (base de données), https://doi.org/10.1787/7f54581d-fr.

StatLink https://doi.org/10.1787/888934282208

Encadré 1.2. **Répartition des ratios impôts/PIB en fonction du niveau de revenu des pays**

Les besoins de financement des pays sont fonction en partie de leur niveau de revenu, ce qui constitue un élément important à prendre en compte pour comprendre les ratios impôts/PIB dans les différents pays. Par exemple, les pays à faible niveau de revenu sont confrontés aux plus grandes difficultés en matière de financement, et la mobilisation des recettes est, en ce qui les concerne, particulièrement importante pour se procurer les ressources dont ils ont besoin pour améliorer les conditions de vie de leurs populations (Gaspar et al., 2019[14]). Si l'on répartit les 30 pays étudiés dans cette publication selon la classification de la Banque mondiale fondée sur le revenu des pays (Banque mondiale, 2021[15]), il est possible de comparer les systèmes fiscaux de pays ayant des niveaux de revenu similaires. Le graphique 1.6 montre la répartition

Encadré 1.2. **Répartition des ratios impôts/PIB en fonction du niveau de revenu des pays** *(suite)*

des ratios impôts/PIB pour trois catégories de revenu en 2019 : les pays à faible revenu, les pays à revenu intermédiaire de la tranche inférieure, ainsi que les pays à revenu intermédiaire de la tranche supérieure et les pays à revenu élevé qui forment une seule catégorie.

Graphique 1.6. **Ratios impôts/PIB par groupes de revenu, 2019**

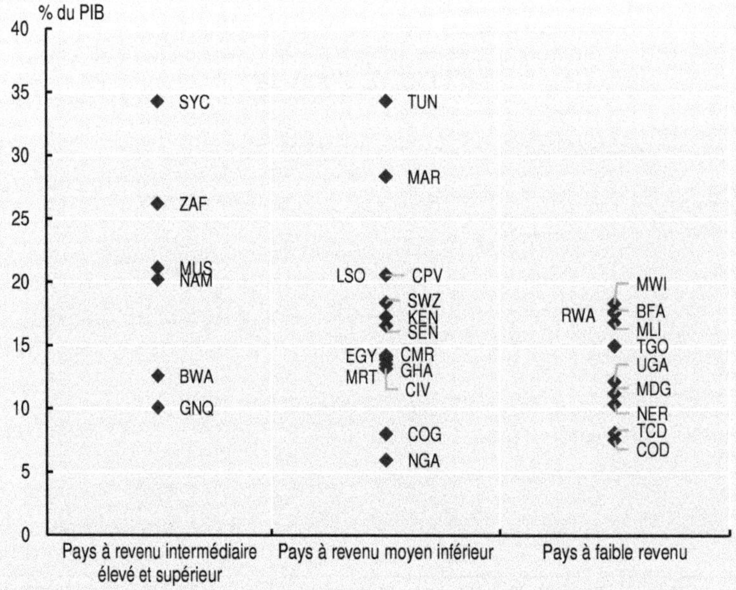

Note : Les chiffres prennent en compte les recettes fiscales des administrations infranationales pour l'Afrique du Sud, l'Eswatini, le Maroc, Maurice, la Mauritanie et le Nigéria (recettes des États uniquement) pour l'année 2019.

Source : Calculs des auteurs basés sur des données figurant dans (OCDE/CUA/ATAF, 2021[4]), « Statistiques des recettes publiques en Afrique : Tableaux comparatifs », *Statistiques fiscales de l'OCDE* (base de données), *https://doi.org/10.1787/7f54581d-fr*. Classification des pays de la Banque mondiale en fonction de leurs revenus (Banque mondiale, 2021[15]).

StatLink https://doi.org/10.1787/888934282227

En 2019, 24 des 30 pays africains figurant dans cette publication étaient classés parmi les pays à faible revenu ou à revenu intermédiaire de la tranche inférieure, dont 10 dans la catégorie des pays à faible revenu. Cette catégorie de pays présente la dispersion la plus faible par rapport aux pays à revenu élevé ; et tous les pays à faible revenu ont enregistré un ratio impôts/PIB inférieur à 20 %. Au sein de cette catégorie, les ratios impôts/PIB variaient de 7.5 % du PIB en République démocratique du Congo à 18.3 % au Malawi, avec une moyenne de 13.5 % en 2019. Dans six des dix pays, les ratios impôts/PIB étaient inférieurs à 16 % en 2019, niveau que le FMI considère comme trop faible pour que les pays à faible revenu puissent financer les dépenses supplémentaires nécessaires pour atteindre les ODD (Gaspar et al., 2019[14]).

Pour les 14 pays à revenu intermédiaire de la tranche inférieure, le ratio moyen impôts/PIB s'élevait à 17.1 % du PIB en 2019. Si ce groupe présente la dispersion la plus forte des ratios impôts/PIB, y compris les ratios impôts/PIB le plus élevé (Tunisie) et le plus faible (Nigéria), 12 d'entre eux affichaient des ratios impôts/PIB proches de 20 % ou inférieurs à ce niveau. Au sein de cette catégorie, le Maroc et la Tunisie se distinguent avec un ratio impôt/PIB supérieur à 28 %. Dans les pays à revenu élevé et à revenu intermédiaire de la tranche supérieure, les recettes fiscales en pourcentage du PIB varient considérablement, de 10.1 % en Guinée équatoriale à 34.3 % pour les Seychelles, avec une moyenne à 20.7 % du PIB.

Encadré 1.2. **Répartition des ratios impôts/PIB en fonction du niveau de revenu des pays** *(suite)*

La moyenne Afrique (30) a augmenté de 1.8 p.p. au cours de la dernière décennie, et les trois groupes ont accru leurs recettes fiscales entre 2010 et 2019. Les augmentations enregistrées entre 2010 et 2019 ont été d'une ampleur similaire. Les pays à revenu intermédiaire de la tranche inférieure étudiés dans les *Statistiques des recettes publiques en Afrique* ont enregistré l'augmentation la plus forte en moyenne (1.9 p.p.) entre 2010 et 2019, suivis des pays à faible revenu (1.7 p.p.), tandis que le groupe des pays à revenu intermédiaire de la tranche supérieure et à revenu élevé a connu une augmentation de 1.6 p.p. en moyenne sur la même période. Dans tous les pays, indépendamment de la catégorie de revenu à laquelle ils appartiennent, l'augmentation des ratios impôts/PIB au cours de la dernière décennie a été inférieure à 5 p.p. en moyenne, un niveau considéré par le FMI – avant la pandémie de COVID-19 – comme un objectif « ambitieux et approprié », nécessaire à de nombreux pays pour atteindre les ODD (Gaspar et al., 2019[14]). Il s'agit d'un objectif ambitieux pour les pays africains, si l'on tient compte des résultats obtenus au cours de la décennie précédente et des conséquences de la pandémie de COVID-19.

Les recettes moyennes de TVA des 30 pays d'Afrique ont le plus contribué à l'augmentation du ratio moyen impôts/PIB de la moyenne Afrique (30), avec une hausse de 1.0 p.p. pour s'établir à 4.9 % du PIB en 2019. La plus forte hausse annuelle des recettes de TVA en pourcentage du PIB s'est produite entre 2012 et 2013 (0.4 % du PIB) après l'introduction de la TVA en 2012 en République démocratique du Congo et en Eswatini. La légère augmentation du taux normal moyen de TVA, qui est passé de 15.9 % en 2010 à 16.1 % en 2019, pourrait aussi avoir contribué à la croissance des recettes moyennes de TVA en pourcentage du PIB sur la même période.

Les impôts sur le revenu et les bénéfices étaient le deuxième principal moteur de l'augmentation du ratio moyen impôts/PIB des pays d'Afrique (30) entre 2010 et 2019, en hausse de 0.6 p.p. pour atteindre 6.3 % du PIB en 2019. Après avoir culminé en 2013 à 6.4 % du PIB, ils ont cependant diminué jusqu'en 2017. Cette baisse est entièrement due aux recettes de l'IS qui ont diminué de 0.5 p.p. sur la période. La baisse des cours du pétrole et des produits miniers entre 2013 et 2016 pourrait avoir contribué à cette diminution. Les impôts sur le revenu et les bénéfices ont de nouveau augmenté en 2018 et 2019. En revanche, au sein de cette catégorie, l'IRPP a progressé régulièrement entre 2010 et 2019, passant de 2.4 % du PIB en 2010 à 3.2 % en 2019, ce qui représente une hausse de 0.8 p.p., sous l'effet de la progression des revenus et d'une imposition plus efficace des particuliers fortunés dans les pays d'Afrique subsaharienne (Moore, Prichard et Fjeldstad, 2018[16]). Il en résulte une évolution de la répartition moyenne des impôts sur le revenu et les bénéfices au cours de la période, avec une part plus importante de l'IRPP. En 2019, les recettes tirées de l'IRPP représentaient 51 % du total des recettes de l'impôt sur le revenu et les bénéfices, contre 42 % en 2010.

Les recettes moyennes provenant des autres taxes sur les biens et services (c'est-à-dire hors TVA), soit l'équivalent de 3.6 % du PIB en 2019, ont légèrement diminué en pourcentage du PIB depuis 2010, en partie en raison de la baisse des recettes provenant des taxes sur les échanges. Cette diminution est associée à la libéralisation des échanges à l'échelle du continent, qui s'est traduite par l'abaissement des droits à l'importation, le rétrécissement de l'assiette des produits et services soumis à des droits d'accise et l'élimination des taxes sur les exportations. Les droits de douane seront de nouveau réduits dans le cadre de la Zone de libre-échange continentale africaine (ZLECAf) (OCDE/CUA/ATAF, 2020[17]).

Les moteurs du changement dans les pays d'Amérique latine et des Caraïbes sont similaires à ceux constatés en Afrique au cours de la même période. À l'instar de la moyenne Afrique (30), les recettes de TVA ont le plus contribué à l'accroissement du ratio moyen impôts/PIB des pays ALC entre 2010 et 2019, puisqu'elles ont progressé de 0.8 p.p. Les hausses des recettes provenant des cotisations de sécurité sociale et des impôts sur le revenu et les bénéfices (0.6 p.p. dans les deux cas) ont également favorisé l'augmentation globale du ratio moyen impôts/PIB de la région ALC. Les niveaux de CSS en pourcentage du PIB diffèrent nettement entre les deux régions : en 2019, les recettes provenant des CSS s'établissaient à 3.9 % du PIB dans la région ALC, contre 1.4 % en moyenne pour les pays d'Afrique (30).

Graphique 1.7. **Recettes tirées des impôts sur le revenu et les bénéfices, de la TVA et d'autres catégories d'impôt, en pourcentage du PIB, 2010-19**

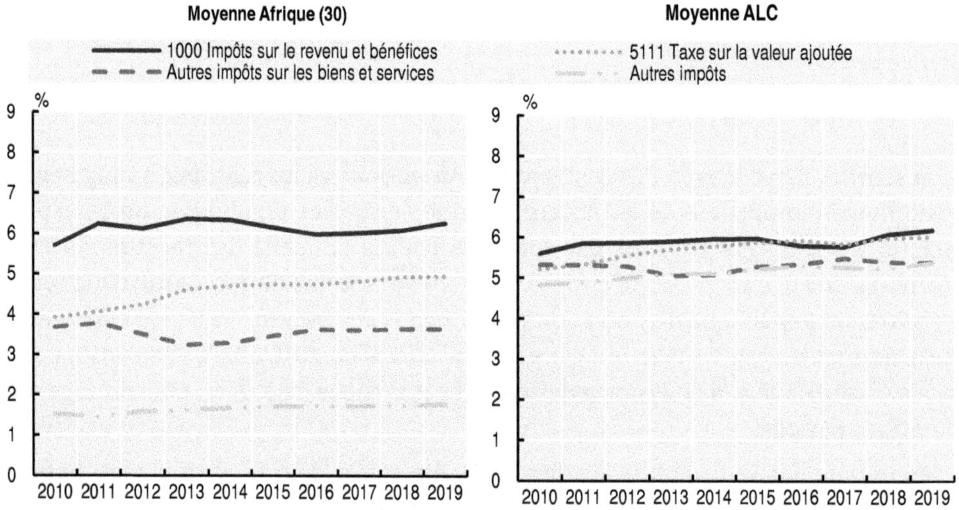

Note : Les chiffres prennent en compte les recettes fiscales des administrations infranationales pour l'Afrique du Sud, l'Eswatini, le Maroc, Maurice, la Mauritanie et le Nigéria (recettes des États uniquement) pour la période 2002-2019.
Source : Calculs des auteurs basés sur (OCDE/CUA/ATAF, 2021[4]), « Statistiques des recettes publiques en Afrique : Tableaux comparatifs », *Statistiques fiscales de l'OCDE* (base de données), *https://doi.org/10.1787/7f54581d-fr*.
StatLink *https://doi.org/10.1787/888934282246*

Les ratios impôts/PIB ont augmenté dans 24 pays entre 2010 et 2019 et ont diminué dans six. Le Rwanda et la Tunisie ont enregistré les plus fortes hausses, respectivement 5.4 et 7.1 p.p., alors que c'est au Tchad que la baisse a été la plus prononcée (6.5 p.p.) (graphique 1.8).

L'augmentation du ratio impôts/PIB de la Tunisie entre 2010 et 2019 s'explique essentiellement par la hausse des recettes provenant de l'IRPP (3.4 p.p.) et des CSS (2.4 p.p.). Au cours de cette période, la Tunisie a entrepris d'importantes réformes de son système fiscal et de son administration fiscale afin de mobiliser des recettes fiscales (voir encadré 1.3).

L'augmentation du ratio impôts/PIB du Rwanda entre 2010 et 2019 s'explique essentiellement par la hausse des recettes provenant des impôts sur le revenu et les bénéfices (2.5 p.p.) et de la TVA (1.9 p.p.). Depuis 2010, les recettes fiscales ont régulièrement augmenté au Rwanda, de 0.6 p.p. par an en moyenne, sous l'effet d'importantes réformes de la politique et de l'administration fiscales visant à compenser la baisse des recettes provenant de l'aide extérieure et des taxes sur les échanges[7]. Les changements administratifs portent notamment sur la dématérialisation des outils destinés aux contribuables, la modernisation des procédures de recouvrement et de contrôle, et un meilleur recouvrement des arriérés de TVA. S'agissant de la politique fiscale, le Rwanda a élargi l'assiette de l'IRPP, instauré des retenues à la source (TVA et impôts sur le revenu), supprimé les exonérations fiscales, et relevé les taux de plusieurs droits d'accise et droits à l'importation au cours de la période considérée. Ces réformes se sont traduites par une amélioration de la discipline fiscale, notamment en ce qui concerne la TVA, et par une augmentation significative des recettes fiscales dans les principales catégories d'impôts (Akitoby et al., 2019[18]), (PwC, 2019[19]) (FMI, 2020[20]). Plus récemment, le Rwanda a adopté en 2018 une nouvelle loi relative à l'impôt sur le revenu qui a levé les ambiguïtés et élargi l'assiette de l'impôt (Economist Intelligence, 2018[21]), et contribué à accroître les recettes de l'impôt sur le revenu de 0.7 p.p. entre 2017 et 2019.

Graphique 1.8. **Variations des ratios impôts/PIB entre 2010 et 2019 (points de pourcentage)**

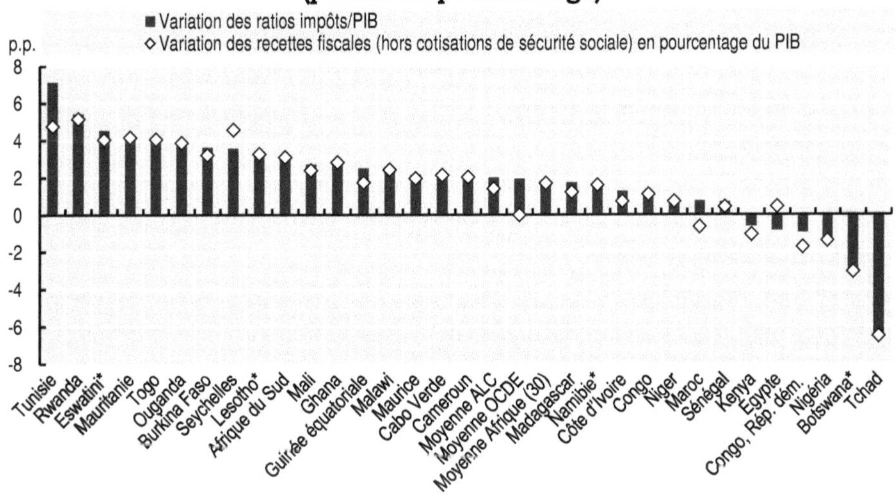

Notes : Les chiffres prennent en compte les recettes fiscales des administrations infranationales pour l'Afrique du Sud, l'Eswatini, le Maroc, Maurice, la Mauritanie et le Nigéria (recettes des États uniquement) pour l'année 2019.

*Au Botswana, en Eswatini, au Lesotho et en Namibie, l'année fiscale court du mois d'avril au mois de mars. Les chiffres de 2019 pour ces pays incluent donc les recettes perçues jusqu'au 31 mars 2020, au moment où la pandémie de COVID-19 s'est déclarée. Veuillez vous reporter aux notes des tableaux par pays au chapitre 5 pour plus d'informations.

La moyenne Afrique (30) et les moyennes ALC (26 pays d'Amérique latine et Caraïbes) et OCDE (37 pays) sont des moyennes non pondérées.

Source : Tableaux 4.1 et 4.2 figurant au chapitre 4 et (OCDE/CUA/ATAF, 2021[4]), « Statistiques des recettes publiques en Afrique : Tableaux comparatifs », *Statistiques fiscales de l'OCDE* (base de données), *https://doi.org/10.1787/7f54581d-fr*.

StatLink https://doi.org/10.1787/888934282265

Encadré 1.3. **Réformes fiscales en Tunisie, 2010-2019**

Depuis 2010, la Tunisie a connu la plus forte croissance des ratios impôts/PIB de tous les pays africains inclus dans la publication *Statistiques des recettes publiques en Afrique*. Le ratio Impôts/PIB a augmenté de 7.1 p.p. entre 2010 et 2019 passant de 27.2 % en 2010 à 34.3 % en 2019. Cette augmentation est principalement attribuable à la hausse des recettes de l'IRPP (3.4 p.p.), des CSS (2.4 p.p.) et de la TVA (0.8 p.p.) au cours de cette période. La forte augmentation de la masse salariale (147 %) entre 2010 et 2019 – suite aux pressions syndicales après la révolution qui ont entrainé des augmentations successives des salaires – a contribué à la hausse des recettes de l'IRPP et des CSS au cours de la période. De vastes réformes de la fiscalité et de l'administration fiscale adoptées par la Tunisie depuis 2010 ont aussi favorisé la hausse de ces recettes entre 2010 et 2019 ainsi que des recettes de la TVA. Plusieurs axes de réformes ont été engagés durant la dernière décennie. Ces axes sont classés comme suit :

Encadré 1.3. **Réformes fiscales en Tunisie, 2010-2019** *(suite)*

L'élargissement de l'assiette imposable :

- Imposition des revenus distribués et des revenus réalisés des jeux de pari, de hasard et de loterie par voie de retenue à la source libératoire. (Lois de Finances 2016 et 2018)
- Élargissement du champ d'application de l'impôt fixé à 35 % (des assurances mutuelles, des fonds des adhérents, des grandes surfaces commerciales, des concessionnaires automobiles, des franchisés d'une marque ou d'une enseigne commerciale étrangère). (Lois de Finances 2018,2019 et 2020)
- Élargissement de l'assiette de la TVA par la suppression de l'exonération de nombreux produits, services et entreprises publiques. (Lois de Finances 2016 et 2017)

La révision des taux d'imposition :

- Révision du barème de l'impôt sur le revenu des personnes physiques par l'élargissement de la 1ère tranche exonérée de TND 1 500 à TND 5 000 et la révision des autres tranches du barème. (Loi de Finances 2017)
- Suppression des différents taux d'impôt sur les sociétés (20 %, 25 %) et instauration d'un seul taux général fixé à 15 %. (Loi de Finances 2021)
- Relèvement des taux de la TVA en 2018 d'un point de pourcentage de 18 % à 19 % pour le taux normal, de 6 % à 7 % pour le taux réduit et de 12 % à 13 % pour le taux intermédiaire. (Loi de Finances 2018)

La rationalisation des avantages fiscaux

- Suppression de plusieurs avantages fiscaux et orientation des dits avantages vers les priorités nationales à savoir le développement régional, l'agriculture, les nouveaux promoteurs, les diplômés de l'enseignement supérieur. (Loi de Finances 2017)
- Suppression du régime fiscal préférentiel de l'exportation et des prestataires des services financiers non-résidents, et ce pour assurer la convergence des régimes fiscaux des sociétés on-shore et off-shore. (Loi de Finances 2017)

Autres

- Promulgation d'un cadre juridique pour lutter contre l'érosion de l'assiette fiscale et le transfert des bénéfices par les prix de transfert conformément aux normes internationales applicables dans ce domaine (programme BEPS qui porte sur l'érosion de la base d'imposition et le transfert de bénéfices). (Loi de Finances 2019)
- Création la Brigade des investigations et de la lutte contre l'évasion fiscale (BILEF). (Loi de Finances 2017)
- La levée du secret bancaire.

L'administration fiscale continue à se transformer pour accroitre la mobilisation des recettes fiscales dans le future et un de ses objectifs est l'amélioration des capacités de l'État à collecter les recettes. Pour atteindre cet objectif, des actions ont été mises en vigueur visant l'amélioration du recouvrement par la promotion de la digitalisation de l'administration fiscale ainsi que l'élargissement de l'assiette fiscale, la lutte contre la fraude et l'évasion fiscale. Ces actions comprennent l'élargissement de l'échange électronique des renseignements entre l'administration fiscale et les citoyens, la mise en œuvre de la facture électronique et de l'enregistrement à distance, l 'amélioration de la gestion du régime forfaitaire, l'élargissement du champ d'application de la TVA et la suppression progressive du régime suspensif de la TVA.

Source : Ministère des Finances de la Tunisie.

Au Tchad, les recettes fiscales en pourcentage du PIB ont sensiblement diminué entre 2010 et 2019 (6.5 p.p.) en raison d'une baisse des recettes de l'IS de 8 p.p. sur la même période. Le pays étant une économie pétrolière, les fluctuations des cours du pétrole ont un impact direct, à la hausse comme à la baisse, sur ses recettes fiscales (Banque mondiale, 2018[22]). Compte tenu des difficultés rencontrées par le Tchad pour mobiliser des recettes fiscales provenant d'autres sources, la Banque mondiale lui a accordé en 2018 un soutien financier pour l'aider à améliorer la mobilisation de ses recettes en renforçant son administration fiscale et en développant des outils de suivi. Par exemple, le ministère du Pétrole verra sa capacité à superviser les opérateurs pétroliers renforcée, et se dotera d'un cadastre pétrolier ainsi que d'un système de gestion des contrats (Banque mondiale, 2018[22]).

Graphique 1.9. **Variations des ratios impôts/PIB par principales rubriques d'impôt entre 2010 et 2019 et par pays (points de pourcentage)**

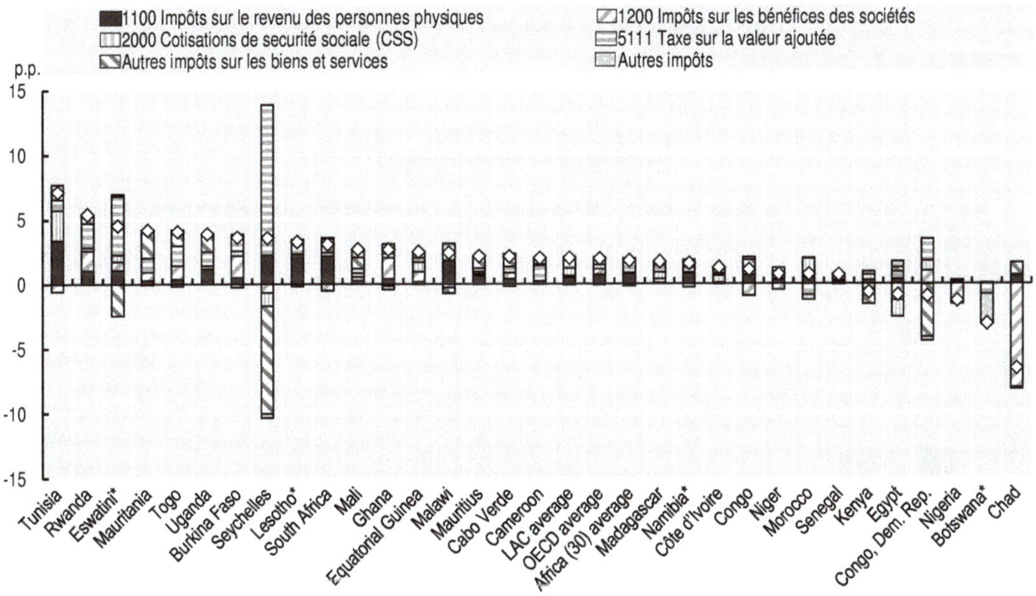

Notes : Les chiffres prennent en compte les recettes fiscales des administrations infranationales pour l'Afrique du Sud, l'Eswatini, le Maroc, Maurice, la Mauritanie et le Nigéria (recettes des États uniquement) pour l'année 2019.
*Au Botswana, en Eswatini, au Lesotho et en Namibie, l'année fiscale court du mois d'avril au mois de mars. Les chiffres de 2019 pour ces pays incluent donc les recettes perçues jusqu'au 31 mars 2020, au début de la pandémie de COVID-19. Veuillez vous reporter aux notes des tableaux par pays au chapitre 5 pour plus d'informations.
La moyenne Afrique (30) et les moyennes ALC (26 pays) et OCDE (37 pays) sont des moyennes non pondérées.
Source : Calculs des auteurs basés sur (OCDE/CUA/ATAF, 2021[4]), « Statistiques des recettes publiques en Afrique : Tableaux comparatifs », *Statistiques fiscales de l'OCDE* (base de données), *https://doi.org/10.1787/7f54581d-fr*.
StatLink https://doi.org/10.1787/888934282284

Encadré 1.4. **Variations des ratios impôts/PIB dans les pays membres de la SACU**

Cinq des 30 pays inclus dans cette publication font partie de l'Union douanière d'Afrique australe (SACU) : Afrique du Sud, Botswana, Eswatini, Lesotho et Namibie. La SACU a été fondée en 1910, ce qui en fait l'union douanière la plus ancienne au monde (SACU, 2020[23]). Les cinq pays membres de la SACU sont liés par un accord de partage des recettes qui prévoit l'application de tarifs extérieurs communs et une répartition des droits de douane et d'accise perçus par les pays membres. Dans la présente publication, les recettes issues des droits de douane et d'accise sont incluses dans les recettes fiscales du pays de la SACU qui les a collectées (Afrique du Sud), et les montants redistribués par le fonds commun des recettes de la SACU sont classés dans les tableaux des recettes non fiscales, sous la rubrique des recettes diverses pour le Botswana, l'Eswatini, le Lesotho, et la Namibie (voir encadré 2.3 au chapitre 2).

En 2019, la moyenne des pays de la SACU (la moyenne SACU) était supérieure d'environ 3 p.p. à celle de l'Afrique (30) et s'élevait à 19.6 %. L'évolution du ratio impôts/PIB entre 2010 et 2019 dans les pays de la SACU a été, en moyenne, similaire à celle de la moyenne de l'Afrique (30) au cours de la même période. Alors que

Encadré 1.4. **Variations des ratios impôts/PIB dans les pays membres de la SACU** *(suite)*

le ratio moyen impôts/PIB de l'Afrique (30) a progressé de 14.8 % du PIB en 2010 à 16.6 % en 2019, la moyenne SACU est passée de 17.7 % du PIB en 2010 à 19.6 % en 2019.

Les recettes de TVA ont été le principal moteur de la progression des deux moyennes au cours de cette période, avec une augmentation de 1.0 p.p. de la moyenne Afrique (30) et de 1.1 p.p. en ce qui concerne la moyenne des pays de la SACU. L'Afrique du Sud, l'Eswatini, le Lesotho et la Namibie ont enregistré une hausse de leur ratio impôts/PIB comprise entre 1.6 p.p. (Namibie) et 4.5 p.p. (Eswatini), tandis que le Botswana a vu son ratio baisser de 3.1 p.p. au cours de la période, sous l'effet d'un repli des recettes tirées de l'impôt sur le revenu (2.3 p.p.) et de la TVA (0.9 p.p.).

Graphique 1.10. **Variation des ratios impôts/PIB par catégories d'impôts dans les pays de la SACU, 2010 à 2019**

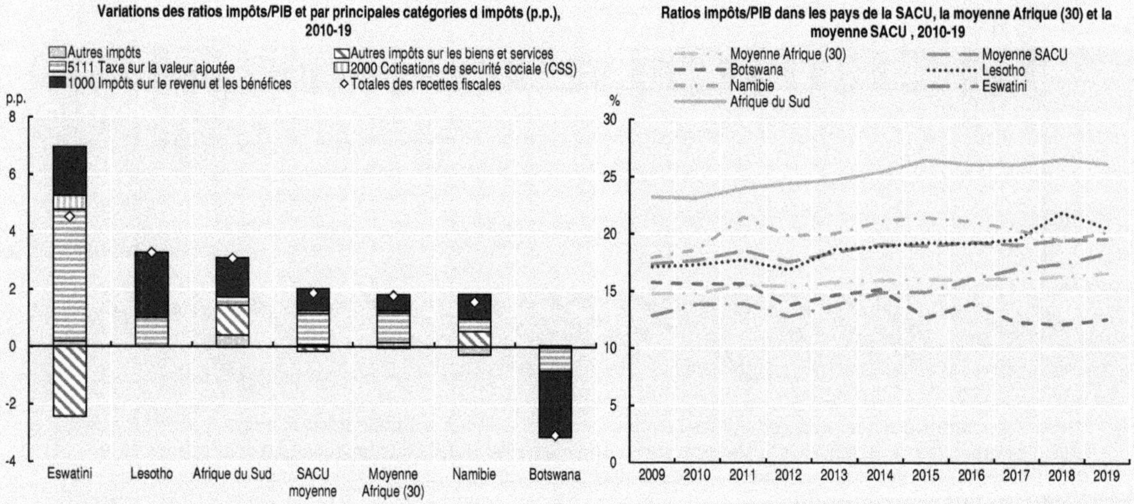

Source : Calculs des auteurs basés sur (OCDE/CUA/ATAF, 2021$_{[4]}$), « Statistiques des recettes publiques en Afrique : Tableaux comparatifs », *Statistiques fiscales de l'OCDE* (base de données), *https://doi.org/10.1787/7f54581d-fr*.

StatLink https://doi.org/10.1787/888934282303

Facteurs ayant un effet sur les ratios impôts/PIB

Les ratios impôts/PIB sont influencés par divers facteurs de portée nationale et internationale. Sur le plan national, il s'agit entre autres des caractéristiques macroéconomiques telles que la diversification d'une économie, l'importance de l'agriculture, les dotations en ressources, l'ouverture aux échanges et la taille de l'économie informelle. L'évolution de la situation politique des pays, telles que les troubles sociaux, de niveau de corruption, peut également influer sur les ratios impôts/PIB. La capacité des administrations fiscales et le civisme fiscal (le consentement à l'impôt) sont aussi étroitement liés au niveau des recettes fiscales (OCDE, 2015$_{[24]}$), (OCDE, 2019$_{[25]}$). L'emplacement géographique peut exercer une influence sur les ratios impôts/PIB: par exemple, les pays enclavés peuvent plus difficilement taxer les biens et services au port d'entrée que les pays ayant un accès à la mer. Enfin, des facteurs internationaux, y compris les politiques fiscales d'autres pays, peuvent se répercuter sur les ratios impôts/PIB.

Les ratios impôts/PIB sont généralement supérieurs dans les pays à haut revenu : en général, les pays de l'OCDE collectent des recettes fiscales plus importantes que les pays hors OCDE, en pourcentage du PIB. La plupart des pays couverts dans cette publication affichent des niveaux de revenu par habitant et des ratios impôts/PIB plus bas que les pays de l'OCDE et de la région ALC. Les niveaux de PIB par habitant varient davantage entre les pays africains qu'entre les pays ALC et les pays de l'OCDE.

Graphique 1.11. **Ratios impôts/PIB et PIB par habitant (en PPA) dans les pays d'Afrique, d'Amérique latine et des Caraïbes, de l'OCDE et dans certaines économies d'Asie et du Pacifique, 2019**

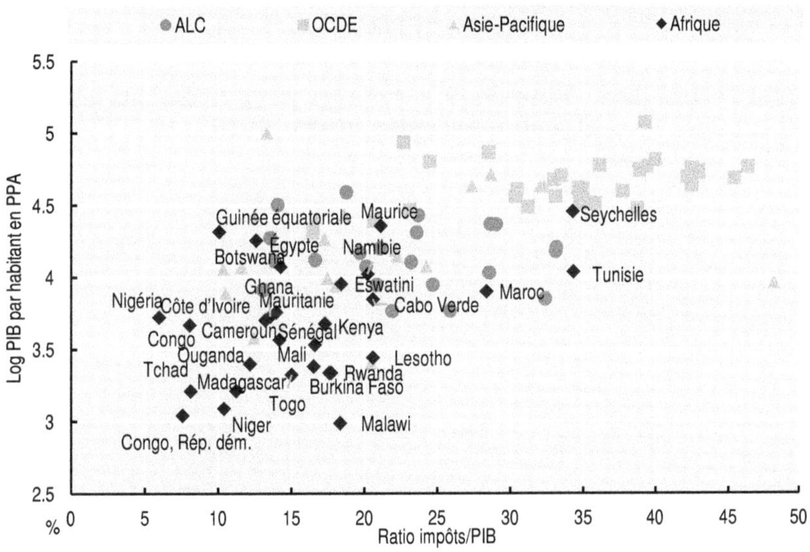

Note : L'axe y est sur une échelle logarithmique. La parité de pouvoir d'achat (PPA) entre deux pays est le taux auquel la monnaie d'un pays doit être convertie dans celle d'un second pays pour qu'un volume donné de monnaie du premier pays permette d'acheter la même quantité de biens et de services dans chaque pays. Le taux de conversion PPA est le taux utilisé pour convertir une monnaie nationale en dollar international courant. Un dollar international a le même pouvoir d'achat que le dollar US aux États-Unis. Un dollar international est une monnaie hypothétique utilisée comme moyen pour convertir et comparer les coûts d'un pays à l'autre grâce à un point de référence commun, le dollar US (définitions issues de (FMI, 2019[26]) et (OMS, 2015[27]).

Source : (FMI, 2021[5]) pour les chiffres du PIB par habitant. Les ratios impôts/PIB proviennent des éditions régionales des *Statistiques des recettes publiques*.

StatLink https://doi.org/10.1787/888934282322

Les pays qui tirent des recettes substantielles des exportations de ressources naturelles affichent souvent un faible ratio impôts/PIB. Ils peuvent avoir recours à des formes d'imposition moins contraignantes d'un point de vue politique (BAfD/OCDE/CEA, 2010[28]), (Mawejje, 2019[29]), et leurs bases d'imposition sont souvent relativement étroites. Le graphique 1.12 montre la répartition des ratios impôts/PIB des pays riches en ressources naturelles par rapport aux pays pauvres en ressources naturelles. Près d'un tiers des pays étudiés dans cette publication sont riches en ressources[8] : la République du Congo, la Guinée équatoriale, le Nigéria et le Tchad sont riches en pétrole[9], et cinq autres pays possèdent des ressources minérales substantielles (des diamants au Botswana ; des diamants, de l'or, du coltan, du cobalt et du cuivre en République démocratique du Congo ; des diamants, de l'or et du cacao au Ghana ; du cuivre, du fer et de l'or en Mauritanie ; du fer et des phosphates au Togo).

Le graphique 1.12 confirme que les pays riches en ressources figurant dans cette publication affichent des ratios impôts/PIB inférieurs à ceux des pays pauvres en ressources naturelles. En 2019, tous les pays riches en ressources naturelles affichaient des ratios impôts/PIB inférieurs à 15 %, alors que tous les pays pauvres en ressources naturelles, sauf cinq, affichaient des ratios supérieurs à ce niveau. En outre, alors que plusieurs pays riches en ressources naturelles affichaient des ratios impôts/PIB inférieurs à 10 %, les ratios impôts/PIB des pays pauvres en ressources étaient tous supérieurs à 10 %. En particulier, les quatre pays riches en pétrole (République du Congo, Guinée équatoriale, Nigéria et Tchad) affichaient des ratios impôts/PIB inférieurs ou proches de 10 %. Les recettes pétrolières proviennent pour l'essentiel des rentes et redevances pétrolières, qui ne sont pas considérées comme des recettes fiscales (voir chapitre 2). Les pays en développement ont beaucoup de mal à imposer les industries extractives en raison d'exonérations fiscales ou de contrats de longue date accordés aux industriels du secteur qui profitent aux élites locales (Gwaindepi, 2021[31]), (Brautigam, Fjeldstad et Moore, 2008[32]).

Graphique 1.12. **Ratios impôts/PIB dans les pays riches en ressources et pauvres en ressources, 2019**

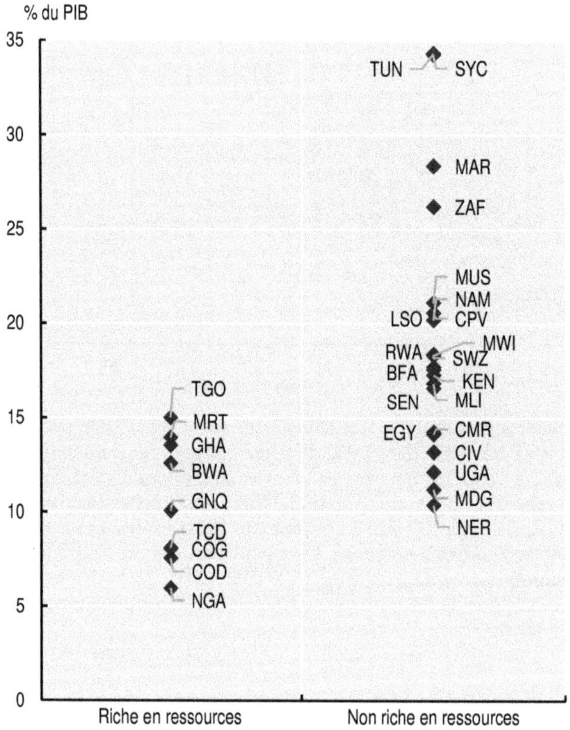

Note : Les chiffres prennent en compte les recettes fiscales des administrations infranationales pour l'Afrique du Sud, l'Eswatini, le Maroc, Maurice, la Mauritanie et le Nigéria (recettes des États uniquement).
Source : Calculs des auteurs basés sur (OCDE/CUA/ATAF, 2021[4]), « Statistiques des recettes publiques en Afrique : Tableaux comparatifs », *Statistiques fiscales de l'OCDE* (base de données), *https://doi.org/10.1787/7f54581d-fr*.
La classification des pays par niveau de ressources est basée sur (CUA/OCDE, 2021[30]).
StatLink *https://doi.org/10.1787/888934282341*

Comme on l'a vu plus haut, le civisme fiscal, à savoir les perceptions et attitudes des contribuables à l'égard du consentement à l'impôt et des pratiques de fraude, peut jouer un rôle dans les ratios impôts/PIB. L'OCDE a analysé le civisme fiscal dans différentes régions et examiné ses déterminants (OCDE, 2019[25]). S'agissant des particuliers, l'attachement à la démocratie, la foi, le niveau d'études et la confiance dans l'administration sont autant de facteurs qui influent sur le civisme fiscal. L'amélioration perçue de la qualité de l'administration de l'impôt, la simplification du paiement de l'impôt et l'offre de services publics de qualité semblent tous exercer une influence sur le civisme fiscal. Le genre peut aussi jouer un rôle : alors que dans la plupart des régions le civisme fiscal est plus élevé chez les femmes que chez les hommes, c'est l'inverse en Afrique. S'agissant des entreprises, l'étude menée par l'OCDE a recours à des données relatives à la sécurité juridique en matière fiscale concernant les entreprises multinationales (EMN)[10]. Dans les pays en développement, y compris en Afrique, la sécurité juridique en matière fiscale semble se répercuter sur l'activité économique, elle entraîne une modification de la structure des activités, une augmentation des coûts et des changements de décision en matière d'investissement. Même s'il existe des variations d'une région à l'autre, la fiscalité internationale et les relations entre les autorités et les entreprises sont des préoccupations communes à tous les pays en développement. En Afrique, la clarté de la législation et la sécurité juridique en matière fiscale représentent les principaux sujets de préoccupation (OCDE, 2019[25]).

Structures fiscales

La structure fiscale d'un pays mesure la composition de ses recettes fiscales en fonction des différents types d'impôts. Il s'agit là d'un indicateur important, car différents impôts ont différents effets économiques et sociaux. La composition des impôts dans les 30 pays étudiés reflète des différences concernant leurs choix politiques, leurs structures et situations économiques, les capacités de leur administration fiscale et d'autres facteurs historiques. Les pays peuvent être divisés en trois grands groupes en fonction de leur principale source de recettes : TVA, autres impôts sur les biens et services et impôts sur le revenu.

Évolution des structures fiscales, 2010-2019

Depuis 2010, la structure fiscale moyenne des pays étudiés a opéré un transfert vers les recettes de l'IRPP et de la TVA, au détriment des impôts sur les biens et services autres que la TVA. Les hausses intervenues dans ces deux catégories d'impôts expliquent également pour beaucoup l'augmentation globale du ratio impôts/PIB en moyenne au cours de la période. Les recettes tirées de l'IRPP ont progressé de 0.8 p.p., tandis que celles issues de la TVA ont augmenté de 1.0 p.p. entre 2010 et 2019, atteignant respectivement 3.9 % et 4.9 % du PIB en 2019 (graphique 1.13).

L'augmentation de la TVA et de l'IRPP en pourcentage du PIB a également contribué à accroître la part de ces deux impôts dans les recettes fiscales totales. La fraction des recettes fiscales provenant de la TVA a crû de 2.2 p.p. pour s'établir à 29.3 % du total en 2019, ce qui traduit la poursuite d'une tendance durable à l'augmentation des recettes de TVA au détriment de celles tirées d'autres impôts sur des biens et services (y compris de la taxe sur les ventes, des accises et des impôts sur des biens et services spécifiques). De même, la part des recettes issues de l'IRPP a augmenté de 2.1 p.p. au cours de cette période, atteignant 17.7 % des recettes fiscales totales en 2019, alors que la part des recettes provenant de l'IS a diminué (2.8 p.p.). Cependant, la part des recettes provenant de l'IRPP reste toujours inférieure à celle des recettes issues de l'IS (18.8 % des recettes fiscales totales en 2019).

Graphique 1.13. **Structure fiscale, moyenne Afrique (30) en pourcentage du total des recettes fiscales et en pourcentage du PIB, 2010 et 2019**

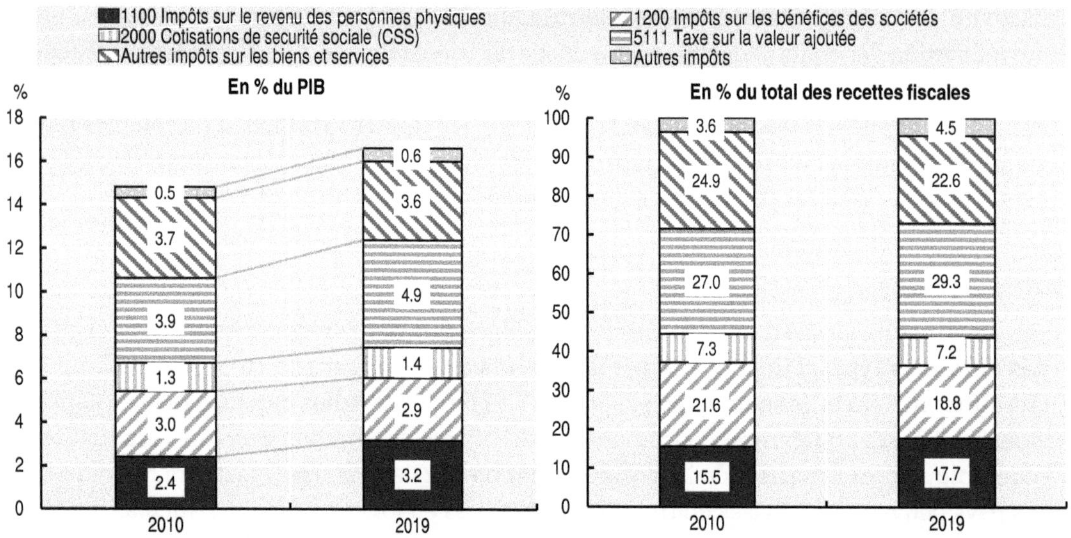

Note : La moyenne Afrique (30) n'est pas pondérée. Il convient d'interpréter la moyenne des pays d'Afrique (30) avec prudence, car les données relatives aux cotisations de sécurité sociale ne sont pas disponibles ou ne sont que partielles pour quelques pays. Pour plus de précisions, se reporter aux tableaux par pays présentés dans le chapitre 5.

Source : Calculs des auteurs basés sur des données figurant dans (OCDE/CUA/ATAF, 2021[4]), « Statistiques des recettes publiques en Afrique : Tableaux comparatifs », *Statistiques fiscales de l'OCDE* (base de données), *https://doi.org/10.1787/7f54581d-fr*.

StatLink *https://doi.org/10.1787/888934282360*

Structures fiscales en 2019

En 2019, les recettes de TVA ont généré la majeure partie des recettes fiscales dans les pays couverts par cette publication (graphique 1.14). Elles ont représenté 29.3 % du total des recettes fiscales en moyenne, soit un pourcentage comparable à la moyenne ALC (27.7 %), environ 9.0 p.p. de plus que la moyenne de l'OCDE (20.4 %, chiffre de 2018), et 7.0 p.p. de plus que la moyenne Asie-Pacifique (24) (22.8 %). Toutefois, les recettes de TVA pour la moyenne des pays d'Afrique (30) sont inférieures aux moyennes ALC et OCDE lorsqu'elles sont mesurées en pourcentage du PIB [4.9 % du PIB en Afrique, contre 6.0 % dans la région ALC et 6.8 % dans la zone OCDE (chiffre de 2018)], et similaires à la moyenne Asie-Pacifique (24) (4.7 % du PIB).

La part moyenne des recettes de l'IS dans le total des recettes fiscales en Afrique s'élevait à 18.8 % en 2019, ce qui est supérieur à la moyenne de la région ALC et de la zone OCDE (respectivement 15.8 % et 10.0 %, chiffre de 2018 pour l'OCDE), mais inférieur à la moyenne Asie-Pacifique (24) (20.1 %). En pourcentage du PIB, les parts moyennes des recettes de l'IS pour les 30 pays d'Afrique et pour l'OCDE étaient similaires [respectivement 2.9 % et 3.1 % du PIB (chiffre de 2018)] ; ces pourcentages sont néanmoins inférieurs à la moyenne ALC et Asie-Pacifique (24) (3.6 % du PIB en 2019) (graphique 1.14).

En revanche, la part moyenne, dans les 30 pays d'Afrique, des recettes de l'IRPP (17.7 % du total des recettes) était similaire à la moyenne de la région Asie-Pacifique (24) (17.0 %), inférieure à moyenne de l'OCDE de 23.5 % (chiffre de 2018), mais supérieure à la moyenne ALC (9.2 %). En pourcentage du PIB, le niveau moyen des recettes de l'IRPP dans la zone OCDE était plus de deux fois supérieur à la moyenne des 30 pays d'Afrique.

Graphique 1.14. **Structure fiscale pour la moyenne des pays d'Afrique (30), ALC et OCDE en pourcentage du total des recettes fiscales et du PIB, 2019**

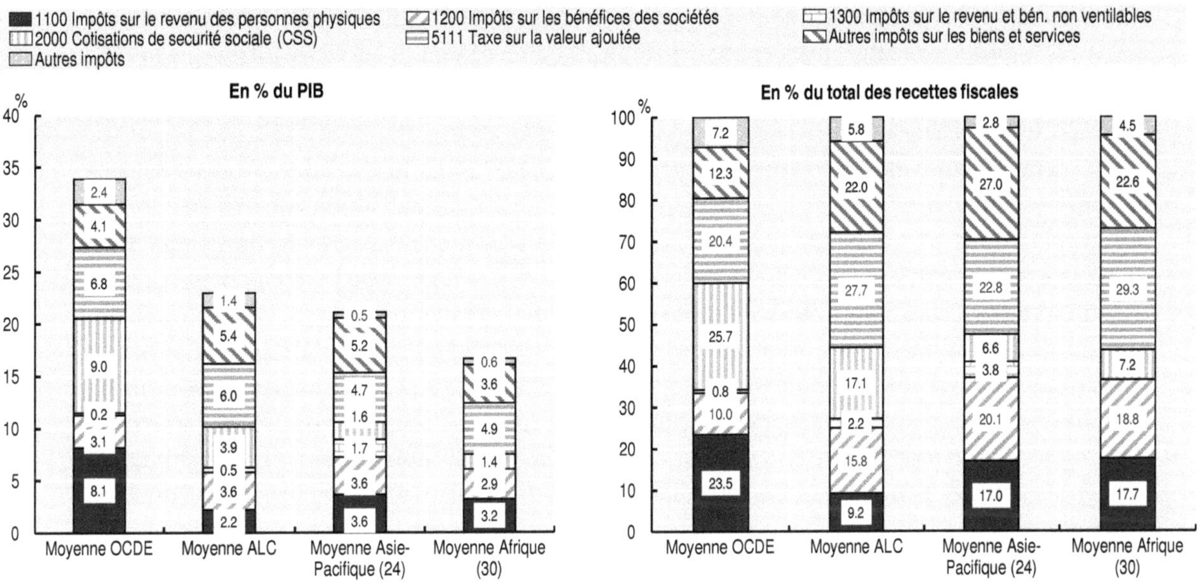

Note : La moyenne Afrique (30) et les moyennes Asie-Pacifique (24 économies), ALC (26 pays) et OCDE (37 pays) sont des moyennes non pondérées.

Il convient d'interpréter la moyenne des pays d'Afrique (30) avec prudence, car les données relatives aux cotisations de sécurité sociale ne sont pas disponibles ou ne sont que partielles pour quelques pays. Pour plus de précisions, se reporter aux tableaux par pays présentés dans le chapitre 5.

Les données concernant l'OCDE portent sur l'année 2018, car les données de 2019 ne sont pas disponibles.

Source : Calculs des auteurs basés sur des données figurant dans (OCDE/CUA/ATAF, 2021[4]), « Statistiques des recettes publiques en Afrique : Tableaux comparatifs », *Statistiques fiscales de l'OCDE* (base de données), *https://doi.org/10.1787/7f54581d-fr*.

StatLink https://doi.org/10.1787/888934282379

Le graphique 1.15 illustre, pour tous les pays de cette publication, la ventilation des recettes fiscales entre impôts sur le revenu (personnes physiques et sociétés), cotisations de sécurité sociale et impôts sur les biens et services (y compris la TVA ainsi que d'autres impôts sur les biens et services).

Les impôts sur les biens et services constituaient la principale source de recettes fiscales pour 22 des 30 pays étudiés (les deux premiers groupes de pays représentés dans le graphique 1.15). Dans ces pays, ils ont généré de 35.6 % des recettes fiscales en Tunisie à 75.9 % au Togo. La TVA y représentait le principal poste de recettes tirées des impôts sur les biens et services, sauf en République du Congo, en Côte d'Ivoire, au Kenya, et en Ouganda.

Dans huit pays (Afrique du Sud, Botswana, Eswatini, Guinée équatoriale, Lesotho, Namibie, Nigéria, Tchad), la plus grande partie des recettes fiscales provient des impôts sur le revenu et les bénéfices. En effet, ils représentaient une part plus importante des recettes fiscales totales que les moyennes OCDE et ALC, allant de 48.2 % des recettes totales en Eswatini à 76.4 % en Guinée équatoriale.

Dans 18 des 30 pays couverts par cette publication, la part des recettes fiscales tirées de l'IRPP est supérieure à celle provenant de l'IS. La part des recettes de l'IS est particulièrement importante au Nigéria et en Guinée équatoriale, où elles représentent respectivement 45.9 % et 67.1 % du total des recettes, tandis qu'au Lesotho et en Namibie, plus de 40 % des recettes totales provenaient de l'IRPP en 2019. Dans 25 pays, les recettes issues de la TVA représentaient une part plus importante des recettes fiscales totales que les recettes provenant d'autres taxes sur les biens et services. Dans cinq pays seulement, la République du Congo, la Côte d'Ivoire, le Kenya, l'Ouganda et le Tchad, la part des recettes fiscales provenant d'autres taxes sur les biens et services était plus élevée. En revanche, le Botswana, le Lesotho et la Namibie, qui sont tous membres de la SACU[11] (voir encadré 2.3), tirent moins de 5.0 % de leurs recettes fiscales totales d'impôts sur les biens et services autres que la TVA. L'accord de partage des recettes entre les pays de la SACU explique cette part relativement faible par rapport aux autres pays.

L'importance des cotisations de sécurité sociale[12] dans le total des recettes fiscales varie considérablement entre les 30 pays étudiés. La part des cotisations de sécurité sociale dans le total des recettes fiscales était la plus élevée au Maroc (21.9 %) et en Tunisie (28.3 %) ; dans les autres pays, elle s'échelonne entre moins de 0.2 % au Cabo Verde à environ 13.0 % en Eswatini. Cette hétérogénéité reflète la diversité des régimes de sécurité sociale et des taux de cotisation, car de nombreux pays utilisent des systèmes différents pour financer les prestations de sécurité sociale. Par exemple, les cotisations de sécurité sociale en Afrique du Sud financent le Fonds d'assurance chômage, tandis que d'autres prestations, comme les programmes d'aide sociale couvrant la vieillesse, la maladie et la maternité, sont financées par les recettes générales. À l'inverse, les régimes de sécurité sociale marocain et tunisien sont calqués sur le système français et couvrent un large éventail de prestations, y compris la vieillesse, l'incapacité, la maladie, la maternité, les accidents du travail (Tunisie), le chômage (Maroc) et les allocations familiales (SSA, 2015[33]).

Graphique 1.15. **Structure fiscale, par pays, 2019**

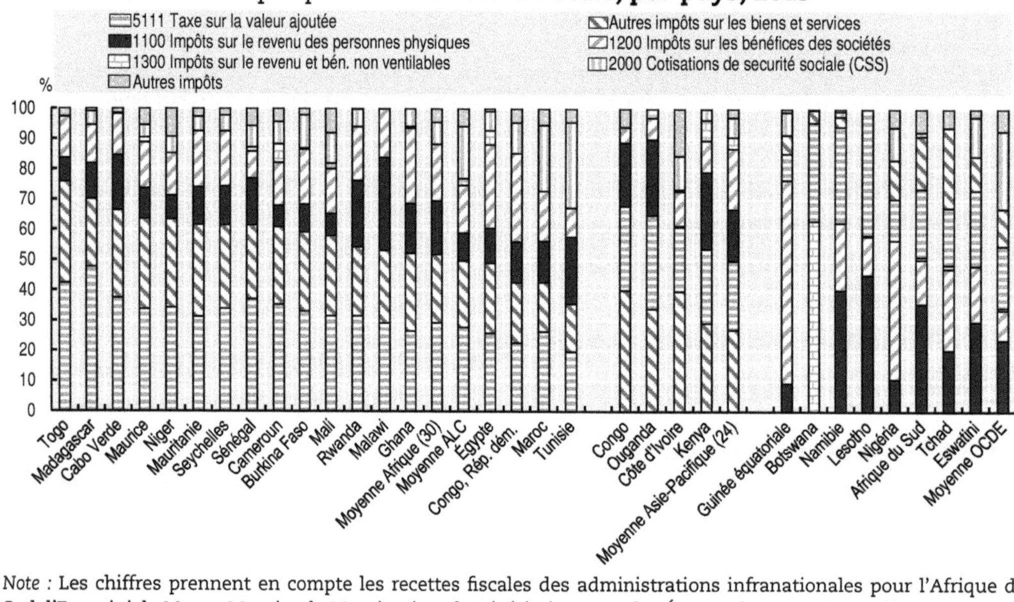

Note : Les chiffres prennent en compte les recettes fiscales des administrations infranationales pour l'Afrique du Sud, l'Eswatini, le Maroc, Maurice, la Mauritanie et le Nigéria (recettes des États uniquement) pour l'année 2019. La moyenne Afrique (30) et les moyennes Asie-Pacifique (24 économies), ALC (26 pays d'Amérique latine et Caraïbes) et OCDE (37 pays) sont des moyennes non pondérées.

Il convient d'interpréter la moyenne des pays d'Afrique (30) avec prudence, car les données relatives aux cotisations de sécurité sociale ne sont pas disponibles ou ne sont que partielles pour quelques pays. Pour plus de précisions, se reporter aux tableaux par pays présentés dans le chapitre 5.

Botswana : la ventilation des recettes tirées des impôts sur le revenu et sur les bénéfices entre la rubrique « 1100 Impôt sur le revenu des personnes physiques » et la rubrique « 1200 Impôt sur les bénéfices des sociétés » n'est pas disponible.

Moyenne OCDE : les données portent sur l'année 2018, car les données de 2019 ne sont pas disponibles.

Source : Calculs des auteurs basés sur des données figurant dans (OCDE/CUA/ATAF, 2021[4]), « Statistiques des recettes publiques en Afrique : Tableaux comparatifs », *Statistiques fiscales de l'OCDE* (base de données), *https://doi.org/10.1787/7f54581d-fr*.

StatLink https://doi.org/10.1787/888934282398

Graphique 1.16. **Recettes provenant de la TVA et d'autres impôts sur les biens et services et recettes tirées de l'IRPP et de l'IS**

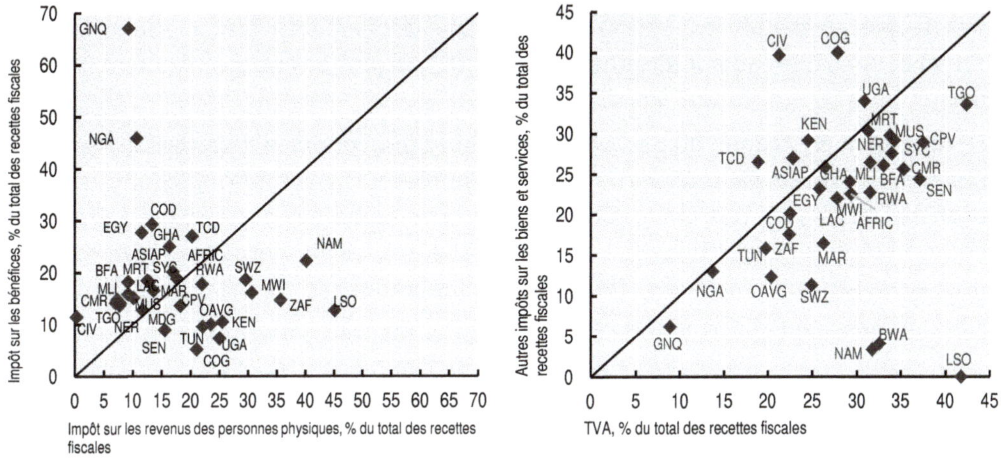

Note : Les chiffres prennent en compte les recettes fiscales des administrations infranationales pour l'Afrique du Sud, l'Eswatini, le Maroc, Maurice, la Mauritanie et le Nigéria (recettes des États uniquement) pour l'année 2019.

Botswana : la ventilation des recettes tirées des impôts sur le revenu et sur les bénéfices entre la rubrique « 1100 Impôt sur le revenu des personnes physiques » et la rubrique « 1200 Impôt sur les bénéfices des sociétés » n'est pas disponible.

Source : Calculs des auteurs basés sur des données figurant dans (OCDE/CUA/ATAF, 2021[4]), « Statistiques des recettes publiques en Afrique : Tableaux comparatifs », *Statistiques fiscales de l'OCDE* (base de données), *https://doi.org/10.1787/7f54581d-fr*.

StatLink https://doi.org/10.1787/888934282417

Ratio des recettes de TVA

Cette section examine le ratio des recettes de TVA (RRT) dans les pays figurant cette publication[13]. Le RRT « mesure l'écart entre les recettes de TVA effectivement collectées et celles qui auraient théoriquement pu être obtenues dans l'hypothèse où l'on aurait appliqué le taux normal à la totalité de la base d'imposition potentielle dans le cadre d'un régime de TVA "pur" et où la totalité de ces recettes aurait été perçue » (OCDE, 2018[34]) (OCDE, 2021[35]). Il correspond au rapport entre les recettes de TVA effectives et le produit de la consommation finale (net des recettes de TVA) et du taux normal de TVA. La formule de calcul est la suivante :

$$\frac{\text{Recettes de TVA}}{(\text{dépenses de consommation finale} - \text{recettes de TVA}) \times \text{taux normal de TVA}}$$

Cet indicateur donne un aperçu de la part des recettes de TVA non recouvrées sous l'effet des exemptions, des taux réduits, des pratiques de fraude et d'optimisation fiscales, ainsi que des défaillances de l'administration fiscale. Néanmoins, cet indicateur doit être interprété avec prudence en se référant aux caractéristiques fondamentales du système de TVA propre à chaque pays, car un RRT élevé peut résulter d'effets de cascade (lorsque l'exemption intervient très en amont dans la chaîne d'approvisionnement, par exemple) ou du non-remboursement de la TVA acquittée sur les intrants. D'autres facteurs peuvent également augmenter le ratio, comme le fait que les règles relatives au lieu d'imposition des ventes internationales dérogent au principe de destination, ou le poids élevé de l'économie informelle dans un pays. Par exemple, en Afrique, de nombreux travailleurs opèrent dans le secteur informel. N'étant pas déclarés à des fins fiscales, ils ne bénéficient pas de remboursements de TVA sur leurs intrants, tandis que les travailleurs et les entreprises du secteur formel peuvent y prétendre (BAD/OCDE/PNUD, 2016[36]).

Le graphique 1.17 rend compte des RRT de 30 pays africains couverts par cette publication. En 2019, le Cabo Verde, l'Afrique du Sud et Maurice affichaient les RRT les plus élevés (respectivement 0.74, 0.58, et 0.56), tandis que la République démocratique du Congo, le Tchad et la Guinée équatoriale affichaient les RRT les plus bas (respectivement 0.12, 0.10, et 0.08).

- Le RRT élevé en Afrique du Sud peut s'expliquer par certaines caractéristiques de son système de TVA. Les exemptions de TVA sont limitées et la gamme des produits et services exonérés de TVA est restreinte, contrairement à de nombreux autres pays d'Afrique. En outre, le seuil d'enregistrement à la TVA y est élevé, ce qui permet à l'administration fiscale sud-africaine d'axer ses efforts sur les plus grandes entreprises (Cnossen, $2015_{[38]}$).
- Le Cabo Verde applique un taux de TVA de 15 %, et a adopté diverses réformes fiscales entre 2013 et 2015 en vue d'augmenter les recettes de TVA (et des impôts sur les sociétés). Il a également automatisé le recouvrement des recettes de TVA en décembre 2017 (CNUCED, $2018_{[39]}$).
- À l'inverse, la République démocratique du Congo affiche un RRT faible de 0.12. Les recettes de TVA ont fortement baissé après la mise en place de cette taxe en 2012, passant de 4.2 % à 1.7 % du PIB en 2019. Cette diminution et le faible niveau du RRT reflètent les difficultés rencontrées par les autorités pour administrer la TVA. Par exemple, la TVA sur les importations des sociétés minières n'est plus perçue en raison de difficultés à rembourser les crédits de TVA. Le FMI a recommandé de renforcer les mécanismes institutionnels afin de recommencer à recouvrer ces recettes (FMI, $2019_{[40]}$).

Graphique 1.17. **Ratio des recettes de TVA par pays, 2019**

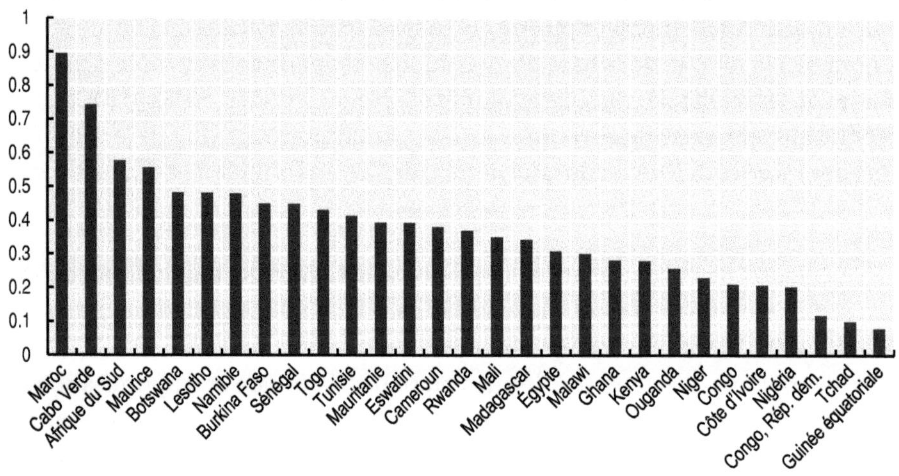

Note : Les Seychelles sont exclues du fait de l'indisponibilité de certaines données.

Source : les taux de TVA proviennent des *Tendances des impôts sur la consommation* (OCDE, $2021_{[35]}$), des sites web de Trading Economics et de Deloitte, les chiffres relatifs aux dépenses de consommation finale de la base de données des *Perspectives de l'économie mondiale* du FMI (FMI, $2020_{[37]}$), et les recettes de TVA des tableaux par pays figurant au chapitre 5.

StatLink https://doi.org/10.1787/888934282436

Recettes des taxes liées à l'environnement

En vertu de l'Accord de Paris de 2016, les pays se sont engagés à décarboner leurs économies d'ici au milieu du siècle, ce qui implique de se détourner des combustibles fossiles comme source d'énergie. Les taxes liées à l'environnement, et plus généralement les instruments fondés sur les prix, jouent un rôle croissant dans de nombreux pays. En intégrant un signal sur les prix dans les décisions des consommateurs, ces taxes mettent en application le principe du pollueur-payeur et incitent les entreprises et les ménages à prendre en compte le coût environnemental de leurs choix.

Une taxe liée à l'environnement est une taxe dont l'assiette est une unité physique (ou une approximation d'une unité physique) de quelque chose qui a un impact négatif spécifique et avéré sur l'environnement, que la taxe vise à changer les comportements ou soit perçue dans un autre but (OCDE, 2005$_{[41]}$). Les recettes tirées des taxes sur l'énergie peuvent augmenter à moyen terme si les pays relèvent les taux effectifs de la taxe sur la teneur en carbone des carburants (Marten et van Dender, 2019$_{[42]}$). Une étude (OCDE/FIT, 2019$_{[43]}$) conjointe du FIT et de l'OCDE montre comment les recettes tirées du transport routier peuvent être stabilisées à long terme en associant des taxes sur les distances parcourues, les véhicules et les carburants.

Bien que les recettes tirées des taxes liées à l'environnement ne ressortent pas de la classification type des recettes fiscales établie par l'OCDE, on peut les identifier en examinant la liste détaillée des taxes spécifiques fournies pour la plupart des pays, qui s'inscrivent dans la classification globale. C'est sur cette base qu'elles ont été intégrées dans la base de données de l'OCDE sur les instruments de la politique de l'environnement (PINE) (OCDE, 2020$_{[44]}$)[14].

Un examen détaillé des taxes prélevées par les 30 pays africains couverts montre qu'en moyenne, les recettes tirées des taxes liées à l'environnement s'élevaient à 1.1 % du PIB en 2019, le même niveau que les moyennes Asie-Pacifique (16 économies)[15] et ALC (respectivement 1.1 % et 1.2 % du PIB), mais moins que la moyenne non pondérée de l'OCDE de 2.2 % du PIB. Les recettes générées par les taxes liées à l'environnement s'échelonnaient entre un peu moins de 0.1 % du PIB en République du Congo et au Nigéria, et 4.7 % aux Seychelles (graphique 1.18). Ces chiffres doivent être interprétés avec prudence, car il n'est pas possible d'identifier précisément le niveau des recettes issues des taxes liées à l'environnement pour chaque pays ; aussi, le niveau des recettes indiqué dans le graphique 1.18 varie en fonction de la granularité des données disponibles.

En 2019, les recettes provenant des taxes sur les produits énergétiques constituaient l'essentiel des recettes tirées des taxes liées à l'environnement dans les pays couverts par cette publication (0.7 % du PIB en moyenne). Les recettes issues des produits énergétiques, généralement des taxes sur le gazole et sur l'essence, représentaient environ les deux tiers du total des recettes générées par les taxes liées à l'environnement en moyenne. Les recettes tirées des taxes sur les transports et sur les véhicules à moteur constituaient l'essentiel du solde, tandis que celles générées par d'autres catégories étaient négligeables, de l'ordre de 0.02 % du total en moyenne. Cette structure est très similaire à la ventilation de ces recettes observée dans les pays de l'OCDE et de la région ALC. En 2019, en revanche, les économies de la région Asie-Pacifique ont davantage recouru aux taxes sur les ressources et les transports qu'aux taxes sur l'énergie.

Les taxes sur les produits énergétiques représentaient la majeure partie des recettes des taxes liées à l'environnement dans tous les pays sauf huit. Les taxes sur les véhicules à moteur et sur les transports constituaient la principale source de recettes liées à l'environnement au Botswana, en Côte d'Ivoire, au Kenya, au Maroc, à Maurice, au Nigéria et en Tunisie. Les recettes provenant des taxes sur les ressources et sur la pollution arrivaient en tête au Cabo Verde, en Guinée équatoriale et au Mali.

Graphique 1.18. **Recettes provenant des taxes liées à l'environnement par pays et par principales catégories de taxe, en pourcentage du PIB, 2019**

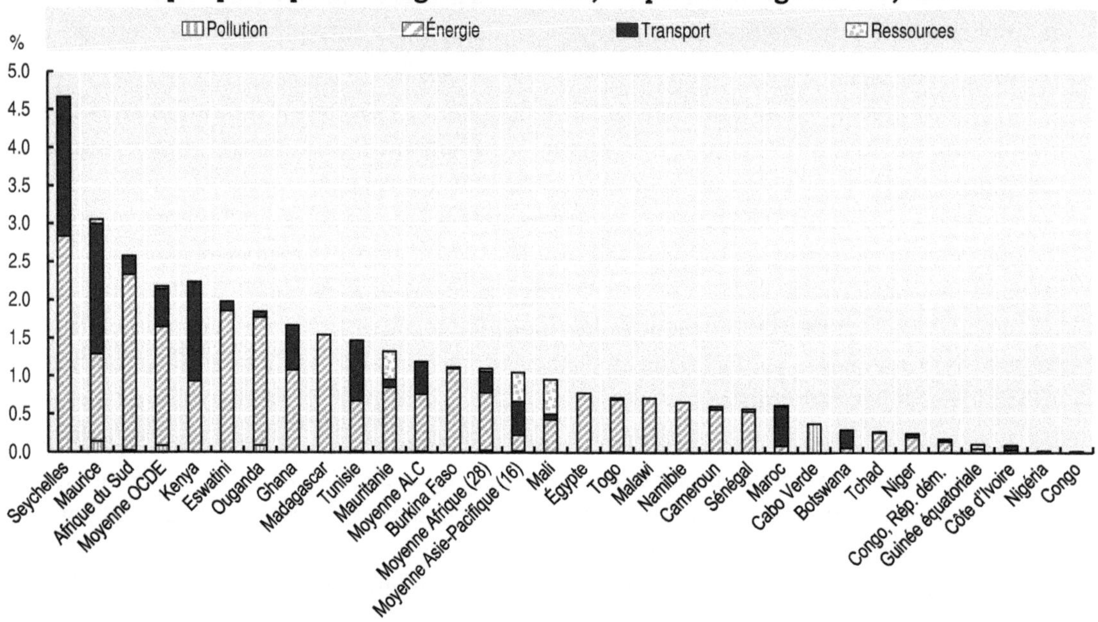

Note : Le Rwanda et le Lesotho sont exclus compte tenu de l'impossibilité d'identifier des recettes tirées de taxes environnementales.
Source : Calculs des auteurs basés sur des données figurant dans (OCDE/CUA/ATAF, 2021[4]), (OCDE, 2020[44]), sur la base de données PINE pour la moyenne de l'OCDE, et dans (OCDE et al., 2021[2]) pour la moyenne ALC.

StatLink https://doi.org/10.1787/888934282455

L'Afrique du Sud affiche l'un des plus hauts niveaux de recettes tirees des taxes liées à l'environnement, soit l'équivalent de 2.8 % du PIB en 2019, la taxe sur les carburants occupant la première place (1.4 % du PIB). Au cours de la dernière décennie, l'Afrique du Sud a mis en place une taxe sur les ampoules incandescentes (2009/10) ; une taxe sur l'électricité (2009/10) ; une taxe sur les émissions de CO_2 des véhicules (2010/11) et une taxe sur les pneus (2016/17). En 2019, le pays a instauré une taxe carbone au taux de 120 rands (8.34 USD) par tonne d'équivalent dioxyde de carbone (SARS, 2020[45]) (Reuters, 2019[46]) (OCDE, 2020[47]).

D'une manière générale, le recours à la fiscalité pour remédier aux problèmes environnementaux est faible dans la région, et il est possible de mobiliser bien davantage ces formes de prélèvements. La sous-utilisation des taxes liées à l'environnement en Afrique doit également s'appréhender dans le contexte de l'utilisation généralisée des subventions aux combustibles fossiles. On estime par exemple que les subventions aux combustibles fossiles en Afrique subsaharienne représentaient 5 % du PIB en 2013 (Coady et al., 2015[48]). Parmi les pays figurant dans cette publication, l'Afrique du Sud, la Côte d'Ivoire et le Nigéria ont accordé des subventions aux combustibles fossiles supérieures à 1 milliard USD en 2015 (Worrall, Whitley et Scott, 2018[49]). La réforme des subventions à l'énergie, parallèlement à la mise en place d'une fiscalité environnementale, pourrait permettre de mobiliser d'importantes recettes publiques et contribuer à la mise en œuvre de l'Agenda 2063 et à la réalisation des Objectifs de développement durable (ODD).

Alors que les États continuent de mettre en place des mesures afin d'aider les entreprises et les contribuables à faire face à la crise du COVID-19, certains gouvernements accordent des allégements fiscaux ou renoncent à certaines taxes. L'ATAF encourage les gouvernements africains à « s'abstenir de suspendre les taxes environnementales pendant cette période, car (...) les allégements fiscaux à court terme ne devraient pas compromettre les objectifs environnementaux à plus long terme » (ATAF, 2020[50]).

Impôts par niveaux d'administration

L'analyse de la répartition des impôts par niveaux d'administration dans les pays couverts par cette publication est limitée par le fait que les données sur les recettes fiscales perçues par les administrations infranationales étaient disponibles pour six pays seulement : Afrique du Sud, Eswatini, Maroc, Maurice[16], Mauritanie et Nigéria[17]. En 2019, les recettes des administrations infranationales étaient inférieures à 1 % du total des recettes fiscales à Maurice, et représentaient 2.0 % en Eswatini, 2.6 % en Mauritanie, 3.1 % au Maroc et 5.2 % en Afrique du Sud. En revanche, les recettes des administrations infranationales s'élevaient à 15.4 % des recettes fiscales totales au Nigéria. Les recettes fiscales des administrations infranationales sont considérées comme faibles dans la région. Selon (BAfD/OCDE/PNUD, 2015[51]), « en Afrique, en moyenne, le poids des recettes des administrations locales équivaut à 7 % des recettes totales perçues par les collectivités locales et régionales et l'administration centrale combinées ».

En général, les compétences fiscales dévolues aux administrations infranationales en Afrique sont limitées. La publication *Perspectives économiques en Afrique 2015* (BAfD/OCDE/PNUD, 2015[51]) observe que « de nombreuses administrations locales perçoivent une fraction importante de leurs recettes totales grâce aux transferts opérés par l'administration centrale ». Les collectivités locales dans la plupart des pays d'Afrique se heurtent à des contraintes de ressources, et les outils dont disposent leurs administrations fiscales sont inadaptés pour recouvrer les impôts et les imputer correctement en comptabilité. Cette situation entraîne des coûts de recouvrement élevés et un grand nombre d'impôts peu productifs. En outre, le traitement des données relatives aux recettes collectées et l'échange de renseignements avec d'autres institutions publiques sont peu développés, et les administrations locales coopèrent généralement peu avec l'administration centrale. Cela se traduit par des impôts en double ou qui vont à l'encontre des objectifs nationaux (comme des taxes locales sur les cultures d'exportation).

Les impôts sur le patrimoine constituent la plus importante source de revenus pour les administrations infranationales en Afrique du Sud, en Eswatini, au Maroc, à Maurice et en Mauritanie. Ils représentent la totalité des recettes fiscales locales recouvrées en Afrique du Sud, en Eswatini, à Maurice et en Mauritanie, et plus de 80 % au Maroc. Le solde se compose principalement des impôts sur les biens et services. À l'inverse, les recettes des administrations infranationales au Nigéria proviennent principalement des impôts sur le revenu.

On observe de grandes disparités en ce qui concerne la fiscalité locale, et de nombreux pays africains ne lèvent aucune taxe locale sur le foncier bâti et non bâti, ni même sur les activités économiques (BAfD/OCDE/PNUD, 2015[51]). À l'exception de l'Afrique du Sud, les registres fonciers en bonne et due forme font défaut ou sont incomplets, ce qui entrave la collecte des impôts fonciers (Fjeldstad, Chambas et Brun, 2014[52]). À Maurice, par exemple, la taxe foncière est peu productive en partie à cause de cadastres périmés et de valeurs de biens qui ne sont plus à jour (FMI, 2014[53]).

Certains pays s'emploient à améliorer leur régime des impôts sur le patrimoine, avec une mise à jour des registres fonciers et des outils administratifs plus efficaces. En 2007, le Maroc a lancé une réforme du système fiscal et des administrations fiscales locales en vue d'augmenter les recettes générées par les impôts locaux (Boisard, de Freitas et Hidouci, 2014[54]). La Côte d'Ivoire a déployé un logiciel SIG pour mieux gérer ses registres fonciers. L'Afrique du Sud a décentralisé avec succès le processus de recouvrement de la taxe foncière urbaine, et a élaboré un système moderne de collecte de cette taxe en utilisant des techniques statistiques afin de réaliser des évaluations de masse assistées par ordinateur (Monkam et Moore, 2015[55]).

Bien que de nombreux pays africains aient entrepris de vastes réformes de leur administration fiscale centrale et de la législation correspondante au cours des dernières décennies, il n'y a guère eu d'initiatives de ce genre au niveau des administrations locales. On a donné la priorité aux recettes perçues par l'administration centrale parce que c'est à cet échelon que la nécessité de réduire les déficits budgétaires s'est fait sentir le plus.

Notes

1 Il convient d'interpréter la moyenne Afrique (30) avec précaution, car des données relatives aux cotisations de sécurité sociale sont indisponibles pour la République du Congo, la République démocratique du Congo (avant 2012), Madagascar (avant 2011), la Namibie, l'Ouganda, le Tchad et le Togo, et sont incomplètes pour le Cameroun et le Sénégal. Les cotisations de sécurité sociale pour le Botswana, le Lesotho et le Malawi sont égales à zéro dans la mesure où elles ne remplissent pas les critères retenus pour être considérées comme des cotisations de sécurité sociale, selon la classification des impôts de l'OCDE figurant dans le Guide d'interprétation. Pour plus de précisions, se reporter aux tableaux par pays présentés dans le chapitre 5.

2 Le Burundi, le Kenya, l'Ouganda, le Rwanda, le Sud-Soudan et la Tanzanie font partie de la Communauté de l'Afrique de l'Est (CAE).

3 Le Burkina Faso, le Bénin, la Côte d'Ivoire, la Guinée-Bissau, le Mali, le Niger, le Sénégal et le Togo adhèrent à l'Union économique et monétaire ouest-africaine (UEMOA).

4 Les cinq pays membres de la SACU sont liés par un accord de partage des recettes qui prévoit l'application de droits de douane extérieurs communs et une répartition des droits de douane et d'accise perçus par les pays membres. Dans la présente publication, les recettes issues des droits de douane et d'accise sont incluses dans les recettes fiscales du pays de la SACU qui les a collectées (Afrique du Sud), et les montants redistribués par le fonds commun des recettes de la SACU sont classés dans les tableaux des recettes non fiscales, sous la rubrique des recettes diverses (Botswana, Eswatini, Lesotho, Namibie).

5 Calculs effectués par l'auteur basés sur (FMI, 2021[5]).

6 Cette information a été communiquée par le ministère des Finances de la Tunisie lors d'échanges avec le Secrétariat de l'OCDE dans le cadre de la préparation de cette publication.

7 À la suite de la création de la Communauté d'Afrique de l'Est (CAE) en 2010, le Rwanda a adopté le cadre relatif aux tarifs extérieurs communs, ce qui s'est traduit par une baisse des recettes tirées des taxes sur les échanges commerciaux de 0.3 p.p. en 2010.

8 Les pays dont plus de 10 % du PIB provenait de la production de pétrole, de gaz, de charbon et de minerais pendant au moins cinq ans entre 2010 et 2019 ont été classés dans la catégorie des pays « riches en ressources » (CUA/OCDE, 2021[30]).

9 Les pays dont plus de 10 % du PIB provenait de la production de pétrole et de gaz naturel pendant au moins cinq ans entre 2010 et 2019 ont été classés dans la catégorie des pays « riches en pétrole » (CUA/OCDE, 2021[30]).

10 L'analyse repose sur une source de données unique, en l'occurrence l'enquête auprès des entreprises réalisée en 2016 par l'OCDE pour obtenir l'avis des équipes dirigeantes de 500 entreprises, en majorité des multinationales, et recueillir ainsi leurs positions sur la sécurité juridique en matière fiscale dans 82 pays en développement.

11 Les cinq pays membres de la SACU sont liés par un accord de partage des recettes qui prévoit l'application de droits de douane extérieurs communs et une répartition des droits de douane et d'accise perçus par les pays membres. Dans la présente publication, les recettes issues des droits de douane et d'accise sont incluses dans les recettes fiscales du pays de la SACU qui les a collectées (Afrique du Sud), et les montants redistribués par le fonds commun des recettes de la SACU sont classés dans les tableaux des recettes non fiscales, sous la rubrique des recettes diverses (Botswana, Eswatini, Lesotho, Namibie).

12 Les données concernant les cotisations de sécurité sociale ne sont pas disponibles pour la République du Congo, la République démocratique du Congo (avant 2012), Madagascar (avant 2011), la Namibie, l'Ouganda, le Tchad et le Togo, et ne sont que partiellement disponibles au Cameroun et au Sénégal. Pour plus de précisions, se reporter aux tableaux par pays présentés dans le chapitre 5.

13 Les Seychelles sont exclues du fait de l'indisponibilité de certaines données.

14 La base de données PINE ventile les taxes liées à l'environnement entre les quatre catégories suivantes :

- Énergie : cette catégorie couvre l'imposition des produits énergétiques tels que les combustibles fossiles et l'électricité, y compris les carburants utilisés pour les transports comme l'essence et le gazole. Toutes les taxes sur les émissions de CO_2 font partie de cette catégorie.
- Véhicules à moteur et services de transport : cette catégorie englobe les taxes sur les importations ou les ventes de matériel de transport, les taxes périodiques sur la propriété, l'immatriculation ou l'usage routier de véhicules à moteur et d'autres taxes liées aux transports.
- Ressources : cette catégorie inclut les taxes sur les industries extractives, l'exploitation forestière, la protection de la vie sauvage et les produits de la pêche.
- Pollution : cette catégorie comprend les taxes sur les substances appauvrissant la couche d'ozone, l'eau et les eaux usées, et la gestion des déchets.

15 La moyenne est calculée pour 16 pays et non 24, car il n'a pas été possible d'identifier les recettes fiscales liées à l'environnement pour huit pays faute de données.

16 Les données concernant Maurice proviennent des états financiers établis par le Bureau des statistiques de Maurice.

17 Les recettes fiscales infranationales intègrent les recettes des États, mais excluent celles des collectivités locales.

Références

Akitoby, B. et al. (2019), *Case Studies in Tax Revenue Mobilization in Low-Income Countries*, *https://www.imf.org/en/Publications/WP/Issues/2019/05/14/Case-Studies-in-Tax-Revenue-Mobilization-in-Low-Income-Countries-46719* (consulté le 20 septembre 2021). [18]

ATAF (2020), *Mining Tax Policy Responses to COVID-19: Webinar Q&A*, *https://www.ataftax.org/mining-tax-policy-responses-to-covid-19-webinar-q-a*. [50]

BAD/OCDE/PNUD (2016), *Perspectives économiques en Afrique 2016 ; Villes durables et transformation structurelle*, Éditions OCDE, Paris, *https://dx.doi.org/10.1787/aeo-2016-fr*. [36]

BAfD (2021), *Equatorial Guinea Economic Outlook, African Development Bank - Building today, a better Africa tomorrow*, *https://www.afdb.org/en/countries/central-africa/equatorial-guinea/equatorial-guinea-economic-outlook* (consulté le 20 septembre 2021). [8]

BAfD/OCDE/CEA (2010), *African Economic Outlook 2010: Domestic Resource Mobilisation and Aid*, Éditions OCDE, Paris, *http://dx.doi.org/10.1787/aeo-2010-en*. [28]

BAfD/OCDE/PNUD (2015), *Perspectives économiques en Afrique 2015 : Développement territorial et inclusion spatiale*, Éditions OCDE, Paris, *https://doi.org/10.1787/aeo-2015-fr*. [51]

Banque centrale de Mauritanie (2019), *Rapport annuel*, *https://www.bcm.mr/IMG/pdf/rapport_anuel_2019.fr.pdf* (consulté le 20 septembre 2021). [12]

Banque mondiale (2021), *World Bank Country and Lending Groups*, *https://datahelpdesk.worldbank.org/knowledgebase/articles/906519* (consulté le 20 septembre 2021). [15]

Banque mondiale (2020), *Mali Economic Update*, *https://documents1.worldbank.org/curated/en/781261603955655796/pdf/Mali-Economic-and-Poverty-Update-during-COVID-19.pdf* (consulté le 20 septembre 2021). [9]

Banque mondiale (2018), *La Banque mondiale aide le Tchad à mobiliser et à améliorer la gestion des ressources intérieures*, *https://www.banquemondiale.org/fr/news/press-release/2018/07/06/chad-world-bank-helps-strengthen-domestic-resource-mobilization-and-management*. [22]

Boisard, S., C. de Freitas et G. Hidouci (2014), *Renforcer les recettes fiscales locales pour financer le développement urbain en Afrique*, Fonds Mondial pour le Développement des Villes (FMDV), Paris, *http://delog.org/web/wp-content/uploads/2016/03/Etude-FMDV-Fiscalite%CC%81-locale-Villes-Afrique-8-Cas.pdf*. [54]

Brautigam, D., O. Fjeldstad et M. Moore (2008), *Taxation and State-Building in Developing Countries: Capacity and Consent – ICTD, CMI*, *https://www.ictd.ac/publication/taxation-and-state-building-in-developing-countries-capacity-and-consent/* (consulté le 20 septembre 2021). [32]

Cnossen, S. (2015), *Mobilizing VAT revenues in African countries*, *https://www.researchgate.net/publication/276344974_Mobilizing_VAT_revenues_in_African_countries*. [38]

CNUCED (2018), *Investment Policy Review of Cabo Verde*, *http://unctad.org/ipr* (consulté le 7 septembre 2020). [39]

Coady, D. et al. (2015), « How Large Are Global Energy Subsidies? », *IMF Working Paper*, *https://www.imf.org/external/pubs/ft/wp/2015/wp15105.pdf*. [48]

CUA/OCDE (2021), *Dynamiques du développement en Afrique 2021 : Transformation digitale et qualité de l'emploi*, Commission de l'Union africaine, Addis Ababa, Éditions OCDE, Paris, *https://dx.doi.org/10.1787/cd08eac8-fr*. [30]

Diallo, M. (2018), « UEMOA : L'optimisation de la mobilisation des recettes fiscales propres, au centre d'un séminaire », *LeFaso.net*, *https://lefaso.net/spip.php?article84079*. [6]

Economist Intelligence (2018), *New income tax law comes into force*, *http://country.eiu.com/article.aspx?articleid=1636776147&Country=Rwanda&topic=Economy&subtopic=Fo_2* (consulté le 20 septembre 2021). [21]

EITI (2021), *Mauritania | Extractive Industries Transparency Initiative*, *https://eiti.org/mauritania* (consulté le 21 septembre 2021). [11]

Fjeldstad, O., G. Chambas et J. Brun (2014), *Local government taxation in Sub-Saharan Africa: a review and an agenda for research*, 2, Chr. Michelsen Institute, Bergen, *http://www.cmi.no/publications/file/5098-local-government-taxation-in-sub-saharan-africa.pdf*. [52]

FMI (2021), *Union économique et monétaire ouest-africaine : Rapport des services du FMI sur les politiques communes des pays membres – communiqué de presse, rapport des services du FMI et déclaration de l'administrateur pour les pays membres de l'UEMOA*, *https://www.imf.org/-/media/Files/Publications/CR/2021/French/1WAUFA2021001.ashx* (consulté le 20 septembre 2021). [7]

FMI (2021), *World Economic Outlook Database, April 2021*, *https://www.imf.org/en/Publications/WEO/weo-database/2021/April* (consulté le 20 septembre 2021). [5]

FMI (2020), *Mali : Demande de décaissement au titre de la facilité de crédit rapide et de rééchelonnement de l'accès au titre de la facilité élargie de crédit – communiqué de presse, rapport des services du FMI et déclaration de l'administrateur pour le Mali*, *https://www.imf.org/-/media/Files/Publications/CR/2020/French/1MLIFA2020002.ashx* (consulté le 20 septembre 2021). [10]

FMI (2020), *The Development Path Less Traveled-The Experience of Rwanda*, *https://www.imf.org/en/Publications/Departmental-Papers-Policy-Papers/Issues/2020/08/17/The-Development-Path-Less-Travelled-The-Experience-of-Rwanda-49609*. [20]

FMI (2020), *World Economic Outlook, April 2020 : The Great Lockdown*. [37]

FMI (2019), *République démocratique du Congo : Consultation de 2019 au titre de l'article iv - communiqué de presse ; rapport des services du FMI ; et déclaration du Directeur exécutif pour la République démocratique du Congo*, *https://www.imf.org/-/media/Files/Publications/CR/2019/French/1CODFA2019001.ashx* (consulté le 8 septembre 2020). [40]

FMI (2019), *World Economic Outlook – Frequently Asked Questions*, *https://www.imf.org/external/pubs/ft/weo/faq.htm#q4d* (consulté le 6 septembre 2019). [26]

FMI (2014), *Mauritius: 2014 article IV consultation-staff report (2014b)*, FMI, *http://www.imf.org/external/pubs/ft/scr/2014/cr14107.pdf*. [53]

Gaspar, V. et al. (2019), *Fiscal Policy and Development : Human, Social, and Physical Investments for the SDGs*, *https://www.imf.org/en/Publications/Staff-Discussion-Notes/Issues/2019/01/18/Fiscal-Policy-and-Development-Human-Social-and-Physical-Investments-for-the-SDGs-46444* (consulté le 20 septembre 2021). [14]

Gwaindepi, A. (2021), « Domestic revenue mobilisation in developing countries: An exploratory analysis of sub-Saharan Africa and Latin America », *Journal of International Development*, vol. 33/2, pp. 396-421, *http://dx.doi.org/10.1002/JID.3528*. [31]

Lesotho Times (2020), « LRA misses revenue target amid COVID-19 economic impact – Lesotho Times », *https://lestimes.com/lra-misses-revenue-target-amid-covid-19-economic-impact/* (consulté le 20 septembre 2021). [13]

Marten, M. et K. van Dender (2019), « The use of revenues from carbon pricing », *Documents de travail de l'OCDE sur la fiscalité*, n° 43, Éditions OCDE, Paris, *https://dx.doi.org/10.1787/3cb265e4-en*. [42]

Mawejje, J. (2019), « Natural resources governance and tax revenue mobilization in sub saharan Africa: The role of EITI », *Resources Policy*, vol. 62, pp. 176-183, *http://dx.doi.org/10.1016/J.RESOURPOL.2019.04.001*. [29]

Monkam, N. et M. Moore (2015), *How Property Tax Would Benefit Africa*, Africa Research Institute, *http://www.africaresearchinstitute.org/publications/property-tax-benefit-africa*. [55]

Moore, M., W. Prichard et O. Fjeldstad (2018), *Taxing Africa: Coercion, Reform and Development – ICTD*, Zed Books, *https://www.ictd.ac/publication/taxing-africa-coercion-reform-and-development/* (consulté le 20 septembre 2021). [16]

OCDE (2021), *Revenue Statistics in Asia and the Pacific 2021: Emerging Challenges for the Asia-Pacific Region in the COVID-19*, Éditions OCDE, Paris, *https://doi.org/10.1787/ed374457-en*. [1]

OCDE (2021), *Tendances des impôts sur la consommation 2020 : TVA/TPS et droits d'accises – taux, tendances et questions stratégiques*, Éditions OCDE, Paris, *https://dx.doi.org/10.1787/3f06ea4d-fr*. [35]

OCDE (2020), « OECD analysis of budgetary support and tax expenditures. 2020 country notes », *Inventory of Support Measures for Fossil Fuels database*, *http://www.oecd.org/fossil-fuels/data/*. [47]

OCDE (2020), *PINE database*, *https://www.oecd.org/fr/environnement/outils-evaluation/environmentaltaxation.htm*. [44]

OCDE (2020), *Statistiques des recettes publiques 2020*, Éditions OCDE, Paris, *https://dx.doi.org/10.1787/c6381ca6-fr*. [3]

OCDE (2019), *Tax Morale: What Drives People and Businesses to Pay Tax?*, Éditions OCDE, *https://doi.org/10.1787/f3d8ea10-en*. [25]

OCDE (2018), *Tendances des impôts sur la consommation 2018 : TVA/TPS et droits d'accise: taux, tendances et questions stratégiques*, Éditions OCDE, Paris, *https://dx.doi.org/10.1787/g2g9fa9e-fr*. [34]

OCDE (2015), *Coopération pour le développement 2014 : Mobiliser les ressources au service du développement durable*, Éditions OCDE, Paris, *https://dx.doi.org/10.1787/dcr-2014-fr*. [24]

OCDE (2005), *Glossary of statistical terms*, *https://stats.oecd.org/glossary/detail.asp?ID=6437*. [41]

OCDE et al. (2021), *Revenue Statistics in Latin America and the Caribbean*, Éditions OCDE, Paris, *https://doi.org/10.1787/96ce5287-en-es*. [2]

OCDE/CUA/ATAF (2021), *Recettes fiscales en Afrique : Tableaux comparatifs*, Éditions OCDE, Paris, *https://doi.org/10.1787/7fb1581d-fr*. [4]

OCDE/CUA/ATAF (2020), *Revenue Statistics in Africa 2020: 1990-2018*, Éditions OCDE, Paris, *https://doi.org/10.1787/14e1edb1-en-fr*. [17]

OCDE/FIT (2019), *Tax revenue implications from the decarbonisation of road transport: Scenarios for Slovenia*, Éditions OCDE, *https://doi.org/10.1787/87b39a2f-en*. [43]

OMS (2015), *Purchasing Power Parity 2005*, Organisation mondiale de la santé, *http://www.who.int/choice/costs/ppp/en/*. [27]

PwC (2019), *Sustaining the momemtum: Rwanda's 2019/20 National Budget Bulletin*, *https://www.pwc.com/rw/en/pdf/rwanda-budget-analysis-2019-20.pdf*. [19]

Reuters (2019), *South African carbon tax finally becomes law*, *https://www.reuters.com/article/us-safrica-carbontax/south-african-carbon-tax-finally-becomes-law-idUSKCN1SW0K6* (consulté le 6 septembre 2019). [46]

SACU (2020), *What is SACU?*, *http://www.sacu.int/about/what_is.html* (consulté le 10 septembre 2020). [23]

SARS (2020), *Tax statistics 2020*, *https://www.sars.gov.za/wp-content/uploads/Docs/TaxStats/2020/Tax-Statistics-2020.pdf*. [45]

SSA (2015), *Social Security Through the World: Africa*, SSA Publication Social Security Administration, Washington, DC, *http://www.ssa.gov/policy/docs/progdesc/ssptw/2014-2015/africa/ssptw15africa.pdf*. [33]

Worrall, L., S. Whitley et A. Scott (2018), « Reforming Africa's Fossil Fuel Subsidies », *sun-connect-news.org*, *https://www.sun-connect-news.org/de/articles/business/details/reforming-africas-fossil-fuel-subsidies/*. [49]

Chapter 2

Non-tax revenue trends, 2000-2019

Chapitre 2

Tendances des recettes non fiscales, 2000-2019

Revenue Statistics in Africa 1990-2019/Statistiques des recettes publiques en Afrique 1990-2019

Chapter 2

Non-tax revenue trends, 2000-2019

Introduction

A complete picture of public finances requires statistics that go beyond taxation, especially in the case of many African countries that obtain substantial revenues in the form of grants or royalties from oil and minerals. *Revenue Statistics in Africa* collects statistics on both tax and non-tax revenues, non-tax revenues being government revenues that do not meet the OECD definition of taxation. Although data on non-tax revenues might not come from the same sources or have the same reliability as tax statistics (see Box 2.1), they need to be included in any accounting of a country's total financial resources. This chapter provides cross-country comparisons of non-tax revenues for the countries in this publication.[1]

The main categories of non-tax revenues[2] reported as part of this project are (see also Annex B):

- grants from foreign governments or international organisations (budget aid, food aid, capital transfers, current transfers, project grants, programme grants, international debt relief, etc.);
- rents and royalties (such as oil or mining royalties);
- other property income (interest, dividends and other returns on government investment);
- sales of goods and services (which include some administrative fees);
- fines and penalties (including fines and penalties due to tax violations);
- miscellaneous and unidentified revenues (non-tax revenues that cannot be classified according to the other categories).

Box 2.1. **Non-tax revenues and data reliability**

Data on non-tax revenues are often less detailed than tax revenue data. Some countries might have aggregate figures for total non-tax revenues in some years but do not break this information down beyond grants and other non-tax revenue categories. This may be because data on non-tax revenues often comes from several different sources. Revenue Statistics in Africa indicates cases where total non-tax revenues are reported but may be incomplete.

Non-tax revenue data are not necessarily subject to the same level of scrutiny as tax revenues. Many types of non-tax revenue are not part of the main budget process, nor are they defined by legislation so they are not subject to the same oversight mechanisms as tax revenues. Non-tax revenues that are not accompanied by legal compulsions do not always require the same documentation.

Non-tax revenues are often under the responsibility of different authorities than tax revenues, so there is not necessarily a separation made between revenues and expenses. Some revenues, such as administrative fees, might be used as cost-recovery mechanisms and subtracted from cost figures rather than reported as revenues. This could be the case for local governments or other public institutions for which data only exists on net transfers of funds to the central government.

Grants, legal settlements and mining and oil contracts also often involve large payments by external entities such as multinational corporations and foreign governments that do not necessarily have incentives to maintain transparency. There could also be incentives to collude with local authorities to conceal costs. In addition, some countries may negotiate large payments from resource extraction payments as a lump sum that bundles together many categories of both tax and non-tax revenue, making detailed breakdowns less feasible.

Non-tax revenues as a percentage of GDP

In 2019, non-tax revenues as a percentage of GDP varied significantly among the 30 countries included in this publication. They ranged from 26.7% of GDP in Lesotho to 0.5% of GDP in South Africa. In every country except Botswana, Lesotho, and the Republic of the Congo, non-tax revenues were lower than tax revenues (Figure 2.1). On average, the amount of non-tax revenue collected in each country was 45.4% of the amount collected in tax revenues.

Figure 2.1. **Total tax and non-tax revenue by country, 2019**

Percentage of GDP

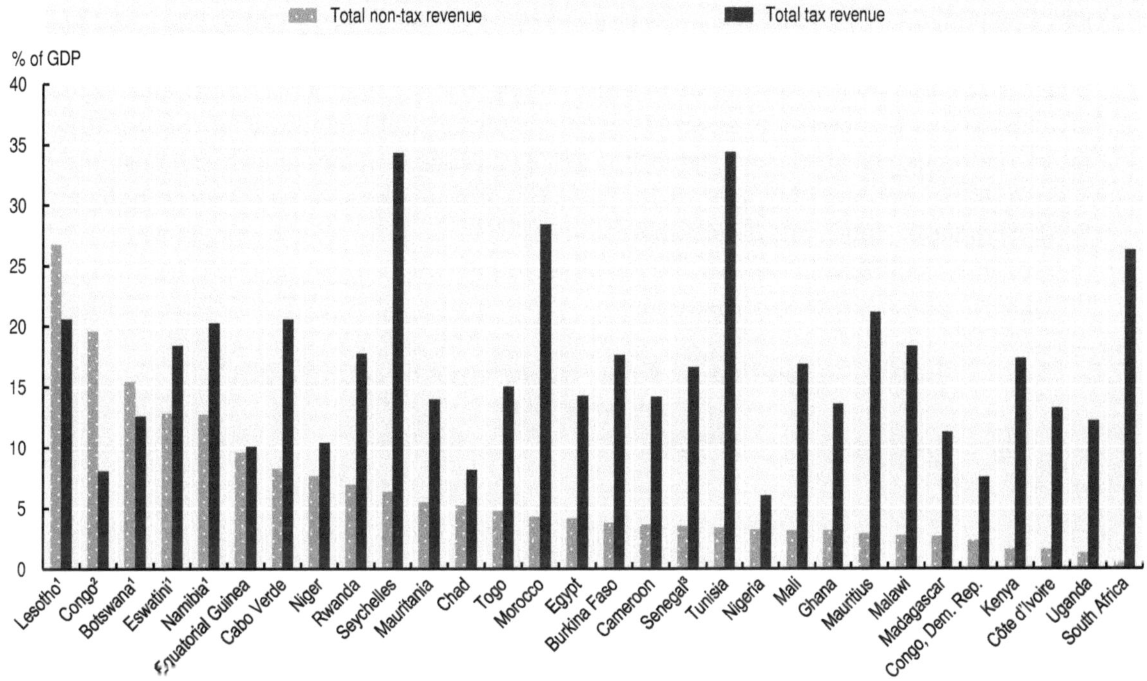

Notes: Non-tax revenue includes sub-national non-tax government revenues for Eswatini, Kenya, Mauritius, and Morocco, the only countries for which such revenues are reported. In 2019, these represented, respectively, 1%, 22%, 5% and 39% of all non-tax revenue collected for each country. Mauritania, Nigeria and South Africa reported some local and regional taxes, but no local and regional non-tax revenues.

1. Non-tax revenues for Botswana, Eswatini, Lesotho, and Namibia include funds from excises and customs duties collected by South Africa and then transferred to them through the Southern African Customs Union (SACU) revenue-sharing agreement.
2. Figures for grant revenues and oil revenues for the Republic of the Congo are those reported by the IMF in its April 2021 *World Economic Outlook*.
3. 2018 figures were used for Senegal since 2019 figures were not available.

The tax-to-GDP ratios and non-tax-to-GDP ratios need to be interpreted with caution for some countries due to incomplete data. See the country tables in Chapters 5 and 6 for further information.

Source: Table 4.1 in Chapter 4 and Table 6.1 in Chapter 6.

StatLink https://doi.org/10.1787/888934282474

As explained in Box 1.1 of Chapter 1, changes to the ratios of revenues to GDP can depend on factors that impact the numerator or the denominator. In many years, an increase in revenue happens at the same time that GDP declines, and vice versa. This is particularly pronounced for grant revenues and rents and royalties. Between 2009 and 2019, 48% of year-over-year changes in grant revenues were accompanied by a change in GDP that went in the opposite direction – that is, either an increase in grants occurred at the same time as a decrease in GDP, or a decrease in grants coincided with an increase in GDP. For rents and royalties, this percentage was 37%. The importance of resource extraction for both revenues and economic growth in some countries can explain some of this difference. The IMF calculated (IMF, 2021[1]) that oil-related GDP was over 30% of total GDP in Equatorial Guinea, and over 19% in Chad in 2019, so an increase in oil production in these two countries in a year could have a significant impact on both oil rents and overall GDP. On the other hand, with grant royalties, there could be lag times between a change in grant levels and its impact on a country's economy so that the annual variance in grant levels might not align with the variance in GDP levels.

Different clusters of countries appear when looking at the relationship between tax revenues and non-tax revenues as a percentage of GDP (Figure 2.2). The three countries with oil and gas production over 15% of GDP (Chad, the Republic of the Congo and Equatorial Guinea) are among those with the lowest tax-to-GDP ratios in this chart. Nine of the countries in this chart are identified as "resource-rich" since over 10% of their GDP came from oil, gas, coal and mineral production for at least 5 years between 2010 and 2019, according to World Bank data. All of these countries (Botswana, Chad, the Democratic Republic of the Congo, Equatorial Guinea, Ghana, Mauritania, Nigeria, the Republic of the Congo, and Togo) are clustered in the lower left hand side of the scatterplot with relatively low tax-to-GDP ratios. Countries that are net recipients of revenues through the Southern African Customs Union (SACU) also have high non-tax revenues (see further explanation in the section on SACU revenues). Upper middle-income countries that are not major oil producers tend to have less of both grant revenues and resource revenues, which may increase the need to mobilise domestic resources via taxation.

Figure 2.2. **Total tax and non-tax revenue by country, 2019**

Percentage of GDP

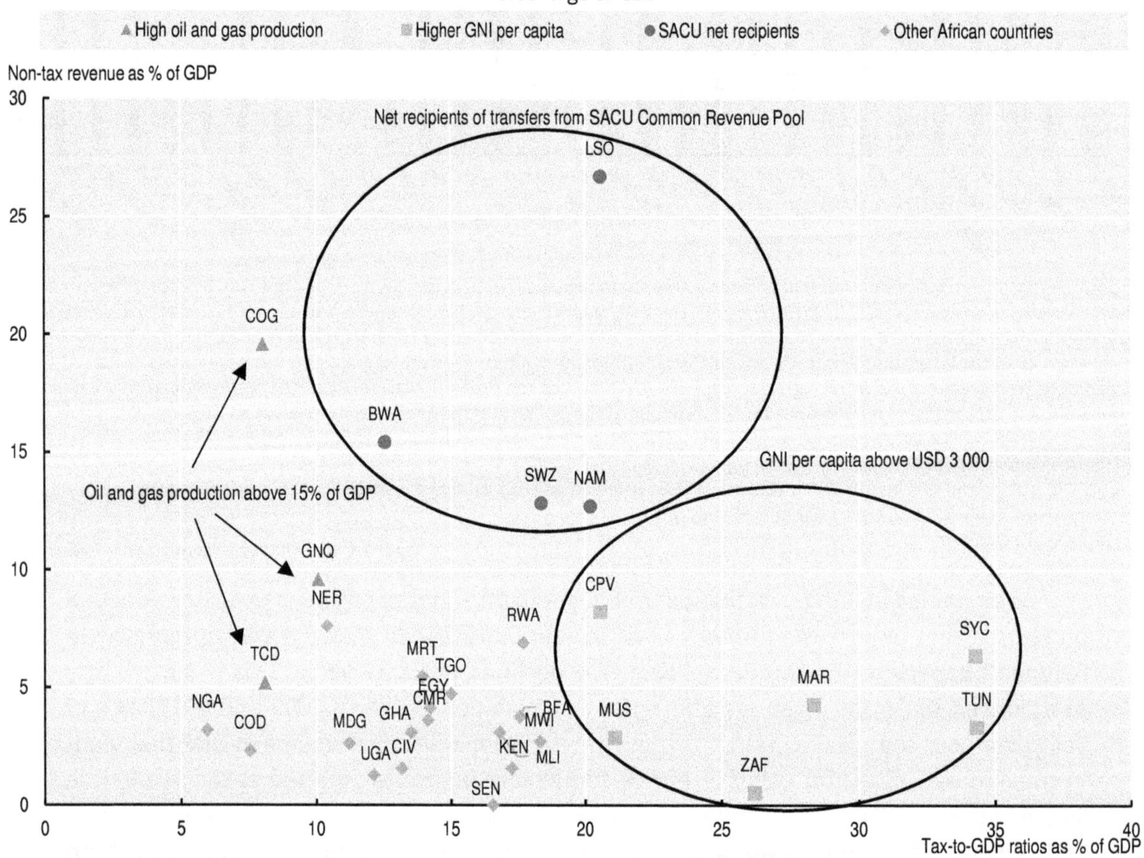

Note: See footnotes to Figure 2.1 and country tables in Chapters 5 and 6 for further information.

Source: Authors' calculations based on data from (OECD/AUC/ATAF, 2021[2]), "Revenue Statistics in Africa: Comparative tables", *OECD Tax Statistics* (database), *https://doi.org/10.1787/be755711-en*, and World Bank *World Development Indicators* (database) (World Bank, 2021[3]) for figures on oil and gas production as a % of GDP and for GNI per capita.

StatLink https://doi.org/10.1787/888934282493

While the Africa (30) average tax-to-GDP ratio rose between 2010 and 2019, average non-tax revenues have declined significantly (Figure 2.3). After peaking in 2012 at 8.6% of GDP, average non-tax revenues dropped to 5.9% in 2016 before reaching 6.3% in 2019. This decline was driven by declines in rents and royalties and in grant revenues as a percentage of GDP. In 2019, grant revenues as a percentage of GDP were at 1.3% of GDP, their lowest point since 2010. Rents and royalties were at 1.7%, 1 percentage point lower than in 2012, after having rebounded only slightly from their 2016 low point. These declines have been enough to cause total revenues to go down over this period, leading to increased deficits and indebtedness (See Chapter 3).

Figure 2.3. **Africa (30) average non-tax revenues, 2010-19**

Percentage of GDP

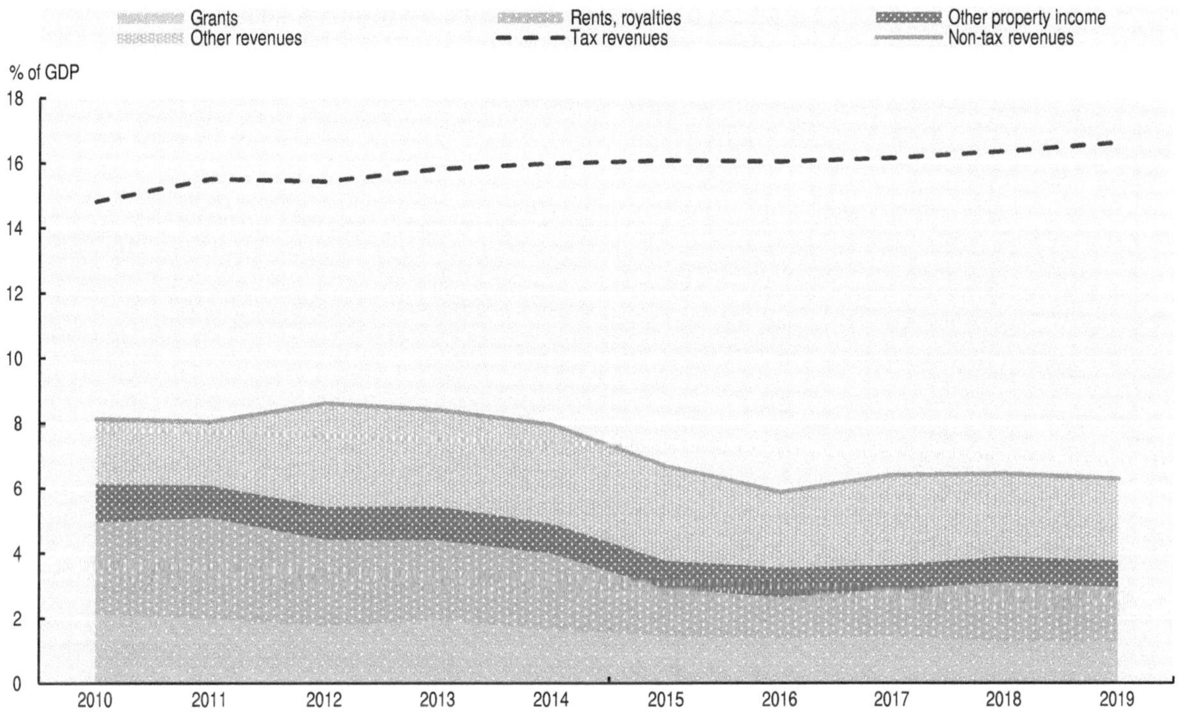

Source: Authors' calculations based on data from (OECD/AUC/ATAF, 2021[2]), "Revenue Statistics in Africa: Comparative tables", *OECD Tax Statistics* (database), *https://doi.org/10.1787/be755711-en*.

StatLink https://doi.org/10.1787/888934282512

Different sources of non-tax revenues are associated with different types of risk, either due to their annual variability, or their vulnerability to economic shocks and political changes. Figure 2.4 shows the contribution of each sub-category to total non-tax revenues for each country. Four distinct groups are apparent in these data:

- Nine countries received a majority of their non-tax revenue in the form of grants in 2019 (in descending order, Niger, Rwanda, Togo, Senegal,[3] Mali, Malawi, Madagascar, Côte d'Ivoire, and Uganda).
- Six countries received most of their non-tax revenues from rents and royalties (in descending order, the Republic of the Congo, Equatorial Guinea, Mauritania, Chad, Cameroon, and Nigeria). For all these countries, oil royalties provided the majority of non-tax revenues.

- Botswana, Eswatini, Lesotho, and Namibia, the four neighbours of South Africa that belong to SACU, received substantial non-tax revenues in terms of transfers from the SACU Common Revenue Pool (Box 2.2).
- For the remaining eleven countries, neither grants, rents and royalties, nor SACU revenues constituted a majority of non-tax revenues. The main sources of non-tax revenues for these countries included: interest and dividends for Seychelles and Tunisia; fees for goods and services for Ghana, Kenya, Mauritius and Morocco; and miscellaneous and unallocated revenues for Egypt. Grants were the largest source of non-tax revenues for Burkina Faso and Cabo Verde, but were less than 50% of non-tax revenues. Similarly, rents and royalties were the largest source of non-tax revenues for the Democratic Republic of the Congo and South Africa, but were less than of their half the non-tax revenues.

Figure 2.4. **Structure of non-tax revenues by country, 2019**

Percentage of GDP

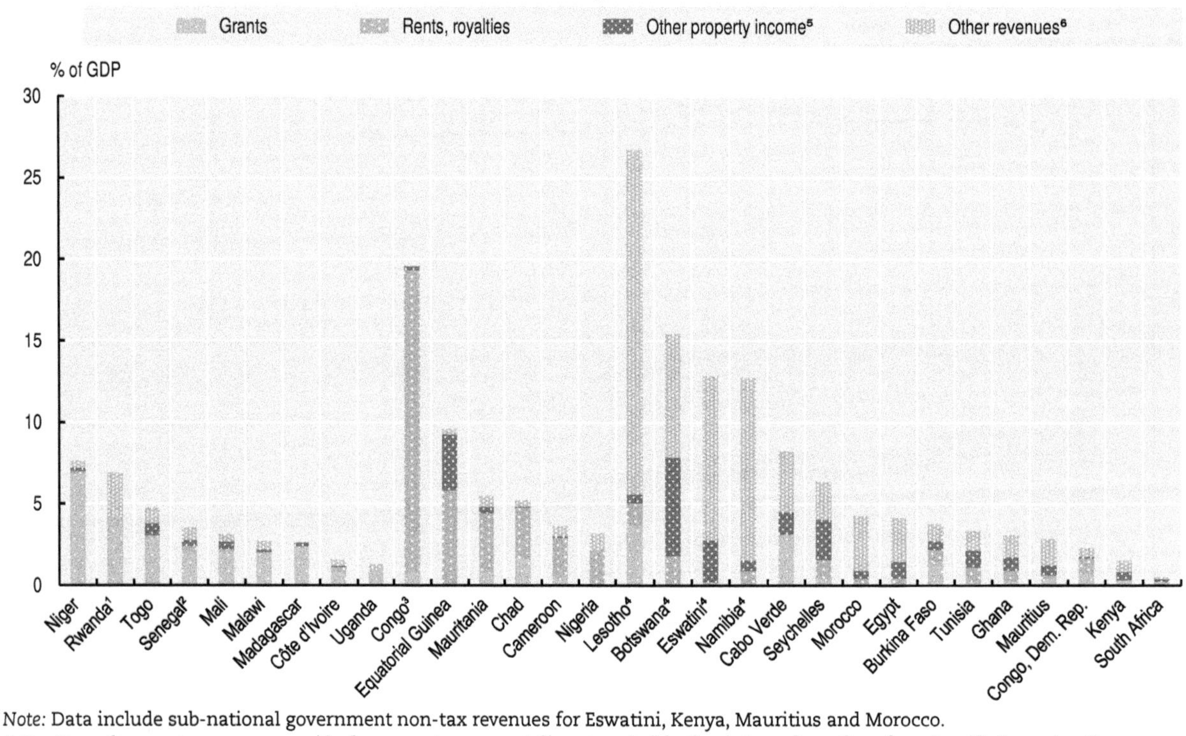

Note: Data include sub-national government non-tax revenues for Eswatini, Kenya, Mauritius and Morocco.

1. For Rwanda, non-tax revenues aside from grants were not disaggregated in the data and are therefore classified as miscellaneous and unidentified revenues.
2. 2018 figures were used for Senegal since 2019 figures were not available.
3. Figures reported here represent mainly grant revenue and oil revenue obtained from the IMF's April 2021 *World Economic Outlook* classified as rents and royalties.
4. For Botswana, Eswatini, Lesotho and Namibia, "Other revenues" include funds from excises and customs duties collected by South Africa and then transferred to these countries through the *Southern African Customs Union* (SACU) revenue-sharing agreement.
5. Interest, dividends, etc.
6. Sales, fines, SACU revenues, etc.

See the footnotes to Figure 2.1 and country tables in Chapters 5 and 6 for further information.

Source: Table 6.2 in Chapter 6.

StatLink https://doi.org/10.1787/888934282531

Different sources of non-tax revenues behave differently over time (Figure 2.5). Many African countries experienced substantial variation in non-tax revenues, regardless of whether they obtained the largest share of their revenues from grants (Burkina Faso and Togo), resource rents (Chad and Mauritania), SACU transfers (Eswatini and Namibia) or other non-tax revenues (Ghana and Mauritius).

Figure 2.5. **Change in the structure of non-tax revenues for selected countries, 2000-19**

Percentage of GDP

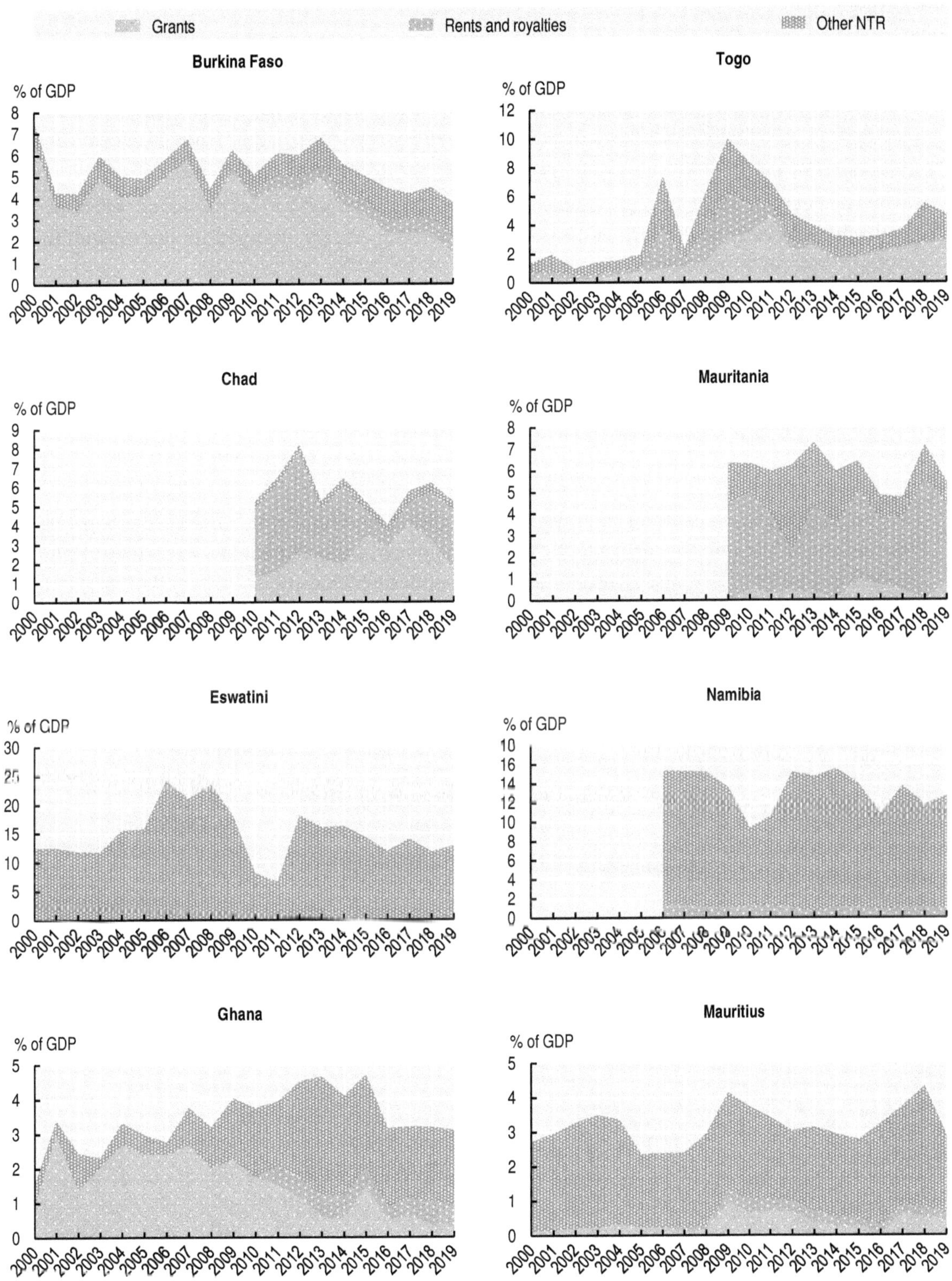

Note: See footnotes to Figure 2.1 and country tables in Chapters 5 and 6 for further information. Charts for all countries in the publication can be found online at the *Statlink* below.

Source: Authors' calculations based on data from (OECD/AUC/ATAF, 2021[2]), "Revenue Statistics in Africa: Comparative tables", *OECD Tax Statistics* (database), *https://doi.org/10.1787/be755711-en.*

StatLink https://doi.org/10.1787/888934282550

Although there are long-term trends in non-tax revenues, these revenues tend to vary more from year to year than do tax revenues. Over the past decade, 15 of the 30 countries in this publication showed at least one year-on-year increase in non-tax revenue equivalent to at least 2% of GDP, while 15 countries registered at least one year-on-year decrease of a similar magnitude. Such fluctuations are often driven by resource rents (caused by swings in commodity prices or production), or by grant revenues (reflecting the shorter duration and lower predictability of grant flows in comparison to tax revenues). Other sources of non-tax revenue, such as Eswatini's SACU revenues, have also proven highly variable.

- In the Republic of the Congo, between 2014 and 2015, after a fall in oil prices, oil revenues dropped from 27.8% of GDP to 10.1% of GDP. In 2015, Congo changed its hydrocarbons code in order to strengthen the national share in oil profits (EIU, 2015$_{[4]}$).
- Between 2011 and 2012, Mali experienced a sudden drop in grant revenues, from 4.5% of GDP down to 0.1% during a year of multiple political crises.
- Eswatini's non-tax revenues fell from 18.2% of GDP to 8.1% between 2009 and 2010, when its SACU revenues as a % of GDP fell by 80% following the collapse in customs and excise taxes in the two years following the global financial crisis.

Grants

This publication contains countries that receive substantial grant revenues alongside some for which grants are negligible. In 2019, 13 countries received grant revenues amounting to less than 0.5% of GDP and 12 received grant revenues which were less than 2% of total tax revenues (Figure 2.6). All of these countries were middle-income or high-income countries, according to the World Bank's classification based on gross national incomes (World Bank, 2021$_{[5]}$). On the other hand, of the ten low-income countries covered by this report, only Uganda received grants amounting to less than 1% of GDP. For six of these countries, grant revenues were equivalent to more than 15% of tax revenues.

Figure 2.6. **Grants by country, 2019**

Percentage of GDP

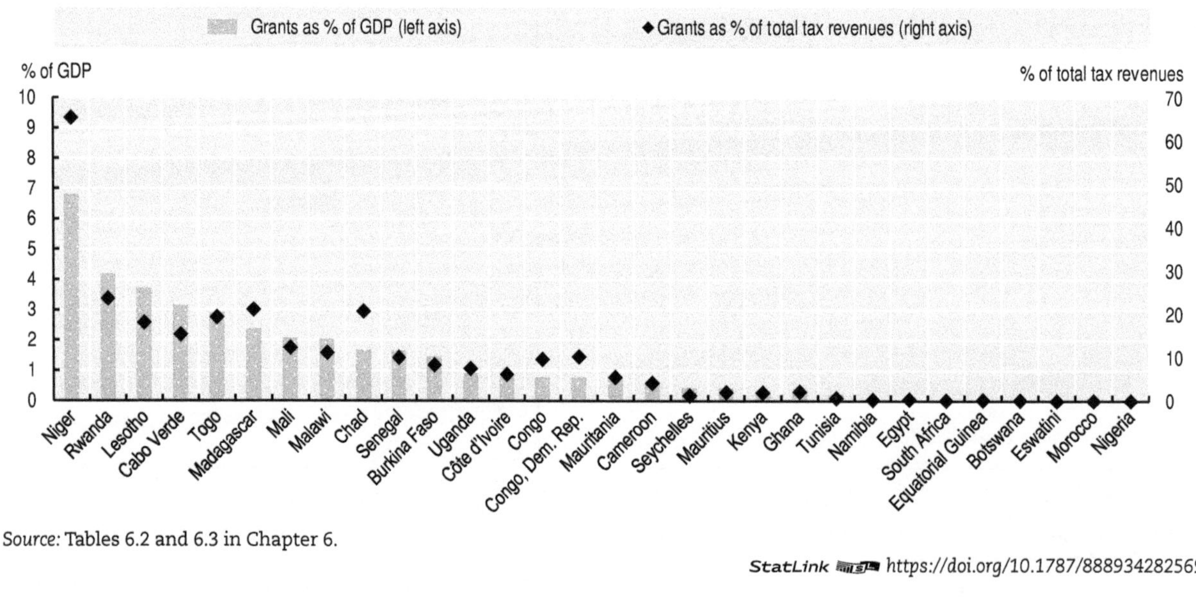

Source: Tables 6.2 and 6.3 in Chapter 6.

StatLink https://doi.org/10.1787/888934282569

Figure 2.7 presents grants as a percentage of GDP received by countries in this publication and their gross national income (GNI) per capita. The figure has an empty upper right-hand quadrant as higher income African countries receive proportionately lower grant revenues. However, many countries occupy the bottom left quadrant of the graph as well, as there are countries with relatively low levels of grant income despite having lower incomes. For example, Burkina Faso, Rwanda and Uganda had GNI per capita in 2019 between USD 780 and USD 830, but they reported grants as a percentage of GDP in that year ranging from 0.9% (Uganda) and 1.5% (Burkina Faso) to 4.2% (Rwanda).

Figure 2.7. **Grants as a percentage of GDP and GNI per capita by country, 2019**

Percentage of GDP

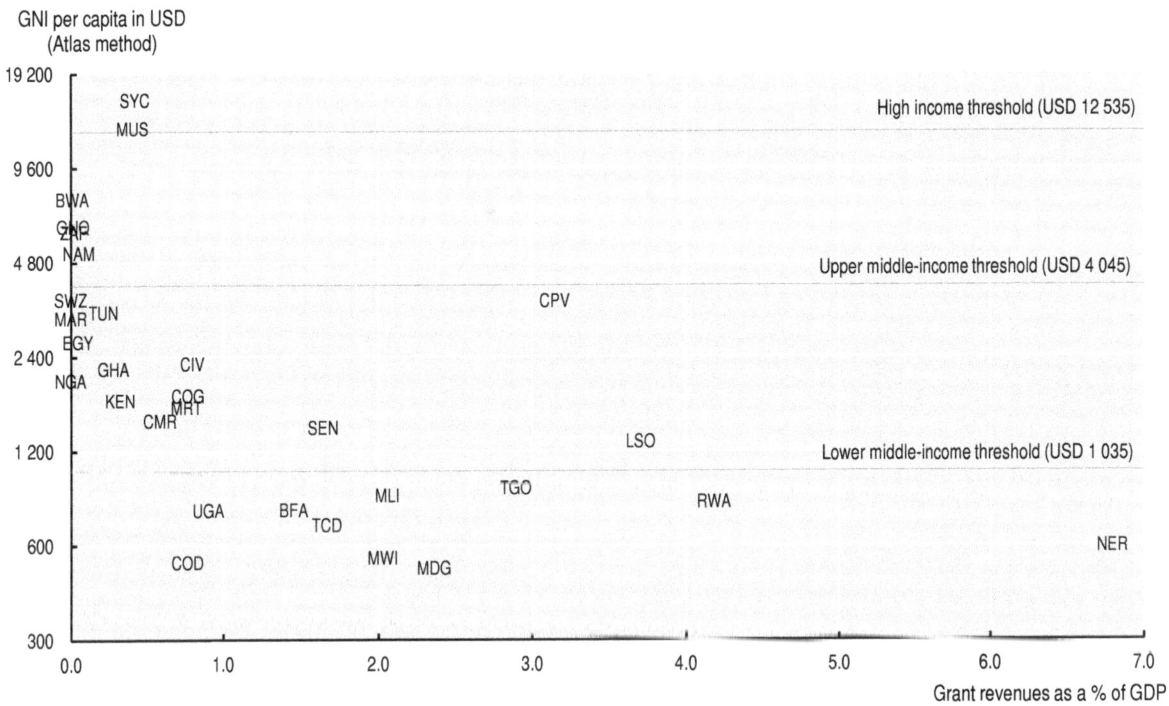

Note: GNI figures are converted to USD using the World Bank Atlas Method.

Source: Table 6.2 in Chapter 6, and World Bank *World Development Indicators* (database) (World Bank, 2021[3]).

StatLink https://doi.org/10.1787/888934282588

Grant revenues and foreign aid are similar concepts, although in practice it is difficult to align aid statistics, as reported by donor countries, with the grant revenues reported by recipient countries, due to data, methodological, and conceptual issues.

Grant revenues have some overlap with official development assistance (ODA), as defined by the OECD Development Assistance Committee (DAC).[3] Grants covered by this publication focus on revenues received by countries from foreign governments and international organisations, whereas ODA is a measure of donor countries' efforts to support development in low- and middle-income countries. ODA not only covers flows captured under "grants" in this publication (budget aid, food aid, capital transfers, current transfers, project grants, programme grants, international debt relief, etc.), but also encompasses concessional loans, in-kind technical assistance, in-donor administrative costs, in-donor refugee costs and scholarships, as well as other activities that do not generate a (net) revenue flow to the country. The volume of ODA received by a given country will thus be different from – and usually higher than – the volume of grants reported in *Revenue Statistics*.

Statistics collected by the DAC on ODA flows to African countries include public flows from all members of the DAC and some countries outside the DAC, as well as multilateral organisations such as the World Bank, the IMF and the UN. Statistics on development co-operation provided by some large non-OECD economies, such as Brazil, China and India, are not included (OECD, 2021[6]).

Comparing grant revenues to net ODA (Figure 2.8) shows that the assistance received by African countries is far greater than the amounts that end up going in to their national budgets. Although the countries receiving the most net ODA tend to receive the most grant revenues, the relationship is not linear and there are notable outliers, such as Malawi, whose net ODA as a percentage of GDP of 15.2% far outstrips all other African countries, but whose grant revenues as a percentage of GDP trail behind 8 other African countries.

Figure 2.8. **Grants and net official development assistance (ODA) received, 2019**

Percentage of GDP

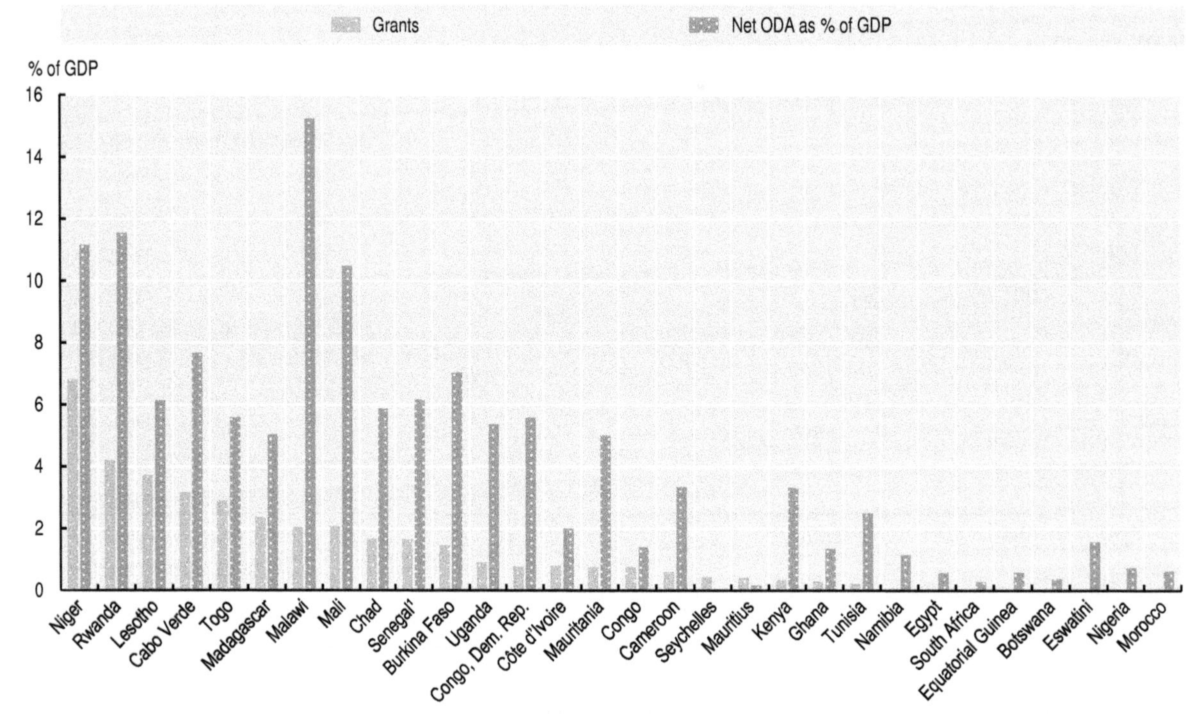

Note: Figures for net ODA include donations from the 30 member countries of the OECD Development Assistance Committee (DAC), the 20 non-DAC countries, as well as multilateral institutions, and private donations. Some major donor countries, such as China are not yet accounted for in these data.

1. 2018 figures were used for Senegal since 2019 figures were not available.

Source: Table 6.2 in Chapter 6 and OECD Development Assistance Committee (DAC) 2021 for the ODA data.

StatLink https://doi.org/10.1787/888934282607

African countries relying on grant revenues often face sudden drops in grants from one year to the next. Eight countries faced a single-year drop in grant revenues of at least 2 percentage points of GDP in at least one year between 2010 and 2019, and for six of these, it was over 3 p.p. Malawi had grants amounting to over 10% of GDP in 2013. They dropped by 65% the following year, in US dollars, the year of the CashGate Scandal (VOANews, 2013[7]). In total, 14 countries among the 30 participating in this publication registered a one-year drop in grant revenues equivalent to at least 1.0% of GDP over the decade.

Average grant revenues as a percentage of GDP for the countries in this publication declined to 1.3% of GDP in 2019 from 2.2% in 2010. Between 2010 and 2019, the only years in which average grants as a percentage of GDP for the countries in this publication increased were 2013 and 2017, with 2014 being the year in which average grants decreased the most. Changes in grant revenues often depend on circumstances unique to the country. Egypt, for example, saw a spike in grant revenues in 2014 following the normalisation of international relations after its internal political crisis, while Mali saw its grant revenues disappear in 2012 with the outbreak of the Mali War before resuming the following year.

The COVID-19 crisis had an impact on aid flows to Africa in order to mitigate the impact of the pandemic. Globally, net ODA from DAC member countries to countries around the world rose by 7% in real terms in 2020 compared with 2019, with aid to multilateral organisations rising by 9% and humanitarian aid rising by 6%. This comes after a decade in which the average annual increase in real terms was 2.0%, with three consecutive years of declines between 2017 and 2019. The increase in net ODA from DAC countries to Africa, by contrast, was more muted, with preliminary data showing a rise of 4.1% in 2020 (OECD, 2021[8]).

Resource revenues and other property income

One of the most important sources of non-tax revenues for governments originates from their status as property owner, especially as land owner. Such revenues are reported as property income in *Revenue Statistics in Africa* and encompass various forms of income (Figure 2.9).

Figure 2.9. **Rents and royalties by country, 2019**

Percentage of GDP

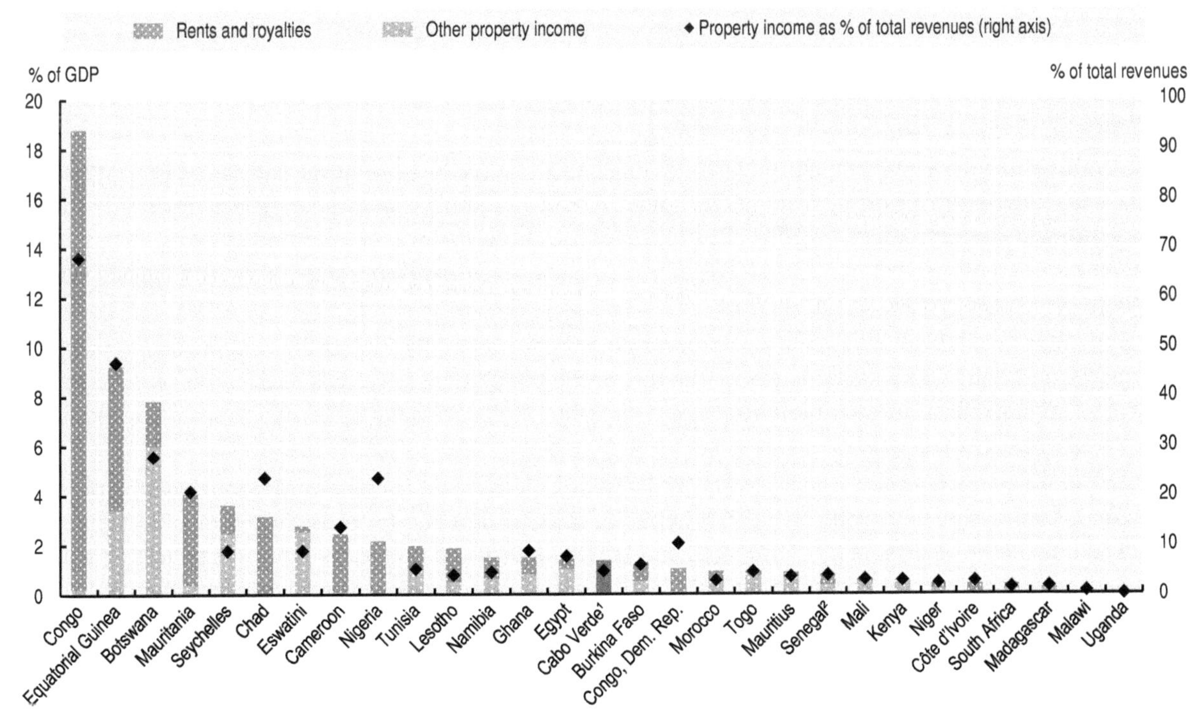

Note: Rwanda is excluded as the data are not available.

1. Cabo Verde property income is not disaggregated.

2. 2018 figures were used for Senegal since 2019 figures were not available.

Source: Authors' calculations based on Tables 6.5-6.34 and Table 4.17.

StatLink https://doi.org/10.1787/888934282626

Rents and royalties are revenues generated from property the government owns, usually by prospecting and extracting non-renewable resources from government land or from harvesting government-owned farms and forests. Interest and dividends are returns on government-owned investments in corporations. In general, royalties from oil and minerals are kept distinct from other forms of investment income, but the issue can become complicated. Many African governments create public corporations that manage oil revenues or maintain revenue-sharing agreements with private corporations that exploit these natural resources. The classification of such funds is not always clear. For example, in Botswana, a significant proportion of property income comes from companies investing in diamond extraction (Box 2.2).

Box 2.2. **Natural resources and public finances**

There are various mechanisms[4] by which natural resources generate revenues or savings for government:

- Rents and royalties are the most direct means of deriving revenue from natural resource wealth. The government charges fees to companies and individuals in exchange for the right to access government lands. It does this in its capacity as landowner and these fees are generally decided through negotiation. These are recorded under property income.
- Payment for services provided by the government is another source of non-tax revenue paid for by businesses in the primary sector. This can include, for example, payments for environmental inspections or for the construction of infrastructure, or, in the case of Mauritius, payment for weather data and maps. These are recorded under sales of goods and services.
- Public ownership (full or partial) of a corporation that exploits natural resources on the government's behalf results in government revenues in the form of profits and dividends. These are recorded under property income. The government of Botswana, for example, collects most of its resource-related revenues from dividends it receives from its 50% stake in Debswana, the company that operates the main diamond mines in Botswana (MiningTechnology, 2020[10]).
- Taxes targeting the activity of natural resource exploitation could be introduced, such as an excise tax on the sale of materials extracted from public lands or a tax on mining that targets the activity, rather than the individual or company exploiting natural resources. These, too, will be recorded as taxes. Such taxes on mining activity exist in Niger and Senegal, who impose taxes on mining activities which are classified under other taxes on goods and services.
- Companies and individuals exploiting natural resources are generally subject to the same taxes (such as income taxes and value-added taxes) as the rest of the population. Revenues from these general taxes will be included in government financial statements, but not necessarily attributed to sectors exploiting natural resources.
- Companies and individuals may use some of the wealth they obtain from natural resource extraction to build infrastructure or provide services. Where this satisfies demand for public investment or services, it could result in savings on government expenditure, but it would not be recorded as revenue. In some cases, as a condition for access to publicly-owned natural resources, governments may demand that companies and individuals provide certain services, for example paying for at least part of the cost of constructing and maintaining roads to mines. An example of this was mining companies participating in a proposed 3 000 km rail link between Benin, Burkina Faso, Niger, Côte d'Ivoire, Ghana, Nigeria and Togo (CNN, 2015[11]).

Revenues from natural resources

Rents and royalties among the 30 countries participating in this publication consist mostly of oil revenues. In 2019, over 79.4% of total rents and royalties in USD were specifically reported as oil revenues (royalties and revenues from revenue-sharing agreements with oil companies), which accounted for a majority of rents and royalties for Cameroon, Chad, the Republic of the Congo, Egypt, Ghana, Equatorial Guinea and Nigeria. Meanwhile, minerals were the source of most rents and royalties for Botswana, Burkina Faso, the Democratic Republic of the Congo, Kenya, Lesotho, Namibia, Niger and Uganda. Fishing accounted for 53% of all revenue recorded as rents and royalties in Seychelles and for 71% in Mauritania in 2019. In Mauritania in 2018, fishing rents were USD 205 million or 2.6% of GDP. Over 88% of total rents and royalties for the 30 countries were resource-related; the remainder included revenues from the construction and operation of airports in Kenya and Togo, for example. Tunisia is only a minor producer of natural gas, but it collects over TND 500 million (Tunisian dinars) each year in rents from the Trans-Mediterranean gas pipeline, which carries Algerian natural gas to Europe (AfricanManager, 2019[9]).

Natural resource revenues tend to be a highly volatile source of financing. Five countries (Chad, Republic of the Congo, Equatorial Guinea, Mauritania and Nigeria) generated rents and royalties equivalent to more than 5% of GDP in at least one of the most recent ten years and they all registered at least one year-over-year decrease in rents and royalties of over 38%. Chad and the Republic of the Congo both saw at least one year with a decrease of over 64%.

As oil royalties are the dominant form of rents and royalties in Africa, these revenues are highly dependent on actual oil prices (Figure 2.10). With or without Nigerian rents and royalties, which, since 2010, have amounted to between 45% and 70% of total rents and royalties collected by African governments, the evolution of African rents and royalties tracks the international crude oil price.

Figure 2.10. **Total rents and royalties in USD and crude oil price in USD, 2010-19**

Percentage of 2010-19 average

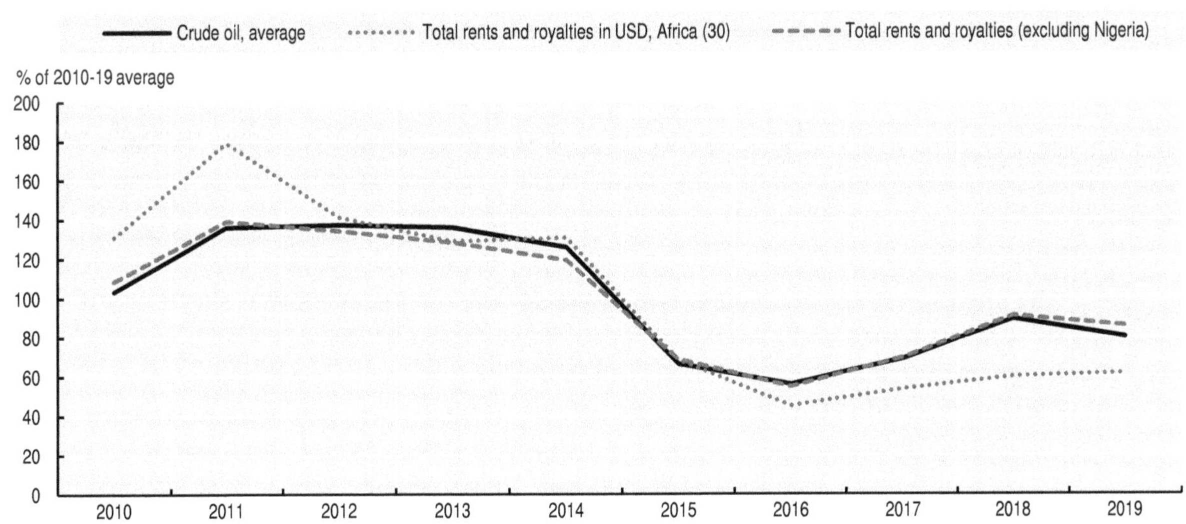

Source: World Bank Commodity Price Data (The Pink Sheet) (World Bank, 2020[12]) and authors' calculations based on data from (OECD/AUC/ATAF, 2021[2]), "Revenue Statistics in Africa: Comparative tables", *OECD Tax Statistics* (database), *https://doi.org/10.1787/be755711-en.*

StatLink *https://doi.org/10.1787/888934282645*

Although resource revenues in African countries are dominated by oil revenues, the countries in this publication have considerable natural resource wealth outside oil, even if, with the exception of Botswana, this generally does not translate into large revenues.

There is a great deal of variation in the size and type of natural resource endowments in African countries. The contribution of this natural wealth to countries' GDP also varies, as does its impact on government budgets. For example, according to World Bank estimates of the contribution of natural resources to economic output (Figure 2.11), Chad, the Republic of the Congo and Equatorial Guinea (mostly oil), and the Democratic Republic of the Congo (mostly minerals) were the four countries for which natural resources contributed an estimated equivalent of 10% of GDP to economic output in 2019 (World Bank, $2021_{[3]}$).[5]

Figure 2.11. **Estimated natural resource extraction, 2019**

Percentage of GDP

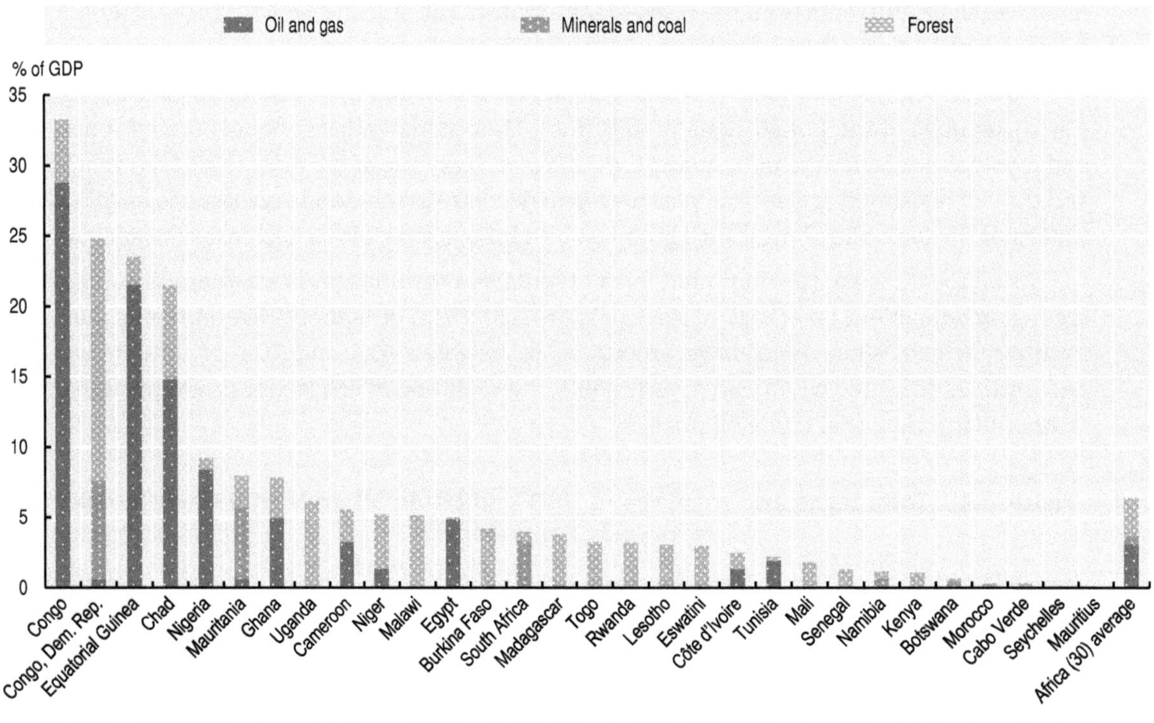

Source: World Bank *World Development Indicators* (database) (World Bank, $2021_{[3]}$) for estimates of the total value of natural resource production in each country.

StatLink https://doi.org/10.1787/888934282664

The impact of countries' natural resource endowment on public finances also varies greatly. Countries such as Chad, the Republic of the Congo, Mauritania and Equatorial Guinea generate significant public revenues from their natural wealth, while South Africa, for example, reported public revenues from natural resource rents equivalent to no more than 0.2% of GDP despite its natural resource wealth production exceeding 3.9% of GDP.

In three countries (the Democratic Republic of the Congo, Malawi and Uganda) wealth generated by forests exceeded 5% of GDP, but did not contribute much to national revenues. Although countries such as Cameroon and Niger did collect some royalties on logging, forest revenues were a small part of the non-tax revenues for the countries in question. Due to the fragility of its Sahel and Saharan ecology, and the importance of wood as an energy source to local communities, Niger has been working with villages on forest management, to establish sustainable forest harvesting practices (Rives, Peltier and Montagne, 2010[13]).

Other non-tax revenues

Certain countries generate substantial non-tax revenues from the normal operations of government. These revenues can be divided into sales of goods and services, fines and penalties, and miscellaneous and unidentified non-tax revenues. The challenges in compiling non-tax revenues outlined in Box 2.3 are often encountered in these kinds of revenues, since they are typically not collected by tax administrations and are often not defined by legislation. They might not even be captured by government budgets.

For all these categories of revenues, there can be arguments about the degree to which they are unrequited or compulsory, and therefore whether they are more properly classified as taxes. The question of which administrative fees are taxes and which are not is discussed in Annexes A and B. However, this is not always clear for the question of fines and penalties.

Institutions and governments that have less authority, and thus less tax collection power, may rely more on these kinds of non-tax revenues. This means that the lack of information in this publication on local government finances might under-estimate the non-tax revenues collected by these institutions.

Sales of goods and services and administrative fees

Governments produce goods and services both as a market- and as a non-market participant. As a market participant, governments sometimes provide goods and services that can also be obtained from private companies (such as selling food or providing transportation). At the same time, they also provide services in the course of administering programmes and executing laws that are unique to the function of government. Fees charged for these non-market services are generally classified as administrative fees.

Administrative fees are often difficult to classify since they occupy a grey area between payments for services (which are non-tax revenues) and compulsory unrequited payments collected during government operations (which are taxes).[6] Court fees and fees for driver's licences, passports, patent registrations and marriage certificates tend to be classified as non-tax revenues. When administrative fees are classified as taxes, they are typically assigned to one of the following categories:

- 4400 Taxes on financial and capital transactions (for example, taxes on sales of land);
- 5200 Taxes on use of goods and performing activities (for example hunting licences, vehicle registrations);
- 6000 Other taxes (for example, sales of fiscal stamps, where stamps are used to pay for taxes and administrative fees).

Six countries generated revenues from sales of goods and services and administrative fees equivalent to at least 1% of GDP in 2019 (Figure 2.12): Cabo Verde (3.1% of GDP), Egypt (1.3% of GDP), Ghana (1.3% of GDP), Lesotho (2.7% of GDP), Morocco (1.8% of GDP) and Seychelles (2.1% of GDP). In the cases of Cabo Verde, these revenues were equivalent to 16.5% of total tax revenues, and for Lesotho, 13.2%.

The composition of these revenues varied by country. In Cabo Verde, 98% of revenues listed under "sales of goods and services" were fees. In Ghana, most revenues listed as sales of goods and services were collected by Municipalities, Departments and Agencies or by Metropolitan, Municipal and District Assemblies. In Morocco, 53% of revenue from government sales of goods and services were collected at the local level.

Figure 2.12. **Sales of goods and services and administrative fees and other revenues related to administration, 2019**

Percentage of GDP

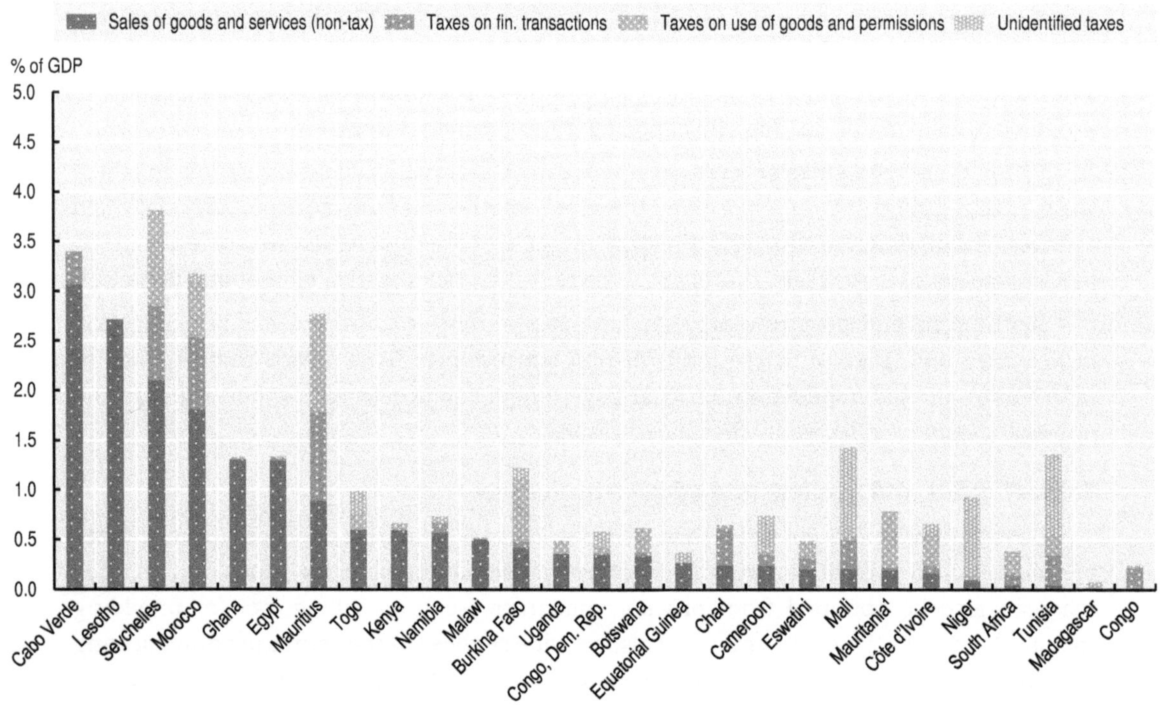

Note: Figures reported here include sub-national tax revenues for Mauritius, Morocco, Nigeria, and South Africa and sub-national non-tax revenues for Eswatini, Kenya, Mauritius, and Morocco, the only countries for which such revenues were reported for 2019. Nigeria, Rwanda, and Senegal are excluded as data are not available.

Source: Authors' calculations based on data from (OECD/AUC/ATAF, 2021[2]), "Revenue Statistics in Africa: Comparative tables", *OECD Tax Statistics* (database), *https://doi.org/10.1787/be755711-en*.

StatLink *https://doi.org/10.1787/888934282683*

Miscellaneous or unidentified revenue

Some notable categories of non-tax revenue do not fit within any of the categories listed above. These include:

- capital transfers not included elsewhere;
- voluntary donations to government agencies from individuals or private corporations (not including donations from international organisations, which are classified as grants);
- private payments to government made as a result of major court settlements or insurance claims (such as the EUR 100 million payment ArcelorMittal agreed to pay to the government of Senegal after a court case following the cancelation of an iron mine (RFI, 2014[14]);
- payments covering different categories in the classification list where a breakdown is not available;
- payments whose proper classification is unknown due to a lack of data. Rwanda did not disaggregate non-tax revenue outside of grants, so these were included in this category;

- SACU revenues to Botswana, Eswatini, Lesotho and Namibia (see Box 2.3).

Miscellaneous and unidentified revenues can be a significant component of non-tax revenues in certain countries. These include exceptional voluntary contributions to government in Tunisia, capital transfers from special statutory funds in Mauritius and, in Morocco, payments made to government in exchange for the right to compete with state institutions in the provision of services.

The volatility of miscellaneous and unidentified revenues may be due to large capital transfers, revenue streams that are short-lived or funds that are reclassified as unidentified due to lack of information. The higher values for this category could reflect uncertainty as to the true amount of revenue within other non-tax revenue classifications.

Box 2.3. **SACU revenue**

The Southern African Customs Union (SACU) incorporates Botswana, Eswatini, Lesotho, Namibia and South Africa. It is headquartered in Windhoek, Namibia. Its vision is "an economic community with equitable and sustainable development, dedicated to the welfare of its people for a common future".

SACU is the oldest customs union in the world, having been founded in 1899 between the British colony of Cape of Good Hope and the Orange Free State Boer Republic. Subsequent agreements in 1910 and 1969 included Botswana, Eswatini and Lesotho. Following Namibia's independence in 1990 and the end of apartheid in South Africa in 1994, new negotiations led to the current SACU agreement, which was signed in 2002.

The SACU agreement provides for free movement of SACU manufactured products within the union, without application of tariffs or duties. It also provides for common external tariffs and for the payment of customs and excise duties into a common pool to be shared between the SACU countries under the revenue-sharing formula set out in the Annex to the agreement.

The revenue-sharing agreement includes three components:

- A customs component, which divides the gross amount of customs duties according to the value of goods each country imports from other SACU countries in a given year (as a percentage of intra-SACU imports).
- An excise component, which divides the gross amount of excise duties according to each country's GDP as a percentage of SACU's combined GDP.
- A development component, which is funded from 15% of the excise component and is weighted toward less developed SACU countries using a formula based on GDP per capita.

In this publication, revenue from excises, tariffs and customs duties are included as tax revenues in the SACU country that collected the revenue. They are included under headings 5121 (Excises) and 5123 (Customs and import duties) in the tax revenue tables. Revenues received from the SACU Common Revenue Pool are included as miscellaneous revenue in the non-tax revenue tables, as seen in Table 6.13 for Eswatini. In the case of South Africa, where payments exceed the revenue share received from the Pool, the payments net of the share received are recorded as a memorandum item in the non-tax revenue table (Table 6.22).

Sources: (SACU, 2017[15]), (SACU, 2014[16]).

Southern African Customs Union revenues

All five members of SACU collect customs and excise taxes under a unified tax regime and then transfer those funds to the SACU Common Revenue Pool. The SACU Revenue Pool in turn redistributes the tax moneys collected under a complex revenue sharing formula. In practice, however, South Africa possesses the main ports of entry into Southern Africa and ends up collecting almost all the customs duties and excises allocated to the SACU Common Revenue Pool. South Africa therefore ends up making net payments into the SACU Revenue Pool, while the other SACU countries are net recipients of funds from the Pool.

SACU revenues to South Africa are negligible but they have a strong impact on the finances of the other members of the customs union (Figure 2.13). In 2019, these revenues boosted the revenues of Botswana, Eswatini, Lesotho and Namibia by 7.2%, 9.8%, 18.4% and 10.5% of GDP, respectively. Besides exogenous economic shocks, member countries also saw their SACU revenues rise and fall due to changes in the parameters used in the SACU revenue-sharing formula. The economic shock of the global financial crisis rendered many economic forecasts of the time inaccurate; because SACU payments were calculated based on these forecasts, major adjustments to SACU payments were required in 2010 and 2011 to compensate for years of overpayments into the SACU pool (Mongardini et al., 2011[17]). A similar situation occurred in 2014, when a slowdown in South Africa's economy again caused forecasts to be revised downward; Eswatini, Lesotho and Namibia's SACU revenues declined as a percentage of GDP in 2015 and 2016, although this trend was reversed in 2017.

Figure 2.13. **Total SACU and other non-tax revenues by country**

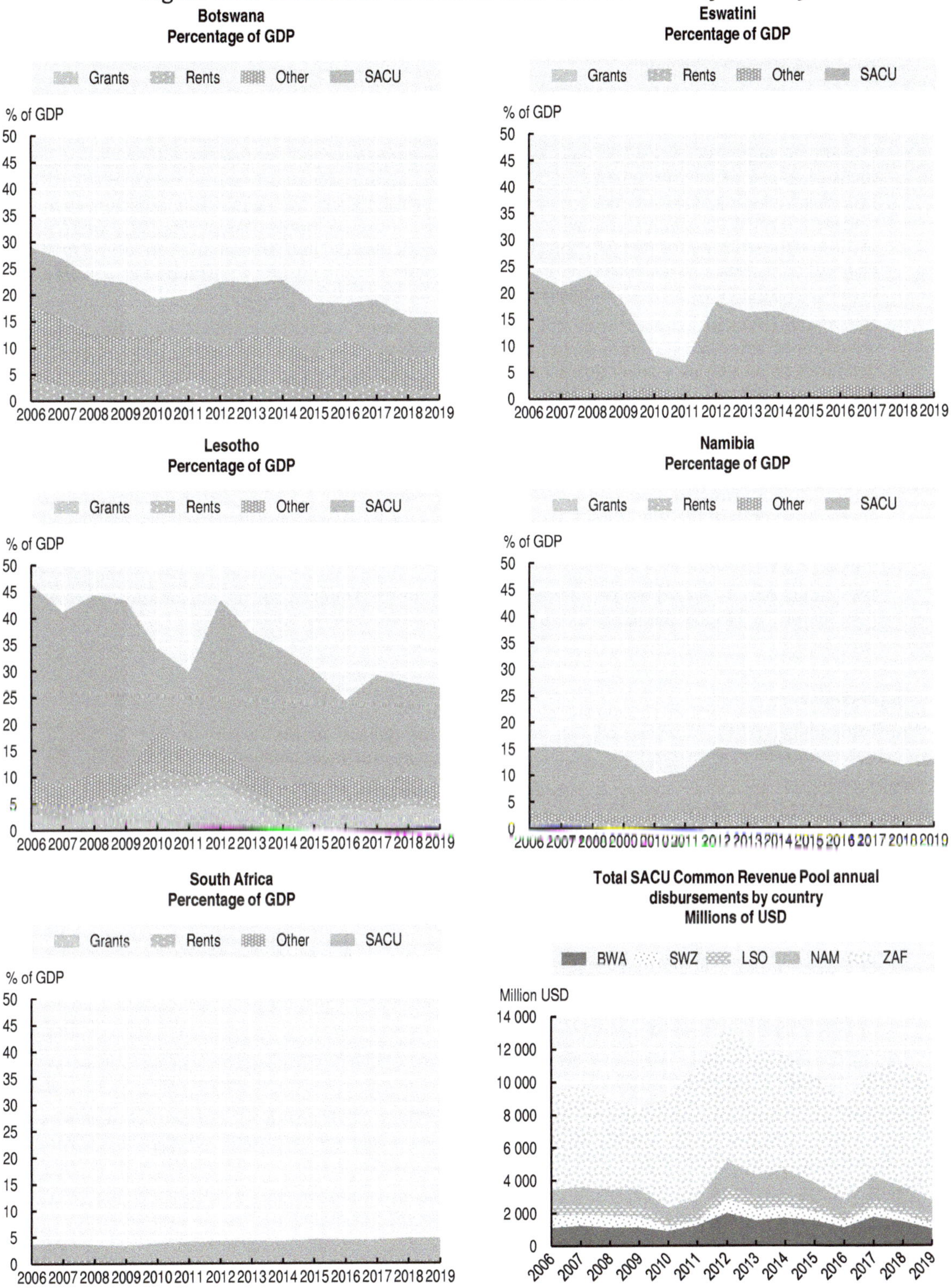

Note: SACU revenues reported here are classified as non-tax revenues for all countries presented here except for South Africa. For South Africa, SACU revenues received by the government of South Africa are classified under customs duties and excise taxes, and not non-tax revenues.

Source: Authors' calculations based on data from (OECD/AUC/ATAF, 2021[2]), "Revenue Statistics in Africa: Comparative tables", *OECD Tax Statistics* (database), *https://doi.org/10.1787/be755711-en*.

StatLink https://doi.org/10.1787/888934282702

Notes

1 There is no comparison with the averages of the 26 Latin American and Caribbean (LAC) countries (see (OECD et al., 2021[20])) and the 37 OECD countries (see (OECD, 2017[18])), as these publications do not cover non-tax revenues.

2 Please see the Interpretative Guide to non-tax revenue in Annex B of this report for the definitions of these revenue categories.

3 The official definition of ODA is: "flows to countries and territories on the Development Assistance Committee List of ODA Recipients and to multilateral institutions which are provided by official agencies, including state and local governments, or by their executive agencies. In addition, each transaction must be administered with the promotion of the economic development and welfare of developing countries as its main objective; and be concessional in character and conveys a grant element of at least 25% (calculated at a rate of discount of 10%)". Further information is available at: *www.oecd.org/dac/financing-sustainable-development/index-terms.htm#ODA*.

4 Note that taxes on oil extraction can include corporate income tax, excise taxes on energy products, un-refunded sales taxes such as VATs and non-tax revenue can include royalties, profit sharing, dividends received from state enterprises, and other investment income received from government direct participation in extractive enterprises (Mansour and Rota-Graziosi, 2013[19]).

5 The World Bank refers to "natural resource rents". This is calculated as the difference between the value of natural resource production in the countries according to commodity prices and the estimated cost of resource extraction. It is not to be confused with the definition of resource rent used by the OECD, for which it is defined as a form of government revenue. Please see the documentation of resource rents in the World Bank World Development Indicators dataset (see *https://databank.worldbank.org/metadataglossary/adjusted-net-savings/series/NY.GDP.TOTL.RT.ZS*) and the Interpretative Guide for more details."

6 See paragraphs 9-13 of the OECD Interpretative Guide in Annex A for an explanation of how administrative fees are classified in this publication.

References

AfricanManager (2019), *Gazoduc-ENI: Des royalties de 500 millions de dinars par an pour la Tunisie*, *https://africanmanager.com/la-tunisie-tirera-500-millions-de-dinars-par-an-du-gazoduc-avec-litalie/*. [9]

CNN (2015), *Mammoth rail network to put West African economies on the right track*, *https://edition.cnn.com/2015/03/05/africa/west-africa-minerals-railway/index.html* (accessed on 21 September 2020).[11]

EIU (2015), *Government approves new hydrocarbons code*, *https://country.eiu.com/article.aspx?articleid=1303035314&Country=Congo%20(Brazzaville)&topic=Eco_9*. [4]

IMF (2021), *World Economic Outlook, April 2021 Edition (database)*, *www.imf.org/en/Publications/WEO/weo-database/2021/April* (accessed on April). [1]

Mansour, M. and G. Rota-Graziosi (2013), "Tax Coordination, Tax Competition, and Revenue Mobilization in the West African Economic and Monetary Union", *IMF Working Paper*, Vol. 13/163, *www.imf.org/en/Publications/WP/Issues/2016/12/31/Tax-Coordination-Tax-Competition-and-Revenue-Mobilization-in-the-West-African-Economic-and-40756*. [19]

MiningTechnology (2020), *Debswana diamond mines*, *www.mining-technology.com/projects/debswana/* (accessed on 20 September 2020). [10]

Mongardini, J. et al. (2011), *In the wake of the global economic crisis: adjusting to lower revenue of the Southern African Customs*, International Monetary Fund, *www.imf.org/external/pubs/ft/dp/2011/afr1101.pdf*. [17]

OECD (2021), *COVID-19 spending helped to lift foreign aid to an all-time high in 2020 – Detailed Note*, *www.oecd.org/dac/financing-sustainable-development/development-finance-data/ODA-2020-detailed-summary.pdf*. [8]

OECD (2021), *DAC Data Submitters*, *www.oecd.org/dac/financing-sustainable-development/development-finance-standards/dacdatasubmitters.htm* (accessed on 20 September 2021). [6]

OECD (2017), *Revenue Statistics 2017*, OECD Publishing, Paris, *https://dx.doi.org/10.1787/9789264283183-en*. [18]

OECD/AUC/ATAF (2021), *Revenue Statistics in Africa: Comparative tables*, OECD Publishing, Paris, *http://dx.doi.org/10.1787/be755711-en*. [2]

OECD et al. (2021), *Revenue Statistics in Latin America and the Caribbean 2021*, OECD Publishing, Paris, *https://doi.org/10.1787/96ce5287-en-es*. [20]

RFI (2014), *Le gros chèque d'Arcelor Mittal au Sénégal*, *www.rfi.fr/economie/20140605-le-gros-cheque-arcelor-mittal-senegal*. [14]

Rives, F., R. Peltier and P. Montagne (2010), *Fifteen years of forest community management in Niger: from a technician's dream to social reality*, CIRAD, *https://agritrop.cirad.fr/555467/1/document_555467.pdf*. [13]

SACU (2017), *Southern African Customs Union Agreement 2002 (As amended on 12 April 2013)*, *www.sacu.int/list.php?type=Agreements*. [15]

SACU (2014), *Implementing a Common Agenda Towards Regional Integration: 2014 Annual Report*, *www.sacu.int/docs/reports_annual/2014/annual_report.pdf*. [16]

VOANews (2013), *Malawi: Donors Withhold Aid Over Cashgate Scandal*, *www.voanews.com/africa/malawi-donors-withhold-aid-over-cashgate-scandal* (accessed on 21 September 2020). [7]

World Bank (2021), *World Bank Country and Lending Groups*, *https://datahelpdesk.worldbank.org/knowledgebase/articles/906519* (accessed in June 2021). [5]

World Bank (2021), *World Development Indicators*, *https://data.worldbank.org/* (accessed on 8 September 2020). [3]

World Bank (2020), *World Bank Commodity Price Data (The Pink Sheet)*, *www.worldbank.org/en/research/commodity-markets* (accessed in August 2020). [12]

Revenue Statistics in Africa 1990-2019/Statistiques des recettes publiques en Afrique 1990-2019

Chapitre 2

Tendances des recettes non fiscales, 2000-2019

Introduction

Les statistiques relatives à la fiscalité ne sauraient suffire pour dresser le panorama complet des finances publiques, en particulier dans le cas de nombreux pays africains, qui perçoivent d'importantes recettes sous la forme de dons ou de redevances pétrolières et minières. Les *Statistiques des recettes publiques en Afrique* présentent des données sur les recettes fiscales et non fiscales, ces dernières étant les recettes des administrations publiques qui ne correspondent pas à la définition des recettes fiscales établie par l'OCDE. Si les données relatives aux recettes non fiscales ne sont pas nécessairement aussi fiables que les statistiques des recettes fiscales ou peuvent provenir de sources différentes (voir encadré 2.1), il n'en convient pas moins de prendre en compte ces recettes dans le total des ressources financières d'un pays. Le présent chapitre livre des comparaisons des recettes non fiscales entre les pays couverts par la présente publication[1].

Les principales catégories de recettes non fiscales[2] examinées dans le cadre de ce projet sont les suivantes (voir également annexe B) :

- dons émanant de pays étrangers ou d'organisations internationales (aide budgétaire, aide alimentaire, transferts de capitaux, transferts courants, subventions de projets, bourses de programme, allégement de la dette internationale, etc.) ;
- loyers et redevances (par exemple, redevances pétrolières ou minières) ;
- autres revenus de la propriété (intérêts, dividendes et autres rémunérations d'investissements publics) ;
- produits de la vente de biens et de services (ce qui inclut certains frais administratifs) ;
- produits des amendes et pénalités (notamment pour infraction à la législation fiscale) ;
- recettes diverses non identifiées (recettes non fiscales qui ne peuvent être classées dans les autres catégories).

Encadré 2.1. **Recettes non fiscales et fiabilité des données**

Les données relatives aux recettes non fiscales sont souvent moins détaillées que celles relatives aux recettes fiscales. Il arrive que, pour certaines années, des pays fournissent un total agrégé de leurs recettes non fiscales, sans autre détail que la répartition entre dons et autres catégories. Cela tient probablement au fait que les données relatives aux recettes non fiscales proviennent souvent d'une multiplicité de sources. Les *Statistiques des recettes publiques en Afrique* contiennent des cas où le montant total des recettes non fiscales indiqué peut être incomplet.

Les données sur les recettes non fiscales ne font pas nécessairement l'objet de vérifications aussi strictes que celles relatives aux recettes fiscales. Un grand nombre de catégories ne sont pas prises en compte dans l'élaboration du budget principal et ne sont pas non plus définies par la loi, en conséquence de quoi elles ne sont pas soumises aux mêmes mécanismes de contrôle que les recettes fiscales. En l'absence de

Encadré 2.1. **Recettes non fiscales et fiabilité des données** *(suite)*

dispositions juridiques contraignantes, les recettes non fiscales ne sont pas toujours soumises aux mêmes obligations documentaires.

Les recettes non fiscales relèvent souvent d'autorités différentes que les recettes fiscales, de sorte que la distinction n'est pas nécessairement faite entre les recettes et les dépenses. Il est possible que certaines recettes, comme les frais administratifs, servent de mécanismes d'amortissement et viennent minorer les coûts au lieu d'être comptabilisées comme recettes. Ce cas de figure peut concerner les collectivités locales et autres institutions publiques pour lesquelles les données disponibles concernent uniquement les transferts nets de fonds à destination de l'administration centrale.

Les dons, les règlements juridiques, les contrats d'exploitation minière ou pétrolière donnent aussi souvent lieu à des versements importants de la part d'entités extérieures telles que des entreprises multinationales ou des administrations étrangères qui ne sont pas toujours incitées à faire preuve de transparence. Il est également possible que ces entités soient tentées de s'entendre avec les autorités locales en vue de masquer les coûts. En outre, il est plus difficile d'établir des ventilations détaillées dès lors qu'un pays négocie en contrepartie de l'extraction de ressources le versement de sommes forfaitaires élevées, qui regroupent plusieurs catégories de recettes, fiscales et non fiscales.

Recettes non fiscales exprimées en pourcentage du PIB

Dans les 30 pays couverts par la présente publication, les recettes non fiscales, exprimées en pourcentage du PIB, ont varié en 2019 à l'intérieur d'une large fourchette, allant de 26.7 % au Lesotho à 0.5 % en Afrique du Sud. Dans tous les pays, à l'exception du Botswana, du Lesotho et de la République du Congo les recettes non fiscales ont été inférieures aux recettes fiscales (graphique 2.1). En moyenne, le montant des recettes non fiscales perçues dans chacun de ces pays a représenté 45.4 % du montant des recettes fiscales recouvrées.

Comme indiqué dans l'encadré 1.1 du Chapitre 1, la variation des ratios de recettes au PIB dépend de facteurs qui influent sur le numérateur comme sur le dénominateur. On observe sur plusieurs années que l'augmentation des recettes coïncide avec une diminution du PIB, et inversement. Cette tendance est particulièrement marquée pour les recettes provenant de dons et les loyers et redevances. Entre 2009 et 2019, 48 % des fluctuations annuelles des recettes sous forme de dons se sont accompagnées d'une évolution en sens inverse du PIB – autrement dit le PIB diminuait lorsque les dons augmentaient et il augmentait lorsque les dons diminuaient. Ce pourcentage était de 37 % pour les loyers et les redevances. Le rôle essentiel joué par l'extraction des ressources dans la mobilisation des recettes et la croissance économique dans certains pays peut expliquer en partie cette différence. Le FMI a calculé (FMI, 2021[1]) que le pétrole était à l'origine de plus de 30 % du total du PIB en Guinée équatoriale et plus de 19 % au Tchad en 2019, de sorte qu'une augmentation de la production pétrolière dans ces deux pays sur une année peut avoir un impact significatif à la fois sur les rentes pétrolières et sur le PIB global. S'agissant des dons, en revanche, il peut y avoir un décalage entre le moment où le niveau des dons varie et son impact sur l'économie d'un pays, de sorte que la variation annuelle du niveau des dons peut ne pas correspondre à celle du PIB.

Graphique 2.1. **Recettes fiscales et non fiscales totales par pays, 2019**

En pourcentage du PIB

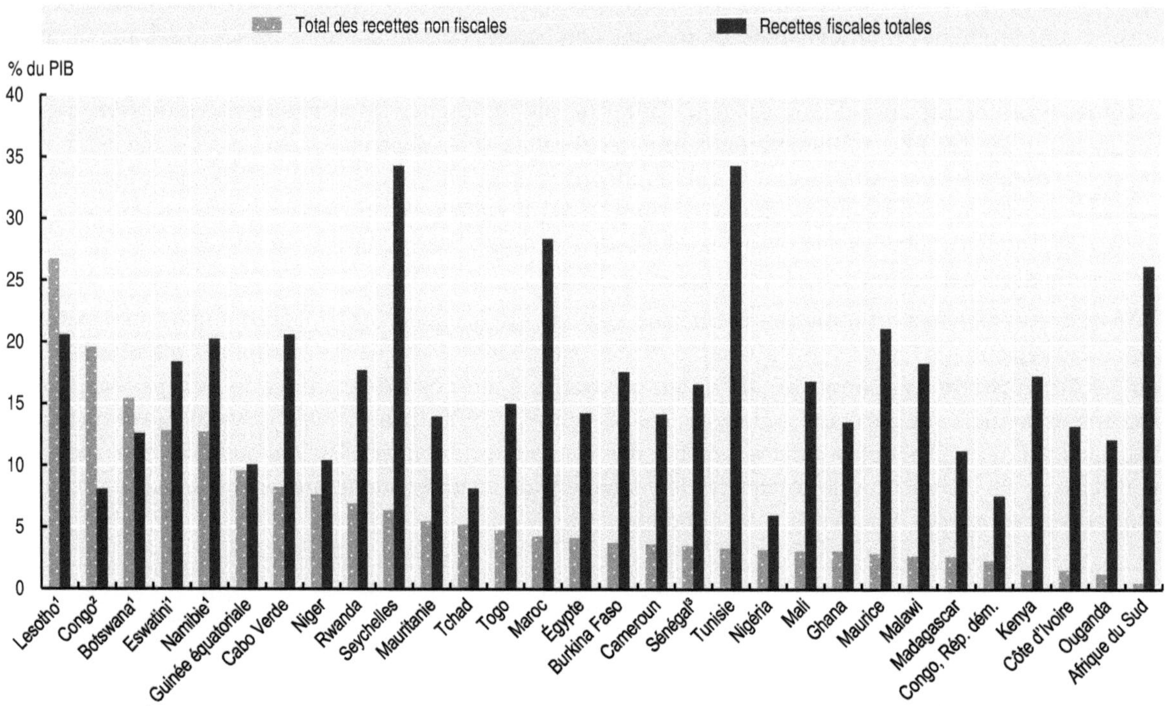

Notes : Les recettes non fiscales incluent celles perçues par les administrations infranationales de l'Eswatini, du Kenya, du Maroc et de Maurice, seuls pays pour lesquels les données correspondantes sont disponibles. En 2019, les recettes non fiscales perçues par les administrations infranationales représentaient, pour chacun de ces pays, respectivement 1 %, 22 %, 5 % et 39 % des recettes non fiscales totales. L'Afrique du Sud, la Mauritanie et le Nigéria ont déclaré percevoir des taxes locales et régionales, mais n'ont pas fait état de recettes non fiscales locales ou régionales.

1. Dans les cas du Botswana, de l'Eswatini, du Lesotho et de la Namibie, les recettes non fiscales incluent les fonds qui leur sont transférés en vertu de l'accord de partage des recettes de l'Union douanière d'Afrique australe (SACU) après perception des droits de douane et d'accise par l'Afrique du Sud.

2. Les montants indiqués ici pour les dons et recettes pétrolières de la République du Congo sont ceux publiés en avril 2021 dans les *Perspectives de l'économie mondiale* du FMI.

3. Les chiffres utilisés pour le Sénégal se rapportent à 2018, car les chiffres pour 2019 n'étaient pas disponibles.

Pour certains pays, les valeurs des ratios recettes fiscales/PIB et recettes non fiscales/PIB sont à interpréter avec prudence car elles reposent sur des données incomplètes. Pour de plus amples informations, se reporter aux tableaux par pays des chapitres 5 et 6.

Source : Tableau 4.1 du chapitre 4 et tableau 6.1 du chapitre 6.

StatLink https://doi.org/10.1787/888934282892

L'examen du rapport entre recettes fiscales et non fiscales exprimées en pourcentage du PIB fait apparaître différents groupes de pays (graphique 2.2). Les trois pays dont la production de pétrole et de gaz dépasse 15 % du PIB (Tchad, République du Congo et Guinée équatoriale) figurent parmi ceux qui affichent les ratios impôts/PIB les plus faibles de ce graphique. Neuf des pays inclus dans ce graphique sont considérés comme « riches en ressources naturelles » puisque plus de 10 % de leur PIB provient de la production de pétrole, de gaz, de charbon et de minerais pendant au moins cinq ans entre 2010 et 2019, selon les données de la Banque mondiale. Tous ces pays (Botswana, Ghana, Guinée équatoriale, Mauritanie, Nigéria, République démocratique du Congo, République du Congo, Tchad et Togo) sont regroupés dans la partie inférieure gauche du diagramme, avec des ratios impôts/PIB relativement faibles. Les pays bénéficiaires nets des recettes redistribuées par l'Union douanière d'Afrique australe (SACU) se caractérisent également par un niveau élevé de recettes non fiscales (se reporter à la section sur les recettes issues de la SACU pour de plus amples explications). En général, les pays à revenu intermédiaire supérieur qui ne sont pas de grands producteurs de pétrole perçoivent moins de dons et de recettes tirées des ressources naturelles, ce qui les contraint davantage à recourir à la fiscalité pour mobiliser des ressources intérieures.

Graphique 2.2. **Recettes fiscales et non fiscales totales par pays, 2019**

En pourcentage du PIB

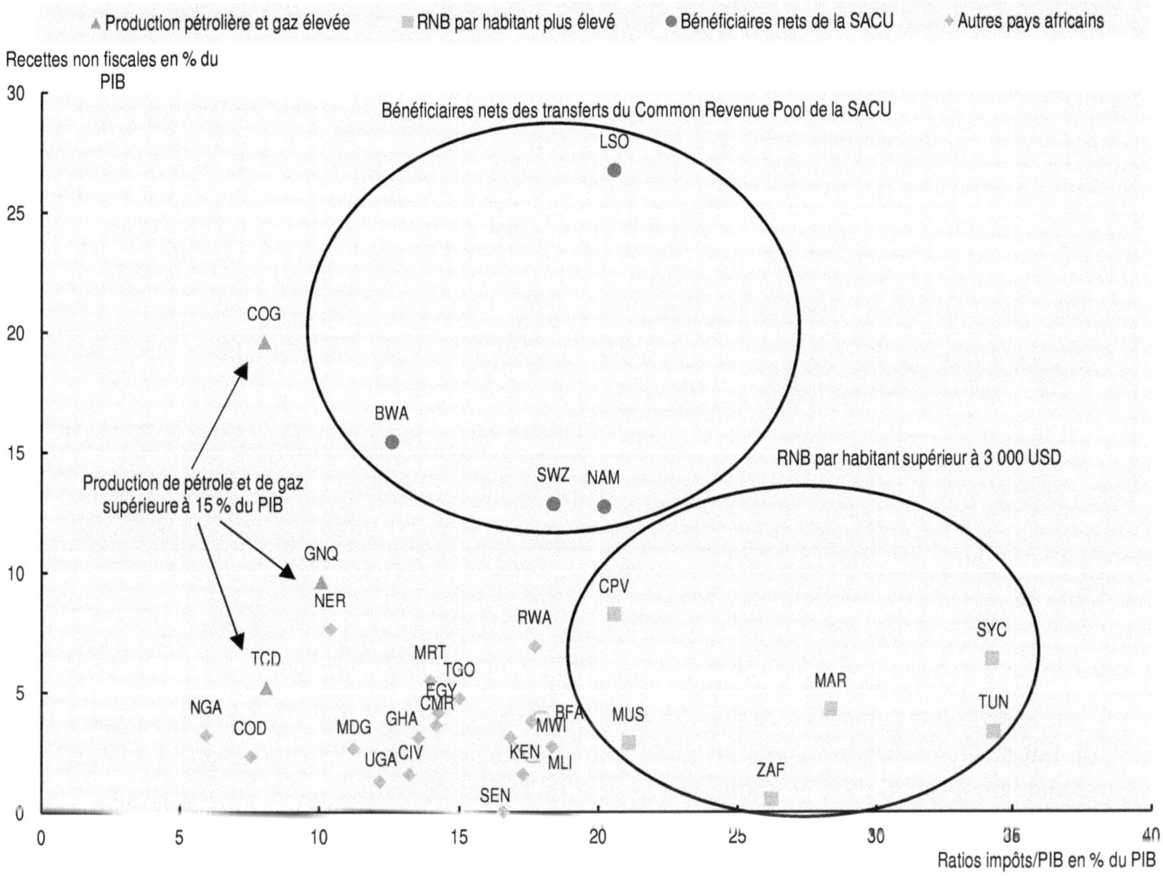

Note : Pour de plus amples informations, se reporter aux notes du graphique 2.1 et aux tableaux par pays présentés dans les chapitres 5 et 6.

Source : Calculs des auteurs basés sur des données figurant dans (OCDE/CUA/ATAF, 2021[2]), « Statistiques des recettes publiques en Afrique : Tableaux comparatifs », *Statistiques fiscales de l'OCDE* (base de données), *https://doi.org/10.1787/7f54581d-fr* et Banque mondiale, *Indicateurs du développement dans le monde* (base de données) (Banque mondiale, 2021[3]) pour les chiffres relatifs à la production de pétrole et de gaz exprimés en pourcentage du PIB et pour le RNB par habitant.

StatLink https://doi.org/10.1787/888934282911

En Afrique (30 pays), le ratio moyen recettes fiscales/PIB a progressé entre 2010 et 2019, tandis que celui des recettes non fiscales a chuté (graphique 2.3). Après avoir culminé en 2012 à 8.6 %, le montant moyen des recettes non fiscales est tombé à 5.9 % en 2016 avant de remonter à 6.3 % en 2019. Cette diminution tient au recul des recettes tirées des loyers et redevances et des recettes perçues sous forme de dons, exprimées en pourcentage du PIB. En 2019, les recettes des dons en pourcentage du PIB étaient de 1.3 % du PIB, atteignant leur point le plus bas depuis 2010. Les loyers et les redevances étaient de 1.7 % en 2019, un point de pourcentage de moins qu'en 2012, après avoir légèrement rebondi depuis le creux de 2016. Ces baisses ont suffi à entraîner une baisse des recettes totales au cours de cette période, entraînant une augmentation des déficits et de l'endettement (voir le chapitre 3).

Graphique 2.3. **Niveau moyen des recettes non fiscales en Afrique (30), 2010-19**

En pourcentage du PIB

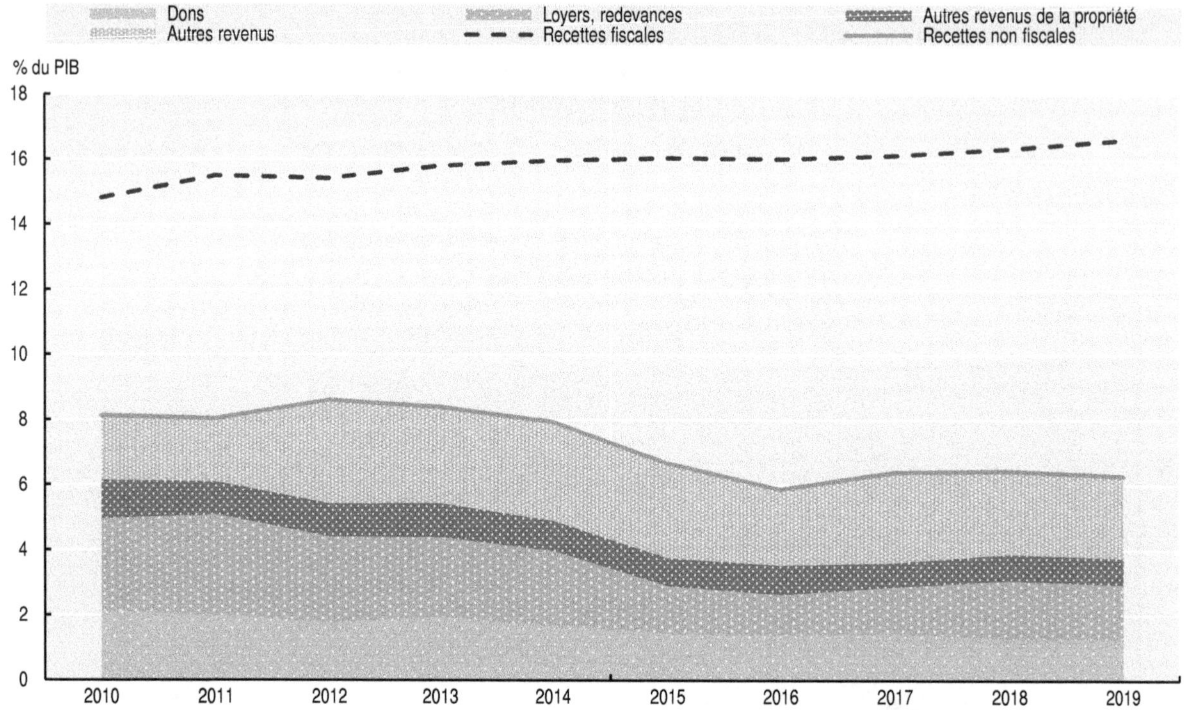

Source : Calculs des auteurs basés sur des données figurant dans (OCDE/CUA/ATAF, 2021[2]), « Statistiques des recettes publiques en Afrique : Tableaux comparatifs », *Statistiques fiscales de l'OCDE* (base de données), *https://doi.org/10.1787/7f54581d-fr*

StatLink https://doi.org/10.1787/888934282930

Selon leur origine, les recettes non fiscales sont associées à différents types de risques, du fait de leur variabilité annuelle ou de leur vulnérabilité aux chocs économiques ou aux changements politiques. Le graphique 2.4 montre la part de chaque sous-catégorie dans le total des recettes non fiscales des pays. Ces données font apparaître quatre groupes distincts :

- Neuf pays ont perçu en 2019 la majorité de leurs recettes non fiscales sous la forme de dons (par ordre décroissant : le Niger, le Rwanda, le Togo, le Sénégal, le Mali, le Malawi, Madagascar, la Côte d'Ivoire et l'Ouganda).
- Six pays ont perçu l'essentiel de leurs recettes non fiscales sous forme de loyers et de redevances (par ordre décroissant la République du Congo, la Guinée équatoriale, la Mauritanie, le Tchad, le Cameroun et le Nigéria). Dans tous ces pays les redevances pétrolières ont représenté l'essentiel des recettes non fiscales.
- Les quatre voisins de l'Afrique du Sud membres la SACU, à savoir le Botswana, le Lesotho, la Namibie et l'Eswatini, ont perçu une grande partie de leurs recettes non fiscales sous la forme de revenus transférés par la SACU (encadré 2.2).
- Pour les onze pays restants, ni les dons, ni les loyers et redevances, ni les recettes de la SACU ne constituaient la majorité des recettes non fiscales. Les principales sources de recettes non fiscales pour ces pays sont les suivantes : intérêts et dividendes pour les Seychelles et la Tunisie ; des produits de la vente de biens et services dans les cas du Ghana, du Kenya, de Maurice et du Maroc ; et de recettes diverses et non affectées dans le cas de l'Égypte. Les dons étaient la principale source de recettes non fiscales pour le Burkina Faso et le Cabo Verde, mais représentaient moins de 50 % des recettes non fiscales. De

même, les loyers et redevances étaient la principale source de recettes non fiscales pour la République démocratique du Congo et l'Afrique du Sud, mais représentaient moins de la moitié de leurs recettes non fiscales.

Graphique 2.4. **Structure des recettes non fiscales par pays, 2019**

En pourcentage du PIB

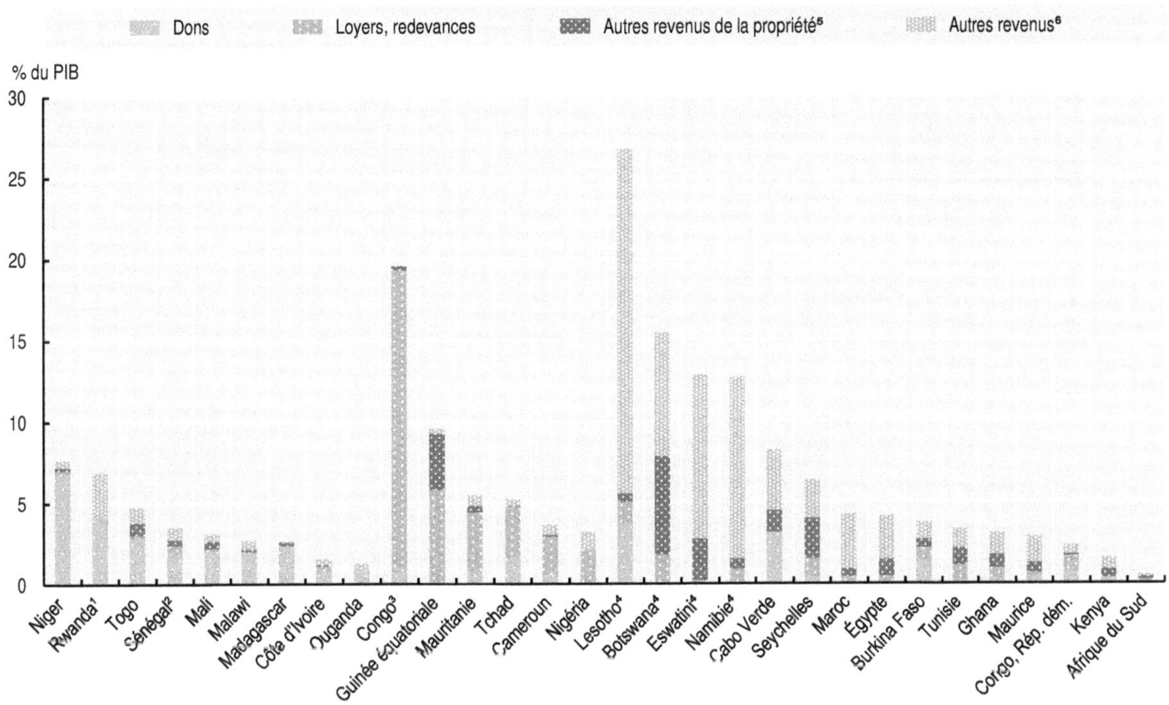

Note : Les données prennent en compte les recettes non fiscales perçues par les administrations infranationales pour l'Eswatini, le Kenya, le Maroc et Maurice.

1. Dans le cas du Rwanda, les recettes non fiscales autres que les dons ne sont pas ventilées par sous-catégorie et sont donc assimilées aux recettes diverses et non identifiées.
2. Faute de données disponibles pour 2019, ce sont les données de 2018 qui ont été utilisées pour le Sénégal.
3. Les chiffres présentés ici correspondent principalement aux dons et recettes pétrolières recensés dans les *Perspectives de l'économie mondiale* du FMI d'avril 2021 au titre des loyers et redevances.
4. Dans les cas du Botswana, de l'Eswatini, du Lesotho et de la Namibie, les « autres recettes » incluent les fonds qui leur sont transférés en vertu de l'accord de partage des recettes de l'Union douanière d'Afrique australe (SACU) après perception des droits de douane et d'accise par l'Afrique du Sud.
5. Intérêts, dividendes, etc.
6. Ventes, amendes, revenus issus de la SACU, etc.

Pour de plus amples informations, se reporter aux notes du graphique 2.1 et aux tableaux par pays présentés dans les chapitres 5 et 6.

Source : Tableau 6.2 du chapitre 6.

StatLink https://doi.org/10.1787/888934282949

La composition des recettes non fiscales a évolué dans le temps (graphique 2.5). De nombreux pays africains ont subi de fortes variations de leurs recettes non fiscales, qu'elles proviennent principalement de dons (Burkina Faso et Togo), de rentes de ressources (Tchad et Mauritanie), des revenus transférés par la SACU (Eswatini et Namibie) ou d'autres sources (Ghana et Maurice).

Graphique 2.5. **Évolution de la structure des recettes non fiscales dans certains pays, 2000-19**

En pourcentage du PIB

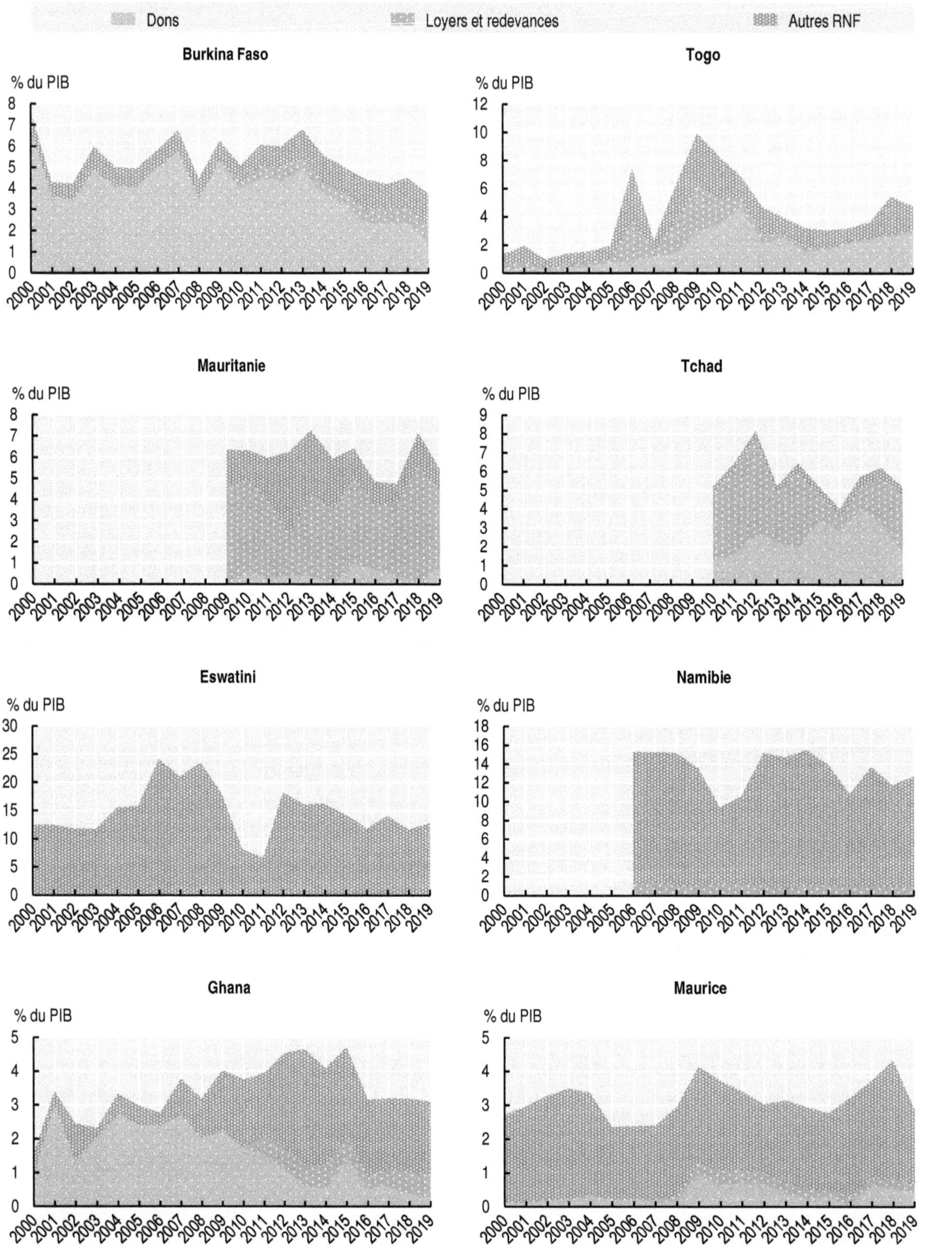

Note : Pour de plus amples informations, se reporter aux notes du graphique 2.1 et aux tableaux par pays présentés dans les chapitres 5 et 6. Les graphiques de tous les pays de la publication sont disponibles en ligne sur le lien *Statlink* ci-dessous.

Source : Calculs des auteurs basés sur des données figurant dans (OCDE/CUA/ATAF, 2021[2]), « Statistiques des recettes publiques en Afrique : Tableaux comparatifs », *Statistiques fiscales de l'OCDE* (base de données), *https://doi.org/10.1787/7f54581d-fr*

StatLink *https://doi.org/10.1787/888934282968*

Malgré les tendances à long terme qui se dégagent, les recettes non fiscales semblent fluctuer davantage d'une année sur l'autre que les recettes fiscales. Ces dix dernières années, 15 des 30 pays couverts par la présente publication ont connu au moins une année où leurs recettes non fiscales ont augmenté d'au moins 2 % du PIB par rapport à l'année précédente, et 15 pays ont connu au moins une année où leurs recettes non fiscales ont enregistré un recul d'une ampleur similaire par rapport à l'année précédente. Ces fluctuations sont souvent imputables aux rentes provenant de ressources (qui subissent les effets des variations des prix des matières premières, ou des variations de la production) ou aux recettes provenant de dons (qui s'inscrivent moins dans la durée et sont moins prévisibles que les recettes fiscales). D'autres sources de recettes non fiscales, notamment les revenus de l'Eswatini issus de la SACU, se sont également révélées sujettes à une grande variabilité.

- En République du Congo, une baisse des prix pétroliers les a fait chuter entre 2014 et 2015, où elles sont passées de 27.8 % à 10.1 % du PIB. En 2015, le Congo a réformé son code des hydrocarbures de manière à accroître la part des bénéfices pétroliers versés à l'État (EIU, 2015[4]).
- Entre 2011 et 2012, les recettes sous forme de dons ont chuté au Mali, passant de 4.5 % à 0.1 % du PIB, en l'espace d'une année marquée par de multiples crises politiques.
- L'Eswatini a vu ses recettes non fiscales passer de 18.2 % à 8.1 % du PIB entre 2009 et 2010 du fait que ses revenus issus de la SACU en % du PIB avaient chuté de 80 %, comme suite à l'effondrement des droits de douane et d'accise durant les deux années qui ont suivi la crise financière mondiale.

Dons

Les dons constituent une source de recettes plus ou moins importante selon les pays étudiés dans la présente publication. En 2019, ils ont représenté moins de 0.5 % du PIB de 13 pays et, dans 12 cas, moins de 2 % du total des recettes fiscales (graphique 2.6). Tous sont des pays à revenu intermédiaire ou à revenu élevé, d'après la classification de la Banque mondiale fondée sur le revenu national brut (Banque mondiale, 2021[5]). À l'inverse, sur les 10 pays à faible revenu considérés dans la présente étude, seul l'Ouganda a perçu un volume de dons équivalant à moins de 1 % de son PIB. Pour six de ces pays, les recettes sous forme de dons ont représenté plus de 15 % des recettes fiscales.

Le graphique 2.7 indique le volume des dons perçus par les pays étudiés dans la présente publication (en pourcentage du PIB) ainsi que le montant de leur revenu national brut (PNB) par habitant. Si la partie supérieure droite est vide, c'est parce que les dons constituent, en proportion, une source de recettes moins importante pour les pays africains dont le revenu est plus élevé. Cela dit, un grand nombre de pays figurent dans la partie inférieure gauche, car il y a des pays qui, malgré un revenu faible, perçoivent proportionnellement peu de recettes sous forme de dons. Par exemple, le Burkina Faso, l'Ouganda et le Rwanda ont enregistré un RNB par habitant compris entre 780 USD et 830 USD en 2019, alors que les dons qu'ils ont déclaré avoir perçus cette même année ont représenté respectivement 0.9 % (Ouganda) 1.5 % (Burkina Faso) et 4.2 % (Rwanda) de leur PIB.

Si les recettes sous forme de dons et l'aide extérieure recouvrent des notions similaires, dans la pratique, la diversité des données, méthodes et concepts employés fait qu'il difficile d'accorder les statistiques de l'aide tirées des déclarations des pays donneurs avec les revenus issus de l'aide dont les pays récipiendaires font état.

Graphique 2.6. **Dons par pays, 2019**

En pourcentage du PIB

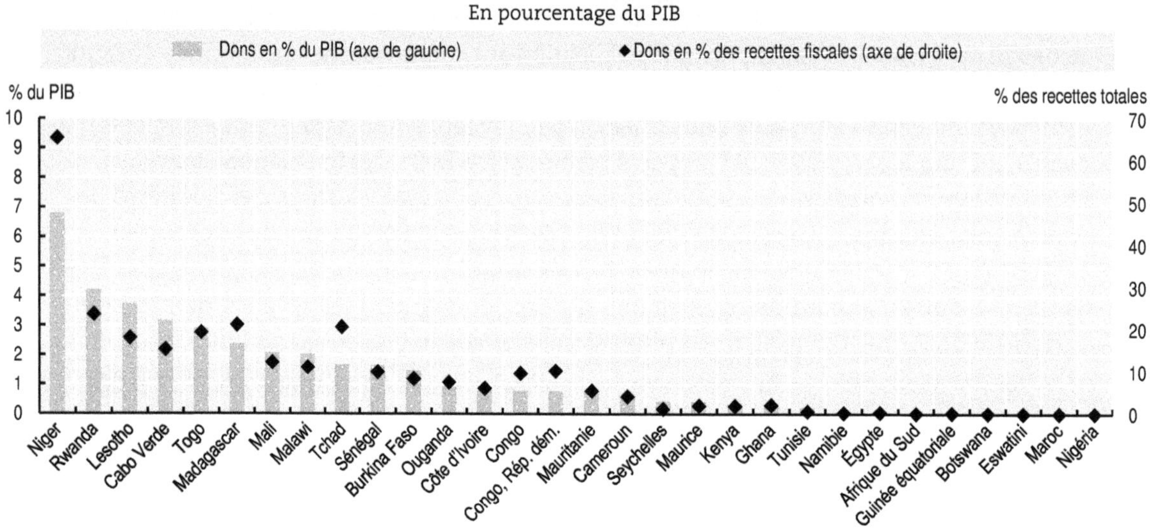

Source : Tableaux 6.2 et 6.3 du chapitre 6.

StatLink https://doi.org/10.1787/888934282987

Graphique 2.7. **Dons en pourcentage du PIB et du PNB par habitant et par pays, 2019**

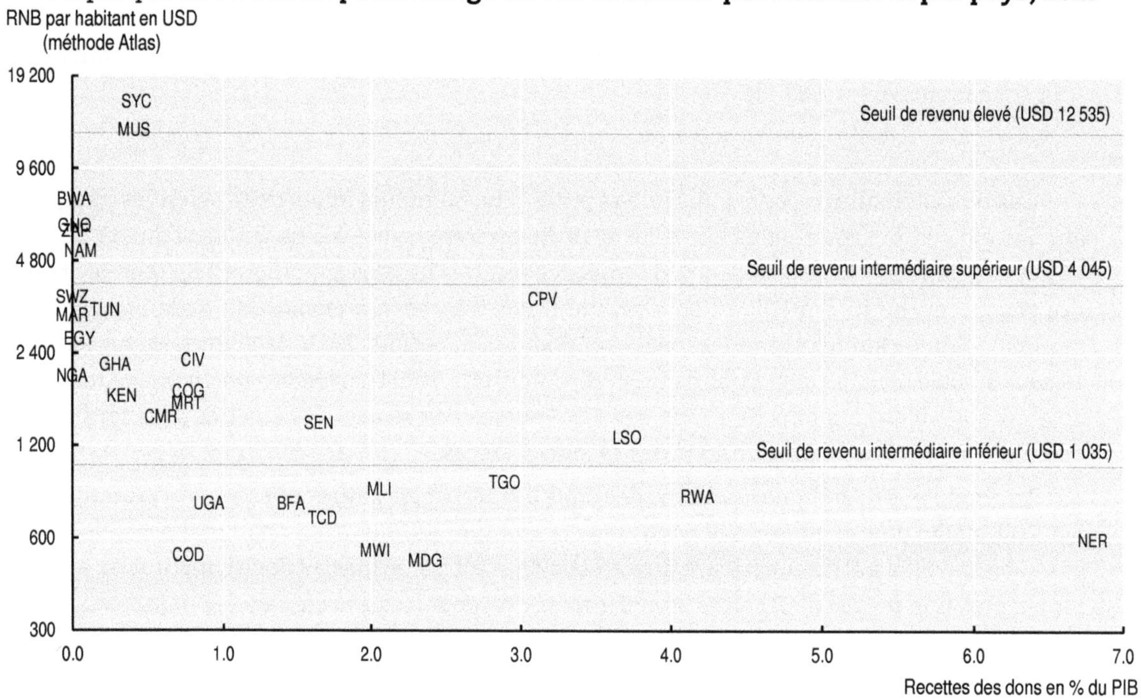

Note : Les chiffres du PNB ont été convertis en USD suivant la méthode Atlas de la Banque mondiale.

Source : Tableau 6.2 du chapitre 6, et Banque mondiale *World Development Indicators* (base de données) (Banque mondiale, 2021[3]).

StatLink https://doi.org/10.1787/888934283006

Les recettes sous forme de dons présentent des éléments communs avec l'aide publique au développement (APD) telle que définie par le Comité d'aide au développement (CAD) de l'OCDE[3]. Les dons couverts par la présente publication correspondent principalement à des recettes perçues d'autres États et d'organisations internationales tandis que l'APD mesure essentiellement les efforts déployés par les pays donneurs en faveur du développement dans les pays à faible revenu et à revenu intermédiaire. L'APD recouvre les apports considérés comme des « dons » dans la présente publication (aide budgétaire, aide alimentaire, transferts de capitaux, transferts courants, subventions de projets, bourses de programme, allégement de la dette internationale, etc.) mais elle englobe également les prêts assortis de conditions libérales, l'assistance technique en nature, les dépenses administratives supportées par les donneurs, le coût des réfugiés dans les pays donneurs et les bourses d'étude ainsi que d'autres activités ne générant pas d'entrées de recettes (nettes) dans le pays. C'est pour cette raison que le volume de l'APD reçue par un pays donné diffère du montant des dons – généralement plus élevé – qui est indiqué dans les *Statistiques des recettes publiques*.

Les statistiques relatives aux apports d'APD à destination de l'Afrique qui sont recueillies par le CAD englobent les apports publics provenant de l'ensemble des membres du CAD et de certains pays non membres du CAD ainsi que des organisations multilatérales comme la Banque mondiale, le FMI et l'ONU. En sont exclues les statistiques relatives à la coopération pour le développement de grandes économies non membres de l'OCDE, comme la Chine, le Brésil et l'Inde (OCDE, 2021[6]).

En comparant les valeurs des recettes sous forme de dons et des apports nets d'APD (graphique 2.8), on constate que le montant de l'assistance perçu par les pays africains dépasse nettement les sommes versées dans leur budget national. Si, en règle générale, les pays qui perçoivent les apports nets d'APD les plus élevés sont aussi ceux dont les recettes sous forme de dons sont les plus importantes, la corrélation n'est pas linéaire et l'on observe des cas atypiques, comme celui du Malawi, dont l'APD nette en pourcentage du PIB (15.2 %) le place loin en tête des pays africains, alors qu'il arrive bon dixième du classement des recettes sous forme de dons exprimées en pourcentage du PIB.

Graphique 2.8. **Dons et apports nets d'aide publique au développement (APD) perçus, 2019**

En pourcentage du PIB

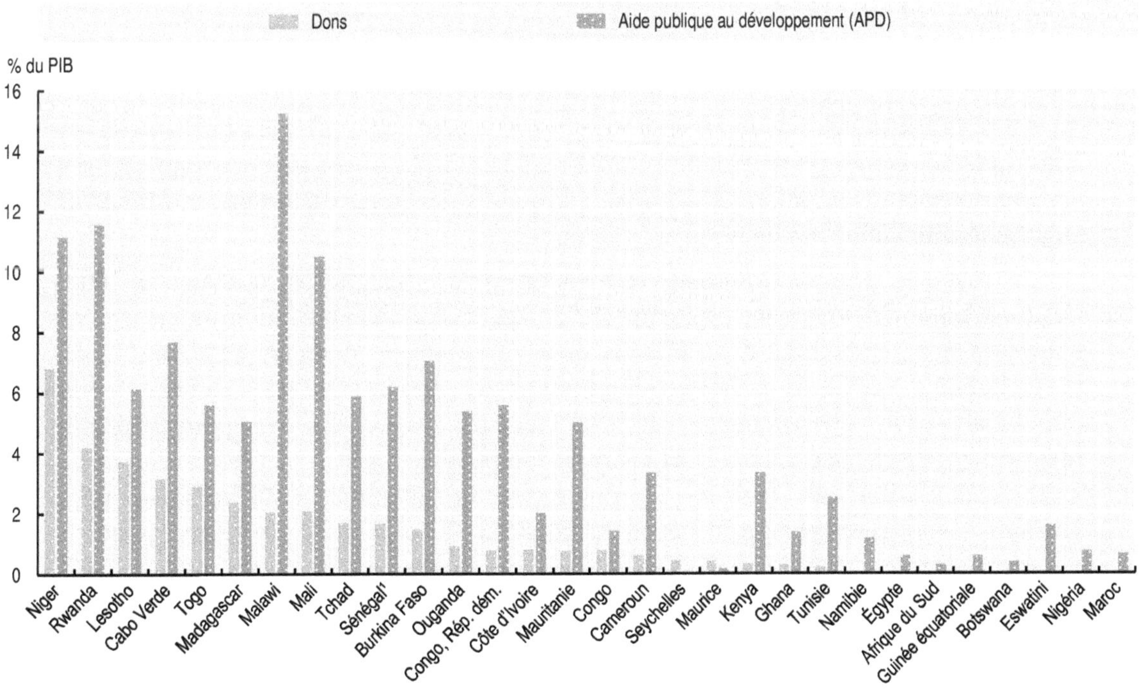

Note : Les valeurs de l'APD nette incluent les dons versés par les 30 pays membres du Comité d'aide au développement (CAD) de l'OCDE, 20 pays non membres du CAD ainsi que des organisations multilatérales et des organismes privés. De grands donneurs, comme la Chine, ne sont pas encore pris en compte.

1. Faute de données disponibles pour 2019, ce sont les données de 2018 qui ont été utilisées pour le Sénégal.

Source : Tableau 6.2 du chapitre 6 et Comité d'aide au développement (CAD) de l'OCDE pour les données relatives à l'APD versée en 2021.

StatLink https://doi.org/10.1787/888934283025

Il n'est pas rare que les pays tributaires des dons se trouvent confrontés à de fortes diminutions annuelles de cette source de recettes. Huit pays ont enregistré entre 2010 et 2019 une ou plusieurs diminutions annuelles de ces recettes d'au moins 2 points de pourcentage, voire de plus de 3 points pour six d'entre eux. Au Malawi, les dons, qui représentaient plus de 10 % du PIB en 2013, ont chuté de 65 %, en USD, l'année suivante, qui a été marquée par le scandale du Cashgate (VOANews, 2013[7]). Au total, 14 pays parmi les 30 étudiés ont enregistré au cours de la décennie écoulée une baisse de leurs recettes annuelles sous forme de dons équivalant à au moins 1.0 % du PIB.

En moyenne, les recettes sous forme de dons perçues par les pays étudiés sont tombées à 1.3 % du PIB en 2019, alors qu'elles se situaient à 2.2 % du PIB en 2010. Entre 2010 et 2019, le niveau moyen des dons, exprimé en pourcentage du PIB, n'a augmenté dans les pays étudiés qu'en 2013 et 2017, et a accusé la plus forte diminution en 2014. Les fluctuations de ces recettes sont souvent liées au contexte national. L'Égypte, par exemple, a vu ses recettes sous forme de dons augmenter brusquement en 2014, dans le contexte de la normalisation des relations internationales qui a suivi sa crise politique interne, tandis que le Mali a vu cette source de recettes se tarir en 2012, avec l'éclatement de la guerre, avant de réapparaître l'année suivante.

La crise du COVID-19 a eu une incidence sur les apports d'aide à l'Afrique qui ont visé à atténuer l'impact de la pandémie. Globalement, l'APD distribuée par les Membres du CAD aux pays du monde entier a progressé de 7 % en termes réels entre 2019 et 2020, l'aide aux organisations multilatérales augmentant de 9 % et l'aide humanitaire de 6 %. Cette évolution fait suite à une décennie de hausse de la croissance annuelle moyenne en termes réels de 2.0 %, avec trois années consécutives de baisse entre 2017 et 2019. En revanche, la hausse des apports d'ADP consentis par les pays du CAD à l'Afrique a été plus modérée, les données préliminaires faisant apparaître une augmentation de 4.1 % en 2020 (OCDE, 2021[8]).

Recettes tirées des ressources et autres revenus de la propriété

C'est en leur qualité de propriétaire, et en particulier de propriétaire terrien, que les États tirent une grande partie de leurs recettes non fiscales. Ces recettes sont comptabilisées comme revenus de la propriété dans les *Statistiques des recettes publiques en Afrique* et englobent différents types de revenus (graphique 2.9).

Les loyers et redevances sont des recettes tirées de l'utilisation du domaine de l'État, habituellement dans le cadre d'activités de prospection et d'exploitation de ressources naturelles non renouvelables sur des terres appartenant au domaine de l'État, ou de l'exploitation de fermes et de forêts détenues par l'État. Les intérêts et dividendes sont la rémunération d'investissements réalisés par l'État dans des sociétés. En règle générale, les redevances pétrolières et minières ne sont pas comptabilisés avec les autres catégories de revenus d'investissement, mais la question peut se révéler complexe. De nombreux pays africains créent des entreprises publiques chargées de gérer les recettes pétrolières ou nouent des accords de partage des recettes avec des entreprises privées qui exploitent ces ressources naturelles. La classification de ces fonds n'est pas toujours claire. À titre d'exemple, au Botswana, une part importante des revenus de la propriété provient des entreprises qui investissent dans l'extraction du diamant (encadré 2.2).

Graphique 2.9. **Loyers et redevances par pays, 2019**

En pourcentage du PIB

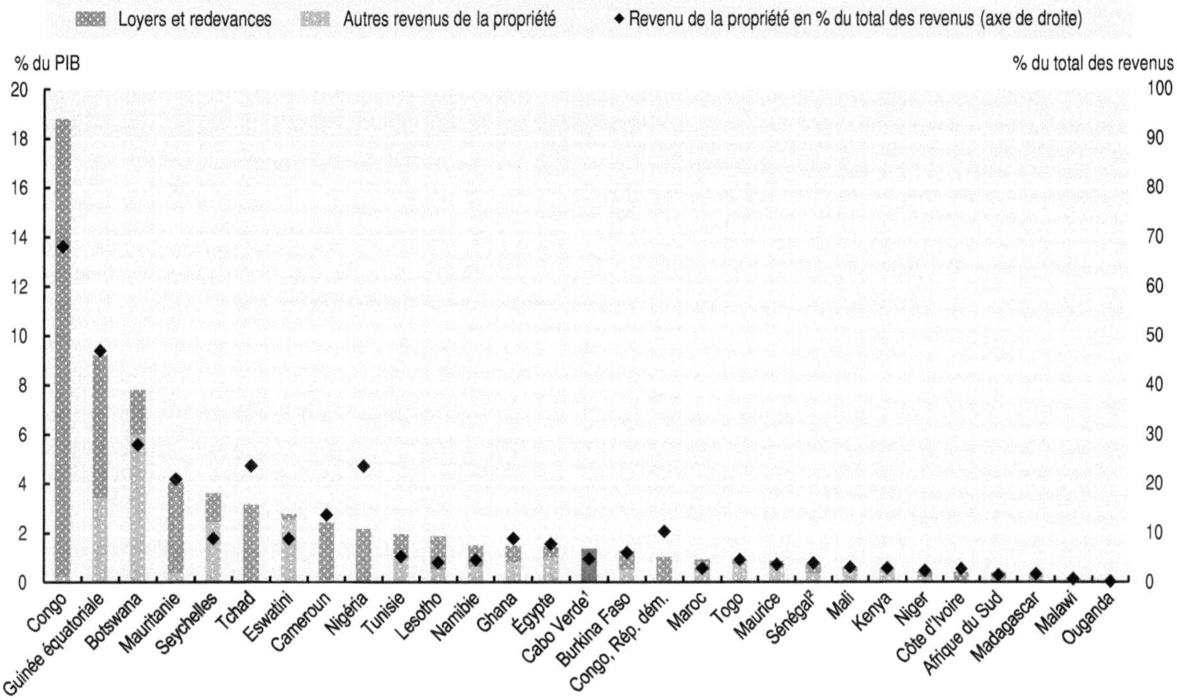

Note : Le Rwanda n'apparaît pas dans ce graphique faute de données disponibles.

1. Les données relatives aux revenus de la propriété pour le Cabo Verde n'ont pas été ventilées.
2. Faute de données disponibles pour 2019, ce sont les données de 2018 qui ont été utilisées pour le Sénégal.

Source : Calculs réalisés par les auteurs à partir des données des tableaux 6.5 6.34 et 4.17.

StatLink https://doi.org/10.1787/888934283044

Encadré 2.2. **Ressources naturelles et finances publiques**

Il existe différentes façons[4] pour les États de dégager des recettes ou des économies à partir des ressources naturelles :

- Le moyen le plus direct réside dans les loyers et redevances. L'État exige des entreprises et particuliers qu'ils s'acquittent de redevances en échange du droit d'accéder aux terres appartenant au domaine public. Il agit en sa qualité de propriétaire des terrains concernés et les montants à verser sont généralement fixés par voie de négociations. Ces redevances sont comptabilisées comme revenus de la propriété.
- Le paiement des services fournis par les administrations publiques constitue une autre source de recettes non fiscales, lesquelles sont versées par des entreprises du secteur primaire. Il peut s'agir des contrôles environnementaux, de la construction d'ouvrages ou, dans le cas de Maurice, de la fourniture de données météorologiques et de cartes. Les recettes correspondantes sont comptabilisées comme produits de la vente de biens et de services.
- Le fait, pour l'État, de détenir une partie ou la totalité du capital d'une société exploitant en son nom des ressources naturelles peut lui procurer des recettes sous forme de bénéfices et de dividendes. Ces redevances sont comptabilisées comme revenus de la propriété. Le Botswana, par exemple, tire l'essentiel de ses recettes liées aux ressources naturelles des dividendes que lui rapporte sa participation de 50 % au capital de la société Debswana, qui exploite les principales mines de diamants du pays (Mining Technology, 2020[10]).

Encadré 2.2. **Ressources naturelles et finances publiques** *(suite)*

- Il est possible de taxer l'exploitation des ressources naturelles, notamment sous la forme de droits d'accise sur les matières premières extraites de terres appartenant au domaine public ou de taxes minières qui ciblant, non pas la personne physique ou morale qui exploite les ressources naturelles, mais l'activité d'exploitation proprement dite. Les revenus correspondants sont alors comptabilisés dans les recettes fiscales. Le Niger et le Sénégal appliquent de telles taxes sur les activités d'extraction, qui relèvent de la catégorie « autres impôts sur des biens et services ».
- Les sociétés et les particuliers qui exploitent des ressources naturelles acquittent le plus souvent les mêmes impôts et taxes (impôts sur le revenu et taxe sur la valeur ajoutée, par exemple) que les autres contribuables. Les recettes tirées de ces impôts et taxes de portée générale figurent bien dans les comptes publics, mais pas nécessairement dans la catégorie spécifique des recettes issues de ressources naturelles.
- Par ailleurs, il arrive que des sociétés et des particuliers consacrent une partie de leur richesse issue de l'extraction de ressources naturelles à la construction d'infrastructures ou à la fourniture de services. Dès lors que ces infrastructures ou services répondent à une demande d'investissements ou de services publics, il peut en résulter une économie sur les dépenses publiques, qui toutefois ne sera pas comptabilisée comme une recette pour l'État. Dans certains cas, l'État impose, comme condition à l'accès aux ressources naturelles dont il est propriétaire, que les entreprises et particuliers concernés fournissent certains services, par exemple en prenant à leur charge une partie au moins du coût de la construction et de l'entretien des routes desservant les mines. Des entreprises minières ont ainsi été mises à contribution dans le financement d'un réseau ferroviaire qui reliera sur 3 000 km le Bénin, le Burkina Faso, le Niger, la Côte d'Ivoire, le Ghana, le Nigéria et le Togo (CNN, 2015$_{[11]}$).

Recettes tirées des ressources naturelles

Dans les 30 pays étudiés ici, les loyers et redevances correspondent principalement à des recettes minières et pétrolières. En 2019, plus de 79.4 % du total des loyers et redevances, exprimés en USD, ont été spécifiquement déclarés comme recettes pétrolières (redevances et recettes perçues au titre d'accords de partage des recettes conclus avec des compagnies pétrolières), celles-ci représentant la majeure partie des loyers et redevances perçus par le Cameroun, l'Égypte, le Ghana, la Guinée équatoriale, le Nigéria, la République du Congo et le Tchad. Parallèlement, les ressources minières ont constitué la source principale de loyers et redevances du Botswana, du Burkina Faso, du Kenya, du Lesotho, de la Namibie, du Niger, de l'Ouganda et de la République démocratique du Congo. En 2019, la pêche a représenté 53 % de l'ensemble des recettes comptabilisées en loyers et redevances aux Seychelles, et 71 % en Mauritanie. Cette même année, en Mauritanie, les rentes de la pêche ont rapporté 205 millions USD, soit 2.6 % du PIB. Plus de 88 % du total des loyers et redevances perçus par les 30 pays étudiés sont liés aux ressources naturelles ; le reste de ces recettes proviennent de la construction et de l'exploitation d'aéroports, comme dans les cas du Kenya et du Togo. Le gazoduc Transméditerranéen, qui achemine du gaz naturel algérien en Europe, rapporte chaque année plus de 500 millions TND (dinars tunisiens) en loyers à la Tunisie, qui n'est pourtant qu'un modeste producteur de gaz naturel (African Manager, 2019$_{[9]}$).

Les recettes tirées des ressources naturelles constituent une source de financement qui se caractérise souvent par une forte volatilité. Cinq pays (Guinée équatoriale, Mauritanie, Nigéria, République du Congo et Tchad) ont perçu des loyers et redevances équivalant à plus de 5 % du PIB au moins une année au cours de la décennie écoulée et tous ont enregistré au moins une baisse annuelle de ces recettes de plus de 38 %. Le Tchad et la République du Congo ont accusé au moins une fois une diminution annuelle de plus de 64 %.

Comme les redevances pétrolières domine dans les rentes et redevances perçues en Afrique, les recettes qu'elles procurent sont fortement tributaires de l'évolution des prix pétroliers (graphique 2.10). Le montant total des rentes et redevances perçues par les États africains – que l'on compte ou non celles du Nigéria, qui représentent entre 45 % et 70 % de ce total depuis 2010 – évolue au même rythme que les cours internationaux du pétrole brut.

Graphique 2.10. **Total des loyers et redevances perçus, en USD, et prix du pétrole brut en USD, 2010-19**

En pourcentage de la moyenne calculée pour la période 2010-19

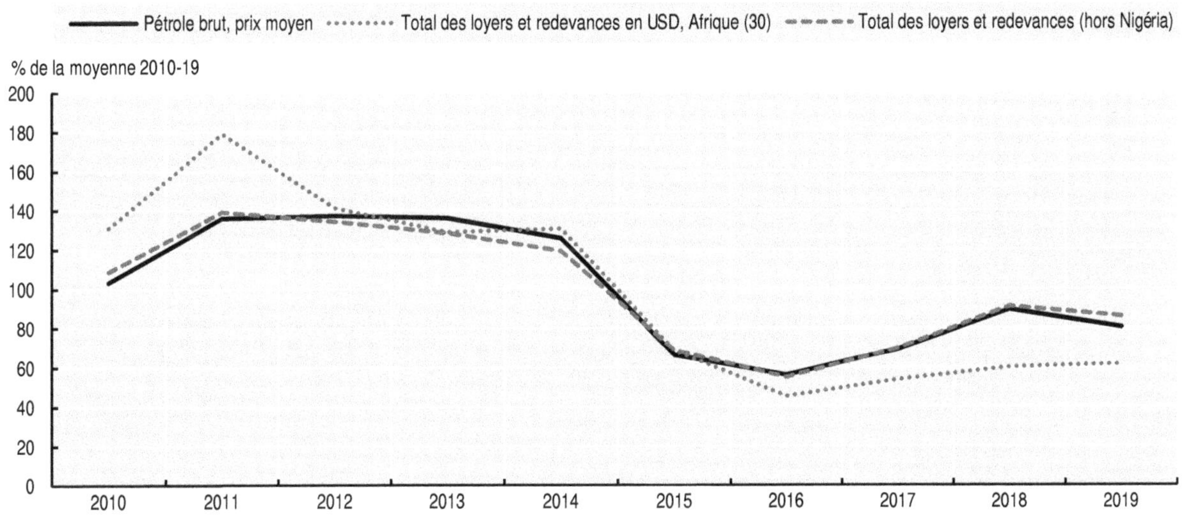

Source : Banque mondiale, Données sur les prix des matières premières (« The Pink Sheet ») (Banque mondiale, 2020[12]) et calculs des auteurs à partir des données figurant dans (OCDE/CUA/ATAF, 2021[2]), « Statistiques des recettes publiques en Afrique : Tableaux comparatifs », *Statistiques fiscales de l'OCDE* (base de données), *https://doi.org/10.1787/be755711-en*.

StatLink *https://doi.org/10.1787/888934283063*

Bien que le pétrole soit la ressource naturelle qui apporte le plus aux caisses des États africains, les pays étudiés ici en possèdent bien d'autres encore, en quantités considérables, sans toutefois en tirer d'importants revenus, sauf dans le cas du Botswana.

On observe des différences marquées entre les pays africains, que l'on considère l'ampleur ou la composition de leurs richesses naturelles. La contribution des richesses naturelles au PIB est également variable selon les pays, de même que leur impact sur les budgets publics. Ainsi, d'après les estimations de la Banque mondiale, eu égard à la contribution des ressources naturelles à la production économique (graphique 2.11), les quatre pays pour lesquels les ressources naturelles ont contribué à la production économique à hauteur de 10 % du PIB en 2019 sont le Tchad, la République du Congo et la Guinée équatoriale (principalement des hydrocarbures), et la République démocratique du Congo (principalement des minerais) (Banque mondiale, 2021[3])[5].

Les effets des ressources naturelles dont dispose chaque pays sur les finances publiques varient aussi considérablement. Des pays comme la Mauritanie, la Guinée équatoriale, la République du Congo et le Tchad tirent des recettes publiques importantes de leurs ressources naturelles tandis que d'autres, comme l'Afrique du Sud, dont la richesse issue de l'exploitation des ressources naturelles représente pourtant plus de 3.9 % du PIB, ont déclaré un montant de recettes publiques au titre des rentes des ressources naturelles inférieur à 0.2 % du PIB.

Graphique 2.11. **Extraction de ressources naturelles, estimations, 2019**

En pourcentage du PIB

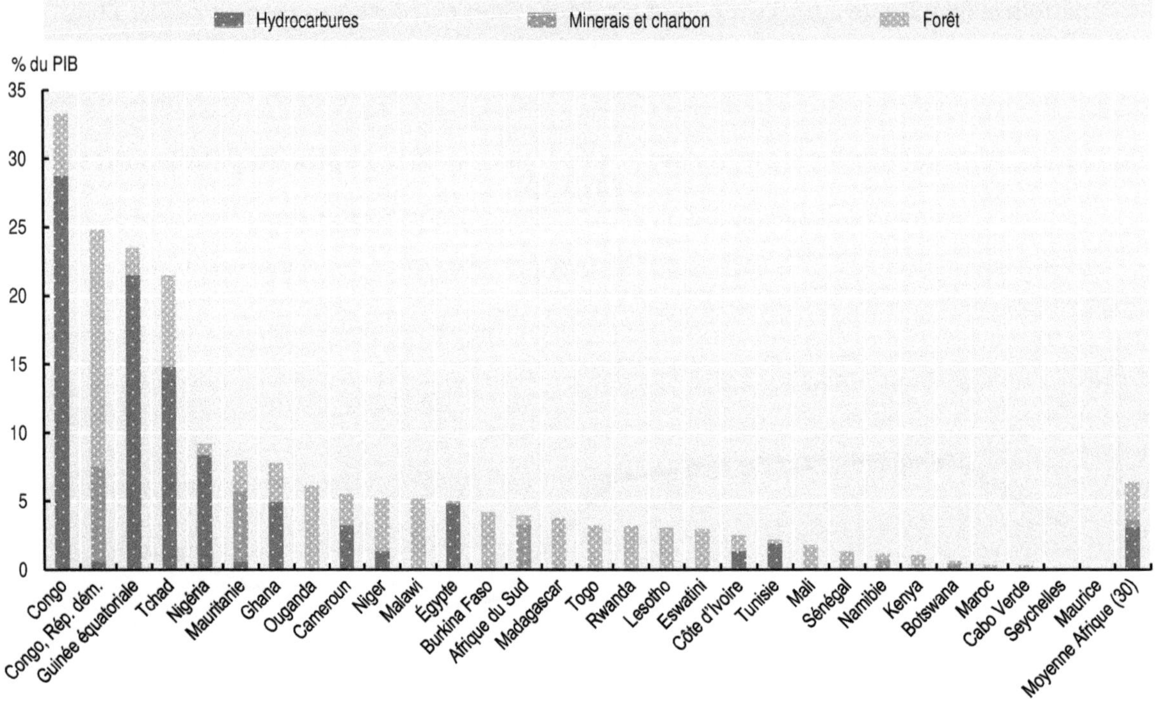

Source : Banque mondiale, *Indicateurs du développement dans le monde* (base de données) (Banque mondiale, 2021[3]) pour les estimations de la valeur totale de la production de ressources naturelles de chaque pays.

StatLink https://doi.org/10.1787/888934283082

Dans trois pays (République démocratique du Congo, Malawi, et Ouganda), la richesse produite à partir des forêts équivaut à plus de 5 % du PIB, mais ne contribue guère aux recettes publiques. Bien que certains pays, comme le Cameroun et le Niger, n'aient pas perçu de redevances au titre de l'exploitation de leurs forêts, les recettes forestières ont tout de même représenté une petite part de leurs recettes non fiscales. Au Niger, vu que l'écologie du Sahel et du Sahara est fragile et que le bois constitue une importance source d'énergie pour les communautés locales, le gouvernement étudie la question de la gestion forestière en partenariat avec les villages en vue de mettre en place des pratiques d'exploitation durables (Rives, Peltier et Montagne, 2010[13]).

Autres recettes non fiscales

Certains pays tirent d'importantes recettes non fiscales du fonctionnement habituel des administrations publiques. Ces recettes peuvent être regroupées en trois catégories : produits de la vente de biens et de services, produits des amendes et pénalités, et recettes diverses et non identifiées. Les difficultés posées par le recueil des recettes non fiscales exposées à l'encadré 2.3 sont fréquemment accentuées avec ce type de recettes, dans la mesure où elles ne sont généralement pas perçues par les administrations fiscales et ne sont, bien souvent, pas définies par la législation. Elles peuvent même ne pas figurer dans les comptes publics.

Pour tous ces types de recettes, on peut se demander s'il s'agit de prélèvements obligatoires effectués sans contrepartie et, par conséquent, dans quelle mesure il ne serait pas plus approprié de les classer dans les recettes fiscales. La question de savoir quels frais administratifs doivent être ou non considérés comme des impôts est examinée dans les annexes A et B. Toutefois, la question de la classification des amendes et des pénalités n'est pas toujours facile à trancher.

Les institutions et administrations publiques qui ont moins de pouvoir, et donc moins d'autorité pour prélever l'impôt, peuvent s'appuyer davantage sur ce type de recettes non fiscales. Autrement dit, le montant de recettes non fiscales perçues par ces collectivités locales peut être sous-estimé dans la présente publication faute d'informations sur leurs finances.

Produits de la vente de biens et de services et frais administratifs

Les administrations peuvent produire des biens et des services relevant aussi bien du secteur marchand que non marchand. Dans le secteur marchand, les administrations publiques proposent parfois des biens et services pouvant être aussi fournis auprès d'entreprises privées (tels que la vente d'aliments ou la prestation de services de transport). Parallèlement, elles assurent, lorsqu'elles gèrent des programmes ou garantissent le respect de la loi, différents services qui sont du seul ressort de l'État. Les frais facturés pour ces services non marchands sont le plus souvent considérés comme des frais administratifs.

Les frais administratifs sont souvent difficiles à classer, car ils se situent dans une zone grise, à mi-chemin entre les rémunérations de services (qui sont des recettes non fiscales) et les prélèvements obligatoires effectués sans contrepartie au profit d'administrations publiques (qui sont des recettes fiscales)[6]. Les frais de justice, ainsi que les frais de dossiers pour les permis de conduire, passeports, enregistrements de brevets et certificats de mariage sont très souvent classés dans les recettes non fiscales. Lorsqu'ils sont considérés comme des recettes fiscales, ils sont en principe rattachés à l'une des catégories suivantes :

- 4400 Impôts sur les transactions mobilières et immobilières (par exemple, taxes sur les transactions foncières) ;
- 5200 Impôts sur l'utilisation des biens et l'autorisation d'exercer des activités (par exemple, permis de chasse, enregistrement des véhicules) ;
- 6000 Autres impôts (par exemple, vente de timbres fiscaux, dans les cas où ces timbres sont utilisés pour le paiement des taxes et frais administratifs).

Dans six des pays étudiés, les recettes tirées de la vente de biens et de services et de la perception de frais administratifs représentaient au moins 1 % du PIB en 2019 (graphique 2.12) : Cabo Verde (3.1 % du PIB), Égypte (1.3 % du PIB), Ghana (1.3 % du PIB), Lesotho (2.7 % du PIB), Maroc (1.8 % du PIB) et Seychelles (2.1 % du PIB). Ces recettes ont représenté 16.5 % du total des recettes fiscales du Cabo Verde, et 13.2 % dans le cas du Lesotho.

La ventilation de ces recettes a été variable selon les pays. Au Cabo Verde, les frais administratifs représentaient 98 % des recettes enregistrées dans la vente de biens et de services. Au Ghana, l'essentiel des recettes tirées de la vente de biens et de services ont été perçues soit au niveau des communes, départements et agences administratives, soit au niveau des districts, assemblées municipales et métropolitaines. Au Maroc, 53 % des recettes issues de la vente de biens et de services par des administrations publiques sont collectées au niveau local.

Graphique 2.12. **Produits de la vente de biens et de services, frais administratifs et autres recettes liées à l'administration, 2019**

En pourcentage du PIB

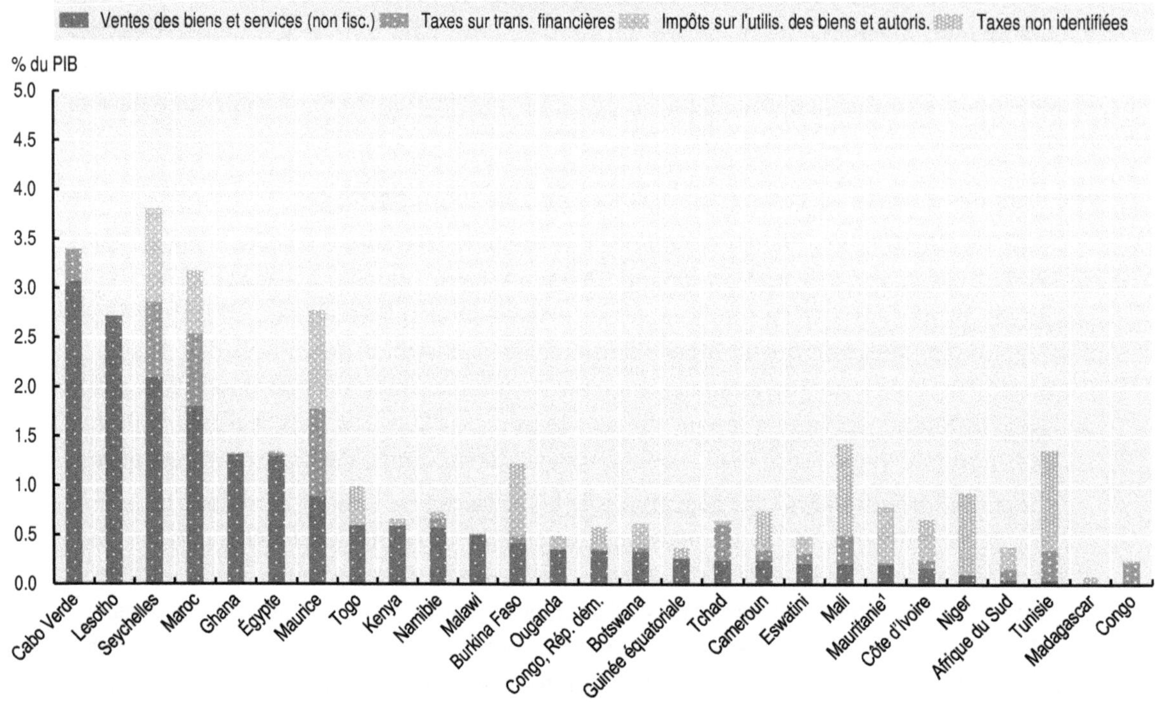

Note : Les montants indiqués ici incluent les recettes fiscales perçues par les administrations infranationales dans les cas de l'Afrique du Sud, du Maroc, de Maurice et du Nigeria, et les recettes non fiscales perçues par les administrations infranationales dans les cas d'Eswatini, du Kenya, du Maroc, et de Maurice, seuls pays pour lesquels les données correspondantes sont disponibles pour 2019. Faute de données, il n'est pas tenu compte du Nigéria, du Rwanda et du Sénégal.

Source : Calculs des auteurs basés sur des données figurant dans (OCDE/CUA/ATAF, 2021[2]), « Statistiques des recettes publiques en Afrique : Tableaux comparatifs », *Statistiques fiscales de l'OCDE* (base de données), *https://doi.org/10.1787/7f54581d-fr*

StatLink *https://doi.org/10.1787/888934283101*

Recettes diverses ou non identifiées

Certaines recettes non fiscales représentent des montants significatifs, mais ne relèvent d'aucune des catégories citées ci-dessus. Il s'agit notamment :

- Des transferts en capital ne rentrant pas dans les principales catégories de recettes non fiscales ;
- Des dons versés par des particuliers ou sociétés à des organismes publics (à l'exception des dons émanant d'organisations internationales comme le FMI, qui relèvent de la catégorie des dons) ;
- des sommes versées par des entités privées aux administrations publiques à l'issue d'importantes procédures judiciaires ou au titre d'indemnités d'assurance (comme les 100 millions EUR d'indemnités qu'ArcelorMittal a dû payer à l'État sénégalais en application de la décision de justice rendue suite à l'annulation d'un projet de mine de fer ((RFI, 2014[14])) ;
- Des versements qui relèvent de différentes catégories de la classification et pour lesquels aucune ventilation n'est disponible ;
- Des versements inclassables faute de données pertinentes. Le Rwanda n'ayant pas donné le détail de ses recettes non fiscales, sauf en ce qui concerne les dons, elles ont été classées dans la catégorie des recettes diverses et non identifiées ;

- Des revenus transférés par la SACU au Botswana, à l'Eswatini, au Lesotho et à la Namibie (voir encadré 2.3).

Encadré 2.3. **Recettes issues de la SACU**

L'Union douanière d'Afrique australe (*South African Customs Union*, SACU) réunit l'Afrique du Sud, le Botswana, l'Eswatini, le Lesotho et la Namibie. Son siège se trouve à Windhoek (Namibie). Cette union douanière vise à établir « une communauté économique qui favorise un développement équitable et durable, au service du bien-être des peuples, pour construire un avenir commun ».

La SACU, qui est la plus ancienne union douanière au monde, a été créée en 1899 entre la colonie britannique du Cap de Bonne-Espérance et la République boer de l'État libre d'Orange. Des accords conclus par la suite, en 1910 puis en 1969, ont marqué l'adhésion du Botswana, de l'Eswatini et du Lesotho. Après l'accession à l'indépendance de la Namibie, en 1990, et la fin de l'apartheid en Afrique du Sud, en 1994, de nouvelles négociations ont été ouvertes pour aboutir, en 2002, à la conclusion de l'accord en vigueur à ce jour.

Cet accord prévoit la libre circulation entre les pays membres de la SACU de tous les produits manufacturés fabriqués dans ces pays, en franchise de droits. Il définit également des tarifs extérieurs communs et la mise en commun des droits de douane et d'accise, en vue de leur partage entre les pays membres de la SACU suivant la formule de répartition des recettes figurant en annexe à l'Accord.

Les règles de partage des recettes comprennent trois composantes :

- Une composante douanière, qui divise le montant brut des droits de douane en fonction de la valeur des marchandises importées par chaque pays depuis les autres pays membres de la SACU au cours de l'année considérée (en pourcentage des importations totales intra-SACU).
- Une composante portant sur les droits d'accise, qui divise le montant brut de ces droits selon le ratio correspondant au PIB de chaque pays rapporté au PIB total de la SACU.
- Une composante de développement, financée par 15 % de la composante liée aux droits d'accise et pondérée en faveur des pays moins développés de la SACU selon une formule fondée sur le PIB par habitant.

Dans la présente publication, les recettes issues des droits de douane et d'accise sont incluses dans les recettes fiscales du pays de la SACU qui les a collectées. Elles sont rapportées dans les rubriques 5121 (accises) et 5123 (droits de douane et droits à l'importation) des tableaux des recettes fiscales. Les montants redistribués par le fonds commun des recettes de la SACU sont classés dans les tableaux des recettes non fiscales, sous la rubrique des recettes diverses et non identifiées, comme indiqué dans le tableau 6.13 à propos de l'Eswatini. En ce qui concerne l'Afrique du Sud, contributeur net au mécanisme de la SACU, les contributions, nettes des reversements perçus, sont indiquées pour mémoire dans le tableau des recettes non fiscales (tableau 6.22).

Source : (SACU, 2017[15]), (SACU, 2014[16]).

Les recettes diverses et non identifiées peuvent représenter une composante non négligeable des recettes non fiscales de certains pays. C'est le cas de la Tunisie (contributions volontaires exceptionnelles versées à l'administration), de Maurice (transferts en capital provenant de fonds statutaires spéciaux) et du Maroc (versements effectués au bénéfice de l'administration en contrepartie du droit à entrer en concurrence avec des institutions publiques pour la fourniture de services).

La variabilité des recettes diverses et non identifiées peut être imputable à des transferts de capitaux importants, à des entrées de recettes éphémères ou à des reclassifications de fonds dans la catégorie des recettes non identifiées en raison de l'absence de données. La présence de montants élevés dans cette rubrique pourrait conduire à s'interroger sur la précision des montants inscrits dans les autres catégories de recettes non fiscales.

Recettes issues de l'Union douanière d'Afrique australe

Les cinq membres de la SACU prélèvent des droits de douane et d'accise dans le cadre d'un régime fiscal uniforme, puis transfèrent les sommes collectées dans le fonds commun de recettes de la SACU. Ce fonds les redistribue ensuite selon une complexe formule de partage des recettes. Dans les faits, toutefois, comme l'Afrique du Sud détient les principaux ports d'entrée de l'Afrique australe, ce pays collecte la quasi-totalité des droits de douane et d'accise destinés au fonds commun de recettes de la SACU. En conséquence, l'Afrique du Sud en est un contributeur net, et les autres pays membres des bénéficiaires nets.

Si les revenus issus la SACU sont quantité négligeable pour l'Afrique du Sud, ils sont en revanche essentiels pour les finances des autres membres de l'Union douanière (graphique 2.13). En 2019, ils ont fait grimper les recettes du Botswana, de l'Eswatini, du Lesotho et de la Namibie, exprimées en pourcentage du PIB, de 7.2 %, 9.8 %, 18.4 % et 10.5 % respectivement. Indépendamment des chocs économiques exogènes, le montant des recettes redistribuées par la SACU a fluctué au gré de l'évolution des paramètres employés dans la formule de partage des recettes. Le choc économique causé par la crise financière mondiale a rendu caduques une grande partie des prévisions économiques d'alors ; les paiements de la SACU étant calculés à partir de ces prévisions, il a fallu procéder à d'importants ajustements en 2010 et 2011 pour compenser les versements excessifs effectués pendant plusieurs années au titre du système de regroupement et de redistribution des recettes de la SACU (Mongardini et al., 2011[17]). Une situation similaire s'est produite en 2014, où le ralentissement de l'économie sud-africaine a de nouveau contraint à corriger les prévisions à la baisse. Les recettes redistribuées par la SACU à l'Eswatini, au Lesotho et à la Namibie, en pourcentage du PIB, ont diminué en 2015 et 2016, mais la tendance s'est inversée en 2017.

Graphique 2.13. **Total des recettes issues de la SACU et autres recettes non fiscales, par pays**

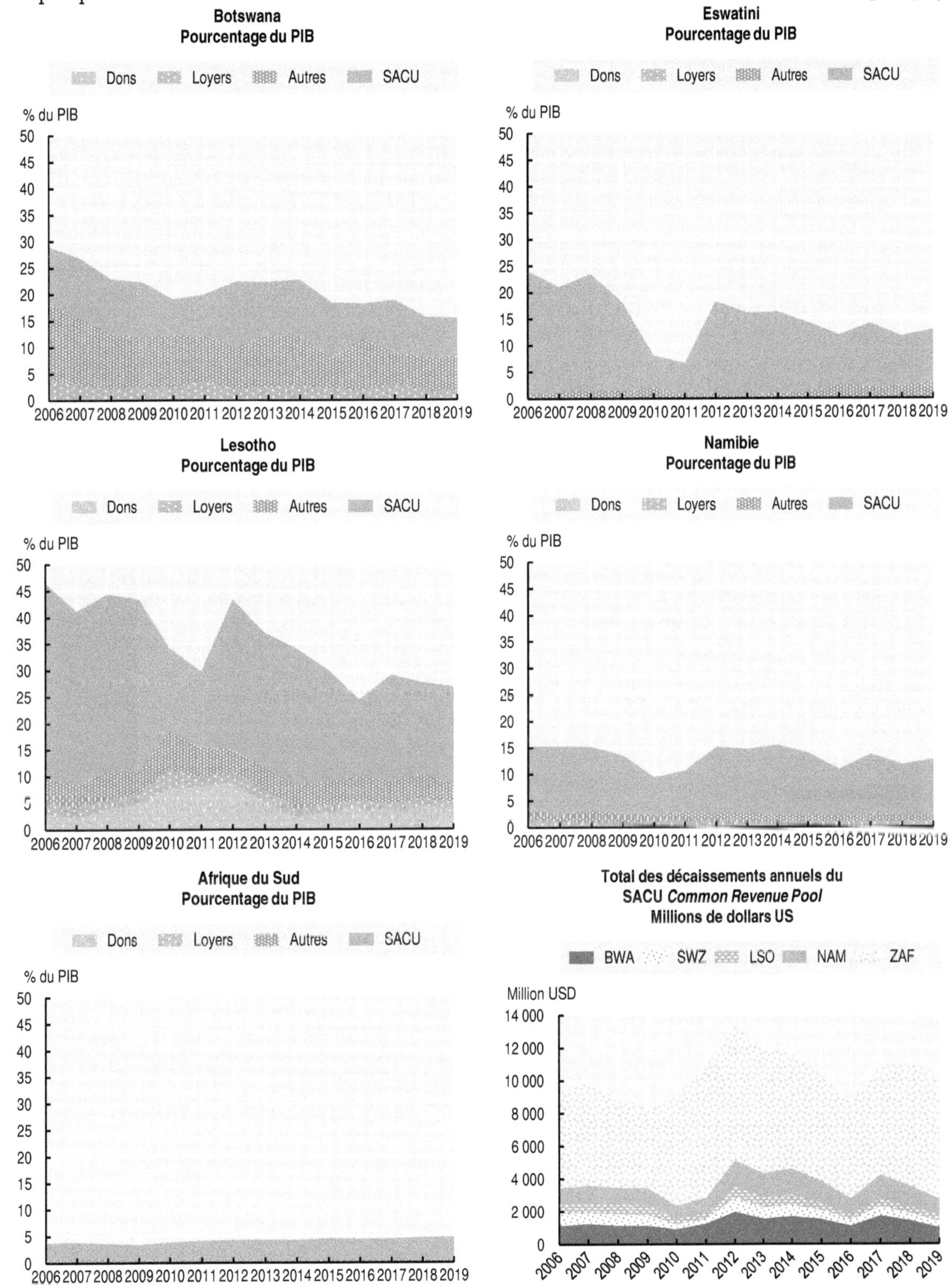

Note : Les recettes issues de la SACU qui sont indiquées ici relèvent des recettes non fiscales pour tous les pays étudiés, sauf l'Afrique du Sud, où elles sont assimilées aux droits de douane et d'accise.

Source : Calculs des auteurs basés sur des données figurant dans (OCDE/CUA/ATAF, 2021[2]), « Statistiques des recettes publiques en Afrique : Tableaux comparatifs », *Statistiques fiscales de l'OCDE* (base de données), *https://doi.org/10.1787/7f54581d-fr*

StatLink *https://doi.org/10.1787/888934283120*

Notes

1 Il n'y a pas de comparaison possible avec les moyennes des 26 pays d'Amérique latine et des Caraïbes (ALC) (voir (OCDE et al., 2021[20])) et des 37 pays de l'OCDE (voir (OCDE, 2017[18])), car les publications correspondantes ne couvrent pas les recettes non fiscales.

2 Voir le Guide d'interprétation sur les recettes non fiscales dans l'annexe B du présent rapport pour la définition de ces catégories de revenus.

3 La définition officielle de l'APD est la suivante : « tous les apports de ressources qui sont fournis aux pays et territoires figurant sur la Liste des bénéficiaires d'APD établie par le Comité d'aide au développement ou à des institutions multilatérales et qui émanent d'organismes publics, y compris des États et des collectivités locales, ou d'organismes agissant pour le compte d'organismes publics, sachant que chaque opération doit en outre avoir pour but essentiel de favoriser le développement économique et l'amélioration du niveau de vie des pays en développement, et être assortie de conditions favorables et comporter un élément de libéralité au moins égal à 25 % (sur la base d'un taux d'actualisation de 10 %) ». Des informations supplémentaires sont disponibles à l'adresse suivante : *www.oecd.org/dac/financing-sustainable-development/index-terms.htm#ODA*.

4 Il convient de noter que les recettes fiscales tirées de l'extraction pétrolière peuvent englober l'impôt sur les bénéfices des sociétés, les droits indirects sur des produits énergétiques ainsi que des taxes sur les ventes non remboursables, telles que la TVA, tandis que les recettes non fiscales peuvent inclure les redevances, les transferts de bénéfices, les dividendes versés par les entreprises publiques et d'autres revenus d'investissements perçus au titre de la participation directe de l'État dans le capital d'entreprises du secteur extractif (Mansour et Rota-Graziosi, 2013[19]).

5 La Banque mondiale utilise l'expression « bénéfices tirés des ressources naturelles ». Ceux-ci correspondent à la différence entre la valeur des ressources naturelles produites dans les pays, qui est fonction des prix des matières premières, et le coût estimé de l'extraction des ressources. À ne pas confondre avec la rente de ressources, que l'OCDE définit comme étant une catégorie de recette publique. Veuillez consulter la documentation sur les rentes de ressources dans l'ensemble de données des indicateurs de développement mondial de la Banque mondiale (voir *https://databank.worldbank.org/metadataglossary/adjusted-net-savings/series/NY.GDP.TOTL.RT.ZS)* et le guide d'interprétation pour plus de détails.

6 Pour de plus amples informations sur la classification des frais administratifs, consulter, à l'annexe A, les paragraphes 9 à 13 du Guide d'interprétation de l'OCDE.

Références

African Manager (2019), *Gazoduc-ENI: Des royalties de 500 millions de dinars par an pour la Tunisie, africanmanager.com/la-tunisie-tirera-500-millions-de-dinars-par-an-du-gazoduc-avec-litalie/.* [9]

Banque mondiale (2021), *Indicateurs du développement dans le monde, https://donnees.banquemondiale.org/indicateur/GC.TAX.TOTL.GD.ZS* (consulté le 8 septembre 2020). [3]

Banque mondiale (2021), *World Bank Country and Lending Groups, https://datahelpdesk.worldbank.org/knowledgebase/articles/906519* (consulté en juin 2021). [5]

Banque mondiale (2020), *Données sur les prix des matières premières (The Pink Sheet), www.worldbank.org/en/research/commodity-markets* (consulté en août 2020). [12]

CNN (2015), *Mammoth rail network to put West African economies on the right track, https://edition.cnn.com/2015/03/05/africa/west-africa-minerals-railway/index.html* (consulté le 21 septembre 2020). [11]

EIU (2015), *Government approves new hydrocarbons code, https://country.eiu.com/article.aspx?articleid=1303035314&Country=Congo%20(Brazzaville)&topic=Eco_9.* [4]

FMI (2021), *Base de données des Perspectives de l'économie mondiale, avril 2021, www.imf.org/external/pubs/ft/weo/2020/01/weodata/index.aspx* (consulté le 8 septembre 2020). [1]

Mansour, M. et G. Rota-Graziosi (2013), « Tax Coordination, Tax Competition, and Revenue Mobilization in the West African Economic and Monetary Union », *IMF Working Paper*, vol. 13/163, *www.imf.org/en/Publications/WP/Issues/2016/12/31/Tax-Coordination-Tax-Competition-and-Revenue-Mobilization-in-the-West-African-Economic-and-40756.* [19]

MiningTechnology (2020), *Debswana diamond mines, www.mining-technology.com/projects/debswana/* (consulté le 20 septembre 2020). [10]

Mongardini, J. et al. (2011), *In the wake of the global economic crisis: adjusting to lower revenue of the Southern African Customs*, Fonds monétaire international, *www.imf.org/external/pubs/ft/dp/2011/afr1101.pdf*. [17]

OCDE (2021), *DAC Data Submitters*, *www.oecd.org/dac/financing-sustainable-development/development-finance-standards/dacdatasubmitters.htm* (consulté le 20 septembre 2021). [6]

OCDE (2021), *Les dépenses liées au COVID-19 ont contribué à hisser l'aide extérieure à un niveau sans précédent en 2020*, *www.oecd.org/fr/developpement/financementpourledeveloppementdurable/statistiques-financement-developpement/APD-2020-detail-resume.pdf*. [8]

OCDE (2017), *Statistiques des recettes publiques 2017*, Éditions OCDE, Paris, *https://dx.doi.org/10.1787/9789264283206-fr*. [18]

OCDE/CUA/ATAF (2021), *Recettes fiscales en Afrique : Tableaux comparatifs*, Éditions OCDE, Paris, *http://dx.doi.org/10.1787/be755711-en*. [2]

OCDE et al. (2021), *Revenue Statistics in Latin America and the Caribbean 2021*, Éditions OCDE, Paris, *https://dx.doi.org/10.1787/96ce5287-en-es*. [20]

RFI (2014), *Le gros chèque d'Arcelor Mittal au Sénégal*, *http://www.rfi.fr/economie/20140605-le-gros-cheque-arcelor-mittal-senegal*. [14]

Rives, F., R. Peltier et P. Montagne (2010), *Fifteen years of forest community management in Niger: from a technician's dream to social reality*, CIRAD, *https://agritrop.cirad.fr/555467/1/document_555467.pdf*. [13]

SACU (2017), *Southern African Customs Union Agreement 2002 (tel qu'amendé le 12 avril 2013)*, *www.sacu.int/list.php?type=Agreements*. [15]

SACU (2014), *Implementing a Common Agenda Towards Regional Integration: 2014 Annual Report*, *www.sacu.int/docs/reports_annual/2014/annual_report.pdf*. [16]

VOANews (2013), *Malawi: Donors Withhold Aid Over Cashgate Scandal*, *www.voanews.com/africa/malawi-donors-withhold-aid-over-cashgate-scandal* (consulté le 21 septembre 2020). [7]

Chapter 3

Public debt in Africa and the impact of the COVID-19 pandemic

Chapitre 3

La dette publique en Afrique et l'impact de la pandémie de COVID-19

Revenue Statistics in Africa 1990-2019/Statistiques des recettes publiques en Afrique 1990-2019

Chapter 3

Public debt in Africa and the impact of the COVID-19 pandemic

Introduction

The COVID-19 pandemic has led to higher debt levels across Africa as countries increased borrowing to finance immediate public health needs and to protect lives and livelihoods. Governments introduced fiscal stimulus packages (including tax and expenditure policies) to support businesses and individuals through lockdowns and the broader economic downturn even as public revenues fell due to declines in economic activity and natural resource prices. The external debt position of many African countries deteriorated in 2020 as a result; as of 30 June, 2021, the International Monetary Fund (IMF) classified seven countries (Burkina Faso, Cameroon, Cabo Verde, Chad, Ghana, Kenya and Mauritania) as being at high risk of debt distress, while the Republic of the Congo was classified as being in debt distress (IMF, 2021[1]). The African Union has proposed several measures spanning the short, medium and long term to assist countries to mitigate the effects of the pandemic on their public finances.

This special feature provides the statistical and policy context around Africa's increased debt vulnerability, using revenue data contained in the *Revenue Statistics in Africa* report. The first section shows the evolution of indicators of debt, debt service[1] and revenues in the ten years prior to the COVID-19 pandemic. The second section explores the evolving composition of African debt over the same period, while the third examines the medium-term outlook for African debt in the aftermath of COVID-19. The chapter closes with recommendations by the African Union to a range of stakeholders to improve management of African countries' debt.

Revenues have not kept pace with debt increases since 2010

For the 30 countries included in this edition of *Revenue Statistics in Africa*, total debt levels and debt service costs have been rising over the past decade (Figure 3.1). In US dollars, both total levels of debt and annual debt service were over two and a half times higher in 2019 than they were ten years previously; in 2019, total revenues in US dollar terms were only 11% higher than they were in 2010. The composition of debt and the structure of revenues have also changed significantly, most notably with respect to increases in bond issuance (discussed in the next section).

Calculating debt service payments as a proportion of government revenues demonstrates the extent to which the costs of servicing debt constrain a government's capacity to finance domestic spending and investment. While this indicator varies greatly across the countries included in *Revenue Statistics in Africa 2021*, debt service payments absorbed a higher proportion of government revenues in the years 2015-19 than in the previous five-year interval in every country except Tunisia. Between 2015 and 2019, debt service costs ranged from 2.1% of total revenues (as recorded in this publication) in Nigeria to 17% of total government revenues in Côte d'Ivoire (Figure 3.2). For many countries, this increase reversed earlier trends: in 16 of the 30 countries, debt service declined as a percentage of total revenues between the period 2005-09 and 2010-14.

Figure 3.1. **Annual general government debt stock, general government debt service, and general government revenues for *Revenue Statistics in Africa* countries in USD billion**

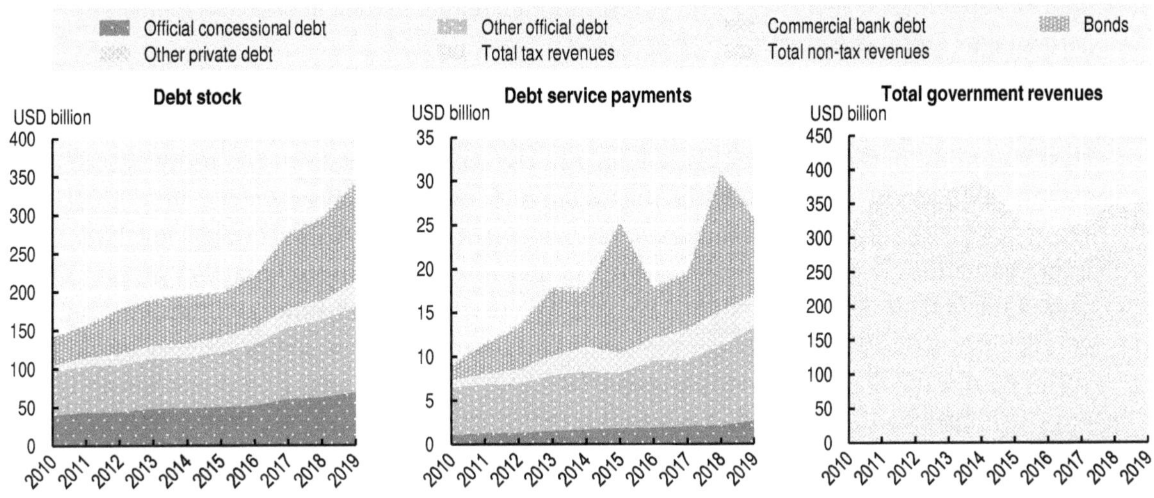

Note: The *International Debt Statistics Database* does not include information on Equatorial Guinea, Mauritius, Namibia or Seychelles. General government debt includes loans from governments and their agencies (including central banks), loans from autonomous bodies, and direct loans from official export credit agencies.

Debt service are the sum of principal repayments and interest payments actually made in the year specified.

Source: Author's calculations based on World Bank *International Debt Statistics* (IDS) database (World Bank, 2021[2]), and tax and non-tax revenues from (OECD/AUC/ATAF, 2021[3]), "Revenue Statistics in Africa: Comparative tables", *OECD Tax Statistics* (database), *http://dx.doi.org/10.1787/be755711-en*.

StatLink https://doi.org/10.1787/888934282721

Figure 3.2. **Average service on external debt for the general government sector as a percentage of total revenues, *Revenue Statistics in Africa* countries**

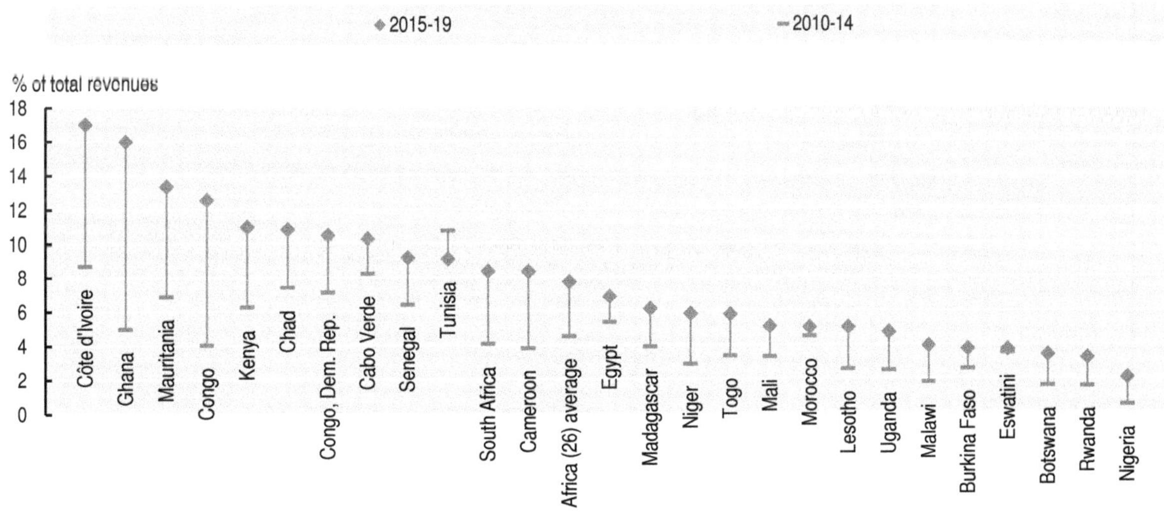

Source: Author's calculations based on from World Bank *International Debt Statistics* (IDS) database (World Bank, 2021[2]), and tax and non-tax revenues from (OECD/AUC/ATAF, 2021[3]), "Revenue Statistics in Africa: Comparative tables", *OECD Tax Statistics* (database), *http://dx.doi.org/10.1787/be755711-en*.

StatLink https://doi.org/10.1787/888934282740

The high dispersion in the ratio of debt service payments to total revenues for the 26 countries in *Revenue Statistics in Africa* for which there is also data within the World Bank debt statistics reflects significant heterogeneity in both numerator and denominator. Figure 3.3 compares average annual revenues and average annual debt service over the period 2010-14 with those in the period 2015-19 (in both cases as a percentage of GDP). For most countries, the values in black and bold (years 2015-19) are located to the right of figures in red italics (years 2010-14), representing increases in debt service payments as a percentage of total revenues.

Some oil-rich countries, such as the Republic of the Congo, saw a large shift downwards between the two periods due to declining oil prices, which caused total revenues to plummet. Most countries, however, moved horizontally in the chart: their total revenues remained steady as a percentage of GDP while debt payments increased, thereby narrowing fiscal space. Countries that made these horizontal movements tended to be relatively insulated from fluctuations in oil and grant revenues and they often experienced improved access to capital markets during a time of increased lending to African governments. Chad was the only country where both debt service payments and government revenues declined between 2010-14 and 2015-19. Debt service payments for Chad were lower after 2015 due to a major principal repayment in 2014, after which it received debt relief from the Highly Indebted Poor Countries Initiative (HIPC) (World Bank, 2015[4]). As a heavily oil-dependent country, Chad also saw lower government revenues after 2015 associated with declines in oil prices.

Figure 3.3. **Average annual general government revenue and average annual general government debt service as a percentage of GDP.**

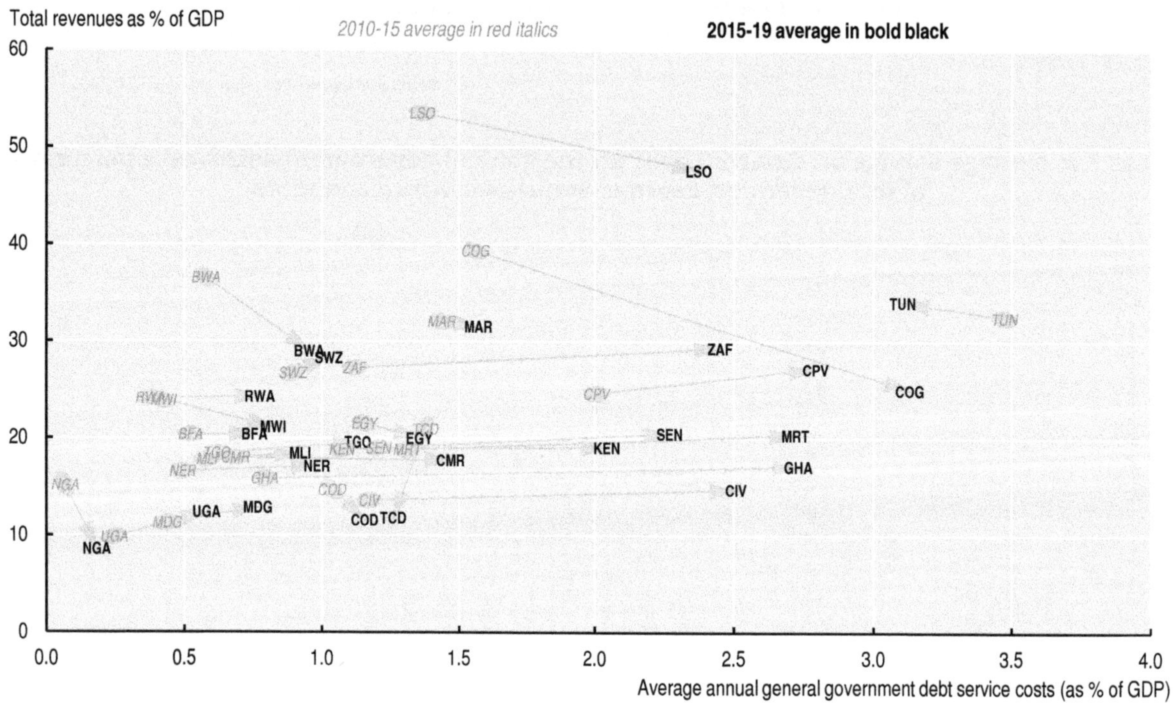

Note: Among the 30 countries included within *Revenue Statistics in Africa 2021*, four were not included in the International Debt Statistics database: Equatorial Guinea, Mauritius, Namibia, and Seychelles.

Source: Author's calculations based on World Bank *International Debt Statistics* (IDS) database (World Bank, 2021[2]), and the IMF *World Economic Outlook* database (IMF, 2021[5]) and from (OECD/AUC/ATAF, 2021[3]), "Revenue Statistics in Africa: Comparative tables", *OECD Tax Statistics* (database), *http://dx.doi.org/10.1787/be755711-en.*

StatLink *https://doi.org/10.1787/888934282759*

Since 2010, almost two-thirds of the increase in tax revenues – and the resultant expansion of fiscal space – has been offset by higher debt service payments. Average interest payments on general government debt rose from 0.3% of GDP in 2010 to 0.7% in 2019, while principal repayments increased from 0.6% of GDP to 1.3% of GDP over the same period (Figure 3.4) adding up to an increase in average debt service payments equivalent to 1.1% of GDP. Over the same period, the increase in tax revenues was equivalent to 1.8% of GDP. Despite the increase, however, debt service payments for these African countries remain lower than the average debt service payments paid by developing countries in Europe (2.7% of GDP) and Latin America and the Caribbean (3.0% of GDP), and they are around the same level as those paid by developing countries in Asia (1.7%) (World Bank, 2021[2]).

Figure 3.4. **Average external debt service and revenue, *Revenue Statistics in Africa* countries**

Percentage of GDP

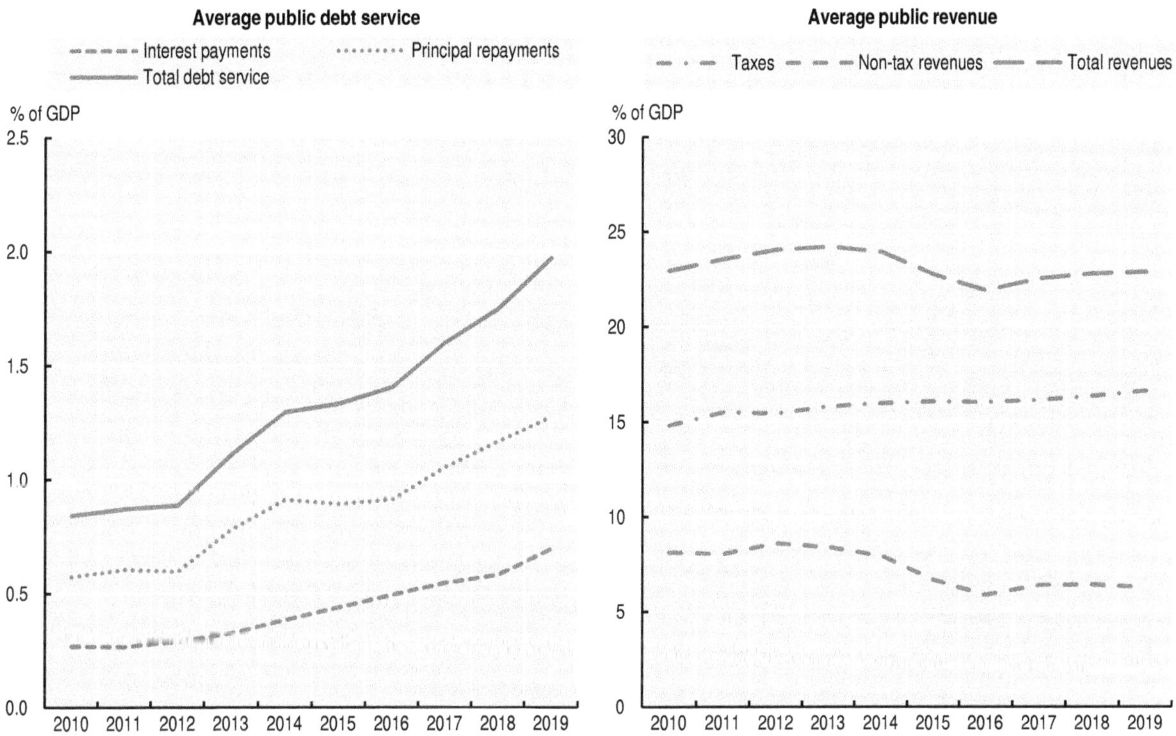

Note: An unweighted average of 26 countries out of the 30 countries reported in *Revenue Statistics in Africa 2021* is presented here. The *International Debt Statistics* database does not include information on Equatorial Guinea, Mauritius, Namibia or Seychelles.

Source: Author's calculations based on World Bank *International Debt Statistics* (IDS) database (World Bank, 2021[2]), and tax and non-tax revenues from (OECD/AUC/ATAF, 2021[3]), "Revenue Statistics in Africa: Comparative tables", *OECD Tax Statistics* (database), *http://dx.doi.org/10.1787/be755711-en* and the IMF *World Economic Outlook* database (IMF, 2021[5]).

StatLink https://doi.org/10.1787/888934282778

African governments have both increased their level of external government debt and seen an increase in borrowing costs. Between 2010 and 2019, among 26 *Revenue Statistics in Africa countries*, 19 registered an increase in their external government debt as a percentage of GDP as well as in the ratio of interest payments paid to debt stock (Figure 3.5). As a result, over this period, the average ratio of debt interest payments to debt stock for these countries rose from 1.6% to 3.1%. As the next section discusses, this increase reflects that African countries are going beyond concessional financing in order to access capital at market rates.

However, an increase in borrowing costs is not necessarily a consequence of greater access to capital at market rates: some countries, such as Botswana and Nigeria, whose arrows in Figure 3.5 are horizontal, saw increases in borrowing costs without an accompanying increase in debt as a percentage of GDP. Although the volume of debt remained steady, the profile of debt evolved over this period, changing the cost of debt service. Others, such as Cabo Verde, saw an increase in debt with a lower accompanying increase in the cost of debt.

Figure 3.5. **Change in annual interest payments as percentage of total external debt stock compared with change in total debt stock as percentage of GDP, *Revenue Statistics in Africa* countries**

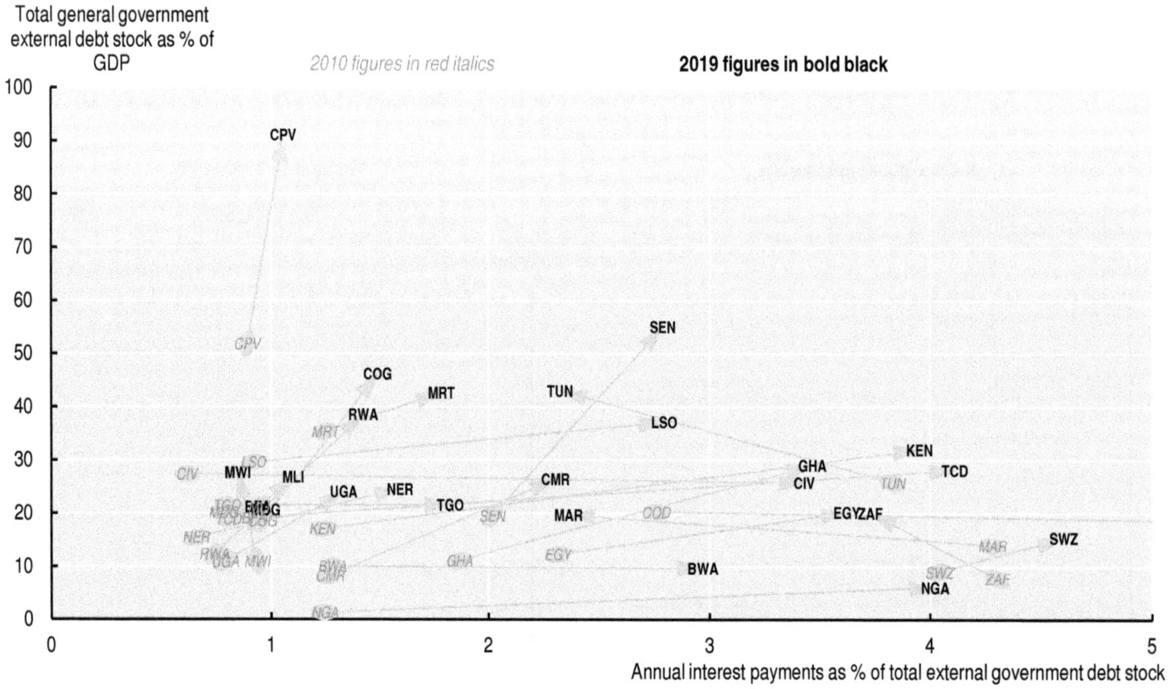

Note: An unweighted average of 26 countries out of the 30 countries reported in *Revenue Statistics in Africa* is presented here. The *International Debt Statistics* database does not include information on Equatorial Guinea, Mauritius, Namibia or Seychelles.

Source: Author's calculations based on World Bank *International Debt Statistics* (IDS) database (World Bank, 2021[2]), and the IMF *World Economic Outlook* database (IMF, 2021[5]).

StatLink https://doi.org/10.1787/888934282797

The composition of Africa's external debt is changing

The increase in the debt service payments of African countries is linked to a shift from traditional creditors like the Paris Club and multilateral development banks to commercial and other private creditors since the turn of the century. The share of bilateral lenders in Africa's external debt stock fell from over 50% in 2000 to just 27% in 2019, with commercial creditors taking up much of the space (AfDB, 2021[6]). The number of African countries borrowing on commercial terms on international capital markets has increased from 3 in 2001 to 21 in 2020.

Between 2009 and 2019, bonds went from 18% to 37% of outstanding debt held by *Revenue Statistics in Africa* countries (Figure 3.1 in the previous section). Over the same period, concessional debt from official creditors declined from 28% of debt to 20%. These changes indicate debt portfolios that are less favourable to borrowers, increasingly based on private, non-concessional sources that tend to be more difficult to renegotiate during periods of financial distress.

It is important to note that the use of bonds to finance public spending has been concentrated in a few African countries. Bonds were only reported for 12 *Revenue Statistics in Africa* countries in 2019 (Figure 3.6); 43% of these bonds were issued by South Africa and constituted 70% of South Africa's outstanding debt in 2019.

Figure 3.6. **Outstanding general government debt for *Revenue Statistics in Africa* countries, 2019, in USD billion, total and bonds**

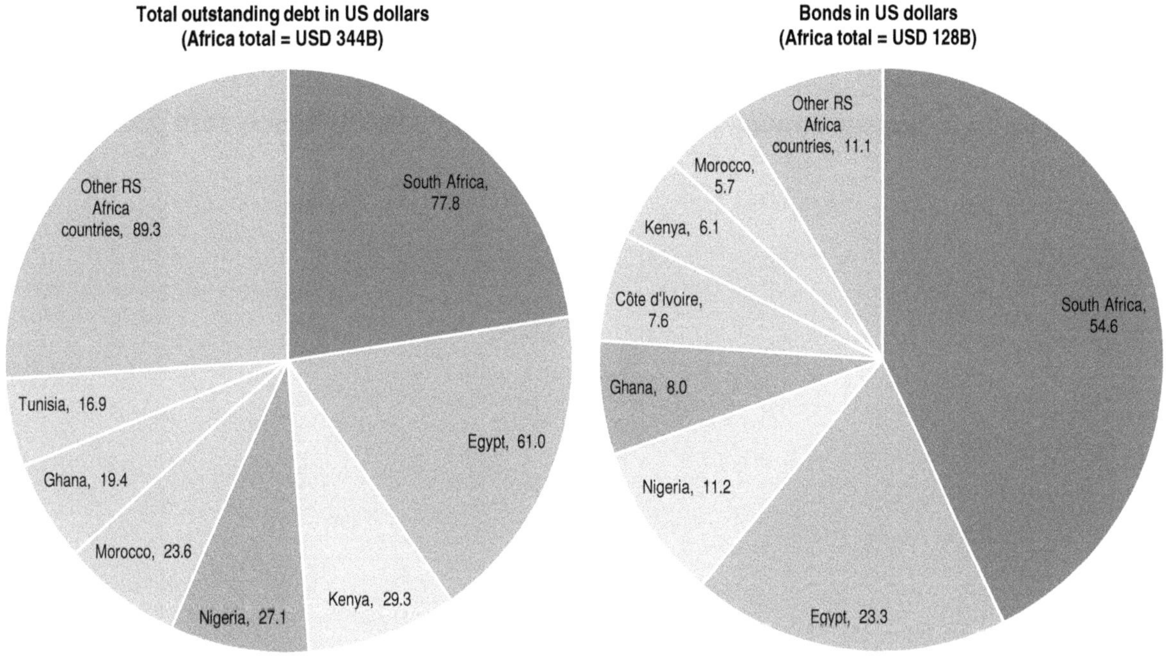

Note: The *International Debt Statistics* database does not include information on Equatorial Guinea, Mauritius, Namibia, or the Seychelles.
Source: Author's calculations based on World Bank *International Debt Statistics* (IDS) database (World Bank, 2021[2]).

StatLink https://doi.org/10.1787/888934282816

The recent tendencies for middle-income countries to raise capital through a few large bonds sales or to seek debt at short maturities have resulted in a bunching of debt repayments in some African countries, leading to large spikes in debt service payments, notably in South Africa and Chad (Figure 3.7). Total debt service payments on bonds by *Revenue Statistics in Africa* countries recorded year-on-year increases of 108%, 137%, and 148% in 2011, 2015, and 2018, respectively. Such spikes, along with the annual variation in revenues in African countries associated with grant and oil revenues, heighten stress on African public finances and can increase the gap between revenue and expenditures that drive further demand for debt financing. Chad, for example, faced significant liquidity challenges in the late 2010s as debt arrears accumulated, requiring the negotiation of debt restructuring with its largest private creditor, Glencore (IMF, 2018[7]), and leading Chad to become the first country to request a debt restructuring under the IMF's Extended Credit and Extended Fund facilities (Reuters, 2021[8]).

Debt increases in African countries have increased their exposure to foreign exchange risk. Every year since 2006, with the exception of the year 2010, between 26 and 28 out of 37 African countries for which there is data have had a majority of their debt denominated in foreign currency.[2] This creates a mismatch between the currency in which a country's debt and interest payments are denominated and the country's revenues, which are predominantly raised in national currency. Governments with foreign currency debt need to access money markets to convert the currency of their revenues in order to make their debt payments. Exchange rates for many African countries are prone to major shocks, which impact the ratio of foreign-denominated debt to GDP, possibly reversing or nullifying any debt reduction in that country. For example, between 2014 and 2015, the amount of foreign-denominated debt owed by the government of Cabo Verde decreased by 6%, when expressed in US dollars. However, due in part to the depreciation of the Cabo Verdean Escudo, which declined 16% compared to the US dollar over that same year, the ratio of foreign-denominated debt to GDP for Cabo Verde actually increased by 10%.

Figure 3.7. **Average annual debt service in Chad and South Africa, 2010-2020**
Percentage of GDP

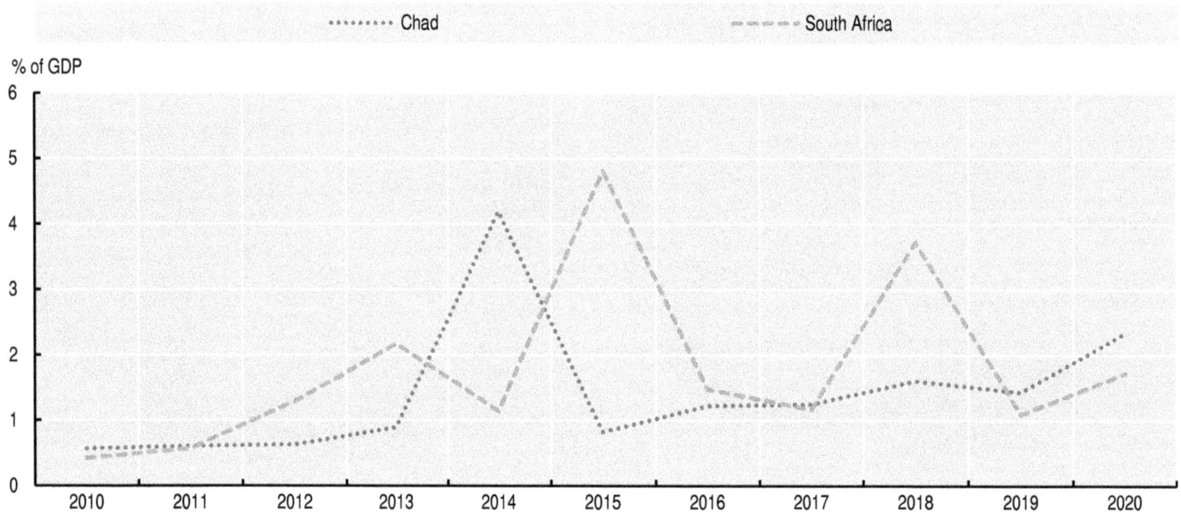

Source: Author's calculations based on World Bank *International Debt Statistics* (IDS) database (World Bank, 2021[2]) and the IMF *World Economic Outlook* database (IMF, 2021[5]).

StatLink *https://doi.org/10.1787/888934282835*

Sixteen out of 27 African countries experienced at least one year in which the impact of the year-over-year change in exchange rate would have had the effect of increasing debt-to-GDP ratios by at least 10% of GDP had all other factors remained equal (Figure 3.8). In some cases, had there been no mitigating factors, exchange rate shocks would have doubled or tripled a country's debt burden within a single year. The African Development Bank (AfDB, 2021[6]) indicated that the outlook for the debt ratios of oil-exporting countries in particular would worsen as a result of currency depreciation. In 2015, when the last major shock to commodity prices occurred, the median impact of currency depreciation on debt burdens was equivalent to 4.4% of GDP.

Figure 3.8. **Maximum year-on-year impact of exchange rate changes on foreign currency debt, 2000-19**

Percentage of GDP

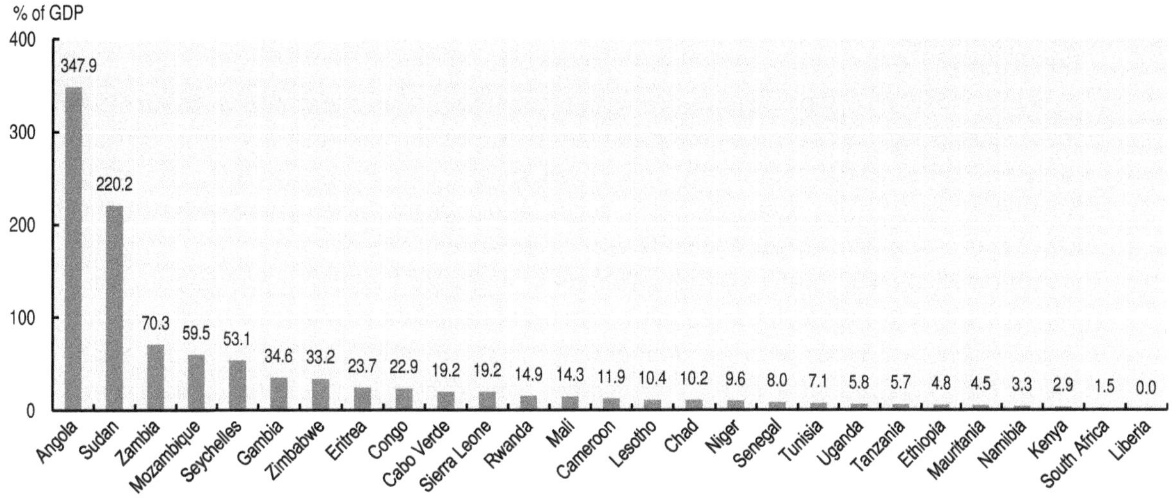

Note: The impact of the exchange rate changes on debt burden for a given year is calculated by taking that year-over-year change in the local-currency to US dollar exchange rate, and multiplying it by the debt-to-GDP ratio recorded for the previous year. This calculation measures the effect of the one-year exchange rate shock in the counterfactual where GDP levels and debt levels remain constant.

Source: Author's calculations based on World Bank *International Debt Statistics* (IDS) database (World Bank, 2021[2]) and the IMF *World Economic Outlook* database (IMF, 2021[5]).

StatLink https://doi.org/10.1787/888934282854

Medium-term debt outlook and COVID-19

As the COVID-19 pandemic continues, debt vulnerabilities in African countries are becoming deeper and more widespread. In 2020, the average African general government gross debt-to-GDP ratio rose to 70.5% in 2020, up from 62.6% in 2019. Africa's GDP contracted by 1.9% in 2020, the most severe economic downturn in the continent since 1991. For the next five years, the debt-to-GDP ratio is projected to decline but remain above the 2019 level. Globally, public debt increased due to the COVID-19 pandemic, reaching approximately 98% of GDP due to a combination of slowdowns in economic activity, lower fiscal revenues, higher spending on health and economic stimulus packages. Many African countries likewise rolled out fiscal stimuli to protect livelihoods that were affected by the closure of businesses resulting from the lockdown measures that were put in place across the continent to curb the spread of the virus.

The growing fiscal requirements of African countries to respond to the pandemic coupled with the economic downturn placed considerable strain on public revenues and countries were compelled to resort to debt financing. Some of the fiscal measures deployed in Africa were tax-based, further putting pressure on public revenues. Tax cuts and tax deferrals for individuals and businesses aimed at ameliorating the burden on citizens were among the measures employed by governments (OECD/AUC/ATAF, 2020[9]). Among 23 African countries examined by (ATAF, 2020), 204 tax-relief measures were reported in response to the COVID-19 pandemic by July 2020 (ATAF, 2020[10]).

Larger debt burdens have increased the likelihood of debt distress. According to the IMF's DSA analysis, eight countries included in *Revenue Statistics in Africa 2021* are in high overall debt distress, 11 are in moderate distress while the Republic of Congo is in debt distress. In 2020, 21 African countries had external debt payments as a share of government revenues that exceeded 14% of GDP, which the IMF has identified as a signal of increased likelihood of debt default in low-income countries (LICs) and lower middle-income countries (LMICs). Five of these countries had external debt payments above 30% of revenues, substantially weakening their ability to respond to the COVID-19 pandemic in terms of strengthening health services, supporting businesses or scaling up social protection to protect the most vulnerable in society.

While the COVID-19 pandemic is expected to continue to put pressure on public debt and fiscal budgets, other risks are projected to undermine debt sustainability across African countries. These include commodity and export shocks, contingent liabilities related to state-owned enterprises, exchange rate shocks, and a high share of commercial debt. Also of concern to African governments are the persistent negative sovereign ratings by the international credit rating agencies. The APRM indicated that seven African countries received a negative outlook from the major international credit rating agencies during the first half of 2021, with only Benin and Mali receiving positive ratings during the same period (UNECA/AUC, 2021[11]). Most of the downgrades were driven by the deteriorating fiscal positions of the countries concerned.

International financial institutions expect debt service payments to increase in the coming years as a consequence of the ongoing pandemic, with a greater increase among LMICs than upper middle-income countries (UMICs). According to projections in the IMF *World Economic Outlook* (IMF, 2021[5]), average annual debt service for UMICs in the years 2021-25 are expected to be 0.3% of GDP higher than their average over the years 2015-19. By contrast, average annual debt service payments are projected to be 1.0% of GDP and 0.6% of GDP higher for LMICs and LICs, respectively. Bhutan and Zambia, two LMICs, are expected to have the highest annual debt service between 2021 and 2025, while annual debt service payments for four countries in this publication (Cabo Verde, Tunisia, Mauritania and Senegal) are projected to exceed 3.5% of GDP (Figure 3.9).

Figure 3.9. **Projected average annual debt service for low and medium income countries around the world, by country, 2021-25**

Percentage of GDP

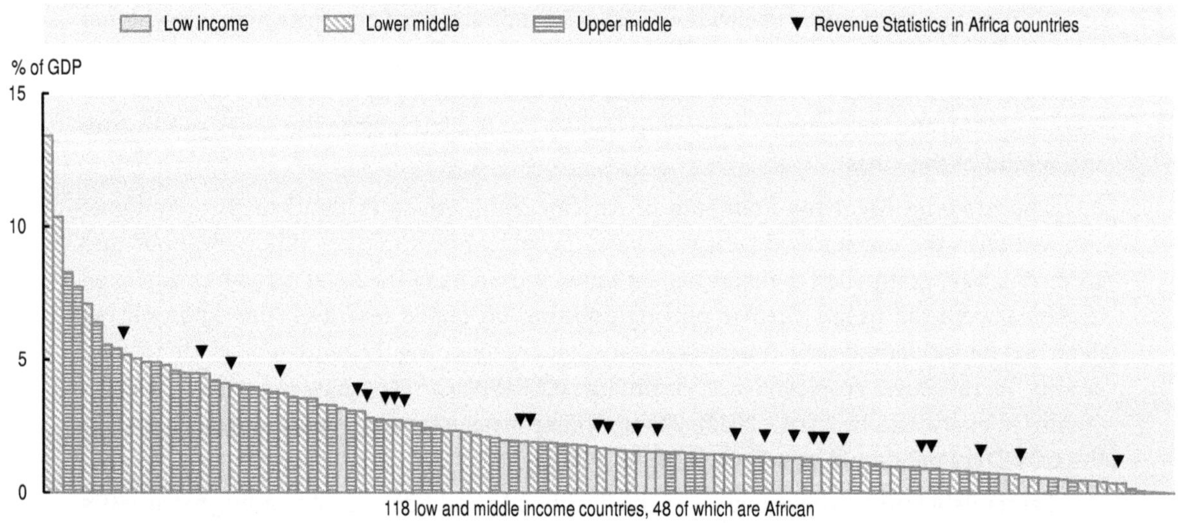

Note: The *International Debt Statistics* database does not include information on Equatorial Guinea, Mauritius, Namibia or Seychelles.
Source: Author's calculations based on World Bank *International Debt Statistics* (IDS) database (World Bank, 2021[2]) and the IMF *World Economic Outlook* database (IMF, 2021[5]).

StatLink https://doi.org/10.1787/888934282873

At the onset of the COVID-19 pandemic, the then Chairperson of the African Union and President of South Africa, H. E. Cyril Matamela Ramaphosa, appointed a group of Special Envoys to mobilise international support for Africa's response. The Special Envoys immediately recognised the imminent debt crisis that would be fuelled by the massive financial resources required to fight the pandemic and the economic fallout from the pandemic. The Special Envoys engaged with African governments, bilateral and multilateral partners, and other stakeholders, in particular international financial institutions, to mobilise the necessary resources for financing the African response to the pandemic.

The G20 Debt Service Suspension Initiative (DSSI) took effect in May 2020 to postpone debt amounting to approximately USD 11.5 billion for qualifying low- and middle-income countries up to December 2021. Of the 73 countries that are eligible for the temporary suspension of debt service under the DSSI, 32 are in Africa. Countries utilising the DSSI have made various pledges, including the use of the freed-up resources to finance social, health, and economic spending to fight the pandemic, disclosing public sector financial spending, and limiting non-concessional borrowing as agreed with the IMF and World Bank (World Bank, 2021$_{[12]}$).

Although the DSSI has released over USD 5 billion to date, the funds that have been freed up are not adequate to meet the financing needs of African countries due to the larger share of Africa's sovereign debt owed to private creditors. Calls by the G20 for private creditors to participate in the DSSI have gone unheeded, further contributing to the challenge for African countries of introducing measures to mitigate the pandemic and promote a sustainable economic recovery.

The Paris Conference on Financing Africa, organised by the President of France, Emmanuel Macron, also called for the implementation of measures aimed at providing sustainable financial support to African countries. Specifically, the Conference called for Africa's closer integration within the international financial architecture through improved access to liquidity and coordinated support by multilateral and bilateral development agencies for African governments. Further, the Conference highlighted the importance of tackling debt vulnerabilities within the Common Framework for Debt Treatments beyond the DSSI.

In line with the recommendations of the African Union, the Conference supported sustainable development financing by creditors and borrowers as a means of avoiding a new cycle of indebtedness based on the G20 Operational Guidelines for Sustainable Financing and supporting the implementation of the Voluntary Principles for Debt Transparency of the Institute for International Finance. Another conclusion of the Conference was to support debtor countries to institute reforms aimed at enhancing public spending efficiency and public financial management, including debt management.

African Union proposals to chart a sustainable debt recovery

Central to the consensus emerging from the consultations of the AU Special Envoys with the various stakeholders was the need to ensure the debt sustainability of African countries and, at the national level, the importance of fiscal reforms that would contribute towards this objective. In an effort to minimise the debt burden for many African countries, avoid future debt distress and support a sustainable debt recovery, the African Union has proposed several measures with implications for the African Union, member states and development partners. The measures proposed by the African Union for each of these groups include:

- ***African Union***
  - Develop a common African position for the reform of the international financial architecture and advocate for this objective.
  - Continue advocacy efforts for debt service suspension beyond December 2021, particularly in view of the COVID-19 pandemic, which continues to demand massive amounts of public revenues.
  - Advocate for the reallocation of a larger share of the USD 650 billion in Special Drawing Rights (SDRs) of the IMF to African countries.
- ***Member states***
  - Accelerate efforts to ratify the legal instruments establishing African Union Financial Institutions, especially the African Monetary Fund and African Financial Stability Mechanism, which would cushion countries from future economic shocks, reduce regional spillover effects, and support macroeconomic and fiscal policy reforms.
  - Implement the recommendations of the Addis Ababa Action Agenda on debt sustainability.
  - Consider the issuance of debt in national currency.
  - Strengthen debt transparency and management.
  - Use debt for productive investment or growth-enhancing investments rather than maintaining spending plans.
  - Improve financial inclusion and access to finance through new financial technologies and other blockchain innovations.
  - Improve domestic savings and domestic private sector credit to GDP to enhance countries' ability to finance Africa's development needs.
  - Focus policies to support diaspora-funded businesses, attract remittances to create a pool of funds to finance major projects and allow governments to borrow from their citizens abroad. Remittances could be a crucial source of capital for small and home-based businesses, and maybe seed money for start-ups.
  - Attract foreign direct investment, an important source of private external finance for countries' development.
  - Improve domestic resource mobilisation to support Africa's development financing by upscaling efforts to curb illicit financial flows and improve revenue collection by strengthening tax administrations.
- ***Development partners***
  - As the pandemic persists, debt pressures are continuing to build. While the Common Framework for Debt Treatment has proven beneficial, it remains insufficient to meet the financing needs of African countries. A new approach in consultation with African Finance Ministers and the G20 is urgently needed to ensure that countries in need of debt restructuring have access to appropriately designed facilities.
  - Support countries to pay back commercial debts through multilateral or regional debt buy-back funds. Such efforts would need to be financed, either bilaterally or multilaterally, for example through new issuance and/ or reallocation of SDRs or other mechanisms, debt swaps (e.g. Debt for Climate Adaptation Swap Initiative), debt exchanges or re-profiling and other instruments.

- Support calls for the reform of the international financial architecture to better involve and support the needs of developing countries.
- Support the reallocation of a larger proportion of the IMF's SDRs - at least an additional USD 100 billion - to African countries by offering a portion of their unused shares to support the post-pandemic recovery of African economies, vaccine capacity, financing the private sector in support of the African Continental Free Trade Area etc.
- Call for private creditors to participate in global efforts aimed at enhancing debt management and sustainability in developing countries.

Notes

1 Within World Bank data, debt service is the sum of principal repayments and interest actually paid in currency, goods or services on long-term obligations.

2 There is more locally-denominated debt than foreign-denominated debt for these countries but two-thirds was held by just three countries: Algeria, Morocco and South Africa.

References

AfDB (2021), *African Economic Outlook 2021 - From Debt Resolution to Growth: The Road Ahead for Africa*, African Development Bank, *www.afdb.org/en/knowledge/publications/african-economic-outlook*. [6]

ATAF (2020), "Tax Administration & Policy Developments in Response to the COVID-19 Pandemic in Africa", *ATAF Research Tax Paper* Issue 01, *https://events.ataftax.org/index.php?page=documents&-func=view&document_id=66&_ga=2.27820600.50862724.1634547789-1908447849.1600676783*. [10]

IMF (2021), *List of LIC DSAs for PRGT-Eligible Countries*, *www.imf.org/external/Pubs/ft/dsa/DSAlist.pdf*. [1]

IMF (2021), *World Economic Outlook, April 2021 Edition (database)*, *www.imf.org/en/Publications/WEO/weo-database/2021/April*. [5]

IMF (2018), *First review under the extended credit facility arrangement request for a waiver of nonobservance of performance criteria, rephasing of disbursements, and financing assurances review-debt sustainability analysis*, International Monetary Fund, *www.imf.org/external/pubs/ft/dsa/pdf/2018/dsacr18108.pdf*. [7]

OECD/AUC/ATAF (2021), *Revenue Statistics in Africa: Comparative tables*, OECD Publishing, Paris, *http://dx.doi.org/10.1787/be755711-en*. [3]

OECD/AUC/ATAF (2020), *Revenue Statistics in Africa 2020: 1990-2018*, OECD Publishing, *https://doi.org/10.1787/14e1edb1-en-fr*. [9]

Reuters (2021), "UPDATE 3-Chad becomes first country to ask for debt overhaul under G20 common framework", *Reuters*, By Andrea Shalal, Karin Strohecker, *www.reuters.com/article/chad-debt-idCNL1N2K21XN*. [8]

UNECA/AUC (2021), *Africa sovereign credit rating review: 2021 MID-YEAR OUTLOOK*, United Nations. Economic Commission for Africa; African Union Commission, *https://hdl.handle.net/10855/45537*. [11]

World Bank (2021), *Debt Service Suspension Initiative Brief*, *www.worldbank.org/en/topic/debt/brief/covid-19-debt-service-suspension-initiative*. [12]

World Bank (2021), *International Debt Statistics Database*, World Bank, *https://databank.worldbank.org/source/international-debt-statistics* (accessed on 26 July 2021). [2]

World Bank (2015), *IMF and World Bank Announce US$1.1 billion Debt Relief for Chad*, *www.worldbank.org/en/news/press-release/2015/04/29/imf-world-bank-debt-relief-chad*. [4]

Revenue Statistics in Africa 1990-2019/Statistiques des recettes publiques en Afrique 1990-2019

Chapitre 3

La dette publique en Afrique et l'impact de la pandémie de COVID-19

Introduction

La pandémie de COVID-19 a entraîné une hausse des niveaux d'endettement en Afrique, les pays ayant dû recourir davantage à l'emprunt pour financer leurs besoins immédiats en matière de santé publique et protéger la vie et les moyens de subsistance de leurs concitoyens. Les États ont adopté des programmes de relance budgétaire (comprenant des mesures fiscales et de dépenses) pour aider les entreprises et les particuliers pendant les périodes de confinement et de ralentissement économique général, alors même que les recettes publiques baissaient sous l'effet du déclin de l'activité économique et de la chute des prix des ressources naturelles. L'encours de la dette extérieure de nombreux pays africains a augmenté en 2020 ; au 30 juin 2021, le Fonds monétaire international (FMI) a classé sept pays (Burkina Faso, Cabo Verde, Cameroun, Ghana, Kenya, Mauritanie et Tchad) dans la catégorie des pays à haut risque de surendettement, tandis que la République du Congo est considérée comme en situation de surendettement (FMI, 2021[1]). L'Union africaine a proposé diverses mesures à court, moyen et long terme afin d'aider les pays à atténuer les répercussions de la pandémie sur leurs finances publiques.

Cette étude spéciale présente le contexte statistique et stratégique dans lequel s'inscrit la fragilité grandissante de l'Afrique vis-à-vis de la dette, en utilisant les données relatives aux recettes publiques figurant dans la publication *Statistiques des recettes publiques en Afrique*. La première section décrit l'évolution des indicateurs de la dette, du service de la dette[1] et des recettes au cours des dix années qui ont précédé la pandémie de COVID-19. La deuxième section analyse l'évolution de la composition de la dette africaine pendant la même période, et la troisième examine les perspectives à moyen terme de la dette africaine dans le sillage de la crise du COVID-19. En conclusion, l'étude énumère les recommandations adressées par l'Union africaine à un ensemble de parties prenantes en vue d'améliorer la gestion de la dette des pays africains.

Depuis 2010, les recettes collectées n'ont pas suivi l'augmentation de l'endettement

Pour les 30 pays couverts par cette édition des *Statistiques des recettes publiques en Afrique*, les niveaux totaux de la dette et les coûts du service de la dette ont augmenté au cours de la dernière décennie, contrairement aux recettes publiques (graphique 3.1). Mesurés en dollars des États-Unis, les niveaux totaux de la dette et du service annuel de la dette en 2019 étaient plus de deux fois et demie supérieurs à ce qu'ils étaient dix ans plus tôt ; en 2019, les recettes totales, libellées en dollars des États-Unis, étaient supérieures de seulement 11 % à leur niveau en 2010. La composition de la dette et la structure des recettes ont elles aussi beaucoup changé, surtout du fait de l'accroissement des émissions d'obligations (abordé à la section suivante).

Graphique 3.1. **Niveaux annuels de l'encours de la dette, du service de la dette et des recettes des administrations publiques dans les pays couverts par les *Statistiques des recettes publiques en Afrique*, en milliards USD**

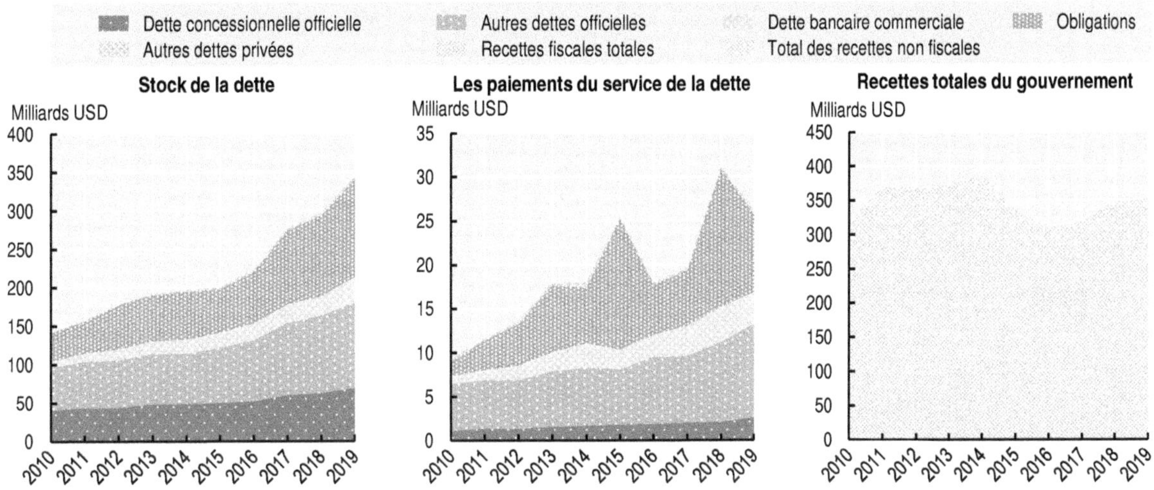

Note : La base de données des *Statistiques sur la dette internationale* ne contient pas d'informations sur la Guinée équatoriale, Maurice, la Namibie ou les Seychelles.

La dette des administrations publiques englobe les prêts accordés par les gouvernements et leurs agences (incluant les banques centrales), les prêts d'institutions publiques autonomes et les prêts directs provenant des organismes publics de crédit à l'exportation. Le service de la dette désigne la somme des remboursements du principal et des paiements d'intérêts effectués au cours de l'année indiquée.

Source : Calculs de l'auteur basés sur la base de données *International Debt Statistics* (IDS) de la Banque mondiale (Banque mondiale, 2021[2]) et les recettes fiscales et non fiscales de (OCDE/CUA/ATAF, 2021[3]), « Recettes publiques en Afrique : Tableaux comparatifs », *Statistiques fiscales de l'OCDE* (base de données), *https://doi.org/10.1787/tax-data-fr*.

StatLink https://doi.org/10.1787/888934283139

Exprimés en pourcentage des recettes publiques, les paiements au titre du service de la dette révèlent dans quelle mesure le coût du remboursement de la dette érode la capacité d'un État à financer ses dépenses et ses investissements. Bien que cet indicateur varie beaucoup dans les pays couverts par les *Statistiques des recettes publiques en Afrique* 2021, les paiements au titre du service de la dette ont absorbé une fraction plus élevée des recettes publiques pendant la période 2015-19 qu'au cours de l'intervalle de cinq ans précédent dans tous les pays, à l'exception de la Tunisie. Entre 2015 et 2019, le coût du service de la dette était compris entre 2.1 % des recettes publiques totales (telles qu'elles ressortent de cette publication) au Nigéria et 17 % en Côte d'Ivoire (graphique 3.2). Pour de nombreux pays, cette augmentation est venue mettre un terme à une tendance inverse : dans 16 des 30 pays, le service de la dette a diminué en pourcentage du total des recettes entre la période 2005-09 et la période 2010-14.

La dispersion importante du ratio des paiements au titre du service de la dette par rapport au total des recettes pour les 26 pays étudiés dans les *Statistiques des recettes publiques en Afrique* (pour lesquels la base de données des statistiques sur la dette de la Banque mondiale contient aussi des données) reflète la forte hétérogénéité du numérateur comme du dénominateur. Le graphique 3.3 compare la moyenne des recettes annuelles et la moyenne du service annuel de la dette entre la période 2010-14 et la période 2015-19 (en pourcentage du PIB). Dans la plupart des pays, les valeurs en caractères gras et noirs (années 2015-19) se situent sur la droite des chiffres en italiques et en rouge (années 2010-14), ce qui correspond à une hausse des paiements du service de la dette en pourcentage du total des recettes.

Graphique 3.2. **Service moyen de la dette extérieure pour le secteur des administrations publiques, en pourcentage du total des recettes, pays couverts par les *Statistiques des recettes publiques en Afrique***

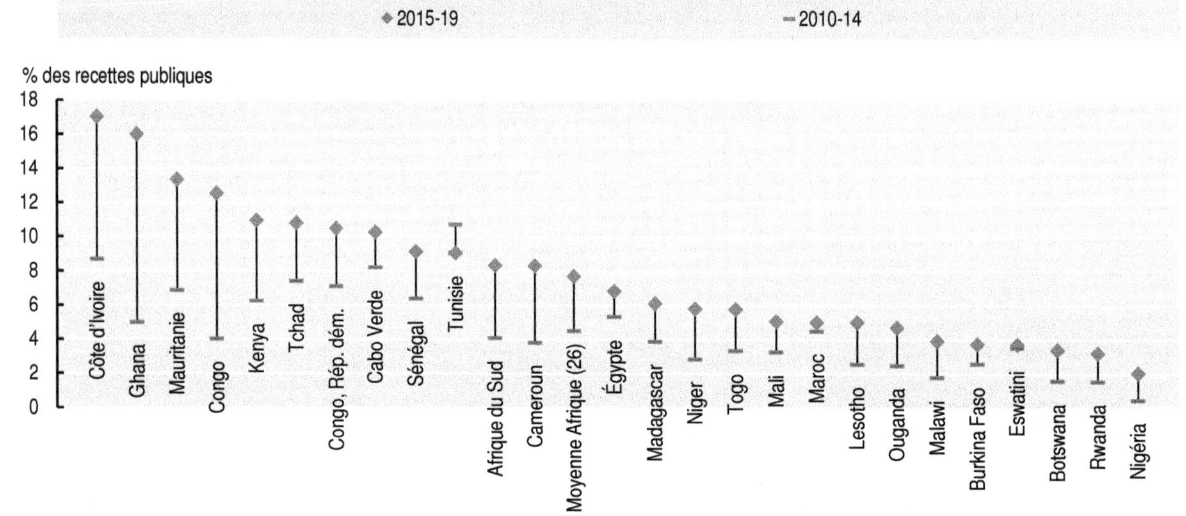

Source : Calculs de l'auteur basés sur la base de données *International Debt Statistics* (IDS) de la Banque mondiale (Banque mondiale, 2021) et les recettes fiscales et non fiscales de (OCDE/CUA/ATAF, 2021[3]), « Recettes publiques en Afrique : Tableaux comparatifs », *Statistiques fiscales de l'OCDE* (base de données), *https://doi.org/10.1787/tax-data-fr*.

StatLink https://doi.org/10.1787/888934283158

Graphique 3.3. **Moyennes annuelles des recettes des administrations publiques et du service de la dette des administrations publiques**

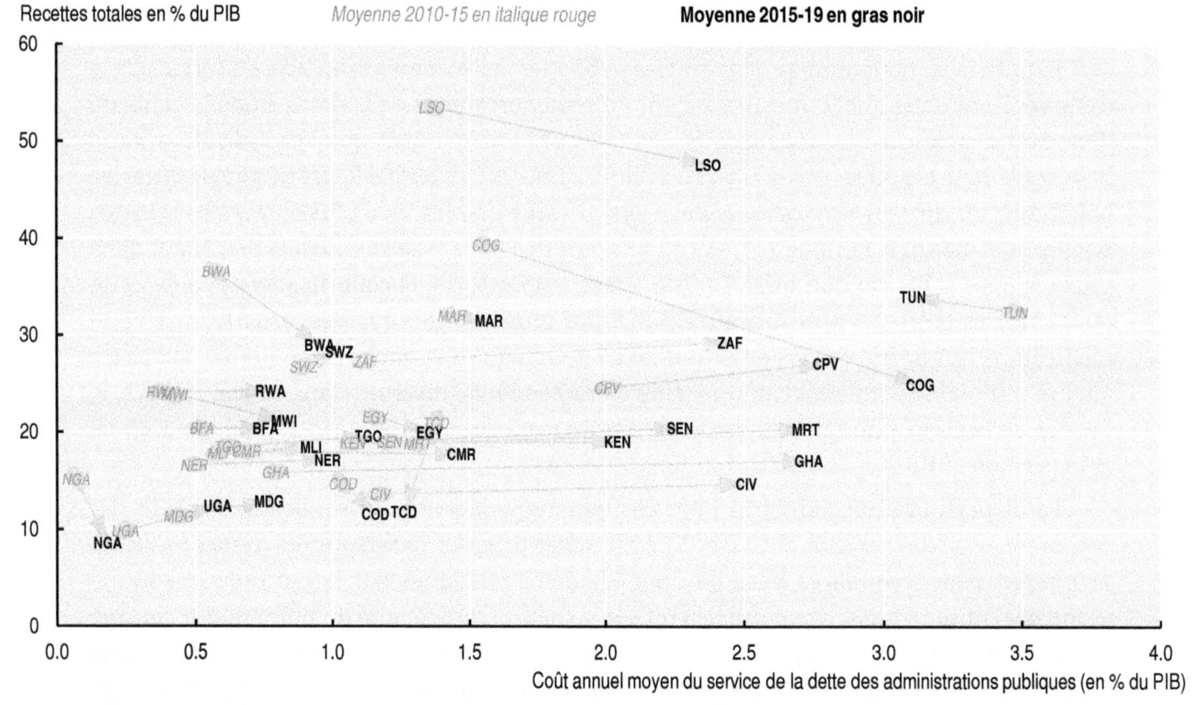

Note : Parmi les 30 pays étudiés dans les *Statistiques des recettes publiques en Afrique 2021*, quatre ne figuraient pas dans la base de données des Statistiques sur la dette internationale : la Guinée équatoriale, Maurice, la Namibie et les Seychelles.
Source : Calculs de l'auteur basés sur la base de données *International Debt Statistics* (IDS) de la Banque mondiale (Banque mondiale, 2021[2]), la base de données des *Perspectives de l'économie mondiale* database (FMI, 2021[5]) et les recettes fiscales et non fiscales de (OCDE/CUA/ATAF, 2021[3]), « Recettes publiques en Afrique : Tableaux comparatifs », *Statistiques fiscales de l'OCDE* (base de données), *https://doi.org/10.1787/tax-data-fr*.

StatLink https://doi.org/10.1787/888934283177

Certains pays riches en pétrole, comme la République du Congo, ont vu leur situation se détériorer fortement entre les deux périodes à cause de la baisse des cours du pétrole, qui a entraîné un effondrement des recettes totales. Toutefois, la plupart des pays se sont déplacés horizontalement sur le graphique : leurs recettes totales sont restées stables, en pourcentage du PIB, tandis que leurs remboursements de la dette ont augmenté, réduisant ainsi leur marge de manœuvre budgétaire. Les pays qui ont opéré ces déplacements horizontaux avaient tendance à être relativement protégés face aux fluctuations des recettes pétrolières et sous forme de dons, et ont souvent bénéficié d'un meilleur accès aux marchés de capitaux durant la période où les prêts aux pays africains étaient plus largement accordés. Le Tchad est le seul pays dans lequel les paiements au titre du service de la dette et les recettes publiques ont baissé entre 2010-2014 et 2015-19. Au Tchad, les paiements au service de la dette ont diminué après 2015 en raison d'un important remboursement du principal intervenu en 2014, à la suite duquel il a bénéficié d'un allègement de la dette au titre de l'Initiative en faveur des pays pauvres très endettés (Initiative PPTE) (Banque mondiale, 2015[4]). En sa qualité de pays très dépendant du pétrole, le Tchad a également subi une baisse des recettes publiques après 2015, sous l'effet de l'érosion des cours du pétrole.

Depuis 2010, près des deux tiers de la progression des recettes fiscales – et de l'élargissement de la marge de manœuvre budgétaire qui en résulte – ont été absorbés par l'augmentation des paiements au titre du service de la dette. Les paiements moyens d'intérêts sur la dette des administrations publiques sont passés de 0.3 % du PIB en 2010 à 0.7 % en 2019, tandis que les remboursements du principal sont passés de 0.6 % du PIB à 1.3 % du PIB au cours de la même période (graphique 3.4), venant s'ajouter à une hausse des paiements moyens au titre du service de la dette équivalente à 1.1 % du PIB. Sur la même période, l'accroissement des recettes fiscales représentait 1.8 % du PIB. Malgré cette hausse, les paiements au titre du service de la dette à la charge de ces pays africains restent néanmoins inférieurs à ceux effectués par les pays en développement en Europe (2.7 % du PIB en moyenne) et dans la région Amérique latine et Caraïbes (3.0 % du PIB), et se situent à peu près au même niveau que ceux réalisés par les pays en développement en Asie (1.7 %) (Banque mondiale, 2021[2]).

Les pays africains ont à la fois accru le niveau de leur dette publique extérieure et subi une hausse de leurs coûts d'emprunt. Entre 2010 et 2019, 19 des 26 pays étudiés ont enregistré une augmentation de leur dette publique extérieure en pourcentage du PIB, et une progression de leur ratio des paiements d'intérêts rapportés à l'encours de la dette (graphique 3.5). Aussi, au cours de cette période, le ratio moyen des paiements d'intérêts de la dette rapportés à l'encours de la dette s'est accru de 1.6 % à 3.1 % pour ces pays. Comme la section suivante l'explique, cette hausse traduit le fait que les pays africains ne se limitent plus aux financements concessionnels, mais souscrivent à des emprunts aux taux du marché.

Toutefois, un relèvement des coûts d'emprunt n'est pas forcément la conséquence d'un plus large accès aux capitaux aux taux du marché : dans certains pays, comme le Botswana et le Nigéria, dont les flèches sont à horizontales dans le graphique 3.5, la hausse des coûts d'emprunt ne s'est pas accompagnée d'une augmentation de la dette en pourcentage du PIB. Bien que le volume de la dette reste stable, son profil a évolué au cours de cette période, avec des répercussions sur le coût du service de la dette. Dans d'autres pays, comme le Cabo Verde, la dette s'est creusée tandis que l'augmentation du coût de la dette a ralenti.

Graphique 3.4. **Moyennes du service de la dette extérieure et des recettes publiques, pays couverts par les *Statistiques des recettes publiques en Afrique***

Pourcentage du PIB

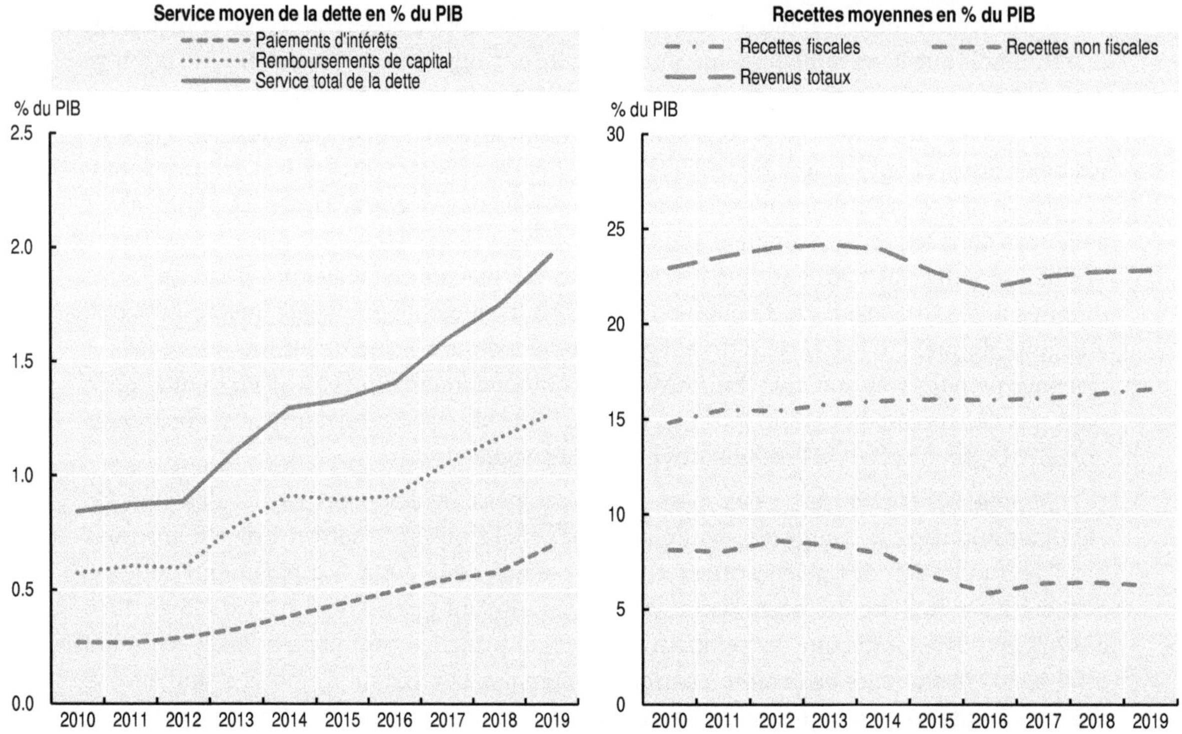

Note : Ce graphique présente une moyenne non pondérée de 26 pays sur les 30 étudiés dans les *Statistiques des recettes publiques en Afrique* 2021. La base de données des *Statistiques sur la dette internationale* ne contient pas d'informations sur la Guinée équatoriale, Maurice, la Namibie ou les Seychelles.

Source : Calculs de l'auteur basés sur la base de données *International Debt Statistics* (IDS) de la Banque mondiale (Banque mondiale, 2021) et les recettes fiscales et non fiscales de (OCDE/CUA/ATAF, 2021[3]), « Recettes publiques en Afrique : Tableaux comparatifs », *Statistiques fiscales de l'OCDE* (base de données), *https://doi.org/10.1787/tax-data-fr*.

StatLink *https://doi.org/10.1787/888934283196*

Graphique 3.5. **Évolution des paiements d'intérêts annuels en pourcentage de l'encours total de la dette extérieure, comparée à l'évolution de l'encours total de la dette en pourcentage du PIB, pays couverts par les *Statistiques des recettes publiques en Afrique***

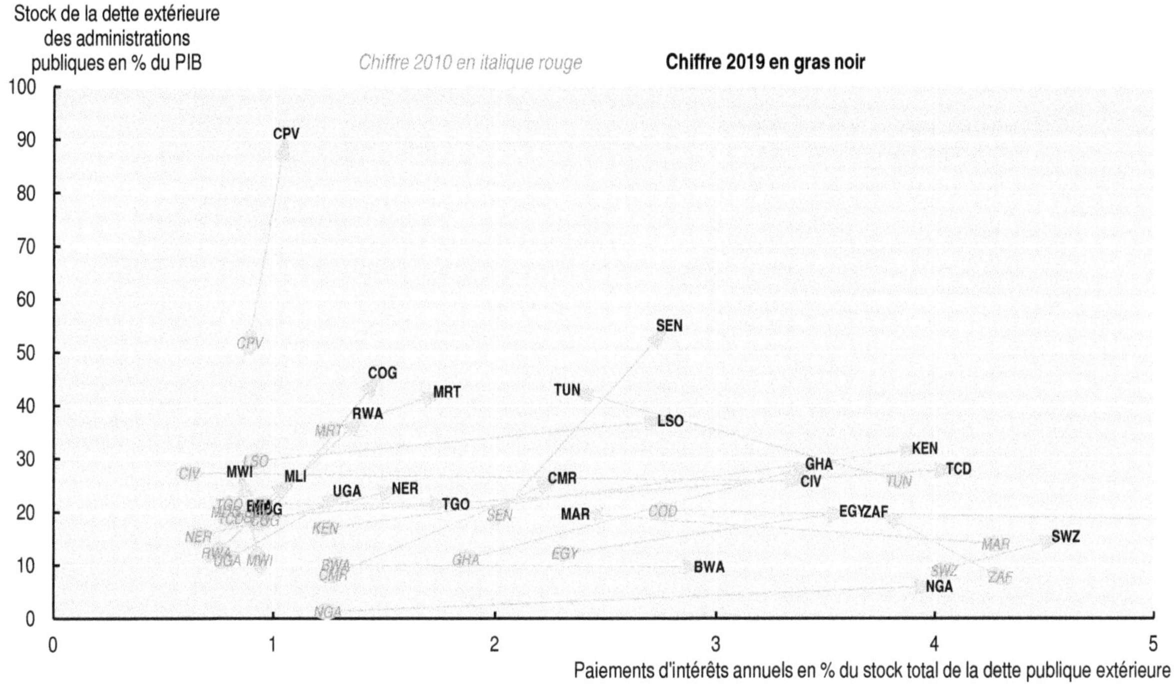

Note : Ce graphique présente une moyenne non pondérée de 26 pays sur les 30 étudiés dans les *Statistiques des recettes publiques en Afrique*. La base de données des *Statistiques sur la dette internationale* ne contient pas d'informations sur la Guinée équatoriale, Maurice, la Namibie ou les Seychelles.

Source : Calculs de l'auteur basés sur la base de données *International Debt Statistics* (IDS) de la Banque mondiale (Banque mondiale, 2021[2]) et la base de données des *Perspectives de l'économie mondiale* database (FMI, 2021[5]).

StatLink https://doi.org/10.1787/888934283215

La composition de la dette extérieure de l'Afrique évolue

L'augmentation des paiements au titre du service de la dette des pays africains est liée au passage de créanciers traditionnels comme le Club de Paris et les banques multilatérales de développement à des créanciers commerciaux et privés depuis le début du siècle. La part des créanciers bilatéraux dans l'encours de la dette extérieure de l'Afrique a baissé de plus de 50 % en 2000 à seulement 27 % en 2019, tandis que les créanciers commerciaux occupent une grande partie de l'espace (BAD, 2021[6]). Le nombre de pays africains qui empruntent à des conditions commerciales sur les marchés internationaux de capitaux a progressé de 3 en 2001 à 21 en 2020.

Entre 2009 et 2019, les obligations sont passées de 18 % à 37 % de l'encours de la dette détenue par les pays couverts par les *Statistiques des recettes publiques en Afrique* (graphique 3.1 à la section précédente). Au cours de la même période, les emprunts concessionnels souscrits auprès de créanciers publics ont baissé de 28 % à 20 % de l'encours total de la dette. Ces changements attestent de portefeuilles de créances moins favorables aux emprunteurs, composés de plus en plus d'emprunts privés non concessionnels qui sont généralement plus difficiles à renégocier pendant les périodes de difficultés financières.

Il est important de remarquer que le recours aux obligations pour financer les dépenses publiques se concentre dans un petit nombre de pays africains. En 2019, les obligations concernaient seulement 12 pays couverts par les *Statistiques des recettes publiques en Afrique* (graphique 3.6) ; 43 % de ces obligations étaient émises par l'Afrique du Sud et représentaient 70 % de l'encours de la dette sud-africaine la même année.

Graphique 3.6. **Encours de la dette des administrations publiques des pays couverts par les *Statistiques des recettes publiques en Afrique*, 2019, en milliards USD, total et obligations**

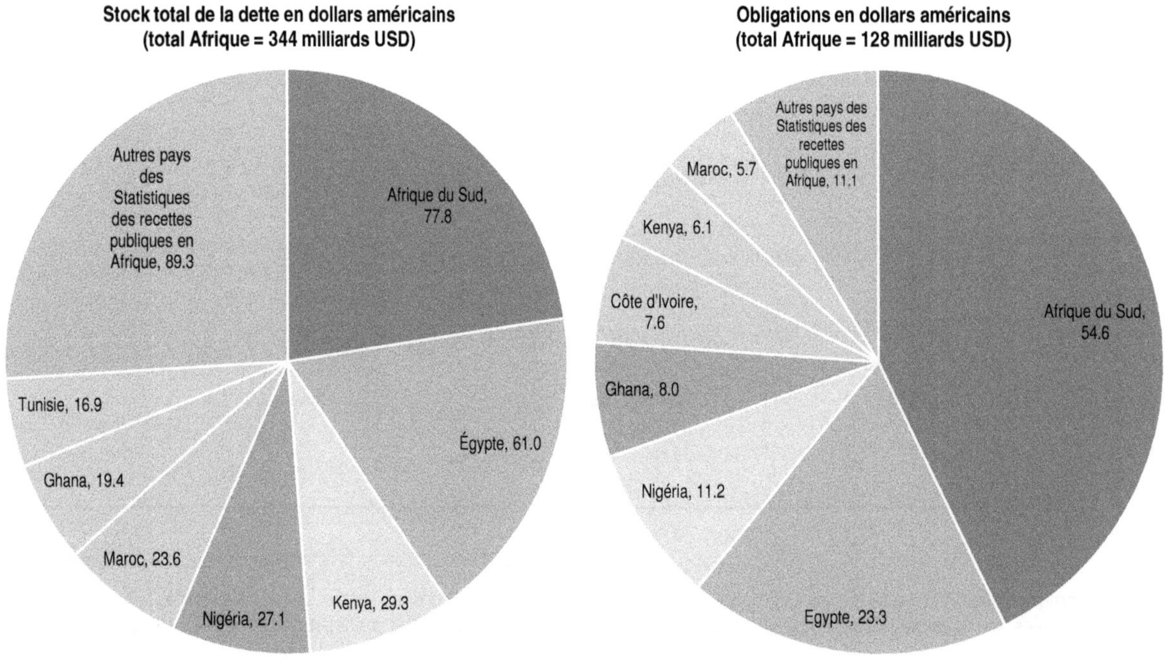

Note : La base de données des *Statistiques sur la dette internationale* ne contient pas d'informations sur la Guinée équatoriale, Maurice, la Namibie ou les Seychelles.
Source : Calculs de l'auteur basés sur la base de données *International Debt Statistics* (IDS) de la Banque mondiale (Banque mondiale, 2021[2]).
StatLink https://doi.org/10.1787/888934283234

La tendance récemment observée dans les pays à revenu intermédiaire à lever des fonds en procédant à un petit nombre d'émissions massives d'obligations ou en souscrivant des emprunts à court terme entraîne une concentration des remboursements de la dette dans certains pays africains, conduisant à de fortes hausses des paiements au titre du service de la dette, notamment en Afrique du Sud et au Tchad (graphique 3.7). Le total des paiements au titre du service de la dette sous forme d'obligations effectués par les pays couverts par les *Statistiques des recettes publiques en Afrique* a enregistré des augmentations en glissement annuel de respectivement 108 %, 137 % et 148 % en 2011, 2015 et 2018. Ces hausses, conjuguées aux fluctuations annuelles des recettes perçues par les pays africains en lien avec les dons et les rentes pétrolières, accentuent les pressions qui s'exercent sur leurs finances publiques et creusent l'écart entre les recettes et les dépenses, alimentant la demande de nouveaux financements par la dette. Par exemple, le Tchad s'est heurté à de graves problèmes de liquidité à la fin des années 2010 à cause de l'accumulation des arriérés de paiement, le contraignant à négocier une restructuration de sa dette avec son principal créancier privé, Glencore (FMI, 2018[7]), et est ainsi devenu le premier pays à solliciter une restructuration de sa dette au titre de la facilité élargie de crédit et du mécanisme élargi de crédit du FMI (Reuters, 2021[8]).

Graphique 3.7. **Service de la dette annuel moyen au Tchad et en Afrique du Sud, 2010-2020**

Pourcentage du PIB

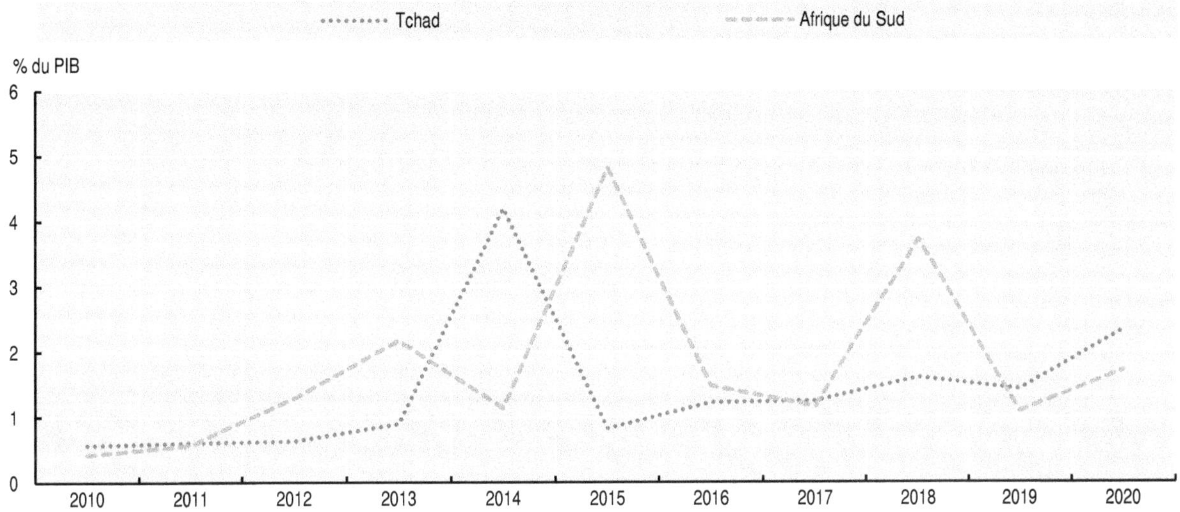

Source : Calculs de l'auteur basés sur la base de données *International Debt Statistics* (IDS) de la Banque mondiale (Banque mondiale, 2021[2]) et la base de données des *Perspectives de l'économie mondiale* database (FMI, 2021[5]).

StatLink https://doi.org/10.1787/888934283253

L'endettement croissant des pays africains les rend plus vulnérables au risque de change. Chaque année depuis 2006, à l'exception de l'année 2010, dans 26 à 28 des 37 pays africains pour lesquels il existe des données, la majorité des titres de créance étaient libellés en monnaies étrangères[2]. Il en résulte un décalage entre la monnaie dans laquelle la dette et les paiements d'intérêts d'un pays sont libellés et les recettes de ce pays, perçues principalement en monnaie nationale. Les États dont la dette est libellée en monnaie étrangère doivent faire des opérations de change sur le marché monétaire afin de procéder à leurs paiements d'intérêts. Les taux de change de nombreux pays africains sont exposés à des chocs de grande ampleur, qui se répercutent sur le ratio de la dette libellée en monnaie étrangère rapportée au PIB, risquant d'interrompre ou de réduire à néant leurs efforts de désendettement. Par exemple, entre 2014 et 2015, le montant de la dette libellée en monnaie étrangère due par les administrations publiques du Cabo Verde a diminué de 6 %, exprimé en dollars US. Cependant, en partie à cause de la dépréciation de l'escudo cap-verdien, qui a perdu 16 % de sa valeur face au dollar US cette même année, le ratio de la dette libellée en monnaie étrangère rapporté au PIB du Cabo Verde a en fait augmenté de 10 %.

16 pays africains sur 27 ont été, au moins une année durant, dans une situation où, tous autres facteurs égaux par ailleurs, la variation en glissement annuel du taux de change aurait eu pour effet d'accroître le ratio dette/PIB d'au moins 10 % du PIB (graphique 3.8). Dans certains cas, en l'absence de circonstances atténuantes, les chocs de change auraient multiplié par deux ou par trois la charge de la dette d'un pays en l'espace d'une seule année. Selon la Banque africaine de développement (BAD, 2021[6]), les perspectives d'évolution des ratios d'endettement des pays exportateurs de pétrole se détérioreront sous l'effet de la dépréciation de la monnaie. En 2015, date du dernier grand choc affectant les prix des matières premières, l'impact médian de la dépréciation monétaire sur la charge de la dette équivalait à 4.4 % du PIB.

Graphique 3.8. **Impact annuel maximum des variations de change sur la dette libellée en monnaie étrangère, 2000-19**

Pourcentage du PIB

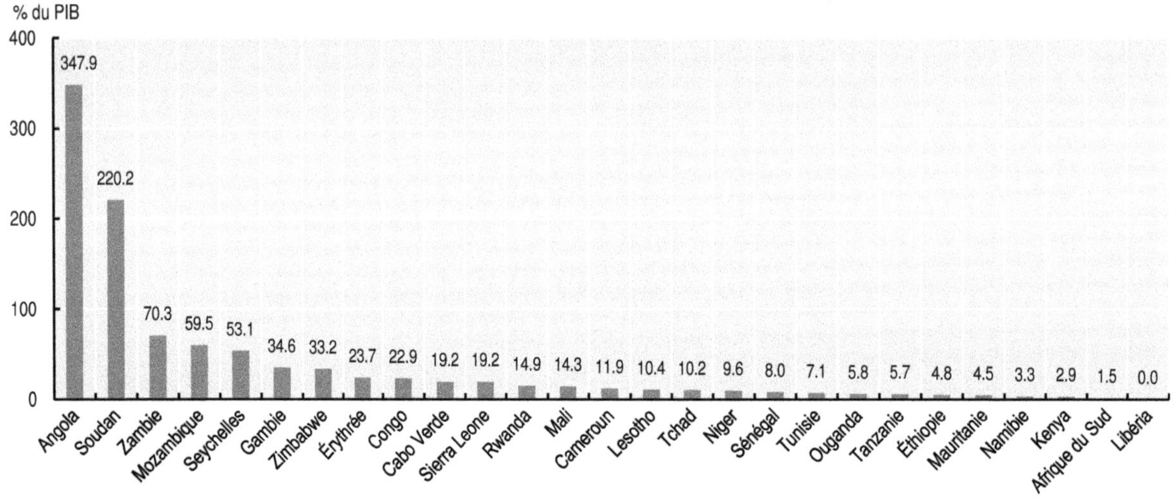

Note : L'impact des variations de taux de change sur la charge de la dette est calculé en partant de la variation annuelle du taux de change entre la monnaie locale et le dollar US, et en la multipliant par le ratio dette/PIB de l'année précédente. Ce calcul appréhende l'effet du choc de change annuel dans l'hypothèse où les niveaux de PIB et d'endettement restent constants.

Source : Calculs de l'auteur basés sur la base de données *International Debt Statistics* (IDS) de la Banque mondiale (Banque mondiale, 2021[2]) et la base de données des *Perspectives de l'économie mondiale* database (FMI, 2021[5]).

StatLink https://doi.org/10.1787/888934283272

Perspectives de la dette à moyen terme et COVID-19

Alors que la pandémie de COVID-19 se poursuit, la vulnérabilité des pays africains à l'égard de la dette s'aggrave et se généralise. En 2020, le ratio moyen dette brute des administrations publiques africaines/PIB a atteint 70.5 % en 2020, contre 62.6 % en 2019. Le PIB de l'Afrique s'est contracté de 1.9 % en 2020, soit la récession la plus grave que le continent ait connue depuis 1991. Sur les cinq prochaines années, le ratio dette/PIB devrait baisser, tout en restant supérieur au niveau de 2019. À l'échelle de l'Afrique, la crise du COVID-19 a gonflé la dette publique, qui avoisine 98 % du PIB sous l'effet conjugué du ralentissement de l'activité économique, de la baisse des recettes budgétaires, de l'augmentation des dépenses de santé et des programmes de relance économique. De nombreux pays africains ont également déployé des programmes de relance budgétaire visant à protéger les moyens de subsistance menacés par la fermeture des entreprises consécutive aux mesures de confinement mises en place à l'échelle du continent pour contrer la propagation du virus.

Les besoins budgétaires grandissants des pays africains pour faire face à la pandémie, associés à la récession économique, ont lourdement pesé sur les recettes publiques, et les pays ont été contraints de recourir à l'endettement. Certaines mesures budgétaires appliquées en Afrique étaient de nature fiscale, érodant un peu plus les recettes publiques. Les baisses et les reports d'impôts en faveur des particuliers et des entreprises visant à alléger la charge pesant sur les citoyens figuraient au nombre de mesures prises par les gouvernements (OCDE/CUA/ATAF, 2021[9]). En date de juillet 2020, les 23 pays africains examinés (ATAF, 2020) avaient signalé 204 mesures d'allègement d'impôt en réponse à la pandémie de COVID-19 (ATAF, 2020[10]).

L'alourdissement de la charge de la dette accroît le risque de surendettement. Selon l'analyse de viabilité de la dette effectuée par le FMI, huit pays couverts par les *Statistiques des recettes publiques en Afrique 2021* connaissent un risque élevé de surendettement, onze un risque modéré de surendettement, tandis que la République du Congo est en situation de surendettement. En 2020, 21 pays africains supportaient des paiements au titre du service de la dette extérieure, rapportés au total des recettes publiques, supérieurs à 14 % du PIB, seuil que le FMI considère comme un signal de risque accru de défaut de paiement dans les pays à faible revenu (PFR) et à revenu intermédiaire de la tranche inférieure (PRITI). Dans cinq de ces pays, les paiements au titre de la dette extérieure dépassaient 30 % des recettes publiques, ce qui réduit considérablement leur capacité à faire face à la pandémie de COVID-19 en étoffant leurs services de santé, soutenant les entreprises ou renforçant la protection sociale afin de venir en aide aux catégories les plus vulnérables de la société.

La pandémie de COVID-19 devrait continuer de peser sur la dette publique et sur les budgets, mais d'autres risques menacent la viabilité de la dette dans les pays africains. Ces risquent incluent les chocs affectant les prix des matières premières et les exportations, les passifs éventuels liés aux entreprises publiques, les chocs de change et le poids élevé de la dette commerciale. Les notations souveraines systématiquement négatives décernées par les agences internationales de notation de crédit constituent un autre problème pour les pays africains. Selon le MAEP (UNECA/CUA, 2021[11]) sept pays d'Afrique ont reçu une notation négative de la part des grandes agences internationales de notation de crédit au premier semestre de 2021, et seuls le Bénin et le Mali ont obtenu des notes positives au cours de la même période. Les dégradations de notes s'expliquaient principalement par la détérioration de la situation budgétaire des pays concernés.

Les institutions financières internationales s'attendent à ce que les paiements au titre du service de la dette augmentent dans les années à venir sous l'effet des répercussions de la pandémie actuelle, la hausse étant plus forte parmi les pays à revenu intermédiaire (PRI) de la tranche inférieure que pour les pays à revenu intermédiaire de la tranche supérieure (PRIT). D'après les prévisions des *Perspectives de l'économie mondiale* du FMI (FMI, 2021[5]), le service de la dette annuel moyen des pays à revenu intermédiaire de la tranche supérieure au cours des années 2021-25 devrait dépasser de l'équivalent de 0.3 % de PIB leur moyenne au cours de la période 2015-19. À l'inverse, la moyenne annuelle des paiements au titre du service de la dette devrait être plus élevée de respectivement 1.0 % et 0.6 % du PIB pour les pays à revenu intermédiaire de la tranche inférieure et les pays à faible revenu. C'est au Bhoutan et en Zambie, deux pays PRITI, que le service annuel de la dette devrait être le plus élevé entre 2021 et 2025, tandis qu'il devrait dépasser 3.5 % du PIB dans quatre pays couverts par cette publication (Cabo Verde, Tunisie, Mauritanie et Sénégal) (graphique 3.9).

Graphique 3.9. **Prévisions du service de la dette annuel moyen, pour les pays à faible revenu et à revenu intermédiaire, par pays, 2021-25**

Pourcentage du PIB

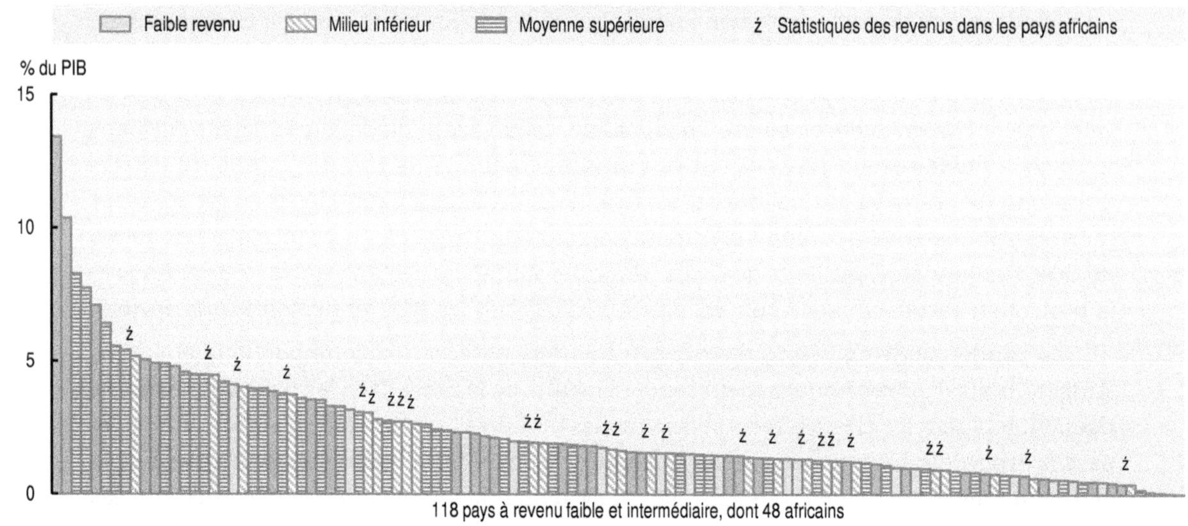

Note : La base de données des *Statistiques sur la dette internationale* ne contient pas d'informations sur la Guinée équatoriale, Maurice, la Namibie ou les Seychelles.

Source : Calculs de l'auteur basés sur la base de données *International Debt Statistics* (IDS) de la Banque mondiale (Banque mondiale, 2021[2]) et la base de données des *Perspectives de l'économie mondiale* database (FMI, 2021[5]).

StatLink https://doi.org/10.1787/888934283291

Au début de la pandémie de COVID-19, Cyril Matamela Ramaphosa, alors président de l'Union africaine et Président de l'Afrique du Sud, a mis en place un groupe d'envoyés spéciaux chargés de mobiliser l'aide internationale en faveur de la réponse africaine à la crise. Les envoyés spéciaux ont immédiatement perçu le risque imminent de crise de la dette, attisé par les besoins financiers considérables pour lutter contre la pandémie et ses répercussions économiques. Ils se sont rapprochés des gouvernements des pays africains, des partenaires bilatéraux et multilatéraux et d'autres parties prenantes, notamment les institutions financières internationales, en vue de trouver les ressources nécessaires au financement de la réponse africaine à la pandémie.

L'initiative de suspension du service de la dette (ISSD) du G20 engagée en mai 2020 vise à reporter jusqu'en décembre 2021 les paiements dus au titre du service de la dette, soit environ 11.5 milliards USD, en faveur des pays éligibles à revenu faible et intermédiaire. Parmi les 73 pays éligibles à la suspension temporaire du service de la dette au titre de l'ISSD, 32 se trouvent en Afrique. Les pays qui bénéficient de l'ISSD ont pris divers engagements, notamment utiliser la marge budgétaire créée pour financer les dépenses sociales, sanitaires ou économiques en réponse à la pandémie, faire connaître les engagements financiers du secteur public et ne contracter de nouveaux emprunts non concessionnels que conformément aux limites convenues avec le FMI et la Banque mondiale (Banque mondiale, 2021[12]).

Bien que l'ISSD ait débloqué plus de 5 milliards USD à ce jour, les fonds ainsi disponibles ne sont pas suffisants pour répondre aux besoins de financement des pays africains en raison de la part élevée de la dette souveraine africaine détenue par des créanciers privés. Les appels du G20 en faveur de la participation de créanciers privés à l'ISSD sont restés lettre morte, compliquant la tâche des pays africains amenés à prendre des mesures pour atténuer la pandémie et promouvoir une reprise économique durable.

La Conférence de Paris sur le financement des économies africaines, organisée par le Président français Emmanuel Macron, a également plaidé pour la mise en œuvre de mesures visant à fournir un appui financier durable aux pays africains. En l'occurrence, la Conférence a lancé un appel pour renforcer l'intégration de l'Afrique dans l'architecture financière internationale grâce à un meilleur accès aux liquidités et à une aide coordonnée des agences de développement bilatérales et multilatérales aux gouvernements des pays africains. En outre, la Conférence a souligné l'importance de s'attaquer aux vulnérabilités liées à la dette dans le respect du Cadre commun pour le traitement de la dette au-delà de l'Initiative ISSD.

Conformément aux recommandations de l'Union africaine, la Conférence a appuyé le financement du développement durable par les créanciers et les emprunteurs comme moyen d'éviter un nouveau cycle d'endettement basé sur les Principes opérationnels du financement soutenable du G20 et en soutenant l'application des Principes volontaires pour la transparence de la dette de l'*Institute for International Finance*. La Conférence a également conclu à la nécessité d'aider les pays débiteurs à engager des réformes visant à accroître l'efficacité des dépenses publiques et à améliorer la gestion des finances publiques, y compris la gestion de la dette.

Propositions de l'Union africaine pour une évolution viable de la dette

L'élément central du consensus qui se dégage des consultations menées entre les envoyés spéciaux de l'UA et les différentes parties prenantes est la nécessité d'assurer la viabilité de la dette des pays africains et, au niveau national, l'importance d'engager les réformes budgétaires concourant à cet objectif. Soucieuse d'alléger la charge de la dette pour de nombreux pays africains, d'éviter les situations de surendettement et d'accompagner une évolution viable de la dette, l'Union africaine a proposé diverses mesures ayant des implications pour l'organisation, ses États membres et les partenaires du développement. Les mesures proposées par l'Union africaine comprennent pour chacun de ces groupes.

- ***Union africaine***
  - Élaborer une position commune à l'ensemble de l'Afrique en matière de réforme de l'architecture financière internationale et promouvoir cet objectif.
  - Continuer à plaider en faveur de la suspension du service de la dette au-delà de décembre 2021, au regard notamment de la pandémie de COVID-19 qui continue d'exiger la mobilisation de recettes publiques considérables.
  - Plaider en faveur de la réattribution d'une fraction plus élevée des 650 milliards USD de droits de tirage spéciaux (DTS) du FMI en faveur des pays africains.
- ***États membres***
  - Accélérer les efforts visant à ratifier les instruments juridiques qui établissent les institutions financières de l'Union africaine, notamment le Fonds monétaire africain et le Mécanisme africain de stabilité financière, qui protégeront les pays des chocs économiques futurs, réduiront les effets de contagion régionaux et favoriseront les réformes des politiques macroéconomique et budgétaire.
  - Mettre en œuvre les recommandations du Programme d'action d'Addis-Abeba en matière de viabilité de la dette.
  - Envisager d'émettre des titres de dette en monnaie nationale.
  - Renforcer la transparence et la gestion de la dette.

- Mobiliser la dette pour générer des investissements productifs ou porteurs de croissance plutôt que pour pérenniser des plans de dépenses.
- Améliorer l'inclusion financière et l'accès aux financements au moyen de nouvelles technologies financières et d'autres innovations de la blockchain.
- Renforcer l'épargne intérieure et l'offre de crédits au secteur privé afin d'accroître la capacité des pays à financer les besoins de développement de l'Afrique.
- Élaborer des politiques visant à soutenir les entreprises financées par la diaspora, mobiliser les envois de fonds pour créer un regroupement de fonds destiné à financer les grands projets et autoriser les États à emprunter auprès de leurs ressortissants vivant à l'étranger. Les envois de fonds pourraient constituer une source de financement précieuse pour les petites entreprises et les entreprises à domicile, et éventuellement aussi pour fournir un capital d'amorçage aux start-ups.
- Attirer l'investissement direct étranger, source importante de financements extérieurs privés pour le développement des pays.
- Améliorer la mobilisation des ressources intérieures pour soutenir le financement du développement de l'Afrique en redoublant d'efforts pour combattre les flux financiers illicites et améliorer la collecte des recettes en renforçant les administrations fiscales.

- ***Partenaires de développement***
  - Alors que la pandémie persiste, les pressions sur la dette continuent de s'accentuer. Si le Cadre commun pour le traitement de la dette s'est avéré bénéfique, il reste insuffisant pour répondre aux besoins de financement des pays africains. Il est urgent d'adopter une nouvelle approche en consultation avec les ministres des finances africains et le G20 pour faire en sorte que les pays qui ont besoin de restructurer leur dette aient accès à des facilités conçues de manière appropriée.
  - Aider les pays à rembourser leurs dettes commerciales au moyen de fonds régionaux ou multilatéraux de rachat de la dette ; financer ces efforts, au niveau bilatéral ou multilatéral, par exemple par l'émission de nouveaux DTS et/ou la réattribution de DTS ou par d'autres mécanismes, des échanges de créances (ex. Initiative en faveur d'échanges de dettes contre des mesures d'adaptation aux changements climatiques, par exemple), des échanges de dette ou sa restructuration, et d'autres instruments.
  - Soutenir les appels en faveur de la réforme de l'architecture financière internationale en vue d'associer davantage les pays en développement et de répondre à leurs besoins.
  - Soutenir la réattribution d'une fraction plus élevée des DTS du FMI – au moins 100 milliards de dollars supplémentaires – en faveur des pays africains en offrant une partie de leurs quote-parts inutilisées pour soutenir la reprise post-pandémique des économies africaines, la capacité de production de vaccins, le financement du secteur privé à l'appui de la zone de libre-échange continentale africaine, etc.
  - Demander aux créanciers privés de prendre part aux efforts mondiaux visant à améliorer la gestion et la viabilité de la dette dans les pays en développement.

Notes

1 Selon les données de la Banque mondiale, le service de la dette désigne la somme des remboursements du principal et des intérêts effectivement payés en devise, biens ou services au titre d'obligations à long terme.

2 Dans ces pays, la dette libellée en monnaie locale est plus élevée que celle libellée en monnaie étrangère, mais les deux tiers de cette dette étaient détenus par seulement trois pays : l'Afrique du Sud, l'Algérie et le Maroc.

Références

ATAF (2020), « Tax Administration & Policy Developments in Response to the COVID-19 Pandemic in Africa », *ATAF Research Tax Paper* Issue 01, *https://events.ataftax.org/index.php?page=documents&func=view&document_id=66&_ga=2.27820600.50862724.1634547789-1908447849.1600676783.* [10]

BAD (2021), *Perspectives économiques en Afrique 2021 - De la résolution de la dette à la croissance - une feuille de route pour l'Afrique*, Banque Africaine de dévloppement, *www.afdb.org/fr/documents-publications/perspectives-economiques-en-afrique.* [6]

Banque mondiale (2021), *Base de données des statistiques de la dette internationale*, World Bank, *https://databank.worldbank.org/source/international-debt-statistics* (consulté le 26 juillet 2021). [2]

Banque mondiale (2021), *Mémoire sur l'initiative de suspension du service de la dette*, *www.banquemondiale.org/fr/topic/debt/brief/covid-19-debt-service-suspension-initiative.* [12]

Banque mondiale (2015), *Le FMI et la Banque mondiale annoncent un allégement de la dette de 1,1 milliard de dollars en faveur du Tchad*, *https://www.banquemondiale.org/fr/news/press-release/2015/04/29/imf-world-bank-debt-relief-chad.* [4]

FMI (2021), *List of LIC DSAs for PRGT-Eligible Countries*, *www.imf.org/external/Pubs/ft/dsa/DSAlist.pdf.* [1]

FMI (2021), *Perspectives de l'économie mondiale, édition d'avril 2021 (base de données)*, *www.imf.org/en/Publications/WEO/weo-database/2021/April*, 2020. [5]

FMI (2018), *First review under the extended credit facility arrangement request for a waiver of nonobservance of performance criteria, rephasing of disbursements, and financing assurances review debt sustainability analysis*, Fond monétaire internationale, *www.imf.org/external/pubs/ft/dsa/pdf/2018/dsacr18108.pdf.* [7]

OCDE/CUA/ATAF (2021), *Statistiques des recettes publiques en Afrique 2021*, OECD Publishing, *doi.org/10.1787/14e1edb1-en-fr.* [9]

OECD/CUA/ATAF (2021), *Revenue Statistics in Africa: Comparative tables*, OECD Publishing, Paris, *http://dx.doi.org/10.1787/be755711-en.* [3]

Reuters (2021), « UPDATE 3-Chad becomes first country to ask for debt overhaul under G20 common framework », *Reuters*, By Andrea Shalal, Karin Strohecker, *www.reuters.com/article/chad-debt-idCNL1N2K21XN.* [8]

UNECA/CUA (2021), *Africa sovereign credit rating review: 2021 MID-YEAR OUTLOOK*, United Nations. Economic Commission for Africa; African Union Commission, *https://hdl.handle.net/10855/45537.* [11]

Chapter 4

Tax levels and tax structures, 1990-2019

Chapitre 4

Niveaux et structures des impôts, 1990-2019

Chapter 4 / Chapitre 4

Comparative tables, 1990-2019

In all of the following tables a ("..") indicates not available. The main series in this volume cover the years 1990 to 2019.

Figures referring to 1991-99 and 2009 in Table 4.1 and 4.2 and figures relating to 1990-98, 2001-08, and 2011-13 in Tables 4.5 to 4.19 have been omitted because of lack of space. Complete series are, however, available on line at OECD/ATAF/AUC (2021), "Revenue Statistics in Africa: Comparative tables", OECD Tax Statistics (database), *http://dx.doi.org/10.1787/be755711-en*.

The OECD average is taken from Revenue Statistics (2020). Costa Rica was not an OECD Member at the time of preparation of this publication. Accordingly, Costa Rica does not appear in the list of OECD Members and is not included in the zone aggregates.

Tableaux comparatifs, 1990-2019

Dans tous les tableaux suivants le symbole («.. ») signifie que l'information n'est pas disponible. La principale série dans ce volume couvre les années 1990 à 2019.

Les années 1991 à 1999 et 2009 dans le tableau 4.1 et 4.2 et les années 1990-98, 2001-08, et 2011-13 dans les tableaux 4.5 à 4.19 ont été omis en raison du manque d'espace. Les séries complètes ont cependant disponibles en ligne sur OCDE/ATAF/CUA (2021), « Statistiques des recettes publiques en Afrique: Tableaux comparatifs », Statistiques fiscales de l'OCDE (base de données), *http://dx.doi.org/10.1787/7f54581d-fr*.

La moyenne de l'OCDE est tirée des Statistiques des recettes publiques (2020). Le Costa Rica n'était pas membre de l'OCDE au moment de la préparation de cette publication. En conséquence, le Costa Rica n'apparaît pas dans la liste des Membres de l'OCDE et n'est pas incluse dans les agrégats de la zone OCDE.

Table 4.1. **Total tax revenue as percentage of GDP, 1990-2019**
Tableau 4.1. **Total des recettes fiscales en pourcentage du PIB, 1990-2019**

	1990	2000	2001	2002	2003	2004	2005	2006	2007	2008
Botswana	..	..	..	..	..	15.5	15.2	15.2	13.7	17.1
Burkina Faso	..	10.2	10.2	10.7	11.3	12.4	11.7	12.1	12.6	11.9
Cabo Verde	10.5	15.6	16.9	19.3	17.7	18.7	19.5	20.9	20.8	21.2
Cameroon / Cameroun	..	11.3	12.6	11.8	12.3	11.3	12.0	12.4	12.8	12.5
Chad / Tchad	..	..	..	..	..	..	..	..	..	..
Congo	..	3.8	5.6	6.5	7.9	7.5	5.9	5.6	5.9	6.0
Congo, Dem. Rep. / Congo, Rép. dém.[1]	..	0.6	2.3	3.0	3.4	4.7	5.2	5.8	6.9	8.5
Côte d'Ivoire	15.6	11.1	11.3	11.5	10.6	11.5	11.3	11.7	12.4	12.2
Egypt / Égypte	..	..	..	15.7	15.5	15.6	15.5	17.2	16.3	16.3
Equatorial Guinea / Guinée équatoriale	..	..	..	..	..	..	8.2	9.7	7.5	7.8
Eswatini	..	10.7	10.5	10.8	11.8	11.4	11.6	11.7	11.8	12.9
Ghana	..	7.8	8.3	8.5	9.7	10.4	10.5	9.9	10.0	10.6
Kenya	..	..	16.6	16.1	16.7	17.1	18.4	17.5	18.1	18.9
Lesotho	..	..	..	..	..	16.7	15.4	14.4	14.6	15.2
Madagascar[2]	..	9.6	8.3	6.5	8.8	9.6	8.9	9.4	10.0	11.4
Malawi	..	..	..	..	..	..	12.6	12.6	13.6	14.6
Mali[3]	..	11.4	11.4	12.3	13.9	14.9	14.5	14.1	14.3	13.3
Mauritania / Mauritanie	..	..	..	..	..	..	..	..	10.0	10.1
Mauritius / Maurice[4]	22.3	18.3	16.3	16.0	17.3	17.4	17.9	17.8	17.0	18.7
Morocco / Maroc[2,5]	..	22.0	22.7	22.7	22.4	22.7	24.9	26.2	28.6	31.1
Namibia / Namibie	..	..	..	..	..	..	..	16.2	17.2	17.7
Niger	..	7.3	7.7	8.2	8.2	8.8	8.3	8.6	9.0	9.0
Nigeria / Nigéria	..	..	..	..	..	..	..	..	..	..
Rwanda[2]	..	10.2	11.3	12.4	12.2	12.1	12.1	11.2	11.5	12.4
Senegal / Sénégal[6]	..	13.1	12.6	13.5	13.9	14.5	15.3	15.7	16.2	15.2
Seychelles	..	..	..	..	..	..	..	..	..	27.9
South Africa / Afrique du Sud[7]	21.8	20.1	21.2	20.7	20.2	21.2	22.8	24.0	25.3	25.3
Togo	..	7.0	8.0	7.1	8.8	9.8	9.9	10.7	11.3	10.7
Tunisia / Tunisie[2]	..	24.4	24.8	24.8	24.2	24.1	24.2	24.4	25.2	26.8
Uganda / Ouganda	..	8.3	8.2	8.5	8.8	9.0	9.3	9.4	9.5	9.3
Africa (30) average / Moyenne Afrique (30)[8]	..	..	..	..	..	..	..	..	..	..
Asia-Pacific (24) average / Moyenne Asie-Pacifique (24)[9]	..	..	..	..	..	..	..	..	..	..
LAC average / Moyenne ALC[10]	**15.7**	**18.2**	**18.4**	**18.5**	**18.9**	**19.3**	**20.1**	**20.7**	**21.3**	**21.4**
OECD average / Moyenne OCDE[11]	**31.1**	**33.3**	**32.8**	**32.6**	**32.5**	**32.5**	**33.0**	**33.1**	**33.2**	**32.6**

	2009	2010	2012	2013	2014	2015	2016	2017	2018	2019
Botswana	15.8	15.6	13.8	14.7	15.2	12.7	14.0	12.3	12.1	12.6
Burkina Faso	12.6	14.0	14.9	15.9	14.3	14.6	15.3	16.1	16.5	17.6
Cabo Verde	18.4	18.4	17.7	17.8	16.9	18.7	18.7	20.2	21.3	20.6
Cameroon / Cameroun	13.1	12.1	13.5	14.1	14.4	14.7	14.2	14.4	14.6	14.2
Chad / Tchad	..	14.6	14.6	15.4	10.6	5.8	4.7	6.2	7.9	8.1
Congo	8.0	6.9	0.9	8.7	9.6	12.8	13.3	10.8	7.6	8.0
Congo, Dem. Rep. / Congo, Rép. dém.[1]	7.9	8.5	10.7	10.1	9.6	9.8	8.6	6.9	7.0	7.5
Côte d'Ivoire	12.2	11.9	12.8	12.7	12.2	12.6	13.1	13.3	13.0	13.2
Egypt / Égypte	16.4	15.1	14.0	15.4	14.2	14.6	14.4	15.2	14.9	14.2
Equatorial Guinea / Guinée équatoriale	12.8	7.6	8.8	8.9	9.8	12.0	7.1	6.6	6.5	10.1
Eswatini	12.9	13.9	12.8	13.7	14.9	15.0	16.1	17.0	17.4	18.4
Ghana	10.5	10.9	12.1	11.4	12.2	13.1	13.7	13.8	14.1	13.5
Kenya	18.2	17.9	17.9	18.0	19.3	18.6	18.5	18.4	17.4	17.3
Lesotho	17.1	17.3	16.9	18.6	18.9	19.3	19.2	19.6	21.9	20.6
Madagascar[2]	9.5	9.5	9.2	9.3	8.9	9.5	10.0	10.9	11.4	11.2
Malawi	15.3	15.9	14.5	16.2	17.9	16.8	16.9	18.7	18.3	18.3
Mali[3]	14.4	14.1	14.0	14.2	13.9	15.2	16.5	16.7	13.3	16.8
Mauritania / Mauritanie	10.4	9.8	13.5	13.3	15.1	14.5	14.2	14.5	16.0	14.0
Mauritius / Maurice[4]	19.2	19.0	19.5	19.2	19.3	19.3	19.5	19.9	20.4	21.1
Morocco / Maroc[2,5]	27.7	27.6	29.5	28.1	27.8	26.8	27.5	28.0	28.2	28.4
Namibia / Namibie	17.9	18.6	19.9	20.0	21.1	21.5	21.1	20.4	19.4	20.2
Niger	10.4	9.6	10.6	12.7	12.4	12.6	10.5	9.5	11.2	10.4
Nigeria / Nigéria	..	7.3	9.4	8.3	7.6	6.1	5.3	5.7	6.3	6.0
Rwanda[2]	12.1	12.3	13.7	15.0	15.3	16.1	16.2	16.2	16.9	17.7
Senegal / Sénégal[6]	15.0	15.9	16.1	15.4	16.2	16.4	17.0	16.3	16.5	16.6
Seychelles	28.8	30.7	31.2	29.3	30.5	29.8	32.2	32.2	34.7	34.3
South Africa / Afrique du Sud[7]	23.2	23.1	24.4	24.8	25.4	26.5	26.1	26.1	26.6	26.2
Togo	10.8	10.9	12.5	14.5	15.5	16.0	16.4	15.8	14.6	15.0
Tunisia / Tunisie[2]	26.8	27.2	29.1	29.8	30.9	30.2	29.6	31.1	31.8	34.3
Uganda / Ouganda	8.5	8.3	8.5	9.0	9.3	10.5	11.1	11.4	11.7	12.1
Africa (30) average / Moyenne Afrique (30)[8]	**14.8**	**14.8**	**15.4**	**15.8**	**16.0**	**16.1**	**16.0**	**16.1**	**16.3**	**16.6**
Asia-Pacific (24) average / Moyenne Asie-Pacifique (24)[9]	..	**18.9**	**20.0**	**20.0**	**19.2**	**19.6**	**19.0**	**20.1**	**20.8**	**21.0**
LAC average / Moyenne ALC[10]	**20.6**	**20.9**	**21.7**	**21.7**	**21.9**	**22.3**	**22.4**	**22.3**	**22.7**	**22.9**
OECD average / Moyenne OCDE[11]	**31.8**	**31.9**	**32.7**	**33.0**	**33.2**	**33.3**	**34.0**	**33.7**	**33.9**	**33.8**

Table 4.1. **Total tax revenue as percentage of GDP, 1990-2019** *(cont.)*
Tableau 4.1. **Total des recettes fiscales en pourcentage du PIB, 1990-2019** *(suite)*

.. Not available

Note: The figures include sub-national government tax revenues for Eswatini, Mauritania (for 2009-19), Mauritius, Morocco, Nigeria (only state revenues) and South Africa (for 2003-19). Sub-national government tax revenues are not available in other countries.

Data on social security contributions are not available for Chad, the Republic of the Congo, the Democratic Republic of the Congo (prior to 2012), Equatorial Guinea (prior to 2013), Madagascar (prior to 2011), Namibia (prior to 2009), Togo and Uganda; and are only partially available in Cameroon and Senegal. Social security contributions for Botswana, Lesotho and Malawi are deemed to be null as they do not meet the criteria to be classified as social security contributions set out in the OECD classification of taxes in the Interpretative Guide.

In Ghana, Lesotho, Malawi, Nigeria and Uganda, revenues from property taxes are mainly levied by local governments for which data on revenue are not available. In the Democratic Republic of the Congo only data for property taxes levied by the Direction Générale des Recettes Administratives, Judiciaires, Domaniales et de Participation (DGRAD) are available for 2010-19.

See the country tables in Chapter 5 for further information on data issues for individual countries.

1. The figures should be interpreted with caution as they are affected by macroeconomic instability in the early 2000s. For the years prior to 2010, the figures exclude some revenues collected by the Direction Générale des Recettes Administratives, Judiciaires, Domaniales et de Participation (DGRAD), which are estimated to be less than 1% of total tax revenue. See Table 5.6 in Chapter 5 for further information.
2. Madagascar, Morocco, Rwanda and Tunisia do not include social security contributions in the tax-to-GDP ratio in their official publications as these countries do not consider them to be taxes. They are included as tax revenue in this publication, following the classification set out in the OECD Interpretative Guide.
3. Part of the figures for social security contributions in Mali for 2019 were not available, and so were assumed to be equal to 2018 figures.
4. The fiscal year for Mauritius changed in 2010 and in 2015. Figures for 2015 needed to be estimated as a result.
5. Social security contributions in Morocco are estimated for years prior to 2002.
6. These figures include contributions to the Senegalese Pension Institute (IPRES) (estimated prior to 2006) and contributions to the social security fund (CSS) (from 2012 as data for previous years are not available). Social security contributions in Senegal are estimated for 2018 and 2019.
7. Includes payments made by South Africa to the Southern African Customs Union (SACU) pool.
8. Represents an unweighted average of the 30 African countries in this publication. In 2009, the Africa (30) average is calculated based on estimated tax-to-GDP ratios for Chad and Nigeria in that year, as data were not available prior to 2010 in these countries. The estimations in 2009 for these two countries are based on data for later years and on IMF figures from the *World Economic Outlook April 2021*. Details of the estimations are available in the metadata. The Africa (30) should be interpreted with caution as data for social security contributions (category 2000) and property taxes (category 4000) are not available or are partial in a few countries. See the country tables in Chapter 5 for further information.
9. Represents an unweighted average for 24 Asian and Pacific economies included in the publication *Revenue Statistics in Asia and the Pacific 2021*.
10. Represents an unweighted average for 26 Latin American and Caribbean (LAC) countries included in the publication *Revenue Statistics in Latin America and the Caribbean 2021*.
11. Represents an unweighted average for 37 OECD countries.

.. Non disponible

Note : Les chiffres incluent les recettes fiscales collectées par les administrations infranationales pour l'Afrique du Sud (pour les années 2003 à 2019), Eswatini, le Maroc, Maurice, la Mauritanie (pour les années 2009 à 2019) et le Nigéria (recettes des administrations régionales). Les données des recettes fiscales collectées par les administrations infranationales ne sont pas disponibles pour les autres pays.

Les données des cotisations de sécurité sociale ne sont pas disponibles pour la République du Congo, la République démocratique du Congo (avant 2012), la Guinée équatoriale (avant 2013), Madagascar (avant 2011), la Namibie (avant 2009), l'Ouganda, le Tchad et le Togo et ne sont que partiellement disponibles au Cameroun et au Sénégal. Les cotisations de sécurité sociale pour le Botswana, le Lesotho et le Malawi sont nulles car elles ne répondent pas aux critères de classification des cotisations de sécurité sociale de la classification des impôts établie dans le Guide d'interprétation de l'OCDE.

Au Ghana, au Lesotho, au Malawi, au Nigéria et en Ouganda, les recettes provenant des impôts sur le patrimoine sont principalement perçues par les administrations locales pour lesquelles les données ne sont pas disponibles. En République démocratique du Congo, seules les données des impôts sur le patrimoine qui sont prélevées par la Direction Générale des Recettes Administratives, Judiciaires, Domaniales et de Participation (DGRAD) sont disponibles pour 2010-19.

Voir les tableaux par pays au chapitre 5 pour plus d'informations sur les problèmes de données pour chaque pays.

1. Les chiffres doivent être interprétés avec prudence car ils sont affectés par une instabilité macroéconomique au début des années 2000. Pour les années antérieures à 2010, les chiffres excluent certaines recettes perçues par la Direction Générale des Recettes Administratives, Judiciaires, Domaniales et de Participation (DGRAD) estimées inférieures à 1 % du total des recettes fiscales. Voir le tableau 5.6 du chapitre 5 pour plus d'informations.
2. Madagascar, le Maroc, le Rwanda et la Tunisie n'incluent pas les cotisations de sécurité sociale dans le ratio impôts/PIB dans leurs publications officielles car ces pays ne les considèrent pas comme des impôts. Elles sont incluses dans les recettes fiscales de cette publication en accordance avec la classification des impôts établie dans le Guide d'interprétation de l'OCDE.
3. Une partie des chiffres des cotisations de sécurité sociale au Mali n'étaient pas disponibles pour 2019 et sont donc supposées être égales aux chiffres de 2018.
4. L'année fiscale pour Maurice a changé en 2010 et en 2015. Les chiffres pour 2015 ont dû être estimés en conséquence.
5. Les cotisations de sécurité sociale au Maroc antérieures à 2002 sont estimées.
6. Les chiffres comprennent les cotisations de sécurité sociale de l'Institution de prévoyance retraite du Sénégal (IPRES) (estimées pour les années antérieures à 2006) et les cotisations de sécurité sociale de la Caisse de Sécurité Sociale (CSS) (à partir de 2012 car les données pour les années précédentes ne sont pas disponibles). Les cotisations de sécurité sociale de 2018 et 2019 sont estimées.
7. Comprend les paiements effectués par l'Afrique du Sud au fond collectif de l'Union douanière d'Afrique australe (SACU).
8. Représente une moyenne non pondérée des 30 pays africains inclus dans cette publication. En 2009, la moyenne de l'Afrique (30) est calculée sur la base des ratios impôts/PIB estimés pour le Nigéria et le Tchad car les données n'étaient pas disponibles avant 2010 dans ces pays. Les estimations en 2009 pour ces deux pays sont basées sur des données des années ultérieures et sur les chiffres du FMI tirés des *Perspectives de l'économie mondiale d'avril* 2021. Les détails des estimations sont disponibles dans les métadonnées. Il convient d'interpréter cette moyenne avec prudence à cause de valeurs manquantes ou incomplètes pour la rubrique 2000 (cotisations de sécurité sociale) et la rubrique 4000 (taxes sur le patrimoine). Voir les tableaux de pays au chapitre 5 pour plus d'informations.
9. Représente la moyenne non pondérée pour 24 économies de l'Asie et du Pacifique incluses dans la publication *Revenue Statistics in Asia and Pacific 2021*.
10. Représente la moyenne non pondérée pour 26 pays d'Amérique latine et des Caraïbes (ALC) inclus dans la publication *Revenue Statistics in La America and the Caribbean 2021*.
11. Représente la moyenne non pondérée pour 37 pays de l'OCDE.

StatLink https://doi.org/10.1787/888934283310

Table 4.2. **Total tax revenue (excluding social security) as percentage of GDP**
Tableau 4.2. **Total des recettes fiscales (sécurité sociale non comprise) en pourcentage du PIB**

	1990	2000	2001	2002	2003	2004	2005	2006	2007	2008
Botswana	..	..	..	..	..	15.5	15.2	15.2	13.7	17.1
Burkina Faso	..	8.6	8.7	9.2	9.7	10.7	10.2	10.5	11.0	10.4
Cabo Verde	10.5	14.8	16.5	18.9	17.2	18.2	18.9	20.4	20.7	21.2
Cameroon / Cameroun	..	10.4	11.6	10.8	11.3	10.3	11.1	11.6	12.0	11.7
Chad / Tchad	..	..	..	..	..	..	..	..	..	..
Congo	..	3.8	5.6	6.5	7.9	7.5	5.9	5.6	5.9	6.0
Congo, Dem. Rep. / Congo, Rép. dém.[1]	..	0.6	2.3	3.0	3.4	4.7	5.2	5.8	6.9	8.5
Côte d'Ivoire	14.6	10.1	10.3	10.5	9.7	10.5	10.4	10.8	11.4	11.3
Egypt / Égypte	..	..	..	12.3	12.1	12.5	12.7	14.4	13.8	13.9
Equatorial Guinea / Guinée équatoriale	..	..	..	..	..	..	8.2	9.7	7.5	7.8
Eswatini	..	9.5	9.3	9.6	10.6	10.1	10.2	10.2	10.2	11.4
Ghana	..	7.1	7.5	7.6	8.8	9.5	9.7	8.8	8.9	9.6
Kenya	..	..	16.4	15.9	16.5	16.9	18.1	17.2	17.9	18.7
Lesotho	..	..	..	..	..	16.7	15.4	14.4	14.6	15.2
Madagascar	..	9.6	8.3	6.5	8.8	9.6	8.9	9.4	10.0	11.4
Malawi	..	..	..	..	..	..	12.6	12.6	13.6	14.6
Mali	..	10.5	10.5	11.3	12.8	13.6	13.1	12.7	12.8	11.9
Mauritania / Mauritanie	..	..	..	..	..	..	..	..	9.4	9.5
Mauritius / Maurice[2]	21.4	17.5	15.5	15.2	16.6	16.7	17.2	17.2	16.4	18.1
Morocco / Maroc	..	19.6	19.5	19.5	19.0	19.2	20.7	21.5	23.8	26.5
Namibia / Namibie	..	..	..	..	..	..	..	16.2	17.2	17.7
Niger	..	6.9	7.4	7.8	7.8	8.4	7.9	8.3	8.7	8.6
Nigeria / Nigéria	..	..	..	..	..	..	..	..	..	..
Rwanda	..	9.7	10.7	11.9	11.6	11.2	11.3	10.6	10.7	11.6
Senegal / Sénégal	..	12.6	12.1	12.9	13.3	13.9	14.7	15.1	15.5	14.5
Seychelles	..	..	..	..	..	..	..	..	..	22.6
South Africa / Afrique du Sud[3]	21.8	20.1	21.2	20.5	19.9	20.9	22.4	23.6	24.9	24.9
Togo	..	7.0	8.0	7.1	8.8	9.8	9.9	10.7	11.3	10.7
Tunisia / Tunisie	..	19.2	19.5	19.3	18.6	18.6	18.7	18.4	19.0	20.4
Uganda / Ouganda	..	8.3	8.2	8.5	8.8	9.0	9.3	9.4	9.5	9.3
Africa (30) average / Moyenne Afrique (30)[4]	..	..	..	..	..	..	..	..	..	..
Asia-Pacific (24) average / Moyenne Asie-Pacifique (24)[5]	..	..	..	..	..	..	..	..	..	..
LAC average / Moyenne ALC[6]	**13.4**	**15.3**	**15.5**	**15.6**	**16.1**	**16.4**	**17.2**	**17.8**	**18.4**	**18.4**
OECD average / Moyenne OCDE[7]	**24.0**	**24.8**	**24.3**	**24.1**	**24.0**	**24.1**	**24.6**	**24.8**	**24.9**	**24.2**

	2009	2010	2012	2013	2014	2015	2016	2017	2018	2019
Botswana	15.8	15.6	13.8	14.7	15.2	12.7	14.0	12.3	12.1	12.6
Burkina Faso	11.1	12.4	13.5	14.3	12.7	12.8	13.5	14.3	14.7	15.7
Cabo Verde	18.4	18.4	17.7	17.7	16.9	18.7	18.7	20.1	21.3	20.5
Cameroon / Cameroun	12.2	11.1	12.5	13.1	13.5	13.8	13.1	13.4	13.6	13.1
Chad / Tchad	..	14.6	14.6	15.4	10.6	5.8	4.7	6.2	7.9	8.1
Congo	8.0	6.0	6.9	8.7	9.6	12.8	13.3	10.8	7.6	8.0
Congo, Dem. Rep. / Congo, Rép. dém.[1]	7.9	8.5	10.3	9.6	9.0	9.2	8.0	8.4	7.2	6.8
Côte d'Ivoire	11.2	11.0	11.6	11.3	10.8	11.2	11.6	11.8	11.5	11.7
Egypt / Égypte	14.3	12.9	11.9	13.1	11.8	12.1	12.6	12.9	13.7	13.3
Equatorial Guinea / Guinée équatoriale	12.8	7.6	8.8	8.4	9.2	11.3	6.3	5.9	5.9	9.3
Eswatini	11.1	12.0	11.3	12.3	13.1	13.0	14.1	14.7	15.0	16.0
Ghana	9.2	9.9	11.1	10.4	11.0	11.9	12.5	12.8	13.3	12.8
Kenya	18.0	17.7	17.7	17.8	19.0	18.3	18.0	18.0	16.8	16.7
Lesotho	17.1	17.3	16.9	18.6	18.9	19.3	19.2	19.6	21.9	20.6
Madagascar	9.5	9.5	8.9	8.9	8.6	9.1	9.7	10.5	10.7	10.7
Malawi	15.3	15.9	14.5	16.2	17.9	16.8	16.9	18.7	18.3	18.3
Mali	12.9	12.8	12.5	12.8	12.4	13.7	14.7	15.0	11.7	15.1
Mauritania / Mauritanie	9.8	9.1	12.8	12.7	14.2	13.6	13.4	13.8	15.2	13.3
Mauritius / Maurice[2]	18.6	18.3	18.8	18.5	18.6	18.5	18.7	19.0	19.6	20.2
Morocco / Maroc	23.0	22.8	24.1	22.8	22.4	21.5	22.0	22.3	22.4	22.2
Namibia / Namibie	17.6	18.3	19.5	19.7	20.8	21.1	20.8	20.0	19.1	19.9
Niger	9.9	9.1	10.1	12.1	11.8	12.0	9.9	8.9	10.6	9.8
Nigeria / Nigéria	..	6.7	8.7	7.6	6.9	5.5	4.7	5.1	5.8	5.3
Rwanda	11.3	11.5	12.8	13.9	14.3	15.2	15.1	15.2	15.9	16.7
Senegal / Sénégal	14.3	15.0	15.1	14.4	15.2	15.3	15.9	15.1	15.4	15.4
Seychelles	23.9	27.9	30.6	28.5	29.5	28.6	31.0	31.0	32.1	32.5
South Africa / Afrique du Sud[3]	22.8	22.8	24.0	24.4	25.0	26.1	25.7	25.8	26.2	25.9
Togo	10.8	10.9	12.5	14.5	15.5	16.0	16.4	15.8	14.6	15.0
Tunisia / Tunisie	19.8	19.8	20.8	21.2	22.4	21.3	20.2	21.4	22.6	24.6
Uganda / Ouganda	8.5	8.3	8.5	9.0	9.3	10.5	11.1	11.4	11.7	12.1
Africa (30) average / Moyenne Afrique (30)[4]	..	**13.5**	**14.2**	**14.6**	**14.7**	**14.7**	**14.7**	**14.8**	**15.0**	**15.2**
Asia-Pacific (24) average / Moyenne Asie-Pacifique (24)[5]	..	**17.7**	**18.6**	**18.7**	**17.9**	**18.4**	**17.7**	**18.8**	**19.4**	**19.4**
LAC average / Moyenne ALC[6]	**17.4**	**17.6**	**18.2**	**18.1**	**18.3**	**18.6**	**18.6**	**18.5**	**18.9**	**19.0**
OECD average / Moyenne OCDE[7]	**23.1**	**23.2**	**23.9**	**24.1**	**24.4**	**24.5**	**25.0**	**24.8**	**24.9**	..

Table 4.2. **Total tax revenue (excluding social security) as percentage of GDP** *(cont.)*
Tableau 4.2. **Total des recettes fiscales (sécurité sociale non comprise) en pourcentage du PIB** *(suite)*

.. Not available

Note: The figures include sub-national government tax revenues for Eswatini, Mauritania (for 2009-19), Mauritius, Morocco, Nigeria (only state revenues) and South Africa (for 2003-19). Sub-national government tax revenues are not available in other countries.

In Ghana, Lesotho, Malawi, Nigeria and Uganda, revenues from property taxes are mainly levied by local governments for which data on revenue are not available. In the Democratic Republic of the Congo only data for property taxes levied by the Direction Générale des Recettes Administratives, Judiciaires, Domaniales et de Participation (DGRAD) are available for 2010-19.

See the country tables in Chapter 5 for further information on data issues for individual countries.

1. The figures should be interpreted with caution as they are affected by macroeconomic instability in the early 2000s. For the years prior to 2010, the figures exclude some revenues collected by the Direction Générale des Recettes Administratives, Judiciaires, Domaniales et de Participation (DGRAD), which are estimated to be less than 1% of total tax revenue. See Table 5.6 in Chapter 5 for further information.
2. The fiscal year for Mauritius changed in 2010 and in 2015. Figures for 2015 needed to be estimated as a result.
3. Includes payments made by South Africa to the Southern African Customs Union (SACU) pool.
4. Represents an unweighted average of the 30 African countries in this publication. In 2009, the Africa (30) average is calculated based on estimated tax-to-GDP ratios for Chad and Nigeria in that year, as data were not available prior to 2010 in these countries. The estimations in 2009 for these two countries are based on data for later years and on IMF figures from the *World Economic Outlook April 2021*. Details of the estimations are available in the metadata. The Africa (30) should be interpreted with caution as data for social security contributions (category 2000) and property taxes (category 4000) are not available or are partial in a few countries. See the country tables in Chapter 5 for further information.
5. Represents an unweighted average for 24 Asian and Pacific economies included in the publication *Revenue Statistics in Asia and the Pacific 2021*.
6. Represents an unweighted average for 26 Latin American and Caribbean (LAC) countries included in the publication *Revenue Statistics in Latin America and the Caribbean 2021*.
7. Represents an unweighted average for 37 OECD countries.

.. Non disponible

Note : Les chiffres incluent les recettes fiscales collectées par les administrations infranationales pour l'Afrique du Sud (pour les années 2003 à 2019), Eswatini, le Maroc, Maurice, la Mauritanie (pour les années 2009 à 2019) et le Nigéria (recettes des administrations régionales). Les données des recettes fiscales collectées par les administrations infranationales ne sont pas disponibles pour les autres pays.

Au Ghana, au Lesotho, au Malawi, au Nigéria et en Ouganda, les recettes provenant des impôts sur le patrimoine sont principalement perçues par les administrations locales pour lesquelles les données ne sont pas disponibles. En République démocratique du Congo, seules les données des impôts sur le patrimoine qui sont prélevées par la Direction Générale des Recettes Administratives, Judiciaires, Domaniales et de Participation (DGRAD) sont disponibles pour 2010-19.

Voir les tableaux par pays au chapitre 5 pour plus d'informations sur les problèmes de données pour chaque pays.

1. Les chiffres doivent être interprétés avec prudence car ils sont affectés par une instabilité macroéconomique au début des années 2000. Pour les années antérieures à 2010, les chiffres excluent certaines recettes perçues par la Direction Générale des Recettes Administratives, Judiciaires, Domaniales et de Participation (DGRAD) estimées inférieures à 1 % du total des recettes fiscales. Voir le tableau 5.6 du chapitre 5 pour plus d'informations.
2. L'année fiscale pour Maurice a changé en 2010 et en 2015. Les chiffres pour 2015 ont dû être estimés en conséquence.
3. Comprend les paiements effectués par l'Afrique du Sud au fond collectif de l'Union douanière d'Afrique australe (SACU).
4. Représente une moyenne non pondérée des 30 pays africains inclus dans cette publication. En 2009, la moyenne de l'Afrique (30) est calculée sur la base des ratios impôts/PIB estimés pour le Nigéria et le Tchad car les données n'étaient pas disponibles avant 2010 dans ces pays. Les estimations en 2009 pour ces deux pays sont basées sur des données des années ultérieures et sur les chiffres du FMI tirés des Perspectives de l'économie mondiale d'avril 2021. Les détails des estimations sont disponibles dans les métadonnées. Il convient d'interpréter cette moyenne avec prudence à cause de valeurs manquantes ou incomplètes pour la rubrique 2000 (cotisations de sécurité sociale) et la rubrique 4000 (taxes sur le patrimoine). Voir les tableaux de pays au chapitre 5 pour plus d'informations.
5. Représente la moyenne non pondérée pour 24 économies de l'Asie et du Pacifique incluses dans la publication *Revenue Statistics in Asia and the Pacific 2021*.
6. Représente la moyenne non pondérée pour 26 pays d'Amérique latine et des Caraïbes (ALC) inclus dans la publication *Revenue Statistics in Latin America and the Caribbean 2021*.
7. Représente la moyenne non pondérée pour 37 pays de l'OCDE.

StatLink https://doi.org/10.1787/888934283329

Table 4.3. **Tax revenue of the main headings as percentage of GDP, 2019**
Tableau 4.3. **Recettes fiscales des principales rubriques en pourcentage du PIB, 2019**

	1000 Income & profits / Impôts & profits	2000 Social security / Sécurité sociale	3000 Payroll / Salaires	4000 Property / Patrimoine	5000 Goods and services / Biens et services	6000 Other taxes / Autres impôts
Botswana	7.9	0.0	0.0	0.0	4.6	0.0
Burkina Faso	4.9	1.9	0.1	0.1	10.4	0.1
Cabo Verde	6.6	0.0	0.0	0.3	13.6	0.0
Cameroon / Cameroun	3.9	1.0	0.2	0.1	8.6	0.3
Chad / Tchad	3.9	..	0.1	0.4	3.7	0.0
Congo	2.1	..	0.3	0.2	5.5	0.0
Congo, Dem. Rep. / Congo, Rép. dém.	3.2	0.8	0.1	0.1	3.2	0.1
Côte d'Ivoire	1.6	1.5	1.5	0.4	8.0	0.1
Egypt / Égypte	6.2	0.9	0.0	0.1	7.0	0.0
Equatorial Guinea / Guinée équatoriale	7.7	0.8	0.0	0.0	1.5	0.1
Eswatini	8.9	2.4	0.0	0.5	6.7	0.0
Ghana	5.7	0.8	0.0	..	7.1	0.0
Kenya	7.4	0.6	0.0	0.0	9.3	0.0
Lesotho	12.0	0.0	0.0	..	8.6	0.0
Madagascar[1]	2.7	0.5	0.0	0.1	7.9	0.1
Malawi	8.6	0.0	0.0	..	9.8	0.0
Mali[2]	4.0	1.7	0.1	0.3	9.8	0.9
Mauritania / Mauritanie[3]	4.3	0.7	0.0	0.4	8.6	0.0
Mauritius / Maurice	5.7	0.9	0.2	1.0	13.4	0.0
Morocco / Maroc[1]	8.5	6.2	0.0	1.4	12.1	0.1
Namibia / Namibie	12.6	0.3	0.0	0.1	7.1	0.1
Niger	2.3	0.6	0.1	0.1	6.6	0.8
Nigeria / Nigéria	3.4	0.6	0.0	..	1.6	0.3
Rwanda[1]	7.0	1.0	0.0	0.0	9.6	0.0
Senegal / Sénégal[4]	4.3	1.2	0.2	0.4	10.2	0.3
Seychelles	10.6	1.8	0.0	0.8	21.1	0.0
South Africa / Afrique du Sud[5]	13.4	0.4	0.3	1.7	10.5	0.0
Togo	3.2	..	0.1	0.1	11.4	0.2
Tunisia / Tunisie[1]	10.9	9.7	0.4	0.3	12.2	0.8
Uganda / Ouganda	4.3	..	0.0	..	7.9	0.0
Africa (30) average / Moyenne Afrique (30)[6]	**6.3**	**1.4**	**0.1**	**0.4**	**8.6**	**0.1**
Asia-Pacific (24) average / Moyenne Asie-Pacifique (24)[7]	**8.6**	**1.6**	**0.1**	**0.7**	**9.9**	**0.2**
LAC average / Moyenne ALC[8]	**6.2**	**3.9**	**0.2**	**0.9**	**11.4**	**0.4**
OECD average / Moyenne OCDE[9]	**11.5**	**9.0**	**0.4**	**1.9**	**10.9**	**0.1**

Table 4.3. **Tax revenue of the main headings as percentage of GDP, 2019** *(cont.)*
Tableau 4.3. **Recettes fiscales des principales rubriques en pourcentage du PIB, 2019** *(suite)*

.. Not available

Note: The figures include sub-national government tax revenues for Eswatini, Mauritania (for 2009-19), Mauritius, Morocco, Nigeria (only state revenues) and South Africa (for 2003-19). Sub-national government tax revenues are not available in other countries.

Data on social security contributions are not available for Chad, the Republic of the Congo, the Democratic Republic of the Congo (prior to 2012), Equatorial Guinea (prior to 2013), Madagascar (prior to 2011), Namibia (prior to 2009), Togo and Uganda; and are only partially available in Cameroon and Senegal. Social security contributions for Botswana, Lesotho and Malawi are deemed to be null as they do not meet the criteria to be classified as social security contributions set out in the OECD classification of taxes in the Interpretative Guide.

In Ghana, Lesotho, Malawi, Nigeria and Uganda, revenues from property taxes are mainly levied by local governments for which data on revenue are not available. In the Democratic Republic of the Congo only data for property taxes levied by the Direction Générale des Recettes Administratives, Judiciaires, Domaniales et de Participation (DGRAD) are available for 2010-19.

See the country tables in Chapter 5 for further information on data issues for individual countries.

1. Madagascar, Morocco, Rwanda and Tunisia do not include social security contributions in the tax-to-GDP ratio in their official publications as these countries do not consider them to be taxes. They are included as tax revenue in this publication, following the classification set out in the OECD Interpretative Guide.
2. Part of the figures for social security contributions in Mali for 2019 were not available, and so were assumed to be equal to 2018 figures.
3. Social security contributions from the Caisse Nationale de Sécurité Sociale are estimated for 2019.
4. Social security contributions are estimated for 2018 and 2019.
5. The figures for heading 5000 goods and services should be interpreted with caution as they include payments made by South Africa to the Southern African Customs Union (SACU) pool.
6. Represents an unweighted average of the 30 African countries in this publication. The Africa (30) should be interpreted with caution as data for social security contributions (category 2000) and property taxes (category 4000) are not available or are partial in a few countries. See the country tables in Chapter 5 for further information.
7. Represents an unweighted average for 24 Asian and Pacific economies included in the publication *Revenue Statistics in Asia and the Pacific 2021*.
8. Represents an unweighted average for 26 Latin American and Caribbean (LAC) countries included in the publication *Revenue Statistics in Latin America and the Caribbean 2021*.
9. Represents an unweighted average for 37 OECD countries. Data are for 2018 as data for 2019 were not available at the date of publication.

.. Non disponible

Note : Les chiffres incluent les recettes fiscales collectées par les administrations infranationales pour l'Afrique du Sud (pour les années 2003 à 2019), Eswatini, le Maroc, Maurice, la Mauritanie (pour les années 2009 à 2019) et le Nigéria (recettes des administrations régionales). Les données des recettes fiscales collectées par les administrations infranationales ne sont pas disponibles pour les autres pays.

Les données des cotisations de sécurité sociale ne sont pas disponibles pour la République du Congo, la République démocratique du Congo (avant 2012), la Guinée équatoriale (avant 2013), Madagascar (avant 2011), la Namibie (avant 2009), l'Ouganda, le Tchad et le Togo et ne sont que partiellement disponibles au Cameroun et au Sénégal. Les cotisations de sécurité sociale pour le Botswana, le Lesotho et le Malawi sont nulles car elles ne répondent pas aux critères de classification des cotisations de sécurité sociale de la classification des impôts établie dans le Guide d'interprétation de l'OCDE.

Au Ghana, au Lesotho, au Malawi, au Nigéria et en Ouganda, les recettes provenant des impôts sur le patrimoine sont principalement perçues par les administrations locales pour lesquelles les données ne sont pas disponibles. En République démocratique du Congo, seules les données des impôts sur le patrimoine qui sont prélevées par la Direction Générale des Recettes Administratives, Judiciaires, Domaniales et de Participation (DGRAD) sont disponibles pour 2010-19.

Voir les tableaux par pays au chapitre 5 pour plus d'informations sur les problèmes de données pour chaque pays.

1. Madagascar, le Maroc, le Rwanda et la Tunisie n'incluent pas les cotisations de sécurité sociale dans le ratio impôts/PIB dans leurs publications officielles car ces pays ne les considèrent pas comme des impôts. Elles sont incluses dans les recettes fiscales de cette publication en accordance avec la classification des impôts établie dans le Guide d'interprétation de l'OCDE.
2. Une partie des chiffres des cotisations de sécurité sociale au Mali n'étaient pas disponibles pour 2019 et sont donc supposées être égales aux chiffres de 2018.
3. Les cotisations de sécurité sociale de la Caisse Nationale de Sécurité Sociale sont estimées pour 2019.
4. Les cotisations de sécurité sociale sont estimées pour 2018 et 2019.
5. Les chiffres relatifs à la rubrique 5000 produits et services doivent être interprétés avec prudence car ils incluent les paiements effectués par l'Afrique du Sud à l'Union douanière d'Afrique australe (SACU).
6. Représente une moyenne non pondérée des 30 pays africains inclus dans cette publication. Il convient d'interpréter cette moyenne avec prudence à cause de valeurs manquantes ou incomplètes pour la rubrique 2000 (cotisations de sécurité sociale) et la rubrique 4000 (taxes sur le patrimoine). Veuillez voir les tableaux des pays au chapitre 5 pour plus d'informations.
7. Représente la moyenne non pondérée pour 24 économies de l'Asie et du Pacifique incluses dans la publication *Revenue Statistics in Asia and the Pacific 2021*.
8. Représente la moyenne non pondérée pour 26 pays d'Amérique latine et des Caraïbes (ALC) inclus dans la publication *Revenue Statistics in Latin America and the Caribbean 2021*.
9. Représente la moyenne non pondérée pour 37 pays de l'OCDE. Les données sont pour 2018 car les données pour 2019 n'étaient pas disponibles à la date de la publication.

StatLink https://doi.org/10.1787/888934283348

Table 4.4. **Tax revenue of the main headings as percentage of total taxation, 2019**

Tableau 4.4. **Recettes fiscales des principales rubriques en pourcentage du total des recettes fiscales, 2019**

	1000 Income & profits / Impôts & profits	2000 Social security / Sécurité sociale	3000 Payroll / Salaires	4000 Property / Patrimoine	5000 Goods and services / Biens et services	6000 Other taxes / Autres impôts
Botswana	63.0	0.0	0.0	0.3	36.7	0.0
Burkina Faso	27.8	10.9	0.8	0.7	59.1	0.7
Cabo Verde	31.9	0.2	0.0	1.6	66.3	0.0
Cameroon / Cameroun	27.4	7.3	1.1	0.8	60.9	2.4
Chad / Tchad	48.5	..	1.6	4.5	45.4	0.0
Congo	26.2	..	3.2	2.8	67.8	0.0
Congo, Dem. Rep. / Congo, Rép. dém.	42.6	10.1	1.9	0.7	42.7	2.0
Côte d'Ivoire	12.3	11.3	11.6	3.1	61.0	0.8
Egypt / Égypte	43.8	6.4	0.0	0.8	49.0	0.0
Equatorial Guinea / Guinée équatoriale	76.4	7.5	0.0	0.0	15.1	1.0
Eswatini	48.2	13.0	0.0	2.6	36.3	0.0
Ghana	42.0	5.8	0.0	..	52.2	0.0
Kenya	42.7	3.6	0.0	0.0	53.7	0.0
Lesotho	58.3	0.0	0.0	..	41.7	0.0
Madagascar[1]	24.4	4.4	0.0	0.5	70.2	0.4
Malawi	46.7	0.0	0.0	..	53.2	0.1
Mali[2]	24.0	10.0	0.9	1.8	58.0	5.3
Mauritania / Mauritanie[3]	30.9	4.8	0.1	2.7	61.5	0.0
Mauritius / Maurice	26.9	4.1	0.8	4.6	63.6	0.1
Morocco / Maroc[1]	30.1	21.9	0.0	5.1	42.7	0.3
Namibia / Namibie	62.4	1.7	0.0	0.5	35.1	0.3
Niger	21.9	5.4	0.6	1.2	63.4	7.5
Nigeria / Nigéria	56.6	10.7	0.6	..	26.7	5.4
Rwanda[1]	39.8	5.9	0.0	0.1	54.2	0.0
Senegal / Sénégal[4]	25.8	7.0	1.5	2.2	61.5	2.0
Seychelles	31.0	5.2	0.0	2.2	61.5	0.0
South Africa / Afrique du Sud[5]	51.1	1.3	1.2	6.3	40.0	0.0
Togo	21.4	..	0.4	0.8	75.9	1.5
Tunisia / Tunisie[1]	31.7	28.3	1.2	0.9	35.6	2.4
Uganda / Ouganda	35.2	..	0.0	..	64.8	0.0
Africa (30) average / Moyenne Afrique (30)[6]	**38.4**	**7.2**	**0.9**	**1.9**	**51.9**	**1.1**
Asia-Pacific (24) average / Moyenne Asie-Pacifique (24)[7]	**39.2**	**6.6**	**0.5**	**3.2**	**49.8**	**1.4**
LAC average / Moyenne ALC[8]	**27.0**	**17.1**	**0.8**	**3.8**	**49.8**	**1.5**
OECD average / Moyenne OCDE[9]	**34.3**	**25.7**	**1.2**	**5.6**	**32.7**	**0.5**

Table 4.4. **Tax revenue of the main headings as percentage of total taxes, 2019** *(cont.)*
Tableau 4.4. **Recettes fiscales des principales rubriques en pourcentage du total des recettes fiscales, 2019** *(suite)*

.. Not available

Note: The figures include sub-national government tax revenues for Eswatini, Mauritania (for 2009-19), Mauritius, Morocco, Nigeria (only state revenues) and South Africa (for 2003-19). Sub-national government tax revenues are not available in other countries.

Data on social security contributions are not available for Chad, the Republic of the Congo, the Democratic Republic of the Congo (prior to 2012), Equatorial Guinea (prior to 2013), Madagascar (prior to 2011), Namibia (prior to 2009), Togo and Uganda; and are only partially available in Cameroon and Senegal. Social security contributions for Botswana, Lesotho and Malawi are deemed to be null as they do not meet the criteria to be classified as social security contributions set out in the OECD classification of taxes in the Interpretative Guide.

In Ghana, Lesotho, Malawi, Nigeria and Uganda, revenues from property taxes are mainly levied by local governments for which data on revenue are not available. In the Democratic Republic of the Congo only data for property taxes levied by the Direction Générale des Recettes Administratives, Judiciaires, Domaniales et de Participation (DGRAD) are available for 2010-19.

See the country tables in Chapter 5 for further information on data issues for individual countries.

1. Madagascar, Morocco, Rwanda and Tunisia do not include social security contributions in the tax-to-GDP ratio in their official publications as these countries do not consider them to be taxes. They are included as tax revenue in this publication, following the classification set out in the OECD Interpretative Guide.
2. Part of the figures for social security contributions in Mali for 2019 were not available, and so were assumed to be equal to 2018 figures.
3. Social security contributions from the Caisse Nationale de Sécurité Sociale are estimated for 2019.
4. Social security contributions are estimated for 2018 and 2019.
5. The figures for heading 5000 goods and services should be interpreted with caution as they include payments made by South Africa to the Southern African Customs Union (SACU) pool.
6. Represents an unweighted average of the 30 African countries in this publication. The Africa (30) should be interpreted with caution as data for social security contributions (category 2000) and property taxes (category 4000) are not available or are partial in a few countries. See the country tables in Chapter 5 for further information.
7. Represents an unweighted average for 24 Asian and Pacific economies included in the publication *Revenue Statistics in Asia and the Pacific 2021.*
8. Represents an unweighted average for 26 Latin American and Caribbean (LAC) countries included in the publication *Revenue Statistics in Latin America and the Caribbean 2021.*
9. Represents an unweighted average for 37 OECD countries. Data are for 2018 as data for 2019 were not available at the date of publication.

.. Non disponible

Note : Les chiffres incluent les recettes fiscales collectées par les administrations infranationales pour l'Afrique du Sud (pour les années 2003 à 2019), Eswatini, le Maroc, Maurice, la Mauritanie (pour les années 2009 à 2019) et le Nigéria (recettes des administrations régionales). Les données des recettes fiscales collectées par les administrations infranationales ne sont pas disponibles pour les autres pays.

Les données des cotisations de sécurité sociale ne sont pas disponibles pour la République du Congo, la République démocratique du Congo (avant 2012), la Guinée équatoriale (avant 2013), Madagascar (avant 2011), la Namibie (avant 2009), l'Ouganda, le Tchad et le Togo et ne sont que partiellement disponibles au Cameroun et au Sénégal. Les cotisations de sécurité sociale pour le Botswana, le Lesotho et le Malawi sont nulles car elles ne répondent pas aux critères de classification des cotisations de sécurité sociale de la classification des impôts établie dans le Guide d'interprétation de l'OCDE.

Au Ghana, au Lesotho, au Malawi, au Nigéria et en Ouganda, les recettes provenant des impôts sur le patrimoine sont principalement perçues par les administrations locales pour lesquelles les données ne sont pas disponibles. En République démocratique du Congo, seules les données des impôts sur le patrimoine qui sont prélevées par la Direction Générale des Recettes Administratives, Judiciaires, Domaniales et de Participation (DGRAD) sont disponibles pour 2010-19.

Voir les tableaux par pays au chapitre 5 pour plus d'informations sur les problèmes de données pour chaque pays.

1. Madagascar, le Maroc, le Rwanda et la Tunisie n'incluent pas les cotisations de sécurité sociale dans le ratio impôts/PIB dans leurs publications officielles car ces pays ne les considèrent pas comme des impôts. Elles sont incluses dans les recettes fiscales de cette publication en accordance avec la classification des impôts établie dans le Guide d'interprétation de l'OCDE.
2. Une partie des chiffres des cotisations de sécurité sociale au Mali n'étaient pas disponibles pour 2019 et sont donc supposées être égales aux chiffres de 2018.
3. Les cotisations de sécurité sociale de la Caisse Nationale de Sécurité Sociale sont estimées pour 2019.
4. Les cotisations de sécurité sociale sont estimées pour 2018 et 2019.
5. Les chiffres relatifs à la rubrique 5000 produits et services doivent être interprétés avec prudence car ils incluent les paiements effectués par l'Afrique du Sud à l'Union douanière d'Afrique australe (SACU).
6. Représente une moyenne non pondérée des 30 pays africains inclus dans cette publication. Il convient d'interpréter cette moyenne avec prudence à cause de valeurs manquantes ou incomplètes pour la rubrique 2000 (cotisations de sécurité sociale) et la rubrique 4000 (taxes sur le patrimoine). Veuillez voir les tableaux des pays au chapitre 5 pour plus d'informations.
7. Représente la moyenne non pondérée pour 24 économies de l'Asie et du Pacifique incluses dans la publication *Revenue Statistics in Asia and the Pacific* 2021.
8. Représente la moyenne non pondérée pour 26 pays d'Amérique latine et des Caraïbes (ALC) inclus dans la publication *Revenue Statistics in Latin America and the Caribbean* 2021.
9. Représente la moyenne non pondérée pour 37 pays de l'OCDE. Les données sont pour 2018 car les données pour 2019 n'étaient pas disponibles à la date de la publication.

StatLink https://doi.org/10.1787/888934283367

Table 4.5. **Taxes on income and profits (1000) as percentage of GDP**
Tableau 4.5. **Impôts sur le revenu et les bénéfices (1000) en pourcentage du PIB**

	1999	2000	2009	2010	2014	2015	2016	2017	2018	2019
Botswana	..	..	10.3	10.2	10.9	8.6	9.7	7.5	7.8	7.9
Burkina Faso	..	2.5	2.4	2.7	3.8	3.4	3.8	4.0	4.2	4.9
Cabo Verde	5.4	5.5	5.9	5.7	5.0	6.1	6.1	6.5	6.7	6.6
Cameroon / Cameroun	2.7	3.2	4.3	3.3	4.5	4.7	4.0	3.6	3.9	3.9
Chad / Tchad	..	..	..	11.3	7.3	3.3	2.1	3.0	4.2	3.9
Congo	3.0	1.8	2.6	2.3	3.3	5.0	5.2	4.3	1.9	2.1
Congo, Dem. Rep. / Congo, Rép. dém.	..	0.2	2.0	2.3	3.0	3.5	2.6	2.5	3.4	3.2
Côte d'Ivoire	2.1	1.8	1.8	1.5	1.7	1.5	1.5	1.6	1.8	1.6
Egypt / Égypte	..	..	7.7	6.8	6.9	6.4	6.6	6.2	6.5	6.2
Equatorial Guinea / Guinée équatoriale	..	..	11.9	6.8	8.3	9.9	4.8	4.6	4.3	7.7
Eswatini	6.3	5.5	7.1	7.2	7.6	7.3	8.1	8.2	8.4	8.9
Ghana	..	2.3	3.5	3.9	4.7	4.2	3.8	4.6	5.4	5.7
Kenya	..	..	7.2	7.3	8.9	8.6	8.4	8.3	7.7	7.4
Lesotho	..	..	10.3	9.7	11.2	12.0	12.0	11.7	12.9	12.0
Madagascar	1.6	1.6	2.5	2.4	2.0	2.1	2.3	2.4	2.5	2.7
Malawi	..	..	6.4	7.0	8.0	8.2	8.2	9.1	8.8	8.6
Mali	1.6	1.6	3.2	3.5	4.2	3.8	3.9	4.4	3.3	4.0
Mauritania / Mauritanie	..	..	3.4	3.4	5.7	4.9	4.4	4.5	4.7	4.3
Mauritius / Maurice[1]	2.5	2.4	5.4	4.9	4.7	4.8	4.8	5.1	5.2	5.7
Morocco / Maroc	..	5.7	9.3	8.0	8.2	8.0	8.3	8.7	8.7	8.5
Namibia / Namibie	..	..	10.6	11.7	12.9	12.8	12.8	12.6	12.1	12.6
Niger	..	1.3	3.3	2.4	3.9	3.1	2.8	2.6	2.4	2.3
Nigeria / Nigéria	..	..	..	4.6	4.8	3.6	2.9	3.2	3.8	3.4
Rwanda	2.8	2.7	4.2	4.5	5.7	6.1	6.3	6.3	6.8	7.0
Senegal / Sénégal	2.5	2.9	3.6	4.1	4.1	4.1	4.6	4.5	4.7	4.3
Seychelles	..	..	7.1	9.1	9.7	9.2	10.4	10.8	10.8	10.6
South Africa / Afrique du Sud	12.2	11.4	12.8	12.0	13.1	13.8	13.5	13.8	13.8	13.4
Togo	..	1.5	2.2	1.8	2.6	2.7	3.2	2.7	3.0	3.2
Tunisia / Tunisie	..	5.5	8.0	8.1	9.8	9.1	8.2	8.9	8.5	10.9
Uganda / Ouganda	1.6	1.5	2.5	2.6	3.2	3.6	3.9	3.9	4.0	4.3
Africa (30) average / Moyenne Afrique (30)[2]	**..**	**..**	**..**	**5.7**	**6.3**	**6.1**	**6.0**	**6.0**	**6.1**	**6.3**
Asia-Pacific (24) average / Moyenne Asie-Pacifique (24)[3]	**..**	**..**	**..**	**7.4**	**7.0**	**7.5**	**7.2**	**7.8**	**8.2**	**8.6**
LAC average / Moyenne ALC[4]	**3.9**	**4.2**	**5.6**	**5.6**	**6.0**	**6.0**	**5.8**	**5.8**	**6.1**	**6.2**
OECD average / Moyenne OCDE[5]	**11.4**	**11.7**	**10.5**	**10.4**	**11.1**	**11.1**	**11.1**	**11.4**	**11.5**	**..**

.. Not available

Note: The figures include sub-national government tax revenues for Eswatini, Mauritania (for 2009-19), Mauritius, Morocco, Nigeria (only state revenues) and South Africa (for 2003-19). Sub-national government tax revenues are not available in other countries.

1. The fiscal year for Mauritius changed in 2010 and in 2015. Figures for 2015 needed to be estimated as a result.
2. Represents an unweighted average of the 30 African countries in this publication.
3. Represents an unweighted average for 24 Asian and Pacific economies included in the publication *Revenue Statistics in Asia and the Pacific 2021*.
4. Represents an unweighted average for 26 Latin American and Caribbean (LAC) countries included in the publication *Revenue Statistics in Latin America and the Caribbean 2021*.
5. Represents an unweighted average for 37 OECD countries.

.. Non disponible

Note : Les chiffres incluent les recettes fiscales collectées par les administrations infranationales pour l'Afrique du Sud (pour les années 2003 à 2019), Eswatini, le Maroc, Maurice, la Mauritanie (pour les années 2009 à 2019) et le Nigéria (recettes des administrations régionales). Les données des recettes fiscales collectées par les administrations infranationales ne sont pas disponibles pour les autres pays.

1. L'année fiscale pour Maurice a changé en 2010 et en 2015. Les chiffres pour 2015 ont dû être estimés en conséquence.
2. Représente une moyenne non pondérée des 30 pays africains inclus dans cette publication.
3. Représente la moyenne non pondérée pour 24 économies de l'Asie et du Pacifique incluses dans la publication *Revenue Statistics in Asia and the Pacific 2021*.
4. Représente la moyenne non pondérée pour 26 pays d'Amérique latine et des Caraïbes (ALC) inclus dans la publication *Revenue Statistics in Latin America and the Caribbean 2021*.
5. Représente la moyenne non pondérée pour 37 pays de l'OCDE.

StatLink https://doi.org/10.1787/888934283386

Table 4.6. **Taxes on income and profits (1000) as percentage of total taxation**
Tableau 4.6. **Impôts sur le revenu et les bénéfices (1000) en pourcentage du total des recettes fiscales**

	1999	2000	2009	2010	2014	2015	2016	2017	2018	2019
Botswana	..	..	65.4	65.3	71.7	67.9	69.5	61.3	64.7	63.0
Burkina Faso	..	24.7	19.3	19.3	26.9	23.2	24.8	24.5	25.4	27.8
Cabo Verde	35.6	35.7	32.2	30.9	29.7	32.6	32.4	32.4	31.4	31.9
Cameroon / Cameroun	25.0	28.1	32.4	27.1	31.5	32.3	28.1	25.3	27.0	27.4
Chad / Tchad	..	..	..	77.6	68.5	56.3	45.6	48.0	53.0	48.5
Congo	48.4	48.2	32.8	33.4	34.1	38.5	39.1	40.0	24.6	26.2
Congo, Dem. Rep. / Congo, Rép. dém.	..	34.0	25.9	26.9	31.8	35.5	30.4	36.6	43.9	42.6
Côte d'Ivoire	17.8	16.4	14.5	12.8	13.6	12.0	11.2	12.2	13.7	12.3
Egypt / Égypte	..	..	46.7	44.8	48.6	44.1	45.9	40.6	43.8	43.8
Equatorial Guinea / Guinée équatoriale	..	..	93.6	89.1	84.7	82.5	67.1	69.4	66.8	76.4
Eswatini	54.7	51.0	55.2	51.7	50.8	48.7	50.2	48.5	48.3	48.2
Ghana	..	28.9	32.9	36.1	38.9	32.1	27.4	33.2	38.6	42.0
Kenya	..	..	39.9	40.6	46.2	46.4	45.6	44.9	44.2	42.7
Lesotho	..	..	60.1	56.3	59.2	62.3	62.4	59.7	58.8	58.3
Madagascar	16.6	17.0	26.1	24.8	22.6	22.5	23.3	22.3	22.2	24.4
Malawi	..	..	41.5	44.2	44.8	48.7	48.4	48.5	48.0	46.7
Mali	14.2	14.5	22.2	24.7	30.0	25.2	23.9	26.2	24.8	24.0
Mauritania / Mauritanie	..	..	32.3	34.8	37.9	33.4	31.3	31.2	29.4	30.9
Mauritius / Maurice[1]	13.8	13.0	28.3	25.7	24.3	25.0	24.8	25.9	25.4	26.9
Morocco / Maroc	..	26.0	33.6	28.9	29.7	29.8	30.2	31.1	30.7	30.1
Namibia / Namibie	..	..	58.9	63.0	61.1	59.4	60.5	61.8	62.1	62.4
Niger	..	18.0	31.9	25.4	31.4	24.7	26.4	27.0	21.1	21.9
Nigeria / Nigéria	..	..	..	63.5	63.4	59.9	55.8	55.7	60.1	56.6
Rwanda	25.7	26.0	34.7	36.2	37.3	38.1	38.6	39.1	40.3	39.8
Senegal / Sénégal	19.6	22.1	24.2	25.9	25.1	25.3	26.9	27.4	28.4	25.8
Seychelles	..	..	24.8	29.5	31.6	31.0	32.2	33.6	31.2	31.0
South Africa / Afrique du Sud	57.8	56.7	55.2	52.1	51.7	51.9	51.8	52.8	51.8	51.1
Togo	..	20.9	20.0	16.5	16.7	16.6	19.2	17.1	20.3	21.4
Tunisia / Tunisie	..	22.6	29.9	29.7	31.8	30.0	27.8	28.5	26.5	31.7
Uganda / Ouganda	18.0	18.2	29.2	31.5	34.0	34.7	34.9	34.7	34.3	35.2
Africa (30) average / Moyenne Afrique (30)[2]	**..**	**..**	**..**	**38.9**	**40.3**	**39.0**	**37.9**	**38.0**	**38.0**	**38.4**
Asia-Pacific (24) average / Moyenne Asie-Pacifique (24)[3]	**..**	**..**	**..**	**39.0**	**36.2**	**38.5**	**38.3**	**38.9**	**39.1**	**39.2**
LAC average / Moyenne ALC[4]	**21.4**	**22.2**	**27.0**	**26.3**	**27.0**	**26.7**	**26.4**	**26.3**	**26.9**	**27.0**
OECD average / Moyenne OCDE[5]	**33.7**	**34.5**	**33.0**	**32.6**	**33.3**	**33.6**	**33.1**	**33.9**	**34.3**	**..**

.. Not available

Note: The figures include sub-national government tax revenues for Eswatini, Mauritania (for 2009-19), Mauritius, Morocco, Nigeria (only state revenues) and South Africa (for 2003-19). Sub-national government tax revenues are not available in other countries.

1. The fiscal year for Mauritius changed in 2010 and in 2015. Figures for 2015 needed to be estimated as a result.
2. Represents an unweighted average of the 30 African countries in this publication.
3. Represents an unweighted average for 24 Asian and Pacific economies included in the publication *Revenue Statistics in Asia and the Pacific 2021.*
4. Represents an unweighted average for 26 Latin American and Caribbean (LAC) countries included in the publication *Revenue Statistics in Latin America and the Caribbean 2021.*
5. Represents an unweighted average for 37 OECD countries.

.. Non disponible

Note : Les chiffres incluent les recettes fiscales collectées par les administrations infranationales pour l'Afrique du Sud (pour les années 2003 à 2019), Eswatini, le Maroc, Maurice, la Mauritanie (pour les années 2009 à 2019) et le Nigéria (recettes des administrations régionales). Les données des recettes fiscales collectées par les administrations infranationales ne sont pas disponibles pour les autres pays.

1. L'année fiscale pour Maurice a changé en 2010 et en 2015. Les chiffres pour 2015 ont dû être estimés en conséquence.
2. Représente une moyenne non pondérée des 30 pays africains inclus dans cette publication.
3. Représente la moyenne non pondérée pour 24 économies de l'Asie et du Pacifique incluses dans la publication *Revenue Statistics in Asia and the Pacific 2021.*
4. Représente la moyenne non pondérée pour 26 pays d'Amérique latine et des Caraïbes (ALC) inclus dans la publication *Revenue Statistics in Latin America and the Caribbean 2021.*
5. Représente la moyenne non pondérée pour 37 pays de l'OCDE.

StatLink https://doi.org/10.1787/888934283405

Table 4.7. **Social security contributions (2000) as percentage of GDP**
Tableau 4.7. **Cotisations de sécurité sociale (2000) en pourcentage du PIB**

	1999	2000	2009	2010	2014	2015	2016	2017	2018	2019
Botswana	..	..	0.0	0.0	0.0	0.0	0.0	0.0	0.0	0.0
Burkina Faso	..	1.6	1.6	1.5	1.5	1.7	1.8	1.8	1.8	1.9
Cabo Verde	0.0	0.8	0.0	0.0	0.0	0.0	0.0	0.0	0.0	0.0
Cameroon / Cameroun	0.8	0.9	0.9	1.0	0.9	0.9	1.0	1.1	1.1	1.0
Chad / Tchad	..	..	..	..	..	..	..	..	..	..
Congo	..	..	..	..	..	..	..	..	..	..
Congo, Dem. Rep. / Congo, Rép. dém.	..	..	..	..	0.6	0.6	0.5	0.5	0.5	0.8
Côte d'Ivoire	0.8	1.0	1.0	1.0	1.4	1.4	1.6	1.5	1.5	1.5
Egypt / Égypte	..	..	2.1	2.2	2.4	2.5	1.8	2.3	1.2	0.9
Equatorial Guinea / Guinée équatoriale	..	..	..	..	0.6	0.8	0.7	0.7	0.6	0.8
Eswatini	1.3	1.2	1.7	1.9	1.8	1.9	2.0	2.3	2.5	2.4
Ghana	..	0.7	1.4	0.9	1.1	1.2	1.2	0.9	0.8	0.8
Kenya	..	..	0.2	0.2	0.3	0.3	0.5	0.5	0.6	0.6
Lesotho	..	..	0.0	0.0	0.0	0.0	0.0	0.0	0.0	0.0
Madagascar[1]	..	..	..	..	0.4	0.4	0.4	0.4	0.6	0.5
Malawi	..	..	0.0	0.0	0.0	0.0	0.0	0.0	0.0	0.0
Mali[2]	0.8	0.9	1.5	1.4	1.6	1.5	1.8	1.8	1.7	1.7
Mauritania / Mauritanie[3]	..	..	0.6	0.7	0.9	0.9	0.8	0.8	0.8	0.7
Mauritius / Maurice[4]	0.8	0.8	0.6	0.7	0.8	0.8	0.8	0.8	0.8	0.9
Morocco / Maroc[1,5]	..	2.4	4.7	4.8	5.4	5.3	5.5	5.7	5.8	6.2
Namibia / Namibie	..	..	0.3	0.4	0.3	0.4	0.3	0.4	0.3	0.3
Niger	..	0.4	0.5	0.5	0.6	0.6	0.6	0.6	0.5	0.6
Nigeria / Nigéria	..	..	..	0.6	0.7	0.6	0.5	0.6	0.5	0.6
Rwanda[1]	0.5	0.5	0.8	0.8	1.0	1.0	1.1	1.0	1.0	1.0
Senegal / Sénégal[6]	0.5	0.5	0.7	0.9	1.1	1.1	1.1	1.2	1.2	1.2
Seychelles	..	..	4.8	2.8	1.1	1.2	1.1	1.2	2.5	1.8
South Africa / Afrique du Sud	0.0	0.0	0.4	0.4	0.4	0.4	0.4	0.4	0.4	0.4
Togo	..	..	..	..	..	..	..	..	..	..
Tunisia / Tunisie[1]	..	5.3	7.0	7.3	8.5	8.9	9.4	9.7	9.2	9.7
Uganda / Ouganda	..	..	..	..	..	..	..	..	..	..
Africa (30) average / Moyenne Afrique (30)[7]	**..**	**..**	**..**	**1.3**	**1.3**	**1.3**	**1.3**	**1.4**	**1.4**	**1.4**
Asia-Pacific (24) average / Moyenne Asie-Pacifique (24)[8]	**..**	**..**	**..**	**1.2**	**1.3**	**1.3**	**1.3**	**1.3**	**1.4**	**1.6**
LAC average / Moyenne ALC[9]	**2.8**	**2.9**	**3.3**	**3.3**	**3.6**	**3.8**	**3.8**	**3.8**	**3.8**	**3.9**
OECD average / Moyenne OCDE[10]	**8.5**	**8.4**	**8.7**	**8.7**	**8.8**	**8.8**	**9.0**	**8.9**	**9.0**	**..**

Table 4.7. **Social security contributions (2000) as percentage of GDP** *(cont.)*
Tableau 4.7. **Cotisations de sécurité sociale (2000) en pourcentage du PIB** *(suite)*

.. Not available

Note: The figures include sub-national government tax revenues for Eswatini, Mauritania (for 2009-19), Mauritius, Morocco, Nigeria (only state revenues) and South Africa (for 2003-19). Sub-national government tax revenues are not available in other countries.

Data on social security contributions are not available for Chad, the Republic of the Congo, the Democratic Republic of the Congo (prior to 2012), Equatorial Guinea (prior to 2013), Madagascar (prior to 2011), Namibia (prior to 2009), Togo and Uganda; and are only partially available in Cameroon and Senegal. Social security contributions for Botswana, Lesotho and Malawi are deemed to be null as they do not meet the criteria to be classified as social security contributions set out in the OECD classification of taxes in the Interpretative Guide.

1. Madagascar, Morocco, Rwanda and Tunisia do not include social security contributions in the tax-to-GDP ratio in their official publications as these countries do not consider them to be taxes. They are included as tax revenue in this publication, following the classification set out in the OECD *Interpretative Guide.*
2. Part of the figures for social security contributions in Mali for 2019 were not available, and so were assumed to be equal to 2018 figures.
3. Social security contributions from the Caisse Nationale de Sécurité Sociale are estimated for 2019.
4. The fiscal year for Mauritius changed in 2010 and in 2015. Figures for 2015 needed to be estimated as a result.
5. Social security contributions in Morocco are estimated for years prior to 2002.
6. These figures include contributions to the Senegalese Pension Institute (IPRES) (estimated prior to 2006) and contributions to the social security fund (CSS) (from 2012 as data for previous years are not available). Social security contributions in Senegal are estimated for 2018 and 2019.
7. Represents an unweighted average of the 30 African countries in this publication. The Africa (30) should be interpreted with caution as data for property taxes (category 4000) are not available or are partial in a few countries. See the country tables in Chapter 5 for further information.
8. Represents an unweighted average for 24 Asian and Pacific economies included in the publication *Revenue Statistics in Asia and the Pacific 2021.*
9. Represents an unweighted average for 26 Latin American and Caribbean (LAC) countries included in the publication *Revenue Statistics in Latin America and the Caribbean 2021.*
10. Represents an unweighted average for 37 OECD countries.

.. Non disponible

Note : Les chiffres incluent les recettes fiscales collectées par les administrations infranationales pour l'Afrique du Sud (pour les années 2003 à 2019), Eswatini, le Maroc, Maurice, la Mauritanie (pour les années 2009 à 2019) et le Nigéria (recettes des administrations régionales). Les données des recettes fiscales collectées par les administrations infranationales ne sont pas disponibles pour les autres pays.

Les données des cotisations de sécurité sociale ne sont pas disponibles pour la République du Congo, la République démocratique du Congo (avant 2012), la Guinée équatoriale (avant 2013), Madagascar (avant 2011), la Namibie (avant 2009), l'Ouganda, le Tchad et le Togo et ne sont que partiellement disponibles au Cameroun et au Sénégal. Les cotisations de sécurité sociale pour le Botswana, le Lesotho et le Malawi sont nulles car elles ne répondent pas aux critères de classification des cotisations de sécurité sociale de la classification des impôts établie dans le Guide d'interprétation de l'OCDE.

1. Madagascar, le Maroc, le Rwanda et la Tunisie n'incluent pas les cotisations de sécurité sociale dans le ratio impôts/PIB dans leurs publications officielles car ces pays ne les considèrent pas comme des impôts. Elles sont incluses dans les recettes fiscales de cette publication en accordance avec la classification des impôts établie dans le *Guide d'interprétation de l'OCDE.*
2. Une partie des chiffres des cotisations de sécurité sociale au Mali n'étaient pas disponibles pour 2019 et sont donc supposées être égales aux chiffres de 2018.
3. Les cotisations de sécurité sociale de la Caisse Nationale de Sécurité Sociale sont estimées pour 2019.
4. L'année fiscale pour Maurice a changé en 2010 et en 2015. Les chiffres pour 2015 ont dû être estimés en conséquence.
5. Les cotisations de sécurité sociale au Maroc antérieures à 2002 sont estimées.
6. Les chiffres comprennent les cotisations de sécurité sociale de l'Institution de prévoyance retraite du Sénégal (IPRES) (estimées pour les années antérieures à 2006) et les cotisations de sécurité sociale de la Caisse de Sécurité Sociale (CSS) (à partir de 2012 car les données pour les années précédentes ne sont pas disponibles). Les cotisations de sécurité sociale de 2018 et 2019 sont estimées.
7. Représente une moyenne non pondérée des 30 pays africains inclus dans cette publication. Il convient d'interpréter cette moyenne avec prudence à cause de valeurs manquantes ou incomplètes pour la rubrique 4000 (taxes sur le patrimoine). Veuillez voir les tableaux de pays au chapitre 5 pour plus d'informations.
8. Représente la moyenne non pondérée pour 24 économies de l'Asie et du Pacifique incluses dans la publication *Revenue Statistics in Asia and the Pacific 2021.*
9. Représente la moyenne non pondérée pour 26 pays d'Amérique latine et des Caraïbes (ALC) inclus dans la publication *Revenue Statistics in Latin America and the Caribbean 2021.*
10. Représente la moyenne non pondérée pour 37 pays de l'OCDE.

StatLink https://doi.org/10.1787/888934283424

Table 4.8. **Social security contributions (2000) as percentage of total taxation**

Tableau 4.8. **Cotisations de sécurité sociale (2000) en pourcentage du total des recettes fiscales**

	1999	2000	2009	2010	2014	2015	2016	2017	2018	2019
Botswana	..	..	0.0	0.0	0.0	0.0	0.0	0.0	0.0	0.0
Burkina Faso	..	15.9	12.5	11.0	10.8	11.8	11.5	11.0	11.1	10.9
Cabo Verde	0.0	5.2	0.2	0.2	0.2	0.2	0.2	0.2	0.2	0.2
Cameroon / Cameroun	7.8	8.1	6.8	8.6	6.2	6.0	7.3	7.3	7.2	7.3
Chad / Tchad	..	..	..	..	..	..	..	..	..	..
Congo	..	..	..	..	..	..	..	..	..	..
Congo, Dem. Rep. / Congo, Rép. dém.	..	..	..	..	6.3	5.9	6.1	7.5	6.1	10.1
Côte d'Ivoire	6.9	8.8	7.8	8.0	11.6	11.2	11.9	11.4	11.4	11.3
Egypt / Égypte	..	..	12.7	14.6	16.9	17.0	12.6	15.1	7.9	6.4
Equatorial Guinea / Guinée équatoriale	..	..	..	..	5.7	6.3	10.5	10.8	9.9	7.5
Eswatini	10.9	11.6	13.4	13.6	12.2	13.0	12.3	13.4	14.1	13.0
Ghana	..	9.4	13.0	8.6	9.4	9.0	8.8	6.6	5.7	5.8
Kenya	..	..	1.0	1.1	1.4	1.5	2.6	2.5	3.2	3.6
Lesotho	..	..	0.0	0.0	0.0	0.0	0.0	0.0	0.0	0.0
Madagascar[1]	..	..	..	..	4.2	4.2	3.5	3.6	5.6	4.4
Malawi	..	..	0.0	0.0	0.0	0.0	0.0	0.0	0.0	0.0
Mali[2]	7.0	7.7	10.7	9.8	11.2	9.9	11.2	10.5	12.5	10.0
Mauritania / Mauritanie[3]	..	..	5.9	6.7	5.8	6.2	5.4	5.3	5.0	4.8
Mauritius / Maurice[4]	4.6	4.5	3.3	3.6	4.0	4.1	4.1	4.1	3.8	4.1
Morocco / Maroc[1,5]	..	11.0	17.1	17.5	19.5	19.8	20.1	20.2	20.7	21.9
Namibia / Namibie	..	..	1.6	1.9	1.6	1.7	1.6	1.8	1.8	1.7
Niger	..	5.4	4.4	5.3	5.1	4.7	5.5	6.1	4.7	5.4
Nigeria / Nigéria	..	..	..	7.6	9.3	9.9	10.2	10.9	8.4	10.7
Rwanda[1]	4.5	5.0	6.6	6.4	6.4	6.0	6.7	6.0	5.9	5.9
Senegal / Sénégal[6]	3.9	4.0	4.7	5.8	6.6	6.7	6.7	7.1	7.1	7.0
Seychelles	..	..	16.8	9.1	3.5	3.9	3.5	3.8	7.2	5.2
South Africa / Afrique du Sud	0.0	0.0	1.6	1.6	1.5	1.5	1.4	1.4	1.3	1.3
Togo	..	..	..	..	..	..	..	..	..	..
Tunisia / Tunisie[1]	..	21.6	26.1	27.0	27.5	29.5	31.6	31.1	29.1	28.3
Uganda / Ouganda	..	..	..	..	..	..	..	..	..	..
Africa (30) average / Moyenne Afrique (30)[7]	**..**	**..**	**..**	**7.3**	**7.2**	**7.3**	**7.5**	**7.6**	**7.3**	**7.2**
Asia-Pacific (24) average / Moyenne Asie-Pacifique (24)[8]	**..**	**..**	**..**	**5.4**	**5.5**	**5.4**	**5.6**	**5.5**	**5.4**	**6.6**
LAC average / Moyenne ALC[9]	**15.5**	**15.8**	**15.7**	**15.7**	**16.5**	**16.6**	**16.7**	**17.0**	**16.9**	**17.1**
OECD average / Moyenne OCDE[10]	**24.8**	**24.8**	**26.6**	**26.4**	**26.0**	**25.7**	**25.7**	**25.6**	**25.7**	**..**

Table 4.8. **Social security contributions (2000) as percentage of total taxation** *(cont.)*
Tableau 4.8. **Cotisations de sécurité sociale (2000) en pourcentage du total des recettes fiscales** *(suite)*

.. Not available

Note: The figures include sub-national government tax revenues for Eswatini, Mauritania (for 2009-19), Mauritius, Morocco, Nigeria (only state revenues) and South Africa (for 2003-19). Sub-national government tax revenues are not available in other countries.

Data on social security contributions are not available for Chad, the Republic of the Congo, the Democratic Republic of the Congo (prior to 2012), Equatorial Guinea (prior to 2013), Madagascar (prior to 2011), Namibia (prior to 2009), Togo and Uganda; and are only partially available in Cameroon and Senegal. Social security contributions for Botswana, Lesotho and Malawi are deemed to be null as they do not meet the criteria to be classified as social security contributions set out in the OECD classification of taxes in the Interpretative Guide.

1. Madagascar, Morocco, Rwanda and Tunisia do not include social security contributions in the tax-to-GDP ratio in their official publications as these countries do not consider them to be taxes. They are included as tax revenue in this publication, following the classification set out in the *OECD Interpretative Guide*.
2. Part of the figures for social security contributions in Mali for 2019 were not available, and so were assumed to be equal to 2018 figures.
3. Social security contributions from the Caisse Nationale de Sécurité Sociale are estimated for 2019.
4. The fiscal year for Mauritius changed in 2010 and in 2015. Figures for 2015 needed to be estimated as a result.
5. Social security contributions in Morocco are estimated for years prior to 2002.
6. These figures include contributions to the Senegalese Pension Institute (IPRES) (estimated prior to 2006) and contributions to the social security fund (CSS) (from 2012 as data for previous years are not available). Social security contributions in Senegal are estimated for 2018 and 2019.
7. Represents an unweighted average of the 30 African countries in this publication. The Africa (30) should be interpreted with caution as data for property taxes (category 4000) are not available or are partial in a few countries. See the country tables in Chapter 5 for further information.
8. Represents an unweighted average for 24 Asian and Pacific economies included in the publication *Revenue Statistics in Asia and the Pacific 2021*.
9. Represents an unweighted average for 26 Latin American and Caribbean (LAC) countries included in the publication *Revenue Statistics in Latin America and the Caribbean 2021*.
10. Represents an unweighted average for 37 OECD countries.

.. Non disponible

Note : Les chiffres incluent les recettes fiscales collectées par les administrations infranationales pour l'Afrique du Sud (pour les années 2003 à 2019), Eswatini, le Maroc, Maurice, la Mauritanie (pour les années 2009 à 2019) et le Nigéria (recettes des administrations régionales). Les données des recettes fiscales collectées par les administrations infranationales ne sont pas disponibles pour les autres pays.

Les données des cotisations de sécurité sociale ne sont pas disponibles pour la République du Congo, la République démocratique du Congo (avant 2012), la Guinée équatoriale (avant 2013), Madagascar (avant 2011), la Namibie (avant 2009), l'Ouganda, le Tchad et le Togo et ne sont que partiellement disponibles au Cameroun et au Sénégal. Les cotisations de sécurité sociale pour le Botswana, le Lesotho et le Malawi sont nulles car elles ne répondent pas aux critères de classification des cotisations de sécurité sociale de la classification des impôts établie dans le Guide d'interprétation de l'OCDE.

1. Madagascar, le Maroc, le Rwanda et la Tunisie n'incluent pas les cotisations de sécurité sociale dans le ratio impôts/PIB dans leurs publications officielles car ces pays ne les considèrent pas comme des impôts. Elles sont incluses dans les recettes fiscales de cette publication en accordance avec la classification des impôts établie dans le *Guide d'interprétation de l'OCDE*.
2. Une partie des chiffres des cotisations de sécurité sociale au Mali n'étaient pas disponibles pour 2019 et sont donc supposées être égales aux chiffres de 2018.
3. Les cotisations de sécurité sociale de la Caisse Nationale de Sécurité Sociale sont estimées pour 2019.
4. L'année fiscale pour Maurice a changé en 2010 et en 2015. Les chiffres pour 2015 ont dû être estimés en conséquence.
5. Les cotisations de sécurité sociale au Maroc antérieures à 2002 sont estimées.
6. Les chiffres comprennent les cotisations de sécurité sociale de l'Institution de prévoyance retraite du Sénégal (IPRES) (estimées pour les années antérieures à 2006) et les cotisations de sécurité sociale de la Caisse de Sécurité Sociale (CSS) (à partir de 2012 car les données pour les années précédentes ne sont pas disponibles). Les cotisations de sécurité sociale de 2018 et 2019 sont estimées.
7. Représente une moyenne non pondérée des 30 pays africains inclus dans cette publication. Il convient d'interpréter cette moyenne avec prudence à cause de valeurs manquantes ou incomplètes pour la rubrique 4000 (taxes sur le patrimoine). Veuillez voir les tableaux de pays au chapitre 5 pour plus d'informations.
8. Représente la moyenne non pondérée pour 24 économies de l'Asie et du Pacifique incluses dans la publication *Revenue Statistics in Asia and the Pacific 2021*.
9. Représente la moyenne non pondérée pour 26 pays d'Amérique latine et des Caraïbes (ALC) inclus dans la publication *Revenue Statistics in Latin America and the Caribbean 2021*.
10. Représente la moyenne non pondérée pour 37 pays de l'OCDE.

StatLink https://doi.org/10.1787/888934283443

Table 4.9. **Taxes on property (4000) as percentage of GDP**
Tableau 4.9. **Impôts sur le patrimoine (4000) en pourcentage du PIB**

	1999	2000	2009	2010	2014	2015	2016	2017	2018	2019
Botswana	..	..	0.0	0.1	0.0	0.0	0.0	0.0	0.0	0.0
Burkina Faso	..	0.0	0.1	0.1	0.2	0.1	0.2	0.1	0.1	0.1
Cabo Verde	0.7	0.8	0.7	0.5	0.4	0.4	0.3	0.3	0.4	0.3
Cameroon / Cameroun	0.1	0.2	0.1	0.1	0.1	0.1	0.2	0.2	0.1	0.1
Chad / Tchad	..	..	..	0.5	0.4	0.2	0.1	0.1	0.1	0.4
Congo	0.0	0.1	0.1	0.0	0.1	0.2	0.1	0.1	0.1	0.2
Congo, Dem. Rep. / Congo, Rép. dém.[1]	..	..	..	0.0	0.0	0.0	0.0	0.0	0.1	0.1
Côte d'Ivoire	0.3	0.3	0.3	0.3	0.3	0.3	0.4	0.3	0.4	0.4
Egypt / Égypte	..	..	0.1	0.1	0.1	0.1	0.1	0.1	0.1	0.1
Equatorial Guinea / Guinée équatoriale	..	..	0.0	0.0	0.0	0.0	0.0	0.0	0.0	0.0
Eswatini	0.2	0.3	0.2	0.3	0.3	0.3	0.3	0.4	0.5	0.5
Ghana	..	..	..	..	..	..	..	..	..	..
Kenya	..	..	0.0	0.0	0.0	0.0	0.0	0.0	0.0	0.0
Lesotho	..	..	..	..	..	..	..	..	..	..
Madagascar	0.1	0.1	0.1	0.1	0.1	0.1	0.1	0.1	0.1	0.1
Malawi	..	..	..	..	..	..	..	..	..	..
Mali	0.2	0.1	0.2	0.2	0.2	0.2	0.3	0.4	0.3	0.3
Mauritania / Mauritanie[2]	..	..	0.5	0.4	0.5	0.7	0.6	0.5	0.5	0.4
Mauritius / Maurice[3]	1.3	1.2	1.1	1.1	1.1	1.0	1.1	1.1	1.0	1.0
Morocco / Maroc	..	1.3	1.5	1.6	1.9	2.0	2.0	1.6	1.5	1.4
Namibia / Namibie	..	..	0.3	0.2	0.2	0.2	0.2	0.2	0.1	0.1
Niger	..	0.1	0.1	0.1	0.0	0.0	0.0	0.0	0.1	0.1
Nigeria / Nigéria[1]	..	..	..	..	..	..	..	..	..	..
Rwanda	0.0	0.0	0.0	0.0	0.0	0.0	0.0	0.0	0.0	0.0
Senegal / Sénégal	0.3	0.3	0.4	0.5	0.4	0.4	0.5	0.4	0.4	0.4
Seychelles	..	..	0.3	1.1	0.5	0.8	0.5	0.5	0.6	0.8
South Africa / Afrique du Sud	0.4	0.4	1.3	1.3	1.4	1.3	1.4	1.6	1.6	1.7
Togo	..	0.0	0.1	0.1	0.1	0.1	0.1	0.1	0.1	0.1
Tunisia / Tunisie	..	0.3	0.3	0.3	0.3	0.3	0.3	0.3	0.3	0.3
Uganda / Ouganda[1]	..	..	..	..	..	..	..	..	..	..
Africa (30) average / Moyenne Afrique (30)[4]	**..**	**..**	**..**	**0.4**	**0.3**	**0.4**	**0.4**	**0.3**	**0.3**	**0.4**
Asia-Pacific (24) average / Moyenne Asie-Pacifique (24)[5]	**..**	**..**	**..**	**0.7**	**0.7**	**0.7**	**0.7**	**0.7**	**0.7**	**0.7**
LAC average / Moyenne ALC[6]	**0.7**	**0.7**	**0.8**	**0.8**	**0.9**	**0.9**	**0.8**	**0.9**	**0.8**	**0.9**
OECD average / Moyenne OCDE[7]	**1.7**	**1.7**	**1.7**	**1.7**	**1.9**	**1.9**	**2.3**	**1.9**	**1.9**	**..**

.. Not available

Note: The figures include sub-national government tax revenues for Eswatini, Mauritania (for 2009-19), Mauritius, Morocco, Nigeria (only state revenues) and South Africa (for 2003-19). Sub-national government tax revenues are not available in other countries.

1. In Ghana, Lesotho, Malawi, Nigeria and Uganda, revenues from property taxes are mainly levied by local governments, for which data are not available. In the Democratic Republic of the Congo, only data for property tax revenues levied by the Direction Générale des Recettes Administratives, Judiciaires, Domaniales et de Participation (DGRAD) are available for 2010-19. See the country tables in Chapter 5 for further information.
2. Data are estimated for 2019.
3. The fiscal year for Mauritius changed in 2010 and in 2015. Figures for 2015 needed to be estimated as a result.
4. Represents an unweighted average of the 30 African countries in this publication. The Africa (30) should be interpreted with caution as data for property taxes (category 4000) are not available or are partial in a few countries. See the country tables in Chapter 5 for further information.
5. Represents an unweighted average for 24 Asian and Pacific economies included in the publication *Revenue Statistics in Asia and the Pacific 2021*.
6. Represents an unweighted average for 26 Latin American and Caribbean (LAC) countries included in the publication *Revenue Statistics in Latin America and the Caribbean 2021*.
7. Represents an unweighted average for 37 OECD countries.

.. Non disponible

Note : Les chiffres incluent les recettes fiscales collectées par les administrations infranationales pour l'Afrique du Sud (pour les années 2003 à 2019), Eswatini, le Maroc, Maurice, la Mauritanie (pour les années 2009 à 2019) et le Nigéria (recettes des administrations régionales). Les données des recettes fiscales collectées par les administrations infranationales ne sont pas disponibles pour les autres pays.

1. Au Ghana, au Lesotho, au Malawi, au Nigéria et en Ouganda, les recettes provenant des impôts sur le patrimoine sont principalement perçues par les administrations locales pour lesquelles les données ne sont pas disponibles. En République démocratique du Congo, seules les données des recettes relatives aux impôts sur le patrimoine qui sont prélevées par la Direction Générale des Recettes Administratives, Judiciaires, Domaniales et de Participation (DGRAD) sont disponibles pour la période 2010-18. Voir les tableaux des pays au chapitre 5 pour plus d'informations.
2. Les données sont estimées pour 2019.
3. L'année fiscale pour Maurice a changé en 2010 et en 2015. Les chiffres pour 2015 ont dû être estimés en conséquence.
4. Représente une moyenne non pondérée des 30 pays africains inclus dans cette publication. Il convient d'interpréter cette moyenne avec prudence à cause de valeurs manquantes ou incomplètes pour la rubrique 4000 (taxes sur le patrimoine). Veuillez voir les tableaux de pays au chapitre 5 pour plus d'informations.
5. Représente la moyenne non pondérée pour 24 économies de l'Asie et du Pacifique incluses dans la publication *Revenue Statistics in Asia and the Pacific 2021*.
6. Représente la moyenne non pondérée pour 26 pays d'Amérique latine et des Caraïbes (ALC) inclus dans la publication *Revenue Statistics in Latin America and the Caribbean 2021*.
7. Représente la moyenne non pondérée pour 37 pays de l'OCDE.

StatLink https://doi.org/10.1787/888934283462

Table 4.10. **Taxes on property (4000) as percentage of total taxation**
Tableau 4.10. **Impôts sur le patrimoine (4000) en pourcentage du total des recettes fiscales**

	1999	2000	2009	2010	2014	2015	2016	2017	2018	2019
Botswana	..	..	0.2	0.4	0.2	0.3	0.3	0.3	0.3	0.3
Burkina Faso	..	0.4	0.8	0.7	1.1	0.8	1.0	0.7	0.7	0.7
Cabo Verde	4.4	5.3	3.8	2.7	2.6	2.0	1.5	1.5	1.9	1.6
Cameroon / Cameroun	1.0	1.6	1.1	1.1	0.8	0.9	1.1	1.1	0.8	0.8
Chad / Tchad	..	..	..	3.1	3.3	3.2	2.8	1.6	1.5	4.5
Congo	0.8	1.3	0.9	0.7	0.7	1.7	0.5	0.7	1.8	2.8
Congo, Dem. Rep. / Congo, Rép. dém.[1]	..	..	..	0.6	0.4	0.4	0.5	0.5	0.7	0.7
Côte d'Ivoire	2.4	2.8	2.5	2.4	2.7	2.6	2.9	2.6	2.9	3.1
Egypt / Égypte	..	..	0.6	0.6	0.4	0.6	0.6	0.6	0.6	0.8
Equatorial Guinea / Guinée équatoriale	..	..	0.0	0.0	0.0	0.0	0.1	0.0	0.1	0.0
Eswatini	2.1	2.6	1.9	2.0	1.7	1.7	1.6	2.3	2.6	2.6
Ghana	..	..	..	..	..	..	..	..	..	..
Kenya	..	..	0.2	0.2	0.1	0.1	0.1	0.1	0.0	0.0
Lesotho	..	..	..	..	..	..	..	..	..	..
Madagascar	0.7	0.7	0.6	0.5	0.7	0.8	0.7	0.6	0.8	0.5
Malawi	..	..	..	..	..	..	..	..	..	..
Mali	2.0	1.3	1.4	1.6	1.7	1.5	2.1	2.2	2.1	1.8
Mauritania / Mauritanie[2]	..	..	5.1	4.3	3.2	4.8	4.1	3.3	2.9	2.7
Mauritius / Maurice[3]	7.1	6.4	5.9	5.7	5.7	5.2	5.7	5.5	4.9	4.6
Morocco / Maroc	..	5.9	5.3	5.9	7.0	7.4	7.2	5.6	5.3	5.1
Namibia / Namibie	..	..	1.6	0.9	1.0	1.0	0.8	0.8	0.6	0.5
Niger	..	1.1	0.5	0.8	0.2	0.4	0.3	0.4	0.7	1.2
Nigeria / Nigéria[1]	..	..	..	..	..	..	..	..	..	..
Rwanda	0.2	0.2	0.0	0.0	0.0	0.1	0.1	0.1	0.1	0.1
Senegal / Sénégal	2.2	2.0	2.9	3.1	2.5	2.4	2.7	2.5	2.5	2.2
Seychelles	..	..	1.1	3.5	1.7	2.6	1.6	1.5	1.7	2.2
South Africa / Afrique du Sud	1.9	1.8	5.5	5.7	5.5	5.0	5.4	6.0	5.9	6.3
Togo	..	0.4	0.8	0.8	0.8	0.8	0.8	0.7	0.8	0.8
Tunisia / Tunisie	..	1.1	1.1	1.0	1.0	1.1	1.1	1.0	0.9	0.9
Uganda / Ouganda[1]	..	..	..	..	..	..	..	..	..	..
Africa (30) average / Moyenne Afrique (30)[4]	**..**	**..**	**..**	**1.9**	**1.8**	**1.9**	**1.8**	**1.7**	**1.7**	**1.9**
Asia-Pacific (24) average / Moyenne Asie-Pacifique (24)[5]	**..**	**..**	**..**	**3.5**	**3.1**	**3.2**	**3.1**	**3.1**	**3.1**	**3.2**
LAC average / Moyenne ALC[6]	**3.9**	**3.7**	**4.2**	**4.0**	**4.1**	**4.0**	**3.8**	**3.8**	**3.7**	**3.8**
OECD average / Moyenne OCDE[7]	**5.5**	**5.5**	**5.6**	**5.5**	**5.8**	**5.8**	**6.6**	**5.9**	**5.6**	**..**

.. Not available

Note: The figures include sub-national government tax revenues for Eswatini, Mauritania (for 2009-19), Mauritius, Morocco, Nigeria (only state revenues) and South Africa (for 2003-19). Sub-national government tax revenues are not available in other countries.

1. In Ghana, Lesotho, Malawi, Nigeria and Uganda, revenues from property taxes are mainly levied by local governments, for which data are not available. In the Democratic Republic of the Congo, only data for property tax revenues levied by the Direction Générale des Recettes Administratives, Judiciaires, Domaniales et de Participation (DGRAD) are available for 2010-19. See the country tables in Chapter 5 for further information.
2. Data are estimated for 2019.
3. The fiscal year for Mauritius changed in 2010 and in 2015. Figures for 2015 needed to be estimated as a result.
4. Represents an unweighted average of the 30 African countries in this publication. The Africa (30) should be interpreted with caution as data for property taxes (category 4000) are not available or are partial in a few countries. See the country tables in Chapter 5 for further information.
5. Represents an unweighted average for 24 Asian and Pacific economies included in the publication *Revenue Statistics in Asia and the Pacific 2021*.
6. Represents an unweighted average for 26 Latin American and Caribbean (LAC) countries included in the publication *Revenue Statistics in Latin America and the Caribbean 2021*.
7. Represents an unweighted average for 37 OECD countries.

.. Non disponible

Note : Les chiffres incluent les recettes fiscales collectées par les administrations infranationales pour l'Afrique du Sud (pour les années 2003 à 2019), Eswatini, le Maroc, Maurice, la Mauritanie (pour les années 2009 à 2019) et le Nigéria (recettes des administrations régionales). Les données des recettes fiscales collectées par les administrations infranationales ne sont pas disponibles pour les autres pays.

1. Au Ghana, au Lesotho, au Malawi, au Nigéria et en Ouganda, les recettes provenant des impôts sur le patrimoine sont principalement perçues par les administrations locales pour lesquelles les données ne sont pas disponibles. En République démocratique du Congo, seules les données des recettes relatives aux impôts sur le patrimoine qui sont prélevées par la Direction Générale des Recettes Administratives, Judiciaires, Domaniales et de Participation (DGRAD) sont disponibles pour la période 2010-19. Voir les tableaux des pays au chapitre 5 pour plus d'informations.
2. Les données sont estimées pour 2019.
3. L'année fiscale pour Maurice a changé en 2010 et en 2015. Les chiffres pour 2015 ont dû être estimés en conséquence.
4. Représente une moyenne non pondérée des 30 pays africains inclus dans cette publication. Il convient d'interpréter cette moyenne avec prudence à cause de valeurs manquantes ou incomplètes pour la rubrique 4000 (taxes sur le patrimoine). Veuillez voir les tableaux de pays au chapitre 5 pour plus d'informations.
5. Représente la moyenne non pondérée pour 24 économies de l'Asie et du Pacifique incluses dans la publication *Revenue Statistics in Asia and the Pacific 2021*.
6. Représente la moyenne non pondérée pour 26 pays d'Amérique latine et des Caraïbes (ALC) inclus dans la publication *Revenue Statistics in Latin America and the Caribbean 2021*.
7. Représente la moyenne non pondérée pour 37 pays de l'OCDE.

StatLink https://doi.org/10.1787/888934283481

Table 4.11. **Taxes on goods and services (5000) as percentage of GDP**
Tableau 4.11. **Impôts sur les biens et services (5000) en pourcentage du PIB**

	1999	2000	2009	2010	2014	2015	2016	2017	2018	2019
Botswana	..	..	5.4	5.4	4.3	4.0	4.2	4.7	4.2	4.6
Burkina Faso	..	5.8	8.3	9.4	8.5	9.1	9.4	10.0	10.1	10.4
Cabo Verde	9.2	8.4	11.7	12.2	11.4	12.2	12.4	13.3	14.2	13.6
Cameroon / Cameroun	7.0	7.0	7.5	7.3	8.4	8.4	8.5	9.1	9.1	8.6
Chad / Tchad	..	..	..	2.7	2.8	2.2	2.3	3.0	3.6	3.7
Congo	2.8	1.7	5.0	4.3	6.0	7.3	7.6	6.0	5.3	5.5
Congo, Dem. Rep. / Congo, Rép. dém.	..	0.4	5.3	5.6	5.3	5.4	5.2	3.6	3.4	3.2
Côte d'Ivoire	7.2	6.6	7.8	7.9	7.4	7.9	8.2	8.2	7.8	8.0
Egypt / Égypte	..	..	6.6	6.0	4.8	5.6	5.9	6.6	7.1	7.0
Equatorial Guinea / Guinée équatoriale	..	..	0.8	0.7	0.8	1.2	1.4	1.2	1.3	1.5
Eswatini	3.7	3.7	3.8	4.5	5.2	5.5	5.8	6.1	6.1	6.7
Ghana	..	4.8	5.7	6.0	6.3	7.7	8.7	8.3	7.9	7.1
Kenya	..	..	10.7	10.4	10.1	9.7	9.6	9.7	9.1	9.3
Lesotho	..	..	6.8	7.6	7.7	7.3	7.2	7.9	9.0	8.6
Madagascar	7.9	7.8	6.9	7.1	6.5	6.9	7.2	8.0	8.1	7.9
Malawi	..	..	8.9	8.8	9.9	8.6	8.7	9.6	9.5	9.8
Mali	8.2	8.2	8.8	8.5	7.4	8.9	9.8	9.8	7.7	9.8
Mauritania / Mauritanie	..	..	5.8	5.3	8.0	8.1	8.4	8.7	10.0	8.6
Mauritius / Maurice[1]	13.1	13.6	11.9	12.2	12.6	12.5	12.6	12.6	13.3	13.4
Morocco / Maroc	..	12.3	11.9	12.9	11.9	11.3	11.3	11.7	12.1	12.1
Namibia / Namibie	..	..	6.6	6.1	7.5	8.0	7.7	7.2	6.8	7.1
Niger	..	5.3	6.0	6.1	6.9	7.5	6.4	5.7	7.4	6.6
Nigeria / Nigéria	..	..	..	1.9	1.8	1.6	1.5	1.6	1.6	1.6
Rwanda	7.5	7.0	7.1	7.1	8.6	9.0	8.9	8.9	9.1	9.6
Senegal / Sénégal	9.0	9.1	9.9	10.1	10.3	10.3	10.5	10.0	10.0	10.2
Seychelles	..	..	16.5	17.8	19.3	18.6	20.2	19.7	20.7	21.1
South Africa / Afrique du Sud	8.3	8.0	8.5	9.1	10.2	10.7	10.5	10.1	10.6	10.5
Togo	..	5.2	8.1	8.6	12.1	12.8	12.7	12.4	11.1	11.4
Tunisia / Tunisie	..	12.7	10.7	10.7	11.3	10.8	10.6	11.1	12.7	12.2
Uganda / Ouganda	7.2	6.8	6.0	5.6	6.1	6.8	7.2	7.4	7.7	7.9
Africa (30) average / Moyenne Afrique (30)[2]	**..**	**..**	**..**	**7.6**	**8.0**	**8.2**	**8.4**	**8.4**	**8.5**	**8.6**
Asia-Pacific (24) average / Moyenne Asie-Pacifique (24)[3]	**..**	**..**	**..**	**9.5**	**10.1**	**10.0**	**9.7**	**10.1**	**10.4**	**9.9**
LAC average / Moyenne ALC[4]	**10.0**	**10.1**	**10.3**	**10.5**	**10.9**	**11.1**	**11.3**	**11.3**	**11.4**	**11.4**
OECD average / Moyenne OCDE[5]	**11.0**	**10.8**	**10.3**	**10.6**	**10.8**	**10.9**	**11.0**	**11.0**	**10.9**	**..**

.. Not available

Note: The figures include sub-national government tax revenues for Eswatini, Mauritania (for 2009-19), Mauritius, Morocco, Nigeria (only state revenues) and South Africa (for 2003-19). Sub-national government tax revenues are not available in other countries.

1. The fiscal year for Mauritius changed in 2010 and in 2015. Figures for 2015 needed to be estimated as a result.
2. Represents an unweighted average of the 30 African countries in this publication.
3. Represents an unweighted average for 24 Asian and Pacific economies included in the publication *Revenue Statistics in Asia and the Pacific 2021*.
4. Represents an unweighted average for 26 Latin American and Caribbean (LAC) countries included in the publication *Revenue Statistics in Latin America and the Caribbean 2021*.
5. Represents an unweighted average for 37 OECD countries.

.. Non disponible

Note : Les chiffres incluent les recettes fiscales collectées par les administrations infranationales pour l'Afrique du Sud (pour les années 2003 à 2019), Eswatini, le Maroc, Maurice, la Mauritanie (pour les années 2009 à 2019) et le Nigéria (recettes des administrations régionales). Les données des recettes fiscales collectées par les administrations infranationales ne sont pas disponibles pour les autres pays.

1. L'année fiscale pour Maurice a changé en 2010 et en 2015. Les chiffres pour 2015 ont dû être estimés en conséquence.
2. Représente une moyenne non pondérée des 30 pays africains inclus dans cette publication.
3. Représente la moyenne non pondérée pour 24 économies de l'Asie et du Pacifique incluses dans la publication *Revenue Statistics in Asia and the Pacific 2021*.
4. Représente la moyenne non pondérée pour 26 pays d'Amérique latine et des Caraïbes (ALC) inclus dans la publication *Revenue Statistics in Latin America and the Caribbean 2021*.
5. Représente la moyenne non pondérée pour 37 pays de l'OCDE.

StatLink https://doi.org/10.1787/888934283500

Table 4.12. **Taxes on goods and services (5000) as percentage of total taxation**
Tableau 4.12. **Impôts sur les biens et services (5000) en pourcentage du total des recettes fiscales**

	1999	2000	2009	2010	2014	2015	2016	2017	2018	2019
Botswana	..	..	34.4	34.3	28.1	31.7	30.2	38.4	35.0	36.7
Burkina Faso	..	57.0	65.6	67.3	59.8	62.8	61.2	62.2	61.4	59.1
Cabo Verde	60.0	53.8	63.8	66.2	67.5	65.3	65.9	66.0	66.5	66.3
Cameroon / Cameroun	64.7	62.2	56.8	60.1	58.3	57.0	59.9	62.8	62.2	60.9
Chad / Tchad	..	..	..	18.3	26.7	37.6	49.2	48.5	45.2	45.4
Congo	45.6	45.5	63.2	62.2	62.5	57.1	57.6	56.0	70.0	67.8
Congo, Dem. Rep. / Congo, Rép. dém.	..	65.3	66.9	65.6	55.3	54.5	60.5	51.9	44.4	42.7
Côte d'Ivoire	62.5	59.8	64.5	66.0	60.6	62.7	62.1	62.0	59.6	61.0
Egypt / Égypte	..	..	40.0	40.0	34.0	38.2	40.8	43.7	47.6	49.0
Equatorial Guinea / Guinée équatoriale	..	..	6.0	9.4	8.1	10.3	20.0	18.7	19.2	15.1
Eswatini	32.2	34.8	29.5	32.6	35.2	36.6	35.8	35.7	35.0	36.3
Ghana	..	61.7	54.2	55.3	51.7	58.9	63.8	60.2	55.8	52.2
Kenya	..	..	58.8	58.1	52.2	52.0	51.7	52.5	52.6	53.7
Lesotho	..	..	39.9	43.7	40.8	37.7	37.6	40.3	41.2	41.7
Madagascar	80.9	81.3	72.8	74.3	72.4	72.4	72.1	73.2	71.1	70.2
Malawi	..	..	58.4	55.6	55.1	51.2	51.5	51.3	51.9	53.2
Mali	71.5	72.0	61.0	60.4	52.8	58.7	59.2	58.6	57.7	58.0
Mauritania / Mauritanie	..	..	56.4	54.0	53.0	55.4	59.2	60.1	62.6	61.5
Mauritius / Maurice[1]	72.9	74.6	61.8	64.4	65.2	64.9	64.6	63.6	65.2	63.6
Morocco / Maroc	..	55.7	43.1	46.8	42.8	42.2	41.2	41.9	42.9	42.7
Namibia / Namibie	..	..	36.7	32.9	35.3	37.2	36.4	35.1	34.9	35.1
Niger	..	72.0	58.3	62.9	55.9	59.8	60.9	60.2	65.9	63.4
Nigeria / Nigéria	..	..	..	25.8	23.3	26.4	29.0	27.8	25.4	26.7
Rwanda	69.6	68.8	58.7	57.4	56.3	55.9	54.7	54.8	53.6	54.2
Senegal / Sénégal	71.5	69.2	66.3	63.4	63.7	63.1	61.9	61.3	60.7	61.5
Seychelles	..	..	57.2	57.8	63.1	62.4	62.7	61.1	59.9	61.5
South Africa / Afrique du Sud	39.4	39.9	36.6	39.5	40.0	40.3	40.1	38.5	39.8	40.0
Togo	..	74.8	75.0	78.4	78.5	80.1	77.5	78.5	76.3	75.9
Tunisia / Tunisie	..	51.8	39.9	39.5	36.4	35.8	35.8	35.8	39.7	35.6
Uganda / Ouganda	81.8	81.6	70.6	67.3	65.7	65.1	65.1	64.9	65.5	64.8
Africa (30) average / Moyenne Afrique (30)[2]	**..**	**..**	**..**	**52.0**	**50.0**	**51.1**	**52.3**	**52.2**	**52.3**	**51.9**
Asia-Pacific (24) average / Moyenne Asie-Pacifique (24)[3]	**..**	**..**	**..**	**51.3**	**54.1**	**51.4**	**51.5**	**51.2**	**50.9**	**49.8**
LAC average / Moyenne ALC[4]	**57.5**	**56.6**	**50.4**	**51.2**	**50.1**	**50.4**	**50.6**	**50.7**	**50.3**	**49.8**
OECD average / Moyenne OCDE[5]	**33.9**	**33.6**	**33.0**	**33.8**	**33.2**	**33.2**	**33.0**	**33.0**	**32.7**	**..**

.. Not available

Note: The figures include sub-national government tax revenues for Eswatini, Mauritania (for 2009-19), Mauritius, Morocco, Nigeria (only state revenues) and South Africa (for 2003-19). Sub-national government tax revenues are not available in other countries.

1. The fiscal year for Mauritius changed in 2010 and in 2015. Figures for 2015 needed to be estimated as a result.
2. Represents an unweighted average of the 30 African countries in this publication.
3. Represents an unweighted average for 24 Asian and Pacific economies included in the publication *Revenue Statistics in Asia and the Pacific 2021*.
4. Represents an unweighted average for 26 Latin American and Caribbean (LAC) countries included in the publication *Revenue Statistics in Latin America and the Caribbean 2021*.
5. Represents an unweighted average for 37 OECD countries.

.. Non disponible

Note : Les chiffres incluent les recettes fiscales collectées par les administrations infranationales pour l'Afrique du Sud (pour les années 2003 à 2019), Eswatini, le Maroc, Maurice, la Mauritanie (pour les années 2009 à 2019) et le Nigéria (recettes des administrations régionales). Les données des recettes fiscales collectées par les administrations infranationales ne sont pas disponibles pour les autres pays.

1. L'année fiscale pour Maurice a changé en 2010 et en 2015. Les chiffres pour 2015 ont dû être estimés en conséquence.
2. Représente une moyenne non pondérée des 30 pays africains inclus dans cette publication.
3. Représente la moyenne non pondérée pour 24 économies de l'Asie et du Pacifique incluses dans la publication *Revenue Statistics in Asia and the Pacific 2021*.
4. Représente la moyenne non pondérée pour 26 pays d'Amérique latine et des Caraïbes (ALC) inclus dans la publication *Revenue Statistics in Latin America and the Caribbean 2021*.
5. Représente la moyenne non pondérée pour 37 pays de l'OCDE.

StatLink https://doi.org/10.1787/888934283519

Table 4.13. **Taxes on general consumption (5110) as percentage of GDP**
Tableau 4.13. **Impôts généraux sur la consommation (5110) en pourcentage du PIB**

	1999	2000	2009	2010	2014	2015	2016	2017	2018	2019
Botswana	..	..	5.0	4.9	3.8	3.6	3.8	4.2	3.8	4.1
Burkina Faso	..	2.9	4.7	4.6	4.6	4.9	5.0	5.4	5.4	5.8
Cabo Verde	0.0	0.0	6.9	7.2	6.1	6.8	6.6	7.3	8.2	7.7
Cameroon / Cameroun	3.4	3.6	4.0	3.8	4.8	4.8	4.8	5.2	5.4	5.0
Chad / Tchad	..	..	..	1.4	1.5	1.0	1.4	1.7	1.2	1.5
Congo	2.5	1.5	2.7	2.4	3.4	4.0	4.2	3.5	3.3	3.2
Congo, Dem. Rep. / Congo, Rép. dém.	..	0.1	3.0	3.0	2.4	2.5	2.8	2.0	1.9	1.7
Côte d'Ivoire	2.5	2.4	2.7	2.9	2.6	2.6	2.5	2.7	2.8	2.9
Egypt / Égypte	..	..	3.3	3.1	2.4	2.7	2.6	3.2	3.5	3.7
Equatorial Guinea / Guinée équatoriale	..	..	0.6	0.6	0.5	0.8	0.8	0.7	0.7	0.9
Eswatini	3.0	3.0	3.2	3.8	3.9	4.0	4.2	4.2	4.3	4.6
Ghana	..	2.0	3.2	3.3	3.6	4.2	4.0	4.0	3.8	3.6
Kenya	..	..	4.8	4.7	4.6	4.5	4.4	4.4	4.2	4.2
Lesotho	..	..	6.8	7.6	7.7	7.3	7.2	7.9	9.0	8.6
Madagascar	4.2	4.5	4.7	4.8	4.5	4.7	4.9	5.5	5.5	5.4
Malawi	..	..	4.3	4.0	5.3	4.8	4.7	5.2	5.2	5.3
Mali	3.6	3.8	5.1	4.9	3.9	4.2	4.7	4.9	3.9	5.3
Mauritania / Mauritanie	..	..	3.4	3.3	5.0	4.7	4.3	4.3	5.0	4.4
Mauritius / Maurice[1]	4.3	4.6	6.6	6.8	6.7	6.8	6.8	6.8	7.0	7.1
Morocco / Maroc	..	5.2	7.4	8.3	8.1	7.6	7.5	7.7	7.8	7.4
Namibia / Namibie	..	..	6.5	6.0	7.4	7.8	7.4	6.9	6.3	6.4
Niger	..	2.0	3.6	3.5	4.2	4.5	3.7	3.2	5.0	3.8
Nigeria / Nigéria	..	..	..	1.0	0.9	0.8	0.8	0.8	0.9	0.8
Rwanda	2.1	2.0	3.9	3.7	4.9	4.9	4.8	5.0	5.1	5.6
Senegal / Sénégal	4.5	5.2	5.7	6.0	5.7	5.9	5.8	5.7	5.6	6.1
Seychelles	..	..	6.7	4.0	11.0	10.3	11.0	10.8	12.1	12.2
South Africa / Afrique du Sud	5.1	4.9	5.3	5.6	6.2	6.3	6.2	5.8	6.1	5.9
Togo	..	2.6	4.6	5.0	7.4	7.5	7.6	7.3	6.5	6.7
Tunisia / Tunisie	..	6.2	5.9	6.1	6.5	6.2	5.9	6.2	7.2	7.0
Uganda / Ouganda	2.8	2.7	2.9	2.7	3.0	3.4	3.6	3.6	3.7	3.7
Africa (30) average / Moyenne Afrique (30)[2]	**..**	**..**	**..**	**4.3**	**4.8**	**4.8**	**4.8**	**4.9**	**5.0**	**5.0**
Asia-Pacific (24) average / Moyenne Asie-Pacifique (24)[3]	**..**	**..**	**..**	**4.5**	**5.0**	**5.1**	**4.9**	**5.0**	**5.1**	**5.0**
LAC average / Moyenne ALC[4]	**5.4**	**5.5**	**6.3**	**6.4**	**7.1**	**7.2**	**7.3**	**7.2**	**7.3**	**7.2**
OECD average / Moyenne OCDE[5]	**6.6**	**6.6**	**6.4**	**6.7**	**6.9**	**6.9**	**7.0**	**7.0**	**7.1**	**..**

.. Not available

Note: The figures include sub-national government tax revenues for Eswatini, Mauritania (for 2009-19), Mauritius, Morocco, Nigeria (only state revenues) and South Africa (for 2003-19). Sub-national government tax revenues are not available in other countries.

1. The fiscal year for Mauritius changed in 2010 and in 2015. Figures for 2015 needed to be estimated as a result.
2. Represents an unweighted average of the 30 African countries in this publication.
3. Represents an unweighted average for 24 Asian and Pacific economies included in the publication *Revenue Statistics in Asia and the Pacific 2021*.
4. Represents an unweighted average for 26 Latin American and Caribbean (LAC) countries included in the publication *Revenue Statistics in Latin America and the Caribbean 2021*.
5. Represents an unweighted average for 37 OECD countries.

.. Non disponible

Note : Les chiffres incluent les recettes fiscales collectées par les administrations infranationales pour l'Afrique du Sud (pour les années 2003 à 2019), Eswatini, le Maroc, Maurice, la Mauritanie (pour les années 2009 à 2019) et le Nigéria (recettes des administrations régionales). Les données des recettes fiscales collectées par les administrations infranationales ne sont pas disponibles pour les autres pays.

1. L'année fiscale pour Maurice a changé en 2010 et en 2015. Les chiffres pour 2015 ont dû être estimés en conséquence.
2. Représente une moyenne non pondérée des 30 pays africains inclus dans cette publication.
3. Représente la moyenne non pondérée pour 24 économies de l'Asie et du Pacifique incluses dans la publication *Revenue Statistics in Asia and the Pacific 2021*.
4. Représente la moyenne non pondérée pour 26 pays d'Amérique latine et des Caraïbes (ALC) inclus dans la publication *Revenue Statistics in Latin America and the Caribbean 2021*.
5. Représente la moyenne non pondérée pour 37 pays de l'OCDE.

StatLink https://doi.org/10.1787/888934283538

Table 4.14. **Taxes on general consumption (5110) as percentage of total taxation**
Tableau 4.14. **Impôts généraux sur la consommation (5110) en pourcentage du total des recettes fiscales**

	1999	2000	2009	2010	2014	2015	2016	2017	2018	2019
Botswana	..	..	31.4	31.3	25.3	28.2	27.1	34.0	31.1	32.6
Burkina Faso	..	28.7	37.2	32.8	32.3	33.7	32.8	33.3	32.9	33.1
Cabo Verde	0.0	0.0	37.6	39.3	36.3	36.5	35.5	36.2	38.7	37.5
Cameroon / Cameroun	31.5	32.2	30.8	31.2	33.2	32.9	33.8	36.3	36.8	35.3
Chad / Tchad	..	..	..	9.9	14.4	17.8	30.5	27.9	14.9	18.9
Congo	40.7	40.2	34.1	35.1	35.3	31.5	31.5	32.0	43.0	39.6
Congo, Dem. Rep. / Congo, Rép. dém.	..	18.4	38.1	35.6	25.3	25.8	32.9	29.2	24.9	22.6
Côte d'Ivoire	21.9	21.8	22.0	24.1	21.0	20.3	19.2	20.3	21.4	21.7
Egypt / Égypte	..	..	20.1	20.6	17.2	18.3	18.2	21.2	23.4	25.8
Equatorial Guinea / Guinée équatoriale	..	..	4.9	7.4	4.8	6.3	11.1	11.0	11.3	8.9
Eswatini	26.2	28.0	25.1	27.4	26.0	26.7	26.4	25.0	24.5	25.0
Ghana	..	26.1	30.8	30.0	29.9	32.1	28.9	29.4	26.7	26.4
Kenya	..	..	26.2	26.1	23.9	24.5	23.6	24.1	24.1	24.6
Lesotho	..	..	39.9	43.7	40.8	37.7	37.6	40.3	41.2	41.7
Madagascar	43.0	46.5	49.5	50.7	50.4	49.1	48.6	50.4	48.4	47.7
Malawi	..	..	27.9	25.4	29.5	28.3	27.6	27.7	28.1	29.2
Mali	30.9	33.7	35.6	34.8	28.2	27.9	28.8	29.4	29.4	31.5
Mauritania / Mauritanie	..	..	33.0	33.4	33.2	32.5	30.4	29.7	31.3	31.2
Mauritius / Maurice[1]	23.7	25.3	34.3	36.1	34.6	35.4	35.0	34.1	34.5	33.8
Morocco / Maroc	..	23.6	26.6	30.1	29.2	28.4	27.2	27.4	27.5	26.2
Namibia / Namibie	..	..	36.0	32.1	35.1	36.5	35.2	33.9	32.6	31.8
Niger	..	27.4	35.0	36.7	34.1	35.6	35.2	34.2	45.1	36.8
Nigeria / Nigéria	..	..	..	14.0	11.7	13.3	15.3	14.9	13.6	13.7
Rwanda	19.8	20.0	32.1	29.9	32.3	30.6	29.5	31.0	30.2	31.5
Senegal / Sénégal	35.6	39.6	38.0	37.7	35.4	35.8	33.9	34.8	33.7	37.1
Seychelles	..	..	23.4	13.0	36.0	34.5	34.1	33.4	34.9	35.5
South Africa / Afrique du Sud	24.3	24.6	22.9	24.1	24.4	23.7	23.7	22.2	22.8	22.4
Togo	..	36.9	42.8	45.9	47.8	46.9	46.2	46.0	44.6	44.5
Tunisia / Tunisie	..	25.2	22.1	22.3	21.1	20.3	19.9	19.9	22.8	20.4
Uganda / Ouganda	32.4	33.0	33.7	32.3	32.4	32.3	32.4	31.6	32.0	30.8
Africa (30) average / Moyenne Afrique (30)[2]	**..**	**..**	**..**	**29.8**	**29.4**	**29.4**	**29.7**	**30.0**	**30.2**	**29.9**
Asia-Pacific (24) average / Moyenne Asie-Pacifique (24)[3]	**..**	**..**	**..**	**21.7**	**24.4**	**24.8**	**24.4**	**24.5**	**24.2**	**24.7**
LAC average / Moyenne ALC[4]	**28.6**	**28.7**	**29.8**	**30.1**	**31.5**	**31.5**	**32.0**	**31.7**	**31.9**	**31.4**
OECD average / Moyenne OCDE[5]	**20.2**	**20.4**	**20.5**	**21.3**	**21.3**	**21.1**	**20.9**	**21.2**	**21.2**	**..**

.. Not available

Note: The figures include sub-national government tax revenues for Eswatini, Mauritania (for 2009-19), Mauritius, Morocco, Nigeria (only state revenues) and South Africa (for 2003-19). Sub-national government tax revenues are not available in other countries.

1. The fiscal year for Mauritius changed in 2010 and in 2015. Figures for 2015 needed to be estimated as a result.
2. Represents an unweighted average of the 30 African countries in this publication.
3. Represents an unweighted average for 24 Asian and Pacific economies included in the publication *Revenue Statistics in Asia and the Pacific 2021*.
4. Represents an unweighted average for 26 Latin American and Caribbean (LAC) countries included in the publication *Revenue Statistics in Latin America and the Caribbean 2021*.
5. Represents an unweighted average for 37 OECD countries.

.. Non disponible

Note : Les chiffres incluent les recettes fiscales collectées par les administrations infranationales pour l'Afrique du Sud (pour les années 2003 à 2019), Eswatini, le Maroc, Maurice, la Mauritanie (pour les années 2009 à 2019) et le Nigéria (recettes des administrations régionales). Les données des recettes fiscales collectées par les administrations infranationales ne sont pas disponibles pour les autres pays.

1. L'année fiscale pour Maurice a changé en 2010 et en 2015. Les chiffres pour 2015 ont dû être estimés en conséquence.
2. Représente une moyenne non pondérée des 30 pays africains inclus dans cette publication.
3. Représente la moyenne non pondérée pour 24 économies de l'Asie et du Pacifique incluses dans la publication *Revenue Statistics in Asia and the Pacific 2021*.
4. Représente la moyenne non pondérée pour 26 pays d'Amérique latine et des Caraïbes (ALC) inclus dans la publication *Revenue Statistics in Latin America and the Caribbean 2021*.
5. Représente la moyenne non pondérée pour 37 pays de l'OCDE.

StatLink https://doi.org/10.1787/888934283557

Table 4.15. **Taxes on specific goods and services (5120) as percentage of GDP**
Tableau 4.15. **Impôts sur les biens et services déterminés (5120) en pourcentage du PIB**

	1999	2000	2009	2010	2014	2015	2016	2017	2018	2019
Botswana	..	..	0.2	0.2	0.2	0.3	0.3	0.3	0.2	0.3
Burkina Faso	..	2.2	2.9	2.8	3.3	3.6	3.7	4.0	4.1	3.9
Cabo Verde	9.2	8.4	4.8	5.0	5.3	5.4	5.7	6.0	5.9	5.9
Cameroon / Cameroun	3.6	3.3	3.3	3.4	3.5	3.5	3.6	3.8	3.7	3.6
Chad / Tchad	..	..	..	1.2	1.3	1.1	0.9	1.3	2.2	2.1
Congo	0.3	0.2	2.3	1.9	2.6	3.3	3.4	2.6	2.0	2.2
Congo, Dem. Rep. / Congo, Rép. dém.	..	0.3	2.3	2.4	2.8	2.8	2.3	1.5	1.4	1.4
Côte d'Ivoire	4.5	4.0	4.9	4.7	4.5	5.0	5.3	5.2	4.7	4.9
Egypt / Égypte	..	..	3.2	2.9	2.4	2.9	3.3	3.4	3.6	3.3
Equatorial Guinea / Guinée équatoriale	..	..	0.1	0.2	0.3	0.5	0.6	0.5	0.5	0.6
Eswatini	0.6	0.6	0.4	0.6	1.2	1.4	1.4	1.7	1.7	1.9
Ghana	..	2.8	2.5	2.8	2.7	3.5	4.8	4.2	4.1	3.5
Kenya	..	..	5.8	5.6	5.3	5.0	5.1	5.2	4.9	5.0
Lesotho	..	..	0.0	0.0	0.0	0.0	0.0	0.0	0.0	0.0
Madagascar	3.7	3.3	2.2	2.2	1.9	2.2	2.3	2.5	2.6	2.5
Malawi	..	..	4.7	4.8	4.6	3.9	4.0	4.4	4.4	4.4
Mali	4.6	4.3	3.6	3.6	3.4	4.6	5.0	4.8	3.7	4.4
Mauritania / Mauritanie	..	..	2.3	1.9	2.8	3.2	3.6	3.9	4.5	3.8
Mauritius / Maurice[1]	8.7	8.8	4.3	4.4	4.9	4.7	4.8	4.9	5.3	5.3
Morocco / Maroc	..	6.8	4.2	4.3	3.5	3.4	3.5	3.7	3.8	4.1
Namibia / Namibie	..	..	0.1	0.1	0.0	0.1	0.3	0.2	0.4	0.7
Niger	..	3.1	2.4	2.5	2.7	3.0	2.7	2.4	2.3	2.7
Nigeria / Nigéria	..	..	..	0.8	0.9	0.8	0.7	0.7	0.7	0.8
Rwanda	5.3	4.9	3.2	3.3	3.7	3.9	4.0	3.8	3.9	3.9
Senegal / Sénégal	4.5	3.8	4.2	4.0	4.5	4.4	4.6	4.2	4.4	4.0
Seychelles	..	..	8.6	12.7	7.4	7.3	8.1	7.9	7.7	8.0
South Africa / Afrique du Sud	3.2	3.1	3.0	3.4	3.8	4.2	4.1	4.1	4.3	4.4
Togo	..	2.6	3.5	3.5	4.7	5.2	5.1	5.1	4.6	4.5
Tunisia / Tunisie	..	6.3	4.5	4.4	4.5	4.4	4.5	4.7	5.2	5.0
Uganda / Ouganda	4.1	3.8	3.0	2.7	2.9	3.3	3.5	3.7	3.8	4.0
Africa (30) average / Moyenne Afrique (30)[2]	..	..	..	**3.1**	**3.1**	**3.2**	**3.4**	**3.4**	**3.3**	**3.4**
Asia-Pacific (24) average / Moyenne Asie-Pacifique (24)[3]	..	..	..	**4.6**	**4.5**	**4.4**	**4.3**	**4.6**	**4.8**	**4.5**
LAC average / Moyenne ALC[4]	**4.4**	**4.3**	**3.6**	**3.7**	**3.4**	**3.6**	**3.6**	**3.7**	**3.7**	**3.8**
OECD average / Moyenne OCDE[5]	**3.8**	**3.6**	**3.3**	**3.3**	**3.3**	**3.3**	**3.4**	**3.3**	**3.2**	..

.. Not available

Note: The figures include sub-national government tax revenues for Eswatini, Mauritania (for 2009-19), Mauritius, Morocco, Nigeria (only state revenues) and South Africa (for 2003-19). Sub-national government tax revenues are not available in other countries.

1. The fiscal year for Mauritius changed in 2010 and in 2015. Figures for 2015 needed to be estimated as a result.
2. Represents an unweighted average of the 30 African countries in this publication.
3. Represents an unweighted average for 24 Asian and Pacific economies included in the publication *Revenue Statistics in Asia and the Pacific 2021*.
4. Represents an unweighted average for 26 Latin American and Caribbean (LAC) countries included in the publication *Revenue Statistics in Latin America and the Caribbean 2021*.
5. Represents an unweighted average for 37 OECD countries.

.. Non disponible

Note : Les chiffres incluent les recettes fiscales collectées par les administrations infranationales pour l'Afrique du Sud (pour les années 2003 à 2019), Eswatini, le Maroc, Maurice, la Mauritanie (pour les années 2009 à 2019) et le Nigéria (recettes des administrations régionales). Les données des recettes fiscales collectées par les administrations infranationales ne sont pas disponibles pour les autres pays

1. L'année fiscale pour Maurice a changé en 2010 et en 2015. Les chiffres pour 2015 ont dû être estimés en conséquence.
2. Représente une moyenne non pondérée des 30 pays africains inclus dans cette publication.
3. Représente la moyenne non pondérée pour 24 économies de l'Asie et du Pacifique incluses dans la publication *Revenue Statistics in Asia and the Pacific 2021*.
4. Représente la moyenne non pondérée pour 26 pays d'Amérique latine et des Caraïbes (ALC) inclus dans la publication *Revenue Statistics in Latin America and the Caribbean 2021*.
5. Représente la moyenne non pondérée pour 37 pays de l'OCDE.

StatLink https://doi.org/10.1787/888934283576

Table 4.16. **Taxes on specific goods and services (5120) as percentage of total taxation**
Tableau 4.16. **Impôts sur les biens et services déterminés (5120) en pourcentage du total des recettes fiscales**

	1999	2000	2009	2010	2014	2015	2016	2017	2018	2019
Botswana	..	..	1.4	1.3	1.6	2.2	1.8	2.5	1.8	2.2
Burkina Faso	..	21.7	22.8	20.3	23.0	25.0	24.3	24.7	24.6	22.1
Cabo Verde	60.0	53.8	26.2	26.9	31.3	28.8	30.5	29.7	27.8	28.9
Cameroon / Cameroun	33.0	29.6	25.5	28.4	24.6	23.8	25.7	26.2	25.1	25.3
Chad / Tchad	..	..	..	8.1	12.0	19.1	18.2	20.3	28.4	26.1
Congo	4.6	5.1	29.0	27.1	27.1	25.4	25.9	23.8	26.5	27.8
Congo, Dem. Rep. / Congo, Rép. dém.	..	45.6	28.7	28.5	29.6	28.3	27.1	22.0	18.3	19.2
Côte d'Ivoire	38.9	35.8	40.0	39.5	37.0	40.0	40.5	39.3	35.7	36.9
Egypt / Égypte	..	..	19.7	19.2	16.7	19.9	22.5	22.5	24.1	23.1
Equatorial Guinea / Guinée équatoriale	..	..	1.1	2.0	3.3	4.0	8.8	7.7	7.9	6.2
Eswatini	5.0	5.9	3.0	4.1	8.3	9.0	8.7	10.0	9.7	10.4
Ghana	..	35.6	23.3	25.3	21.8	26.9	34.9	30.8	29.0	25.7
Kenya	..	..	31.8	31.2	27.7	26.9	27.5	28.0	27.9	28.7
Lesotho	..	..	0.0	0.0	0.0	0.0	0.0	0.0	0.0	0.0
Madagascar	37.7	34.4	23.1	23.4	21.8	23.1	23.3	22.6	22.5	22.3
Malawi	..	..	30.5	30.2	25.6	22.9	23.9	23.6	23.8	24.0
Mali	40.2	37.9	25.2	25.3	24.4	30.6	30.1	29.0	27.9	26.2
Mauritania / Mauritanie	..	..	22.3	19.2	18.7	21.8	25.8	26.7	27.8	27.0
Mauritius / Maurice[1]	48.2	48.3	22.2	23.4	25.2	24.3	24.5	24.8	26.2	25.2
Morocco / Maroc	..	30.9	15.3	15.6	12.5	12.7	12.8	13.3	13.5	14.5
Namibia / Namibie	..	..	0.7	0.7	0.2	0.7	1.2	1.1	2.3	3.4
Niger	..	42.9	22.9	25.8	21.5	23.9	25.3	25.5	20.4	26.1
Nigeria / Nigéria	..	..	..	11.6	11.5	12.7	13.3	12.6	11.5	12.6
Rwanda	48.9	47.9	26.3	26.9	23.9	24.4	24.4	23.3	22.9	22.3
Senegal / Sénégal	35.5	29.2	27.8	25.4	27.8	26.8	27.3	26.0	26.5	23.9
Seychelles	..	..	29.8	41.4	24.4	24.4	25.3	24.6	22.3	23.3
South Africa / Afrique du Sud	15.1	15.3	13.0	14.6	14.9	15.9	15.7	15.6	16.2	16.7
Togo	..	37.7	32.0	32.2	30.4	32.8	30.9	32.1	31.2	30.3
Tunisia / Tunisie	..	25.7	17.0	16.3	14.5	14.7	15.1	15.2	16.3	14.6
Uganda / Ouganda	47.1	46.4	35.0	32.9	31.6	31.2	31.4	32.1	32.3	32.9
Africa (30) average / Moyenne Afrique (30)[2]	**..**	**..**	**..**	**20.9**	**19.8**	**20.7**	**21.6**	**21.2**	**21.0**	**20.9**
Asia-Pacific (24) average / Moyenne Asie-Pacifique (24)[3]	**..**	**..**	**..**	**27.1**	**26.6**	**23.8**	**24.2**	**23.9**	**24.2**	**22.6**
LAC average / Moyenne ALC[4]	**27.3**	**26.4**	**18.8**	**19.2**	**16.6**	**17.0**	**16.8**	**17.2**	**16.7**	**16.6**
OECD average / Moyenne OCDE[5]	**11.8**	**11.4**	**10.5**	**10.6**	**10.0**	**10.1**	**10.1**	**9.9**	**9.6**	**..**

.. Not available

Note: The figures include sub-national government tax revenues for Eswatini, Mauritania (for 2009-19), Mauritius, Morocco, Nigeria (only state revenues) and South Africa (for 2003-19). Sub-national government tax revenues are not available in other countries.

1. The fiscal year for Mauritius changed in 2010 and in 2015. Figures for 2015 needed to be estimated as a result.
2. Represents an unweighted average of the 30 African countries in this publication.
3. Represents an unweighted average for 24 Asian and Pacific economies included in the publication *Revenue Statistics in Asia and the Pacific 2021.*
4. Represents an unweighted average for 26 Latin American and Caribbean (LAC) countries included in the publication *Revenue Statistics in Latin America and the Caribbean 2021.*
5. Represents an unweighted average for 37 OECD countries.

.. Non disponible

Note : Les chiffres incluent les recettes fiscales collectées par les administrations infranationales pour l'Afrique du Sud (pour les années 2003 à 2019), Eswatini, le Maroc, Maurice, la Mauritanie (pour les années 2009 à 2019) et le Nigéria (recettes des administrations régionales). Les données des recettes fiscales collectées par les administrations infranationales ne sont pas disponibles pour les autres pays.

1. L'année fiscale pour Maurice a changé en 2010 et en 2015. Les chiffres pour 2015 ont dû être estimés en conséquence.
2. Représente une moyenne non pondérée des 30 pays africains inclus dans cette publication.
3. Représente la moyenne non pondérée pour 24 économies de l'Asie et du Pacifique incluses dans la publication *Revenue Statistics in Asia and the Pacific 2021.*
4. Représente la moyenne non pondérée pour 26 pays d'Amérique latine et des Caraïbes (ALC) inclus dans la publication *Revenue Statistics in Latin America and the Caribbean 2021.*
5. Représente la moyenne non pondérée pour 37 pays de l'OCDE.

StatLink https://doi.org/10.1787/888934283595

Table 4.17. **Gross domestic product for tax reporting years at current prices, in national currency units**

Tableau 4.17. **Produit intérieur brut pour les années de déclaration fiscale à prix courants, en monnaie nationale**

	1999	2000	2009	2010	2014	2015	2016	2017	2018	2019
Botswana[1]	26 404	30 165	76 814	91 395	145 918	152 191	172 949	182 669	192 091	193 515
Burkina Faso	2 086 188	2 108 160	4 444 601	5 002 182	6 884 466	6 995 311	7 598 720	8 227 851	8 997 919	9 225 643
Cabo Verde	67 501	70 536	135 879	138 569	154 436	158 699	165 782	173 097	183 698	195 202
Cameroon / Cameroun	6 589 531	7 179 525	12 285 308	12 948 432	17 276 469	18 285 382	19 344 838	20 328 363	21 492 534	22 769 258
Chad / Tchad	1 069 308	1 115 969	4 385 556	5 290 608	6 912 490	6 474 073	6 047 146	5 854 572	6 127 318	6 406 367
Congo	1 627 099	2 580 266	4 572 805	6 505 751	8 844 629	7 029 660	6 021 964	6 453 235	7 440 618	7 347 988
Congo, Dem. Rep. / Congo, Rép. dém.	229 768	1 317 075	15 101 188	19 536 677	33 223 988	35 111 226	37 517 392	55 676 093	76 495 500	83 190 159
Côte d'Ivoire	10 533 309	10 547 104	15 845 677	17 036 122	24 135 859	27 086 150	28 423 874	29 955 010	32 222 266	34 298 893
Egypt / Égypte[2]	323 434	357 607	1 095 848	1 268 711	2 130 000	2 443 900	2 709 400	3 470 000	4 437 400	5 322 100
Equatorial Guinea / Guinée équatoriale	454 391	822 850	7 095 919	8 072 293	10 746 852	7 795 420	6 661 365	7 084 543	7 375 490	6 459 504
Eswatini[1]	11 102	12 366	30 879	33 123	48 941	52 871	56 771	59 459	62 482	64 716
Ghana	4 735	6 249	48 989	61 596	155 433	180 399	215 077	256 671	300 596	349 480
Kenya[2]	979 764	1 043 127	2 673 373	3 016 495	5 073 867	5 843 416	6 653 575	7 594 403	8 528 977	9 316 235
Lesotho[1]	5 320	5 876	15 153	16 950	27 396	30 419	31 197	30 627	31 914	33 840
Madagascar	5 376 277	6 265 668	18 812 596	20 863 367	30 240 588	33 216 184	37 637 590	41 058 841	46 600 692	52 532 775
Malawi[2]	115 049	157 897	810 853	960 659	2 290 405	2 884 126	3 570 895	4 246 475	4 804 999	5 385 478
Mali	2 117 674	2 103 270	4 812 025	5 288 939	7 093 033	7 747 730	8 311 926	8 922 038	9 481 956	10 140 292
Mauritania / Mauritanie	41 608	42 517	123 695	155 297	199 573	200 221	225 473	241 913	251 497	290 978
Mauritius / Maurice[2]	108 648	121 023	288 005	307 957	392 062	409 893	422 329	445 983	469 229	489 802
Morocco / Maroc	408 177	412 897	748 483	784 624	925 376	987 950	1 013 229	1 063 045	1 108 463	1 151 170
Namibia / Namibie[1]	22 295	27 979	77 060	84 476	137 632	148 941	161 173	173 930	181 065	179 407
Niger	1 556 847	1 586 921	3 448 075	3 875 000	5 346 046	5 724 873	6 135 410	6 497 014	7 134 254	7 564 953
Nigeria / Nigéria	5 307 362	6 897 482	44 285 561	55 469 351	90 136 985	95 177 736	102 575 419	114 899 251	129 086 908	145 639 140
Rwanda	607 000	676 000	3 236 000	3 585 000	5 645 000	6 178 000	6 876 000	7 694 000	8 291 000	9 105 000
Senegal / Sénégal	4 057 714	4 270 612	7 593 295	7 976 735	9 775 039	10 508 650	11 283 396	12 191 796	12 840 090	13 655 367
Seychelles	3 328	3 513	11 533	11 705	17 119	18 340	18 989	20 858	21 540	22 192
South Africa / Afrique du Sud[3]	925 690	1 053 138	2 794 228	3 055 613	4 133 873	4 420 793	4 759 555	5 078 190	5 357 640	5 605 034
Togo	1 456 906	1 429 225	2 144 003	2 289 158	3 047 841	3 334 957	3 574 400	3 713 600	3 951 400	4 230 600
Tunisia / Tunisie	27 216	29 433	58 677	63 055	80 866	84 689	89 789	95 865	106 242	114 939
Uganda / Ouganda[2]	10 794 382	12 067 688	43 759 280	51 348 000	86 994 500	92 874 000	99 889 500	109 205 000	120 330 500	132 780 000

1. The GDP for Botswana, Eswatini and Namibia are adjusted using the following formula: GDP(n)*3/4+GDP(n+1))/4 in order to make them correspond more closely to an April(n)-to-March(n+1) fiscal year. The GDP for Lesotho is not adjusted because it is already reported on an April-March fiscal year basis in the *IMF World Economic Outlook*.
2. The GDP for Kenya, Malawi and Uganda in all years and for Mauritius in the years preceding 2010 and from 2016 are adjusted using the formula GDP(n)/2+GDP(n-1)/2. This is done in order to make the value of the GDP correspond more closely to a July(n-1)-to-June(n) fiscal year. The GDP for Egypt is not adjusted because it is already reported on a July-June fiscal year basis in the IMF World Economic Outlook. The GDP for Mauritius is not adjusted from 2010 to 2015 because public finance data are reported on a calendar year for those years.
3. Statistics South Africa released new GDP estimates in August 2021 that took into account updates and re-basing of its national accounting methodology. These new figures are between 8.6% and 12.4% higher than the GDP figures used in the 2020 edition. The total tax-to-GDP ratios for South Africa in the 2021 edition are therefore between 1.9 p.p. and 2.8 p.p. lower than they would had they been calculated using the same GDP figures used in the 2020 edition.

Source: IMF, *World Economic Outlook*, April 2021; South Africa: Statistics South Africa.

1. Le PIB pour Botswana, Eswatini, et la Namibie est ajusté selon la formule PIB(n)*3/4+PIB(n+1))/4 afin de le faire correspondre le mieux possible à une année fiscale de avril (n) à mars (n+1). Le PIB du Lesotho n'est pas ajusté car il est déjà publié sur la base d'un exercice fiscal avril-mars dans les *Perspectives de l'économie mondiale du FMI*.
2. Le PIB pour le Kenya, le Malawi et l'Ouganda, pour toutes les années et pour Maurice dans les années antérieures à 2010 et à partir de 2016, est ajusté selon la formule suivante : PIB(n)/2+PIB(n-1)/2 afin de le faire correspondre le mieux possible à une année fiscale de juillet (n-1) à juin (n). Le PIB de l'Égypte n'est pas ajusté car il est déjà publié sur la base de l'exercice juillet-juin dans les Perspectives de l'économie mondiale du FMI. Le PIB de Maurice n'est pas ajusté de 2010 à 2015 car les données de finances publiques sont reportées sur une année civile pour ces années.
3. Statistics South Africa a publié de nouvelles estimations du PIB qui tiennent compte des mises à jour et du re-basement de sa méthodologie de comptabilité nationale en août 2021. Ces nouveaux chiffres sont entre 8.6 % et 12.4 % plus élevés que les chiffres du PIB de l'édition 2020. Les ratios impôt total/PIB de l'Afrique du Sud dans l'édition 2021 sont donc inférieurs de 1.9 à 2.8 p.p. à ce qu'ils auraient été s'ils avaient été calculés à partir du PIB utilisé dans l'édition 2020.

Source : FMI, *Perspectives de l'économie mondiale, avril 2021*; Afrique du Sud : Statistics South Africa.

StatLink https://doi.org/10.1787/888934283614

Table 4.18. **Gross domestic product for tax reporting years at current prices, in millions of US dollars at market exchange rates**

Tableau 4.18. **Produit intérieur brut pour les années de déclaration fiscale à prix courants, en monnaie millions de dollars US aux taux de change du marché**

	1999	2000	2009	2010	2014	2015	2016	2017	2018	2019
Botswana[1]	5 564	5 731	10 902	13 444	15 806	14 748	16 089	17 703	18 582	13 754
Burkina Faso	3 388	2 961	9 440	10 118	13 947	11 833	12 819	14 165	16 207	15 746
Cabo Verde	657	609	1 698	1 664	1 860	1 597	1 663	1 770	1 967	1 982
Cameroon / Cameroun	10 695	9 802	26 094	26 191	34 999	30 932	32 635	34 997	38 712	38 863
Chad / Tchad	1 739	1 572	9 315	10 701	14 003	10 952	10 202	10 079	11 036	10 934
Congo	2 646	3 624	9 713	13 159	17 918	11 891	10 159	11 110	13 402	12 542
Congo, Dem. Rep. / Congo, Rép. dém.	19 147	19 077	18 495	21 541	35 911	37 915	36 640	37 615	47 099	50 418
Côte d'Ivoire	17 114	14 851	33 693	34 431	48 882	45 815	47 964	51 588	58 011	58 539
Egypt / Égypte[2]	95 039	104 752	198 316	230 024	305 567	332 075	332 484	236 528	250 253	302 335
Equatorial Guinea / Guinée équatoriale	738	1 159	15 088	16 314	21 765	13 185	11 241	12 201	13 278	11 025
Eswatini[1]	1 758	1 690	3 807	4 535	4 334	3 999	3 963	4 472	4 617	3 353
Ghana	17 756	11 467	34 254	43 043	53 173	48 595	54 989	58 978	65 518	66 998
Kenya[2]	15 046	14 245	36 458	38 511	58 336	62 891	66 713	74 043	83 349	91 606
Lesotho[1]	871	847	1 937	2 356	2 477	2 207	2 219	2 356	2 320	2 289
Madagascar	4 278	4 629	9 617	9 983	12 523	11 323	11 849	13 176	13 974	14 519
Malawi[2]	3 058	3 051	5 758	6 576	5 744	6 229	5 947	5 861	6 571	7 287
Mali	3 444	2 963	10 221	10 698	14 369	13 106	14 022	15 360	17 079	17 308
Mauritania / Mauritanie	1 986	1 780	4 725	5 637	6 615	6 182	6 414	6 784	7 048	7 930
Mauritius / Maurice[2]	4 416	4 702	9 560	10 004	12 803	11 692	11 962	12 746	13 721	14 115
Morocco / Maroc	41 632	38 859	92 897	93 217	110 081	101 179	103 312	109 683	118 096	119 701
Namibia / Namibie[1]	3 515	3 821	9 506	11 566	12 188	11 267	11 260	13 080	13 389	9 406
Niger	2 532	2 235	7 324	7 838	10 830	9 684	10 350	11 185	12 850	12 912
Nigeria / Nigéria	57 477	67 824	297 458	369 062	568 499	492 437	404 649	375 745	421 737	448 120
Rwanda	1 797	1 718	5 694	6 148	8 272	8 585	8 734	9 253	9 629	10 123
Senegal / Sénégal	6 599	6 016	16 128	16 134	19 802	17 777	19 035	20 989	23 127	23 307
Seychelles	623	615	847	970	1 343	1 377	1 426	1 528	1 542	1 580
South Africa / Afrique du Sud[3]	151 426	151 855	331 184	417 315	381 195	346 663	323 493	381 317	404 673	387 849
Togo	2 370	2 014	4 554	4 630	6 174	5 641	6 030	6 393	7 117	7 221
Tunisia / Tunisie	22 943	21 474	43 466	44 054	47 634	43 172	41 801	39 627	40 139	39 169
Uganda / Ouganda[2]	8 027	7 789	23 263	24 395	32 727	30 284	28 501	30 470	32 739	35 942

1. The GDP for Botswana, Eswatini and Namibia are adjusted using the following formula: GDP(n)*3/4+GDP(n+1))/4 in order to make them correspond more closely to an April(n)-to-March(n+1) fiscal year. The GDP for Lesotho is not adjusted because it is already reported on an April-March fiscal year basis in the *IMF World Economic Outlook*.
2. The GDP for Kenya, Malawi and Uganda in all years and for Mauritius in the years preceding 2010 and from 2016 are adjusted using the formula GDP(n)/2+GDP(n-1)/2. This is done in order to make the value of the GDP correspond more closely to a July(n-1)-to-June(n) fiscal year. The GDP for Egypt is not adjusted because it is already reported on a July-June fiscal year basis in the IMF World Economic Outlook. The GDP for Mauritius is not adjusted from 2010 to 2015 because public finance data are reported on a calendar year for those years.
3. Statistics South Africa released new GDP estimates in August 2021 that took into account updates and re-basing of its national accounting methodology. These new figures are between 8.6% and 12.4% higher than the GDP figures used in the 2020 edition. The total tax-to-GDP ratios for South Africa in the 2021 edition are therefore between 1.9 p.p. and 2.8 p.p. lower than they would had they been calculated using the same GDP figures used in the 2020 edition.

Source: IMF, *World Economic Outlook*, April 2021; South Africa: Statistics South Africa.

1. Le PIB pour Botswana, Eswatini, et la Namibie est ajusté selon la formule PIB(n)*3/4+PIB(n+1))/4 afin de le faire correspondre le mieux possible à une année fiscale de avril (n) à mars (n+1). Le PIB du Lesotho n'est pas ajusté car il est déjà publié sur la base d'un exercice fiscal avril-mars dans les *Perspectives de l'économie mondiale du FMI*.
2. Le PIB pour le Kenya, le Malawi et l'Ouganda, pour toutes les années et pour Maurice dans les années antérieures à 2010 et à partir de 2016, est ajusté selon la formule suivante : PIB(n)/2+PIB(n-1)/2 afin de le faire correspondre le mieux possible à une année fiscale de juillet (n-1) à juin (n). Le PIB de l'Égypte n'est pas ajusté car il est déjà publié sur la base de l'exercice juillet-juin dans les Perspectives de l'économie mondiale du FMI. Le PIB de Maurice n'est pas ajusté de 2010 à 2015 car les données de finances publiques sont reportées sur une année civile pour ces années.
3. Statistics South Africa a publié de nouvelles estimations du PIB qui tiennent compte des mises à jour et du re-basement de sa méthodologie de comptabilité nationale en août 2021. Ces nouveaux chiffres sont entre 8.6 % et 12.4 % plus élevés que les chiffres du PIB de l'édition 2020. Les ratios impôt total/PIB de l'Afrique du Sud dans l'édition 2021 sont donc inférieurs de 1.9 à 2.8 p.p. à ce qu'ils auraient été s'ils avaient été calculés à partir du PIB utilisé dans l'édition 2020.

Source : FMI, *Perspectives de l'économie mondiale, avril 2021*; Afrique du Sud : Statistics South Africa.

StatLink https://doi.org/10.1787/888934283633

Table 4.19. **Exchange rates used, national currency per US dollar**
Tableau 4.19. **Taux de change utilisés, unités de monnaie nationale par dollar US**

	1999	2000	2009	2010	2014	2015	2016	2017	2018	2019
Botswana	4.75	5.26	7.05	6.80	9.23	10.32	10.75	10.32	10.34	14.07
Burkina Faso	615.70	711.98	470.80	494.39	493.63	591.15	592.77	580.86	555.19	585.89
Cabo Verde	102.70	115.88	80.04	83.28	83.03	99.39	99.69	97.81	93.41	98.50
Cameroon / Cameroun	616.15	732.49	470.80	494.39	493.63	591.15	592.77	580.86	555.19	585.89
Chad / Tchad	614.87	709.89	470.80	494.39	493.63	591.15	592.77	580.86	555.19	585.89
Congo	614.86	711.98	470.80	494.39	493.63	591.15	592.77	580.86	555.19	585.89
Congo, Dem. Rep. / Congo, Rép. dém.	12.00	69.04	816.49	906.96	925.17	926.06	1 023.96	1 480.15	1 624.13	1 650.00
Côte d'Ivoire	615.47	710.21	470.29	494.79	493.76	591.21	592.61	580.66	555.45	585.91
Egypt / Égypte	3.40	3.41	5.53	5.52	6.97	7.36	8.15	14.67	17.73	17.60
Equatorial Guinea / Guinée équatoriale	615.70	710.21	470.29	494.79	493.76	591.21	592.61	580.66	555.45	585.91
Eswatini	6.32	7.32	8.11	7.30	11.29	13.22	14.33	13.30	13.53	19.30
Ghana	0.27	0.54	1.43	1.43	2.92	3.71	3.91	4.35	4.59	5.22
Kenya	65.12	73.23	73.33	78.33	86.98	92.91	99.73	102.57	102.33	101.70
Lesotho	6.11	6.94	7.82	7.19	11.06	13.78	14.06	13.00	13.75	14.79
Madagascar	1 256.76	1 353.50	1 956.21	2 089.95	2 414.81	2 933.51	3 176.54	3 116.11	3 334.75	3 618.32
Malawi	37.62	51.75	140.82	146.08	398.77	463.04	600.45	724.53	731.30	739.03
Mali	614.86	709.89	470.80	494.39	493.63	591.15	592.77	580.86	555.19	585.89
Mauritania / Mauritanie	20.95	23.89	26.18	27.55	30.17	32.39	35.15	35.66	35.68	36.69
Mauritius / Maurice	24.61	25.74	30.13	30.78	30.62	35.06	35.30	34.99	34.20	34.70
Morocco / Maroc	9.80	10.63	8.06	8.42	8.41	9.76	9.81	9.69	9.39	9.62
Namibia / Namibie	6.34	7.32	8.11	7.30	11.29	13.22	14.31	13.30	13.52	19.07
Niger	614.86	709.89	470.81	494.39	493.63	591.15	592.77	580.86	555.20	585.89
Nigeria / Nigéria	92.34	101.70	148.88	150.30	158.55	193.28	253.49	305.79	306.08	325.00
Rwanda	337.83	393.44	568.29	583.12	682.43	719.60	787.25	831.53	861.08	899.45
Senegal / Sénégal	614.86	709.89	470.80	494.39	493.63	591.15	592.77	580.86	555.19	585.89
Seychelles	5.34	5.71	13.61	12.07	12.75	13.32	13.32	13.65	13.97	14.05
South Africa / Afrique du Sud	6.11	6.94	8.44	7.32	10.84	12.75	14.71	13.32	13.24	14.45
Togo	614.70	709.60	470.80	494.39	493.63	591.15	592.77	580.86	555.19	585.89
Tunisia / Tunisie	1.19	1.37	1.35	1.43	1.70	1.96	2.15	2.42	2.65	2.93
Uganda / Ouganda	1 344.84	1 549.25	1 881.09	2 104.89	2 658.22	3 066.79	3 504.72	3 583.97	3 675.41	3 694.34

Note: The exchange rate is calculated by taking the ratio of the estimated fiscal year GDP in national currency for Table 4.17 to the estimated fiscal year GDP in US dollars in Table 4.18.

Note : Le taux de change est calculé en prenant le rapport entre le PIB estimé de l'année fiscale en monnaie nationale du tableau 4.17 et le PIB estimé de l'année fiscale en dollars US du tableau 4.18.

StatLink https://doi.org/10.1787/888934283652

Chapter 5

Country tables, tax revenues, 1999-2019

Chapitre 5

Tableaux pays, recettes fiscales, 1999-2019

Chapter 5 / Chapitre 5

Country tables, 1999-2019

In all of the following tables a ("..") indicates not available or not applicable. The main series in this volume cover the years 1999 to 2019.

Figures referring to 1990-98, 2001-08, and 2011-13 in Tables 5.1 to 5.30 have been omitted because of lack of space. Complete series are, however, available on line at *http://dx.doi.org/10.1787/93add7a4-en*.

Tableaux pays, 1999-2019

Dans tous les tableaux suivants le symbole («..») signifie que l'information n'est pas disponible ou qu'elle n'est pas applicable. La principale série dans ce volume couvre les années 1999 à 2019.

Les années 1990-98, 2001-08, et 2011-13 dans les tableaux 5.1 à 5.30 ont été omis en raison du manque d'espace. Les séries complètes sont cependant disponibles en ligne sur *http://dx.doi.org/10.1787/ef1bbbc4-fr*.

Table 5.1. **Botswana**

Details of tax revenue / Recettes fiscales détaillées

Million BWP

	1999	2000	2009	2010	2014	2015	2016	2017	2018	2019
Total tax revenue	..	..	**12 107**	**14 300**	**22 160**	**19 332**	**24 139**	**22 470**	**23 287**	**24 357**
1000 Taxes on income, profits and capital gains	..	..	**7 918**	**9 345**	**15 882**	**13 134**	**16 777**	**13 772**	**15 069**	**15 341**
1100 Of individuals	..	..	..	..	..	..	..	..	..	..
1110 On income and profits	..	..	..	..	..	..	..	..	..	..
1120 On capital gains	..	..	..	..	..	..	..	..	..	..
1200 Corporate	..	..	..	..	..	..	..	..	..	..
1210 On profits	..	..	..	..	..	..	..	..	..	..
1220 On capital gains	..	..	..	..	..	..	..	..	..	..
1300 Unallocable between 1100 and 1200	..	..	7 918	9 345	15 882	13 134	16 777	13 772	15 069	15 341
Assessed income tax	..	..	4 342	5 168	9 365	6 825	9 454	6 894	7 661	6 501
Income tax arrears and deductions	..	..	2 853	3 114	5 185	5 259	5 172	4 948	5 349	7 187
Withholding tax	..	..	724	1 062	1 332	1 050	2 152	1 930	2 059	1 653
PAYE taxes	..	..	0	0	0	0	0	0	0	0
2000 Social security contributions	..	..	**0**	**0**	**0**	**0**	**0**	**0**	**0**	**0**
2100 Employees	..	..	..	..	..	..	..	..	..	..
2110 On a payroll basis	..	..	..	..	..	..	..	..	..	..
2120 On an income tax basis	..	..	..	..	..	..	..	..	..	..
2200 Employers	..	..	..	..	..	..	..	..	..	..
2210 On a payroll basis	..	..	..	..	..	..	..	..	..	..
2220 On an income tax basis	..	..	..	..	..	..	..	..	..	..
2300 Self-employed or non-employed	..	..	..	..	..	..	..	..	..	..
2310 On a payroll basis	..	..	..	..	..	..	..	..	..	..
2320 On an income tax basis	..	..	..	..	..	..	..	..	..	..
2400 Unallocable between 2100, 2200 and 2300	..	..	..	..	..	..	..	..	..	..
2410 On a payroll basis	..	..	..	..	..	..	..	..	..	..
2420 On an income tax basis	..	..	..	..	..	..	..	..	..	..
3000 Taxes on payroll and workforce	..	..	**0**	**0**	**0**	**0**	**0**	**0**	**0**	**0**
4000 Taxes on property	..	..	**29**	**52**	**54**	**66**	**62**	**63**	**78**	**71**
4100 Recurrent taxes on immovable property	..	..	0	0	0	0	0	0	0	0
4110 Households	..	..	..	..	..	..	..	..	..	..
4120 Others	..	..	..	..	..	..	..	..	..	..
4200 Recurrent taxes on net wealth	..	..	0	0	0	0	0	0	0	0
4210 Individual	..	..	..	..	..	..	..	..	..	..
4220 Corporate	..	..	..	..	..	..	..	..	..	..
4300 Estate, inheritance and gift taxes	..	..	0	0	0	0	0	0	0	0
4310 Estate and inheritance taxes	..	..	..	..	..	..	..	..	..	..
4320 Gift taxes	..	..	..	..	..	..	..	..	..	..
4400 Taxes on financial and capital transactions	..	..	29	52	54	66	62	63	78	71
4500 Non-recurrent taxes	..	..	0	0	0	0	0	0	0	0
4510 On net wealth	..	..	..	..	..	..	..	..	..	..
4520 Other non-recurrent taxes	..	..	..	..	..	..	..	..	..	..
4600 Other recurrent taxes on property	..	..	0	0	0	0	0	0	0	0
5000 Taxes on goods and services	..	..	**4 160**	**4 903**	**6 223**	**6 132**	**7 300**	**8 635**	**8 140**	**8 944**
5100 Taxes on production, sale, transfer, etc.	..	..	3 969	4 669	5 955	5 870	6 981	8 207	7 661	8 475
5110 General taxes	..	..	3 805	4 401	5 606	5 448	6 535	7 650	7 253	7 939
5111 Value added taxes	..	..	3 805	4 481	5 606	5 448	6 535	7 650	7 253	7 939
VAT revenues (gross)	..	..	3 805	4 481	5 606	5 448	6 535	7 650	7 253	7 939
VAT accrued interest	..	..	0	0	0	0	0	0	0	0
VAT refunds	..	..	0	0	0	0	0	0	0	0
5112 Sales tax	..	..	0	0	0	0	0	0	0	0
5113 Other	..	..	0	0	0	0	0	0	0	0
5120 Taxes on specific goods and services	..	..	164	188	349	422	446	557	408	536
5121 Excises	..	..	138	157	318	393	435	553	405	531
Alcohol levy	..	..	0	0	214	284	327	427	284	401
Fuel levy	..	..	138	157	104	109	107	126	121	130
5122 Profits of fiscal monopolies	..	..	0	0	0	0	0	0	0	0
5123 Customs and import duties	..	..	6	9	2	4	6	2	1	1
5124 Taxes on exports	..	..	1	2	2	2	3	2	2	3
5125 Taxes on investment goods	..	..	0	0	0	0	0	0	0	0
5126 Taxes on specific services	..	..	18	20	28	23	2	0	0	1
5127 Other taxes on internat. trade and transactions	..	..	0	0	0	0	0	0	0	0
5128 Other taxes	..	..	0	0	0	0	0	0	0	0
5130 Unallocable between 5110 and 5120	..	..	0	0	0	0	0	0	0	0
5200 Taxes on use of goods and perform activities	..	..	191	234	268	262	319	428	479	469

Table 5.1. **Botswana** *(cont.)*

Details of tax revenue / Recettes fiscales détaillées

Million BWP

	1999	2000	2009	2010	2014	2015	2016	2017	2018	2019
5210 Recurrent taxes	..	..	191	234	268	262	319	428	479	469
5211 Paid by households: motor vehicles	..	..	61	62	73	77	85	110	115	118
5212 Paid by others: motor vehicles	..	..	103	144	161	180	193	270	317	346
5213 Paid in respect of other goods	..	..	28	29	34	5	40	48	46	5
5220 Non-recurrent taxes	..	..	0	0	0	0	0	0	0	0
5300 Unallocable between 5100 and 5200	..	..	0	0	0	0	0	0	0	0
6000 Other taxes	**..**	**..**	**0**	**0**	**0**	**0**	**0**	**0**	**0**	**0**
6100 Paid solely by business	..	..	..	..	..	..	..	..	..	..
6200 Other	..	..	..	..	..	..	..	..	..	..

.. Not available

Note: Data are on a fiscal year basis beginning 1st April. For example, the data for 2019 represent April 2019 to March 2020.

Figures exclude tax revenues collected by sub-national governments as the data are not available.

Heading 2000: Social security contributions for Botswana are deemed to be null as they do not meet the criteria to be classified as social security contributions set out in the OECD classification of taxes in the Interpretative Guide.

Source: Botswana Ministry of Finance and Economic Development, and Statistics Botswana.

StatLink https://doi.org/10.1787/888934283671

Table 5.2. **Burkina Faso**

Details of tax revenue / Recettes fiscales détaillées

Million XOF

	1999	2000	2009	2010	2014	2015	2016	2017	2018	2019
Recettes fiscales totales	**..**	**214 601**	**561 956**	**698 853**	**982 743**	**1 018 759**	**1 161 369**	**1 326 065**	**1 484 685**	**1 621 604**
1000 Impôts sur revenu, bénéfices et gains en capital	**..**	**53 109**	**108 384**	**135 056**	**264 278**	**236 193**	**287 770**	**325 403**	**377 120**	**450 579**
1100 Des personnes physiques	..	15 371	46 966	56 429	71 703	75 300	88 707	102 422	125 405	149 467
1110 Sur le revenu et les bénéfices	..	15 371	46 966	56 429	71 703	75 300	88 707	102 422	125 405	149 467
Impôt sur les revenus	..	0	60	84	19	18	14	49	1	0
Impôt sur les bénéfices industriels, commerciaux et agricoles (pers. phys.)	..	1 235	2 519	3 133	4 242	4 828	4 884	6 888	16 128	26 249
Impôt sur les bénéfices non commerciaux (pers. phys.)	..	754	2 067	2 404	3 959	4 809	5 492	5 821	8 008	9 479
Impôt unique sur les traitements et salaires	..	13 382	42 320	50 809	63 483	65 646	78 317	89 665	101 268	113 738
1120 Sur les gains en capital	..	..	..	..	..	..	..	..	..	..
1200 Des sociétés	..	36 190	58 815	76 008	189 457	157 319	194 665	217 472	246 558	295 436
1210 Sur les bénéfices	..	36 190	58 815	76 008	189 457	157 319	194 665	217 472	246 558	295 436
Impôt sur les sociétés	..	0	0	67 027	162 667	132 050	163 454	186 641	209 595	249 434
Contribution du secteur informel et des micro-entreprises	..	0	1 646	1 475	1 664	1 638	1 938	1 926	2 244	2 082
Impôt sur les bénéfices industriels, commerciaux et agricoles (pers. mor.)	..	32 221	48 896	0	0	0	0	0	0	0
Impôts sur le revenu des créances	..	548	1 600	1 622	3 746	4 698	5 463	6 155	0	0
Impôts sur le revenu des valeurs mobilières	..	3 420	6 673	5 884	21 380	18 932	23 810	22 750	0	0
Impôts sur le revenu des capitaux mobiliers	..	0	0	0	0	0	0	0	34 719	43 920
1220 Sur les gains en capital	..	..	..	..	..	..	..	..	..	..
1300 Non ventilables entre 1100 et 1200	..	1 549	2 603	2 619	3 118	3 574	4 399	5 509	5 157	5 675
Impôts sur les revenus fonciers	..	1 402	2 268	2 337	2 925	3 206	3 668	4 175	4 813	4 874
Reversement des honoraires	..	91	69	19	0	0	0	0	0	0
Taxes sur les plus-values	..	56	266	263	193	367	731	1 334	345	801
2000 Cotisations de sécurité sociale	**..**	**34 142**	**70 090**	**76 584**	**105 729**	**120 046**	**133 708**	**145 635**	**164 195**	**177 435**
2100 A la charge des salariés	..	10 332	21 612	23 424	31 521	35 064	34 204	37 255	42 003	45 391
2110 Sur la base du salaire	..	10 332	21 612	23 424	31 521	35 064	34 204	37 255	42 003	45 391
2120 Sur la base de l'impôt sur le revenu	..	0	0	0	0	0	0	0	0	0
2200 A la charge des employeurs	..	23 810	48 479	53 160	74 208	84 983	99 504	108 380	122 192	132 044
2210 Sur la base du salaire	..	23 810	48 479	53 160	74 208	84 983	99 504	108 380	122 192	132 044
2220 Sur la base de l'impôt sur le revenu	..	0	0	0	0	0	0	0	0	0
2300 A charge des travailleurs indép. ou sans emploi	..	0	0	0	0	0	0	0	0	0
2310 Sur la base du salaire	..	..	..	..	..	..	..	..	..	..
2320 Sur la base de l'impôt sur le revenu	..	..	..	..	..	..	..	..	..	..
2400 Non ventilables entre 2100, 2200 et 2300	..	0	0	0	0	0	0	0	0	0
2410 Sur la base du salaire	..	..	..	..	..	..	..	..	..	..
2420 Sur la base de l'impôt sur le revenu	..	..	..	..	..	..	..	..	..	..
3000 Sur salaires ou main d'oeuvre	**..**	**2 678**	**6 196**	**5 479**	**7 407**	**7 009**	**8 762**	**10 013**	**12 331**	**13 210**
4000 Impôts sur le patrimoine	**..**	**938**	**4 236**	**4 778**	**10 516**	**8 529**	**12 061**	**9 784**	**9 982**	**11 025**
4100 Impôts périodiques sur la propriété immobilière	..	54	543	615	1 092	1 011	1 366	1 359	2 013	2 438
Contribution foncière	..	0	0	0	0	0	0	75	169	232
Taxe de résidence	..	8	399	460	558	469	749	624	681	781
Taxe sur les biens de mainmorte	..	45	144	155	534	542	617	659	1 163	1 425
4110 Ménages	..	0	0	0	0	0	0	0	0	0
4120 Autres agents	..	0	0	0	0	0	0	0	0	0
4200 Impôts périodiques sur l'actif net	..	0	0	0	0	0	0	0	0	0
4210 Personnes physiques	..	..	..	..	..	..	..	..	..	..
4220 Sociétés	..	..	..	..	..	..	..	..	..	..
4300 Impôts sur mut. par décès, succ. et donations	..	73	54	41	148	200	188	101	170	317
4310 Impôts sur mut. par décès et successions	..	66	49	28	132	179	169	95	156	265
4320 Impôts sur les donations	..	7	5	13	15	21	19	5	13	52
4400 Impôts sur transact. mobilières et immob.	..	646	2 309	2 803	7 673	6 160	8 836	6 702	5 818	5 778
4500 Impôts non-périodiques	..	165	1 329	1 318	1 604	1 158	1 671	1 621	1 981	2 492
4510 Sur l'actif net	..	0	0	0	0	0	0	0	0	0
4520 Autres non-périodiques	..	165	1 329	1 318	1 604	1 158	1 671	1 621	1 981	2 492
4600 Autres impôts périodiques sur patrimoine	..	0	0	0	0	0	0	0	0	0
5000 Impôts sur les biens et services	**..**	**122 232**	**368 699**	**470 504**	**587 826**	**639 524**	**710 978**	**824 168**	**911 247**	**958 660**
5100 Impôts sur production, vente, transfert, etc.	..	108 003	337 493	370 927	543 782	598 102	662 383	769 064	852 880	895 777
5110 Impôts généraux	..	61 497	209 124	229 176	317 347	343 378	380 664	441 791	487 799	536 770
5111 Taxes sur la valeur ajoutée	..	61 497	208 622	228 498	316 600	342 660	379 986	440 983	486 929	535 895
Recettes TVA (brute)	..	62 566	214 091	236 198	389 950	393 160	440 486	511 508	537 954	586 658
Remboursements de la TVA	..	-1 068	-5 469	-7 700	-73 350	-50 500	-60 500	-70 525	-51 025	-50 763
5112 Impôts sur les ventes	..	0	0	0	0	0	0	0	0	0

Table 5.2. **Burkina Faso** *(cont.)*

Details of tax revenue / Recettes fiscales détaillées

Million XOF

	1999	2000	2009	2010	2014	2015	2016	2017	2018	2019
5113 Autres impôts	..	0	502	678	746	719	678	808	870	874
Taxe sur chiffre d'affaires	..	0	0	0	0	0	0	0	0	0
Taxe de développement touristique	..	0	502	678	746	719	678	808	870	874
5120 Impôts sur biens et services déterminés	..	46 506	128 369	141 750	226 435	254 723	281 719	327 273	365 080	359 007
5121 Accises	..	16 129	40 742	46 912	77 469	94 105	105 434	129 214	140 930	137 505
Boissons	..	4 954	11 902	13 887	24 434	26 202	30 596	35 726	36 685	30 097
Taxes sur le café, le thé et les noix de cola	..	549	625	938	1 098	1 603	1 417	1 380	1 500	1 832
Taxe sur les produits pétroliers	..	10 515	27 925	31 710	50 988	65 266	71 818	90 167	100 432	102 918
Taxe sur les tabacs et allumettes	..	111	171	139	691	789	1 187	1 279	1 839	1 712
Autres accises	..	0	119	239	257	246	415	662	474	947
5122 Bénéfices des monopoles fiscaux	..	2 912	6 214	7 234	11 831	15 212	17 668	18 360	22 259	24 158
Monopole des tabacs	..	2 912	6 214	7 234	11 831	15 212	17 668	18 360	22 259	24 158
5123 Droits de douane et droits à l'importation	..	25 242	78 936	85 075	130 085	128 465	140 632	161 095	182 180	176 799
Redevance informatique et statistique	..	3 574	8 786	10 030	15 435	16 218	17 484	20 852	22 277	22 581
Droits de douanes	..	21 589	70 150	75 045	114 649	112 247	123 148	140 243	159 903	154 217
Taxe dégressive de protection	..	79	0	0	0	0	0	0	0	0
5124 Taxes à l'exportation	..	572	441	434	685	601	416	455	454	422
Contribution du secteur élevage	..	572	441	434	685	601	416	455	454	422
5125 Impôts sur biens d'équipement	..	0	0	0	0	0	0	0	0	0
5126 Impôts sur services déterminés	..	1 651	2 037	2 096	6 366	16 339	17 570	18 149	19 139	19 560
Taxe sur billets avions	..	3	450	349	608	563	671	697	645	509
Taxe spécifique sur les entreprises de télécommunication	..	0	0	0	1 980	11 970	11 965	12 268	13 152	13 796
Taxe sur les contrats d'assurance	..	1 648	1 587	1 748	3 777	3 806	4 373	4 338	4 007	4 404
Taxe sur les jeux de hasard	..	0	0	0	0	0	561	847	1 335	851
5127 Autres impôts sur commerce et transact. internat.	..	0	0	0	0	0	0	0	0	0
5128 Autres impôts	..	0	0	0	0	0	0	0	119	563
5130 Non ventilables entre 5110 et 5120	..	0	0	0	0	0	0	0	0	0
5200 Impôts sur utilisation des biens et exerc. activites	..	10 503	29 166	98 077	43 335	38 970	45 082	52 634	53 794	57 470
5210 Impôts périodiques	..	3 837	7 337	70 529	11 136	12 022	14 361	16 270	19 339	20 101
5211 A la charge des ménages: véhicules à moteur	..	0	0	0	0	0	0	0	0	0
5212 A la charge autres agents: véhicules à moteur	..	0	0	0	0	0	0	0	0	0
5213 Autres impôts périodiques	..	3 837	7 337	70 529	11 136	12 022	14 361	16 270	19 339	20 101
Taxe sur les armes	..	0	42	32	31	30	34	36	38	41
Contribution des patentes	..	3 347	5 965	7 218	9 802	10 736	13 087	13 557	18 186	19 128
Taxe de visionnement et de vérification	..	9	70	82	93	0	0	0	0	0
Matière forestière, faune sauvage et pêche	..	461	1 118	1 215	1 190	1 239	1 183	1 159	1 093	874
Recettes en matière d'hydraulique	..	0	6	0	0	0	0	0	0	0
Autorisation d'exploiter les hôtels et les restaurants	..	0	0	0	0	0	0	1	4	1
Licence de téléphonie mobile	..	0	0	61 793	0	0	0	1 500	0	0
Licence - vente à la consommation	..	20	137	190	20	18	56	16	17	56
5220 Impôts non-périodiques	..	6 666	21 829	27 547	32 199	26 948	30 721	36 365	34 456	37 369
Autres droits d'enregistrement	..	4 418	16 654	22 202	24 689	21 309	24 410	31 001	29 372	32 219
Taxe de jouissance	..	2 241	5 165	5 327	7 505	5 637	6 302	5 339	5 066	5 132
Licences d'agences et de guides touristiques	..	0	1	3	0	0	3	17	17	12
Agrément armes à feu	..	0	0	0	1	0	2	0	1	0
Agréments au code des investissements	..	7	9	14	4	2	3	8	0	6
5300 Non ventilables entre 5100 et 5200	..	3 726	2 040	1 501	709	2 452	3 514	2 470	4 573	5 413
Autres impôts non ventilables	..	74	256	169	253	264	668	641	734	1 323
Taxe préférentielle communautaire	..	3 154	278	0	0	0	0	0	0	0
Taxe pour le développement de la télévision	..	498	1 506	1 332	456	2 188	2 846	1 829	3 839	4 090
6000 Autres impôts	**..**	**1 502**	**4 351**	**6 452**	**6 988**	**6 579**	**8 089**	**10 262**	**9 810**	**10 695**
Droits de timbre	..	1 436	4 193	5 678	6 885	6 538	7 995	10 191	9 770	9 963
Autres recettes fiscales	..	66	157	774	102	41	94	71	39	732
6100 A la charge exclusive des entreprises	..	..	..	..	..	..	..	..	..	..
6200 A la charge d'autres agents	..	..	..	..	..	..	..	..	..	..

.. Non disponible

Note : Année civile se terminant le 31 décembre.

Les données sont sur la base des encaissements.

Les chiffres n'incluent pas les recettes fiscales collectées par les collectivités locales car elles ne sont pas disponibles. Cependant, ils incluent des recettes collectées par l'administration centrale au profit des collectivités locales.

Les recettes provenant de la taxe de location de biens, des droits sur les titres miniers, des redevances minières et des frais administratifs sont incluses dans les recettes non fiscales comme le préconise la classification OCDE (voir le guide d'interprétation en Annexe A). La classification nationale du Burkina Faso les comptabilise comme des recettes fiscales.

À partir de 2018, les impôts sur le revenu des créances et les impôts sur le revenu des valeurs mobilières sont rapportés ensemble sous la rubrique des impôts sur le revenu des capitaux mobiliers.

Source : Ministère de l'Économie, des Finances et du Développement du Burkina Faso.

StatLink https://doi.org/10.1787/888934283690

Table 5.3. **Cabo Verde**

Details of tax revenue / Recettes fiscales détaillées

Million CVE

	1999	2000	2009	2010	2014	2015	2016	2017	2018	2019
Recettes fiscales totales	**10 318**	**10 974**	**25 008**	**25 552**	**26 088**	**29 667**	**31 056**	**34 885**	**39 159**	**40 159**
1000 Impôts sur revenu, bénéfices et gains en capital	**3 674**	**3 913**	**8 061**	**7 892**	**7 747**	**9 669**	**10 050**	**11 292**	**12 300**	**12 806**
1100 Des personnes physiques	2 756	2 958	4 453	4 645	4 998	5 327	6 317	7 062	6 927	7 334
1110 Sur le revenu et les bénéfices	..	..	..	..	..	..	..	..	..	..
1120 Sur les gains en capital	..	..	..	..	..	..	..	..	..	..
1200 Des sociétés	919	955	3 607	3 247	2 749	4 342	3 733	4 230	5 374	5 472
1210 Sur les bénéfices	..	..	..	..	..	..	..	..	..	..
1220 Sur les gains en capital	..	..	..	..	..	..	..	..	..	..
1300 Non ventilables entre 1100 et 1200	0	0	0	0	0	0	0	0	0	0
2000 Cotisations de sécurité sociale	**0**	**569**	**46**	**42**	**56**	**46**	**56**	**60**	**77**	**76**
2100 A la charge des salariés	..	..	..	..	..	..	..	..	..	..
2110 Sur la base du salaire	..	..	..	..	..	..	..	..	..	..
2120 Sur la base de l'impôt sur le revenu	..	..	..	..	..	..	..	..	..	..
2200 A la charge des employeurs	..	..	..	..	..	..	..	..	..	..
2210 Sur la base du salaire	..	..	..	..	..	..	..	..	..	..
2220 Sur la base de l'impôt sur le revenu	..	..	..	..	..	..	..	..	..	..
2300 A charge des travailleurs indép. ou sans emploi	..	..	..	..	..	..	..	..	..	..
2310 Sur la base du salaire	..	..	..	..	..	..	..	..	..	..
2320 Sur la base de l'impôt sur le revenu	..	..	..	..	..	..	..	..	..	..
2400 Non ventilables entre 2100, 2200 et 2300	..	569	46	42	56	46	56	60	77	76
2410 Sur la base du salaire	..	569	46	42	56	46	56	60	77	76
Contributions pour la sécurité sociale	..	11	27	28	49	40	56	60	77	76
Taxe sociale unique	..	558	19	14	7	5	0	0	0	0
2420 Sur la base de l'impôt sur le revenu	..	0	0	0	0	0	0	0	0	0
3000 Sur salaires ou main d'oeuvre	**0**	**0**	**0**	**0**	**0**	**0**	**0**	**0**	**0**	**0**
4000 Impôts sur le patrimoine	**457**	**584**	**951**	**701**	**668**	**582**	**472**	**509**	**742**	**634**
4100 Impôts périodiques sur la propriété immobilière	0	0	0	0	0	0	0	0	0	0
4110 Ménages	..	..	..	..	..	..	..	..	..	..
4120 Autres agents	..	..	..	..	..	..	..	..	..	..
4200 Impôts périodiques sur l'actif net	0	0	0	0	0	0	0	0	0	0
4210 Personnes physiques	..	..	..	..	..	..	..	..	..	..
4220 Sociétés	..	..	..	..	..	..	..	..	..	..
4300 Impôts sur mut. par décès, succ. et donations	0	0	0	0	0	0	0	0	0	0
4310 Impôts sur mut. par décès et successions	..	..	..	..	..	..	..	..	..	..
4320 Impôts sur les donations	..	..	..	..	..	..	..	..	..	..
4400 Impôts sur transact. mobilières et immob.	457	584	951	701	668	582	472	509	742	634
4500 Impôts non-périodiques	0	0	0	0	0	0	0	0	0	0
4510 Sur l'actif net	..	..	..	..	..	..	..	..	..	..
4520 Autres non-périodiques	..	..	..	..	..	..	..	..	..	..
4600 Autres impôts périodiques sur patrimoine	0	0	0	0	0	0	0	0	0	0
5000 Impôts sur les biens et services	**6 187**	**5 908**	**15 950**	**16 917**	**17 618**	**19 370**	**20 479**	**23 023**	**26 039**	**26 643**
5100 Impôts sur production, vente, transfert, etc.	6 187	5 908	15 950	16 917	17 618	19 370	20 479	23 023	26 039	26 643
5110 Impôts généraux	0	0	9 397	10 035	9 458	10 824	11 017	12 646	15 139	15 048
5111 Taxes sur la valeur ajoutée	..	..	9 397	10 035	9 458	10 824	11 017	12 646	15 139	15 048
TVA à l'importation (brute) - DGA	..	..	5 900	6 180	6 253	6 358	6 601	7 260	7 801	8 260
TVA intérieure (brute) - DGCI	..	..	3 847	4 341	3 917	4 935	5 385	6 046	8 412	8 468
Remboursements de la TVA	..	..	-349	-486	-712	-469	-969	-661	-1 074	-1 679
5112 Impôts sur les ventes	..	..	0	0	0	0	0	0	0	0
5113 Autres impôts	..	..	0	0	0	0	0	0	0	0
5120 Impôts sur biens et services déterminés	6 187	5 908	6 553	6 882	8 160	8 546	9 462	10 377	10 900	11 595
5121 Accises	2 192	1 938	1 334	1 494	2 065	2 073	2 228	2 621	2 680	2 931
Taxe spéciale sur la consommation	2 192	1 812	1 147	1 227	1 507	1 478	1 550	1 937	1 963	2 192
Taxe écologique	0	126	187	267	558	595	678	684	717	739
5122 Bénéfices des monopoles fiscaux	0	0	0	0	0	0	0	0	0	0
5123 Droits de douane et droits à l'importation	3 995	3 971	5 219	5 388	5 497	5 827	6 523	6 906	7 409	7 672
5124 Taxes à l'exportation	0	0	0	0	0	0	0	0	0	0
5125 Impôts sur biens d'équipement	0	0	0	0	0	0	0	0	0	0
5126 Impôts sur services déterminés	0	0	0	0	598	645	711	849	811	992
Contribution touristique	..	..	..	..	598	645	711	849	811	992
Autres (taxe incendie, taxe touristique)	..	..	..	..	0	0	0	0	0	0
5127 Autres impôts sur commerce et transact. internat.	0	0	0	0	0	0	0	0	0	0
5128 Autres impôts	0	0	0	0	0	0	0	0	0	0
5130 Non ventilables entre 5110 et 5120	0	0	0	0	0	0	0	0	0	0
5200 Impôts sur utilisation des biens et exerc. activites	0	0	0	0	0	0	0	0	0	0

Table 5.3. **Cabo Verde** *(cont.)*

Details of tax revenue / Recettes fiscales détaillées

Million CVE

	1999	2000	2009	2010	2014	2015	2016	2017	2018	2019
5210 Impôts périodiques	..	..	..	..	..	..	..	..	..	..
5211 A la charge des ménages: véhicules à moteur	..	..	..	..	..	..	..	..	..	..
5212 A la charge autres agents: véhicules à moteur	..	..	..	..	..	..	..	..	..	..
5213 Autres impôts périodiques	..	..	..	..	..	..	..	..	..	..
5220 Impôts non-périodiques	..	..	..	..	..	..	..	..	..	..
5300 Non ventilables entre 5100 et 5200	0	0	0	0	0	0	0	0	0	0
6000 Autres impôts	**0**	**0**	**0**	**0**	**0**	**0**	**0**	**0**	**0**	**0**
6100 A la charge exclusive des entreprises	..	..	..	..	..	..	..	..	..	..
6200 A la charge d'autres agents	..	..	..	..	..	..	..	..	..	..

.. Non disponible

Note : Année civile se terminant le 31 décembre.

Les données sont sur la base des encaissements.

Les chiffres n'incluent pas les données des recettes fiscales collectées par les collectivités locales car elles ne sont pas disponibles.

Le prélèvement communautaire de la CEDEAO (Communauté économique des États de l'Afrique de l'Ouest) n'est pas compris parmi les impôts selon le guide d'interprétation de l'OCDE (voir § 4). La classification nationale du Cabo Verde le compte comme une recette fiscale. Cette recette qui n'est pas comprise dans le total des recettes fiscales ou des recettes non fiscales est présentée à titre de rubrique « Pour mémoire » dans le tableau 6.7 du chapitre 6.

Rubrique 4400 : Cette rubrique comprend les droits de timbre, classifiés au Cabo Verde dans la rubrique « autres impôts ».

Rubrique 5126 : La taxe incendie et la taxe touristique sont classifiées dans la rubrique « autres impôts » au Cabo Verde.

Source : Ministère des Finances et du Plan du Cabo Verde.

StatLink https://doi.org/10.1787/888934283709

Table 5.4. **Cameroon / Cameroun**

Details of tax revenue / Recettes fiscales détaillées

Million XAF

	1999	2000	2009	2010	2014	2015	2016	2017	2018	2019
Recettes fiscales totales	**710 067**	**810 500**	**1 611 401**	**1 571 695**	**2 486 045**	**2 687 926**	**2 743 908**	**2 935 179**	**3 146 494**	**3 222 162**
1000 Impôts sur revenu, bénéfices et gains en capital	**177 700**	**228 100**	**522 719**	**425 741**	**784 122**	**867 834**	**771 155**	**741 551**	**848 398**	**882 190**
1100 Des personnes physiques	76 700	87 100	97 774	102 793	175 021	185 512	179 475	200 845	247 546	226 293
1110 Sur le revenu et les bénéfices	76 700	87 100	97 743	102 728	174 190	184 213	177 669	199 386	246 321	225 213
Traitements, salaires, pensions et rentes viagères	52 100	60 800	80 469	86 440	127 331	135 738	131 524	139 280	165 187	150 396
Revenus fonciers	0	0	2 715	2 402	13 247	12 405	12 716	13 058	14 401	12 442
Bénéfices artisanaux, industriels et commerciaux	0	0	6 115	5 342	13 648	21 010	15 689	26 107	29 610	35 745
Bénéfices agricoles	0	0	29	47	27	56	31	30	161	253
Bénéfices des professions non commerciales	0	0	462	295	592	2 875	5 687	9 750	24 643	14 865
Autres impôts sur le revenu	24 600	26 300	7 952	8 202	19 345	12 130	12 022	11 162	12 319	11 511
1120 Sur les gains en capital	..	..	31	65	831	1 299	1 806	1 459	1 225	1 079
Impôts sur plus-values sur cession immobilière	..	..	29	46	830	1 297	1 803	1 440	1 223	1 079
Impôts sur les autres gains en capital	..	..	2	19	1	2	3	19	2	0
1200 Des sociétés	82 500	119 400	362 677	256 404	460 571	538 969	460 785	385 971	441 882	457 428
1210 Sur les bénéfices	82 500	119 400	362 677	256 404	460 571	538 969	460 785	385 971	441 882	457 428
Bénéfices des sociétés pétrolières	20 300	39 000	188 766	83 764	161 724	171 891	108 966	66 471	86 948	113 018
Bénéfices des sociétés non pétrolières	62 200	80 400	173 911	172 639	298 847	367 078	351 818	319 500	354 934	344 410
1220 Sur les gains en capital	..	..	..	..	..	..	..	..	..	..
1300 Non ventilables entre 1100 et 1200	18 500	21 600	62 268	66 544	148 530	143 352	130 896	154 735	158 970	198 470
Taxe spéciale sur les revenus payés à l'étranger	11 200	12 400	34 250	38 877	97 511	84 412	68 691	62 806	67 809	91 879
Impôts sur les revenus des capitaux mobiliers	7 300	9 200	27 218	27 629	44 489	48 774	39 350	42 155	42 715	47 612
Centimes communaux sur l'impôt sur le revenu	0	0	800	39	6 530	10 166	22 855	49 774	48 446	58 978
2000 Cotisations de sécurité sociale	**55 300**	**65 500**	**109 161**	**135 747**	**153 707**	**160 992**	**200 960**	**213 796**	**226 610**	**235 937**
2100 A la charge des salariés	18 353	19 747	31 477	33 297	40 917	44 669	44 655	45 763	48 105	45 565
2110 Sur la base du salaire	18 353	19 747	31 477	33 297	40 917	44 669	44 655	45 763	48 105	45 565
2120 Sur la base de l'impôt sur le revenu	0	0	0	0	0	0	0	0	0	0
2200 A la charge des employeurs	..	..	..	..	..	..	..	..	..	..
2210 Sur la base du salaire	..	..	..	..	..	..	..	..	..	..
2220 Sur la base de l'impôt sur le revenu	..	..	..	..	..	..	..	..	..	..
2300 A charge des travailleurs indép. ou sans emploi	..	..	..	..	..	..	..	..	..	..
2310 Sur la base du salaire	..	..	..	..	..	..	..	..	..	..
2320 Sur la base de l'impôt sur le revenu	..	..	..	..	..	..	..	..	..	..
2400 Non ventilables entre 2100, 2200 et 2300	36 947	45 753	77 684	102 450	112 790	116 323	156 305	168 033	178 505	190 372
2410 Sur la base du salaire	36 947	45 753	77 684	102 450	112 790	116 323	156 305	168 033	178 505	190 372
2420 Sur la base de l'impôt sur le revenu	0	0	0	0	0	0	0	0	0	0
3000 Sur salaires ou main d'oeuvre	**9 467**	**0**	**18 063**	**17 860**	**46 902**	**53 572**	**52 826**	**54 350**	**32 131**	**36 046**
4000 Impôts sur le patrimoine	**7 300**	**13 100**	**17 896**	**18 003**	**21 024**	**25 437**	**30 471**	**33 393**	**25 311**	**27 113**
4100 Impôts périodiques sur la propriété immobilière	200	500	1 716	1 552	1 692	1 743	3 905	3 652	2 443	2 249
4110 Ménages	..	..	..	..	..	..	..	..	..	..
4120 Autres agents	..	..	..	..	..	..	..	..	..	..
4200 Impôts périodiques sur l'actif net	0	0	0	0	0	0	0	0	0	0
4210 Personnes physiques	..	..	..	..	..	..	..	..	..	..
4220 Sociétés	..	..	..	..	..	..	..	..	..	..
4300 Impôts sur mut. par décès, succ. et donations	0	0	25	39	214	62	160	60	86	38
4310 Impôts sur mut. par décès et successions	..	..	25	39	214	62	160	60	86	38
4320 Impôts sur les donations	..	..	0	0	0	0	0	0	0	0
4400 Impôts sur transact. mobilières et immob.	7 100	12 600	16 156	16 412	19 117	23 632	26 406	29 681	22 782	24 827
Droits d'enregistrement sur les mutations entre vifs	..	..	50	32	586	391	376	577	76	301
Droits d'enrgmnt. sur les mutations immob.	..	..	2 052	2 747	3 250	3 080	2 921	3 107	3 924	4 991
Droits de bail	..	..	4 147	4 602	2 725	2 364	2 425	2 452	2 395	2 802
Droits autres mutations et transactions	..	..	9 907	9 031	12 556	17 797	20 685	23 545	16 388	16 733
4500 Impôts non-périodiques	0	0	0	0	0	0	0	0	0	0
4510 Sur l'actif net	..	..	..	..	..	..	..	..	..	..
4520 Autres non-périodiques	..	..	..	..	..	..	..	..	..	..
4600 Autres impôts périodiques sur patrimoine	0	0	0	0	0	0	0	0	0	0
5000 Impôts sur les biens et services	**459 400**	**503 800**	**915 617**	**944 412**	**1 448 405**	**1 532 668**	**1 642 804**	**1 844 728**	**1 958 026**	**1 963 031**
5100 Impôts sur production, vente, transfert, etc.	457 700	501 100	908 175	936 564	1 438 522	1 522 834	1 632 420	1 834 787	1 948 068	1 952 839
5110 Impôts généraux	223 400	260 900	496 721	490 521	826 250	883 618	928 368	1 066 216	1 158 458	1 138 354
5111 Taxes sur la valeur ajoutée	223 400	260 900	496 717	490 513	826 225	883 580	928 368	1 066 216	1 158 458	1 138 354
TVA intérieure (brute)	150 300	186 500	303 271	299 504	532 980	604 046	629 355	803 903	846 136	810 285
TVA à la porte (brute)	94 600	107 300	234 156	259 343	358 184	354 701	355 033	344 389	384 310	394 070
Remboursements de la TVA	-21 500	-32 900	-40 711	-68 333	-64 938	-75 167	-56 020	-82 076	-71 988	-66 002
5112 Impôts sur les ventes	0	0	0	0	0	0	0	0	0	0
5113 Autres impôts	0	0	4	8	25	39	0	0	0	0

Table 5.4. **Cameroon / Cameroun** *(cont.)*

Details of tax revenue / Recettes fiscales détaillées

Million XAF

	1999	2000	2009	2010	2014	2015	2016	2017	2018	2019
5120 Impôts sur biens et services déterminés	234 300	240 200	411 454	446 043	612 272	639 216	704 052	768 571	789 609	814 485
5121 Accises	88 700	84 000	158 910	164 943	240 269	289 280	323 562	334 313	337 533	380 616
Droits d'accises intérieure	25 200	26 500	80 572	68 414	98 327	170 164	204 785	193 857	192 954	217 381
Droits d'accises à la porte	1 500	1 900	317	12 936	14 762	14 608	12 662	17 872	16 655	33 798
Taxe spéciale sur les produits pétroliers	62 000	55 600	78 019	82 962	118 515	103 773	105 579	122 036	127 456	128 709
Vignette sur tabac et produits manufacturés	0	0	2	632	8 665	736	537	548	469	728
5122 Bénéfices des monopoles fiscaux	0	0	0	0	0	0	0	0	0	0
5123 Droits de douane et droits à l'importation	102 300	119 900	240 690	261 731	345 511	320 314	350 705	397 478	394 169	386 778
5124 Taxes à l'exportation	31 900	24 300	6 174	8 793	15 089	17 133	16 330	22 654	36 581	31 799
5125 Impôts sur biens d'équipement	0	0	0	0	0	0	0	0	0	0
5126 Impôts sur services déterminés	1 300	1 100	107	3 600	5 238	5 035	6 387	6 059	12 271	13 889
5127 Autres impôts sur commerce et transact. internat.	0	0	0	0	0	0	0	0	0	0
5128 Autres impôts	10 100	10 900	5 574	6 977	6 165	7 454	7 068	8 068	9 054	1 403
5130 Non ventilables entre 5110 et 5120	0	0	0	0	0	0	0	0	0	0
5200 Impôts sur utilisation des biens et exerc. activités	1 700	2 700	7 442	7 848	9 883	9 835	10 385	9 940	9 959	10 193
5210 Impôts périodiques	1 700	2 700	7 442	7 848	9 883	9 835	10 385	9 940	9 959	10 193
5211 A la charge des ménages: véhicules à moteur	600	1 600	5 622	6 111	7 819	7 539	8 050	7 386	7 000	7 000
5212 A la charge autres agents: véhicules à moteur	1 100	1 100	1 669	1 663	1 985	2 213	2 205	2 451	2 710	2 859
5213 Autres impôts périodiques	0	0	151	74	79	83	130	103	248	334
5220 Impôts non-périodiques	0	0	0	0	0	0	0	0	0	0
5300 Non ventilables entre 5100 et 5200	0	0	0	0	0	0	0	0	0	0
6000 Autres impôts	**900**	**0**	**27 946**	**29 932**	**31 885**	**47 424**	**45 692**	**47 360**	**56 018**	**77 845**
6100 A la charge exclusive des entreprises	..	..	..	..	..	..	..	..	..	..
6200 A la charge d'autres agents	..	..	..	..	..	..	..	..	..	..

.. Non disponible

Note : Année civile se terminant le 31 décembre.

Les données sont sur la base des encaissements.

Les chiffres n'incluent pas les recettes fiscales collectées par les collectivités locales car elles ne sont pas disponibles.

Rubrique 2000 : Les cotisations de sécurité sociale du secteur public (APU) incluent uniquement les cotisations pour les retraites et ne couvrent pas les prestations familiales et d'invalidité.

Rubrique 5111 : Les données antérieures à 1999 correspondent aux recettes de la taxe sur le chiffre d'affaires (TCA) et ont été reclassées dans la rubrique 5113 « Autres impôts généraux sur les biens et services » La TVA a été introduite au Cameroun en 1999. Dans cette édition, les données des recettes TVA sont présentées nettes des remboursements TVA comme le préconise la classification OCDE (voir le Guide d'interprétation en Annexe A).

Source : Ministère des Finances du Cameroun.

StatLink https://doi.org/10.1787/888934283728

Table 5.5. **Chad / Tchad**

Details of tax revenue / Recettes fiscales détaillées

Million XAF

	1999	2000	2009	2010	2014	2015	2016	2017	2018	2019
Recettes fiscales totales	..	..	..	**773 265**	**736 089**	**374 178**	**284 409**	**361 952**	**482 781**	**519 374**
1000 Impôts sur revenu, bénéfices et gains en capital	..	..	..	**599 849**	**504 190**	**210 813**	**129 769**	**173 818**	**255 820**	**251 862**
1100 Des personnes physiques	..	..	..	55 020	97 997	94 216	86 497	88 590	88 445	105 077
1110 Sur le revenu et les bénéfices	..	..	..	55 020	97 997	94 216	86 497	88 590	88 445	105 077
Salariés, Bénéficiaires des pensions et rentes viagères	..	..	..	45 127	67 134	62 041	61 862	62 232	45 048	75 996
Bénéfice des proféssions libérales (non commerciales)	..	..	..	4 877	18 395	21 221	14 983	13 095	18 587	19 740
Bénéfice industriel et commercial	..	..	..	0	123	82	1 093	1 644	1 059	96
Propriétaires fonciers	..	..	..	1 470	1 817	2 434	281	1 094	7 077	2 098
Revenus des capitaux et valeurs mobilières	..	..	..	3 546	10 528	8 438	8 278	10 526	16 674	7 147
1120 Sur les gains en capital	..	..	..	0	0	0	0	0	0	0
1200 Des sociétés	..	..	..	539 410	404 027	114 480	41 350	83 464	165 042	140 200
1210 Sur les bénéfices	..	..	..	539 410	404 027	114 480	41 350	83 464	165 042	140 200
Impots sur les bénéfices des sociétés pétrolières	..	..	..	464 428	314 448	41 797	4 620	32 339	115 930	93 866
Impots sur les bénéfices des sociétés non-pétrolières	..	..	..	53 381	58 520	60 901	29 937	43 741	39 784	30 091
Autres impôts sur les sociétés	..	..	..	21 601	31 059	11 782	6 794	7 384	9 329	16 243
1220 Sur les gains en capital	..	..	..	0	0	0	0	0	0	0
1300 Non ventilables entre 1100 et 1200	..	..	..	5 418	2 166	2 118	1 921	1 763	2 333	6 585
2000 Cotisations de sécurité sociale	..	..	..	..	..	..	..	..	..	..
2100 A la charge des salariés	..	..	..	..	..	..	..	..	..	..
2110 Sur la base du salaire	..	..	..	..	..	..	..	..	..	..
2120 Sur la base de l'impôt sur les revenus	..	..	..	..	..	..	..	..	..	..
2200 A la charge des employeurs	..	..	..	..	..	..	..	..	..	..
2210 Sur la base du salaire	..	..	..	..	..	..	..	..	..	..
2220 Sur la base de l'impôt sur le revenu	..	..	..	..	..	..	..	..	..	..
2300 A charge des travailleurs indép. ou sans emploi	..	..	..	..	..	..	..	..	..	..
2310 Sur la base du salaire	..	..	..	..	..	..	..	..	..	..
2320 Sur la base de l'impôt sur le revenu	..	..	..	..	..	..	..	..	..	..
2400 Non ventilables entre 2100, 2200 et 2300	..	..	..	..	..	..	..	..	..	..
2410 Sur la base du salaire	..	..	..	..	..	..	..	..	..	..
2420 Sur la base de l'impôt sur le revenu	..	..	..	..	..	..	..	..	..	..
3000 Sur salaires ou main d'oeuvre	..	..	..	**8 304**	**11 322**	**10 856**	**6 703**	**6 860**	**1 512**	**8 050**
4000 Impôts sur le patrimoine	..	..	..	**23 875**	**24 268**	**11 922**	**7 909**	**5 740**	**7 041**	**23 620**
4100 Impôts périodiques sur la propriété immobilière	..	..	..	0	0	0	0	0	0	0
4110 Ménages	..	..	..	..	..	..	..	..	..	..
4120 Autres agents	..	..	..	..	..	..	..	..	..	..
4200 Impôts périodiques sur l'actif net	..	..	..	0	0	0	0	0	0	0
4210 Personnes physiques	..	..	..	..	..	..	..	..	..	..
4220 Sociétés	..	..	..	..	..	..	..	..	..	..
4300 Impôts sur mut. par décès, succ. et donations	..	..	..	71	0	0	0	1	12	1
4310 Impôts sur mut. par décès et successions	..	..	..	8	0	0	0	0	1	0
4320 Impôts sur les donations	..	..	..	63	0	0	0	1	12	1
4400 Impôts sur transact. mobilières et immob.	..	..	..	23 651	24 055	11 473	7 713	5 630	6 911	23 386
4500 Impôts non-périodiques	..	..	..	153	213	449	197	109	118	233
4510 Sur l'actif net	..	..	..	0	0	0	0	0	0	0
4520 Autres non-périodiques	..	..	..	153	213	449	197	109	118	233
4600 Autres impôts périodiques sur patrimoine	..	..	..	0	0	0	0	0	0	0
5000 Impôts sur les biens et services	..	..	..	**141 171**	**196 224**	**140 525**	**139 995**	**175 473**	**218 349**	**235 751**
5100 Impôts sur production, vente, transfert, etc.	..	..	..	139 026	194 627	138 375	138 379	174 252	209 235	233 597
5110 Impôts généraux	..	..	..	76 549	106 240	66 730	86 646	100 815	72 160	98 038
5111 Taxes sur la valeur ajoutée	..	..	..	76 549	106 240	66 730	86 646	100 815	72 160	98 038
Taxe sur la valeur ajoutée intérieure	..	..	..	46 148	65 241	45 476	56 619	69 912	39 374	55 598
TVA a l'importation	..	..	..	30 401	40 999	21 254	30 027	30 903	32 786	42 440
5112 Impôts sur les ventes	..	..	..	0	0	0	0	0	0	0
5113 Autres impôts	..	..	..	0	0	0	0	0	0	0
5120 Impôts sur biens et services déterminés	..	..	..	62 477	88 387	71 644	51 733	73 437	137 075	135 559
5121 Accises	..	..	..	9 387	8 704	10 161	11 436	22 541	31 307	34 947
Droit d'accises intérieurs	..	..	..	2 356	6 359	7 045	7 921	15 678	7 111	11 575
Droit d'accises importation	..	..	..	243	246	125	733	2 460	1 261	3 917
Carburants et lubrifiants	..	..	..	6 168	1 334	1 814	1 538	2 544	16 888	13 751
Taxe sur vente de bétail	..	..	..	621	765	1 177	1 243	1 859	1 581	1 734
Taxe intérieure sur les produits pétroliers	..	..	..	0	0	0	1	0	4 466	3 970
5122 Bénéfices de monopoles fiscaux	..	..	..	0	0	0	0	0	0	0

Table 5.5. **Chad / Tchad** *(cont.)*

Details of tax revenue / Recettes fiscales détaillées

Million XAF

	1999	2000	2009	2010	2014	2015	2016	2017	2018	2019
5123 Droits de douane et droits à l'importation	..	..	..	33 151	57 285	48 642	35 700	44 570	79 650	82 129
Droits de douane	..	..	..	26 441	49 339	44 056	31 167	31 229	51 448	54 869
Redevance statistique	..	..	..	6 709	7 947	4 586	4 533	13 341	28 202	27 260
5124 Taxes à l'exportation	..	..	..	19 078	21 945	12 375	3 832	5 683	8 152	5 224
Redevance statistique consortium	..	..	..	16 821	19 419	9 611	2 052	1 860	3 816	2 505
Droits de sortie	..	..	..	2 257	2 526	2 764	1 780	3 823	4 336	2 719
5125 Impôts sur biens d'équipement	..	..	..	0	0	0	0	0	0	0
5126 Impôts sur services déterminés	..	..	..	775	420	431	535	614	17 851	13 126
5127 Autres impôts sur commerce et transact. internat.	..	..	..	0	0	0	0	0	0	0
5128 Autres impôts	..	..	..	86	33	35	230	30	115	133
5130 Non ventilables entre 5110 et 5120	..	..	..	0	0	0	0	0	0	0
5200 Impôts sur utilisation des biens et exerc. activites	..	..	..	2 145	1 597	2 150	1 617	1 221	9 114	2 154
5210 Impôts périodiques	..	..	..	2 145	1 597	2 150	1 617	1 221	9 114	2 154
5211 A la charge des ménages: véhicules à moteur	..	..	..	1 567	1 096	1 929	1 355	694	8 829	519
5212 A la charge autres agents: véhicules à moteur	..	..	..	204	427	144	135	395	74	313
5213 Autres impôts périodiques	..	..	..	374	74	77	127	132	211	1 322
5220 Impôts non-périodiques	..	..	..	0	0	0	0	0	0	0
5300 Non ventilables entre 5100 et 5200	..	..	..	0	0	0	0	0	0	0
6000 Autres impôts	**..**	**..**	**..**	**67**	**85**	**62**	**33**	**61**	**59**	**83**
6100 A la charge exclusive des entreprises	..	..	..	..	..	..	..	..	..	..
6200 A la charge d'autres agents	..	..	..	..	..	..	..	..	..	..

.. Non disponible

Note : Année civile se terminant le 31 décembre.

Les données sont sur la base des encaissements.

Les chiffres n'incluent pas les recettes fiscales collectées par les collectivités locales car elles ne sont pas disponibles.

Les données 2010-18 ont été révisées.

Les recettes provenant des amendes fiscales, des recettes des valeurs mobilières de l'État et de la redevance audiovisuelle sont incluses dans les recettes non fiscales comme le préconise la classification OCDE (voir le guide d'interprétation en Annexe A). La classification nationale du Tchad les comptabilise comme des recettes fiscales.

Source : Ministère des Finances et du Budget du Tchad.

StatLink https://doi.org/10.1787/888934283747

Table 5.6. **Congo**

Details of tax revenue / Recettes fiscales détaillées

Million XAF

	1999	2000	2009	2010	2014	2015	2016	2017	2018	2019
Recettes fiscales totales	**99 782**	**98 684**	**363 985**	**451 987**	**853 192**	**902 868**	**798 829**	**695 816**	**564 871**	**590 712**
1000 Impôts sur revenu, bénéfices et gains en capital	**48 269**	**47 544**	**119 481**	**151 128**	**290 874**	**348 011**	**312 146**	**278 082**	**138 956**	**154 855**
1100 Des personnes physiques	26 300	22 850	55 380	64 700	151 089	150 869	152 392	154 434	114 722	124 272
1110 Sur le revenu et les bénéfices	26 300	22 850	55 380	64 700	151 089	150 869	152 392	154 434	114 722	124 272
Traitements et salaires	25 185	21 836	48 152	54 763	107 791	103 818	99 671	113 244	103 858	109 419
Revenus fonciers	772	549	2 197	2 259	4 752	5 531	6 020	3 534	3 658	3 517
Bénéfices non commerciaux (BNC)	0	0	14	112	50	50	19	37	1 377	2 497
Bénéfices industriels et commerciaux (BIC)	0	0	174	25	67	152	307	143	175	1 127
Revenu des valeurs mobilières (IRVM)	343	466	4 843	7 176	37 120	35 441	41 625	35 517	5 427	4 360
Retenue à la source sur marchés publics et sous-traitant BTP	0	0	0	0	858	471	407	313	221	1 106
Autres recettes sur le revenu des personnes physiques	0	0	0	365	451	5 406	4 345	1 646	6	2 247
1120 Sur les gains en capital	0	0	0	0	0	0	0	0	0	0
1200 Des sociétés	21 968	24 694	64 101	86 428	139 786	197 141	159 753	123 648	24 233	30 583
1210 Sur les bénéfices	21 968	24 694	64 101	86 428	139 786	197 141	159 753	123 648	24 233	30 583
1220 Sur les gains en capital	0	0	0	0	0	0	0	0	0	0
1300 Non ventilables entre 1100 et 1200	0	0	0	0	0	0	0	0	0	0
2000 Cotisations de sécurité sociale	..	..	..	..	..	..	..	..	..	..
2100 A la charge des salariés	..	..	..	..	..	..	..	..	..	..
2110 Sur la base du salaire	..	..	..	..	..	..	..	..	..	..
2120 Sur la base de l'impôt sur le revenu	..	..	..	..	..	..	..	..	..	..
2200 A la charge des employeurs	..	..	..	..	..	..	..	..	..	..
2210 Sur la base du salaire	..	..	..	..	..	..	..	..	..	..
2220 Sur la base de l'impôt sur le revenu	..	..	..	..	..	..	..	..	..	..
2300 A charge des travailleurs indép. ou sans emploi	..	..	..	..	..	..	..	..	..	..
2310 Sur la base du salaire	..	..	..	..	..	..	..	..	..	..
2320 Sur la base de l'impôt sur le revenu	..	..	..	..	..	..	..	..	..	..
2400 Non ventilables entre 2100, 2200 et 2300	..	..	..	..	..	..	..	..	..	..
2410 Sur la base du salaire	..	..	..	..	..	..	..	..	..	..
2420 Sur la base de l'impôt sur le revenu	..	..	..	..	..	..	..	..	..	..
3000 Sur salaires ou main d'oeuvre	**5 272**	**4 965**	**11 257**	**16 585**	**22 650**	**24 528**	**22 754**	**22 962**	**20 436**	**18 720**
4000 Impôts sur le patrimoine	**776**	**1 299**	**3 112**	**3 052**	**6 010**	**15 070**	**4 145**	**5 021**	**10 110**	**16 608**
4100 Impôts périodiques sur la propriété immobilière	0	0	0	0	0	0	0	0	0	0
4110 Ménages	..	..	..	..	..	..	..	..	..	..
4120 Autres agents	..	..	..	..	..	..	..	..	..	..
4200 Impôts périodiques sur l'actif net	0	0	0	0	0	0	0	0	0	0
4210 Personnes physiques	..	..	..	..	..	..	..	..	..	..
4220 Sociétés	..	..	..	..	..	..	..	..	..	..
4300 Impôts sur mut. par décès, succ. et donations	0	0	0	0	0	0	0	0	0	0
4310 Impôts sur mut. par décès et successions	..	..	..	..	..	..	..	..	..	..
4320 Impôts sur les donations	..	..	..	..	..	..	..	..	..	..
4400 Impôts sur transact. mobilières et immob.	776	1 299	3 112	3 052	6 010	15 070	4 145	5 021	10 110	16 608
4500 Impôts non-périodiques	0	0	0	0	0	0	0	0	0	0
4510 Sur l'actif net	..	..	..	..	..	..	..	..	..	..
4520 Autres non-périodiques	..	..	..	..	..	..	..	..	..	..
4600 Autres impôts périodiques sur patrimoine	0	0	0	0	0	0	0	0	0	0
5000 Impôts sur les biens et services	**45 466**	**44 876**	**230 136**	**281 222**	**533 657**	**515 259**	**459 785**	**389 751**	**395 369**	**400 529**
5100 Impôts sur production, vente, transfert, etc.	45 466	44 809	229 889	280 869	532 874	513 854	458 170	388 864	394 360	399 435
5110 Impôts généraux	40 579	39 641	123 997	158 512	301 410	284 586	251 308	222 924	242 924	234 201
5111 Taxes sur la valeur ajoutée	37 632	36 889	117 715	147 032	273 943	253 875	221 768	191 438	149 926	164 276
TVA Intérieure (brute)	38 279	38 962	66 138	92 054	177 038	163 875	140 255	125 630	95 165	101 543
TVA Douane (brute)	0	0	54 134	57 110	96 905	90 000	81 512	67 756	54 761	62 733
Remboursements de la TVA	-647	-2 073	-2 557	-2 132	0	0	0	-1 948	0	0
5112 Impôts sur les ventes	0	0	0	1 742	2 352	2 214	2 175	2 145	2 568	2 184
ASDI (Acompte sur divers impôts)	0	0	0	1 742	2 352	2 214	2 175	2 145	2 568	2 184
5113 Autres impôts	2 947	2 753	6 282	9 738	25 114	28 497	27 366	29 340	90 430	67 741
Taxe spéciale sur les societés (TSS)	2 947	2 753	6 282	9 738	22 830	26 248	25 999	28 288	23 758	25 511
Impôt global forfaitaire	0	0	0	0	2 285	2 250	1 366	1 052	830	858
Impôt forfaitaire sur les sociétés	0	0	0	0	0	0	0	0	57 916	36 860
Impôt forfaitaire sur le revenu des valeurs mobilières	0	0	0	0	0	0	0	0	7 925	4 513
5120 Impôts sur biens et services déterminés	4 587	5 059	105 538	122 357	231 464	229 268	206 862	165 940	149 746	164 126
5121 Accises	4 565	4 966	13 003	17 603	23 896	24 337	24 112	24 311	22 207	22 957
Taxe speciale sur les boissons alcoolisées et le tabac	0	0	0	0	10 862	11 140	11 320	10 114	9 351	9 363

Table 5.6. **Congo** *(cont.)*

Details of tax revenue / Recettes fiscales détaillées

Million XAF

	1999	2000	2009	2010	2014	2015	2016	2017	2018	2019
Droits d'accises	4 565	4 966	13 083	17 603	13 035	13 197	12 792	14 197	12 855	13 454
Taxe spécif. sur les boissons (TSB) - douanes	0	0	0	0	0	0	0	0	0	140
Taxe spécifique sur le tabac (TST) - douanes	0	0	0	0	0	0	0	0	0	1
5122 Bénéfices des monopoles fiscaux	0	0	0	0	0	0	0	0	0	0
5123 Droits de douane et droits à l'importation	0	0	74 610	85 775	172 774	166 613	139 716	106 503	91 286	104 670
Recettes importation	..	0	66 545	77 852	155 030	148 444	125 944	94 833	80 210	92 640
Recettes communautaires	..	0	8 065	7 923	17 745	18 169	13 771	11 670	11 076	12 030
5124 Taxes à l'exportation	0	0	0	0	0	0	0	617	5 380	3 220
5125 Impôts sur biens d'équipement	0	0	0	0	0	0	0	0	0	0
5126 Impôts sur services déterminés	22	93	17 844	18 979	34 793	38 318	43 034	34 509	30 873	33 279
Taxe sur les billets d'avion	0	0	327	597	780	849	791	721	634	640
Taxe sur les télécommunications électroniques	0	0	0	0	0	0	3 596	4 306	5 564	6 940
Taxe sur les assurances	22	93	1 037	1 526	2 009	2 703	2 250	2 418	2 741	3 735
Taxe sur le transfert de fonds	0	0	16 481	16 856	32 004	34 766	36 394	27 049	21 906	21 890
Taxe sur les jeux de hasard	0	0	0	0	0	0	3	14	27	75
5127 Autres impôts sur commerce et transact. internat.	0	0	0	0	0	0	0	0	0	0
5128 Autres impôts	0	0	0	0	0	0	0	0	0	0
5130 Non ventilables entre 5110 et 5120	300	109	354	0	0	0	0	0	1 690	1 108
5200 Impôts sur utilisation des biens et exerc. activites	0	67	246	353	783	1 405	1 615	887	1 009	1 094
5210 Impôts périodiques	..	67	246	353	783	1 405	1 615	887	834	750
5211 A la charge des ménages: véhicules à moteur	..	0	0	0	0	0	0	0	0	0
5212 A la charge autres agents: véhicules à moteur	..	67	246	343	736	1 405	1 006	887	814	750
5213 Autres impôts périodiques	..	0	0	10	47	0	608	0	20	0
5220 Impôts non-périodiques	..	0	0	0	0	0	0	0	176	345
Timbres sur les véhicules automobiles	..	0	0	0	0	0	0	0	176	345
5300 Non ventilables entre 5100 et 5200	0	0	0	0	0	0	0	0	0	0
6000 Autres impôts	**0**	**0**	**0**	**0**	**0**	**0**	**0**	**0**	**0**	**0**
6100 A la charge exclusive des entreprises	..	..	..	..	..	..	..	..	..	..
6200 A la charge d'autres agents	..	..	..	..	..	..	..	..	..	..

.. Non disponible

Note : Année civile se terminant le 31 décembre.

Les données sont sur la base des encaissements.

Les chiffres n'incluent pas les recettes fiscales collectées par les collectivités locales car elles ne sont pas disponibles.

Les données de 2018 et 2019 ont été revisées et une meilleure ventilation a été obtenue dans la rubrique 5113.

Rubrique 1210 : Cette rubrique inclut les recettes de l'impôt forfaitaire sur les sociétés et de l'impôt forfaitaire sur le revenu des valeurs mobilières des sociétés pour les années 1998 à 2019 car il n'a pas été possible de les distinguer des recettes de l'impôt sur les sociétés.

Rubrique 5113 : Cette rubrique inclut les recettes de l'impôt forfaitaire sur les sociétés et de l'impôt forfaitaire sur le revenu des valeurs mobilières des sociétés pour 2018 et 2019 comme le préconise la classification OCDE (voir le guide d'interprétation en Annexe A). La classification nationale de la république du Congo les comptabilise comme des recettes sur les bénéfices des sociétés.

Rubrique 5123 : Les droits d'exportation et des accises perçues à la douane sont inclus dans les données pour la période 2002-2016 car il n'a pas été possible de ventiler ces recettes.

Rubrique 5123 : Les droits d'exportation pour la période 2002-2016 sont inclus dans la rubrique 5123 car il n'a pas été possible de ventiler ces recettes.

Source : Ministère des Finances de la République du Congo.

StatLink https://doi.org/10.1787/888934283766

Table 5.7. **Congo, Dem. Rep. / Congo, Rép. dém.**

Details of tax revenue / Recettes fiscales détaillées

Million CDF

	1999	2000	2009	2010	2014	2015	2016	2017	2018	2019
Recettes fiscales totales	**..**	**7 551**	**1 185 787**	**1 661 159**	**3 182 256**	**3 450 697**	**3 211 131**	**3 860 919**	**5 848 641**	**6 279 193**
1000 Impôts sur revenu, bénéfices et gains en capital	**..**	**2 565**	**307 575**	**447 039**	**1 012 377**	**1 225 021**	**976 671**	**1 411 916**	**2 564 782**	**2 673 855**
1100 Des personnes physiques	..	996	154 403	208 715	516 536	515 851	509 354	660 669	821 801	834 587
1110 Sur le revenu et les bénéfices	..	996	154 403	208 715	516 536	515 851	509 354	660 669	821 801	834 587
Impôt sur les revenus des nationaux	..	899	121 919	162 931	421 427	417 442	409 977	507 845	589 377	631 366
Impôt sur les revenus - Institutions politiques	..	0	3 336	1 842	20 027	16 698	18 828	17 190	21 901	27 224
Impôt sur les revenus - Fonctionnaires et agents publics	..	0	0	0	9 298	12 825	12 789	9 632	10 968	8 855
Impôt sur les revenus - Régies financières	..	0	0	0	9 727	8 186	5 094	5 022	27 654	18 094
Impôt sur les revenus - Expatriés	..	81	29 024	43 779	55 507	59 921	62 241	119 707	170 926	148 489
Impôt sur les revenus - Profésssions libérales	..	15	124	44	0	0	0	0	0	0
Taxe ad valorem sur les gains des parieurs (DGRAD)	..	0	0	119	548	779	424	1 274	975	558
1120 Sur les gains en capital	..	..	..	..	..	..	..	..	..	..
1200 Des sociétés	..	1 569	153 172	237 937	495 784	709 095	467 230	751 074	1 742 853	1 838 845
Impôts sur les revenus des capitaux mobiliers	..	30	15 501	23 356	49 931	53 212	53 445	65 017	164 586	130 849
1210 Sur les bénéfices	..	1 539	137 671	214 582	445 853	655 884	413 785	686 057	1 578 267	1 707 995
Impôt sur les bénéfices - Sociétés non pétrolières	..	1 061	120 382	194 758	390 544	607 004	365 466	604 456	1 466 176	1 603 430
Impôt sur les bénéfices - Non résidents	..	0	0	0	42 882	46 124	45 450	75 010	102 597	97 818
Impôt sur les bénéfices - Entreprises individuelles	..	410	17 289	19 823	12 426	2 756	2 869	6 590	9 494	6 747
Impôts sur les revenus locatifs	..	69	0	0	0	0	0	0	0	0
1220 Sur les gains en capital	..	..	..	..	..	..	..	..	..	..
1300 Non ventilables entre 1100 et 1200	..	..	..	386	57	75	87	173	128	424
2000 Cotisations de sécurité sociale	**..**	**..**	**..**	**..**	**201 049**	**204 103**	**195 756**	**291 371**	**358 466**	**635 957**
2100 A la charge des salariés	..	..	..	..	55 885	56 493	77 021	114 904	117 412	176 369
2110 Sur la base du salaire	..	..	..	..	55 885	56 493	77 021	114 904	117 412	176 369
2120 Sur la base de l'impôt sur le revenu	..	..	..	..	0	0	0	0	0	0
2200 A la charge des employeurs	..	..	..	..	145 101	147 566	118 672	176 313	240 968	459 282
2210 Sur la base du salaire	..	..	..	..	145 101	147 566	118 672	176 313	240 968	459 282
2220 Sur la base de l'impôt sur le revenu	..	..	..	..	0	0	0	0	0	0
2300 A charge des travailleurs indép. ou sans emploi	..	..	..	..	0	0	0	0	0	0
2310 Sur la base du salaire	..	..	..	..	..	..	..	..	..	..
2320 Sur la base de l'impôt sur le revenu	..	..	..	..	..	..	..	..	..	..
2400 Non ventilables entre 2100, 2200 et 2300	..	..	..	..	63	44	64	154	86	307
2410 Sur la base du salaire	..	..	..	..	..	..	..	..	..	..
2420 Sur la base de l'impôt sur le revenu	..	..	..	..	..	..	..	..	..	..
3000 Sur salaires ou main d'oeuvre	**..**	**56**	**13 576**	**15 370**	**49 047**	**48 503**	**43 343**	**59 173**	**91 777**	**121 128**
Impôt sur les rémunérations des expatriés (IERE)	..	56	13 576	15 370	49 047	48 503	43 343	59 173	91 777	121 128
4000 Impôts sur le patrimoine	**..**	**..**	**..**	**9 644**	**13 731**	**12 983**	**14 854**	**19 593**	**38 796**	**44 567**
4100 Impôts périodiques sur la propriété immobilière	..	..	..	3 695	9 743	8 817	9 254	10 546	20 710	31 985
4110 Ménages	..	..	..	..	..	..	..	..	..	..
4120 Autres agents	..	..	..	..	..	..	..	..	..	..
4200 Impôts périodiques sur l'actif net	..	..	..	..	..	..	..	..	..	..
4210 Personnes physiques	..	..	..	..	..	..	..	..	..	..
4220 Sociétés	..	..	..	..	..	..	..	..	..	..
4300 Impôts sur mut. par décès, succ. et donations	..	..	..	..	..	..	..	..	..	..
4310 Impôts sur mut. par décès et successions	..	..	..	..	..	..	..	..	..	..
4320 Impôts sur les donations	..	..	..	..	..	..	..	..	..	..
4400 Impôts sur transact. mobilières et immob.	..	..	..	5 949	3 988	4 166	5 600	9 047	10 078	12 582
4500 Impôts non-périodiques	..	..	..	..	..	..	..	..	..	..
4510 Sur l'actif net	..	..	..	..	..	..	..	..	..	..
4520 Autres non-périodiques	..	..	..	..	..	..	..	..	..	..
4600 Autres impôts périodiques sur patrimoine	..	..	..	..	..	..	..	..	..	..
5000 Impôts sur les biens et services	**..**	**4 931**	**793 401**	**1 090 021**	**1 759 710**	**1 881 272**	**1 943 164**	**2 003 566**	**2 594 311**	**2 680 969**
5100 Impôts sur production, vente, transfert, etc.	..	4 833	791 107	1 064 245	1 745 202	1 866 774	1 925 628	1 977 784	2 525 463	2 622 648
5110 Impôts généraux	..	1 390	451 325	590 594	804 138	891 546	1 056 005	1 127 384	1 456 884	1 417 107
5111 Taxes sur la valeur ajoutée	..	0	0	0	802 236	891 404	1 055 955	1 127 186	1 456 766	1 417 090
TVA intérieure (brute)	..	..	..	..	585 321	639 995	619 212	705 628	939 202	1 055 667
TVA à l'importation (brute)	..	..	..	..	873 055	879 549	561 978	538 173	766 232	803 860
Remboursements TVA	..	..	..	..	-656 140	-628 140	-125 234	-116 616	-248 668	-442 438
5112 Impôts sur les ventes	..	..	..	110	0	0	0	0	0	0

Table 5.7. **Congo, Dem. Rep. / Congo, Rép. dém.** *(cont.)*

Details of tax revenue / Recettes fiscales détaillées

Million CDF

	1999	2000	2009	2010	2014	2015	2016	2017	2018	2019
5113 Autres impôts	..	1 390	451 325	590 484	1 903	143	50	199	119	18
Impôt sur le chiffre d'affaires (ICA) - ventes locales	..	194	90 125	110 004	405	143	47	196	118	14
Impôt sur le chiffre d'affaires (ICA) - Prestations de services	..	409	135 850	181 338	1 310	0	0	0	0	0
Impôt sur le chiffre d'affaires (ICA) - Travaux immobiliers	..	14	5 897	5 969	186	0	0	0	0	0
Impôt sur le chiffre d'affaires (ICA) - Exportation produits miniers	..	0	0	0	0	0	0	0	0	0
Impôt sur le chiffre d'affaires (ICA) - Exportation hors produits miniers	..	6	0	0	0	0	0	0	0	0
ICA/ Importation	..	768	219 453	291 557	0	0	0	0	0	0
Autres impôts géneraux sur les biens et services (DGRAD)	..	0	0	1 616	2	0	2	3	0	3
5120 Impôts sur biens et services déterminés	..	3 442	339 782	473 651	941 064	975 227	869 623	850 400	1 068 579	1 205 541
5121 Accises	..	1 417	122 581	195 837	353 073	409 441	440 387	414 521	482 304	526 419
Redevances sur produits spécifiques (DGRAD)	..	0	0	12 259	807	3 256	1 303	502	563	630
Droits d'accises perçus en régime intérieur	..	1 380	85 692	153 005	249 131	241 476	236 188	301 406	352 244	387 547
Accises (intérieur) - Boissons	..	..	45 424	62 785	145 392	148 179	133 236	178 344	198 758	204 002
Accises (intérieur) - Tabacs et allumettes	..	..	24 624	40 034	14 316	2 643	9 149	3 875	4 901	10 448
Accises (intérieur) - Télécommunication	..	..	15 203	49 338	78 063	86 315	88 198	116 686	145 710	168 852
Accises (intérieur) - Autres produits	..	..	441	848	11 360	4 339	5 605	2 501	2 875	4 245
Droits d'accises perçus à l'importation	..	37	36 888	30 573	103 135	164 710	202 895	112 613	129 497	138 242
Accises (importation) - Boissons	..	..	1 680	2 431	10 474	13 556	13 847	11 696	20 712	11 987
Accises (importation) - Tabacs et allumettes	..	..	3 019	4 739	35 609	59 422	46 449	60 476	54 475	66 304
Accises (importation) - Produits pétroliers	..	..	18 963	9 257	12 671	53 350	102 829	0	0	0
Accises (importation) - Véhicules	..	..	10 813	9 901	11 961	15 878	12 022	15 444	23 427	22 940
Accises (importation) - Autres produits	..	..	2 414	4 246	32 421	22 504	27 749	24 997	30 883	37 011
5122 Bénéfices des monopoles fiscaux	..	0	0	0	0	0	0	0	0	0
5123 Droits de douane et droits à l'importation	..	1 942	209 159	270 089	580 820	560 340	420 432	423 341	569 751	670 378
5124 Taxes à l'exportation	..	83	8 042	7 725	7 171	5 446	4 529	7 413	9 505	7 984
Droits de sortie sur les minerais	..	82	5 731	3 850	2 791	3 238	2 774	5 391	4 780	2 713
Droits de sortie sur les produits agricoles	..	1	2 007	3 046	4 379	2 208	1 755	2 022	4 725	5 271
Droits de sortie sur les autres produits	..	0	304	829	0	0	0	0	0	0
5125 Impôts sur biens d'équipement	..	0	0	0	0	0	0	0	0	0
5126 Impôts sur services déterminés	..	0	0	0	0	0	4 275	5 126	7 019	759
5127 Autres impôts sur commerce et transact. internat.	..	0	0	0	0	0	0	0	0	0
5128 Autres impôts	..	0	0	0	0	0	0	0	0	0
5130 Non ventilables entre 5110 et 5120	..	0	0	0	0	0	0	0	0	0
5200 Impôts sur utilisation des biens et exerc. activites	..	98	2 294	25 776	14 508	14 499	17 536	25 781	68 848	58 321
5210 Impôts périodiques	..	0	0	1 564	947	881	2 443	1 191	2 309	3 163
5211 A la charge des ménages: véhicules à moteur	..	..	..	0	0	0	0	0	0	0
5212 A la charge autres agents: véhicules à moteur	..	..	..	3	37	7	0	16	8	28
5213 Autres impôts périodiques	..	..	..	1 561	910	874	2 443	1 175	2 301	3 135
5220 Impôts non-périodiques	..	98	2 294	24 212	13 561	13 617	15 093	24 591	66 539	55 158
Immatriculation des véhicules routiers (plaques)	..	98	2 294	2 681	2 507	1 366	1 373	2 425	3 734	3 476
Autorisations d'exportation et d'importation	..	0	0	2 909	1 791	3 567	2 642	4 013	4 561	4 018
Taxe d'implantation établisssements dangereux, insalubres et incommodes	..	0	0	1 203	3 079	2 849	3 184	3 148	45 849	32 801
Autres autorisations (DGRAD)	..	0	0	17 419	6 184	5 835	7 894	15 005	12 394	14 863
5300 Non ventilables entre 5100 et 5200	..	0	0	0	0	0	0	0	0	0
6000 Autres impôts	**..**	**0**	**71 236**	**99 085**	**146 341**	**78 815**	**37 342**	**75 301**	**200 509**	**122 716**
Recettes des produits pétroliers	..	..	71 236	98 431	144 910	78 417	35 540	74 389	106 245	121 703
Droits proportionnels sur les S.A.R.L. (DGRAD)	..	..	0	654	1 431	398	1 803	912	94 264	1 013
6100 A la charge exclusive des entreprises	..	..	..	..	..	..	..	..	..	..
6200 A la charge d'autres agents	..	..	..	..	..	..	..	..	..	..

Table 5.7. **Congo, Dem. Rep. / Congo, Rép. dém.** *(cont.)*

Details of tax revenue / Recettes fiscales détaillées

.. Non disponible

Note : Année civile se terminant le 31 décembre.

Les données sont sur la base des encaissements.

Les chiffres n'incluent pas les données des recettes fiscales collectées par les collectivités locales car elles ne sont pas disponibles.

Les données entre 2000 à 2003 doivent être interprétées avec prudence car elles sont largement affectées par des taux d'inflation élevés.

Les recettes provenant de la vente des imprimés sont incluses dans les recettes non fiscales (Ventes de biens et services) comme le préconise la classification OCDE (voir le guide d'interprétation en Annexe A). Elles sont considérées comme des recettes fiscales en République démocratique du Congo.

Rubrique 2000 : Cette rubrique inclut les cotisations à la Caisse Nationale de Sécurité Sociale (CNSS) pour 2012-19 et pour la première fois dans cette édition les cotisations à l' Office national de l'emploi pour 2013-19.

Rubriques 1110, 5113, 5121, 5220, 6000 : Pour la période 2010-19, ces rubriques contiennent des recettes provenant de la Direction Générale des Recettes Administratives, Judiciaires, Domaniales et de Participation (DGRAD) et sont annotées comme telles. Elles sont incluses dans les recettes fiscales comme le préconise la classification OCDE (voir le guide d'interprétation en Annexe A) mais considérées comme des recettes non fiscales en République démocratique du Congo.

Rubriques 1300, 4100, 4400, 5112, 5126, 5128, 5212, 5213 : Pour la période 2010-19, ces rubriques contiennent des recettes provenant exclusivement de la DGRAD. Elles sont incluses dans les recettes fiscales comme le préconise la classification OCDE (voir le guide d'interprétation en Annexe A) mais considérées comme des recettes non fiscales en République démocratique du Congo. Le total des recettes provenant de la DGRAD considérées comme recettes fiscales représente en moyenne 1 % du total des recettes fiscales.

Source : Ministère des Finances de la République démocratique du Congo.

StatLink https://doi.org/10.1787/888934283785

Table 5.8. **Côte d'Ivoire**

Details of tax revenue / Recettes fiscales détaillées

Million XOF

	1999	2000	2009	2010	2014	2015	2016	2017	2018	2019
Recettes fiscales totales	**1 212 095**	**1 169 607**	**1 927 829**	**2 035 468**	**2 946 104**	**3 414 418**	**3 736 455**	**3 983 683**	**4 194 689**	**4 527 842**
1000 Impôts sur revenu, bénéfices et gains en capital	**216 337**	**192 282**	**278 665**	**260 799**	**401 740**	**408 880**	**419 405**	**484 103**	**574 179**	**557 445**
1100 Des personnes physiques	5 161	5 108	6 189	6 970	9 430	10 054	10 762	12 199	13 894	13 089
1110 Sur le revenu et les bénéfices	5 145	5 093	6 164	6 937	9 388	10 011	10 711	12 147	13 822	13 023
Impôt général sur le revenu	0	0	336	1 420	635	817	663	283	114	57
Impôt BIC hors pétrole-gaz (personnes physiques)	5 091	5 045	5 738	5 431	8 610	9 008	9 859	11 660	13 457	12 760
IR des valeurs mobilières (pers. physiques)	54	48	90	86	143	186	189	204	252	206
1120 Sur les gains en capital	16	16	25	33	42	42	51	52	72	67
IR des capitaux (pers. physiques)	16	16	25	33	42	42	51	52	72	67
1200 Des sociétés	152 152	148 900	260 251	240 768	371 821	375 893	384 251	444 595	534 279	517 653
1210 Sur les bénéfices	146 705	143 602	251 941	229 732	357 867	361 782	367 300	427 439	510 483	495 535
Impôt BIC pétrole-gaz	0	0	76 872	63 649	92 389	71 985	54 962	64 392	86 071	104 181
Impôt BIC hors pétrole-gaz (personnes morales)	128 883	127 710	145 264	137 500	217 980	228 043	249 588	295 180	340 667	323 022
IR des valeurs mobilieres (pers. morales)	17 822	15 892	29 805	28 583	47 499	61 753	62 750	67 868	83 745	68 332
1220 Sur les gains en capital	5 447	5 297	8 311	11 036	13 954	14 111	16 951	17 155	23 796	22 118
Impôt sur le revenu des capitaux (personnes morales)	5 447	5 297	8 311	11 036	13 954	14 111	16 951	17 155	23 796	22 118
1300 Non ventilables entre 1100 et 1200	59 024	38 274	12 225	13 061	20 489	22 934	24 392	27 310	26 006	26 703
L'acompte d'impôt sur le revenu du secteur informel (ex ASDI)	55 092	33 983	6 713	7 624	12 509	14 637	16 380	18 567	15 845	16 023
Impôt synthétique	3 932	4 291	5 512	5 437	7 980	8 296	8 011	8 744	10 162	10 680
2000 Cotisations de sécurité sociale	**83 693**	**102 700**	**151 180**	**162 754**	**340 667**	**383 540**	**443 310**	**455 744**	**479 197**	**509 592**
2100 A la charge des salariés	..	..	..	64 364	135 406	151 728	177 045	180 368	189 616	201 522
CNPS	..	..	..	39 044	84 360	92 206	113 016	109 856	115 381	122 230
CGRAE	..	..	..	25 320	51 046	59 522	64 029	70 512	74 235	79 292
2110 Sur la base du salaire	..	..	..	0	0	0	0	0	0	0
2120 Sur la base de l'impôt sur le revenu	..	..	..	0	0	0	0	0	0	0
2200 A la charge des employeurs	..	..	..	98 390	205 261	231 812	266 265	275 376	289 581	308 070
CNPS	..	..	..	47 721	103 107	112 697	138 130	134 268	141 022	149 392
CGRAE	..	..	..	50 669	102 154	119 115	128 135	141 108	148 559	158 678
2210 Sur la base du salaire	..	..	..	0	0	0	0	0	0	0
2220 Sur la base de l'impôt sur le revenu	..	..	..	0	0	0	0	0	0	0
2300 A charge des travailleurs indép. ou sans emploi	..	..	..	0	0	0	0	0	0	0
2310 Sur la base du salaire	..	..	..	..	..	..	..	..	..	..
2320 Sur la base de l'impôt sur le revenu	..	..	..	..	..	..	..	..	..	..
2400 Non ventilables entre 2100, 2200 et 2300	83 693	102 700	151 180	0	0	0	0	0	0	0
2410 Sur la base du salaire	..	..	..	..	..	..	..	..	..	..
2420 Sur la base de l'impôt sur le revenu	..	..	..	..	..	..	..	..	..	..
3000 Sur salaires ou main d'oeuvre	**120 476**	**138 023**	**196 175**	**207 243**	**322 884**	**372 524**	**424 516**	**448 740**	**497 124**	**527 045**
Fonds de formation professionnelle	6 977	6 990	8 702	9 776	12 483	11 805	13 336	18 439	22 674	23 966
Impôt sur traitements et salaires (ITS), solde	113 499	131 033	187 473	197 467	310 400	360 719	411 180	430 301	474 449	503 079
4000 Impôts sur le patrimoine	**29 308**	**32 732**	**48 123**	**49 706**	**79 839**	**89 040**	**106 691**	**102 450**	**120 153**	**139 654**
4100 Impôts périodiques sur la propriété immobilière	20 350	24 664	37 316	38 009	64 645	72 299	79 627	83 394	99 417	113 362
4110 Ménages	..	..	..	..	..	..	..	..	..	..
4120 Autres agents	..	..	..	..	..	..	..	..	..	..
4200 Impôts périodiques sur l'actif net	0	0	0	0	0	0	0	0	0	0
4210 Personnes physiques	..	..	..	..	..	..	..	..	..	..
4220 Sociétés	..	..	..	..	..	..	..	..	..	..
4300 Impôts sur mut. par décès, succ. et donations	0	0	0	0	0	0	0	0	0	0
4310 Impôts sur mut. par décès et successions	..	..	..	..	..	..	..	..	..	..
4320 Impôts sur les donations	..	..	..	..	..	..	..	..	..	..
4400 Impôts sur transact. mobilières et immob.	8 958	8 068	10 807	11 697	15 194	16 741	27 064	19 055	20 735	26 292
4500 Impôts non-périodiques	0	0	0	0	0	0	0	0	0	0
4510 Sur l'actif net	..	..	..	..	..	..	..	..	..	..
4520 Autres non-périodiques	..	..	..	..	..	..	..	..	..	..
4600 Autres impôts périodiques sur patrimoine	0	0	0	0	0	0	0	0	0	0
5000 Impôts sur les biens et services	**758 138**	**699 518**	**1 242 967**	**1 344 201**	**1 783 892**	**2 139 379**	**2 319 981**	**2 470 069**	**2 499 839**	**2 760 029**
5100 Impôts sur production, vente, transfert, etc.	736 778	674 206	1 195 902	1 294 835	1 710 242	2 057 991	2 229 495	2 375 614	2 396 326	2 650 639
5110 Impôts généraux	265 144	255 297	424 588	490 521	619 101	692 417	717 607	809 711	897 334	982 115
5111 Taxes sur la valeur ajoutée	265 144	255 297	401 133	473 712	610 021	680 081	703 826	795 366	883 175	963 541
Recettes TVA (brute) - DGI	94 044	106 797	191 564	194 241	280 819	327 995	354 521	422 679	471 327	516 161
Remboursements credits de TVA (DGI)	0	0	-18 315	-15 480	-25 355	-41 825	-38 159	-43 107	-42 599	-49 349
Recettes TVA (brute) - DGD	171 100	148 500	250 268	313 870	385 546	445 028	446 235	469 599	504 893	547 827
Remboursements credits de TVA (DGD)	0	0	-22 384	-18 919	-30 988	-51 118	-58 771	-53 805	-50 446	-51 099
5112 Impôts sur les ventes	0	0	0	0	0	0	0	0	0	0

Table 5.8. **Côte d'Ivoire** *(cont.)*

Details of tax revenue / Recettes fiscales détaillées

Million XOF

	1999	2000	2009	2010	2014	2015	2016	2017	2018	2019
5113 Autres impôts	0	0	23 455	16 809	9 080	12 336	13 782	14 345	14 159	18 575
Taxe ad-valorem (taxe domaniale)	..	..	0	0	8 760	12 185	13 679	14 293	13 932	18 565
Contribution à la reconstitution nationale	..	..	23 455	1 567	63	71	68	42	98	10
Taxe de solidarité pour la sortie de crise	..	..	0	15 243	257	80	35	10	128	0
5120 Impôts sur biens et services déterminés	471 634	418 909	771 314	804 314	1 091 140	1 365 574	1 511 888	1 565 903	1 498 991	1 668 523
5121 Accises	79 978	74 908	120 478	128 698	130 450	243 151	307 895	310 893	308 095	376 839
Taxe SIDA	0	0	385	740	908	821	621	781	1 048	1 299
Taxe sur le caoutchouc	0	0	0	0	3 124	78	168	5 075	5	66
Taxe sur le tabac pour le dévelopment du sport	0	0	1 505	1 708	2 158	2 029	1 529	1 955	2 621	3 246
Taxe sur les sacs et sachets en matière plastique	0	0	0	0	172	113	37	71	107	122
Taxe sur les boissons	2 041	3 642	4 014	5 050	14 563	18 213	19 084	21 695	24 536	25 343
Taxes sur le carburant	258	290	91	81	95	105	123	130	173	310
Taxes sur le tabac	15 379	15 518	10 877	12 040	19 817	14 771	10 731	13 554	18 786	23 971
Diverses taxes spécifiques à la DGD	62 300	50 300	95 347	96 560	72 567	183 719	242 824	232 598	224 397	281 613
Diverses accises spécifiques à la DGD	0	5 158	8 258	12 520	17 046	23 302	32 777	35 034	36 420	40 803
Taxe spéciale pour la préseration et développement forestier (TSPDF)	0	0	0	0	0	0	0	0	0	66
5122 Bénéfices des monopoles fiscaux	0	0	0	0	0	0	0	0	0	0
5123 Droits de douane et droits à l'importation	175 500	126 512	213 444	288 039	459 674	486 862	500 772	540 927	586 581	607 626
5124 Taxes à l'exportation	181 754	185 114	377 133	331 261	363 222	473 333	520 798	535 512	417 137	477 488
Droits d'enregistrement du café et cacao	4 954	21 114	150 610	103 669	38 033	86 244	128 522	80 719	12 901	39 240
Taxe sur le cacao et café (DGD)	169 800	156 700	217 587	221 180	316 371	377 418	383 637	436 999	343 058	394 161
Taxe sur le bois et autres produits (DGD)	7 000	7 300	8 936	6 412	8 819	9 671	8 639	8 574	2 103	2 236
Dus Anacarde (DGD)	0	0	0	0	0	0	0	9 220	59 076	41 850
5125 Impôts sur biens d'équipement	0	0	0	0	0	0	0	0	0	0
5126 Impôts sur services déterminés	34 402	32 375	60 259	56 315	137 794	162 229	182 423	178 571	187 178	206 570
Contribution de solidarité sur les billets d'avion	0	0	234	216	1 273	3 088	488	100	47	0
Taxe sur le transport aérien	0	0	718	799	2 054	2 569	2 434	1 651	2 101	2 014
Taxe pour la promotion de la culture	0	0	1 613	1 598	2 279	1 884	1 855	1 881	1 849	2 169
Taxe développement des NTICs en zone rurale	0	0	17 538	11 486	16 528	16 977	17 318	20 424	20 318	20 830
Taxe sur les télécommunications	0	0	0	0	43 080	50 618	62 459	47 238	46 893	52 160
Taxes sur les transports urbains	0	0	868	1 019	174	3	7	0	0	0
Prélèvement aux jeux de casino	357	168	286	378	273	163	7	444	1 080	2 324
Taxe d'abattage	2 443	2 434	937	1 125	1 280	1 299	1 354	1 315	659	1 309
Taxe sur la publicité	87	137	251	300	411	437	258	510	1 051	940
Taxe pour le développement touristique	0	0	0	0	1 001	1 298	1 420	1 569	1 609	1 908
Communications téléphoniques	0	0	0	0	16 667	20 425	23 395	23 694	20 659	20 091
Taxe sur les assurances	8 791	6 942	8 757	7 739	12 214	14 435	15 076	17 295	19 228	20 445
Taxe sur les encours bancaires	2 001	2 002	2 992	3 627	3	0	581	0	0	0
Taxe sur les opérations bancaires	20 723	20 692	26 066	28 028	40 554	49 023	55 770	62 449	66 122	70 418
Taxe Salubrité et Protection de l'Environnement	0	0	0	0	2	11	0	1	2	2
Taxe pour l'enlèvement des ordures menagères	0	0	0	0	0	0	0	0	5 559	11 307
Taxe portuaire et aéroportuaire	0	0	0	0	0	0	0	0	0	655
5127 Autres impôts sur commerce et transact. internat.	0	0	0	0	0	0	0	0	0	0
5128 Autres impôts	0	0	0	0	0	0	0	0	0	0
5130 Non ventilables entre 5110 et 5120	0	0	0	0	0	0	0	0	0	0
5200 Impôts sur utilisation des biens et exerc. activites	21 360	25 312	47 065	49 366	73 651	81 388	90 486	94 456	103 513	109 390
5210 Impôts périodiques	21 360	25 312	47 065	49 366	73 651	81 388	90 486	94 456	103 513	109 390
5211 A la charge des ménages: véhicules à moteur	4 317	4 176	7 928	9 171	13 403	14 926	16 103	17 206	18 423	17 592
5212 A la charge autres agents: véhicules à moteur	0	0	0	0	0	0	0	0	0	0
5213 Autres impôts périodiques	17 043	21 136	39 137	40 195	60 248	66 462	74 383	77 250	85 091	91 798
5220 Impôts non-périodiques	0	0	0	0	0	0	0	0	0	0
5300 Non ventilables entre 5100 et 5200	0	0	0	0	0	0	0	0	0	0
6000 Autres impôts	**4 143**	**4 352**	**10 719**	**10 765**	**17 082**	**21 055**	**22 551**	**22 577**	**24 197**	**34 077**
6100 A la charge exclusive des entreprises	0	0	3 823	3 732	5 622	6 979	7 719	9 414	10 275	10 657
Fonds de soutien à l'habitat	..	..	266	45	0	0	0	0	0	0
Fonds interprofessionnel	..	..	3 556	3 687	5 622	6 979	7 719	9 414	10 275	10 657
6200 A la charge d'autres agents	4 143	4 352	6 896	7 033	11 460	14 076	14 833	13 163	13 922	23 420

Table 5.8. **Côte d'Ivoire** *(cont.)*

Details of tax revenue / Recettes fiscales détaillées

.. Non disponible

Note : Année civile se terminant le 31 décembre.

Les données sont sur la base des encaissements.

Les chiffres n'incluent pas les recettes fiscales collectées par les collectivités locales.

Rubrique 2000 : Des données plus détaillées sont disponibles pour la première fois pour cette édition.

La rubrique 5113 comprend la taxe ad-valorem, une taxe domaniale. Les recettes autres que celles de la taxe ad-valorem sont considérées comme des recettes non fiscales selon la classification OCDE (voir le guide d'interprétation en Annexe A). La classification nationale de la Côte d'Ivoire les comptabilise comme des recettes fiscales.

La rubrique 5113 comprend la Contribution à la reconstruction nationale (CRN) instituée en 2004 pour cinq ans et arrivée à expiration en 2009. Elle a été remplacée par la Contribution pour la sortie de crise. Celle-ci était basée sur les charges d'exploitation des entreprises réalisant un chiffre d'affaires annuel supérieur ou égal à 1 milliard de francs, au titre de l'exercice clos au 31 décembre 2009.

La rubrique 6100 comprend le Fonds de soutien à l'habitat (FSH) alimenté par des recettes fiscales affectées (contribution patronale sur la masse salariale, taxes sur services déterminés et taxe sur le carburant). Il n'est pas possible de distinguer ces différents éléments d'où sa classification dans la rubrique 6100. Cette taxe a été supprimée en 2010.

Les recettes de la taxe audiovisuelle et la redevance radiodiffusion télévision ivoirienne (RTI) sont considérées comme des recettes non fiscales selon la classification OCDE (voir le guide d'interprétation en Annexe A) et ont été classifiées dans la rubrique « vente de biens et services». La classification nationale de la Côte d'Ivoire les comptabilise comme des recettes fiscales.

Source : Ministère de l'Économie et des Finances.

StatLink https://doi.org/10.1787/888934283804

Table 5.9. **Egypt / Égypte**

Details of tax revenue / Recettes fiscales détaillées

Million EGP

	1999	2000	2009	2010	2014	2015	2016	2017	2018	2019
Total tax revenue	..	..	**179 630**	**191 492**	**302 070**	**356 096**	**391 033**	**526 741**	**661 558**	**758 065**
1000 Taxes on income, profits and capital gains	..	..	**83 874**	**85 767**	**146 954**	**157 032**	**179 538**	**213 744**	**289 850**	**332 133**
1100 Of individuals	..	..	14 282	16 368	31 411	38 213	42 352	51 011	64 525	87 212
1110 On income and profits	..	..	14 222	16 285	31 193	37 934	42 009	50 627	64 125	86 345
Tax on domestic salaries	..	..	8 270	9 623	19 336	23 803	28 098	34 189	40 976	56 938
Taxes on industrial & commercial profits	..	..	4 688	4 570	8 431	10 589	9 247	11 508	16 815	24 657
Stamp duty on salaries	..	..	874	1 778	2 916	2 998	3 933	3 776	4 683	2 243
Tax on professionals income	..	..	390	314	509	544	731	1 154	1 650	2 506
1120 On capital gains	..	..	60	84	218	279	343	384	400	867
1200 Corporate	..	..	65 971	66 022	104 768	108 285	125 457	146 747	186 374	209 702
1210 On profits	..	..	65 971	66 022	104 768	108 285	125 457	146 747	186 374	209 702
EGPC & foreign partner	..	..	34 135	32 181	46 060	36 000	37 313	42 464	51 976	42 532
Suez Canal Authority	..	..	10 391	9 443	14 312	13 400	14 903	22 300	29 900	34 480
Central Bank of Egypt	..	..	0	0	4 042	3 691	13 245	3 860	0	0
Other companies	..	..	21 445	18 591	25 099	38 512	36 926	47 259	60 776	85 763
Interest income from T-Bills and Bonds	..	..	0	5 808	15 256	16 682	23 069	30 864	43 722	46 928
1220 On capital gains	..	..	..	..	..	..	..	..	..	..
1300 Unallocable between 1100 and 1200	..	..	3 622	3 377	10 775	10 534	11 729	15 987	38 952	35 219
Tax on movable capital revenues from C.B.E	..	..	3 367	3 243	10 604	10 228	10 965	15 691	38 497	34 526
Delayed tax income	..	..	254	134	171	306	765	296	455	693
2000 Social security contributions	..	..	**22 809**	**28 032**	**51 139**	**60 693**	**49 331**	**79 454**	**52 500**	**48 500**
2100 Employees	..	..	0	0	0	0	0	0	0	0
2110 On a payroll basis	..	..	..	..	..	..	..	..	..	..
2120 On an income tax basis	..	..	..	..	..	..	..	..	..	..
2200 Employers	..	..	0	0	0	0	0	0	0	0
2210 On a payroll basis	..	..	..	..	..	..	..	..	..	..
2220 On an income tax basis	..	..	..	..	..	..	..	..	..	..
2300 Self-employed or non-employed	..	..	0	0	0	0	0	0	0	0
2310 On a payroll basis	..	..	..	..	..	..	..	..	..	..
2320 On an income tax basis	..	..	..	..	..	..	..	..	..	..
2400 Unallocable between 2100, 2200 and 2300	..	..	22 809	28 032	51 139	60 693	49 331	79 454	52 500	48 500
2410 On a payroll basis	..	..	..	..	..	..	..	..	..	..
2420 On an income tax basis	..	..	..	..	..	..	..	..	..	..
3000 Taxes on payroll and workforce	..	..	**0**	**0**	**0**	**0**	**0**	**0**	**0**	**0**
4000 Taxes on property	..	..	**1 160**	**1 128**	**1 237**	**2 224**	**2 484**	**3 237**	**4 214**	**6 266**
4100 Recurrent taxes on immovable property	..	..	612	518	428	637	1 172	2 055	2 976	4 856
4110 Households	..	..	..	..	..	..	..	..	..	..
4120 Others	..	..	..	..	..	..	..	..	..	..
4200 Recurrent taxes on net wealth	..	..	0	0	0	0	0	0	0	0
4210 Individual	..	..	..	..	..	..	..	..	..	..
4220 Corporate	..	..	..	..	..	..	..	..	..	..
4300 Estate, inheritance and gift taxes	..	..	0	0	0	0	0	0	0	0
4310 Estate and inheritance taxes	..	..	..	..	..	..	..	..	..	..
4320 Gift taxes	..	..	..	..	..	..	..	..	..	..
4400 Taxes on financial and capital transactions	..	..	548	610	809	1 588	1 312	1 182	1 238	1 410
Property transferring fees	..	..	546	607	799	948	1 002	1 134	1 235	1 407
Stamps taxes	..	..	2	3	10	640	310	49	3	3
4500 Non-recurrent taxes	..	..	..	..	..	..	..	..	..	..
4510 On net wealth	..	..	..	..	..	..	..	..	..	..
4520 Other non-recurrent taxes	..	..	..	..	..	..	..	..	..	..
4600 Other recurrent taxes on property	..	..	0	0	0	0	0	0	0	0
5000 Taxes on goods and services	..	..	**71 787**	**76 564**	**102 741**	**136 146**	**159 680**	**230 306**	**314 993**	**371 166**
5100 Taxes on production, sale, transfer, etc.	..	..	71 474	76 232	102 459	135 761	159 187	229 874	314 484	370 495
5110 General taxes	..	..	36 081	39 519	51 997	64 996	71 015	111 607	154 816	195 441
5111 Value added taxes	..	..	36 081	39 519	51 997	64 996	71 015	111 607	154 816	195 441
Local commodities	..	..	9 542	11 735	14 577	18 415	21 102	32 690	43 100	50 351
Imported goods	..	..	18 063	18 977	28 398	35 010	36 352	61 694	83 939	105 000
Hotel and restaurant services for tourists	..	..	2 211	2 172	1 704	2 334	2 157	3 061	5 894	7 127
Operating services for others	..	..	2 582	2 936	3 442	4 844	6 845	9 563	15 819	24 048
International and local communication services	..	..	3 684	3 700	3 877	4 393	4 559	4 599	6 065	8 915
5112 Sales tax	..	..	0	0	0	0	0	0	0	0
5113 Other	..	..	0	0	0	0	0	0	0	0
5120 Taxes on specific goods and services	..	..	35 393	36 713	50 462	70 765	88 172	118 267	159 667	175 054

Table 5.9. **Egypt / Égypte** *(cont.)*

Details of tax revenue / Recettes fiscales détaillées

Million EGP

	1999	2000	2009	2010	2014	2015	2016	2017	2018	2019
5121 Excises	..	..	15 597	17 170	25 822	41 207	49 468	72 730	106 447	114 977
Tobacco & cigarettes	..	..	6 689	6 997	19 588	26 463	33 584	35 412	51 654	56 389
Petroleum products	..	..	6 991	7 563	3 934	12 004	13 181	33 072	40 470	41 484
Stamp taxes on specific goods	..	..	1 123	1 603	1 258	1 198	948	1 782	1 214	3 687
Other excises	..	..	795	1 006	1 042	1 543	1 755	2 465	13 109	13 417
5122 Profits of fiscal monopolies	..	..	0	0	0	0	0	0	0	0
5123 Customs and import duties	..	..	13 496	13 733	17 352	21 460	27 534	33 411	36 848	40 995
5124 Taxes on exports	..	..	461	819	183	180	216	258	429	427
5125 Taxes on investment goods	..	..	0	0	0	0	0	0	0	0
5126 Taxes on specific services	..	..	3 188	3 074	5 030	4 226	5 377	5 655	8 873	7 269
Stamp taxes on specific services	..	..	2 070	1 950	3 685	2 700	3 361	3 286	5 487	3 517
Other taxes on specific services	..	..	1 118	1 123	1 345	1 526	2 017	2 369	3 386	3 752
5127 Other taxes on internat. trade and transactions	..	..	0	0	0	0	0	0	0	0
5128 Other taxes	..	..	2 651	1 919	2 075	3 690	5 576	6 213	7 070	11 386
5130 Unallocable between 5110 and 5120	..	..	0	0	0	0	0	0	0	0
5200 Taxes on use of goods and perform activities	..	..	313	332	281	386	494	432	509	672
5210 Recurrent taxes	..	..	313	332	281	386	494	432	509	672
5211 Paid by households: motor vehicles	..	..	0	0	0	0	0	0	0	0
5212 Paid by others: motor vehicles	..	..	0	0	0	0	0	0	0	0
5213 Paid in respect of other goods	..	..	313	332	281	386	494	432	509	672
5220 Non-recurrent taxes	..	..	0	0	0	0	0	0	0	0
5300 Unallocable between 5100 and 5200	..	..	0	0	0	0	0	0	0	0
6000 Other taxes	**..**	**..**	**0**	**0**	**0**	**0**	**0**	**0**	**0**	**0**
6100 Paid solely by business	..	..	..	..	..	..	..	..	..	..
6200 Other	..	..	..	..	..	..	..	..	..	..
Memo items:										
VAT revenues	..	..	36 081	39 519	51 997	64 996	71 015	111 607	154 816	195 441
VAT revenues (gross)	..	..	36 925	40 142	52 537	65 708	71 785	112 323	155 565	196 638
VAT refunds	..	..	-843	-623	-540	-712	-770	-716	-749	-1 197

.. Not available

Note: Fiscal year ends on 30 June. For example, the data for 2019 represent July 2018 to June 2019.

The data are on a cash basis.

Figures exclude tax revenues collected by sub-national governments as the data are not available.

Heading 2000: Egypt does not include social security contributions in its tax revenue data as the Egyptian authorities do not consider them as taxes.

Royalties on the Suez Canal as well as other royalties and administrative fees are reported as taxes in Egypt. These revenues are considered as non-tax revenues according to the OECD classification, described in the Interpretative Guide in Annex A.

Source: Ministry of Finance.

StatLink https://doi.org/10.1787/888934283823

Table 5.10. **Equatorial Guinea / Guinée équatoriale**

Details of tax revenue / Recettes fiscales détaillées

Million XAF

	1999	2000	2009	2010	2014	2015	2016	2017	2018	2019
Total tax revenue	..	..	**905 659**	**612 377**	**1 050 252**	**935 907**	**472 214**	**471 096**	**480 100**	**650 848**
1000 Taxes on income, profits and capital gains	..	..	**847 508**	**545 376**	**889 915**	**772 421**	**316 872**	**326 993**	**320 639**	**497 079**
1100 Of individuals	..	..	60 101	59 938	80 236	85 021	67 146	48 799	57 188	60 285
1110 On income and profits	..	..	60 101	59 938	80 236	85 021	67 146	48 799	57 188	60 285
Petroleum tax on physical persons	..	..	43 312	44 339	57 583	64 217	48 186	33 101	39 652	41 720
Personal income tax	..	..	15 672	15 325	22 175	20 421	18 581	15 456	17 201	18 245
Taxes on urban farms	..	..	1 053	129	400	379	369	235	305	297
Taxes on rural farms	..	..	64	145	77	4	10	7	30	22
1120 On capital gains	..	..	0	0	0	0	0	0	0	0
1200 Corporate	..	..	787 407	485 438	809 679	687 400	249 726	278 194	263 451	436 794
1210 On profits	..	..	787 407	485 438	809 679	687 400	249 726	278 194	263 451	436 794
Oil companies - Contractors	..	..	679 928	406 163	660 251	546 181	175 230	167 822	184 343	331 801
Oil companies - Subcontractors	..	..	66 791	29 619	81 686	51 317	31 498	13 841	36 969	52 261
Non-Oil companies - Taxes on companies	..	..	33 960	38 659	56 508	86 658	38 744	34 795	36 571	51 395
Oil companies - Year end (PNT)	..	..	6 488	9 765	9 402	573	1 180	58 081	609	172
OCIPEF Tax on wood exporters	..	..	242	1 233	1 830	2 671	3 074	3 655	4 958	1 166
1220 On capital gains	..	..	0	0	0	0	0	0	0	0
1300 Unallocable between 1100 and 1200	..	..	0	0	0	0	0	0	0	0
2000 Social security contributions	..	..	..	..	**60 033**	**58 868**	**49 766**	**51 009**	**47 725**	**48 714**
2100 Employees	..	..	..	..	8 091	7 935	6 481	6 575	7 054	7 200
2110 On a payroll basis	..	..	..	..	0	0	0	0	0	0
2120 On an income tax basis	..	..	..	..	8 091	7 935	6 481	6 575	7 054	7 200
2200 Employers	..	..	..	..	42 700	41 793	33 954	34 339	36 711	37 472
2210 On a payroll basis	..	..	..	..	0	0	0	0	0	0
2220 On an income tax basis	..	..	..	..	42 700	41 793	33 954	34 339	36 711	37 472
2300 Self-employed or non-employed	..	..	..	..	0	0	0	0	0	0
2310 On a payroll basis	..	..	..	..	..	..	..	..	..	..
2320 On an income tax basis	..	..	..	..	..	..	..	..	..	..
2400 Unallocable between 2100, 2200 and 2300	..	..	..	..	9 241	9 140	9 331	10 094	3 960	4 042
2410 On a payroll basis	..	..	..	..	0	0	0	0	0	0
2420 On an income tax basis	..	..	..	..	9 241	9 140	9 331	10 094	3 960	4 042
3000 Taxes on payroll and workforce	..	..	**0**	**0**	**0**	**0**	**0**	**0**	**0**	**0**
4000 Taxes on property	..	..	**95**	**160**	**367**	**211**	**352**	**192**	**278**	**227**
4100 Recurrent taxes on immovable property	..	..	0	0	0	0	0	0	0	0
4110 Households	..	..	..	..	..	..	..	..	..	..
4120 Others	..	..	..	..	..	..	..	..	..	..
4200 Recurrent taxes on net wealth	..	..	0	0	0	0	0	0	0	0
4210 Individual	..	..	..	..	..	..	..	..	..	..
4220 Corporate	..	..	..	..	..	..	..	..	..	..
4300 Estate, inheritance and gift taxes	..	..	0	0	0	0	0	0	0	0
4310 Estate and inheritance taxes	..	..	..	..	..	..	..	..	..	..
4320 Gift taxes	..	..	..	..	..	..	..	..	..	..
4400 Taxes on financial and capital transactions	..	..	95	160	367	211	352	192	278	227
4500 Non-recurrent taxes	..	..	0	0	0	0	0	0	0	0
4510 On net wealth	..	..	..	..	..	..	..	..	..	..
4520 Other non-recurrent taxes	..	..	..	..	..	..	..	..	..	..
4600 Other recurrent taxes on property	..	..	0	0	0	0	0	0	0	0
5000 Taxes on goods and services	..	..	**54 062**	**57 852**	**84 881**	**96 353**	**94 252**	**88 168**	**92 399**	**98 289**
5100 Taxes on production, sale, transfer, etc.	..	..	54 062	57 852	84 881	96 353	94 252	88 168	92 399	98 289
5110 General taxes	..	..	44 000	45 607	50 409	58 761	52 501	51 978	54 466	57 859
5111 Value added taxes	..	..	44 000	45 607	50 409	58 761	52 501	51 978	54 466	57 859
VAT revenues on petroleum products	..	..	11 490	15 066	2 672	6 799	4 705	3 826	2 355	2 160
VAT revenues other products and services	..	..	32 510	30 541	47 738	51 962	47 796	48 152	52 111	55 699
5112 Sales tax	..	..	0	0	0	0	0	0	0	0
5113 Other	..	..	0	0	0	0	0	0	0	0
5120 Taxes on specific goods and services	..	..	10 062	12 245	34 471	37 592	41 751	36 190	37 933	40 430
5121 Excises	..	..	0	0	14 653	19 961	21 041	15 824	18 570	20 498
Taxes on petroleum products	..	..	0	0	12 749	19 961	21 041	15 824	18 570	17 604
Special excise taxes	..	..	0	0	1 904	0	0	0	0	2 894
5122 Profits of fiscal monopolies	..	..	0	0	0	0	0	0	0	0
5123 Customs and import duties	..	..	9 404	9 667	14 699	13 434	15 854	12 292	13 015	15 438
Imports of petroleum products	..	..	1 146	1 446	1 318	2 009	1 865	1 309	1 448	1 297
Imports of other products	..	..	8 258	8 221	13 381	11 425	13 989	10 983	11 567	14 141

Table 5.10. **Equatorial Guinea / Guinée équatoriale** *(cont.)*

Details of tax revenue / Recettes fiscales détaillées

Million XAF

	1999	2000	2009	2010	2014	2015	2016	2017	2018	2019
5124 Taxes on exports	..	..	657	2 578	3 290	4 197	4 856	8 074	6 348	4 494
Wood exports	..	..	587	2 517	3 152	4 088	4 772	7 956	6 253	4 294
Exports of other products	..	..	9	21	107	91	84	116	89	193
Re-exports	..	..	61	40	31	18	0	3	6	6
5125 Taxes on investment goods	..	..	0	0	0	0	0	0	0	0
5126 Taxes on specific services	..	..	0	0	1 830	0	0	0	0	0
5127 Other taxes on internat. trade and transactions	..	..	0	0	0	0	0	0	0	0
5128 Other taxes	..	..	0	0	0	0	0	0	0	0
5130 Unallocable between 5110 and 5120	..	..	0	0	0	0	0	0	0	0
5200 Taxes on use of goods and perform activities	..	..	0	0	0	0	0	0	0	0
5210 Recurrent taxes	..	..	..	..	..	..	..	..	..	..
5211 Paid by households: motor vehicles	..	..	..	..	..	..	..	..	..	..
5212 Paid by others: motor vehicles	..	..	..	..	..	..	..	..	..	..
5213 Paid in respect of other goods	..	..	..	..	..	..	..	..	..	..
5220 Non-recurrent taxes	..	..	..	..	..	..	..	..	..	..
5300 Unallocable between 5100 and 5200	..	..	0	0	0	0	0	0	0	0
6000 Other taxes	**..**	**..**	**3 994**	**8 989**	**15 058**	**8 054**	**10 972**	**4 733**	**19 060**	**6 538**
6100 Paid solely by business	..	..	..	..	..	..	..	..	..	..
6200 Other	..	..	..	..	..	..	..	..	..	..

.. Not available

Note: Year ending 31st December.

The data are on a cash basis.

Heading 2000: Social security contributions to the Instituto Nacional de Seguridad Social de Guinea Ecuatorial (INSESO) are reported under this heading for the years 2013-19. Disaggregated figures for INSESO revenues in 2019 were not available, so individual line items under this heading were estimated by applying the revenue breakdown for 2018 to the known total INSESO revenus for 2019.

Source: Ministry of Finance, Economy and Planning; Instituto Nacional de Seguridad Social de Guinea Ecuatorial (INSESO).

StatLink https://doi.org/10.1787/888934283842

Table 5.11. **Eswatini**

Details of tax revenue / Recettes fiscales détaillées

Million SZL

	1999	2000	2009	2010	2014	2015	2016	2017	2018	2019
Total tax revenue	**1 271**	**1 327**	**3 975**	**4 588**	**7 295**	**7 907**	**9 140**	**10 101**	**10 891**	**11 893**
1000 Taxes on income, profits and capital gains	**696**	**677**	**2 196**	**2 373**	**3 707**	**3 854**	**4 590**	**4 897**	**5 259**	**5 732**
1100 Of individuals	393	428	1 368	1 449	2 093	2 278	2 766	3 071	3 289	3 513
1110 On income and profits	393	428	1 368	1 449	2 093	2 278	2 766	3 071	3 289	3 513
Pay-as-you-earn tax (PAYE)	386	421	1 254	1 321	2 049	2 176	2 662	2 976	3 181	3 407
Provisional income tax	1	2	12	75	31	24	31	32	44	38
Taxes on interest, dividends and trust income	0	0	16	35	0	1	1	0	0	0
Personal income tax on non-residents	0	0	73	3	1	1	2	0	0	0
Tax on benefits	0	0	11	11	10	15	15	17	18	18
Withholding tax on resident suppliers	0	0	0	0	0	0	0	0	0	0
Personal income tax on the self employed	5	4	1	1	0	59	52	43	43	47
Lottery levy	1	1	2	2	2	2	3	4	3	3
1120 On capital gains	0	0	0	0	0	0	0	0	0	0
1200 Corporate	278	236	809	905	1 570	1 507	1 730	1 825	1 969	2 218
1210 On profits	278	236	809	905	1 570	1 507	1 730	1 825	1 969	2 218
Corporate income tax on resident companies	276	233	674	739	1 468	1 358	1 527	1 388	1 479	1 734
Taxes on royalties	0	0	110	144	27	42	58	0	0	0
Corporate income tax on non-resident companies	2	3	24	22	75	107	145	438	490	483
1220 On capital gains	0	0	0	0	0	0	0	0	0	0
1300 Unallocable between 1100 and 1200	25	14	20	20	44	68	95	1	1	1
Income taxes on non-residents	22	11	15	15	43	67	93	0	0	0
Other taxes on income	2	3	4	4	1	2	2	1	1	1
2000 Social security contributions	**139**	**154**	**532**	**626**	**893**	**1 028**	**1 126**	**1 357**	**1 536**	**1 542**
2100 Employees	35	38	127	157	269	309	342	407	472	475
2110 On a payroll basis	..	..	..	..	..	..	..	..	..	..
2120 On an income tax basis	..	..	..	..	..	..	..	..	..	..
2200 Employers	104	115	405	469	624	719	785	950	1 065	1 067
2210 On a payroll basis	..	..	..	..	..	..	..	..	..	..
2220 On an income tax basis	..	..	..	..	..	..	..	..	..	..
2300 Self-employed or non-employed	0	0	0	0	0	0	0	0	0	0
2310 On a payroll basis	..	..	..	..	..	..	..	..	..	..
2320 On an income tax basis	..	..	..	..	..	..	..	..	..	..
2400 Unallocable between 2100, 2200 and 2300	0	0	0	0	0	0	0	0	0	0
2410 On a payroll basis	..	..	..	..	..	..	..	..	..	..
2420 On an income tax basis	..	..	..	..	..	..	..	..	..	..
3000 Taxes on payroll and workforce	**0**	**0**	**0**	**0**	**0**	**0**	**0**	**0**	**0**	**0**
4000 Taxes on property	**27**	**34**	**74**	**92**	**128**	**133**	**147**	**237**	**285**	**306**
4100 Recurrent taxes on immovable property	20	24	44	54	71	78	77	165	212	236
Local property taxes	20	24	44	54	71	78	77	165	212	236
4110 Households	0	0	0	0	0	0	0	0	0	0
4120 Others	0	0	0	0	0	0	0	0	0	0
4200 Recurrent taxes on net wealth	0	0	0	0	0	0	0	0	0	0
4210 Individual	..	..	..	..	..	..	..	..	..	..
4220 Corporate	..	..	..	..	..	..	..	..	..	..
4300 Estate, inheritance and gift taxes	0	0	0	0	0	0	0	0	0	0
4310 Estate and inheritance taxes	..	..	..	..	..	..	..	..	..	..
Tax on trust beneficiaries	..	..	..	..	..	..	..	..	..	..
4320 Gift taxes	..	..	..	..	..	..	..	..	..	..
4400 Taxes on financial and capital transactions	7	10	30	39	57	56	70	72	73	70
Transfer duties	4	5	18	26	33	30	46	42	49	37
Stamp duties	4	5	12	12	23	25	24	30	23	34
4500 Non-recurrent taxes	0	0	0	0	0	0	0	0	0	0
4510 On net wealth	..	..	..	..	..	..	..	..	..	..
4520 Other non-recurrent taxes	..	..	..	..	..	..	..	..	..	..
4600 Other recurrent taxes on property	0	0	0	0	0	0	0	0	0	0
5000 Taxes on goods and services	**410**	**462**	**1 173**	**1 496**	**2 567**	**2 892**	**3 276**	**3 609**	**3 811**	**4 313**
5100 Taxes on production, sale, transfer, etc.	397	449	1 115	1 442	2 499	2 823	3 202	3 532	3 729	4 205
5110 General taxes	334	372	998	1 255	1 895	2 109	2 409	2 521	2 668	2 972
5111 Value added taxes	0	0	0	0	1 883	2 107	2 407	2 520	2 668	2 965
VAT revenues (gross)	..	..	..	..	2 787	3 048	3 337	3 584	3 753	4 349
VAT refunds	..	..	..	..	-904	-941	-929	-1 063	-1 085	-1 384
5112 Sales tax	334	372	998	1 255	12	2	1	1	0	7
5113 Other	0	0	0	0	0	0	0	0	0	0
5120 Taxes on specific goods and services	63	78	117	186	604	714	793	1 011	1 061	1 232

Table 5.11. **Eswatini** *(cont.)*

Details of tax revenue / Recettes fiscales détaillées

Million SZL

	1999	2000	2009	2010	2014	2015	2016	2017	2018	2019
5121 Excises	61	75	91	148	573	667	732	1 005	1 050	1 218
Fuel taxes	61	75	91	148	573	667	732	1 005	1 050	1 202
Levy on alcohol and tobacco	0	0	0	0	0	0	0	0	0	16
5122 Profits of fiscal monopolies	0	0	0	0	0	0	0	0	0	0
5123 Customs and import duties	0	0	0	0	0	0	0	0	5	9
5124 Taxes on exports	0	0	0	0	0	0	0	0	0	0
Cattle export tax	0	0	0	0	0	0	0	0	0	0
5125 Taxes on investment goods	0	0	0	0	0	0	0	0	0	0
5126 Taxes on specific services	2	2	26	39	31	47	61	6	5	6
Tax on management fees	0	0	24	37	27	42	58	0	0	0
Taxes on lotteries, gaming and betting	2	2	2	2	4	5	3	6	5	6
Other taxes on services and hospitality	0	0	0	0	0	0	0	0	0	0
5127 Other taxes on internat. trade and transactions	0	0	0	0	0	0	0	0	0	0
5128 Other taxes	0	0	0	0	0	0	0	0	0	0
5130 Unallocable between 5110 and 5120	0	0	0	0	0	0	0	0	0	0
5200 Taxes on use of goods and perform activities	13	12	58	54	68	68	74	77	82	108
5210 Recurrent taxes	7	8	30	30	38	38	43	45	48	51
5211 Paid by households: motor vehicles	4	4	11	11	15	16	18	19	20	22
5212 Paid by others: motor vehicles	0	0	0	0	0	0	0	0	0	0
5213 Paid in respect of other goods	3	3	19	19	23	22	25	26	28	29
Trading licences	1	1	13	11	14	14	16	16	18	19
Company licences	1	1	6	7	8	7	8	8	9	9
Special licences	0	1	1	1	1	1	1	1	1	1
5220 Non-recurrent taxes	5	5	27	25	31	31	31	32	34	57
Road tolls	5	4	27	24	30	30	30	32	33	56
Firearm registration fees	0	0	1	1	1	1	1	1	1	1
5300 Unallocable between 5100 and 5200	0	0	0	0	0	0	0	0	0	0
6000 Other taxes	**0**	**0**	**0**	**0**	**0**	**0**	**0**	**0**	**0**	**0**
6100 Paid solely by business	..	..	..	..	..	..	..	..	..	..
6200 Other	..	..	..	..	..	..	..	..	..	..

.. Not available

Note: Data are reported on a fiscal year basis beginning 1st April. For example, the data for 2019 represents April 2019 to March 2020.

The data are on a cash basis.

Heading 5211: This heading includes revenue from motor vehicle licences, the change of ownership fees and the registration of new motor vehicles. These revenues are considered as tax revenue according to the OECD classification, described in the Interpretative Guide in Annex A. The national classification of Eswatini classifies these revenues as non-tax revenues.

Heading 5213: This heading includes revenue from business and sundry licences. These revenues are considered as tax revenues according to the OECD classification, described in the Interpretative Guide in Annex A. The national classification of Eswatini classifies them as nontax revenues.

Heading 5220: This heading includes revenue from the registrations of specific goods (e.g firearms). These revenues are considered as tax revenues under the OECD classification, as set out in the Interpretative Guide in Annex A. The national classification of Eswatini classifies these revenues as non-tax revenues. Revenue from PAYE Penalties, tax interest and penalties on taxes are considered as non-tax revenue under the OECD classification, as set out in the Interpretative Guide in Annex A. The national classification of Eswatini classifies these revenues as tax revenues.

Source: Eswatini Revenue Authority; Local Government; Eswatini National Provident Fund and Public Service Pension Fund; Ministry of Economic Planning and Development; Central Government.

StatLink https://doi.org/10.1787/888934283861

Table 5.12. **Ghana**

Details of tax revenue / Recettes fiscales détaillées

Million GHS

	1999	2000	2009	2010	2014	2015	2016	2017	2018	2019
Total tax revenue	..	**487**	**5 153**	**6 695**	**18 944**	**23 592**	**29 495**	**35 300**	**42 370**	**47 313**
1000 Taxes on income, profits and capital gains	..	**141**	**1 695**	**2 417**	**7 360**	**7 570**	**8 084**	**11 712**	**16 344**	**19 853**
1100 Of individuals	..	56	846	1 115	3 219	3 570	3 702	5 191	6 649	7 734
1110 On income and profits	..	56	846	1 115	3 219	3 570	3 702	5 191	6 649	7 734
Employees income tax	..	48	773	1 015	3 000	3 310	3 466	4 859	6 270	7 313
Self employers income/profit tax	..	8	73	100	219	260	237	332	379	421
1120 On capital gains	..	..	..	..	..	..	..	..	..	..
1200 Corporate	..	70	692	1 080	3 992	3 837	4 233	6 214	9 563	11 833
1210 On profits	..	70	692	1 080	3 992	3 837	4 233	6 214	9 563	11 833
Income/profit tax on companies (excl. oil)	..	70	662	988	3 034	3 620	4 052	5 793	8 528	10 567
Income/profit tax on oil companies	..	0	0	0	797	45	42	225	736	926
National Fiscal Stabilisation Levy (NFSL)	..	0	30	85	162	172	139	196	299	340
National Reconstruction Levy (NRL)	..	0	0	7	0	0	0	0	0	0
1220 On capital gains	..	..	..	..	..	..	..	..	..	..
1300 Unallocable between 1100 and 1200	..	15	157	222	149	163	148	307	132	286
Other direct taxes aside from oil and mineral royalties	..	15	157	222	149	163	148	307	132	286
2000 Social security contributions	..	**46**	**668**	**577**	**1 784**	**2 122**	**2 593**	**2 331**	**2 399**	**2 740**
2100 Employees	..	..	..	..	..	..	..	..	..	..
2110 On a payroll basis	..	..	..	..	..	..	..	..	..	..
2120 On an income tax basis	..	..	..	..	..	..	..	..	..	..
2200 Employers	..	..	..	..	..	..	..	..	..	..
2210 On a payroll basis	..	..	..	..	..	..	..	..	..	..
2220 On an income tax basis	..	..	..	..	..	..	..	..	..	..
2300 Self-employed or non-employed	..	..	..	..	..	..	..	..	..	..
2310 On a payroll basis	..	..	..	..	..	..	..	..	..	..
2320 On an income tax basis	..	..	..	..	..	..	..	..	..	..
2400 Unallocable between 2100, 2200 and 2300	..	46	668	577	1 784	2 122	2 593	2 331	2 399	2 740
2410 On a payroll basis	..	..	..	..	..	..	..	..	..	..
2420 On an income tax basis	..	..	..	..	..	..	..	..	..	..
3000 Taxes on payroll and workforce	..	**0**	**0**	**0**	**0**	**0**	**0**	**0**	**0**	**0**
4000 Taxes on property	..	..	..	..	..	..	..	..	..	..
4100 Recurrent taxes on immovable property	..	..	..	..	..	..	..	..	..	..
4110 Households	..	..	..	..	..	..	..	..	..	..
4120 Others	..	..	..	..	..	..	..	..	..	..
4200 Recurrent taxes on net wealth	..	..	..	..	..	..	..	..	..	..
4210 Individual	..	..	..	..	..	..	..	..	..	..
4220 Corporate	..	..	..	..	..	..	..	..	..	..
4300 Estate, inheritance and gift taxes	..	..	..	..	..	..	..	..	..	..
4310 Estate and inheritance taxes	..	..	..	..	..	..	..	..	..	..
4320 Gift taxes	..	..	..	..	..	..	..	..	..	..
4400 Taxes on financial and capital transactions	..	..	..	..	..	..	..	..	..	..
4500 Non-recurrent taxes	..	..	..	..	..	..	..	..	..	..
4510 On net wealth	..	..	..	..	..	..	..	..	..	..
4520 Other non-recurrent taxes	..	..	..	..	..	..	..	..	..	..
4600 Other recurrent taxes on property	..	..	..	..	..	..	..	..	..	..
5000 Taxes on goods and services	..	**301**	**2 790**	**3 701**	**9 799**	**13 900**	**18 817**	**21 256**	**23 627**	**24 720**
5100 Taxes on production, sale, transfer, etc.	..	301	2 790	3 701	9 799	13 900	18 817	21 256	23 606	24 659
5110 General taxes	..	127	1 587	2 006	5 672	7 562	8 530	10 366	11 326	12 498
5111 Value added taxes	..	127	1 587	2 006	5 672	7 562	8 530	10 366	11 326	12 498
VAT revenues (external collection)	..	89	796	970	2 757	3 489	4 108	4 992	4 912	4 121
VAT revenues (domestic)	..	39	473	649	1 915	2 766	3 022	3 557	3 980	5 209
National Health Insurance Levy (NHIL - customs collection)	..	0	170	183	463	558	613	778	810	715
National Health Insurance Levy (NHIL domestic)	..	0	91	133	319	461	506	598	691	1 030
Social Security and National Insurance Trust (SSNIT) contributions to the National Health Insurance Scheme (NHIS)	..	0	58	72	218	289	280	440	377	153
GETFund Levy (external collection)	..	0	0	0	0	0	0	0	289	834
GETFund Levy (domestic)	..	0	0	0	0	0	0	0	267	435
5112 Sales tax	..	0	0	0	0	0	0	0	0	0
5113 Other	..	0	0	0	0	0	0	0	0	0
5120 Taxes on specific goods and services	..	173	1 203	1 695	4 127	6 337	10 287	10 890	12 279	12 161

Table 5.12. **Ghana** *(cont.)*

Details of tax revenue / Recettes fiscales détaillées

Million GHS

	1999	2000	2009	2010	2014	2015	2016	2017	2018	2019
5121 Excises	..	75	330	374	764	2 402	5 289	4 729	5 282	5 817
Petroleum taxes aside from EFL and RFL	..	53	211	221	617	2 163	2 319	1 665	1 975	1 952
Energy Fund Levy (EFL)	..	0	68	36	0	0	25	28	35	39
Road Fund Levy (RFL)	..	0	0	0	0	0	1 002	1 058	1 331	1 541
Energy Debt Recovery Levy	..	0	0	0	0	0	1 264	962	876	1 665
Price Stabilisation and Recovery Levy	..	0	0	0	0	0	326	346	548	125
Public Lighting Levy (PLL)	..	0	0	0	0	0	23	180	119	63
National Electrification Scheme Levy (NESL)	..	0	0	0	0	0	33	151	78	44
Other excise duties	..	21	51	118	147	239	297	339	319	387
5122 Profits of fiscal monopolies	..	0	0	0	0	0	0	0	0	0
5123 Customs and import duties	..	81	746	1 051	2 773	3 078	4 122	5 485	6 102	5 410
5124 Taxes on exports	..	18	17	95	319	371	269	0	0	0
Levies on cocoa exports	..	18	17	95	319	371	269	..	..	..
5125 Taxes on investment goods	..	0	0	0	0	0	0	0	0	0
5126 Taxes on specific services	..	0	110	174	272	486	608	676	896	934
Communication service tax	..	..	88	137	217	252	339	329	420	412
Airport tax	..	..	22	37	55	235	269	347	476	521
5127 Other taxes on internat. trade and transactions	..	0	0	0	0	0	0	0	0	0
5128 Other taxes	..	0	0	0	0	0	0	0	0	0
5130 Unallocable between 5110 and 5120	..	0	0	0	0	0	0	0	0	0
5200 Taxes on use of goods and perform activities	..	0	0	0	0	0	0	0	21	61
5210 Recurrent taxes	..	..	..	..	..	..	..	..	21	61
5211 Paid by households: motor vehicles	..	..	..	..	..	..	..	..	21	61
Luxury Vehicle Levy	..	..	..	..	..	..	..	..	21	61
5212 Paid by others: motor vehicles	..	..	..	..	..	..	..	..	0	0
5213 Paid in respect of other goods	..	..	..	..	..	..	..	..	0	0
5220 Non-recurrent taxes	..	..	..	..	..	..	..	..	..	..
5300 Unallocable between 5100 and 5200	..	0	0	0	0	0	0	0	0	0
6000 Other taxes	..	**0**	**0**	**0**	**0**	**0**	**0**	**0**	**0**	**0**
6100 Paid solely by business	..	..	..	..	..	..	..	..	..	..
6200 Other	..	..	..	..	..	..	..	..	..	..
Memo items: *VAT refunds*	..	0	31	45	157	627	1 445	1 803	2 125	2 470

.. Not available

Note: Year ending 31st December.

The data are on a cash basis.

Figures exclude tax revenues collected by sub-national governments as the data are not available.

Heading 2000: The data are not available from 2000 to 2007.

Heading 4000: Property tax is levied annually by local authorities and data on these revenues are not available for this report.

Heading 5111: The national health insurance levy is a tax on goods and services whose funds are allocated to the National Health Insurance Scheme (NHIS). The division of GETFund Levy revenues between domestic and external collections are estimates based on programmed budget figures for 2019.

Heading 5121: In previous editions, revenues under the Public Lighting Levy (PLL) and the National Electrification Scheme Levy (NESL) were grouped together with the Energy Debt Recovery Levy (EDRL). These are now reported as separate revenues.

Heading 5211: The Luxury Vehicle Levy has been added to the classification in this edition.

Source: Ghana Statistical Service.

StatLink https://doi.org/10.1787/888934283880

Table 5.13. **Kenya**

Details of tax revenue / Recettes fiscales détaillées

Million KES

	1999	2000	2009	2010	2014	2015	2016	2017	2018	2019
Total tax revenue	..	..	**485 442**	**540 164**	**976 914**	**1 085 219**	**1 231 771**	**1 399 657**	**1 482 598**	**1 609 745**
1000 Taxes on income, profits and capital gains	..	..	**193 745**	**219 227**	**451 793**	**504 077**	**561 792**	**628 373**	**654 675**	**687 183**
1100 Of individuals	..	..	106 856	124 392	259 007	284 222	322 885	348 783	377 353	410 193
1110 On income and profits	..	..	106 856	124 392	259 007	284 222	322 885	348 783	377 353	410 193
Paye As You Earn (PAYE)	..	..	103 413	120 593	252 974	277 068	312 032	336 596	364 104	392 693
Individual income tax	..	..	3 443	3 799	6 033	7 154	8 821	8 179	7 191	8 916
Tax on rental income	..	..	0	0	0	0	2 033	4 007	6 058	8 584
1120 On capital gains	..	..	..	..	..	..	..	..	..	..
1200 Corporate	..	..	62 633	67 661	135 971	126 541	152 407	180 162	160 059	168 783
1210 On profits	..	..	62 633	67 661	135 971	126 541	152 407	180 162	160 059	168 783
Corporation tax	..	..	62 633	67 661	135 971	126 541	152 407	180 162	160 059	168 783
1220 On capital gains	..	..	..	..	..	..	..	..	..	..
1300 Unallocable between 1100 and 1200	..	..	24 256	27 174	56 816	93 313	86 500	99 427	117 263	108 207
Withholding tax	..	..	24 256	27 174	56 816	92 678	82 690	97 009	100 623	105 256
Capital gains tax	..	..	0	0	0	636	3 811	2 419	16 640	2 951
2000 Social security contributions	..	..	**5 079**	**6 026**	**13 629**	**15 826**	**31 996**	**34 978**	**47 889**	**58 081**
2100 Employees	..	..	..	..	..	..	..	..	..	..
Women and children's pension	..	..	..	..	..	..	..	..	..	..
2110 On a payroll basis	..	..	..	..	..	..	..	..	..	..
2120 On an income tax basis	..	..	..	..	..	..	..	..	..	..
2200 Employers	..	..	..	..	..	..	..	..	..	..
2210 On a payroll basis	..	..	..	..	..	..	..	..	..	..
2220 On an income tax basis	..	..	..	..	..	..	..	..	..	..
2300 Self-employed or non-employed	..	..	..	..	..	..	..	..	..	..
2310 On a payroll basis	..	..	..	..	..	..	..	..	..	..
2320 On an income tax basis	..	..	..	..	..	..	..	..	..	..
2400 Unallocable between 2100, 2200 and 2300	..	..	5 079	6 026	13 629	15 826	31 996	34 978	47 889	58 081
2410 On a payroll basis	..	..	..	..	..	..	..	..	..	..
2420 On an income tax basis	..	..	..	..	..	..	..	..	..	..
3000 Taxes on payroll and workforce	..	..	**0**	**0**	**0**	**0**	**0**	**0**	**0**	**0**
4000 Taxes on property	..	..	**1 149**	**1 133**	**1 133**	**1 051**	**1 237**	**940**	**629**	**682**
4100 Recurrent taxes on immovable property	..	..	1 149	1 133	1 133	1 051	1 237	940	629	682
Immovable property (Stand premia on town plots)	..	..	63	86	63	0	36	79	28	94
Land rates	..	..	0	0	0	0	0	0	0	0
Land rent	..	..	1 086	1 047	1 071	1 045	1 201	861	601	588
4110 Households	..	..	..	..	..	..	..	..	..	..
4120 Others	..	..	..	..	..	..	..	..	..	..
4200 Recurrent taxes on net wealth	..	..	0	0	0	0	0	0	0	0
4210 Individual	..	..	..	..	..	..	..	..	..	..
4220 Corporate	..	..	..	..	..	..	..	..	..	..
4300 Estate, inheritance and gift taxes	..	..	0	0	0	0	0	0	0	0
4310 Estate and inheritance taxes	..	..	..	..	..	..	..	..	..	..
4320 Gift taxes	..	..	..	..	..	..	..	..	..	..
4400 Taxes on financial and capital transactions	..	..	0	0	0	0	0	0	0	0
4500 Non-recurrent taxes	..	..	0	0	0	0	0	0	0	0
4510 On net wealth	..	..	..	..	..	..	..	..	..	..
4520 Other non-recurrent taxes	..	..	..	..	..	..	..	..	..	..
4600 Other recurrent taxes on property	..	..	0	0	0	0	0	0	0	0
5000 Taxes on goods and services	..	..	**285 206**	**313 615**	**510 108**	**564 115**	**636 585**	**735 283**	**779 319**	**863 733**
5100 Taxes on production, sale, transfer, etc.	..	..	281 608	309 829	504 197	557 630	629 546	728 596	771 150	857 748
5110 General taxes	..	..	127 008	141 152	233 724	265 501	291 229	336 674	356 881	395 215
5111 Value added taxes	..	..	126 878	141 041	233 558	264 872	290 843	336 572	356 777	395 127
VAT - Ordinary imports	..	..	55 557	57 594	114 556	127 744	125 105	137 232	144 035	157 496
VAT - Oil imports	..	..	4 851	5 352	10 621	7 894	6 368	6 260	7 643	21 683
VAT - Domestic (Gross)	..	..	80 630	92 255	123 068	143 922	174 051	206 545	219 499	230 348
VAT - Domestic (Refunds)	..	..	-14 160	-14 160	-14 688	-14 688	-14 681	-13 464	-14 400	-14 400
5112 Sales tax	..	..	0	0	0	0	0	0	0	0
5113 Other	..	..	131	111	166	630	385	102	103	88
Turnover tax	..	..	131	111	166	630	385	102	103	88
5120 Taxes on specific goods and services	..	..	154 600	168 677	270 473	292 129	338 317	391 923	414 270	462 533

Table 5.13. **Kenya** *(cont.)*

Details of tax revenue / Recettes fiscales détaillées

Million KES

	1999	2000	2009	2010	2014	2015	2016	2017	2018	2019
5121 Excises	..	..	92 675	99 135	129 192	142 489	178 703	215 753	225 319	241 816
Excise duty - Oil	..	..	32 675	35 780	38 416	42 687	51 611	59 502	61 216	63 834
Excise duty - Domestic	..	..	23 785	23 755	35 855	38 246	48 986	55 499	53 011	59 509
Road maintenance levy	..	..	21 570	23 780	28 163	30 890	45 407	69 557	73 668	80 459
Excise duty - Imports	..	..	6 814	6 994	13 151	15 175	18 096	19 696	22 311	24 622
Sugar levy	..	..	1 270	1 590	1 585	1 329	1 357	115	16	0
Petroleum development levy	..	..	1 415	1 585	1 794	1 817	1 974	2 168	2 262	2 165
Petroleum regulatory levy	..	..	122	134	158	301	485	498	521	1 087
Second hand motor vehicles purchase tax	..	..	265	183	0	466	369	166	171	192
Stamp duty-domestic taxes	..	..	4 761	5 332	10 069	11 579	10 417	8 553	12 143	9 947
5122 Profits of fiscal monopolies	..	..	0	0	0	0	0	0	0	0
5123 Customs and import duties	..	..	51 184	57 047	113 701	120 612	125 025	131 577	142 194	154 748
Import duty - Ordinary	..	..	35 325	40 382	65 580	72 346	79 372	85 532	92 076	103 511
Import declaration fees	..	..	14 970	15 836	26 627	27 119	25 851	24 486	26 189	26 782
Railway development levy	..	..	0	0	19 721	18 940	17 273	18 903	20 780	21 303
Import duty - Oil	..	..	888	797	1 016	1 387	1 595	1 329	1 638	1 698
Merchant superintendent shipping levy	..	..	0	32	757	820	934	1 328	1 512	1 454
Stamp duty-customs services	..	..	0	0	0	0	0	0	0	0
5124 Taxes on exports	..	..	0	0	0	0	0	0	0	0
5125 Taxes on investment goods	..	..	0	0	0	0	0	0	0	0
5126 Taxes on specific services	..	..	10 741	12 495	27 580	29 028	34 589	44 592	46 756	65 969
Excise on air time	..	..	6 630	7 893	12 302	13 122	14 884	15 964	15 626	25 120
Airport revenue	..	..	2 144	2 464	6 837	6 619	6 570	11 199	10 414	12 291
Aviation revenue	..	..	1 966	2 138	3 468	3 565	4 122	4 854	4 819	5 912
Excise on financial services	..	..	0	0	4 973	5 722	9 013	12 575	15 898	22 646
5127 Other taxes on internat. trade and transactions	..	..	0	0	0	0	0	0	0	0
5128 Other taxes	..	..	0	0	0	0	0	0	0	0
5130 Unallocable between 5110 and 5120	..	..	0	0	0	0	0	0	0	0
5200 Taxes on use of goods and perform activities	..	..	3 598	3 786	5 911	6 485	7 039	6 687	8 169	5 985
5210 Recurrent taxes	..	..	3 598	3 786	5 911	6 485	7 039	6 687	8 169	5 985
5211 Paid by households: motor vehicles	..	..	3 209	3 367	5 415	6 010	6 564	6 185	7 678	5 474
Road transport fees	..	..	2 409	2 499	3 691	3 947	3 911	4 100	3 366	4 302
Foreign motor vehicles tax	..	..	0	0	0	0	0	93	69	0
Advance and other taxes	..	..	800	868	1 725	2 064	2 653	1 993	4 243	1 172
5212 Paid by others: motor vehicles	..	..	0	0	0	0	0	0	0	0
5213 Paid in respect of other goods	..	..	389	419	496	475	475	501	491	511
Kenya Bureau of Standards (KEBS) tax	..	..	389	419	496	475	475	501	491	511
5220 Non-recurrent taxes	..	..	0	0	0	0	0	0	0	0
5300 Unallocable between 5100 and 5200	..	..	0	0	0	0	0	0	0	0
6000 Other taxes	..	..	**264**	**164**	**250**	**150**	**161**	**83**	**86**	**66**
Other taxes	..	..	264	164	250	150	161	83	86	66
6100 Paid solely by business	..	..	..	..	..	..	..	..	..	..
6200 Other	..	..	..	..	..	..	..	..	..	..

.. Not available

Note: Data are reported on a fiscal year basis beginning 1st July. For example, the data for 2019 represent July 2018 to June 2019

The data are on a cash basis.

Figures exclude tax revenues collected by sub-national governments as the data are not available.

Heading 2000: Data on social security contributions are not readily available but are deemed to be minimal.

Heading 4100: The data for the immovable property (Stand premia on town plots) tax are not readily available for the years 2001-04 and 2006. No estimation was undertaken given the magnitude of the figures.

Source: Kenya Revenue Authority (KRA).

StatLink https://doi.org/10.1787/888934283899

Table 5.14. **Lesotho**

Details of tax revenue / Recettes fiscales détaillées

Million LSL

	1999	2000	2009	2010	2014	2015	2016	2017	2018	2019
Total tax revenue	..	..	**2 595**	**2 933**	**5 182**	**5 861**	**5 988**	**5 990**	**6 984**	**6 962**
1000 Taxes on income, profits and capital gains	..	..	**1 560**	**1 652**	**3 066**	**3 651**	**3 734**	**3 576**	**4 103**	**4 056**
1100 Of individuals	..	..	866	1 180	2 159	2 484	2 695	2 751	3 112	3 142
1110 On income and profits	..	..	866	1 180	2 159	2 484	2 695	2 751	3 112	3 142
Personal income tax	..	..	866	1 180	1 651	1 737	1 965	1 977	2 212	2 296
Withholding tax	..	..	0	0	507	748	730	774	900	847
1120 On capital gains	..	..	0	0	0	0	0	0	0	0
1200 Corporate	..	..	694	472	884	1 133	991	791	959	884
1210 On profits	..	..	694	472	884	1 133	991	791	959	884
Corporate income tax	..	..	694	472	877	1 126	983	784	955	877
Gambling levy	..	..	0	0	7	8	8	7	4	7
1220 On capital gains of corporates	..	..	0	0	0	0	0	0	0	0
1300 Unallocable between 1100 and 1200	..	..	0	0	23	34	48	33	33	29
2000 Social security contributions	..	..	**0**	**0**	**0**	**0**	**0**	**0**	**0**	**0**
2100 Employees	..	..	..	..	..	..	..	..	..	..
2110 On a payroll basis	..	..	..	..	..	..	..	..	..	..
2120 On an income tax basis	..	..	..	..	..	..	..	..	..	..
2200 Employers	..	..	..	..	..	..	..	..	..	..
2210 On a payroll basis	..	..	..	..	..	..	..	..	..	..
2220 On an income tax basis	..	..	..	..	..	..	..	..	..	..
2300 Self-employed or non-employed	..	..	..	..	..	..	..	..	..	..
2310 On a payroll basis	..	..	..	..	..	..	..	..	..	..
2320 On an income tax basis	..	..	..	..	..	..	..	..	..	..
2400 Unallocable between 2100, 2200 and 2300	..	..	..	..	..	..	..	..	..	..
2410 On a payroll basis	..	..	..	..	..	..	..	..	..	..
2420 On an income tax basis	..	..	..	..	..	..	..	..	..	..
3000 Taxes on payroll and workforce	..	..	**0**	**0**	**0**	**0**	**0**	**0**	**0**	**0**
4000 Taxes on property	..	..	..	..	..	..	..	..	..	..
4100 Recurrent taxes on immovable property	..	..	..	..	..	..	..	..	..	..
4110 Households	..	..	..	..	..	..	..	..	..	..
4120 Others	..	..	..	..	..	..	..	..	..	..
4200 Recurrent taxes on net wealth	..	..	..	..	..	..	..	..	..	..
4210 Individual	..	..	..	..	..	..	..	..	..	..
4220 Corporate	..	..	..	..	..	..	..	..	..	..
4300 Estate, inheritance and gift taxes	..	..	..	..	..	..	..	..	..	..
4310 Estate and inheritance taxes	..	..	..	..	..	..	..	..	..	..
4320 Gift taxes	..	..	..	..	..	..	..	..	..	..
4400 Taxes on financial and capital transactions	..	..	..	..	..	..	..	..	..	..
4500 Other non-reccurrent taxes on property	..	..	..	..	..	..	..	..	..	..
4510 On net wealth	..	..	..	..	..	..	..	..	..	..
4520 Other non-recurrent taxes	..	..	..	..	..	..	..	..	..	..
4600 Other recurrent taxes on property	..	..	..	..	..	..	..	..	..	..
5000 Taxes on goods and services	..	..	**1 035**	**1 281**	**2 117**	**2 210**	**2 254**	**2 414**	**2 880**	**2 907**
5100 Taxes on production, sale, transfer, etc	..	..	1 035	1 281	2 117	2 210	2 254	2 414	2 880	2 907
5110 General taxes on goods and services	..	..	1 035	1 281	2 117	2 210	2 254	2 414	2 880	2 907
5111 Value added taxes	..	..	1 035	1 281	2 117	2 210	2 254	2 414	2 880	2 907
VAT on imports	..	..	363	473	705	780	798	795	880	896
VAT - Domestic (Net)	..	..	672	808	1 412	1 430	1 456	1 619	2 000	2 011
VAT - Domestic (Gross)	..	..	837	1 046	1 806	1 996	2 131	2 250	2 681	2 877
VAT - Domestic (Refunds)	..	..	-165	-238	-394	-566	-675	-632	-682	-867
5112 Sales tax	..	..	0	0	0	0	0	0	0	0
5113 Other	..	..	0	0	0	0	0	0	0	0
5120 Taxes on specific goods and services	..	..	0	0	0	0	0	0	0	0
5121 Excises	..	..	..	..	..	..	..	..	..	..
5122 Profits of fiscal monopolies	..	..	..	..	..	..	..	..	..	..
5123 Customs and import duties	..	..	..	..	..	..	..	..	..	..
5124 Taxes on exports	..	..	..	..	..	..	..	..	..	..
5125 Taxes on investment goods	..	..	..	..	..	..	..	..	..	..
5126 Taxes on specific services	..	..	..	..	..	..	..	..	..	..
5127 Other taxes on internat. trade and transactions	..	..	..	..	..	..	..	..	..	..
5128 Other taxes	..	..	..	..	..	..	..	..	..	..
5130 Unallocable between 5110 and 5120	..	..	0	0	0	0	0	0	0	0
5200 Taxes on use of goods and to perform activities	..	..	0	0	0	0	0	0	0	0
5210 Recurrent taxes	..	..	..	..	..	..	..	..	..	..

Table 5.14. **Lesotho** *(cont.)*

Details of tax revenue / Recettes fiscales détaillées

Million LSL

	1999	2000	2009	2010	2014	2015	2016	2017	2018	2019
5211 Paid by households: motor vehicles	..	..	..	..	..	..	..	..	..	..
5212 Paid by others: motor vehicles	..	..	..	..	..	..	..	..	..	..
5213 Paid in respect of other goods	..	..	..	..	..	..	..	..	..	..
5220 Non-recurrent taxes	..	..	..	..	..	..	..	..	..	..
5300 Unallocable between 5100 and 5200	..	..	0	0	0	0	0	0	0	0
6000 Other taxes	**..**	**..**	**0**	**0**	**0**	**0**	**0**	**0**	**0**	**0**
6100 Paid solely by business	..	..	..	..	..	..	..	..	..	..
6200 Other	..	..	..	..	..	..	..	..	..	..

.. Not available

Note: Data are on a fiscal year basis beginning 1st April. For example, the data for 2019 represent April 2019 to March 2020.

Data are reported on a cash basis.

Heading 2000: Social security contributions for Lesotho are deemed to be null as they do not meet the criteria to be classified as social security contributions set out in the OECD classification of taxes in the Interpretative Guide.

Source: Lesotho Revenue Authority for all revenues except for transfers from the SACU Common Revenue Pool. Lesotho Ministry of Finance budget reports for SACU revenues.

StatLink https://doi.org/10.1787/888934283918

Table 5.15. **Madagascar**

Details of tax revenue / Recettes fiscales détaillées

Million MGA

	1999	2000	2009	2010	2014	2015	2016	2017	2018	2019
Recettes fiscales totales	**523 080**	**603 200**	**1 785 190**	**1 980 849**	**2 701 917**	**3 146 042**	**3 780 986**	**4 487 041**	**5 298 756**	**5 888 872**
1000 Impôts sur revenu, bénéfices et gains en capital	**86 580**	**102 580**	**466 047**	**490 294**	**611 375**	**706 750**	**882 598**	**1 002 793**	**1 174 764**	**1 437 601**
1100 Des personnes physiques	30 180	36 080	198 751	253 868	306 645	366 600	429 165	474 685	547 816	687 985
1110 Sur le revenu et les bénéfices	21 860	25 800	166 090	216 415	280 558	338 560	387 703	430 830	492 008	626 286
Traitements et salaires	21 100	25 260	152 264	201 077	260 818	315 570	359 334	398 027	446 571	549 317
Bénéfices non commerciaux (BNC)	760	540	1 729	1 841	2 420	3 850	5 994	6 874	6 094	7 802
Bénéfices industriels et commerciaux (BIC)	0	0	12 097	13 497	17 320	19 140	22 376	25 930	39 344	69 167
1120 Sur les gains en capital	8 320	10 280	32 661	37 453	26 087	28 040	41 461	43 855	55 807	61 699
1200 Des sociétés	53 460	62 240	267 188	236 426	304 730	340 150	453 433	528 108	626 948	749 616
1210 Sur les bénéfices	48 920	56 880	264 145	236 426	304 730	340 150	453 433	528 108	626 948	749 616
1220 Sur les gains en capital	4 540	5 360	3 043	0	0	0	0	0	0	0
1300 Non ventilables entre 1100 et 1200	2 940	4 260	108	0	0	0	0	0	0	0
2000 Cotisations de sécurité sociale	**..**	**..**	**..**	**..**	**113 099**	**133 072**	**132 033**	**159 300**	**295 800**	**260 981**
2100 A la charge des salariés	..	..	..	..	0	0	0	0	0	0
2110 Sur la base du salaire	..	..	..	..	..	..	..	..	..	..
2120 Sur la base de l'impôt sur le revenu	..	..	..	..	..	..	..	..	..	..
2200 A la charge des employeurs	..	..	..	..	0	0	0	0	0	0
2210 Sur la base du salaire	..	..	..	..	..	..	..	..	..	..
2220 Sur la base de l'impôt sur le revenu	..	..	..	..	..	..	..	..	..	..
2300 A charge des travailleurs indép. ou sans emploi	..	..	..	..	0	0	0	0	0	0
2310 Sur la base du salaire	..	..	..	..	..	..	..	..	..	..
2320 Sur la base de l'impôt sur le revenu	..	..	..	..	..	..	..	..	..	..
2400 Non ventilables entre 2100, 2200 et 2300	..	..	..	..	113 099	133 072	132 033	159 300	295 800	260 981
2410 Sur la base du salaire	..	..	..	..	..	..	..	..	..	..
2420 Sur la base de l'impôt sur le revenu	..	..	..	..	..	..	..	..	..	..
3000 Sur salaires ou main d'oeuvre	**0**	**0**	**0**	**0**	**0**	**0**	**0**	**0**	**0**	**0**
4000 Impôts sur le patrimoine	**3 840**	**4 340**	**10 615**	**10 560**	**18 577**	**24 150**	**25 056**	**25 784**	**41 045**	**31 454**
4100 Impôts périodiques sur la propriété immobilière	0	0	0	0	0	0	0	0	0	0
4110 Ménages	..	..	..	..	..	..	..	..	..	..
4120 Autres agents	..	..	..	..	..	..	..	..	..	..
4200 Impôts périodiques sur l'actif net	0	0	0	0	0	0	0	0	0	0
4210 Personnes physiques	..	..	..	..	..	..	..	..	..	..
4220 Sociétés	..	..	..	..	..	..	..	..	..	..
4300 Impôts sur mut. par décès, succ. et donations	0	0	0	0	0	0	0	0	0	0
4310 Impôts sur mut. par décès et successions	..	..	..	..	..	..	..	..	..	..
4320 Impôts sur les donations	..	..	..	..	..	..	..	..	..	..
4400 Impôts sur transact. mobilières et immob.	0	0	0	0	0	0	0	0	0	0
4500 Impôts non-périodiques	0	0	0	0	0	0	0	0	0	0
4510 Sur l'actif net	..	..	..	..	..	..	..	..	..	..
4520 Autres non-périodiques	..	..	..	..	..	..	..	..	..	..
4600 Autres impôts périodiques sur patrimoine	3 840	4 340	10 615	10 560	18 577	24 150	25 056	25 784	41 045	31 454
5000 Impôts sur les biens et services	**423 400**	**490 160**	**1 299 160**	**1 472 696**	**1 955 776**	**2 278 920**	**2 726 608**	**3 283 931**	**3 766 695**	**4 132 535**
5100 Impôts sur production, vente, transfert, etc.	421 840	488 480	1 294 815	1 468 130	1 949 239	2 271 820	2 718 859	3 276 204	3 757 003	4 123 057
5110 Impôts généraux	224 880	280 700	883 255	1 004 032	1 360 458	1 545 130	1 837 385	2 262 049	2 566 967	2 811 054
5111 Taxes sur la valeur ajoutée	202 600	244 860	883 130	1 004 032	1 360 458	1 545 130	1 837 385	2 262 049	2 566 967	2 811 054
TVA Intérieure	77 780	102 560	383 663	437 348	457 308	544 130	693 241	843 911	906 711	953 565
TVA Douane import	124 820	142 300	362 762	387 092	611 850	728 300	881 624	1 088 765	1 232 623	1 346 233
TVA Douane sur les produits pétroliers	0	0	136 705	179 592	291 300	272 700	262 520	329 373	427 632	511 256
5112 Impôts sur les ventes	0	0	0	0	0	0	0	0	0	0
5113 Autres impôts	22 280	35 840	125	0	0	0	0	0	0	0
5120 Impôts sur biens et services déterminés	196 960	207 780	411 560	464 098	588 781	726 690	881 474	1 014 155	1 190 036	1 312 003
5121 Accises	43 280	43 700	157 595	201 039	236 881	268 490	342 945	385 177	422 353	421 151
Accises domestiques	25 500	31 920	157 595	201 039	236 881	268 490	342 945	385 177	422 353	421 151
Accises à la douane	17 780	11 780	0	0	0	0	0	0	0	0
5122 Bénéfices des monopoles fiscaux	0	0	0	0	0	0	0	0	0	0
5123 Droits de douane et droits à l'importation	150 660	152 380	253 840	262 726	351 860	458 100	538 485	628 505	767 173	890 053
Droit de douanes	29 820	24 700	163 181	172 369	264 310	331 400	412 085	493 156	535 458	604 739
Taxe d'importation	52 900	48 140	0	0	0	0	0	0	0	0
Taxes s/ prod. Pétroliers (total)	67 940	79 540	90 659	90 357	87 550	126 700	126 400	135 349	231 715	285 314
5124 Taxes à l'exportation	0	0	0	0	0	0	0	0	0	0
5125 Impôts sur biens d'équipement	0	0	0	0	0	0	0	0	0	0
5126 Impôts sur services déterminés	0	0	0	0	0	0	0	0	0	0

Table 5.15. **Madagascar** *(cont.)*

Details of tax revenue / Recettes fiscales détaillées

Million MGA

	1999	2000	2009	2010	2014	2015	2016	2017	2018	2019
5127 Autres impôts sur commerce et transact. internat.	3 020	11 700	125	333	40	100	44	473	510	799
Taxe statistique s/ import	0	8 040	0	0	0	0	0	0	0	0
Autres	3 020	3 660	125	333	40	100	44	473	510	799
5128 Autres impôts	0	0	0	0	0	0	0	0	0	0
5130 Non ventilables entre 5110 et 5120	0	0	0	0	0	0	0	0	0	0
5200 Impôts sur utilisation des biens et exerc. activités	1 560	1 680	4 345	4 566	6 537	7 100	7 750	7 727	8 692	9 479
5210 Impôts périodiques	1 560	1 680	4 345	4 566	6 537	7 100	7 750	7 727	8 692	9 479
5211 A la charge des ménages: véhicules à moteur	0	0	0	0	0	0	0	0	0	0
5212 A la charge autres agents: véhicules à moteur	0	0	0	0	0	0	0	0	0	0
5213 Autres impôts périodiques	1 560	1 680	4 345	4 566	6 537	7 100	7 750	7 727	8 692	9 479
5220 Impôts non-périodiques	0	0	0	0	0	0	0	0	0	0
5300 Non ventilables entre 5100 et 5200	0	0	0	0	0	0	0	0	0	0
6000 Autres impôts	**9 260**	**6 120**	**9 368**	**7 299**	**3 090**	**3 150**	**14 690**	**15 233**	**21 453**	**26 300**
6100 A la charge exclusive des entreprises	6 440	2 540	3 490	3 739	470	650	1 004	944	687	1 178
6200 A la charge d'autres agents	2 820	3 580	5 878	3 560	2 620	2 500	13 686	14 289	20 766	25 123

.. Non disponible

Note : Année civile se terminant le 31 décembre.

Les données sont sur la base des encaissements.

Les chiffres n'incluent pas les recettes fiscales collectées par les collectivités locales car elles ne sont pas disponibles.

Les cotisations de sécurité sociale sous la rubrique 2000 ne sont pas considérées comme des recettes fiscales au Madagascar

Source : Ministère de l'économie et des Finances de Madagascar.

StatLink https://doi.org/10.1787/888934283937

Table 5.16. **Malawi**

Details of tax revenue / Recettes fiscales détaillées

Million MWK

	1999	2000	2009	2010	2014	2015	2016	2017	2018	2019
Total tax revenue	..	..	**124 263**	**152 744**	**409 458**	**485 326**	**604 221**	**795 784**	**880 895**	**986 710**
1000 Taxes on income, profits and capital gains	..	..	**51 588**	**67 576**	**183 316**	**236 126**	**292 729**	**386 078**	**423 259**	**460 724**
1100 Of individuals	..	..	28 839	36 525	101 902	139 074	186 751	224 334	256 576	302 061
1110 On income and profits	..	..	28 839	36 525	101 902	139 074	186 751	224 334	256 576	302 061
Pay as you earn tax (PAYE)	..	..	25 843	32 849	91 442	126 367	166 855	199 315	228 697	269 244
Fringe benefits	..	..	1 366	1 675	4 495	5 350	7 506	8 981	10 749	12 111
Non-resident tax	..	..	590	835	3 320	4 585	8 488	13 153	13 116	16 350
Dividends	..	..	1 040	1 165	2 645	2 772	3 901	2 885	4 013	4 355
1120 On capital gains	..	..	0	0	0	0	0	0	0	0
1200 Corporate	..	..	22 749	31 051	81 414	97 052	105 978	161 744	166 683	158 664
1210 On profits	..	..	22 749	31 051	81 414	97 052	105 978	161 744	166 683	158 664
Company assessments	..	..	3 787	6 981	8 092	14 186	14 753	21 125	28 858	19 619
Provisional corporate income tax	..	..	12 633	16 253	39 606	43 723	42 897	64 656	64 987	55 936
Withholding tax on corporations	..	..	6 329	7 817	33 715	39 143	48 328	64 041	72 839	83 109
Capital gains tax	..	..	0	0	0	0	0	11 923	0	0
1220 On capital gains of corporates	..	..	0	0	0	0	0	0	0	0
1300 Unallocable between 1100 and 1200	..	..	0	0	0	0	0	0	0	0
2000 Social security contributions	..	..	**0**	**0**	**0**	**0**	**0**	**0**	**0**	**0**
2100 Employees	..	..	..	..	..	..	..	..	..	..
2110 On a payroll basis	..	..	..	..	..	..	..	..	..	..
2120 On an income tax basis	..	..	..	..	..	..	..	..	..	..
2200 Employers	..	..	..	..	..	..	..	..	..	..
2210 On a payroll basis	..	..	..	..	..	..	..	..	..	..
2220 On an income tax basis	..	..	..	..	..	..	..	..	..	..
2300 Self-employed or non-employed	..	..	..	..	..	..	..	..	..	..
2310 On a payroll basis	..	..	..	..	..	..	..	..	..	..
2320 On an income tax basis	..	..	..	..	..	..	..	..	..	..
2400 Unallocable between 2100, 2200 and 2300	..	..	..	..	..	..	..	..	..	..
2410 On a payroll basis	..	..	..	..	..	..	..	..	..	..
2420 On an income tax basis	..	..	..	..	..	..	..	..	..	..
3000 Taxes on payroll and workforce	..	..	**0**	**0**	**0**	**0**	**0**	**0**	**0**	**0**
4000 Taxes on property	..	..	..	..	..	..	..	..	..	..
4100 Recurrent taxes on immovable property	..	..	..	..	..	..	..	..	..	..
4110 Households	..	..	..	..	..	..	..	..	..	..
4120 Others	..	..	..	..	..	..	..	..	..	..
4200 Recurrent taxes on net wealth	..	..	..	..	..	..	..	..	..	..
4210 Individual	..	..	..	..	..	..	..	..	..	..
4220 Corporate	..	..	..	..	..	..	..	..	..	..
4300 Estate, inheritance and gift taxes	..	..	..	..	..	..	..	..	..	..
4310 Estate and inheritance taxes	..	..	..	..	..	..	..	..	..	..
4320 Gift taxes	..	..	..	..	..	..	..	..	..	..
4400 Taxes on financial and capital transactions	..	..	..	..	..	..	..	..	..	..
4500 Other non-reccurrent taxes on property	..	..	..	..	..	..	..	..	..	..
4510 On net wealth	..	..	..	..	..	..	..	..	..	..
4520 Other non-recurrent taxes	..	..	..	..	..	..	..	..	..	..
4600 Other recurrent taxes on property	..	..	..	..	..	..	..	..	..	..
5000 Taxes on goods and services	..	..	**72 548**	**84 865**	**225 687**	**248 646**	**310 922**	**408 050**	**457 223**	**525 273**
5100 Taxes on production, sale, transfer, etc	..	..	72 548	84 865	225 687	248 646	310 922	408 050	457 223	525 273
5110 General taxes on goods and services	..	..	34 709	38 751	120 888	137 551	166 781	220 278	247 658	287 974
5111 Value added taxes	..	..	34 709	38 751	120 878	137 539	166 761	220 266	247 632	287 926
VAT revenues (domestic)	..	..	18 625	21 932	56 454	67 149	75 727	108 064	132 750	163 852
VAT on imports	..	..	20 262	22 482	69 595	80 007	99 900	129 668	139 080	152 835
VAT refunds	..	..	-4 178	-5 663	-5 171	-9 618	-8 866	-17 466	-24 199	-28 761
5112 Sales tax	..	..	0	0	0	0	0	0	0	0
5113 Other	..	..	0	0	9	12	20	13	26	48
Turnover tax	..	..	..	..	9	12	20	13	26	48
5120 Taxes on specific goods and services	..	..	37 839	46 115	104 799	111 094	144 141	187 771	209 565	237 299
5121 Excises	..	..	24 269	31 122	63 738	64 856	91 580	117 941	133 326	149 006
Local excise taxes	..	..	4 980	5 805	13 746	15 368	19 860	28 389	32 208	36 215
Excise taxes on imports	..	..	13 977	14 233	28 511	26 419	29 981	41 714	48 544	55 172
Road Levy (fuel tax)	..	..	5 311	7 507	8 281	9 312	19 619	24 002	26 277	31 218
Road tax (fuel tax)	..	..	0	0	3 617	3 837	4 425	4 717	5 580	6 662
Rural Electrification Levy (fuel tax)	..	..	0	3 577	8 368	8 681	16 255	17 530	18 950	17 781
Storage Levy (fuel tax)	..	..	0	0	1 214	1 240	1 441	1 500	1 768	1 958

Table 5.16. **Malawi** *(cont.)*

Details of tax revenue / Recettes fiscales détaillées

Million MWK

	1999	2000	2009	2010	2014	2015	2016	2017	2018	2019
5122 Profits of fiscal monopolies	..	..	0	0	0	0	0	0	0	0
5123 Customs and import duties	..	..	13 570	14 993	41 061	46 238	52 562	69 830	76 239	88 292
Import duty	..	..	13 287	15 775	41 115	46 121	52 197	69 773	76 179	88 213
Prepayments collected on import duties	..	..	283	-783	-53	117	365	57	60	79
5124 Taxes on exports	..	..	0	0	0	0	0	0	0	0
5125 Taxes on investment goods	..	..	0	0	0	0	0	0	0	0
5126 Taxes on specific services	..	..	0	0	0	0	0	0	0	0
5127 Other taxes on internat. trade and transactions	..	..	0	0	0	0	0	0	0	0
5128 Other taxes	..	..	0	0	0	0	0	0	0	0
5130 Unallocable between 5110 and 5120	..	..	0	0	0	0	0	0	0	0
5200 Taxes on use of goods and to perform activities	..	..	0	0	0	0	0	0	0	0
5210 Recurrent taxes	..	..	..	..	..	..	..	..	..	..
5211 Paid by households: motor vehicles	..	..	..	..	..	..	..	..	..	..
5212 Paid by others: motor vehicles	..	..	..	..	..	..	..	..	..	..
5213 Paid in respect of other goods	..	..	..	..	..	..	..	..	..	..
5220 Non-recurrent taxes	..	..	..	..	..	..	..	..	..	..
5300 Unallocable between 5100 and 5200	..	..	0	0	0	0	0	0	0	0
6000 Other taxes	**..**	**..**	**128**	**303**	**455**	**554**	**570**	**1 656**	**413**	**714**
6100 Paid solely by business	..	..	128	303	455	554	570	1 656	413	714
6200 Other	..	..	0	0	0	0	0	0	0	0

.. Not available

Note: Data are on a fiscal year basis beginning 1st July. For example, the data for 2019 represent July 1, 2018 to June 30, 2019. 2018 and 2019 figures are projections.

Figures exclude revenues from business licenses and permits collected by city and district councils from business entities within their jurisdictions.

Heading 2000: Social security contributions for Malawi are deemed to be null as they do not meet the criteria to be classified as social security contributions set out in the OECD classification of taxes in the Interpretative Guide.

Heading 4000: Revenues from property taxes are mainly levied by local governments for which data on revenue are not available.

Source: Ministry of Finance, Economic Planning and Development of Malawi.

StatLink https://doi.org/10.1787/888934283956

Table 5.17. **Mali**

Details of tax revenue / Recettes fiscales détaillées

Million XOF

	1999	2000	2009	2010	2014	2015	2016	2017	2018	2019
Recettes fiscales totales	**243 171**	**239 362**	**692 578**	**748 245**	**988 961**	**1 174 860**	**1 371 149**	**1 491 790**	**1 263 918**	**1 707 227**
1000 Impôts sur revenu, bénéfices et gains en capital	**34 528**	**34 698**	**153 948**	**184 760**	**296 685**	**296 284**	**327 103**	**391 107**	**313 752**	**410 014**
1100 Des personnes physiques	14 860	16 061	46 003	50 375	75 185	88 233	94 711	111 698	90 875	125 158
1110 Sur le revenu et les bénéfices	14 860	16 061	46 003	50 375	75 185	88 233	94 711	111 698	90 875	125 158
ITS retenue, secteur privé	11 607	12 374	35 458	39 859	63 658	71 153	76 734	91 859	74 395	101 950
ITS retenue, secteur public	2 868	3 311	9 037	8 624	8 797	13 904	13 882	15 677	12 004	18 066
Taxe sur les plus-values de cession	0	0	0	0	818	862	1 042	1 137	1 371	1 599
Impôts sur les revenus fonciers	385	376	1 508	1 892	1 912	2 314	3 053	3 025	3 105	3 543
1120 Sur les gains en capital	0	0	0	0	0	0	0	0	0	0
1200 Des sociétés	17 404	16 034	99 367	118 346	196 451	179 458	206 698	250 612	201 763	253 131
1210 Sur les bénéfices	17 404	16 034	99 367	118 346	196 451	179 458	206 698	250 612	201 763	253 131
Impôt sur les societés (IS privé)	..	..	93 580	107 582	182 231	174 433	199 055	246 446	197 499	249 245
Impôt sur les societés (IS état)	..	..	0	121	49	1	0	3	157	26
BIC secteur privé	16 986	15 996	5 787	10 643	14 171	5 024	7 643	4 163	4 107	3 859
BIC secteur état	418	38	0	0	0	0	0	0	0	0
1220 Sur les gains en capital	..	..	..	..	..	..	..	..	..	..
1300 Non ventilables entre 1100 et 1200	2 264	2 603	8 578	16 039	25 049	28 593	25 694	28 797	21 115	31 725
Taxe synthétique	0	480	1 369	1 212	1 449	1 441	1 503	1 503	1 469	1 486
Impôt sur le revenu des valeurs mobilières	2 264	2 123	7 209	14 827	23 600	27 152	24 191	27 294	19 646	30 239
2000 Cotisations de sécurité sociale	**17 125**	**18 442**	**73 868**	**73 600**	**110 925**	**116 702**	**153 398**	**156 268**	**158 559**	**171 250**
2100 A la charge des salariés	..	..	..	..	..	..	..	..	..	..
2110 Sur la base du salaire	..	..	..	..	..	..	..	..	..	..
2120 Sur la base de l'impôt sur le revenu	..	..	..	..	..	..	..	..	..	..
2200 A la charge des employeurs	..	..	..	..	..	..	..	..	..	..
2210 Sur la base du salaire	..	..	..	..	..	..	..	..	..	..
2220 Sur la base de l'impôt sur le revenu	..	..	..	..	..	..	..	..	..	..
2300 A charge des travailleurs indép. ou sans emploi	..	..	..	..	..	..	..	..	..	..
2310 Sur la base du salaire	..	..	..	..	..	..	..	..	..	..
2320 Sur la base de l'impôt sur le revenu	..	..	..	..	..	..	..	..	..	..
2400 Non ventilables entre 2100, 2200 et 2300	17 125	18 442	73 868	73 600	110 925	116 702	153 398	156 268	158 559	171 250
Cotisations sécurité sociale (CMSS)	..	..	13 659	12 834	24 444	26 550	45 311	41 985	34 758	34 758
Cotisations sécurité sociale (INPS)	17 125	18 442	60 209	60 766	86 481	90 152	108 086	114 283	123 801	136 492
2410 Sur la base du salaire	..	..	..	..	..	..	..	..	..	..
2420 Sur la base de l'impôt sur le revenu	..	..	..	..	..	..	..	..	..	..
3000 Sur salaires ou main d'oeuvre	**4 721**	**4 671**	**5 449**	**6 278**	**9 881**	**11 567**	**13 192**	**13 685**	**11 938**	**14 737**
4000 Impôts sur le patrimoine	**4 783**	**3 149**	**9 411**	**12 062**	**16 512**	**17 933**	**28 489**	**32 171**	**26 353**	**30 862**
4100 Impôts périodiques sur la propriété immobilière	207	119	718	979	1 380	1 561	1 590	2 156	1 779	1 957
Droits de conservation de la propriété	207	119	718	979	1 341	1 549	1 572	2 139	1 764	1 914
Taxe sur les locations des particuliers	0	0	0	0	39	12	18	17	15	42
4110 Ménages	..	..	..	..	..	..	..	..	..	..
4120 Autres agents	..	..	..	..	..	..	..	..	..	..
4200 Impôts périodiques sur l'actif net	0	0	0	0	0	0	0	0	0	0
4210 Personnes physiques	..	..	..	..	..	..	..	..	..	..
4220 Sociétés	..	..	..	..	..	..	..	..	..	..
4300 Impôts sur mut. par décès, succ. et donations	0	0	0	0	0	0	0	0	0	0
4310 Impôts sur mut. par décès et successions	..	..	..	..	..	..	..	..	..	..
4320 Impôts sur les donations	..	..	..	..	..	..	..	..	..	..
4400 Impôts sur transact. mobilières et immob.	4 576	3 030	8 693	11 083	15 132	16 372	26 899	30 015	24 573	28 905
Droits d'enregistrements (DGI)	4 556	2 934	4 706	6 928	8 726	11 023	18 390	19 941	16 754	13 027
Droits d'enregistrements (DND)	0	0	3 882	4 107	6 150	5 321	8 436	9 815	7 499	15 583
Transfert lettre et permis OCC en TF	20	96	0	0	0	0	0	0	0	0
Taxe sur les frais d'édilité	0	0	105	48	256	28	73	259	320	295
4500 Impôts non-périodiques	0	0	0	0	0	0	0	0	0	0
4510 Sur l'actif net	..	..	..	..	..	..	..	..	..	..
4520 Autres non-périodiques	..	..	..	..	..	..	..	..	..	..
4600 Autres impôts périodiques sur patrimoine	0	0	0	0	0	0	0	0	0	0
5000 Impôts sur les biens et services	**173 869**	**172 271**	**422 414**	**451 942**	**522 430**	**689 931**	**811 118**	**874 248**	**728 932**	**989 465**
5100 Impôts sur production, vente, transfert, etc.	173 079	171 443	421 031	450 213	520 077	687 273	807 832	871 041	724 619	985 878
5110 Impôts généraux	75 206	80 633	246 514	260 599	279 167	328 157	394 552	438 914	371 539	537 907
5111 Taxes sur la valeur ajoutée	75 206	80 633	246 514	260 599	279 167	328 157	394 552	438 914	371 539	537 907
TVA à l'importation	45 107	46 622	153 154	161 656	176 270	210 431	232 434	282 199	268 881	316 487
Recettes TVA (privé)	27 718	31 218	91 565	95 383	99 994	113 512	150 102	153 442	100 982	220 473
Recettes TVA (gouvernement)	2 381	2 793	1 795	3 560	2 903	4 214	12 016	3 273	1 677	947
5112 Impôts sur les ventes	0	0	0	0	0	0	0	0	0	0

Table 5.17. **Mali** *(cont.)*

Details of tax revenue / Recettes fiscales détaillées

Million XOF

	1999	2000	2009	2010	2014	2015	2016	2017	2018	2019
5113 Autres impôts	0	0	0	0	0	0	0	0	0	0
5120 Impôts sur biens et services déterminés	97 873	90 810	174 517	189 614	240 910	359 116	413 280	432 127	353 080	447 970
5121 Accises	64 592	45 791	51 945	56 909	68 459	136 898	159 013	148 200	103 676	118 607
Taxes intérieures sur produits petroliers (TIPP)	48 315	33 694	22 999	25 660	27 793	93 264	100 648	87 789	48 611	43 626
Taxe Ad Valorem (entreprises minières) (DNDC)	5 287	4 233	20 550	20 479	25 474	25 253	30 605	30 681	27 246	45 845
Taxes locales sur les tabacs	384	816	4 875	5 385	6 445	8 264	12 787	14 725	14 405	13 420
Taxes sur les boissons alcoolisés	1 025	1 169	2 650	1 777	2 880	3 611	3 672	4 806	4 750	6 037
Impôt spécial sur les boissons	1 624	1 519	500	2 088	3 473	4 237	5 431	6 755	5 459	5 144
Taxe sur autres produits	7 957	4 360	371	1 520	2 394	2 269	5 870	3 444	3 205	4 535
5122 Bénéfices des monopoles fiscaux	0	0	0	0	0	0	0	0	0	0
5123 Droits de douane et droits à l'importation	25 972	30 734	82 268	86 853	105 683	124 049	139 263	161 928	147 355	173 683
Droits de douanes	24 363	29 328	73 902	76 287	93 480	111 062	124 320	144 024	129 869	154 469
Redevance Statistique	0	315	7 748	9 702	11 125	12 940	14 803	17 804	16 939	19 148
Taxe degréssive de protection (TDP)	0	6	582	831	969	0	0	0	0	0
Taxe conjoncturelle à l'importation	1 609	1 085	36	33	109	47	140	100	547	67
5124 Taxes à l'exportation	2 975	4 046	18 589	20 503	26 407	30 243	29 288	37 421	33 887	53 055
CPS sur l'or	2 975	4 046	18 589	20 503	26 407	30 243	29 288	37 421	33 887	53 055
5125 Impôts sur biens d'équipement	0	0	0	0	0	0	0	0	0	0
5126 Impôts sur services déterminés	4 334	10 239	21 715	25 349	40 361	67 926	85 716	84 578	68 162	102 625
Taxes sur les Activités Financières	0	5 785	14 184	17 828	23 112	39 608	41 562	43 886	32 993	59 838
Ristournes sur PMU et CASINO	1 660	1 515	2 909	3 061	5 173	5 966	6 821	6 832	7 069	7 478
Taxes sur les transporteurs routiers	1 544	1 676	2 532	2 659	3 243	3 499	4 890	4 072	4 212	3 505
Taxes sur les contrats d'assurances	1 128	1 261	2 065	1 787	3 465	3 321	4 783	4 454	4 066	4 852
Autres taxes sur les services déterminés	2	2	25	14	3	2	10	1	1	3
Taxe sur Accès au Reseau de Télécom Ouvert au Public (TARTOP)	0	0	0	0	5 365	15 530	27 650	25 333	19 822	26 950
5127 Autres impôts sur commerce et transact. internat.	0	0	0	0	0	0	0	0	0	0
5128 Autres impôts	0	0	0	0	0	0	0	0	0	0
5130 Non ventilables entre 5110 et 5120	0	0	0	0	0	0	0	0	0	0
5200 Impôts sur utilisation des biens et exerc. activites	790	828	1 383	1 729	2 353	2 658	3 286	3 207	4 313	3 588
5210 Impôts périodiques	790	828	1 383	1 729	2 353	2 658	3 286	3 207	4 313	3 588
5211 A la charge des ménages: véhicules à moteur	664	716	1 365	1 715	2 336	2 658	3 286	3 207	3 389	3 588
5212 A la charge autres agents: véhicules à moteur	0	0	0	0	0	0	0	0	0	..
5213 Autres impôts périodiques	126	112	18	14	17	0	0	0	924	..
5220 Impôts non-périodiques	0	0	0	0	0	0	0	0	0	0
5300 Non ventilables entre 5100 et 5200	0	0	0	0	0	0	0	0	0	0
6000 Autres impôts	**8 145**	**6 131**	**27 488**	**19 603**	**32 528**	**42 443**	**37 849**	**24 311**	**24 385**	**90 899**
Droits de Timbres (DGI)	5 751	4 188	9 515	10 797	15 000	16 840	18 821	16 502	17 702	20 027
Droits de timbres (DND)	0	0	163	143	500	235	277	455	406	550
Recettes sur exercices antérieurs	2 394	1 943	17 810	8 663	17 028	25 368	18 751	7 354	6 277	70 323
6100 A la charge exclusive des entreprises	..	..	..	..	..	..	..	..	..	..
6200 A la charge d'autres agents	..	..	..	..	..	..	..	..	..	..
Pour mémoire : *Prélevement communautaire (PC) (taxe UEMOA)*	1 326	1 394	0	0	0	0	0	0	0	0

.. Non disponible

Note : Année civile se terminant le 31 décembre.

Les données sont sur la base des encaissements.

Les chiffres n'incluent pas les recettes fiscales collectées par les collectivités locales car elles ne sont pas disponibles.

Les recettes de la Caisse Nationale d'Assurance Maladie (CANAM) ne sont pas disponibles. Les données sur les cotisations de la Caisse Malienne de Sécurité Sociale (CMSS) et les données de l'Institut National de Prévoyance Sociale (INPS) ne sont disponibles qu'à partir de 2004 et 2006 respectivement. Ces recettes ne sont pas incluses dans les recettes de l'État du Mali.

Rubrique 1100 : La taxe sur les plus-values de cessions était sous la rubrique 1300 dans les éditions précédentes.

Rubrique 1200 : Les recettes sur les BIC étaient sous la rubrique 1100 dans les éditions précédentes.

Rubrique 1300 : La taxe synthétique était sous la rubrique 5113 dans les éditions précédentes.

Rubrique 2000 : Les chiffres sur les cotisations de sécurité sociale de la CMSS n'étaient pas disponibles pour 2019. Pour 2019, la valeur pour 2018 a été utilisée à la place.

Rubrique 5111 : Les recettes de TVA ne comprennent plus les recettes de TVA des comptes spéciaux du Trésor remboursés aux contribuables.

Rubrique 5123 : Les recettes de la CEDEAO (Communauté économique des États de l'Afrique de l'Ouest), y compris les redevances statistiques, le prélèvement communautaire, et la taxe dégressive de protection, ne sont pas considérés comme des recettes fiscales ou des recettes non fiscales selon le guide d'interprétation de l'OCDE (voir § 4).

Rubrique 5126 : Les recettes de TARTOP étaient incluses dans les recettes non fiscales (Ventes de biens et services) dans les éditions précédentes.

Rubriques 5212 et 5213 : Les chiffres sur les recettes du Mali ne sont pas disponibles pour 2019.

Source : Ministère de l'Économie et des Finances et la Direction Nationale du Trésor et de la Comptabilité Publique du Mali.

StatLink https://doi.org/10.1787/888934283975

Table 5.18. **Mauritania / Mauritanie**

Details of tax revenue / Recettes fiscales détaillées

Million MRU

	1999	2000	2009	2010	2014	2015	2016	2017	2018	2019
Recettes fiscales totales	..	..	**12 823**	**15 175**	**30 165**	**29 070**	**31 922**	**35 128**	**40 318**	**40 604**
1000 Impôts sur revenu, bénéfices et gains en capital	..	..	**4 146**	**5 282**	**11 442**	**9 722**	**9 980**	**10 971**	**11 853**	**12 543**
1100 Des personnes physiques	..	..	1 678	2 266	4 847	4 324	4 088	4 110	4 586	5 073
1110 Sur le revenu et les bénéfices	..	..	1 678	2 266	4 847	4 324	4 088	4 110	4 586	5 073
Impôt sur le traitement de salaires	..	..	1 200	1 396	3 901	3 819	3 588	3 635	3 936	4 321
Dont: ITS Pétrole	..	..	147	94	229	129	196	258	342	..
impot sur le revenu des capitaux mobiliers	..	..	311	777	724	400	379	352	526	635
Impôt sur les revenus fonciers	..	..	124	45	142	101	121	119	124	116
Impôt général sur le revenu	..	..	43	48	80	4	0	4	0	0
1120 Sur les gains en capital	..	..	0	0	0	0	0	0	0	0
1200 Des sociétés	..	..	2 468	3 015	6 595	5 398	5 892	6 861	7 267	7 470
1210 Sur les bénéfices	..	..	2 468	3 015	6 595	5 398	5 892	6 861	7 267	7 470
Bénéfices industriels et commerciaux (BIC), non commerciaux (BNC) et impôt minimum forfaitaire (IMF)	..	..	800	1 400	3 195	3 400	3 324	3 025	3 398	3 744
Dont: BIC Pétrole	..	..	201	144	72	43	103	238	296	..
Taxe unique de la SNIM (Société Nationale Industrielle et Minière de Mauritanie)	..	..	1 015	921	1 583	223	430	1 249	408	1 196
IMF Douanes	..	..	653	695	1 466	1 452	1 378	1 590	1 850	1 946
Régime simplifié d'imposition	..	..	0	0	351	323	760	998	1 610	584
1220 Sur les gains en capital	..	..	0	0	0	0	0	0	0	0
1300 Non ventilables entre 1100 et 1200	..	..	0	0	0	0	0	0	0	0
2000 Cotisations de sécurité sociale	..	..	**756**	**1 019**	**1 753**	**1 796**	**1 721**	**1 865**	**2 025**	**1 959**
2100 A la charge des salariés	..	..	..	..	..	..	..	..	..	..
2110 Sur la base du salaire	..	..	..	..	..	..	..	..	..	..
2120 Sur la base de l'impôt sur le revenu	..	..	..	..	..	..	..	..	..	..
2200 A la charge des employeurs	..	..	..	..	..	..	..	..	..	..
2210 Sur la base du salaire	..	..	..	..	..	..	..	..	..	..
2220 Sur la base de l'impôt sur le revenu	..	..	..	..	..	..	..	..	..	..
2300 A charge des travailleurs indép. ou sans emploi	..	..	..	..	..	..	..	..	..	..
2310 Sur la base du salaire	..	..	..	..	..	..	..	..	..	..
2320 Sur la base de l'impôt sur le revenu	..	..	..	..	..	..	..	..	..	..
2400 Non ventilables entre 2100, 2200 et 2300	..	..	756	1 019	1 753	1 796	1 721	1 865	2 025	1 959
Cotisations CNSS	..	..	391	424	587	592	622	646	650	670
Cotisations CNAM	..	..	365	595	1 166	1 204	1 099	1 219	1 376	1 289
2410 Sur la base du salaire	..	..	..	..	..	..	..	..	..	..
2420 Sur la base de l'impôt sur le revenu	..	..	..	..	..	..	..	..	..	..
3000 Sur salaires ou main-d'oeuvre	..	..	**32**	**32**	**32**	**48**	**40**	**42**	**41**	**50**
4000 Impôts sur le patrimoine	..		**653**	**646**	**953**	**1 387**	**1 294**	**1 155**	**1 172**	**1 091**
4100 Impôts périodiques sur la propriété immobilière	..	..	628	622	902	1 346	1 251	1 097	1 113	1 046
4110 Ménages	..	..	..	..	..	..	..	..	..	..
4120 Autres agents	..	..	..	..	..	..	..	..	..	..
4200 Impôts périodiques sur l'actif net	..	..	0	0	0	0	0	0	0	0
4210 Personnes physiques	..	..	..	..	..	..	..	..	..	..
4220 Sociétés	..	..	..	..	..	..	..	..	..	..
4300 Impôts sur mut. par décès, succ. et donations	..	..	0	0	0	0	0	0	0	0
4310 Impôts sur mut. par décès et successions	..	..	..	..	..	..	..	..	..	..
4320 Impôts sur les donations	..	..	..	..	..	..	..	..	..	..
4400 Impôts sur transact. mobilières et immob.	..	..	26	25	51	41	43	58	59	45
Droits de conservation foncière	..	..	26	25	51	41	43	58	59	45
4500 Impôts non-périodiques	..	..	0	0	0	0	0	0	0	0
4510 Sur l'actif net	..	..	..	..	..	..	..	..	..	..
4520 Autres non-périodiques	..	..	..	..	..	..	..	..	..	..
4600 Autres impôts périodiques sur patrimoine	..	..	0	0	0	0	0	0	0	0
5000 Impôts sur les biens et services	..	..	**7 236**	**8 196**	**15 985**	**16 118**	**18 888**	**21 096**	**25 226**	**24 962**
5100 Impôts sur production, vente, transfert, etc.	..	..	7 095	7 983	15 652	15 785	17 916	19 822	23 812	23 651
5110 Impôts généraux	..	..	4 236	5 069	10 007	9 454	9 691	10 428	12 605	12 676
5111 Taxes sur la valeur ajoutée	..	..	4 236	5 069	10 007	9 454	9 691	10 428	12 605	12 676
Recettes TVA intérieur	..	..	900	1 290	3 284	3 500	3 481	3 264	3 643	3 662
Recettes TVA à l'importation	..	..	3 336	3 779	6 723	5 954	6 210	7 164	8 963	9 014
5112 Impôts sur les ventes	..	..	0	0	0	0	0	0	0	0
5113 Autres impôts	..	..	0	0	0	0	0	0	0	0
5120 Impôts sur biens et services déterminés	..	..	2 859	2 915	5 646	6 330	8 224	9 394	11 207	10 975
5121 Accises	..	..	0	0	0	0	0	0	0	0
5122 Bénéfices des monopoles fiscaux	..	..	0	0	0	0	0	0	0	0

Table 5.18. **Mauritania / Mauritanie** *(cont.)*

Details of tax revenue / Recettes fiscales détaillées

Million MRU

	1999	2000	2009	2010	2014	2015	2016	2017	2018	2019
5123 Droits de douane et droits à l'importation	..	..	2 622	2 631	5 092	5 692	7 502	8 358	10 111	9 849
Droit Fiscal à l'importation	..	..	1 636	1 631	3 143	3 313	4 143	4 716	5 502	5 381
Taxe sur les prod. pétroliers	..	..	498	494	664	1 042	1 653	1 735	2 277	2 369
Taxes de consommation	..	..	195	188	471	586	982	1 047	1 256	1 027
Taxe statistique	..	..	294	319	561	553	539	657	810	808
Taxe pour la promotion de la culture et du sport	..	..	0	0	253	199	186	203	266	264
5124 Taxes à l'exportation	..	..	14	20	61	39	45	410	395	328
5125 Impôts sur biens d'équipement	..	..	0	0	0	0	0	0	0	0
5126 Impôts sur services déterminés	..	..	224	264	492	599	677	626	701	799
Taxe sur les les operations financieres	..	..	181	208	430	538	611	561	628	722
Taxe d'aéroport et destination à létranger	..	..	43	56	62	61	66	65	72	76
5127 Autres impôts sur commerce et transact. internat.	..	..	0	0	0	0	0	0	0	0
5128 Autres impôts	..	..	0	0	0	0	0	0	0	0
5130 Non ventilables entre 5110 et 5120	..	..	0	0	0	0	0	0	0	0
5200 Impôts sur utilisation des biens et exerc. activités	..	..	141	213	333	333	972	1 274	1 414	1 311
5210 Impôts périodiques	..	..	141	213	333	333	972	1 274	1 414	1 311
5211 A la charge des ménages: véhicules à moteur	..	..	107	153	234	236	245	247	235	211
5212 A la charge autres agents: véhicules à moteur	..	..	0	0	0	0	0	0	0	0
5213 Autres impôts périodiques	..	..	35	60	99	97	727	1 028	1 179	1 100
Patente	..	..	0	0	78	76	77	77	80	73
Droit de pêche	..	..	35	60	21	21	650	951	1 098	1 027
5220 Impôts non-périodiques	..	..	0	0	0	0	0	0	0	0
5300 Non ventilables entre 5100 et 5200	..	..	0	0	0	0	0	0	0	0
6000 Autres impôts	**..**	**..**	**0**	**0**	**0**	**0**	**0**	**0**	**0**	**0**
6100 A la charge exclusive des entreprises	..	..	..	..	..	..	..	..	..	..
6200 A la charge d'autres agents	..	..	..	..	..	..	..	..	..	..

.. Non disponible

Note : Année civile se terminant le 31 décembre.

Les données sont sur la base des encaissements.

Les données de cette édition sont en monnaie MRU, devise officielle de la Mauritanie depuis le 1er janvier 2018. Elle remplace la monnaie MRO, devise utilisée dans les éditions précédentes.

Rubrique 2000 : Les cotisations de sécurité sociale de la CNSS sont estimées pour 2019.

Rubrique 4100 : Cette rubrique inclut les recettes communales. Ces recettes proviennent des différents impôts communaux et taxes municipales qui comprennent notamment la contribution foncière sur les propriétés bâties, la contribution foncière sur les terrains agricoles affectés à des cultures, la taxe d'habitation, la contribution communale, la patente, la taxe communale et les redevances et les droits domaniaux sur l'occupation du domaine public. Il n'a pas été possible de distinguer chacune de ces recettes ainsi la totalité de ces recettes sont classifiés dans la présente rubrique compte tenu que la majorité provient des impôts sur la propriété immobilière; Ces recettes sont estimées en 2019.

Rubrique 4400 : Cette rubrique inclut les recettes des droits de conservation foncière. Elles sont incluses dans les recettes fiscales comme le préconise la classification OCDE (voir le guide d'interprétation en Annexe A) mais considérées comme des recettes non fiscales en Mauritanie.

Source : Ministère des Finances de la Mauritanie.

StatLink https://doi.org/10.1787/888934283994

Table 5.19. **Mauritius / Maurice**

Details of tax revenue / Recettes fiscales détaillées

Million MUR

	1999	2000	2009	2010	2014	2015	2016	2017	2018	2019
Total tax revenue	**19 590**	**22 146**	**55 277**	**58 404**	**75 777**	**79 225**	**82 339**	**88 584**	**95 752**	**103 385**
1000 Taxes on income, profits and capital gains	**2 700**	**2 881**	**15 629**	**15 005**	**18 385**	**19 793**	**20 403**	**22 938**	**24 325**	**27 810**
1100 Of individuals	1 363	1 540	4 175	4 583	7 049	7 614	7 621	8 661	9 527	10 453
1110 On income and profits	..	..	..	..	..	..	..	..	..	..
1120 On capital gains	..	..	..	..	..	..	..	..	..	..
1200 Corporate	1 337	1 341	10 592	9 457	10 268	10 993	11 686	13 040	13 407	15 648
1210 On profits	1 337	1 341	10 592	9 457	10 268	10 993	11 686	13 040	13 407	15 648
Income tax - companies & corporate bodies	..	..	10 259	8 428	8 972	9 788	10 459	11 881	12 403	14 556
Special levy on banks	..	..	333	455	772	748	771	846	846	934
Solidarity levy on telecommunication companies	..	..	0	424	358	331	308	313	158	158
Corporate social responsibility	..	..	0	150	166	126	147	0	0	0
Special contribution from hotels	..	..	0	0	0	0	0	0	0	0
1220 On capital gains	..	..	..	..	..	..	..	..	..	..
1300 Unallocable between 1100 and 1200	..	..	862	965	1 068	1 186	1 096	1 236	1 392	1 709
Tax deduction at source	..	..	862	965	1 068	1 186	1 096	1 236	1 392	1 709
2000 Social security contributions	**898**	**986**	**1 845**	**2 113**	**3 019**	**3 252**	**3 380**	**3 648**	**3 630**	**4 239**
2100 Employees	299	329	615	704	1 006	1 084	1 127	1 216	1 210	1 413
2110 On a payroll basis	..	..	..	..	..	..	..	..	..	..
2120 On an income tax basis	..	..	..	..	..	..	..	..	..	..
2200 Employers	599	657	1 230	1 408	2 012	2 168	2 253	2 432	2 420	2 826
2210 On a payroll basis	..	..	..	..	..	..	..	..	..	..
2220 On an income tax basis	..	..	..	..	..	..	..	..	..	..
2300 Self-employed or non-employed	0	0	0	0	0	0	0	0	0	0
2310 On a payroll basis	..	..	..	..	..	..	..	..	..	..
2320 On an income tax basis	..	..	..	..	..	..	..	..	..	..
2400 Unallocable between 2100, 2200 and 2300	0	0	0	0	0	0	0	0	0	0
2410 On a payroll basis	..	..	..	..	..	..	..	..	..	..
2420 On an income tax basis	..	..	..	..	..	..	..	..	..	..
3000 Taxes on payroll and workforce	**123**	**140**	**263**	**176**	**507**	**474**	**592**	**638**	**549**	**777**
Extra-budgetary taxes on payroll and workforce	123	140	263	176	507	474	592	638	549	777
4000 Taxes on property	**1 390**	**1 411**	**3 245**	**3 328**	**4 299**	**4 095**	**4 680**	**4 894**	**4 711**	**4 706**
4100 Recurrent taxes on immovable property	181	205	347	417	279	146	296	318	306	294
4110 Households	0	0	0	0	0	0	0	0	0	0
4120 Others	181	205	347	417	279	146	296	318	306	294
Local taxes on immovable property	181	205	337	410	275	143	292	314	299	288
Campement taxes	0	0	10	6	4	3	4	4	7	6
4200 Recurrent taxes on net wealth	0	0	0	0	0	0	0	0	0	0
4210 Individual	..	..	..	..	..	..	..	..	..	..
4220 Corporate	..	..	..	..	..	..	..	..	..	..
4300 Estate, inheritance and gift taxes	0	0	0	0	0	0	0	0	0	0
4310 Estate and inheritance taxes	..	..	..	..	..	..	..	..	..	..
4320 Gift taxes	..	..	..	..	..	..	..	..	..	..
4400 Taxes on financial and capital transactions	1 209	1 206	2 891	2 902	4 000	3 907	4 337	4 543	4 385	4 376
Land transfer tax	..	..	1 348	1 190	1 652	1 650	1 831	2 016	1 971	1 964
Registration duty on transfer of immovable property	..	..	1 053	1 180	1 522	1 708	1 943	1 951	1 884	1 859
Tax on transfer of leasehold rights in state lands	..	..	161	175	374	157	119	258	168	164
Registration duty on transfer of shares	..	..	78	84	182	122	174	44	50	53
Registration duty on fixed and floating charges	..	..	161	180	162	157	164	162	204	220
Stamp duties	..	..	71	75	109	112	105	113	109	115
Registration duty on loans	..	..	7	9	0	0	0	0	0	0
Mortgages, inscriptions and transcriptions	..	..	12	11	0	0	0	0	0	0
Other taxes on financial and capital transactions	..	..	0	0	0	0	0	0	0	0
4500 Non-recurrent taxes	0	0	6	10	20	42	47	33	20	36
4510 On net wealth	..	..	0	0	0	0	0	0	0	0
4520 Other non-recurrent taxes	..	..	6	10	20	42	47	33	20	36
4600 Other recurrent taxes on property	0	0	0	0	0	0	0	0	0	0
5000 Taxes on goods and services	**14 278**	**16 514**	**34 145**	**37 618**	**49 379**	**51 422**	**53 173**	**56 355**	**62 410**	**65 719**
5100 Taxes on production, sale, transfer, etc.	14 090	16 312	31 262	34 755	45 300	47 254	48 943	52 228	58 041	61 018
5110 General taxes	4 639	5 604	18 980	21 094	26 225	28 036	28 805	30 231	32 989	34 941
5111 Value added taxes	4 639	5 604	18 980	21 094	26 060	28 036	28 805	30 231	32 989	34 941
VAT revenues (gross)	..	..	24 298	26 590	32 853	33 302	34 142	36 555	39 176	41 948
VAT refunds	..	..	-5 318	-5 495	-6 794	-5 267	-5 337	-6 324	-6 187	-7 007
5112 Sales tax	0	0	0	0	0	0	0	0	0	0

Table 5.19. **Mauritius / Maurice** *(cont.)*

Details of tax revenue / Recettes fiscales détaillées

Million MUR

	1999	2000	2009	2010	2014	2015	2016	2017	2018	2019
5113 Other	0	0	0	0	165	0	0	0	0	0
Extra-budgetary taxes on goods and services	..	..	..	..	165	..	..	..	..	..
Local taxes on goods and services	..	..	..	..	0	..	..	..	..	..
5120 Taxes on specific goods and services	9 452	10 707	12 282	13 660	19 075	19 218	20 138	21 996	25 052	26 077
Unallocated budgetary taxes on goods and services	..	..	0	0	0	0	0	0	0	0
5121 Excises	..	..	8 506	9 331	14 423	14 834	15 633	17 277	20 109	20 871
Spirits, liquors and alcoholic beverages	..	..	2 124	2 351	4 170	4 448	4 603	4 900	5 349	5 221
Tobacco products	..	..	2 098	2 371	3 823	3 851	4 196	4 735	5 333	5 233
Motor vehicles and motor cycles	..	..	1 852	1 928	2 400	2 471	2 582	3 126	3 384	3 756
Petro. products (incl. MIDL)	..	..	2 213	2 421	3 219	3 292	3 438	3 642	5 141	5 700
PET bottles and other plastic products	..	..	124	159	242	250	235	232	252	270
Sugar content of soft drinks	..	..	0	0	330	344	345	374	404	445
Energy inefficient products	..	..	0	0	5	3	2	12	4	4
Sugar brokerage	..	..	0	0	0	0	0	0	0	0
Extra-budgetary excise taxes	..	..	0	0	0	0	0	0	0	0
Other excises	..	..	96	101	233	175	231	255	241	242
5122 Profits of fiscal monopolies	..	..	0	0	0	0	0	0	0	0
5123 Customs and import duties	..	..	1 501	1 525	1 239	1 302	1 343	1 177	1 344	1 379
5124 Taxes on exports	..	..	0	0	0	0	0	0	0	0
5125 Taxes on investment goods	..	..	0	0	0	0	0	0	0	0
5126 Taxes on specific services	..	..	2 137	2 731	3 413	3 083	3 163	3 543	3 599	3 827
Taxes on the national lottery and other lotteries	..	..	16	693	652	436	387	242	221	309
Betting taxes on horse racing, football, etc.	..	..	569	658	934	837	887	944	971	1 047
Gaming taxes on casinos and gaming houses	..	..	962	818	529	591	652	706	778	797
Passenger fee on air tickets	..	..	591	561	1 213	1 173	1 230	1 652	1 630	1 673
Levy on messaging services	..	..	0	0	85	46	7	0	0	0
Hotel and restaurant tax	..	..	0	0	0	0	0	0	0	0
5127 Other taxes on internat. trade and transactions	..	..	0	0	0	0	0	0	0	0
5128 Other taxes	..	..	138	73	0	0	0	0	0	0
Temporary solidarity tax on hotels	..	..	101	0	..	..	..	..	..	..
Local government taxes on goods and services	..	..	37	73	..	..	..	..	..	..
5130 Unallocable between 5110 and 5120	..	..	0	0	0	0	0	0	0	0
5200 Taxes on use of goods and perform activities	188	203	2 749	2 765	4 080	4 168	4 230	4 128	4 369	4 701
5210 Recurrent taxes	188	203	1 861	1 934	2 363	2 702	2 795	2 762	2 922	3 019
5211 Paid by households: motor vehicles	0	0	1 023	1 117	1 345	1 362	1 430	1 463	1 526	1 604
5212 Paid by others: motor vehicles	0	0	0	0	0	0	0	0	0	0
5213 Paid in respect of other goods	188	203	838	816	1 018	1 341	1 366	1 299	1 396	1 415
Company licences	..	..	154	148	235	306	196	198	200	200
Incorporation & lodging fees, search duty, etc.	..	..	9	9	18	18	16	12	14	13
Tourist enterprise licences	..	..	69	74	85	91	110	99	104	112
Gambling licences	..	..	89	100	317	368	438	411	465	439
Liquor licences	..	..	11	10	23	25	23	23	23	23
Freeport licences	..	..	5	0	7	6	7	7	7	1
Pharmacy licences	..	..	5	1	1	2	1	1	1	1
Fishing vessel licences	..	..	32	52	54	43	53	59	63	82
Registration of factories	..	..	2	2	3	3	3	3	3	3
Registration of associations	..	..	2	2	0	1	1	1	1	1
Recruitment licences	..	..	0	2	0	0	1	0	0	0
Environment protection fee	..	..	159	141	159	391	403	383	400	424
Advertising structure fee	..	..	0	0	67	63	64	58	52	58
Regional taxes on permission to use goods	0	0	2	2	3	2	2	3	3	0
Local taxes on permission to use goods	188	203	281	255	0	0	0	0	21	21
Other recurrent taxes on goods and activities	..	..	19	20	45	23	48	42	39	36
5220 Non-recurrent taxes	0	0	888	832	1 716	1 466	1 434	1 366	1 447	1 682
Processing fee on acquisitions schemes	..	..	0	0	3	4	5	4	5	1
Registration duty on transfer of motor vehicles	..	..	792	794	1 195	1 277	1 266	1 335	1 378	1 462
Land conversion tax	..	..	96	38	518	185	163	26	64	219
5300 Unallocable between 5100 and 5200	0	0	134	98	0	0	0	0	0	0
Extra-budgetary taxes on goods and services	..	..	134	98	..	..	..	..	..	..
6000 Other taxes	**201**	**215**	**150**	**164**	**189**	**188**	**111**	**110**	**126**	**134**
Mauritius Revenue Authority penalties	0	0	0	0	59	74	22	24	24	36
Unidentified local government taxes	0	0	0	0	0	0	0	0	0	0
Unidentified taxes	201	215	150	164	130	114	89	86	102	98
6100 Paid solely by business	..	..	..	..	..	..	..	..	..	..
6200 Other	..	..	..	..	..	..	..	..	..	..

Table 5.19. **Mauritius / Maurice** *(cont.)*

Details of tax revenue / Recettes fiscales détaillées

.. Not available

Note: Data for 2016 onwards and for years prior to 2010 are on a fiscal year basis beginning 1st July. For example, the data for 2009 represent July 2008 to June 2009 and 2019 represents July 2018 to June 2019. The data for years 2010-15 are on a calendar year (January-December) basis.

Mauritius' budget statements cover January-June 2015 and July 2015 to June 2016, but neither the fiscal nor the calendar year for 2015. Figures for 2015 are therefore estimated using quarterly revenue figures at the aggregate level and fiscal year revenue data.

Data for the central government budgetary tax prior to 2007 and all extra-budgetary, regional and local data were classified according to the IMF Government Finance Statistics Manual. The 1986 manual was used for data up to 2009 and the 2001 manual for data up to 2009 onwards. Data from 2007 onwards are classified under the OECD classification, as set out in the Interpretative Guide in Annex A.

The Ministry of Social Services (MSS) collects National Pension Fund (NPF) contributions, National Savings Fund (NSF) contributions, the Training Levy and the Recycling Fee. The contributions to the NSF are part of a compulsory savings scheme, and are not classified as revenue in the Revenue Statistics in Africa project. Training Levy and Recycling Fee revenues could not be reported separately due to insufficient data and might be included within the extra-budgetary taxes on payroll and workforce under Heading 3000. In the calendar year 2018, there were a total of 7.1 billion rupees collected under these four MSS funds, of which 4.1 billion were collected for the NPF, 1.9 for the NSF, 1.0 for the Training Levy, and 0.7 billion for the Recycling Fee.

Heading 2000: Revenues under this heading refer only to contributions to the National Pension Fund (NPF). Employer contributions and employee contributions are calculated by taking respectively one third and two thirds of total NPF contributions since employer contributions rates are set at twice those of employees. Other funds labelled as social security contributions in Mauritius financial statements are not included since there is not enough information in order to ensure that they conformed to the definition of social security used in this publication.

Heading 3000: Revenues under this heading include revenues collected by the Ministry of Social Services under the Training Levy.

Heading 1210: The solidarity levy on telecommunications companies, the corporate social responsibility tax and the special contribution from hotels are classified as "other taxes" by the Mauritius Revenue Authority.

Heading 5213: The Environment protection fee and advertising structure fee are classified as other taxes by the Mauritius Revenue Authority.

Heading 5220: Includes the registration duty on transfer of motor vehicles and the land conversion tax that are classified as taxes on property by the Mauritius Revenue Authority.

Source: Mauritius Revenue Authority for the central government budgetary tax data from 2007 to 2014. Statistics Mauritius for extra-budgetary, local government, regional government and social security revenues from 1990 to 2019, as well as for budgetary central government tax revenues up to 2006; Ministry of Finance budget estimates for detailed revenue figures for the periods July 2005-June 2008, for 2016-19, and for the figures used to estimate calendar year 2015 revenues.

StatLink https://doi.org/10.1787/888934284013

Table 5.20. **Morocco / Maroc**

Details of tax revenue / Recettes fiscales détaillées

Million MAD

	1999	2000	2009	2010	2014	2015	2016	2017	2018	2019
Recettes fiscales totales	..	**90 900**	**207 357**	**216 769**	**256 922**	**265 069**	**278 423**	**297 181**	**312 696**	**326 526**
1000 Impôts sur revenu, bénéfices et gains en capital	..	**23 656**	**69 769**	**62 646**	**76 342**	**78 952**	**84 111**	**92 372**	**96 026**	**98 277**
1100 Des personnes physiques	..	14 540	27 116	26 598	34 573	37 214	39 792	40 686	43 889	44 353
1110 Sur le revenu et les bénéfices	..	12 473	23 324	22 391	30 651	32 797	35 082	40 135	43 462	42 823
Salaires	..	10 829	19 396	19 409	26 452	28 277	30 833	31 440	32 561	32 865
Revenus professionnels	..	1 645	3 928	2 982	4 199	4 519	4 249	3 296	6 374	6 112
Autres types d'impôts sur le revenu	..	0	0	0	0	0	0	5 398	4 527	3 846
1120 Sur les gains en capital	..	2 067	3 793	4 207	3 922	4 417	4 710	552	427	1 530
1200 Des sociétés	..	9 116	42 653	36 049	41 769	41 738	44 319	51 686	52 137	53 924
1210 Sur les bénéfices	..	8 330	38 808	31 164	34 327	32 693	44 319	51 607	52 130	53 920
Bénéfices	..	8 084	36 943	29 381	31 017	30 553	42 303	49 410	49 529	51 396
Produits bruts versés aux sociétés étrangères	..	246	1 865	1 783	3 310	2 140	2 016	2 197	2 601	2 524
1220 Sur les gains en capital	..	786	3 845	4 884	7 442	9 045	0	78	7	4
1300 Non ventilables entre 1100 et 1200	..	0	0	0	0	0	0	0	0	0
2000 Cotisations de sécurité sociale	..	**9 982**	**35 415**	**37 924**	**49 976**	**52 418**	**55 998**	**60 112**	**64 622**	**71 422**
2100 A la charge des salariés	..	..	..	..	..	..	..	..	..	..
2110 Sur la base du salaire	..	..	..	..	..	..	..	..	..	..
2120 Sur la base de l'impôt sur le revenu	..	..	..	..	..	..	..	..	..	..
2200 A la charge des employeurs	..	..	..	..	..	..	..	..	..	..
2210 Sur la base du salaire	..	..	..	..	..	..	..	..	..	..
2220 Sur la base de l'impôt sur le revenu	..	..	..	..	..	..	..	..	..	..
2300 A charge des travailleurs indép. ou sans emploi	..	..	..	..	..	..	..	..	..	..
2310 Sur la base du salaire	..	..	..	..	..	..	..	..	..	..
2320 Sur la base de l'impôt sur le revenu	..	..	..	..	..	..	..	..	..	..
2400 Non ventilables entre 2100, 2200 et 2300	..	0	176	192	280	302	377	405	432	505
2410 Sur la base du salaire	..	..	..	..	..	..	..	..	..	..
2420 Sur la base de l'impôt sur le revenu	..	..	..	..	..	..	..	..	..	..
3000 Sur salaires ou main d'oeuvre	..	**0**	**0**	**0**	**0**	**0**	**0**	**0**	**0**	**0**
4000 Impôts sur le patrimoine	..	**5 405**	**10 988**	**12 702**	**17 926**	**19 536**	**20 182**	**16 693**	**16 679**	**16 536**
4100 Impôts périodiques sur la propriété immobilière	..	3 340	4 983	5 740	6 101	6 859	7 477	7 712	7 947	8 182
4110 Ménages	..	1 989	3 282	3 898	3 888	4 414	4 781	4 962	5 143	5 324
Taxe d'habitation	..	517	295	382	301	364	320	361	402	443
Taxe sur les terrains non bâtis	..	135	717	839	901	1 113	1 163	1 301	1 439	1 577
Taxe de services communaux	..	1 337	2 270	2 677	2 685	2 937	3 298	3 300	3 302	3 304
4120 Autres agents	..	1 351	1 701	1 842	2 213	2 445	2 696	2 750	2 804	2 858
4200 Impôts périodiques sur l'actif net	..	0	0	0	0	0	0	0	0	0
4210 Personnes physiques	..	..	..	..	..	..	..	..	..	..
4220 Sociétés	..	..	..	..	..	..	..	..	..	..
4300 Impôts sur mut. par décès, succ. et donations	..	0	0	0	0	0	0	0	0	0
4310 Impôts sur mut. par décès et successions	..	..	..	..	..	..	..	..	..	..
4320 Impôts sur les donations	..	..	..	..	..	..	..	..	..	..
4400 Impôts sur transact. mobilières et immob.	..	2 065	6 005	6 962	11 825	12 677	12 705	8 981	8 732	8 354
4500 Impôts non-périodiques	..	0	0	0	0	0	0	0	0	0
4510 Sur l'actif net	..	..	..	..	..	..	..	..	..	..
4520 Autres non-périodiques	..	..	..	..	..	..	..	..	..	..
4600 Autres impôts périodiques sur patrimoine	..	0	0	0	0	0	0	0	0	0
5000 Impôts sur les biens et services	..	**50 655**	**89 282**	**101 384**	**110 024**	**111 766**	**114 743**	**124 441**	**134 189**	**139 319**
5100 Impôts sur production, vente, transfert, etc.	..	49 539	86 882	99 056	107 068	108 848	111 457	121 108	128 153	132 920
5110 Impôts généraux	..	21 476	55 077	65 247	74 995	75 271	75 735	81 479	86 024	85 707
5111 Taxes sur la valeur ajoutée	..	21 476	55 077	65 247	74 995	75 271	75 735	81 479	86 024	85 707
5112 Impôts sur les ventes	..	0	0	0	0	0	0	0	0	0
5113 Autres impôts	..	0	0	0	0	0	0	0	0	0
5120 Impôts sur biens et services déterminés	..	28 063	31 805	33 809	32 073	33 577	35 722	39 629	42 128	47 212
5121 Accises	..	15 223	19 843	21 382	24 119	25 661	26 451	27 720	28 674	30 276
Taxes intérieures de consommation	..	15 183	19 629	21 132	23 849	25 366	26 134	27 383	28 318	29 900
Taxe sur la vente de produits forestiers	..	4	22	26	20	29	29	18	8	-3
Taxe sur les débits de boissons	..	23	122	143	156	162	167	185	203	221
Taxe sur les eaux minerales et de table	..	13	70	81	94	104	121	133	145	157
5122 Bénéfices des monopoles fiscaux	..	0	0	0	0	0	0	0	0	0
5123 Droits de douane et droits à l'importation	..	12 810	11 805	12 242	7 738	7 715	9 074	8 610	9 693	9 768
5124 Taxes à l'exportation	..	0	0	0	0	0	0	0	0	0
5125 Impôts sur biens d'équipement	..	0	0	0	0	0	0	0	0	0

Table 5.20. **Morocco / Maroc** *(cont.)*

Details of tax revenue / Recettes fiscales détaillées

Million MAD

	1999	2000	2009	2010	2014	2015	2016	2017	2018	2019
5126 Impôts sur services déterminés	..	30	157	184	216	201	197	3 299	3 762	7 169
Taxe de séjour	..	26	137	160	191	173	168	198	228	258
Taxe sur le transport public de voyageurs	..	4	20	24	25	28	29	32	35	3 108
Droit de timbre sur les annonces publicitaires sur écran	..	0	0	0	0	0	0	3 070	3 499	3 803
5127 Autres impôts sur commerce et transact. internat.	..	0	0	0	0	0	0	0	0	0
5128 Autres impôts	..	0	0	0	0	0	0	0	0	0
5130 Non ventilables entre 5110 et 5120	..	0	0	0	0	0	0	0	0	0
5200 Impôts sur utilisation des biens et exerc. activites	..	1 116	2 400	2 328	2 956	2 918	3 286	3 333	6 036	6 399
5210 Impôts périodiques	..	964	1 594	1 385	1 973	1 955	2 348	2 360	3 158	3 459
5211 A la charge des ménages: véhicules à moteur	..	959	1 566	1 351	1 937	1 920	2 310	2 325	2 570	2 846
5212 A la charge autres agents: véhicules à moteur	..	0	0	0	0	0	0	0	556	583
5213 Autres impôts périodiques	..	5	28	33	36	35	38	35	32	29
Taxe sur les permis de chasse	..	5	28	33	36	35	38	35	32	29
5220 Impôts non-périodiques	..	152	805	943	983	963	938	973	2 878	2 941
Taxe sur les opérations de construction	..	113	600	703	718	709	709	716	723	730
Taxe sur les opérations de lotissement	..	39	205	240	265	254	229	257	285	313
Autres	..	0	0	0	0	0	0	0	1 870	1 898
5300 Non ventilables entre 5100 et 5200	..	0	0	0	0	0	0	0	0	0
6000 Autres impôts	**..**	**1 201**	**1 903**	**2 112**	**2 654**	**2 398**	**3 390**	**3 562**	**1 179**	**972**
Droits de timbres	..	1 132	1 537	1 683	2 010	2 092	3 090	3 305	965	801
Taxes locales	..	69	366	429	644	306	300	257	214	171
6100 A la charge exclusive des entreprises	..	..	..	..	..	..	..	..	..	..
6200 A la charge d'autres agents	..	..	..	..	..	..	..	..	..	..

.. Non disponible

Note : Année civile se terminant le 31 décembre.

Les données sont sur la base des encaissements.

Les impôts affectés aux Fonds Spéciaux du Trésor sont compris dans les données.

Rubrique 2000 : Les données de cotisations de sécurité sociales sont estimées pour les années 2000 et 2001. Les recettes des majorations et pénalités relatives aux impôts sont désormais considérées comme des recettes non fiscales. La classification nationale du Maroc les compte comme des recettes fiscales.

Source : Ministère de l'Économie et des Finances.

StatLink https://doi.org/10.1787/888934284032

Table 5.21. **Namibia / Namibie**

Details of tax revenue / Recettes fiscales détaillées

Million NAD

	1999	2000	2009	2010	2014	2015	2016	2017	2018	2019
Total tax revenue	..	..	**13 821**	**15 734**	**29 077**	**31 974**	**34 043**	**35 494**	**35 168**	**36 247**
1000 Taxes on income, profits and capital gains	..	..	**8 137**	**9 912**	**17 780**	**19 006**	**20 607**	**21 946**	**21 855**	**22 611**
1100 Of individuals	..	..	5 218	6 156	10 476	10 982	12 355	13 546	13 923	14 557
1110 On income and profits	..	..	5 218	6 156	10 476	10 982	12 355	13 546	13 923	14 557
Income tax on individuals	..	..	5 084	5 945	10 197	10 794	12 002	13 267	13 588	14 147
Non-resident shareholders tax	..	..	106	189	77	147	266	183	265	307
Tax on royalty	..	..	28	21	202	41	87	96	70	103
1120 On capital gains	..	..	0	0	0	0	0	0	0	0
1200 Corporate	..	..	2 918	3 756	7 304	8 024	8 252	8 400	7 932	8 054
1210 On profits	..	..	2 918	3 756	7 304	8 024	8 252	8 400	7 932	8 054
Diamond mining companies	..	..	511	354	1 980	2 199	1 611	1 654	1 496	1 143
Other mining companies	..	..	61	213	94	99	92	256	445	187
Non-mining companies	..	..	2 279	3 018	4 945	5 425	6 006	5 950	5 384	5 927
Withholding taxes	..	..	53	156	264	280	522	510	607	797
Annual levy on gambling income	..	..	14	15	21	21	21	30	0	0
1220 On capital gains	..	..	0	0	0	0	0	0	0	0
1300 Unallocable between 1100 and 1200	..	..	0	0	0	0	0	0	0	0
2000 Social security contributions	..	..	**226**	**305**	**462**	**537**	**547**	**649**	**621**	**621**
2100 Employees	..	..	..	..	..	..	..	..	..	..
2110 On a payroll basis	..	..	..	..	..	..	..	..	..	..
2120 On an income tax basis	..	..	..	..	..	..	..	..	..	..
2200 Employers	..	..	..	..	..	..	..	..	..	..
2210 On a payroll basis	..	..	..	..	..	..	..	..	..	..
2220 On an income tax basis	..	..	..	..	..	..	..	..	..	..
2300 Self-employed or non-employed	..	..	..	..	..	..	..	..	..	..
2310 On a payroll basis	..	..	..	..	..	..	..	..	..	..
2320 On an income tax basis	..	..	..	..	..	..	..	..	..	..
2400 Unallocable between 2100, 2200 and 2300	..	..	226	305	462	537	547	649	621	621
2410 On a payroll basis	..	..	..	..	..	..	..	..	..	..
2420 On an income tax basis	..	..	..	..	..	..	..	..	..	..
3000 Taxes on payroll and workforce	..	..	**0**	**0**	**0**	**0**	**0**	**0**	**0**	**0**
4000 Taxes on property	..	..	**222**	**139**	**289**	**313**	**284**	**270**	**221**	**174**
4100 Recurrent taxes on immovable property	..	..	0	0	0	0	0	0	0	0
4110 Households	..	..	..	..	..	..	..	..	..	..
4120 Others	..	..	..	..	..	..	..	..	..	..
4200 Recurrent taxes on net wealth	..	..	0	0	0	0	0	0	0	0
4210 Individual	..	..	..	..	..	..	..	..	..	..
4220 Corporate	..	..	..	..	..	..	..	..	..	..
4300 Estate, inheritance and gift taxes	..	..	0	0	0	0	0	0	0	0
4310 Estate and inheritance taxes	..	..	..	..	..	..	..	..	..	..
4320 Gift taxes	..	..	..	..	..	..	..	..	..	..
4400 Taxes on financial and capital transactions	..	..	222	139	289	313	284	270	221	174
4500 Non-recurrent taxes	..	..	0	0	0	0	0	0	0	0
4510 On net wealth	..	..	..	..	..	..	..	..	..	..
4520 Other non-recurrent taxes	..	..	..	..	..	..	..	..	..	..
4600 Other recurrent taxes on property	..	..	0	0	0	0	0	0	0	0
5000 Taxes on goods and services	..	..	**5 070**	**5 169**	**10 272**	**11 902**	**12 389**	**12 458**	**12 274**	**12 732**
5100 Taxes on production, sale, transfer, etc.	..	..	5 070	5 169	10 271	11 901	12 387	12 454	12 274	12 732
5110 General taxes	..	..	4 976	5 057	10 208	11 678	11 978	12 049	11 461	11 516
5111 Value added taxes	..	..	4 976	5 057	10 208	11 678	11 978	12 049	11 461	11 516
5112 Sales tax	..	..	0	0	0	0	0	0	0	0
5113 Other	..	..	0	0	0	0	0	0	0	0
5120 Taxes on specific goods and services	..	..	93	113	63	223	409	405	813	1 216
5121 Excises	..	..	0	0	0	0	0	0	0	0
5122 Profits of fiscal monopolies	..	..	0	0	0	0	0	0	0	0
5123 Customs and import duties	..	..	82	102	44	209	382	342	813	1 201
Levy on fuel	..	..	82	102	44	209	315	342	730	1 107
Environmental levies and carbon emission taxes	..	..	0	0	0	0	67	0	83	94
5124 Taxes on exports	..	..	0	0	0	0	0	0	0	0
5125 Taxes on investment goods	..	..	0	0	0	0	0	0	0	0
5126 Taxes on specific services	..	..	0	0	0	0	0	0	0	0
5127 Other taxes on internat. trade and transactions	..	..	0	0	0	0	0	0	0	0
5128 Other taxes	..	..	12	11	19	14	27	63	0	15
5130 Unallocable between 5110 and 5120	..	..	0	0	0	0	0	0	0	0

Table 5.21. **Namibia / Namibie** *(cont.)*

Details of tax revenue / Recettes fiscales détaillées

Million NAD

	1999	2000	2009	2010	2014	2015	2016	2017	2018	2019
5200 Taxes on use of goods and perform activities	..	..	0	0	1	1	2	4	0	0
5210 Recurrent taxes	..	..	0	0	1	1	2	4	0	0
5211 Paid by households: motor vehicles	..	..	0	0	0	0	0	0	0	0
5212 Paid by others: motor vehicles	..	..	0	0	0	0	0	0	0	0
5213 Paid in respect of other goods	..	..	0	0	1	1	2	4	0	0
5220 Non-recurrent taxes	..	..	0	0	0	0	0	0	0	0
5300 Unallocable between 5100 and 5200	..	..	0	0	0	0	0	0	0	0
6000 Other taxes	**..**	**..**	**167**	**208**	**274**	**216**	**216**	**171**	**197**	**109**
6100 Paid solely by business	..	..	..	..	..	..	..	..	..	..
6200 Other	..	..	..	..	..	..	..	..	..	..

.. Not available

Note: Data are on a cash basis.

Data are on a fiscal year basis beginning 1st April. For example, the data for 2019 represent April 2019 to March 2020.

Figures exclude tax revenues collected by sub-national governments as the data are not available.

Heading 2000: Data are not available prior to 2009.

Heading 5111: Value added taxes: this category includes revenue from VAT, additional sales tax and the general sales tax.

Source: Ministry of Finance of Namibia.

StatLink https://doi.org/10.1787/888934284051

Table 5.22. **Niger**

Details of tax revenue / Recettes fiscales détaillées

Million XOF

	1999	2000	2009	2010	2014	2015	2016	2017	2018	2019
Recettes fiscales totales	**..**	**115 819**	**357 448**	**373 461**	**663 171**	**720 540**	**644 899**	**615 444**	**796 671**	**786 351**
1000 Impôts sur revenu, bénéfices et gains en capital	**..**	**20 891**	**114 008**	**94 839**	**208 402**	**177 695**	**170 506**	**166 432**	**167 981**	**172 209**
1100 Des personnes physiques	..	9 634	21 910	19 756	45 697	45 501	50 942	55 054	55 069	61 154
1110 Sur le revenu et les bénéfices	..	9 634	21 857	19 623	45 468	45 294	50 508	54 667	54 567	60 807
Impôt sur les traitements et salaires	..	8 000	20 905	18 575	44 638	44 198	49 415	53 542	51 539	58 686
Impôt synthétique	..	1 530	879	974	762	1 030	1 047	1 079	2 775	2 060
Impôt général sur le revenu (IGR)	..	103	74	74	68	66	47	46	253	62
1120 Sur les gains en capital	..	0	53	133	229	208	434	387	502	347
Plus-values de cessions. immob. (IPVCI)	..	0	53	133	229	208	434	387	502	347
1200 Des sociétés	..	11 257	92 098	75 083	162 705	132 194	119 564	111 379	112 913	111 055
1210 Sur les bénéfices	..	11 257	92 098	75 083	162 705	132 194	119 564	111 379	112 913	111 055
Impôt sur les bénéfices (ISB)	..	10 933	82 554	67 863	146 385	121 448	109 509	101 156	102 484	102 851
Bénéfices non commerciaux (BNC) (arriérés)	..	126	0	0	0	0	0	0	140	217
Impôt sur le revenu des valeurs mobilières (IRVM)	..	198	6 590	5 695	11 484	7 900	7 966	8 357	8 665	7 776
Recettes portuaires	..	0	2 954	1 525	4 836	2 846	2 089	1 866	1 623	212
1220 Sur les gains en capital	..	0	0	0	0	0	0	0	0	0
1300 Non ventilables entre 1100 et 1200	..	0	0	0	0	0	0	0	0	0
2000 Cotisations de sécurité sociale	**..**	**6 216**	**15 851**	**19 950**	**33 610**	**34 117**	**35 453**	**37 261**	**37 840**	**42 272**
2100 A la charge des salariés	..	..	..	..	..	..	..	..	..	..
2110 Sur la base du salaire	..	..	..	..	..	..	..	..	..	..
2120 Sur la base de l'impôt sur le revenu	..	..	..	..	..	..	..	..	..	..
2200 A la charge des employeurs	..	..	..	..	..	..	..	..	..	..
2210 Sur la base du salaire	..	..	..	..	..	..	..	..	..	..
2220 Sur la base de l'impôt sur le revenu	..	..	..	..	..	..	..	..	..	..
2300 A charge des travailleurs indép. ou sans emploi	..	..	..	..	..	..	..	..	..	..
2310 Sur la base du salaire	..	..	..	..	..	..	..	..	..	..
2320 Sur la base de l'impôt sur le revenu	..	..	..	..	..	..	..	..	..	..
2400 Non ventilables entre 2100, 2200 et 2300	..	6 216	15 851	19 950	33 610	34 117	35 453	37 261	37 840	42 272
2410 Sur la base du salaire	..	..	..	..	..	..	..	..	..	..
2420 Sur la base de l'impôt sur le revenu	..	..	..	..	..	..	..	..	..	..
3000 Sur salaires ou main d'oeuvre	**..**	**401**	**762**	**1 121**	**3 478**	**3 978**	**3 472**	**3 223**	**3 726**	**4 348**
Taxe d'apprentissage (TAP)	..	401	762	1 121	3 478	3 978	3 472	3 223	3 726	4 348
4000 Impôts sur le patrimoine	**..**	**1 252**	**1 866**	**2 906**	**1 612**	**2 742**	**2 117**	**2 318**	**5 564**	**9 804**
4100 Impôts périodiques sur la propriété immobilière	..	1 252	1 866	2 906	1 612	2 742	2 117	2 318	5 564	9 804
Taxe immobilière	..	1 015	1 860	2 904	1 612	2 742	2 117	2 318	2 366	1 684
Taxe foncière	..	238	0	0	0	0	0	0	2	0
Impôt forfaitaire de droit de propriétés	..	0	6	2	0	0	0	0	25	5
Impôt sur le revenu des baux d'habitation	..	0	0	0	0	0	0	0	207	386
Impôt sur le revenu des baux professionnels	..	0	0	0	0	0	0	0	704	1 548
Taxe d'habitation	..	0	0	0	0	0	0	0	2 184	3 141
4110 Ménages	..	..	..	..	..	..	..	..	..	..
4120 Autres agents	..	0	0	0	0	0	0	0	77	3 040
Taxe immobilière des personnes morales	..	0	0	0	0	0	0	0	77	3 040
4200 Impôts périodiques sur l'actif net	..	0	0	0	0	0	0	0	0	0
4210 Personnes physiques	..	..	..	..	..	..	..	..	..	..
4220 Sociétés	..	..	..	..	..	..	..	..	..	..
4300 Impôts sur mut. par décès, succ. et donations	..	0	0	0	0	0	0	0	0	0
4310 Impôts sur mut. par décès et successions	..	..	..	..	..	..	..	..	..	..
4320 Impôts sur les donations	..	..	..	..	..	..	..	..	..	..
4400 Impôts sur transact. mobilières et immob.	..	0	0	0	0	0	0	0	0	0
4500 Impôts non-périodiques	..	0	0	0	0	0	0	0	0	0
4510 Sur l'actif net	..	..	..	..	..	..	..	..	..	..
4520 Autres non-périodiques	..	..	..	..	..	..	..	..	..	..
4600 Autres impôts périodiques sur patrimoine	..	0	0	0	0	0	0	0	0	0
5000 Impôts sur les biens et services	**..**	**83 383**	**208 312**	**234 839**	**370 745**	**431 233**	**392 894**	**370 521**	**525 172**	**498 790**
5100 Impôts sur production, vente, transfert, etc.	..	81 489	207 154	233 477	368 641	428 892	390 385	367 939	521 777	494 738
5110 Impôts généraux	..	31 766	125 164	136 966	225 855	256 546	227 121	210 787	359 611	289 733
5111 Taxes sur la valeur ajoutée	..	31 766	125 164	136 966	197 683	237 621	204 248	190 420	341 450	269 488
TVA intérieure (brute)	..	12 375	71 387	76 999	130 060	145 529	123 186	127 968	259 228	183 386
TVA à l'importation (brute)	..	19 391	53 777	59 967	67 623	92 092	81 062	62 453	82 222	86 103
5112 Impôts sur les ventes	..	..	..	..	0	0	0	0	0	0
5113 Autres impôts	..	0	0	0	28 171	18 925	22 873	20 367	18 161	20 245
Redevance ad valorem	..	0	0	0	28 171	18 925	22 873	20 367	18 161	20 245
5120 Impôts sur biens et services déterminés	..	49 722	81 990	96 511	142 787	172 345	163 263	157 152	162 166	205 004

Table 5.22. **Niger** *(cont.)*

Details of tax revenue / Recettes fiscales détaillées

Million XOF

	1999	2000	2009	2010	2014	2015	2016	2017	2018	2019
5121 Accises	..	13 754	25 936	28 505	39 124	51 081	46 307	29 660	41 203	36 661
Taxe intérieure sur les produits pétroliers (TIPP) (y compris DGD)	..	4 313	9 552	11 694	11 913	19 375	12 703	10 691	18 804	15 673
Taxe sur les tabacs et les cigarettes	..	4 600	10 224	11 279	14 001	17 926	20 295	10 177	11 451	10 795
Taxe sur les boissons alcoolisés (TBA)	..	882	1 132	1 263	1 817	2 684	2 345	1 097	1 074	1 036
Taxe d'exploitation artisanale (TEA)	..	0	0	0	2	22	44	29	182	390
Autres droits d'accises	..	3 959	5 029	4 269	11 391	11 074	10 919	7 665	9 693	8 767
5122 Bénéfices des monopoles fiscaux	..	0	0	0	0	0	0	0	0	0
5123 Droits de douane et droits à l'importation	..	22 930	28 635	36 286	46 536	59 517	53 482	51 104	62 450	72 842
Droits de douane	..	14 722	23 925	28 141	40 976	53 226	48 392	45 933	56 383	64 396
Redevance statistique à l'importation	..	1 652	4 687	8 144	5 558	6 283	5 087	5 167	6 026	8 255
Droits Divers (y compris T.C.I)	..	6 556	23	0	1	8	3	5	41	192
5124 Taxes à l'exportation	..	11 671	24 645	27 567	37 377	31 025	27 590	43 958	48 130	48 086
Taxes sur les réexportations	..	9 997	23 197	25 405	30 923	25 657	23 056	36 838	41 097	41 039
Redevance statistique à l'exportation	..	1 673	1 213	1 465	6 340	5 342	4 524	7 117	6 671	6 982
Taxe forfaitaire sur la réexportation et/ou transit de tabacs et cigarettes (TFEAR)	..	0	235	696	113	25	10	3	363	64
5125 Impôts sur biens d'équipement	..	0	0	0	0	0	0	0	0	0
5126 Impôts sur services déterminés	..	1 238	2 601	3 080	19 074	30 399	35 691	32 096	10 224	46 982
Taxe sur la terminaison du trafic international entrant (TATTIE)	..	0	0	0	12 184	18 666	25 706	22 101	1 452	18 419
Taxe sur l'utilisation du réseau de télécommunication (TURTEL)	..	0	0	0	2 332	5 349	4 973	5 417	4 220	5 853
Taxe sur les recettes des loteries	..	877	1 276	1 303	2 238	3 377	2 474	2 292	1 778	2 716
Taxe unique sur les assurances (TUA)	..	361	1 263	1 490	2 007	2 310	2 291	2 275	2 338	2 852
Impôt sur les gains des loteries	..	0	0	0	25	550	7	1	0	31
Taxe sur les jeux de hasard (TJH)	..	0	38	246	284	140	240	11	435	33
Taxe sur la publicité commerciale extérieure (TPCE)	..	0	23	41	3	8	0	0	1	0
Taxe sur les activités financières (TAFI)	..	0	0	0	0	0	0	0	0	17 078
5127 Autres impôts sur commerce et transact. internat.	..	0	0	0	0	0	0	0	0	0
5128 Autres impôts	..	130	172	1 074	677	324	193	333	158	433
Droits miniers	..	130	172	1 074	667	295	120	25	3	2
Droit fixe mine	..	0	0	0	9	28	67	307	155	428
Droit fixe pétrole	..	0	0	0	0	1	6	0	0	3
5130 Non ventilables entre 5110 et 5120	..	0	0	0	0	0	0	0	0	0
5200 Impôts sur utilisation des biens et exerc. activites	..	894	1 158	1 362	2 104	2 341	2 509	2 582	3 394	4 052
5210 Impôts périodiques	..	529	1 158	1 362	2 073	2 316	2 474	2 562	3 390	4 050
Vignette	..	520	1 149	1 354	2 054	2 310	2 471	2 558	2 918	3 072
5211 A la charge des ménages: véhicules à moteur	..	0	0	0	0	0	0	0	0	0
5212 A la charge autres agents: véhicules à moteur	..	0	0	0	0	0	0	0	0	0
5213 Autres impôts périodiques	..	9	10	8	18	6	3	4	472	977
Permis de chasse et visite	..	0	0	0	9	2	0	0	3	18
Taxe sur les armes à feu (TAF)	..	9	9	8	9	4	3	4	4	13
Taxe sur les abonnements audiovisuels	..	0	0	0	0	0	0	0	465	946
5220 Impôts non-périodiques	..	365	0	0	31	25	35	20	5	3
Péage routier	..	365	..	..	0	0	0	0	0	0
Redevance plaque d'immatriculation	..	0	..	..	31	25	35	20	5	3
5300 Non ventilables entre 5100 et 5200	..	1 000	0	0	0	0	0	0	0	0
6000 Autres impôts	**..**	**3 676**	**16 649**	**19 807**	**45 324**	**70 775**	**40 457**	**35 690**	**56 389**	**58 927**
Droits d'enregistrement	..	2 166	8 474	8 048	29 642	51 113	24 353	18 750	34 344	35 469
Prélèvement pour cpte des collectivités locales	..	0	4 021	6 512	8 161	11 727	8 577	9 283	12 312	12 304
Taxe sur certains frais généraux des entreprises (TCFGE)	..	310	1 729	1 963	4 060	4 132	4 045	4 314	4 729	5 788
Droits de timbre	..	1 201	2 426	3 283	3 460	3 803	3 481	3 343	5 003	5 366
6100 A la charge exclusive des entreprises	..	..	..	..	..	..	..	..	..	..
6200 A la charge d'autres agents	..	..	..	..	..	..	..	..	..	..

Table 5.22. **Niger** *(cont.)*

Details of tax revenue / Recettes fiscales détaillées

.. Non disponible

Note : Année civile se terminant le 31 décembre.

Les données sont sur la base des encaissements.

Les chiffres n'incluent pas les données des recettes fiscales collectées par les collectivités locales car elles ne sont pas disponibles.

Les recettes provenant du domaine public, des redevances minières, des redevances superficiaires des mines et du pétrole et des amendes et pénalités relatives aux impôts sont incluses dans les recettes non fiscales dans cette publication comme le préconise la classification OCDE (voir le guide d'interprétation en Annexe A). La classification du Niger compte ces recettes comme des recettes fiscales.

Rubriques 5111 et 5121 : Ces rubriques contiennent des recettes provenant de la Direction Générale des Douanes (DGD) et sont annotées comme telles.

Rubrique 5220 : Cette rubrique comprend les recettes de la redevance plaques d'immatriculation collectées par la Direction Générale du Trésor et de la Comptabilité Publique (DGTCP) entre 2005 et 2018 comme le préconise la classification OCDE (voir le guide d'interprétation en Annexe A). La classification du Niger compte ces recettes comme des recettes non fiscales.

Source : Direction Générale des Impôts.

StatLink https://doi.org/10.1787/888934284070

Table 5.23. **Nigeria / Nigéria**

Details of tax revenue / Recettes fiscales détaillées

Million NGN

	1999	2000	2009	2010	2014	2015	2016	2017	2018	2019
Total tax revenue	..	..	..	**4 023 597**	**6 886 137**	**5 761 425**	**5 413 912**	**6 547 014**	**8 167 037**	**8 679 676**
1000 Taxes on income, profits and capital gains	..	..	..	**2 555 738**	**4 367 593**	**3 453 159**	**3 018 256**	**3 649 715**	**4 910 261**	**4 910 410**
1100 Of individuals	..	..	..	320 771	520 233	543 561	604 759	711 067	798 630	927 297
1110 On income and profits	..	..	..	320 771	520 233	543 561	604 759	711 067	798 630	927 297
Personal Income Tax (Federal)	..	..	..	32 564	52 846	57 377	59 469	107 682	85 146	70 307
State PAYE ("Pay as You Earn") Tax	..	..	..	268 821	434 006	456 595	511 911	566 212	669 218	809 320
Personal Income Tax (State)	..	..	..	19 386	33 382	29 589	33 379	37 172	44 266	47 670
1120 On capital gains	..	..	..	0	0	0	0	0	0	0
1200 Corporate	..	..	..	2 234 967	3 847 360	2 909 598	2 413 498	2 938 649	4 111 631	3 983 113
1210 On profits	..	..	..	2 233 931	3 844 710	2 892 796	2 314 094	2 935 469	4 099 036	3 977 136
Petroleum Profits Tax	..	..	..	1 480 364	2 453 947	1 289 961	1 157 808	1 520 482	2 467 581	2 114 268
Companies Income Tax	..	..	..	658 503	1 173 491	1 268 977	933 537	1 215 057	1 340 329	1 604 699
Education Tax	..	..	..	89 178	189 614	206 040	130 123	154 957	203 285	221 058
Income tax on gas exploration companies	..	..	..	0	17 750	115 569	85 878	34 839	75 988	21 930
National Information Technology Development Fund	..	..	..	5 886	9 908	12 249	6 748	10 134	11 853	15 181
1220 On capital gains	..	..	..	1 037	2 650	16 802	99 403	3 180	12 595	5 977
1300 Unallocable between 1100 and 1200	..	..	..	0	0	0	0	0	0	0
2000 Social security contributions	..	..	..	**305 163**	**643 447**	**569 879**	**550 052**	**714 218**	**687 080**	**931 600**
2100 Employees	..	..	..	172 418	333 268	269 328	261 414	332 914	324 012	430 691
2110 On a payroll basis	..	..	..	172 418	333 268	269 328	261 414	332 914	324 012	430 691
National Pension Commission (employee-side)	..	..	..	132 745	290 690	226 596	216 978	291 111	270 022	378 511
National Health Insurance Scheme	..	..	..	39 673	42 578	42 732	44 437	41 803	53 990	52 180
2120 On an income tax basis	..	..	..	0	0	0	0	0	0	0
2200 Employers	..	..	..	132 745	310 178	300 551	288 637	381 304	363 068	500 909
2210 On a payroll basis	..	..	..	132 745	310 178	300 551	288 637	381 304	363 068	500 909
National Pension Commission (employer-side)	..	..	..	132 745	290 690	283 244	271 222	363 889	337 528	473 139
Nigerian Social Insurance Trust Fund	..	..	..	0	19 488	17 307	17 415	17 415	25 540	27 770
2220 On an income tax basis	..	..	..	0	0	0	0	0	0	0
2300 Self-employed or non-employed	..	..	..	0	0	0	0	0	0	0
2310 On a payroll basis	..	..	..	..	..	..	..	..	..	..
2320 On an income tax basis	..	..	..	..	..	..	..	..	..	..
2400 Unallocable between 2100, 2200 and 2300	..	..	..	0	0	0	0	0	0	0
2410 On a payroll basis	..	..	..	..	..	..	..	..	..	..
2420 On an income tax basis	..	..	..	..	..	..	..	..	..	..
3000 Taxes on payroll and workforce	..	..	..	**12 610**	**29 980**	**32 766**	**31 704**	**40 890**	**50 310**	**54 760**
4000 Taxes on property	..	..	..	..	..	..	..	..	..	..
4100 Recurrent taxes on immovable property	..	..	..	..	..	..	..	..	..	..
4110 Households	..	..	..	..	..	..	..	..	..	..
4120 Others	..	..	..	..	..	..	..	..	..	..
4200 Recurrent taxes on net wealth	..	..	..	..	..	..	..	..	..	..
4210 Individual	..	..	..	..	..	..	..	..	..	..
4220 Corporate	..	..	..	..	..	..	..	..	..	..
4300 Estate, inheritance and gift taxes	..	..	..	..	..	..	..	..	..	..
4310 Estate and inheritance taxes	..	..	..	..	..	..	..	..	..	..
4320 Gift taxes	..	..	..	..	..	..	..	..	..	..
4400 Taxes on financial and capital transactions	..	..	..	..	..	..	..	..	..	..
4500 Non-recurrent taxes	..	..	..	..	..	..	..	..	..	..
4510 On net wealth	..	..	..	..	..	..	..	..	..	..
4520 Other non-recurrent taxes	..	..	..	..	..	..	..	..	..	..
4600 Other recurrent taxes on property	..	..	..	..	..	..	..	..	..	..
5000 Taxes on goods and services	..	..	..	**1 036 386**	**1 606 272**	**1 520 489**	**1 569 281**	**1 821 381**	**2 072 094**	**2 317 754**
5100 Taxes on production, sale, transfer, etc.	..	..	..	1 029 896	1 593 257	1 501 713	1 548 943	1 799 838	2 047 860	2 287 161
5110 General taxes	..	..	..	564 892	802 965	767 334	828 199	972 348	1 108 040	1 189 981
5111 Value added taxes	..	..	..	564 892	802 965	767 334	828 199	972 348	1 108 040	1 189 981
VAT revenues (domestic)	..	..	..	436 610	616 885	597 412	650 344	770 348	859 018	945 464
VAT revenues (imports)	..	..	..	128 281	186 080	169 921	177 855	202 001	249 022	244 517
5112 Sales tax	..	..	..	0	0	0	0	0	0	0
5113 Other	..	..	..	0	0	0	0	0	0	0
5120 Taxes on specific goods and services	..	..	..	465 005	790 292	734 380	720 743	827 490	939 820	1 097 180
5121 Excises	..	..	..	35 449	39 763	39 784	41 258	41 600	55 060	91 690
5122 Profits of fiscal monopolies	..	..	..	0	0	0	0	0	0	0
5123 Customs and import duties	..	..	..	429 555	750 530	694 596	679 485	785 890	884 760	1 005 490
Import duties	..	..	..	272 248	511 548	468 382	462 058	533 560	604 990	693 490
Other customs taxes	..	..	..	157 307	238 982	226 214	217 428	252 330	279 770	312 000

Table 5.23. **Nigeria / Nigéria** *(cont.)*

Details of tax revenue / Recettes fiscales détaillées

Million NGN

	1999	2000	2009	2010	2014	2015	2016	2017	2018	2019
5124 Taxes on exports	..	..	..	0	0	0	0	0	0	0
5125 Taxes on investment goods	..	..	..	0	0	0	0	0	0	0
5126 Taxes on specific services	..	..	..	0	0	0	0	0	0	0
5127 Other taxes on internat. trade and transactions	..	..	..	0	0	0	0	0	0	0
5128 Other taxes	..	..	..	0	0	0	0	0	0	0
5130 Unallocable between 5110 and 5120	..	..	..	0	0	0	0	0	0	0
5200 Taxes on use of goods and perform activities	..	..	..	6 490	13 015	18 775	20 339	21 542	24 234	30 593
5210 Recurrent taxes	..	..	..	6 490	13 015	18 775	20 339	21 542	24 234	30 593
5211 Paid by households: motor vehicles	..	..	..	6 121	12 568	18 412	19 948	21 214	23 957	30 270
5212 Paid by others: motor vehicles	..	..	..	0	0	0	0	0	0	0
5213 Paid in respect of other goods	..	..	..	368	447	364	391	328	277	323
5220 Non-recurrent taxes	..	..	..	0	0	0	0	0	0	0
5300 Unallocable between 5100 and 5200	..	..	..	0	0	0	0	0	0	0
6000 Other taxes	**..**	**..**	**..**	**113 700**	**238 846**	**185 133**	**244 619**	**320 811**	**447 292**	**465 152**
6100 Paid solely by business	..	..	..	0	0	0	0	0	0	0
6200 Other	..	..	..	113 700	238 846	185 133	244 619	320 811	447 292	465 152
Other tax revenue from states	..	..	..	107 106	227 902	178 048	238 714	311 873	431 493	446 960
Stamp duties	..	..	..	6 593	10 944	7 085	5 905	8 938	15 798	18 192

.. Not available

Note: Year ending 31st December.

The data are on a cash basis.

Some personal income taxes, capital gains taxes, road taxes, and other taxes are collected at the state level.

Statistics on state level revenues were not available in disaggregated form for 2017 and 2018. For these years, revenues for the categories State PAYE ("Pay as You Earn") Tax, Personal Income Tax (State), Other tax revenue from states were estimations.

Heading 1110: State level income taxes on individuals on paid employment are collected on a PAYE ("Pay as you earn") basis, while those who are self-employed or receive business income on a non-salary basis are charged under direct assessment. These are reported separately in this table, but the tax basis is the same for both cases.

Heading 1210: The Petroleum Profits Tax includes all tax revenue payments by oil exploration companies irrespective of the type of exploration arrangement (production sharing, joint ventures, etc) despite the fact that different types of arrangements could give rise to different tax rates. This heading does not include the government's share of company revenue arising from the revenue-sharing component of the exploration arrangements. These latter funds are reported as oil revenues in the non-tax revenue table.

Heading 1220: Capital gains tax for resident companies and non-residents is collected at the federal level while capital gains tax for individuals is collected at the state level.

Heading 2000: The Pension Reform Act was passed in 2004 and mandated both employees and employers to contribute 7.5% each to the pension retirement savings account. However, in 2014 there was an amendment after which the employee was mandated to contribute 8% while the employer contributed a minimum of 10% thereby bringing the total contribution to at leat 18%. For the years up to and including 2014, therefore, 50% of social security contributions are reported under Heading 2110 and the other half under Heading 2210. Starting in 2015, 4/9 of total pension contributions are reported under Heading 2110 and 5/9 of total pension contributions are reported under Heading 2210.

Heading 3000: This heading consists of a 2.5% payroll tax that is used to finance the National Housing Fund.

Heading 5211: Road Taxes, or taxes charged on the issuance of motor vehicle licenses, are collected at the state level.

Heading 5213: This heading contains taxes collected under the Pre-Operational Levy. This is a tax charged each year to companies that, more than 18 months after being registered, still have not commenced operations.

Heading 6000: Other state taxes include stamp duties, capital gains taxes, business premise registration, Land Use Charge, market taxes, and levies that are collected by state governments.

Source: Federal Inland Revenue Service.

StatLink https://doi.org/10.1787/888934284089

Table 5.24. **Rwanda**

Details of tax revenue / Recettes fiscales détaillées

Million RWF

	1999	2000	2009	2010	2014	2015	2016	2017	2018	2019
Total tax revenue	**65 379**	**68 909**	**389 939**	**440 724**	**865 554**	**997 232**	**1 115 636**	**1 248 017**	**1 401 503**	**1 611 730**
1000 Taxes on income, profits and capital gains	**16 820**	**17 943**	**135 218**	**159 567**	**322 827**	**379 676**	**430 431**	**488 184**	**565 235**	**640 854**
1100 Of individuals	5 761	6 621	81 595	102 037	193 212	224 553	253 893	278 076	312 070	354 545
1110 On income and profits	5 761	6 621	81 595	102 037	193 212	224 553	253 893	278 076	312 070	354 545
Pay As You Earn	..	..	..	..	..	216 750	245 138	267 311	300 751	343 064
Rental income tax	..	..	..	..	..	7 803	8 754	10 765	11 319	11 481
1120 On capital gains	0	0	0	0	0	0	0	0	0	0
1200 Corporate	11 059	11 322	53 623	57 530	129 615	155 123	176 538	210 108	253 165	286 309
1210 On profits	11 059	11 322	53 623	57 530	129 615	155 123	176 538	210 108	253 165	286 309
Corporation income tax	7 629	3 603	27 881	26 459	39 157	49 571	58 645	70 053	94 656	95 881
Withholding tax	64	59	6 932	10 764	49 948	58 422	71 929	84 786	71 474	96 990
Personal income tax	1 153	868	6 558	7 316	6 950	7 358	8 752	10 012	10 991	10 291
Other taxes on profits	2 214	6 792	12 253	12 991	33 561	39 772	37 212	45 257	76 044	83 147
1220 On capital gains	0	0	0	0	0	0	0	0	0	0
1300 Unallocable between 1100 and 1200	0	0	0	0	0	0	0	0	0	0
2000 Social security contributions	**2 925**	**3 423**	**25 741**	**28 235**	**55 530**	**59 687**	**74 717**	**74 897**	**83 344**	**94 371**
2100 Employees	1 096	1 283	9 652	10 586	20 820	22 379	28 014	28 082	31 249	35 384
2110 On a payroll basis	1 096	1 283	9 652	10 586	20 820	22 379	28 014	28 082	31 249	35 384
2120 On an income tax basis	0	0	0	0	0	0	0	0	0	0
2200 Employers	1 826	2 138	16 086	17 644	34 701	37 299	46 691	46 803	52 082	58 973
2210 On a payroll basis	1 826	2 138	16 086	17 644	34 701	37 299	46 691	46 803	52 082	58 973
2220 On an income tax basis	0	0	0	0	0	0	0	0	0	0
2300 Self-employed or non-employed	2	3	4	4	9	9	11	11	13	14
2310 On a payroll basis	2	3	4	4	9	9	11	11	13	14
2320 On an income tax basis	0	0	0	0	0	0	0	0	0	0
2400 Unallocable between 2100, 2200 and 2300	0	0	0	0	0	0	0	0	0	0
2410 On a payroll basis	..	..	..	..	..	..	..	..	..	..
2420 On an income tax basis	..	..	..	..	..	..	..	..	..	..
3000 Taxes on payroll and workforce	**0**	**0**	**0**	**0**	**0**	**0**	**0**	**0**	**0**	**0**
4000 Taxes on property	**141**	**130**	**79**	**97**	**19**	**632**	**779**	**1 156**	**1 293**	**2 142**
4100 Recurrent taxes on immovable property	141	130	78	96	19	632	779	1 156	1 293	2 142
4110 Households	141	130	78	96	19	632	779	1 156	1 293	2 142
4120 Others	0	0	0	0	0	0	0	0	0	0
4200 Recurrent taxes on net wealth	0	0	0	0	0	0	0	0	0	0
4210 Individual	..	..	..	..	..	..	..	..	..	..
4220 Corporate	..	..	..	..	..	..	..	..	..	..
4300 Estate, inheritance and gift taxes	0	0	0	0	0	0	0	0	0	0
4310 Estate and inheritance taxes	..	..	..	..	..	..	..	..	..	..
4320 Gift taxes	..	..	..	..	..	..	..	..	..	..
4400 Taxes on financial and capital transactions	0	0	0	0	0	0	0	0	0	0
4500 Non-recurrent taxes	0	0	0	0	0	0	0	0	0	0
4510 On net wealth	..	..	..	..	..	..	..	..	..	..
4520 Other non-recurrent taxes	..	..	..	..	..	..	..	..	..	..
4600 Other recurrent taxes on property	0	0	1	0	0	0	0	0	0	0
5000 Taxes on goods and services	**45 493**	**47 413**	**228 901**	**252 826**	**487 178**	**557 238**	**609 709**	**683 780**	**751 631**	**874 363**
5100 Taxes on production, sale, transfer, etc.	44 867	46 777	227 785	250 214	485 735	549 277	601 651	676 883	744 296	867 102
5110 General taxes	12 919	13 777	125 055	131 665	279 275	305 544	329 331	386 484	422 903	507 719
5111 Value added taxes	12 919	13 777	125 055	131 665	279 275	305 544	329 331	386 484	422 903	507 719
VAT revenues (gross)	..	..	138 950	146 295	310 305	339 493	365 923	429 748	476 671	576 953
VAT Refunds	..	..	-13 895	-14 629	-31 031	-33 949	-36 592	-43 264	-53 768	-69 234
5112 Sales tax	0	0	0	0	0	0	0	0	0	0
5113 Other	0	0	0	0	0	0	0	0	0	0
5120 Taxes on specific goods and services	31 949	32 999	102 730	118 548	206 461	243 733	272 320	290 399	321 393	359 383
5121 Excises	17 932	18 849	55 078	75 236	121 220	138 261	143 701	148 561	169 237	183 714
Excise tax on beers	7 710	7 146	19 311	22 548	36 872	45 950	42 510	47 862	54 801	61 170
Excise tax on petroleum	6 742	7 857	16 605	30 941	37 283	47 043	49 761	50 013	55 791	59 311
Strategic reserves levy	0	0	0	0	0	4 185	9 485	10 355	10 502	11 386
Other excises taxes	3 481	3 846	19 162	21 746	47 065	41 084	41 946	40 331	48 143	51 848
5122 Profits of fiscal monopolies	0	0	0	0	0	0	0	0	0	0

Table 5.24. **Rwanda** *(cont.)*

Details of tax revenue / Recettes fiscales détaillées

Million RWF

	1999	2000	2009	2010	2014	2015	2016	2017	2018	2019
5123 Customs and import duties	14 016	14 151	47 620	43 313	85 241	105 472	128 620	141 838	152 155	175 669
Import duties	8 682	9 260	35 303	26 215	55 106	69 731	72 062	80 738	83 601	100 742
Rwanda road maintenance fund	2 743	2 531	9 833	14 843	25 167	29 620	43 062	45 768	48 805	53 109
Infrastructure development levy	0	0	0	0	0	3 837	10 069	11 164	12 228	14 039
African Union Levy	0	0	0	0	0	0	0	721	1 579	1 835
Other customs and import duties	2 591	2 360	2 484	2 254	4 968	2 284	3 426	3 448	5 942	5 943
5124 Taxes on exports	0	0	33	0	0	0	0	0	0	0
5125 Taxes on investment goods	0	0	0	0	0	0	0	0	0	0
5126 Taxes on specific services	0	0	0	0	0	0	0	0	0	0
5127 Other taxes on internat. trade and transactions	0	0	0	0	0	0	0	0	0	0
5128 Other taxes	0	0	0	0	0	0	0	0	0	0
5130 Unallocable between 5110 and 5120	0	0	0	0	0	0	0	0	0	0
5200 Taxes on use of goods and perform activities	626	636	1 116	2 612	1 442	7 961	8 058	6 897	7 335	7 261
5210 Recurrent taxes	626	636	1 116	2 612	1 442	7 961	8 058	6 897	7 335	7 261
5211 Paid by households: motor vehicles	626	636	1 116	2 612	1 442	3 252	2 947	2 691	2 269	3 473
5212 Paid by others: motor vehicles	0	0	0	0	0	0	0	0	0	0
5213 Paid in respect of other goods	0	0	0	0	0	4 709	5 111	4 206	5 066	3 788
5220 Non-recurrent taxes	0	0	0	0	0	0	0	0	0	0
5300 Unallocable between 5100 and 5200	0	0	0	0	0	0	0	0	0	0
6000 Other taxes	**0**	**0**	**0**	**0**	**0**	**0**	**0**	**0**	**0**	**0**
6100 Paid solely by business	..	..	..	..	..	..	..	..	..	..
6200 Other	..	..	..	..	..	..	..	..	..	..

.. Not available

Note: Year ending 31st December. From 2008, the figures for social security contributions are on a fiscal year basis beginning 1st July. For example, data for 2019 represent July 2018 to June 2019.

The data are on a cash basis.

Figures exclude tax revenues collected by sub-national governments as the data are not available.

Figures include fines related to tax revenues as it is not possible to split these out from tax revenues. These revenues are now classified as non-tax revenues following a change in the OECD classification. Rwanda considers these revenues as tax revenues.

Heading 2000: Rwanda does not include social security contributions in their tax revenue data as the Rwandan authorities do not consider them as taxes.

Source: Rwanda Revenue Authority.

StatLink https://doi.org/10.1787/888934284108

Table 5.25. **Senegal / Sénégal**

Details of tax revenue / Recettes fiscales détaillées

Million XOF

	1999	2000	2009	2010	2014	2015	2016	2017	2018	2019
Recettes fiscales totales	**511 248**	**559 295**	**1 138 498**	**1 267 799**	**1 586 865**	**1 723 131**	**1 920 344**	**1 987 098**	**2 123 504**	**2 263 843**
1000 Impôts sur revenu, bénéfices et gains en capital	**100 300**	**123 771**	**275 078**	**328 200**	**398 500**	**435 600**	**516 600**	**544 800**	**603 022**	**584 000**
1100 Des personnes physiques	54 700	64 021	175 378	192 900	238 200	261 000	314 500	307 700	371 635	352 200
1110 Sur le revenu et les bénéfices	54 200	63 370	173 578	191 000	234 700	257 900	310 800	304 000	366 904	350 700
1120 Sur les gains en capital	500	651	1 800	1 900	3 500	3 100	3 700	3 700	4 731	1 500
1200 Des sociétés	38 700	49 418	78 000	106 100	133 800	147 300	165 500	191 700	189 986	201 300
1210 Sur les bénéfices	38 700	49 418	78 000	106 100	133 800	147 300	165 500	191 700	189 986	201 300
1220 Sur les gains en capital	..	..	..	..	..	..	..	..	..	..
1300 Non ventilables entre 1100 et 1200	6 900	10 332	21 700	29 200	26 500	27 300	36 600	45 400	41 400	30 500
2000 Cotisations de sécurité sociale	**20 108**	**22 215**	**53 889**	**72 999**	**104 381**	**116 260**	**128 210**	**142 070**	**150 000**	**159 423**
2100 A la charge des salariés	..	..	..	..	..	..	..	..	..	..
2110 Sur la base du salaire	..	..	..	..	..	..	..	..	..	..
2120 Sur la base de l'impôt sur le revenu	..	..	..	..	..	..	..	..	..	..
2200 A la charge des employeurs	..	..	..	..	..	..	..	..	..	..
2210 Sur la base du salaire	..	..	..	..	..	..	..	..	..	..
2220 Sur la base de l'impôt sur le revenu	..	..	..	..	..	..	..	..	..	..
2300 A charge des travailleurs indép. ou sans emploi	..	..	..	..	..	..	..	..	..	..
2310 Sur la base du salaire	..	..	..	..	..	..	..	..	..	..
2320 Sur la base de l'impôt sur le revenu	..	..	..	..	..	..	..	..	..	..
2400 Non ventilables entre 2100, 2200 et 2300	20 108	22 215	53 889	72 999	104 381	116 260	128 210	142 070	150 000	159 423
Institution de Prévoyance Retraite du Sénégal (IPRES)	20 108	22 215	53 889	72 999	77 930	93 400	103 510	115 670	..	..
Caisse de Sécurité Sociale (CSS)	0	0	0	0	26 451	22 860	24 700	26 400	..	..
2410 Sur la base du salaire	..	..	..	..	..	..	..	..	..	..
2420 Sur la base de l'impôt sur le revenu	..	..	..	..	..	..	..	..	..	..
3000 Sur salaires ou main d'oeuvre	**6 300**	**6 668**	**10 000**	**10 800**	**16 900**	**20 200**	**17 310**	**13 900**	**7 007**	**33 400**
4000 Impôts sur le patrimoine	**11 500**	**11 200**	**33 200**	**39 100**	**39 606**	**41 500**	**51 984**	**48 730**	**52 291**	**49 077**
4100 Impôts périodiques sur la propriété immobilière	0	0	0	0	0	0	0	0	0	0
4110 Ménages	..	..	..	..	..	..	..	..	..	..
4120 Autres agents	..	..	..	..	..	..	..	..	..	..
4200 Impôts périodiques sur l'actif net	0	0	0	0	0	0	0	0	0	0
4210 Personnes physiques	..	..	..	..	..	..	..	..	..	..
4220 Sociétés	..	..	..	..	..	..	..	..	..	..
4300 Impôts sur mut. par décès, succ. et donations	2 530	2 464	5 481	12 445	8 086	8 465	11 564	9 699	3 594	9 982
4310 Impôts sur mut. par décès et successions	..	..	..	..	..	..	..	..	..	..
4320 Impôts sur les donations	..	..	..	..	..	..	..	..	..	..
4400 Impôts sur transact. mobilières et immob.	8 970	8 736	27 719	26 655	31 520	33 035	40 419	39 031	48 697	39 095
Droits de mutation (immeubles)	..	..	16 388	15 418	18 352	15 863	14 995	15 916	23 636	5 906
Droits d'enregistrement autre que patrimoine	..	..	11 331	11 237	13 167	17 172	25 424	23 115	25 061	33 188
4500 Impôts non-périodiques	0	0	0	0	0	0	0	0	0	0
4510 Sur l'actif net	..	..	..	..	..	..	..	..	..	..
4520 Autres non-périodiques	..	..	..	..	..	..	..	..	..	..
4600 Autres impôts périodiques sur patrimoine	0	0	0	0	0	0	0	0	0	0
5000 Impôts sur les biens et services	**365 740**	**386 940**	**754 431**	**804 400**	**1 010 678**	**1 086 871**	**1 187 941**	**1 218 798**	**1 289 460**	**1 391 643**
5100 Impôts sur production, vente, transfert, etc.	363 540	384 590	749 731	799 400	1 002 678	1 078 171	1 175 841	1 207 498	1 278 189	1 380 143
5110 Impôts généraux	181 900	221 410	432 821	478 000	561 400	617 000	651 300	691 700	715 700	839 400
5111 Taxes sur la valeur ajoutée	181 900	221 410	432 821	478 000	561 400	617 000	651 300	691 700	715 700	839 400
5112 Impôts sur les ventes	0	0	0	0	0	0	0	0	0	0
5113 Autres impôts	0	0	0	0	0	0	0	0	0	0
5120 Impôts sur biens et services déterminés	181 640	163 180	316 910	321 400	441 278	461 171	524 541	515 798	562 489	540 743
5121 Accises	55 200	61 100	83 600	82 600	84 078	88 821	107 441	125 998	148 561	107 789
Taxe spécifique sur les produits pétroliers	..	..	59 300	63 900	59 579	61 520	74 600	83 600	91 039	69 286
Taxes sur les tabacs	..	..	9 016	9 647	13 289	14 565	15 252	13 660	16 403	19 672
Taxes sur les corps gras	..	..	1 745	978	1 447	1 964	4 712	4 330	6 413	4 034
Taxes sur les alcools	..	..	5 987	5 297	5 382	5 516	6 824	6 609	7 854	6 056
Taxe sur la cola	..	..	439	273	25	19	8	4	19	-6
Taxe sur les thés	..	..	334	154	124	153	228	118	70	269
Taxe sur le café	..	..	502	175	367	428	441	335	442	673
Taxe sur les produits comestiques	..	..	0	0	1 400	1 465	1 604	1 795	2 544	1 725
Taxe spéciale sur le ciment	..	..	0	0	0	0	0	10 700	14 087	0
Accises non classées ailleurs	..	..	6 277	2 176	2 466	3 189	3 771	4 848	9 690	6 082
5122 Bénéfices des monopoles fiscaux	0	0	0	0	0	0	0	0	0	0
5123 Droits de douane et droits à l'importation	116 500	90 340	163 810	181 600	221 100	227 600	234 600	263 500	290 400	253 600
5124 Taxes à l'exportation	0	0	0	0	0	0	0	2 900	0	0
5125 Impôts sur biens d'équipement	0	0	0	0	0	0	0	0	0	0

Table 5.25. **Senegal / Sénégal** *(cont.)*

Details of tax revenue / Recettes fiscales détaillées

Million XOF

	1999	2000	2009	2010	2014	2015	2016	2017	2018	2019
5126 Impôts sur services déterminés	9 940	11 740	37 600	45 000	69 500	71 200	76 100	95 500	105 378	78 000
Taxe sur les activités financières (TAF)	8 000	9 340	28 500	30 600	45 800	47 700	51 600	55 400	62 534	55 300
Redevance d'utilisation des télécommunications	0	0	5 100	10 000	18 700	19 500	18 600	19 600	22 289	22 700
Taxe sur les contrats d'assurances	1 940	2 400	4 000	4 400	5 000	4 000	5 900	6 300	6 905	0
Contribution au développement économique (CODEC)	0	0	0	0	0	0	0	14 200	13 649	0
5127 Autres impôts sur commerce et transact. internat.	0	0	0	0	0	0	0	0	0	0
5128 Autres impôts	0	0	31 900	12 200	66 600	73 551	106 400	27 900	18 150	101 354
Fonds de sécurisation des importations de produits pétroliers	..	..	31 900	12 200	62 600	69 451	104 600	26 400	17 266	96 854
Contributions spéciales (mines et carrières)	..	..	0	0	4 000	4 100	1 800	1 500	884	4 500
5130 Non ventilables entre 5110 et 5120	0	0	0	0	0	0	0	0	0	0
5200 Impôts sur utilisation des biens et exerc. activites	2 200	2 350	4 700	5 000	8 000	8 700	12 100	11 300	11 271	11 500
5210 Impôts périodiques	2 200	2 350	4 700	5 000	8 000	8 700	12 100	11 300	11 271	11 500
5211 A la charge des ménages: véhicules à moteur	..	..	..	..	..	..	..	..	..	..
5212 A la charge autres agents: véhicules à moteur	..	..	..	..	..	..	..	..	..	..
5213 Autres impôts périodiques	..	..	..	..	..	..	..	..	..	..
5220 Impôts non-périodiques	0	0	0	0	0	0	0	0	0	0
5300 Non ventilables entre 5100 et 5200	0	0	0	0	0	0	0	0	0	0
6000 Autres impôts	**7 300**	**8 500**	**11 900**	**12 300**	**16 800**	**22 700**	**18 300**	**18 800**	**21 725**	**46 300**
6100 A la charge exclusive des entreprises	..	..	..	..	..	..	..	..	..	..
6200 A la charge d'autres agents	..	..	..	..	..	..	..	..	..	..

.. Non disponible

Note : Année civile se terminant le 31 décembre.

Les données sont sur la base des encaissements.

Les chiffres n'incluent pas les données des recettes fiscales collectées par les collectivités locales car elles ne sont pas disponibles.

Les chiffres ne comprennent pas les taxes parafiscales car elles ne sont pas disponibles.

La rubrique 2000 comprend les cotisations de sécurité sociale de l'Institution de prévoyance retraite du Sénégal (IPRES) à partir de 2006 et les cotisations de sécurité sociale de la Caisse de Sécurité Sociale (CSS) à partir de 2012. Les cotisations de sécurité sociale au Sénégal antérieures à 2006 sont estimées.

La rubrique 5126 comprend la redevance sur l'accès ou l'utilisation du réseau des télécommunications publiques (RUTEL) classifiée comme accise au Sénégal.

Les recettes fiscales incluent les amendes et pénalités sur impôts et taxes considérées comme des recettes non fiscales. Il n'a pas été possible pour cette édition de séparer le versement des amendes et pénalités des recettes correspondant aux impôts auxquels ces amendes et pénalités se rattachent. La classification nationale du Sénégal les compte comme des recettes fiscales.

Source : Ministère de l'Économie, des Finances et du Plan.

StatLink https://doi.org/10.1787/888934284127

Table 5.26. **Seychelles**

Details of tax revenue / Recettes fiscales détaillées

Million SCR

	1999	2000	2009	2010	2014	2015	2016	2017	2018	2019
Total tax revenue	..	..	**3 317**	**3 595**	**5 226**	**5 464**	**6 108**	**6 713**	**7 464**	**7 605**
1000 Taxes on income, profits and capital gains	..	..	**823**	**1 062**	**1 653**	**1 696**	**1 967**	**2 255**	**2 329**	**2 360**
1100 Of individuals	..	..	0	254	878	948	939	901	965	975
1110 On income and profits	..	..	..	254	878	948	939	901	965	975
1120 On capital gains	..	..	..	0	0	0	0	0	0	0
1200 Corporate	..	..	823	808	776	748	1 029	1 354	1 364	1 385
1210 On profits	..	..	823	808	776	748	1 029	1 354	1 364	1 385
Companies	..	..	673	703	639	563	853	1 112	1 155	1 160
Sole traders	..	..	16	14	23	43	32	47	37	38
Partnerships	..	..	6	9	9	11	13	14	16	18
Witholding tax	..	..	109	58	67	88	83	127	96	104
Residential dwellings	..	..	0	0	37	43	47	54	59	65
Others	..	..	0	0	0	0	0	0	0	0
G&S Tax on rental income	..	..	19	24	0	0	0	0	0	0
1220 On capital gains	..	..	0	0	0	0	0	0	0	0
1300 Unallocable between 1100 and 1200	..	..	0	0	0	0	0	0	0	0
2000 Social security contributions	..	..	**558**	**329**	**184**	**215**	**212**	**255**	**540**	**398**
2100 Employees	..	..	19	21	82	93	106	140	185	199
2110 On a payroll basis	..	..	19	21	82	93	106	140	185	199
SPF - Mandatory employee contributions	..	..	19	21	82	93	106	140	185	199
2120 On an income tax basis	..	..	0	0	0	0	0	0	0	0
2200 Employers	..	..	19	21	90	102	106	115	148	196
2210 On a payroll basis	..	..	19	21	90	102	106	115	148	196
SPF - Mandatory employer contributions	..	..	19	21	90	102	106	115	148	196
2220 On an income tax basis	..	..	0	0	0	0	0	0	0	0
2300 Self-employed or non-employed	..	..	0	0	0	0	0	0	0	0
2310 On a payroll basis	..	..	..	..	..	..	..	..	..	..
2320 On an income tax basis	..	..	..	..	..	..	..	..	..	..
2400 Unallocable between 2100, 2200 and 2300	..	..	519	287	12	20	0	0	208	3
2410 On a payroll basis	..	..	0	0	0	0	0	0	0	0
2420 On an income tax basis	..	..	519	287	12	20	0	0	208	3
3000 Taxes on payroll and workforce	..	..	**0**	**0**	**0**	**0**	**0**	**0**	**0**	**0**
4000 Taxes on property	..	..	**38**	**126**	**91**	**140**	**99**	**99**	**126**	**168**
4100 Recurrent taxes on immovable property	..	..	0	0	0	0	0	0	0	0
4110 Households	..	..	..	..	..	..	..	..	..	..
4120 Others	..	..	..	..	..	..	..	..	..	..
4200 Recurrent taxes on net wealth	..	..	0	0	0	0	0	0	0	0
4210 Individual	..	..	..	..	..	..	..	..	..	..
4220 Corporate	..	..	..	..	..	..	..	..	..	..
4300 Estate, inheritance and gift taxes	..	..	0	0	0	0	0	0	0	0
4310 Estate and inheritance taxes	..	..	..	..	..	..	..	..	..	..
4320 Gift taxes	..	..	..	..	..	..	..	..	..	..
4400 Taxes on financial and capital transactions	..	..	38	126	91	140	99	99	126	168
4500 Non-recurrent taxes	..	..	0	0	0	0	0	0	0	0
4510 On net wealth	..	..	..	..	..	..	..	..	..	..
4520 Other non-recurrent taxes	..	..	..	..	..	..	..	..	..	..
4600 Other recurrent taxes on property	..	..	0	0	0	0	0	0	0	0
5000 Taxes on goods and services	..	..	**1 898**	**2 079**	**3 297**	**3 412**	**3 830**	**4 104**	**4 470**	**4 679**
5100 Taxes on production, sale, transfer, etc.	..	..	1 767	1 958	3 157	3 215	3 631	3 896	4 267	4 468
5110 General taxes	..	..	777	468	1 883	1 883	2 084	2 245	2 602	2 697
5111 Value added taxes	..	..	0	0	1 792	1 799	1 996	2 133	2 493	2 586
VAT - Domestic	..	..	..	..	1 011	990	1 070	1 294	1 550	1 587
VAT - Imported goods	..	..	..	..	803	833	950	910	968	1 003
VAT - Exemptions	..	..	..	..	-22	-24	-24	-71	-25	-4
5112 Sales tax	..	..	777	468	6	4	1	17	3	3
G&S Tax on locally manufactured goods (Alcohol)	..	..	165	27	0	0	0	0	0	0
G&S Tax on locally manufactured goods (tobacco)	..	..	89	12	0	0	0	0	0	0
G&S Tax on locally manufactured goods (other)	..	..	43	42	0	0	0	0	0	0
G&S Tax - Fuel/petroleum products	..	..	102	10	0	0	0	0	0	0
G&S Tax - Imported goods	..	..	378	377	0	0	0	0	0	0
G&S Tax - Arrears	..	..	0	0	6	4	1	17	3	3
5113 Other	..	..	0	0	84	79	87	95	106	109
Corporate Social Responsibility Tax (CSR)	..	..	..	..	84	79	87	95	106	109
5120 Taxes on specific goods and services	..	..	989	1 490	1 274	1 333	1 547	1 651	1 666	1 770

Table 5.26. **Seychelles** *(cont.)*

Details of tax revenue / Recettes fiscales détaillées

Million SCR

	1999	2000	2009	2010	2014	2015	2016	2017	2018	2019
5121 Excises	..	..	0	570	858	961	1 144	1 308	1 281	1 385
Alcohol (beverages spirits and vinegar)	..	..	..	180	225	278	356	363	382	419
Petroleum (mineral products)	..	..	..	242	459	493	531	655	609	628
Motor Vehicles (vehicles, aircraft, vessels)	..	..	..	47	61	44	99	135	123	148
Tobacco	..	..	..	102	114	146	157	155	166	164
Sugar tax on beverages	..	..	..	0	0	0	0	0	0	25
5122 Profits of fiscal monopolies	..	..	0	0	0	0	0	0	0	0
5123 Customs and import duties	..	..	437	355	376	326	359	283	315	313
Alcohol (beverages spirits and vinegar)	..	..	62	29	108	97	146	128	128	110
Petroleum (mineral products)	..	..	215	151	14	0	0	0	0	0
Textiles and textile articles	..	..	12	11	27	26	22	20	15	7
Motor Vehicles (vehicles, aircraft, vessels)	..	..	49	63	72	57	40	0	1	0
Tobacco (tobacco and manufactured tobacco)	..	..	4	2	1	2	2	2	2	2
Prepared Food (prepared foodstuffs)	..	..	23	19	20	19	18	11	11	13
Documentary Charges	..	..	2	2	2	2	3	2	2	3
Livestock Trust Fund	..	..	0	0	0	0	0	0	0	22
Other customs duties	..	..	70	79	137	128	133	130	160	160
Custom duties exemptions	..	..	0	-3	-5	-5	-6	-10	-4	-4
5124 Taxes on exports	..	..	0	0	0	0	0	0	0	0
5125 Taxes on investment goods	..	..	0	0	0	0	0	0	0	0
5126 Taxes on specific services	..	..	552	565	40	45	45	60	70	71
Gaming Tax (casino)	..	..	8	6	0	0	0	0	0	0
Tourism Marketing Tax (TMT)	..	..	0	0	40	45	45	60	70	71
G&S Tax - Professional services	..	..	18	27	0	0	0	0	0	0
G&S Tax - Tourism	..	..	404	411	0	0	0	0	0	0
G&S Tax - Telecom and utilities	..	..	93	97	0	0	0	0	0	0
G&S Tax - Insurance	..	..	29	22	0	0	0	0	0	0
5127 Other taxes on internat. trade and transactions	..	..	0	0	0	0	0	0	0	0
5128 Other taxes	..	..	0	0	0	0	0	0	0	0
5130 Unallocable between 5110 and 5120	..	..	0	0	0	0	0	0	0	0
5200 Taxes on use of goods and perform activities	..	..	131	121	140	197	198	208	202	211
5210 Recurrent taxes	..	..	131	121	140	197	198	208	202	211
5211 Paid by households: motor vehicles	..	..	43	42	63	95	102	118	117	129
Road tax and other licences	..	..	42	42	59	88	95	110	108	120
Vehicle testing	..	..	1	0	3	7	7	8	8	9
5212 Paid by others: motor vehicles	..	..	0	0	0	0	0	0	0	0
5213 Paid in respect of other goods	..	..	88	79	78	102	96	90	85	82
Trade/industry licences	..	..	8	8	7	8	9	11	10	10
Licences and other licence registration	..	..	7	5	2	3	3	6	4	6
Telecommunications and radio broadcasting licences	..	..	68	62	64	88	83	72	71	66
Casino and hotel licences	..	..	5	3	3	3	1	1	1	0
Liquor and toddy licences	..	..	0	0	0	0	0	0	0	0
5220 Non-recurrent taxes	..	..	0	0	0	0	0	0	0	0
5300 Unallocable between 5100 and 5200	..	..	0	0	0	0	0	0	0	0
6000 Other taxes	**..**	**..**	**0**	**0**	**0**	**0**	**0**	**0**	**0**	**0**
6100 Paid solely by business	..	..	..	..	..	..	..	..	..	..
6200 Other	..	..	..	..	..	..	..	..	..	..

Table 5.26. **Seychelles** *(cont.)*

Details of tax revenue / Recettes fiscales détaillées

.. Not available

Note: Year ending 31st December.

The data are on a cash basis.

Heading 1210: The Goods and Services Tax in Seychelles was also applied to rental payments, which according to Revenue Statistics in Africa definitions are properly classified as business taxes. These revenues are reported under the Goods and Services Tax heading in budget documents for the Seychelles.

Heading 2000: For the first time, this edition includes revenues collected by the Seychelles Pensions Fund (SPF), which includes mandatory contributions classified by the OECD as social security contributions (reported under Headings 2110 and 2210). Seychelles also collected a social security tax based on income (reported under Heading 2420) which was phased out in 2010, but with a significant collection of arrears in 2018. SPF revenues are not reported as government revenues in Seychelles government documents.

Heading 5112: The Goods and Services Tax in Seychelles existed until it was replaced by a VAT in 2013. This tax imposed a 15% tax rate on sales of products and services in a long list of items enumerated in the Goods and Services Tax Act. Arrears on the Goods and Services Tax includes arrears on goods and services taxes professional services, tourism, telecom and utilities and insurance, which are reported under Heading 5126.

Heading 5121: A new sugar tax on beverages was introduced in 2019.

Heading 5123: "Other customs duties" includes the Levy on Pet Bottles, the Levy on Poultry, the Levy on Cans, and the Levy on Glass Bottles. Collections of revenues for the Livestock Trust Fund began in 2019.

Heading 5126: Goods and services taxes on professional services, tourism, telecom and utilities, and insurance are now classified as taxes on services. These were reported under Heading 5112 in previous editions.

Figures exclude tax revenues collected by sub-national governments as the data are not available.

The various fishing licences fees are not included in tax revenues (about 0.6% of GDP in 2019). These revenues are considered as non-tax revenues in accordance with the OECD classication, as set out in the Interpretative Guide in Annex A.

Source: Seychelles Revenue Commission; Seychelles Ministry of Finance, Economic Planning and Trade; Financial Services Authority Seychelles Annual Reports; and Seychelles Pension Fund Annual Reports.

StatLink https://doi.org/10.1787/888934284146

Table 5.27. **South Africa / Afrique du Sud**

Details of tax revenue / Recettes fiscales détaillées

Million ZAR

	1999	2000	2009	2010	2014	2015	2016	2017	2018	2019
Total tax revenue	**195 773**	**211 561**	**648 312**	**706 530**	**1 050 814**	**1 170 870**	**1 242 774**	**1 326 511**	**1 423 346**	**1 468 889**
1000 Taxes on income, profits and capital gains	**113 084**	**119 979**	**357 739**	**368 118**	**543 216**	**608 229**	**644 259**	**700 574**	**736 734**	**751 182**
1100 Of individuals	83 687	87 105	198 117	219 886	340 708	393 232	418 548	453 768	489 733	523 624
1110 On income and profits	83 687	87 105	198 117	219 886	340 708	393 232	418 548	453 768	489 733	523 624
Employees tax	..	..	188 658	213 113	334 863	382 883	407 105	440 141	475 337	513 613
Employment Incentive Tax (ETI) refunds	..	..	0	0	-2 000	-3 349	-4 905	-4 672	-4 275	-4 590
PIT Provisional tax	..	..	15 680	15 719	19 944	24 200	27 313	29 427	33 426	32 138
PIT Assessment payments	..	..	9 283	7 425	8 682	9 970	11 594	15 011	16 230	13 158
PIT Refunds	..	..	-15 504	-16 372	-20 781	-20 474	-22 559	-26 139	-30 986	-30 695
1120 On capital gains	..	..	..	..	..	..	..	..	..	..
1200 Corporate	21 007	23 987	142 319	132 275	182 022	191 348	200 765	214 316	215 939	215 346
1210 On profits	21 007	23 987	142 319	132 275	182 022	191 348	200 765	214 316	215 939	215 346
CIT Provisional tax	..	..	140 895	136 615	181 491	190 437	202 636	214 097	222 178	221 026
CIT Assessment payments	..	..	12 017	9 051	12 040	11 119	10 291	12 888	13 714	11 953
Royalties	..	..	249	161	276	369	544	434	676	633
CIT Refunds	..	..	-10 842	-13 552	-11 784	-10 577	-12 706	-13 103	-20 630	-18 266
1220 On capital gains	..	..	..	..	..	..	..	..	..	..
1300 Unallocable between 1100 and 1200	8 390	8 887	17 303	15 957	20 486	23 649	24 946	32 489	31 062	12 211
2000 Social security contributions	**0**	**0**	**10 594**	**11 117**	**15 604**	**17 139**	**17 787**	**18 652**	**19 026**	**19 796**
2100 Employees	..	..	5 366	5 740	7 935	8 725	9 051	9 483	9 566	9 954
2110 On a payroll basis	..	..	139	363	267	311	314	314	106	112
2120 On an income tax basis	..	..	5 227	5 377	7 668	8 414	8 737	9 169	9 460	9 842
2200 Employers	..	..	5 227	5 377	7 668	8 414	8 737	9 169	9 460	9 842
2210 On a payroll basis	..	..	0	0	0	0	0	0	0	0
2220 On an income tax basis	..	..	5 227	5 377	7 668	8 414	8 737	9 169	9 460	9 842
2300 Self-employed or non-employed	..	..	0	0	0	0	0	0	0	0
2310 On a payroll basis	..	..	..	..	..	..	..	..	..	..
2320 On an income tax basis	..	..	..	..	..	..	..	..	..	..
2400 Unallocable between 2100, 2200 and 2300	..	..	0	0	0	0	0	0	0	0
2410 On a payroll basis	..	..	..	..	..	..	..	..	..	..
2420 On an income tax basis	..	..	..	..	..	..	..	..	..	..
3000 Taxes on payroll and workforce	**0**	**870**	**7 737**	**8 240**	**13 264**	**15 111**	**15 092**	**15 891**	**17 265**	**18 062**
4000 Taxes on property	**3 710**	**3 829**	**35 732**	**40 108**	**58 303**	**59 110**	**67 554**	**80 044**	**83 554**	**93 022**
4100 Recurrent taxes on immovable property	0	0	27 190	31 041	46 291	44 618	51 668	64 262	67 373	76 806
4110 Households	..	..	26 694	30 533	45 807	44 169	51 133	63 806	66 824	76 279
4120 Others	..	..	496	508	484	449	535	456	549	528
4200 Recurrent taxes on net wealth	0	0	0	0	0	0	0	0	0	0
4210 Individual	..	..	..	..	..	..	..	..	..	..
4220 Corporate	..	..	..	..	..	..	..	..	..	..
4300 Estate, inheritance and gift taxes	287	436	888	855	1 519	2 065	1 832	2 667	2 740	2 780
4310 Estate and inheritance taxes	272	417	815	794	1 349	1 918	1 612	2 303	1 894	2 174
4320 Gift taxes	15	19	73	61	170	147	220	364	846	605
4400 Taxes on financial and capital transactions	1 810	1 094	3 294	2 912	4 098	5 069	6 081	5 248	5 967	6 235
4500 Non-recurrent taxes	1 613	2 299	4 359	5 300	6 394	7 358	7 974	7 868	7 474	7 201
4510 On net wealth	0	0	0	0	0	0	0	0	0	0
4520 Other non-recurrent taxes	1 613	2 299	4 359	5 300	6 394	7 358	7 974	7 868	7 474	7 201
4600 Other recurrent taxes on property	0	0	0	0	0	0	0	0	0	0
5000 Taxes on goods and services	**77 102**	**84 462**	**237 451**	**278 924**	**420 457**	**471 281**	**498 073**	**511 366**	**566 777**	**586 828**
5100 Taxes on production, sale, transfer, etc.	77 102	84 462	233 027	273 602	412 874	463 423	489 342	500 917	555 577	574 093
5110 General taxes	47 564	52 054	148 721	170 548	256 482	277 551	294 694	293 900	324 702	329 415
5111 Value added taxes	47 564	52 054	148 708	170 552	256 464	277 530	294 674	293 864	324 682	329 397
Domestic VAT	26 316	52 547	191 271	202 483	281 168	303 210	314 674	333 647	368 766	392 919
VAT on Imports	21 248	25 148	73 969	78 697	134 603	148 467	151 046	150 841	169 018	181 777
VAT Refunds	0	-25 641	-116 533	-110 627	-159 307	-174 147	-171 046	-190 624	-213 103	-245 298
5112 Sales tax	0	0	13	-5	17	21	20	36	20	18
5113 Other	0	0	0	0	0	0	0	0	0	0
5120 Taxes on specific goods and services	29 537	32 408	84 306	103 054	156 392	185 872	194 647	207 017	230 875	244 679

Table 5.27. **South Africa / Afrique du Sud** *(cont.)*

Details of tax revenue / Recettes fiscales détaillées

Million ZAR

	1999	2000	2009	2010	2014	2015	2016	2017	2018	2019
5121 Excises	23 153	24 341	63 158	76 239	112 440	137 859	143 337	155 062	172 198	183 860
Specific excise tax - Domestic	..	..	20 480	22 448	31 400	34 918	35 714	36 731	41 568	47 811
Ad valorem excise - Domestic	..	..	1 132	1 569	2 848	3 295	3 238	3 652	4 163	4 274
Fuel levy	..	..	28 047	32 758	46 802	56 694	61 064	68 608	74 376	78 361
Plastic bags	..	..	112	177	139	213	221	238	287	328
Electricity levy	..	..	2 102	5 065	8 541	8 481	8 507	8 495	8 448	8 315
Incandescent light bulb levy	..	..	0	180	68	52	66	62	46	34
CO_2 tax - motor vehicle emissions	..	..	0	205	1 591	1 429	1 177	1 347	1 376	1 355
RAF	..	..	11 285	13 837	21 051	32 778	33 350	35 336	41 189	42 658
Tyre Levy	..	..	0	0	0	0	0	593	744	724
5122 Profits of fiscal monopolies	0	0	0	0	0	0	0	0	0	0
5123 Customs and import duties	6 158	7 714	19 134	25 196	41 857	43 965	47 438	47 367	53 936	55 752
Import duties	..	..	..	..	31 616	32 130	33 855	32 742	37 649	37 595
Ad valorem Imported	..	..	..	..	7 573	8 495	8 701	5 668	10 091	10 580
Excise Imported	..	..	..	..	2 668	3 340	4 882	8 954	6 191	7 575
International Oil Pollution Levy	..	..	..	..	0	0	0	3	5	3
5124 Taxes on exports	0	0	19	61	118	121	116	103	62	94
5125 Taxes on investment goods	0	0	0	0	0	0	0	0	0	0
5126 Taxes on specific services	0	0	1 922	2 252	2 992	3 224	3 401	3 775	3 943	4 170
5127 Other taxes on internat. trade and transactions	227	353	73	-695	-1 015	703	355	709	736	804
5128 Other taxes	0	0	0	0	0	0	0	0	0	0
5130 Unallocable between 5110 and 5120	0	0	0	0	0	0	0	0	0	0
5200 Taxes on use of goods and perform activities	0	0	4 424	5 322	7 583	7 858	8 732	10 450	11 199	12 734
5210 Recurrent taxes	..	..	4 424	5 322	7 583	7 858	8 732	10 450	11 199	12 734
5211 Paid by households: motor vehicles	..	..	3 321	4 046	5 879	6 234	6 565	8 120	8 706	9 938
5212 Paid by others: motor vehicles	..	..	830	1 012	1 470	1 558	1 641	2 030	2 176	2 484
5213 Paid in respect of other goods	..	..	273	264	234	66	525	299	317	312
5220 Non-recurrent taxes	..	..	0	0	0	0	0	0	0	0
5300 Unallocable between 5100 and 5200	0	0	0	0	0	0	0	0	0	0
6000 Other taxes	**1 877**	**2 420**	**-941**	**23**	**-29**	**-1**	**9**	**-17**	**-11**	**-1**
6100 Paid solely by business	0	0	0	0	0	0	0	0	0	0
6200 Other	1 877	2 420	-941	23	-29	-1	9	-17	-11	-1
Stamp duties and fees	..	..	102	9	0	0	0	0	0	0
Unallocated Tax Revenue	..	..	-1 043	14	-29	-1	9	-17	-11	-1

Table 5.27. **South Africa / Afrique du Sud** *(cont.)*

Details of tax revenue / Recettes fiscales détaillées

.. Not available

Note: Year ending 31st December. Some fiscal year data have been adjusted to align to calendar years. Social security contributions and taxes at provincial and local levels are reported on a fiscal year basis beginning 1st April. For example, the data for 2019 represent April 2019 to March 2020. Data prior to 1995/96 were restated retrospectively to aggregate the revenues from TBVC States and Self-Governing Territories.

With the adoption of the interim Constitution in 1994, these were abolished.

-TBVC States: Transkei, Bophuthatswana, Venda and Ciskei.

-Self-Governing Territories: Gazankulu, Kangwane, Kwandebele, Kwazulu, Lebowa and Qwaqwa.

Tax revenues on national and provincial government level in South Africa are on a cash basis, while local authorities and public entities are on an accrual basis. Data on provincial and local government revenues were not available for the year 2019/20, so for that year, projections based on the previous three years of data were used.

Tax revenues at the local and provincial levels are only available from 2003 (representing fiscal year 2003/04).

For the year 2018/19, figures for the Road Accident Fund Levy, provincial and local taxes, and contributions to the unemployment insurance funds are projected figures. This affects headings 2000, 5121, 5126, and 5200.

Headings 1110 and 1120: The figures include Capital Gains Tax (CGT). CGT cannot been listed separately under 1120 and 1220 because the data that South African Revenue Service (SARS) collated for CGT are for liability raised and not actual CGT collections received. The figures exclude interest and fines from 1994 onwards. Figures on ETI refunds, which started being collected in 2014, are now reported under 1110. These were included as part of Employees tax in previous editions.

Heading 2000: the social security contributions in South Africa consist of contributions to the Unemployment Insurance Fund (UIF). Standard practice in South Africa is to classify UIF under non-tax revenue. The methodology applied in the compilation of the data was to allocate 50% of the total social security contributions (UIF) to each of employees and employers.

Headings 4110 and 4120: These are local government revenues for which 2019 figures are missing and have been replaced with projections based on the previous three years of data. Recurrent taxes on immovable property were divided into collections onhouseholds (4110) and penalties and collection charges (4120).

Heading 4120: the figures refer to penalties and collection charges on property rates.

Heading 5111: includes interests and fines.

Heading 5121: Following the OECD classification, the Road Accident Fund (RAF) is classified as an excise. The national classification of South Africa classifies this revenue as a social security contribution.

Headings 5121 and 5123: The data for customs duties and excise include revenue on import duties plus specific and ad valorem excise duties that will be paid to Botswana, Eswatini, Lesotho and Namibia (BELN) through the revenue sharing agreement.

Heading 5123: SARS only started separately reporting ordinary custom duties on imported goods, specific excise duties on imported goods and ad valorem duties on imported goods from April 2012. From April 2014 onwards, the Customs Duty amounts for the specific tariff headings under chapter 27 (Mineral Fuels) were treated as fuel levies (5121 Excises). Some estimation was used for the year 2012 due to missing information.

Heading 5124: Revenues from the International Pollution Levy were reported for the first time in this edition of Revenue Statistics in Africa.

Heading 5126: These revenues mostly come from provincial taxes on casinos and horse racing for which 2019 figures are missing and have been replaced with projections based on the previous three years of data.

Headings 5127 and 6200: include negative figures due to refund accounting adjustments.

Heading 5211: an 80:20 ratio was used to split provincial recurrent motor vehicle taxes based on research about South Africa's commercial and private household motor vehicle fleet.

Headings 5211, 5212, and 5213: These revenues mostly come from provincial liquor and motor vehicle licences for which 2019 figures are missing and have been replaced with projections based on the previous three years of data.

Heading 6200: Includes stamp duties and fees plus unallocated tax revenue.

Taxes that were discontinued and introduced (causing breaks in the data) include the following:

a. Ordinary levy discontinued in March 2003 (Heading 5127).

b. Demutualisation charge has been included in Heading 4400. There were two collections in March 1999 and August 1999.

c. Secondary Tax on Companies (STC) in Heading 1300 effective from July 1993 and changed to Dividends Tax (DT) in April 2012.

d. Small business tax amnesty (Heading 1300) effective from March 2007.

e. VAT (Heading 5111) effective from September 1991 at a rate of 10% and increased to 14% in 1993. Prior to that, sales tax data was restated to VAT.

f. Levy on financial services (Heading 4400) effective from January 1992.

g. Skills development levy (Heading 3000) effective from May 2000.

h. Excises (5121)

- Plastic bags effective from June 2005.
- Electricity levy effective from August 2009.
- Incandescent light bulbs effective from March 2010.
- CO_2 tax effective from September 2010.

i. Air departure tax (Heading 5126) effective from December 2000.

j. Universal services fund (Heading 5213 paid in respect of other goods) effective from March 2006.

Source: Data on national government taxation from the South African Revenue Service (SARS); data on social security contributions, and taxes levied at the provincial and local level from the National Treasury of South Africa.

StatLink https://doi.org/10.1787/888934284165

Table 5.28. **Togo**

Details of tax revenue / Recettes fiscales détaillées

Million XOF

	1999	2000	2009	2010	2014	2015	2016	2017	2018	2019
Recettes fiscales totales	..	**99 994**	**232 557**	**250 441**	**471 498**	**533 556**	**586 813**	**585 660**	**576 528**	**634 515**
1000 Impôts sur revenu, bénéfices et gains en capital	..	**20 928**	**46 576**	**41 200**	**78 972**	**88 658**	**112 797**	**100 214**	**117 078**	**136 035**
1100 Des personnes physiques	..	9 440	17 724	18 000	22 700	30 791	39 703	40 826	44 595	48 979
1110 Sur le revenu et les bénéfices	..	9 440	17 724	18 000	22 700	30 791	39 703	40 826	44 595	48 979
Impôt sur le revenu (IR) des transporteurs routiers	..	452	481	393	272	379	500	366	368	261
Retenue sur les revenus des capitaux mobiliers	..	1 185	3 022	6 106	6 199	8 365	12 222	9 882	11 183	11 687
IR des personnes physiques	..	7 804	14 221	11 500	16 229	22 046	26 976	30 571	33 043	36 890
IR des personnes physiques (transferts aux collectivités locales)	..	..	0	1	0	0	5	8	0	0
Taxe foncière sur les propriétés non bâties (TFPNB) - gouv central	..	0	0	0	0	0	0	0	0	56
Taxe foncière sur les propriétés non bâties (TFPNB) - collectivités	..	0	0	0	0	0	0	0	0	84
1120 Sur les gains en capital	..	0	0	0	0	0	0	0	0	0
1200 Des sociétés	..	11 488	28 852	23 200	56 272	57 867	73 094	59 388	72 483	87 056
1210 Sur les bénéfices	..	11 488	28 852	23 200	56 272	57 867	73 094	59 388	72 483	87 056
Impôt sur les sociétés	..	8 997	23 618	18 280	50 496	51 177	64 564	52 080	64 851	76 670
Prélèvement bénéf. industriels et commerciaux (BIC)	..	2 490	5 234	4 920	5 776	6 691	8 530	7 309	7 632	10 387
1220 Sur les gains en capital	..	0	0	0	0	0	0	0	0	0
1300 Non ventilables entre 1100 et 1200	..	0	0	0	0	0	0	0	0	0
2000 Cotisations de sécurité sociale	..	..	..	..	..	..	..	..	..	..
2100 A la charge des salariés	..	..	..	..	..	..	..	..	..	..
2110 Sur la base du salaire	..	..	..	..	..	..	..	..	..	..
2120 Sur la base de l'impôt sur le revenu	..	..	..	..	..	..	..	..	..	..
2200 A la charge des employeurs	..	..	..	..	..	..	..	..	..	..
2210 Sur la base du salaire	..	..	..	..	..	..	..	..	..	..
2220 Sur la base de l'impôt sur le revenu	..	..	..	..	..	..	..	..	..	..
2300 A charge des travailleurs indép. ou sans emploi	..	..	..	..	..	..	..	..	..	..
2310 Sur la base du salaire	..	..	..	..	..	..	..	..	..	..
2320 Sur la base de l'impôt sur le revenu	..	..	..	..	..	..	..	..	..	..
2400 Non ventilables entre 2100, 2200 et 2300	..	..	..	..	..	..	..	..	..	..
2410 Sur la base du salaire	..	..	..	..	..	..	..	..	..	..
2420 Sur la base de l'impôt sur le revenu	..	..	..	..	..	..	..	..	..	..
3000 Sur salaires ou main d'oeuvre	..	**1 973**	**4 604**	**5 491**	**9 155**	**4 551**	**5 599**	**5 018**	**4 757**	**2 262**
Taxe complémentaire à l'impôt sur le revenu	..	79	627	1 220	5 887	956	1 246	1 256	1 042	953
Taxes/salaires	..	1 894	3 851	4 137	2 956	3 284	3 963	3 274	3 253	1 119
Taxe complémentaire à l'Impôt sur le revenu (transferts aux collectivités locales)	..	..	126	134	312	311	389	488	463	190
4000 Impôts sur le patrimoine	..	**374**	**1 881**	**1 898**	**3 826**	**4 360**	**4 766**	**4 256**	**4 819**	**5 048**
4100 Impôts périodiques sur la propriété immobilière	..	374	1 881	1 898	3 826	4 360	4 766	4 256	4 819	5 048
Taxe foncière sur les propriétés bâties	..	278	647	655	1 078	1 465	1 507	1 315	1 410	1 531
Droits d'immatriculation des propriétés foncières	..	96	320	335	521	613	783	228	334	345
Taxe d'enlèvement des ordures (transferts aux collectivités locales)	..	..	122	129	288	315	360	331	407	360
Taxe foncière sur les propriétés bâties (transferts aux collectivités locales)	..	..	599	553	1 551	1 404	1 494	1 783	2 032	2 078
4110 Ménages	..	..	193	226	388	563	623	599	636	735
Taxe d'habitation (transferts aux collectivités locales)	..	..	193	226	388	563	623	599	636	735
4120 Autres agents	..	0	0	0	0	0	0	0	0	0
4200 Impôts périodiques sur l'actif net	..	0	0	0	0	0	0	0	0	0
4210 Personnes physiques	..	..	..	..	..	..	..	..	..	..
4220 Sociétés	..	..	..	..	..	..	..	..	..	..
4300 Impôts sur mut. par décès, succ. et donations	..	0	0	0	0	0	0	0	0	0
4310 Impôts sur mut. par décès et successions	..	..	..	..	..	..	..	..	..	..
4320 Impôts sur les donations	..	..	..	..	..	..	..	..	..	..
4400 Impôts sur transact. mobilières et immob.	..	0	0	0	0	0	0	0	0	0
4500 Impôts non-périodiques	..	0	0	0	0	0	0	0	0	0
4510 Sur l'actif net	..	..	..	..	..	..	..	..	..	..
4520 Autres non-périodiques	..	..	..	..	..	..	..	..	..	..
4600 Autres impôts périodiques sur patrimoine	..	0	0	0	0	0	0	0	0	0
5000 Impôts sur les biens et services	..	**74 771**	**174 376**	**196 239**	**370 207**	**427 424**	**454 604**	**459 815**	**439 693**	**481 493**
5100 Impôts sur production, vente, transfert, etc.	..	74 662	173 896	195 813	368 570	425 367	452 380	457 429	437 006	474 721
5110 Impôts généraux	..	36 941	99 492	115 056	225 401	250 410	271 347	269 266	256 847	282 656

Table 5.28. **Togo** *(cont.)*

Details of tax revenue / Recettes fiscales détaillées

Million XOF

	1999	2000	2009	2010	2014	2015	2016	2017	2018	2019
5111 Taxes sur la valeur ajoutée	..	36 073	94 792	110 316	213 671	236 011	255 323	253 663	237 537	268 602
Recettes TVA (douanes)	..	25 101	65 170	69 840	142 840	167 228	172 435	138 802	142 211	160 514
Recettes TVA (intérieure)	..	10 972	29 622	40 476	70 830	68 783	82 888	114 861	95 325	108 088
5112 Impôts sur les ventes	..	0	0	0	0	0	0	0	0	0
5113 Autres impôts	..	868	4 701	4 740	11 731	14 399	16 024	15 602	19 311	14 054
Taxe professionnelle unique	..	146	343	334	381	507	515	485	537	593
Taxe professionnelle	..	722	1 484	1 587	4 371	6 693	7 943	5 831	7 270	5 060
Taxe professionnelle unique (transferts aux collectivités locales)	..	..	189	206	423	507	572	539	597	810
Taxe professionnelle (transferts aux collectivités locales)	..	..	2 685	2 613	6 556	6 693	6 995	8 747	10 906	7 591
5120 Impôts sur biens et services déterminés	..	37 696	74 372	80 724	143 168	174 957	181 033	188 164	180 159	192 064
5121 Accises	..	12 785	15 441	16 360	29 369	35 150	43 686	43 471	44 429	38 206
Droits d'accises/produits pétroliers	..	11 773	10 557	11 738	16 861	17 972	20 945	20 337	22 978	20 614
Autres droits d'accises	..	1 012	4 885	4 622	7 033	8 246	10 906	10 955	11 835	16 237
Prélèvement pour apurement de la dette du secteur pétrolier (PADSP)	..	0	0	0	5 474	8 932	11 836	12 179	9 616	1 356
5122 Bénéfices des monopoles fiscaux	..	0	0	0	0	0	0	0	0	0
5123 Droits de douane et droits à l'importation	..	22 559	56 751	61 676	99 201	122 750	119 825	127 065	117 608	135 991
Droits de douane	..	18 519	48 761	52 941	83 234	101 730	98 020	86 383	90 186	103 536
Redevance statistique	..	2 717	6 096	6 763	12 740	13 578	14 021	32 653	18 447	23 012
Timbre douanier	..	94	227	297	359	424	298	283	285	290
Cartes et vignettes	..	186	246	237	385	369	600	609	872	919
Taxe de protection et d'entretien des infrastructures	..	1 039	1 418	1 434	2 476	2 958	3 252	3 575	3 917	3 942
Produits des crédits en douane	..	2	1	2	6	5	9	8	8	9
Prélèvement national de solidarité	..	0	0	0	0	3 686	3 625	3 555	3 893	4 284
Remises	..	1	0	0	0	0	0	0	0	0
Entrepôts fictifs	..	1	1	2	1	0	0	0	0	0
5124 Taxes à l'exportation	..	302	1 041	1 430	2 544	2 728	2 476	2 737	2 977	3 104
Taxe spéciale de réexportation	..	302	1 041	1 430	1 947	2 260	2 015	2 156	2 685	3 104
Redevance minière (66,67%)	..	0	0	0	597	468	461	580	292	0
5125 Impôts sur biens d'équipement	..	0	0	0	0	0	0	0	0	0
5126 Impôts sur services déterminés	..	2 049	1 138	1 258	12 055	14 329	15 046	14 891	15 146	14 763
Taxe sur les produits des jeux de hasard	..	151	229	347	682	913	1 047	1 185	1 184	1 343
Taxe/convention d'assurance	..	227	798	815	1 396	2 035	2 365	2 205	2 158	2 248
Taxe sur les activités financières	..	1 671	26	0	9 793	11 140	11 372	11 204	11 508	10 466
Taxe sur les produits des jeux de hasard (transferts aux collectivités locales)	..	..	81	94	171	228	262	296	296	336
Taxe sur les spectacles (transferts aux collectivités locales)	..	..	5	2	13	13	0	0	0	28
Taxe à l'émission des billets d'avion (TEBA)	..	0	0	0	0	0	0	0	0	342
5127 Autres impôts sur commerce et transact. internat.	..	0	0	0	0	0	0	0	0	0
5128 Autres impôts	..	0	0	0	0	0	0	0	0	0
5130 Non ventilables entre 5110 et 5120	..	25	32	33	0	0	0	0	0	0
5200 Impôts sur utilisation des biens et exerc. activites	..	108	480	426	1 637	2 057	2 224	2 386	2 687	6 772
5210 Impôts périodiques	..	108	480	426	1 637	2 057	2 224	2 386	2 687	6 772
5211 A la charge des ménages: véhicules à moteur	..	0	0	0	0	0	0	0	0	223
Taxe sur les véhicules à moteur (TVM)	..	..	..	..	..	..	..	..	..	223
5212 A la charge autres agents: véhicules à moteur	..	2	11	0	185	287	308	311	312	260
5213 Autres impôts périodiques	..	106	470	426	1 452	1 770	1 915	2 076	2 375	6 290
Taxe spéc. sur la fabric. et le commerce des boissons	..	106	220	162	843	1 145	1 158	1 300	1 521	482
Taxe spéc. sur la fabric. et le commerce des boissons (transferts aux collectivités locales)	..	..	250	264	609	625	757	776	855	697
Patente sur activités économiques non-salariaux des pers. phys. (gouv. central)	..	0	0	0	0	0	0	0	0	1 916
Patente sur activités économiques non-salariaux des pers. phys. (collectivités)	..	0	0	0	0	0	0	0	0	3 194
5220 Impôts non-périodiques	..	0	0	0	0	0	0	0	0	0
5300 Non ventilables entre 5100 et 5200	..	0	0	0	0	0	0	0	0	0
6000 Autres impôts	**..**	**1 949**	**5 120**	**5 612**	**9 338**	**8 563**	**9 048**	**16 356**	**10 180**	**9 676**
Droits de timbres	..	1 471	2 444	3 135	2 862	3 612	3 676	3 338	3 258	3 072
Droits d'enregistrement	..	478	2 674	2 436	6 469	4 949	5 158	12 498	6 553	6 392
Taxe d'enregistrement (transferts aux collectivités locales)	..	..	2	41	6	2	214	521	369	213
6100 A la charge exclusive des entreprises	..	..	..	..	..	..	..	..	..	..

Table 5.28. **Togo** *(cont.)*

Details of tax revenue / Recettes fiscales détaillées

Million XOF

	1999	2000	2009	2010	2014	2015	2016	2017	2018	2019
6200 A la charge d'autres agents	..	..	..	..	..	..	..	..	..	..
Pour mémoire :										
Soutien à la politique pétrolière	..	0	2 064	3 700	13 976	5 748	4 077	6 075	13 332	7 048
Droits d'accise et taxes sur prod. pétr. allant à la Société autonome de financement de l'entretien routier (SAFER)	..	5 519	7 007	7 339	7 988	9 495	9 890	11 732	13 820	10 999

.. Non disponible

Note : Année civile se terminant le 31 décembre.

Les données sont sur la base des encaissements.

Les chiffres sous les rubriques 1110, 3000, 4100, 5113, 5126, 5213 et 6000 incluent les recettes recouvrées par l'administration fiscale togolaise pour le compte des collectivités locales. Ce traitement s'applique sur la période 2008-19 et les lignes concernées sont mises en exergue avec la mention « transferts aux collectivités locales ». Ces recettes sont classifiées comme des recettes du gouvernement central conformément au guide d'interprétation de l'OCDE. Le Togo ne les comptabilise pas dans les recettes du budget de l'État.

Rubrique 1110 : La collecte des recettes des taxes foncières sur les propriétés non bâties (TFPNB) a démarré en 2019.

Rubrique 1120 : La collecte des recettes de la taxe sur les plus-values de cession (TPV) a démarré en 2019. La collecte des recettes des patentes sur les activités économiques non-salariaux des personnes physiques a démarré en 2019.

Rubrique 2000 : Les données de cotisations de sécurité sociale ne sont pas disponibles.

Rubrique 5121 : Le prélèvement pour l'apurement de la dette du secteur pétrolier (PADSP) est considéré comme une recette fiscale dans cette publication comme le préconise la classification OCDE (voir le guide d'interprétation en Annexe A). La classification nationale du Togo considère ces recettes comme des recettes non fiscales.

Rubrique 5126 : La collecte des recettes de la taxe à l'émission des billets d'avion (TEBA) a demarré en 2019.

Rubrique 5211 : La collecte des recettes de la taxe sur les véhicules à moteur (TVM) a démarré en 2019.

Les données sur les remboursements de TVA ne sont pas disponibles car au Togo, les crédits de TVA ne font pas l'objet de remboursement avec les moyens classiques de paiement (virement, chèque, espèces, etc.). Lorsqu'un contribuable dispose d'un crédit de TVA, il adresse une demande de remboursement à l'administration fiscale qui lui délivre un certificat de détaxe. Ce certificat lui permet de payer non seulement ses déclarations ultérieures de TVA mais aussi les autres impôts.

La classification nationale du Togo considère les amendes et pénalités relatives aux impôts, les confiscations et ventes en douane et les remboursements du prélèvement communautaire de solidarité comme des recettes fiscales. Ces recettes sont classifiées comme des recettes non fiscales dans cette publication comme le préconise la classification OCDE (voir le guide d'interprétation en Annexe A).

Le Soutien à la politique pétrolière (SPP) est un fond financé par un prélèvement effectué sur la TVA recouvrée par la douane, sauf pour les années 2010-12 quand le SPP était financé par une subvention de l'état.

Source : Office Togolais des Recettes.

StatLink https://doi.org/10.1787/888934284184

Table 5.29. **Tunisia / Tunisie**

Details of tax revenue / Recettes fiscales détaillées

Million TND

	1999	2000	2009	2010	2014	2015	2016	2017	2018	2019
Recettes fiscales totales	..	**7 196**	**15 700**	**17 143**	**24 998**	**25 613**	**26 596**	**29 810**	**33 824**	**39 450**
1000 Impôts sur revenu, bénéfices et gains en capital	..	**1 624**	**4 701**	**5 091**	**7 955**	**7 678**	**7 384**	**8 506**	**8 979**	**12 486**
1100 Des personnes physiques	..	1 049	2 435	2 658	4 096	5 003	5 931	6 191	6 359	8 713
1110 Sur le revenu et les bénéfices	..	1 037	2 423	2 644	4 058	4 965	5 887	6 139	6 311	8 658
Traitements et salaires	..	742	1 843	2 006	3 260	3 549	4 107	4 029	4 054	5 800
Honoraires, commissions, courtage et loyers (personnes physiques)	..	20	158	184	236	364	483	541	508	665
Intérêts dépôts des comptes spéciaux d'épargne	..	65	61	68	125	159	176	199	270	315
Revenus des capitaux mobiliers (personnes physiques)	..	32	79	75	87	212	269	272	310	498
Avances sur les marchés (personnes physiques)	..	27	48	50	56	313	508	624	720	821
Bénéfices industriels et commerciaux	..	43	89	94	98	119	142	146	154	201
Bénéfices non commerciaux	..	17	39	49	71	76	79	81	98	123
Impôt forfaitaire	..	14	23	25	31	36	37	39	48	64
Revenus agricoles	..	5	8	8	15	19	22	26	26	33
Revenus fonciers et autres	..	5	6	8	12	14	22	27	30	40
Autres impôts sur le revenu et bénéfices	..	66	69	78	67	105	42	156	93	99
1120 Sur les gains en capital	..	12	12	13	38	39	45	52	48	54
1200 Des sociétés	..	575	2 264	2 432	3 855	2 673	1 450	2 315	2 620	3 774
1210 Sur les bénéfices	..	575	2 253	2 424	3 848	2 658	1 442	2 295	2 613	3 763
Sociétés pétrolières	..	96	647	813	1 575	950	346	527	709	959
Sociétés non-pétrolières	..	359	926	864	1 137	1 088	806	1 299	1 149	1 984
Avances sur les marchés (sociétés)	..	33	309	356	478	222	46	47	57	48
Avance au titre des importations	..	7	97	111	184	198	198	268	430	468
Revenus des capitaux mobiliers (sociétés)	..	58	114	113	215	72	27	106	226	269
Honoraires, commissions, courtage et loyers (sociétés)	..	16	128	125	183	86	2	1	5	4
Redevances servies aux non résidents	..	3	30	39	53	18	9	7	4	18
Autres impôts sur les bénéfices	..	3	2	3	22	25	9	40	33	12
1220 Sur les gains en capital	..	0	12	7	7	14	7	19	7	11
1300 Non ventilables entre 1100 et 1200	..	0	2	2	4	2	4	0	0	0
2000 Cotisations de sécurité sociale	..	**1 551**	**4 098**	**4 629**	**6 882**	**7 549**	**8 415**	**9 259**	**9 826**	**11 172**
2100 A la charge des salariés	..	..	..	..	..	..	..	..	..	..
2110 Sur la base du salaire	..	..	..	..	..	..	..	..	..	..
2120 Sur la base de l'impôt sur le revenu	..	..	..	..	..	..	..	..	..	..
2200 A la charge des employeurs	..	..	..	..	..	..	..	..	..	..
2210 Sur la base du salaire	..	..	..	..	..	..	..	..	..	..
2220 Sur la base de l'impôt sur le revenu	..	..	..	..	..	..	..	..	..	..
2300 A charge des travailleurs indép. ou sans emploi	..	..	..	..	..	..	..	..	..	..
2310 Sur la base du salaire	..	..	..	..	..	..	..	..	..	..
2320 Sur la base de l'impôt sur le revenu	..	..	..	..	..	..	..	..	..	..
2400 Non ventilables entre 2100, 2200 et 2300	..	1 551	4 098	4 629	6 882	7 549	8 415	9 259	9 826	11 172
2410 Sur la base du salaire	..	..	..	..	..	..	..	..	..	..
2420 Sur la base de l'impôt sur le revenu	..	..	..	..	..	..	..	..	..	..
3000 Sur salaires ou main d'oeuvre	..	**107**	**171**	**199**	**285**	**315**	**345**	**375**	**405**	**457**
Fond de promotion des logements	..	71	115	124	177	191	215	231	246	278
Taxe de formation professionnelle	..	35	56	75	107	124	130	143	159	179
4000 Impôts sur le patrimoine	..	**81**	**172**	**177**	**257**	**282**	**299**	**303**	**308**	**371**
4100 Impôts périodiques sur la propriété immobilière	..	7	9	10	8	11	11	12	13	18
4110 Ménages	..	7	9	10	8	11	11	12	13	18
4120 Autres agents	..	0	0	0	0	0	0	0	0	0
4200 Impôts périodiques sur l'actif net	..	0	0	0	0	0	0	0	0	0
4210 Personnes physiques	..	..	..	..	..	..	..	..	..	..
4220 Sociétés	..	..	..	..	..	..	..	..	..	..
4300 Impôts sur mut. par décès, succ. et donations	..	0	0	0	0	0	0	0	0	0
4310 Impôts sur mut. par décès et successions	..	..	..	..	..	..	..	..	..	..
4320 Impôts sur les donations	..	..	..	..	..	..	..	..	..	..
4400 Impôts sur transact. mobilières et immob.	..	74	164	168	248	271	288	291	295	353
4500 Impôts non-périodiques	..	0	0	0	0	0	0	0	0	0
4510 Sur l'actif net	..	..	..	..	..	..	..	..	..	..
4520 Autres non-périodiques	..	..	..	..	..	..	..	..	..	..
4600 Autres impôts périodiques sur patrimoine	..	0	0	0	0	0	0	0	0	0
5000 Impôts sur les biens et services	..	**3 729**	**6 266**	**6 768**	**9 099**	**9 168**	**9 523**	**10 666**	**13 444**	**14 026**
5100 Impôts sur production, vente, transfert, etc.	..	3 665	6 131	6 612	8 903	8 977	9 300	10 442	13 222	13 803
5110 Impôts généraux	..	1 814	3 468	3 819	5 267	5 211	5 288	5 918	7 696	8 044

Table 5.29. **Tunisia / Tunisie** (*cont.*)

Details of tax revenue / Recettes fiscales détaillées

Million TND

	1999	2000	2009	2010	2014	2015	2016	2017	2018	2019
5111 Taxes sur la valeur ajoutée	..	1 792	3 400	3 750	5 117	5 068	5 118	5 722	7 425	7 797
Recettes TVA (brute)	..	..	3 816	4 163	5 544	5 684	5 771	6 106	7 787	8 093
Remboursements de la TVA	..	..	-416	-413	-427	-617	-653	-384	-362	-296
5112 Impôts sur les ventes	..	0	0	0	0	0	0	0	0	0
5113 Autres impôts	..	21	69	69	150	144	170	196	271	246
5120 Impôts sur biens et services déterminés	..	1 851	2 663	2 793	3 637	3 765	4 012	4 523	5 527	5 760
5121 Accises	..	1 023	1 781	1 814	2 315	2 397	2 876	3 226	3 621	3 692
Tabac	..	371	826	799	1 085	1 087	1 248	1 397	1 490	1 633
Boissons alcoolisées	..	147	154	174	303	290	336	363	431	408
Essences et huiles	..	260	257	268	279	305	649	705	757	760
Voitures	..	86	180	242	251	289	285	333	338	299
Produits alimentaires	..	19	34	31	45	41	44	50	60	66
Ciment	..	11	15	17	20	17	15	15	17	17
Autres accises	..	131	314	282	332	369	299	362	528	509
5122 Bénéfices des monopoles fiscaux	..	0	0	0	0	0	0	0	0	0
5123 Droits de douane et droits à l'importation	..	654	578	620	882	918	742	799	1 235	1 335
Hors tabac	..	565	401	428	603	639	429	486	894	948
Redevances sur prestations douanières à l'importation	..	68	115	142	182	155	188	204	221	234
Taxe conjoncturelle sur ventes du ciment importé	..	0	0	0	41	61	28	0	0	0
Droits de douane - Tabacs	..	9	21	23	31	27	37	51	57	71
Autres droits de douane	..	0	3	4	2	1	0	0	0	0
Prélèvements à l'importation	..	12	34	20	18	29	45	42	46	51
Autres taxes et prélèvements à l'importation	..	1	4	3	5	7	15	16	17	32
5124 Taxes à l'exportation	..	11	19	27	38	41	30	43	72	101
5125 Impôts sur biens d'équipement	..	0	0	0	0	0	0	0	0	0
5126 Impôts sur services déterminés	..	162	283	330	401	409	363	455	599	633
Taxe sur les télécommunications	..	72	103	136	151	147	153	150	178	179
Taxe de compensation sur les transports	..	55	97	105	123	126	67	138	141	142
Taxe sur les assurances	..	33	79	86	120	129	138	156	197	210
Autres impôts sur services déterminés	..	2	3	3	8	7	5	11	82	102
5127 Autres impôts sur commerce et transact. internat.	..	0	0	0	0	0	0	0	0	0
5128 Autres impôts	..	0	1	1	1	1	0	0	0	0
5130 Non ventilables entre 5110 et 5120	..	0	0	0	0	0	0	0	0	0
5200 Impôts sur utilisation des biens et exerc. activites	..	64	135	156	196	191	223	224	222	222
5210 Impôts périodiques	..	55	94	103	124	134	160	160	167	167
5211 A la charge des ménages: véhicules à moteur	..	35	55	60	74	81	91	96	101	105
5212 A la charge autres agents: véhicules à moteur	..	18	39	43	49	53	69	64	67	62
5213 Autres impôts périodiques	..	1	0	0	0	0	0	0	0	0
5220 Impôts non-périodiques	..	9	41	53	72	57	63	64	54	55
5300 Non ventilables entre 5100 et 5200	..	0	0	0	0	0	0	0	0	0
6000 Autres impôts	..	**104**	**292**	**279**	**520**	**622**	**630**	**702**	**862**	**938**
Droits de timbres	..	25	157	133	288	334	350	370	447	484
Droits d'enregistrements	..	40	95	107	146	181	201	214	248	256
Droit sur les voyages à l'étranger	..	12	10	21	30	33	35	38	42	43
Autres impôts - divers	..	28	22	17	57	75	43	81	125	156
6100 A la charge exclusive des entreprises	..	..	..	..	..	..	..	..	..	..
6200 A la charge d'autres agents	..	..	..	..	..	..	..	..	..	..

.. Non disponible

Note : Année civile se terminant le 31 décembre.

Les données sont sur la base des encaissements.

Les chiffres n'incluent pas les données des recettes fiscales collectées par les collectivités locales car elles ne sont pas disponibles.

Les impôts affectés aux Fonds spéciaux du Trésor et aux Fonds de concours sont compris dans les données pour la période 2000-19.

La rubrique 1210 exclut les redevances des compagnies pétrolières. En Tunisie, elles sont considérées comme un complément de l'impôt sur les sociétés depuis avril 2012.

Les cotisations de sécurité sociale sous la rubrique 2000 ne sont pas considérées comme des recettes fiscales en Tunisie.

Source : Ministère des Finances pour toutes les données des recettes fiscales, Ministère des Affaires Sociales pour les données de cotisations de sécurité sociale.

StatLink https://doi.org/10.1787/888934284203

Table 5.30. **Uganda / Ouganda**

Details of tax revenue / Recettes fiscales détaillées

Million UGX

	1999	2000	2009	2010	2014	2015	2016	2017	2018	2019
Total tax revenue	**944 904**	**999 659**	**3 737 567**	**4 252 022**	**8 065 069**	**9 761 430**	**11 042 361**	**12 431 314**	**14 067 590**	**16 130 637**
1000 Taxes on income, profits and capital gains	**170 032**	**181 905**	**1 092 461**	**1 340 327**	**2 744 735**	**3 387 902**	**3 854 687**	**4 308 416**	**4 821 107**	**5 677 950**
1100 Of individuals	120 551	136 806	800 683	958 294	1 989 167	2 382 729	2 767 373	3 070 385	3 479 276	4 033 859
1110 On income and profits	120 551	136 806	800 683	958 294	1 989 167	2 382 729	2 767 373	3 070 385	3 479 276	4 033 859
PAYE	67 651	83 471	555 710	657 920	1 397 556	1 613 243	1 803 532	2 114 995	2 396 113	2 811 297
Rental income tax	0	0	0	0	0	27 649	55 034	71 738	88 747	115 229
Other income tax (not counting WHT)	10 180	11 220	21 626	19 001	53 616	42 189	44 322	50 766	60 485	66 505
WHT on imports	21 812	23 349	64 606	68 581	131 294	152 787	165 145	154 953	179 643	194 169
WHT on general supplies	0	0	78 082	120 061	232 028	282 825	330 729	299 594	337 521	434 281
WHT on government payments	0	0	19 914	44 446	60 016	89 367	150 824	109 882	73 824	75 775
WHT management and professional fees	0	0	44 510	24 886	35 883	45 447	61 860	65 631	89 563	116 368
WHT on dividends	0	0	9 259	11 237	33 926	61 823	69 110	126 912	87 745	74 635
WHT non residents	0	0	4 510	1 356	44 832	57 106	79 583	69 924	152 988	102 942
Other WHT or unclassified	20 908	18 766	2 466	10 806	16	10 293	7 234	5 989	12 646	42 657
1120 On capital gains	..	..	..	..	..	..	..	..	..	..
1200 Corporate	44 305	40 891	229 959	315 379	486 636	714 772	732 159	764 273	884 802	1 167 745
1210 On profits	44 305	40 891	229 959	315 379	486 636	714 772	732 159	764 273	884 802	1 167 745
1220 On capital gains	..	..	..	..	..	..	..	..	..	..
1300 Unallocable between 1100 and 1200	5 176	4 207	61 819	66 654	268 932	290 401	355 154	473 758	457 028	476 346
2000 Social security contributions	..	..	..	..	..	..	..	..	..	..
2100 Employees	..	..	..	..	..	..	..	..	..	..
2110 On a payroll basis	..	..	..	..	..	..	..	..	..	..
2120 On an income tax basis	..	..	..	..	..	..	..	..	..	..
2200 Employers	..	..	..	..	..	..	..	..	..	..
2210 On a payroll basis	..	..	..	..	..	..	..	..	..	..
2220 On an income tax basis	..	..	..	..	..	..	..	..	..	..
2300 Self-employed or non-employed	..	..	..	..	..	..	..	..	..	..
2310 On a payroll basis	..	..	..	..	..	..	..	..	..	..
2320 On an income tax basis	..	..	..	..	..	..	..	..	..	..
2400 Unallocable between 2100, 2200 and 2300	..	..	..	..	..	..	..	..	..	..
2410 On a payroll basis	..	..	..	..	..	..	..	..	..	..
2420 On an income tax basis	..	..	..	..	..	..	..	..	..	..
3000 Taxes on payroll and workforce	**0**	**0**	**0**	**0**	**0**	**0**	**0**	**0**	**0**	**0**
4000 Taxes on property	..	..	..	..	..	..	..	..	..	..
4100 Recurrent taxes on immovable property	..	..	..	..	..	..	..	..	..	..
4110 Households	..	..	..	..	..	..	..	..	..	..
4120 Others	..	..	..	..	..	..	..	..	..	..
4200 Recurrent taxes on net wealth	..	..	..	..	..	..	..	..	..	..
4210 Individual	..	..	..	..	..	..	..	..	..	..
4220 Corporate	..	..	..	..	..	..	..	..	..	..
4300 Estate, inheritance and gift taxes	..	..	..	..	..	..	..	..	..	..
4310 Estate and inheritance taxes	..	..	..	..	..	..	..	..	..	..
4320 Gift taxes	..	..	..	..	..	..	..	..	..	..
4400 Taxes on financial and capital transactions	..	..	..	..	..	..	..	..	..	..
4500 Non-recurrent taxes	..	..	..	..	..	..	..	..	..	..
4510 On net wealth	..	..	..	..	..	..	..	..	..	..
4520 Other non-recurrent taxes	..	..	..	..	..	..	..	..	..	..
4600 Other recurrent taxes on property	..	..	..	..	..	..	..	..	..	..
5000 Taxes on goods and services	**772 546**	**815 835**	**2 639 574**	**2 861 862**	**5 301 667**	**6 350 601**	**7 184 686**	**8 062 848**	**9 213 966**	**10 457 661**
5100 Taxes on production, sale, transfer, etc.	750 617	793 285	2 568 187	2 772 331	5 158 322	6 201 129	7 053 042	7 920 341	9 043 466	10 285 737
5110 General taxes	305 694	329 755	1 259 732	1 371 561	2 611 779	3 150 723	3 580 634	3 933 633	4 503 033	4 976 108
5111 Value added taxes	305 694	329 755	1 259 732	1 371 561	2 611 779	3 150 723	3 580 634	3 933 633	4 503 033	4 976 108
VAT on imports (government taxes)	7 154	16 628	55 742	35 775	20 344	0	0	0	0	0
VAT on imports (non-government taxes)	181 245	178 868	763 635	763 398	1 404 415	1 783 518	1 952 821	2 057 107	2 416 568	2 664 812
VAT on phone talk time	0	0	54 628	93 277	141 352	151 747	181 944	205 342	213 549	200 283
VAT on beer	12 636	11 586	24 542	37 034	96 412	108 831	120 513	126 862	145 809	122 117
VAT on electricity	0	0	54 520	74 584	162 673	112 811	114 679	128 080	170 471	170 536
VAT on sugar	0	0	46 346	64 276	71 294	110 801	120 363	139 657	149 558	120 790
VAT on soft drinks	2 977	5 139	16 665	15 846	30 268	32 385	35 449	43 023	42 791	76 960
VAT on cement	0	0	21 712	25 161	37 356	53 086	72 014	66 491	81 095	87 557
VAT on cigarettes	7 733	6 904	1 382	1 411	6 767	16 759	9 366	9 042	9 522	4 295
Other VAT	116 670	140 630	306 155	359 821	807 772	923 754	1 117 807	1 303 951	1 407 037	1 756 848
VAT refunds	-22 720	-30 000	-85 595	-99 023	-166 874	-142 970	-144 324	-145 923	-133 368	-228 090
5112 Sales tax	0	0	0	0	0	0	0	0	0	0

Table 5.30. **Uganda / Ouganda** *(cont.)*

Details of tax revenue / Recettes fiscales détaillées

Million UGX

	1999	2000	2009	2010	2014	2015	2016	2017	2018	2019
5113 Other	0	0	0	0	0	0	0	0	0	0
5120 Taxes on specific goods and services	444 923	463 530	1 308 455	1 400 770	2 546 543	3 050 407	3 472 408	3 986 708	4 540 433	5 309 629
5121 Excises	130 892	132 953	256 213	275 929	700 426	834 589	878 166	1 018 677	1 122 066	1 257 253
Excise tax on beer	57 209	59 938	85 183	98 864	144 222	146 853	177 678	216 717	263 072	269 276
Excise tax on phone talk time	0	0	88 729	99 490	170 432	184 175	166 780	194 297	178 966	211 878
Excise tax on soft drinks	13 094	13 348	24 560	27 907	59 338	71 799	83 125	90 009	118 869	125 992
Excise tax on cigarettes	32 305	33 572	7 308	7 698	14 246	14 979	12 617	12 072	15 591	14 912
Excise tax on spirits / waragi	2 031	915	11 955	10 376	45 555	53 331	58 203	98 886	157 512	155 648
Excise on international calls	0	0	0	0	68 162	65 142	34 230	33 971	33 341	34 937
Excise tax on sugar	0	0	13 004	17 187	7 479	17 854	18 220	37 973	30 277	35 526
Excise tax on cement	1	1	8 296	8 228	15 729	17 773	20 784	23 729	26 741	32 089
Other excise taxes	26 252	25 180	83 287	84 179	175 262	262 684	306 530	311 024	282 714	361 930
Tax refunds due to diesel tax exemption	0	0	-66 110	-77 999	0	0	0	0	14 982	15 065
5122 Profits of fiscal monopolies	0	0	0	0	0	0	0	0	0	0
5123 Customs and import duties	313 823	330 339	1 050 037	1 122 850	1 831 978	2 188 774	2 522 234	2 886 974	3 333 021	3 712 469
Petroleum duty	193 208	197 202	632 319	716 234	984 245	1 197 749	1 382 952	1 609 602	1 811 817	2 038 658
Surcharge on used imports	0	0	32 867	38 621	72 889	95 895	136 280	164 612	209 782	230 784
Non-oil imports	2 884	5 301	25 050	21 651	27 702	0	0	0	0	0
Commission on imports	21 246	22 746	0	2	0	0	0	0	0	0
Infrastructure Levy	0	0	0	0	0	57 268	62 936	69 107	87 669	92 569
Other import duties	96 485	105 090	360 071	346 621	747 533	841 381	940 066	1 043 652	1 223 753	1 350 458
Fixed duty drawbacks	0	0	-270	-280	-390	-3 520	0	0	0	0
5124 Taxes on exports	0	0	1 137	122	3 126	13 186	15 878	13 968	12 442	20 604
5125 Taxes on investment goods	0	0	0	0	0	0	0	0	0	0
5126 Taxes on specific services	208	238	1 068	1 869	11 012	13 858	56 130	67 089	72 904	319 302
Casino and lottery tax	208	238	1 068	1 869	11 012	13 858	17 416	26 590	29 216	27 896
Bank charges	0	0	0	0	0	0	38 714	40 499	43 688	84 650
Levy on mobile money	0	0	0	0	0	0	0	0	0	49 525
Tax on over-the-top internet services	0	0	0	0	0	0	0	0	0	157 231
5127 Other taxes on internat. trade and transactions	0	0	0	0	0	0	0	0	0	0
5128 Other taxes	0	0	0	0	0	0	0	0	0	0
5130 Unallocable between 5110 and 5120	0	0	0	0	0	0	0	0	0	0
5200 Taxes on use of goods and perform activities	21 929	22 551	71 387	89 531	143 345	149 472	131 645	142 507	170 499	171 924
5210 Recurrent taxes	17 417	17 890	47 834	64 096	92 857	91 886	73 351	80 344	98 194	96 556
5211 Paid by households: motor vehicles	17 417	17 890	47 834	64 096	92 857	91 886	73 351	80 344	98 194	96 556
Fees and licences	17 417	17 890	47 834	64 096	92 857	91 886	73 351	80 344	98 194	96 556
Road user charges	0	0	0	0	0	0	0	0	0	0
5212 Paid by others: motor vehicles	0	0	0	0	0	0	0	0	0	0
5213 Paid in respect of other goods	0	0	0	0	0	0	0	0	0	0
5220 Non-recurrent taxes	4 511	4 660	23 554	25 434	50 488	57 586	58 294	62 164	72 305	75 068
5300 Unallocable between 5100 and 5200	0	0	0	0	0	0	0	0	0	0
6000 Other taxes	**2 326**	**1 919**	**5 532**	**49 833**	**18 668**	**22 927**	**2 988**	**60 050**	**32 518**	**-4 974**
6100 Paid solely by business	0	0	0	0	0	0	0	0	0	0
6200 Other	2 326	1 919	5 532	49 833	18 668	22 927	2 988	60 050	32 518	-4 974
Stamp duties and embossing fees	2 279	1 919	20 952	26 256	39 558	48 557	60 129	88 019	73 945	100 337
Coffee stabilisation tax	48	0	0	0	0	0	0	0	0	0
Government payments on behalf of private companies	0	0	0	0	0	0	0	0	0	0
Agricultural products	0	0	0	0	0	0	0	0	0	0
Un-allocated revenue	0	0	0	29 457	0	0	0	0	0	0
Tax refunds	0	0	-15 420	-5 880	-20 890	-25 630	-57 141	-27 968	-41 428	-105 311
Memo items:										
Gross domestic VAT	140 015	164 259	525 950	671 411	1 353 894	1 510 175	1 772 137	2 022 448	2 234 815	2 554 451
VAT on imports (non-government taxes)	181 245	178 868	763 635	763 398	1 404 415	1 783 518	1 952 821	2 057 107	2 416 568	2 664 812
VAT on imports (government taxes)	7 154	16 628	55 742	35 775	20 344	0	0	0	0	0

.. Not available

Note: Data are reported on a fiscal year basis beginning 1st July. For example, the data for 2019 represent July 2018 to June 2019.

The data are on a cash basis.

Figures exclude tax revenues collected by sub-national governments as the data are not available.

Heading 1110: Subtotals for WHT were removed from this heading in this edition in order to make the presentation clearer.

Heading 4000: Property tax is levied annually by local authorities. Revenue from property tax is not available.

Heading 5121: The "other excises taxes" category combines excise revenues from bottled water, cosmetics and mobile money transfers (all three in the "Indirect Domestic Taxes: excises" section of the Uganda Revenue Authority's budget document) with revenue from the excise duty (in the "taxes on international trade" section) and the excise duty (in the "government taxes" section).

Revenue from driver permits are considered non-tax revenue under the OECD classification, as set out in the Interpretative Guide in Annex A. The national classification of Uganda classifies this revenue as tax revenue.

Source: Uganda Revenue Authority.

StatLink https://doi.org/10.1787/888934284222

Chapter 6

Non-tax revenue tables, 1999-2019

Chapitre 6

Tableaux des recettes non fiscales, 1999-2019

Chapter 6 / Chapitre 6

Non-tax revenue tables, 1999-2019

In all of the following tables a ("..") indicates not available or not applicable. The main series in this volume cover the years 1990 to 2019.

Figures referring to 2001-08, and 2011-13, in Table 6.1 and Tables 6.4 to 6.34 have been omitted because of lack of space. Complete series are, however, available on line at *http://dx.doi.org/10.1787/93add7a4-en*.

Tableaux des recettes non fiscales, 1999-2019

Dans tous les tableaux suivants le symbole («..») signifie que l'information n'est pas disponible ou qu'elle n'est pas applicable. La principale série dans ce volume couvre les années 1990 à 2018.

Les années 2001-08, et 2011-13 dans le tableau 6.1 et les tableaux 6.4 à 6.34 ont été omis en raison du manque d'espace. Les séries complètes sont cependant disponibles en ligne sur *http://dx.doi.org/10.1787/ef1bbbc4-fr*.

Table 6.1. **Total non-tax revenue as percentage of GDP, 1999-2019**
Tableau 6.1. **Total des recettes non fiscales en pourcentage du PIB, 1999-2019**

	1999	2000	2009	2010	2014	2015	2016	2017	2018	2019
Botswana	..	..	22.3	19.1	22.8	18.4	18.2	18.8	15.6	15.4
Burkina Faso	..	7.6	6.3	5.1	5.6	5.0	4.4	4.2	4.5	3.8
Cabo Verde	10.8	7.6	8.8	9.7	5.3	7.6	7.1	7.7	5.6	8.2
Cameroon / Cameroun	3.7	7.3	4.1	4.3	3.9	3.9	2.6	3.1	3.3	3.6
Chad / Tchad	..	..	..	5.2	6.4	5.2	4.0	5.8	6.2	5.2
Congo	0.4	18.4	20.8	31.4	28.2	10.8	12.6	11.6	17.8	19.6
Congo, Dem. Rep. / Congo, Rép. dém.[1]	..	..	..	6.2	6.4	4.7	4.1	3.5	2.7	2.3
Côte d'Ivoire	1.0	0.8	2.6	1.2	1.9	2.4	1.4	1.6	1.5	1.6
Egypt / Égypte	..	..	11.2	8.0	9.5	6.7	5.3	5.9	4.6	4.1
Equatorial Guinea / Guinée équatoriale	..	..	20.4	18.8	14.7	15.0	10.3	11.2	13.4	9.6
Eswatini	12.6	12.5	18.2	8.1	16.3	14.3	11.9	14.1	11.7	12.8
Ghana	..	1.6	4.0	3.7	4.1	4.7	3.2	3.2	3.2	3.1
Kenya	..	..	2.4	1.1	1.5	1.9	1.8	2.1	1.9	1.6
Lesotho	..	..	43.4	34.1	34.0	30.0	24.4	29.1	27.6	26.7
Madagascar	0.0	2.8	1.9	3.0	2.2	1.5	1.9	2.3	2.9	2.6
Malawi	..	..	11.1	11.0	4.9	4.3	4.5	4.8	2.6	2.7
Mali	2.9	5.8	7.1	4.9	3.2	2.5	2.1	3.5	2.4	3.1
Mauritania / Mauritanie[1]	..	..	6.3	6.3	6.0	6.4	4.8	4.7	7.2	5.5
Mauritius / Maurice[2]	3.0	2.7	4.1	3.7	2.9	2.8	3.2	3.7	4.3	2.9
Morocco / Maroc	..	2.2	3.7	3.6	3.8	3.9	3.5	3.5	3.7	4.3
Namibia / Namibie	..	..	13.6	9.4	15.5	14.0	10.8	13.7	11.8	12.7
Niger	..	4.1	4.6	4.6	6.1	5.7	5.1	6.0	7.2	7.6
Nigeria / Nigéria	..	..	..	7.7	4.8	2.9	2.1	2.5	2.9	3.2
Rwanda	11.1	11.8	11.2	11.6	9.1	8.6	7.6	7.2	7.8	6.9
Senegal / Sénégal[1]	1.6	1.6	2.9	2.6	4.0	3.5	4.6	4.1	3.5	..
Seychelles	..	..	9.2	6.2	8.3	6.7	7.8	6.0	7.0	6.3
South Africa / Afrique du Sud	0.5	0.4	0.5	0.5	0.5	0.4	0.4	0.4	0.5	0.5
Togo	..	1.3	10.0	8.3	3.2	3.1	3.2	3.7	5.5	4.7
Tunisia / Tunisie	..	2.5	3.2	2.9	2.4	2.1	1.7	2.9	3.1	3.3
Uganda / Ouganda	3.8	4.7	2.1	1.8	1.0	1.2	1.4	1.1	1.0	1.3
Africa (30) average / Moyenne Afrique (30)[3]	**..**	**..**	**..**	**8.1**	**7.9**	**6.7**	**5.9**	**6.4**	**6.4**	**6.3**

.. Not available

Note: The figures include sub-national government non-tax revenues for Eswatini, Kenya (2014-19), Mauritius and Morocco. Sub-national government non-tax revenues are not available in other countries. See the country tables in Chapter 6 for further information.

1. The data are incomplete and a figure for total non-tax revenue is not included for 2011-12 (Democratic Republic of the Congo) and for 2019 (Senegal).
2. Data for Mauritius are on a July-June fiscal year basis except for the years 2010-15 when they were reported on a calendar year basis. Please see Chapter 5 for more details.
3. Represents an unweighted average of the 30 African countries in this publication.

.. Non disponible

Note : Les chiffres incluent les recettes non fiscales collectées par les administrations infranationales pour l'Eswatini, le Kenya (2014-19), le Maroc et Maurice. Les données des recettes non fiscales collectées par les administrations infranationales ne sont pas disponibles pour les autres pays.Voir les tableaux par pays au chapitre 6 pour plus d'informations.

1. Les données sont incomplètes et le montant des recettes non fiscales totales n'est pas inclus pour 2011-12 (République démocratique du Congo) et pour 2019 (Sénégal).
2. Les données pour Maurice sont sur la base de l'année fiscale juillet-juin sauf pour les années 2010-15 où elles ont été déclarées sur la base de l'année civile. Veuillez consulter le chapitre 5 pour plus de détails.
3. Représente une moyenne non pondérée des 30 pays africains inclus dans cette publication.

StatLink https://doi.org/10.1787/888934284241

Table 6.2. **Non-tax revenue of main headings as percentage of GDP, 2019**
Tableau 6.2. **Recettes fiscales des principales rubriques en pourcentage du PIB, 2019**

	Grants / Dons	Property income / Revenus de la propriété				Sales of goods and services / Ventes de biens et de services	Fines, penalties and forfeits / Amendes, pénalités et confiscations	Miscellaneous and unidentified revenue / Recettes diverses et non identifiées
		Total	Rents and royalties / Loyers et redevances	Interest and dividends / Intérêts et dividendes	Other property income / Autres revenus de la propriété			
Botswana	0.0	7.8	1.8	6.0	0.0	0.3	0.0	7.2
Burkina Faso	1.5	1.3	0.7	0.5	0.0	0.4	0.2	0.4
Cabo Verde	3.1	1.3	..	..	..	3.1	0.2	0.4
Cameroon / Cameroun	0.6	2.4	2.3	0.1	0.0	0.2	0.3	0.1
Chad / Tchad	1.7	3.1	3.1	0.0	0.0	0.2	0.1	0.1
Congo	0.8	18.8	18.5	0.0	0.2	0.0	0.0	0.0
Congo, Dem. Rep. / Congo, Rép. dém.	0.8	1.0	0.9	0.1	0.0	0.3	0.2	0.0
Côte d'Ivoire	0.8	0.4	0.3	0.1	0.0	0.2	0.0	0.2
Egypt / Égypte	0.0	1.4	0.4	1.0	0.0	1.3	0.0	1.4
Equatorial Guinea / Guinée équatoriale	0.0	9.2	5.8	3.2	0.2	0.3	0.0	0.1
Eswatini	0.0	2.8	0.2	2.4	0.1	0.2	0.1	9.8
Ghana	0.3	1.5	0.7	0.8	0.0	1.3	0.0	0.0
Kenya	0.3	0.5	0.0	0.4	0.1	0.6	0.0	0.1
Lesotho	3.7	1.9	1.3	0.5	0.0	2.7	0.0	18.4
Madagascar	2.4	0.2	0.0	0.2	0.0	0.0	0.0	0.0
Malawi	2.0	0.1	0.0	0.1	0.0	0.5	0.0	0.0
Mali	2.1	0.6	0.2	0.4	0.0	0.2	0.2	0.1
Mauritania / Mauritanie	0.8	4.0	3.6	0.4	0.0	0.2	0.2	0.3
Mauritius / Maurice	0.4	0.8	0.2	0.1	0.5	0.9	0.1	0.7
Morocco / Maroc	0.0	0.9	0.4	0.5	0.0	1.8	0.5	1.0
Namibia / Namibie	0.1	1.5	0.8	0.6	0.0	0.6	0.1	10.5
Niger	6.8	0.4	0.2	0.2	0.0	0.1	0.1	0.2
Nigeria / Nigéria	0.0	2.1	2.1	0.0	0.0	0.0	0.0	1.0
Rwanda[1]	4.2	..	..	..	..	..	..	2.7
Senegal / Sénégal	1.6	..	0.5	..	..	0.0	0.1	..
Seychelles	0.4	3.6	1.1	2.5	0.0	2.1	0.0	0.2
South Africa / Afrique du Sud	0.0	0.4	0.2	0.2	0.0	0.0	0.1	0.0
Togo	2.9	0.9	0.2	0.7	0.0	0.6	0.0	0.3
Tunisia / Tunisie	0.2	1.9	0.9	1.0	0.0	0.0	0.9	0.3
Uganda / Ouganda	0.9	0.0	0.0	0.0	0.0	0.4	0.0	0.0
Africa (30) average / Moyenne Afrique (30)[2]	**1.3**	**2.5**	**1.7**	**0.8**	**..**	**0.6**	**0.1**	**1.9**

.. Not available

Note: The figures include sub-national government non-tax revenues for Eswatini, Kenya (2014-19), Mauritius and Morocco. Sub-national government non-tax revenues are not available in other countries. See the country tables in Chapter 6 for further information.

1. Data for property income, sales of goods and services and fines, penalties and forfeits are included in miscellaneous and unidentified revenue.
2. Represents an unweighted average of the 30 African countries in this publication.

.. Non disponible

Note : Les chiffres incluent les recettes non fiscales collectées par les administrations infranationales pour l'Eswatini, le Kenya (2014-19), le Maroc et Maurice. Les données des recettes non fiscales collectées par les administrations infranationales ne sont pas disponibles pour les autres pays.Voir les tableaux par pays au chapitre 6 pour plus d'informations.

1. Les données relatives aux revenus de propriété, les ventes de biens et de services, les amendes, les pénalités et les confiscations sont incluses dans la rubrique « recettes diverses et non identifiées ».
2. Représente une moyenne non pondérée des 30 pays africains inclus dans cette publication.

StatLink https://doi.org/10.1787/888934284260

Table 6.3. **Non-tax revenue of main headings as percentage of total non-tax revenues, 2019**

Tableau 6.3. **Recettes fiscales des principales rubriques en pourcentage du total des recettes non fiscales, 2019**

	Grants / Dons	Property income / Revenus de la propriété				Sales of goods and services / Ventes de biens et de services	Fines, penalties and forfeits / Amendes, pénalités et confiscations	Miscellaneous and unidentified revenue / Recettes diverses et non identifiées
		Total	Rents and royalties / Loyers et redevances	Interest and dividends / Intérêts et dividendes	Other property income / Autres revenus de la propriété			
Botswana	0.1	50.6	11.6	39.0	0.0	2.2	0.2	46.9
Burkina Faso	38.6	33.6	19.8	13.8	0.0	11.2	5.2	11.3
Cabo Verde	38.3	16.4	..	..	..	37.3	2.7	5.2
Cameroon / Cameroun	16.2	66.9	64.0	2.9	0.0	6.8	7.4	2.7
Chad / Tchad	32.1	60.4	59.7	0.0	0.7	4.8	1.3	1.4
Congo	3.9	96.0	94.8	0.0	1.2	0.0	0.0	0.0
Congo, Dem. Rep. / Congo, Rép. dém.	33.2	43.8	39.8	3.9	0.1	15.1	7.8	0.1
Côte d'Ivoire	51.5	25.3	20.1	5.3	0.0	10.9	0.0	12.3
Egypt / Égypte	1.2	34.2	9.5	24.4	0.3	31.3	0.4	32.9
Equatorial Guinea / Guinée équatoriale	0.2	96.3	60.4	33.4	2.4	2.8	0.1	0.7
Eswatini	0.0	21.5	1.7	18.6	1.1	1.6	0.6	76.3
Ghana	9.1	47.4	21.6	25.9	0.0	42.4	0.0	1.1
Kenya	20.7	33.7	1.1	27.2	5.5	37.9	1.1	6.6
Lesotho	13.9	6.9	5.0	1.9	0.0	10.1	0.2	68.9
Madagascar	89.6	8.6	0.9	7.7	0.0	0.3	0.0	1.4
Malawi	74.9	5.2	0.0	5.2	0.0	18.6	1.3	0.0
Mali	66.5	19.3	5.1	13.9	0.3	6.8	5.2	2.2
Mauritania / Mauritanie	13.9	74.3	66.9	7.4	0.0	2.9	3.0	5.9
Mauritius / Maurice	14.2	29.5	8.5	3.1	18.0	31.0	2.6	22.8
Morocco / Maroc	0.0	21.2	9.9	11.3	0.0	42.4	12.0	24.5
Namibia / Namibie	0.4	11.6	6.7	5.0	0.0	4.5	0.4	83.0
Niger	89.2	5.4	2.8	2.5	0.1	1.3	1.9	2.2
Nigeria / Nigéria	0.0	67.4	67.4	0.0	0.0	0.0	0.0	32.6
Rwanda[1]	60.6	..	..	..	..	..	..	39.4
Senegal / Sénégal	..	..	..	..	..	..	..	..
Seychelles	6.7	56.7	17.9	38.8	0.0	33.0	0.0	3.6
South Africa / Afrique du Sud	3.9	71.4	40.2	31.1	0.0	9.2	14.1	1.4
Togo	61.1	18.9	3.4	15.5	0.0	12.6	0.8	6.5
Tunisia / Tunisie	6.5	58.4	27.2	31.2	0.0	1.4	26.1	7.6
Uganda / Ouganda	70.9	1.0	1.0	0.0	0.0	28.1	0.0	0.0
Africa (30) average / Moyenne Afrique (30)[2]	**28.9**	**38.2**	**24.4**	**13.5**	**..**	**14.0**	**3.4**	**17.4**

.. Not available

Note: The figures include sub-national government non-tax revenues for Eswatini, Kenya (2014-19), Mauritius and Morocco. Sub-national government non-tax revenues are not available in other countries. See the country tables in Chapter 6 for further information.

1. Data for property income, sales of goods and services and fines, penalties and forfeits are included in miscellaneous and unidentified revenue.
2. Represents an unweighted average of the 30 African countries in this publication.

.. Non disponible

Note : Les chiffres incluent les recettes non fiscales collectées par les administrations infranationales pour l'Eswatini, le Kenya (2014-19), le Maroc et Maurice. Les données des recettes non fiscales collectées par les administrations infranationales ne sont pas disponibles pour les autres pays.Voir les tableaux par pays au chapitre 6 pour plus d'informations.

1. Les données relatives aux revenus de propriété, les ventes de biens et de services, les amendes, les pénalités et les confiscations sont incluses dans la rubrique « recettes diverses et non identifiées ».
2. Représente une moyenne non pondérée des 30 pays africains inclus dans cette publication.

StatLink https://doi.org/10.1787/888934284279

Table 6.4. **Total non-tax revenue in millions of US dollars at market exchange rates, 1999-2019**

Tableau 6.4. **Total des recettes non fiscales en millions de dollars américains au taux de change du marché, 1999-2019**

	1999	2000	2009	2010	2014	2015	2016	2017	2018	2019
Botswana	..	..	2 434	2 561	3 596	2 709	2 922	3 330	2 896	2 121
Burkina Faso	..	225	591	514	776	594	569	594	725	593
Cabo Verde	71	46	149	161	99	122	118	137	111	163
Cameroon / Cameroun	394	720	1 070	1 134	1 351	1 220	860	1 078	1 293	1 407
Chad / Tchad	..	..	..	561	903	572	411	582	685	568
Congo	10	667	2 015	4 126	5 062	1 279	1 284	1 284	2 388	2 453
Congo, Dem. Rep. / Congo, Rép. dém.	..	..	..	1 339	2 300	1 788	1 504	1 324	1 282	1 166
Côte d'Ivoire	175	121	884	414	905	1 108	677	808	879	910
Egypt / Égypte	..	..	22 137	18 318	28 878	22 274	17 646	13 975	11 414	12 527
Equatorial Guinea / Guinée équatoriale	..	..	3 081	3 062	3 199	1 978	1 157	1 369	1 785	1 056
Eswatini	222	211	692	365	705	570	470	630	539	430
Ghana	..	178	1 379	1 612	2 179	2 293	1 733	1 884	2 091	2 071
Kenya	..	..	891	430	880	1 224	1 199	1 530	1 607	1 437
Lesotho	..	..	841	804	842	661	541	685	641	612
Madagascar	0	128	181	297	272	172	229	298	402	383
Malawi	..	..	637	723	283	268	265	279	173	197
Mali	99	173	724	519	461	334	297	537	404	536
Mauritania / Mauritanie	..	..	300	357	394	397	310	322	505	432
Mauritius / Maurice	133	128	395	372	376	323	386	475	593	405
Morocco / Maroc	..	873	3 430	3 323	4 153	3 961	3 592	3 809	4 311	5 104
Namibia / Namibie	..	..	1 290	1 088	1 890	1 572	1 219	1 791	1 578	1 195
Niger	..	93	336	363	662	548	528	669	920	983
Nigeria / Nigéria	..	..	..	28 431	27 414	14 055	8 508	9 392	12 285	14 279
Rwanda	199	203	640	712	754	736	661	670	756	698
Senegal / Sénégal	103	96	467	412	800	621	882	862	811	..
Seychelles	..	..	78	60	112	93	112	91	108	100
South Africa / Afrique du Sud	700	596	1 528	2 211	1 837	1 406	1 375	1 643	2 093	2 034
Togo	..	27	453	384	197	174	193	234	391	342
Tunisia / Tunisie	..	529	1 405	1 257	1 121	891	716	1 145	1 229	1 305
Uganda / Ouganda	304	367	493	438	311	362	400	346	324	459

.. Not available

Note: This table is derived by dividing the total non-tax revenue figures for each country (in millions of national currency) in Table 6.1 by the exchange rate figures shown in Table 4.19.

.. Non disponible

Note : Ce tableau est obtenu en divisant les chiffres des recettes non fiscales en millions de monnaie nationale du tableau 6.1 pour chaque pays par les taux de change du tableau 4.19.

StatLink https://doi.org/10.1787/888934284298

Table 6.5. **Botswana**

Details of non-tax revenue / Recettes non fiscales détaillées

Million BWP

	1999	2000	2009	2010	2014	2015	2016	2017	2018	2019
Total non-tax revenue	**..**	**..**	**17 152**	**17 412**	**33 197**	**27 953**	**31 412**	**34 363**	**29 941**	**29 841**
Grants	..	..	121	210	316	74	1	170	1	24
Grants	..	..	121	210	316	74	1	170	1	24
IMF Gold Sales	..	..	0	0	0	0	0	0	0	0
Property income	..	..	7 869	9 914	16 402	11 152	18 424	15 092	14 171	15 114
Rents and royalties	..	..	1 820	2 071	3 775	3 223	3 320	5 648	3 403	3 476
Mineral Royalties	..	..	1 809	2 057	3 766	3 215	3 307	5 638	3 383	3 463
Royalties and Dividends	..	..	0	0	0	0	0	0	0	0
Rent of Land	..	..	11	14	9	8	13	10	20	13
Interest and dividends	..	..	6 050	7 842	12 627	7 929	15 104	9 444	10 768	11 638
Mineral Dividends	..	..	4 920	7 054	10 267	6 766	11 976	7 740	9 905	6 547
Bank of Botswana Revenue	..	..	1 000	700	2 079	1 133	2 842	1 573	740	5 049
Profits From Public Enterprises	..	..	108	61	48	18	67	107	117	10
Interest: Parastatals (DDF)	..	..	12	20	229	8	215	19	1	29
Interest: Local Authorities	..	..	0	0	0	0	0	0	0	0
Interest: Deposits	..	..	10	8	4	4	4	4	5	3
Other property income	..	..	0	0	0	0	0	0	0	0
Sales of goods and services	..	..	1 179	1 047	715	811	1 137	1 183	930	653
Motor vehicle revenues	..	..	336	363	49	50	40	44	36	40
Petrol, Oil and Lubricants - Revenue	..	..	186	182	158	231	259	184	217	111
Water revenues	..	..	123	42	1	2	2	2	2	2
Fees and charges	..	..	115	107	133	129	123	599	123	137
Rent of Buildings & Equipment	..	..	83	86	93	97	95	97	97	99
Sale of Livestock	..	..	2	5	2	2	1	4	2	1
Registrations, licences and certificates	..	..	21	22	37	33	34	29	33	38
Other sales of goods and services	..	..	313	242	242	269	583	225	419	226
Fines, penalties and forfeits	..	..	49	31	67	93	65	46	42	60
Traffic fines	..	..	0	0	0	44	25	1	0	0
Court fines	..	..	37	20	52	38	23	22	22	23
Bond revenues	..	..	1	1	1	1	3	3	1	2
Income tax penalty	..	..	0	0	0	0	0	0	0	0
Other fines, penalties and forfeits	..	..	11	10	14	11	14	20	19	36
Miscellaneous and unidentified revenue	..	..	7 934	6 210	15 697	15 823	11 784	17 071	14 797	13 991
SACU Revenue	..	..	7 931	6 207	15 691	15 818	11 773	17 864	14 789	13 976
Recovery of Arrears of Revenue	..	..	2	3	6	5	10	6	8	14
Revenue from Local Authorities	..	..	0	0	0	0	0	0	0	0
Reimbursement of Medical Claims (Revenue)	..	..	1	1	0	1	1	1	1	1
Total tax and non-tax revenue		..	29 260	31 712	55 357	47 285	55 551	56 833	53 229	54 198

.. Not available

Note: Data are on a fiscal year basis beginning 1st April. For example, the data for 2019 represent April 2019 to March 2020.

Figures exclude non-tax revenues collected by sub-national governments as the data are not available.

Source: Botswana Ministry of Finance and Economic Development, and Statistics Botswana.

StatLink https://doi.org/10.1787/888934284317

Table 6.6. **Burkina Faso**

Details of non-tax revenue / Recettes non fiscales détaillées

Millions XOF

	1999	2000	2009	2010	2014	2015	2016	2017	2018	2019
Total des recettes non fiscales	**..**	**160 511**	**278 083**	**254 019**	**382 954**	**351 209**	**337 426**	**345 257**	**402 658**	**347 502**
Dons	..	143 716	232 428	198 940	256 447	230 041	180 190	194 303	215 091	134 275
Revenus de la propriété	..	6 326	15 170	15 447	66 261	57 875	74 704	87 166	104 718	116 802
Loyers et redevances	..	411	5 605	12 453	36 225	37 938	45 182	53 727	65 780	68 748
Droits sur les titres miniers et redevances minières	..	324	5 605	12 453	36 225	37 938	45 182	53 727	65 780	68 748
Redevance sûrété	..	87	0	0	0	0	0	0	0	0
Intérêts et dividendes	..	5 915	9 565	2 993	30 036	19 937	29 522	33 438	38 937	48 054
Intérêts en douane	..	42	17	40	223	493	295	212	124	2 023
Portefeuille de l'Etat et plus value	..	5 873	9 549	2 954	29 813	19 443	29 227	33 227	38 813	46 032
Autres revenus de la propriété	..	0	0	0	0	0	0	0	0	0
Ventes de biens et de services	..	6 408	17 163	24 510	41 957	39 979	44 358	40 816	38 088	38 838
Diverses prestations de services	..	2 364	6 637	10 831	22 054	19 016	20 865	15 311	11 448	9 946
Location de biens	..	8	32	398	159	76	57	222	254	161
Frais douanes	..	2 493	6 737	6 667	9 166	9 795	12 533	14 121	14 173	13 952
Frais visas, papiers d'identite et permis de conduire	..	431	1 575	2 986	4 605	4 582	5 201	5 072	4 793	5 094
Autres frais administratifs	..	1 113	2 182	3 629	5 971	6 511	5 702	6 089	7 421	9 685
Amendes, pénalités et confiscations	..	1 272	3 901	4 505	6 153	8 863	19 025	3 033	4 225	18 162
Recettes diverses et non identifiées	..	2 790	9 420	10 618	12 137	14 451	19 148	19 939	40 536	39 424
Reversement des intérêts	..	2 382	2 943	3 618	3 570	2 534	785	5 309	4 133	2 088
Autres produits	..	408	6 477	7 000	8 568	11 917	18 363	14 629	36 404	37 336
Total des recettes fiscales et non fiscales	..	375 113	840 039	952 872	1 365 697	1 369 969	1 498 795	1 671 321	1 887 343	1 969 106
Pour mémoire :										
Prélèvement communautaire de solidarité (UEMOA)	..	1	7	6	9 003	9 855	11 433	11 884	11 035	10 394
Prélèvement communautaire (CEDEAO)	..	1 144	3 726	4 243	6 734	7 018	7 504	8 705	9 504	9 325

.. Non disponible

Note : Année civile se terminant le 31 décembre.

Les chiffres n'incluent pas les recettes non fiscales collectées par les collectivités locales car elles ne sont pas disponibles. Cependant, ils incluent des recettes collectées par l'administration centrale au profit des collectivités locales.

Les recettes provenant de la taxe de location de biens, des droits sur les titres miniers, redevances minières et des frais administratifs sont incluses dans les recettes non fiscales comme le préconise la classification OCDE (voir le guide d'interprétation en Annexe A). La classification nationale du Burkina Faso les comptabilise comme des recettes fiscales.

Source : Ministère de l'Économie, des Finances et du Développement du Burkina Faso.

StatLink https://doi.org/10.1787/888934284336

Table 6.7. **Cabo Verde**

Details of non-tax revenue / Recettes non fiscales détaillées

Million CVE

	1999	2000	2009	2010	2014	2015	2016	2017	2018	2019
Total des recettes non fiscales	**7 312**	**5 372**	**11 945**	**13 396**	**8 211**	**12 116**	**11 777**	**13 405**	**10 368**	**16 034**
Dons	4 416	3 931	7 536	9 440	2 787	3 958	4 507	6 193	2 265	6 145
Transferts courants de gouvernements étrangers	4 416	0	0	0	228	370	461	278	851	551
Aide budgétaire	0	..	..	..	0	0	0	0	0	0
Aide alimentaire	755	..	..	..	0	0	0	0	0	0
Dons directs	3 661	..	..	..	228	353	449	266	846	548
Autre transfert courants	0	..	..	..	0	17	13	12	5	4
Transferts en capital de gouvernements étrangers	0	3 931	7 536	9 440	2 559	3 588	4 046	5 914	1 414	5 594
Aide budgétaire	..	0	2 180	3 085	1 041	1 282	1 312	2 701	1 103	2 006
Aide alimentaire	..	672	317	338	17	0	60	283	154	231
Dons directs	..	3 259	5 039	6 018	1 501	2 048	2 542	2 930	158	3 357
Autre dons en capital	..	0	0	0	0	259	132	0	0	0
Revenus de la propriété	959	364	904	316	209	1 022	1 083	976	1 793	2 632
Loyers et redevances	..	..	..	..	..	..	..	..	..	..
Intérêts et dividendes	..	..	..	..	..	..	..	..	..	..
Autres revenus de la propriété	..	..	..	..	..	..	..	..	..	..
Ventes de biens et de services	483	592	3 063	3 077	4 010	4 652	5 042	5 189	5 509	5 987
Taux	337	448	3 005	3 003	3 823	4 492	4 738	4 995	5 293	5 841
Ventes	146	144	59	74	187	160	303	194	216	146
Amendes, pénalités et confiscations	112	54	270	376	706	404	679	498	369	433
Recettes diverses et non identifiées	1 342	431	171	187	499	2 079	467	550	431	838
Autres transferts	687	413	58	41	128	36	35	28	24	242
Autres recettes diverses et non spécifiées	655	18	113	146	371	2 043	432	521	407	595
Total des recettes fiscales et non fiscales	17 630	16 346	36 953	38 948	34 299	41 783	42 833	48 290	49 526	56 193
Pour mémoire : *Prélèvement communautaire de la CEDEAO*	0	67	219	245	258	254	290	317	324	339

.. Non disponible

Note : Année civile se terminant le 31 décembre.

Les données sont sur la base des encaissements.

Les chiffres n'incluent pas les données des recettes non fiscales collectées par les collectivités locales car elles ne sont pas disponibles.

La présente publication n'inclut pas le produit de la vente d'actifs non financiers rapporté dans les documents budgétaires du Cabo Verde. La classification nationale du Cabo Verde compte le produit de la vente d'actifs non financiers comme une recette non fiscale. Selon la classification de l'OCDE (voir le guide d'interprétation en Annexe B), le produit de la vente d'actifs n'est pas considéré comme une recette (fiscale ou non fiscale) car il ne représente pas une augmentation de la valeur nette résultant d'une transaction.

Le prélèvement communautaire de la CEDEAO (Communauté économique des États de l'Afrique de l'Ouest) n'est pas compris dans le total des recettes non fiscales ou fiscales et est présenté à titre de rubrique « Pour mémoire ». Le prélèvement communautaire de la CEDEAO est considéré comme une recette fiscale au Cabo Verde. Selon la classification de l'OCDE (voir le guide d'interprétation en Annexe A § 4), ce paiement n'est pas compris parmi les impôts.

Source : Ministère des Finances et du Plan du Cabo Verde.

StatLink https://doi.org/10.1787/888934284355

Table 6.8. **Cameroon / Cameroun**

Details of non-tax revenue / Recettes non fiscales détaillées

Million XAF

	1999	2000	2009	2010	2014	2015	2016	2017	2018	2019
Total des recettes non fiscales	**242 647**	**527 053**	**503 912**	**560 690**	**666 820**	**721 082**	**509 962**	**626 311**	**717 707**	**824 233**
Dons	0	6 900	118 471	78 805	23 813	18 089	54 100	64 800	86 700	133 300
Revenus de la propriété	176 000	404 500	343 193	442 296	580 497	465 541	396 033	398 521	510 077	551 526
Loyers et redevances	176 000	404 500	337 442	437 650	570 574	445 587	376 734	388 483	499 042	527 789
Redevance pétrolière	174 200	399 300	318 528	418 971	517 040	384 630	316 005	319 434	413 325	471 518
Droits de passage du pipeline	0	0	8 344	9 080	24 675	36 201	31 953	27 891	29 543	35 013
Autres loyers et redevances	1 800	5 200	10 570	9 599	28 860	24 756	28 776	41 158	56 175	21 257
Intérêts et dividendes	..	..	5 751	4 646	9 922	19 954	19 299	10 038	11 035	23 737
Autres revenus de la propriété	..	..	0	0	0	0	0	0	0	0
Ventes de biens et de services	34 900	33 500	37 810	37 732	52 990	188 402	29 094	21 737	48 055	56 291
Amendes, pénalités et confiscations	0	0	2 401	1 857	3 975	26 849	15 487	43 386	57 334	61 259
Recettes diverses et non identifiées	31 747	82 153	2 037	0	5 546	22 201	15 248	97 867	15 541	21 857
Total des recettes fiscales et non fiscales	952 714	1 337 553	2 115 314	2 132 385	3 152 865	3 409 008	3 253 870	3 561 490	3 864 201	4 046 395

.. Non disponible

Note : Année civile se terminant le 31 décembre.

Les données sont sur la base des encaissements.

Les chiffres n'incluent pas les recettes non fiscales collectées par les collectivités locales car elles ne sont pas disponibles.

Revenus de la propriété : Cette rubrique inclut les taxes domaniales, la taxe à l'extraction des carrières et la redevance à la production des eaux comme le préconise la classification OCDE (voir le guide d'interprétation en Annexe B). La classification nationale du Cameroun les comptabilise comme des recettes fiscales.

Recettes diverses et non identifiées : Y compris transferts de capitaux non compris ailleurs et transferts volontaires autres que les dons.

Source : Ministère des Finances du Cameroun.

StatLink https://doi.org/10.1787/888934284374

Table 6.9. **Chad / Tchad**

Details of non-tax revenue / Recettes non fiscales détaillées

Million XAF

	1999	2000	2009	2010	2014	2015	2016	2017	2018	2019
Total des recettes non fiscales	..	..	..	**277 272**	**445 658**	**337 904**	**243 337**	**337 881**	**380 062**	**332 670**
Dons	..	..	..	68 799	135 891	221 884	175 497	235 922	199 244	106 891
Revenus de la propriété	..	..	..	193 129	281 907	87 733	44 164	69 280	149 077	200 942
Loyers et redevances	..	..	..	190 753	279 795	86 094	43 333	66 082	146 899	198 643
Redevances et dividendes pétroliers	..	..	..	185 445	231 676	86 094	20 363	56 138	58 653	88 201
Autres recettes pétrolières	..	..	..	5 308	48 119	0	22 970	9 944	88 246	110 442
Intérêts et dividendes	..	..	..	0	0	0	0	0	0	0
Autres revenus de la propriété	..	..	..	2 377	2 112	1 639	831	3 198	2 178	2 299
Ventes de biens et de services	..	..	..	4 162	10 334	10 591	6 837	3 694	2 416	15 873
Amendes, pénalités et confiscations	..	..	..	6 474	7 219	1 528	4 038	2 759	5 678	4 419
Recettes diverses et non identifiées	..	..	..	4 708	10 308	16 168	12 801	26 226	23 648	4 545
Total des recettes fiscales et non fiscales	..	..	..	1 050 538	1 181 747	712 081	527 746	699 833	862 843	852 043

.. Non disponible

Note : Année civile se terminant le 31 décembre.

Les données sont sur la base des encaissements.

Les chiffres n'incluent pas les recettes fiscales collectées par les collectivités locales car elles ne sont pas disponibles.

Les données 2010-18 ont été révisées.

Les données des dons sont issues du FMI.

Les recettes provenant des amendes fiscales, des valeurs mobilières de l'État et de la redevance audiovisuelle incluses dans les recettes non fiscales comme le préconise la classification OCDE (voir le guide d'interprétation en Annexe A). La classification nationale du Tchad les comptabilise comme des recettes fiscales.Les recettes provenant des amendes fiscales sont comptabilisées dans la rubrique amendes, pénalités et confiscations. Les recettes provenant des valeurs mobilières de l'État et de la redevance audiovisuelle sont comptabilisées dans la rubrique dans la rubrique ventes de biens et de services.

Source : Ministère des Finances et du Budget du Tchad; FMI (2021), *Perspectives de l'économie mondiale (PEM) d'avril* 2021.

StatLink https://doi.org/10.1787/888934284393

Table 6.10. **Congo**

Details of non-tax revenue / Recettes non fiscales détaillées

Million XAF

	1999	2000	2009	2010	2014	2015	2016	2017	2018	2019
Total des recettes non fiscales	**6 300**	**474 909**	**948 875**	**2 039 759**	**2 498 538**	**756 377**	**761 392**	**745 852**	**1 325 687**	**1 437 196**
Dons	6 300	6 800	14 500	4 100	31 100	41 400	40 400	29 600	5 900	56 600
Revenus de la propriété	..	468 109	934 375	2 034 514	2 466 650	713 099	720 025	715 490	1 318 180	1 380 212
Loyers et redevances	..	468 109	934 375	2 034 462	2 463 172	707 304	704 803	708 108	1 305 772	1 362 886
Recettes pétrolières	..	468 109	934 375	2 032 755	2 456 307	699 478	699 937	679 323	1 288 100	1 346 809
Redevance pétrolière	..	..	..	0	15	70	118	71	77	13
Redevance minière	..	..	..	2	405	60	12	42	1	1
Redevance forestière	..	..	..	1 705	6 445	7 696	4 735	28 673	17 594	16 063
Intérêts et dividendes	..	..	..	0	0	0	0	0	0	0
Autres revenus de la propriété	..	..	..	53	3 478	5 796	15 223	7 382	12 407	17 326
Ventes de biens et de services	..	..	..	68	245	156	94	597	812	336
Amendes, pénalités et confiscations	..	..	..	1 077	543	1 721	872	165	795	48
Recettes diverses et non identifiées	..	..	..	0	0	0	0	0	0	0
Total des recettes fiscales et non fiscales	106 082	573 593	1 312 860	2 491 746	3 351 730	1 659 245	1 560 221	1 441 669	1 890 558	2 027 908

.. Non disponible

Note : Année civile se terminant le 31 décembre.

Les données sont sur la base des encaissements.

Les données des dons et des recettes pétrolières sont issues de la base de données de la publication FMI (2021), *Perspectives de l'économie mondiale (PEM) d'avril 2021*.

Rubrique Loyers et redevances : À partir de 2017, cette rubrique inclut la redevance bois et la redevance diamant collectées par la Direction Générale des douanes et des droits indirects.

Source : Ministère des Finances et du Budget de la République du Congo, FMI.

StatLink https://doi.org/10.1787/888934284412

Table 6.11. **Congo, Dem. Rep. / Congo, Rép. dém.**

Details of non-tax revenue / Recettes non fiscales détaillées

Million CDF

	1999	2000	2009	2010	2014	2015	2016	2017	2018	2019
Total des recettes non fiscales	**..**	**..**	**..**	**1 213 982**	**2 127 683**	**1 656 103**	**1 539 532**	**1 959 056**	**2 081 663**	**1 924 282**
Dons	..	0	433 338	656 421	1 444 380	1 108 062	1 050 733	1 095 000	851 000	639 651
Revenus de la propriété	..	..	..	397 774	464 141	330 992	264 009	603 407	797 136	842 050
Loyers et redevances	..	..	..	358 125	400 379	292 678	241 690	558 096	735 360	765 716
Royalties des sociétés pétrolières	..	..	..	39 705	38 717	19 050	15 218	29 084	41 483	34 353
Redevance et royalty minières	..	..	..	65 476	148 882	138 244	114 681	279 462	408 754	385 847
Droits superficie annuels	..	..	..	25 340	20 172	20 102	18 930	46 295	13 970	10 199
Bonus de signature - renouvellement (hydrocarbures)	..	..	..	4 566	820	624	1 015	31 462	736	1 041
Redevance annuelle sur l'exploitation et autres	..	..	..	50 599	37 086	38 632	50 465	55 098	53 316	94 512
Autorisation de concessions, extractions et autres autorisations	..	..	..	9 126	18 639	5 789	113	31	131 631	101 098
Permis ressources forestières et faune	..	..	..	3 541	1 730	387	638	6 566	771	2 171
Marge distribuable (recettes pétrolières)	..	..	..	84 491	123 433	52 694	34 918	102 933	83 408	127 330
Redevances superficiaires sur permis d'exploration et sur concession	..	..	..	10	4 197	8 791	4 280	5 878	30	8 502
Autres loyers	..	..	..	75 272	6 703	8 365	1 432	1 286	1 261	662
Intérêts et dividendes	..	..	..	39 301	62 272	37 159	22 228	45 162	40 811	75 305
Dividendes on shore (recettes pétrolières)	..	..	..	8 068	17 375	14 665	3 916	5 867	10 994	20 246
Participations off shore (recettes pétrolières)	..	..	..	25 347	36 372	15 806	10 463	30 839	24 271	41 892
Autres dividendes et participations	..	..	..	5 886	8 524	6 688	7 848	8 457	5 546	13 167
Autres revenus de la propriété	..	..	..	348	1 490	1 155	92	149	20 965	1 029
Ventes de biens et de services	..	..	..	123 659	146 328	164 250	159 245	185 679	331 134	290 935
Vente des imprimés	..	158	431	1 106	1 881	690	218	52	219	75
Taxe de numérotation	..	..	..	16 464	21 121	26 110	26 898	40 126	51 014	45 573
Taxe de régulation et taxe de modification des titres obtenus / télécommunications	..	..	..	13 180	28 709	36 198	38 820	21 884	20 191	18 050
Passeport, visa et carte de travail	..	..	..	20 344	26 288	30 957	26 057	32 248	45 946	42 369
Taxes sur le gardiennage par la Police Nationale Congolaise	..	..	..	4 247	10 346	11 337	10 597	16 059	23 016	34 594
Contrôle des produits d'origine toxique, soporifique et stupéfiante	..	..	..	647	7 699	7 328	6 862	6 248	7 736	7 075
Redevance sur la désinfection et le contrôle sanitaire des friperies	..	..	..	3 828	2 292	3 111	2 586	3 081	14 156	53 800
Agréments	..	..	..	1 359	1 340	1 045	404	733	1 307	1 802
Autres	..	..	..	62 483	44 827	44 950	45 702	62 917	163 082	82 838
Loyers, Institut National de Sécurité Sociale (CNSS)	..	..	..	0	1 825	2 524	1 101	2 331	4 468	4 759
Amendes, pénalités et confiscations	..	..	..	35 378	71 428	50 772	64 951	74 007	101 256	150 665
Amendes et pénalités (Direction générale des impôts)	..	418	8 704	15 455	42 138	15 160	40 058	18 504	65 525	90 865
Amendes et pénalités (DGDA)	..	2	657	1 561	1 615	4 093	2 525	3 492	1 910	1 633
Amendes et pénalités (DGRAD)	..	..	..	18 363	27 676	31 518	22 367	52 011	33 821	58 167
Recettes diverses et non identifiées	..	..	..	750	1 407	2 027	594	964	1 136	982
Total des recettes fiscales et non fiscales	..	7 551	1 185 787	2 875 141	5 309 939	5 106 800	4 750 663	5 819 976	7 930 304	8 203 475

.. Non disponible

Note : Année civile se terminant le 31 décembre.

Les données sont sur la base des encaissements.

Les chiffres n'incluent pas les données des recettes non fiscales collectées par les collectivités locales car elles ne sont pas disponibles.

Les données des dons sont issues de la base de données de la publication FMI (2021), *Perspectives de l'économie mondiale (PEM) d'avril* 2021.

Les données autres que les dons sont disponibles qu'à partir de 2010. Pour la période 2010-18, 5 % en moyenne des recettes considérées comme non fiscales par la République démocratique du Congo ont été classifiées comme recettes fiscales dans cette publication comme le préconise la classification OCDE (voir le guide d'interprétation en Annexe A). Ces recettes collectées par la DGRAD (Direction Générale des Recettes Administratives, Judiciaires, Domaniales et de Participations) sont entre autres les redevances sur produits spécifiques, les droits proportionnels sur les S.A.R.L, la taxe ad valorem sur les gains des parieurs, les autorisations d'exportation et d'importation, la taxe d'implémentation des établissements dangereux/insalubres/incommodes et diverses autorisations.

Les recettes provenant de la vente des imprimés sont incluses dans les recettes non fiscales comme le préconise la classification OCDE (voir le guide d'interprétation en Annexe B). La classification nationale en République démocratique du Congo classifie les recettes de la vente des imprimés comme des recettes fiscales.

Certaines recettes – considérées comme des taxes en République démocratique du Congo – sont considérées comme des frais administratifs et sont classifiées comme des recettes non fiscales comme le préconise la classification OCDE (voir le guide d'interprétation en Annexe B).

Source : Ministère des Finances de la République démocratique du Congo.

StatLink https://doi.org/10.1787/888934284431

Table 6.12. **Côte d'Ivoire**

Details of non-tax revenue / Recettes non fiscales détaillées

Million XOF

	1999	2000	2009	2010	2014	2015	2016	2017	2018	2019
Total des recettes non fiscales	**107 846**	**86 004**	**415 830**	**205 073**	**447 046**	**654 836**	**401 313**	**469 133**	**488 004**	**533 356**
Dons	64 901	33 500	310 928	106 540	303 989	282 200	253 518	266 126	246 158	274 912
Revenus de la propriété	5 188	4 204	80 859	76 308	91 828	285 955	68 211	135 029	145 071	135 074
Loyers et redevances	5 188	4 204	51 869	44 902	82 046	255 515	57 736	119 272	121 350	107 057
Revenus du domaine	0	0	186	283	1 363	2 111	2 972	2 152	2 160	3 578
Taxe d'exploitation pétrolière	0	0	32 945	27 275	39 595	30 851	23 555	27 595	36 888	44 522
Bonus de signature pétrolière	0	0	0	0	0	0	0	0	6 039	8 088
Taxes domaniales (hors taxe ad-valorem 2012-2019)	5 188	4 204	7 910	7 696	31 737	37 224	25 697	24 251	31 812	23 425
Autres loyers et redevances	0	0	10 827	9 647	9 351	185 329	5 512	65 273	44 451	27 444
Intérêts et dividendes	0	0	28 969	27 981	9 693	30 440	10 475	15 757	23 721	28 017
Autres revenus de la propriété	0	0	21	3 426	89	0	0	0	0	0
Ventes de biens et de services	0	0	18 944	21 700	31 556	35 414	43 920	27 870	47 111	57 937
Redevance Radiodiffusion Télévision Ivoirienne (RTI)	..	..	4 173	4 107	6 021	6 244	7 275	8 270	8 587	10 342
Taxe audiovisuelle	..	..	6	0	0	0	0	0	0	0
Autres ventes de biens et de services	..	..	14 766	17 592	25 535	29 170	36 645	19 600	38 524	47 595
Amendes, pénalités et confiscations	0	0	200	173	291	0	0	0	0	0
Recettes diverses et non identifiées	37 757	48 300	4 898	353	19 382	51 267	35 664	40 108	49 664	65 433
Total des recettes fiscales et non fiscales	1 319 941	1 255 611	2 343 659	2 240 542	3 393 149	4 069 254	4 137 768	4 452 816	4 682 693	5 061 198

.. Non disponible

Note : Année civile se terminant le 31 décembre. Les données sont sur la base des encaissements. Les chiffres n'incluent pas les données des recettes non fiscales collectées par les collectivités locales car elles ne sont pas disponibles.

Les recettes des taxes domaniales, la taxe ad valorem et la taxe d'exploitation sont considérées comme des recettes non fiscales selon la classification OCDE (voir le guide d'interprétation en Annexe B). La classification nationale de la Côte d'Ivoire les compte comme des recettes fiscales.

Les recettes des taxes domaniales sont hors taxe ad-valorem pour la période 2012 à 2019, période pour laquelle il a été possible de distinguer ces recettes.

La taxe audiovisuelle et la redevance radiodiffusion télévision ivoirienne (RTI) sont considérées comme des recettes non fiscales selon la classification OCDE (voir le guide d'interprétation en Annexe B). La classification nationale de la Côte d'Ivoire les compte comme des recettes fiscales.

Les recettes diverses et non identifiées comprennent les transferts de capitaux non compris ailleurs et les transferts volontaires autres que les dons.

Source : Ministère de l'Économie et des Finances.

StatLink https://doi.org/10.1787/888934284450

Table 6.13. **Egypt / Égypte**

Details of non-tax revenue / Recettes non fiscales détaillées

Million EGP

	1999	2000	2009	2010	2014	2015	2016	2017	2018	2019
Total non-tax revenue	..	..	**122 322**	**101 032**	**201 296**	**163 927**	**143 795**	**205 018**	**202 382**	**220 509**
Grants	..	..	7 984	4 333	95 856	25 437	3 543	17 683	3 194	2 609
Property income	..	..	54 549	55 890	58 856	83 412	71 503	94 498	74 274	75 499
Rents and royalties	..	..	8 683	7 216	3 898	8 252	6 890	11 917	18 262	20 964
Royalties on petroleum	..	..	3 662	2 750	1 737	5 964	4 139	7 372	11 610	14 148
Royalties on Suez Canal	..	..	1 231	1 354	1 867	1 945	2 059	3 360	5 163	5 157
Other royalties	..	..	3 791	3 112	293	343	693	1 185	1 489	1 659
Interest and dividends	..	..	45 204	47 115	54 709	74 894	64 264	75 244	55 616	53 812
SCA	..	..	13 573	12 729	18 084	19 214	14 755	29 381	23 718	30 308
C.B.E.	..	..	0	205	9 283	13 417	29 462	19 427	5 233	0
Economic authorities	..	..	1 245	1 431	1 630	10 093	7 820	10 989	8 297	10 817
Public and private companies and enterprises	..	..	3 894	3 272	3 157	3 295	3 433	5 230	6 867	5 408
EGPC	..	..	21 637	25 546	21 809	25 414	7 820	5 944	8 144	1 278
Other dividends and interests	..	..	4 855	3 930	747	3 460	974	4 273	3 358	6 001
Other property income	..	..	662	1 559	250	265	350	7 337	396	723
Sales of goods and services	..	..	16 365	24 037	20 624	25 722	28 481	44 150	58 364	68 965
Administrative fees	..	..	2 490	2 681	3 745	4 482	4 453	7 559	10 437	12 520
Development fees	..	..	796	841	742	931	920	534	403	1 991
Service fees	..	..	3 591	3 505	10 001	6 620	7 168	9 010	11 588	13 046
Capital revenues	..	..	9 443	16 962	6 029	13 610	15 824	26 934	35 803	41 252
Other sales of goods and services	..	..	45	49	108	80	116	113	134	156
Fines, penalties and forfeits	..	..	197	234	285	422	671	935	574	900
Miscellaneous and unidentified revenue	..	..	43 228	16 538	25 674	28 934	39 597	47 753	65 977	72 537
Current revenues from special accounts and funds	..	..	11 468	12 268	17 052	17 797	19 627	26 223	35 732	36 128
Voluntary transfers other than grants	..	..	514	684	1 061	901	1 455	2 956	2 143	2 316
Current revenues	..	..	31 008	3 312	7 215	9 827	17 968	17 964	27 576	33 685
Other revenues	..	..	238	275	346	408	547	610	525	409
Total tax and non-tax revenue	..	..	301 952	292 524	503 366	520 022	534 828	731 759	863 940	978 574

.. Not available

Note: Fiscal year ends on 30 June. For example, the data for 2019 represent July 2018 to June 2019.

The data are on a cash basis.

Figures exclude non-tax revenues collected by sub-national governments as the data are not available.

Royalties on the Suez Canal as well as other royalties and administrative fees are reported as tax revenues in Egypt. In accordance with the OECD classification, as set out in the Interpetative Guide in Annex A, these revenues are considered non-tax revenues.

Source: Ministry of Finance.

StatLink https://doi.org/10.1787/888934284469

Table 6.14. **Equatorial Guinea / Guinée équatoriale**

Details of non-tax revenue / Recettes non fiscales détaillées

Million XAF

	1999	2000	2009	2010	2014	2015	2016	2017	2018	2019
Total non-tax revenue	..	..	**1 448 954**	**1 515 259**	**1 579 336**	**1 169 328**	**685 668**	**794 644**	**991 641**	**618 854**
Grants	..	..	0	0	0	0	0	0	0	1 071
Property income	..	..	1 415 224	1 489 017	1 524 837	1 087 688	649 765	742 191	962 877	595 653
Rents and royalties	..	..	763 847	957 200	1 028 514	688 968	421 568	484 757	604 305	373 890
Petroleum royalties	..	..	760 042	951 507	1 022 254	680 217	415 597	478 744	590 596	355 668
Surface royalties	..	..	425	844	766	1 842	619	530	1 794	400
Fishing and concessional royalties	..	..	3 380	4 850	5 493	6 909	5 352	5 483	11 915	17 822
GEOGAM gas sales	..	..	0	0	0	0	0	0	0	0
Interest and dividends	..	..	218 849	437 662	491 591	380 575	206 307	244 266	328 453	206 720
Shareholder participation in oil revenues	..	..	156 003	257 392	325 264	237 800	103 899	99 609	134 422	108 655
Oil dividends	..	..	42 987	146 345	144 237	134 965	84 190	132 925	185 706	93 018
Non-oil dividends	..	..	2 581	17 314	15 601	7 538	17 339	11 522	7 794	1 454
Interest on reserve funds	..	..	16 334	6 977	489	43	45	12	498	3 561
Other interest (banking, deferrals)	..	..	944	9 635	5 674	52	43	8	1	0
INSESO: Interest and dividends	..	..	..	..	326	178	792	191	32	33
Other property income	..	..	432 528	94 155	4 732	18 145	21 889	13 168	30 119	15 043
Contributions of public companies and independent entitites	..	..	20	1 624	3 773	4 149	21 889	9 744	26 104	15 037
Other oil-related property income	..	..	432 507	92 531	959	13 997	0	3 424	4 015	6
Sales of goods and services	..	..	11 350	15 935	26 515	24 901	27 212	20 154	17 470	17 384
Administrative fees and government services	..	..	9 932	13 975	21 821	19 669	19 335	15 052	14 234	13 929
Consular fees	..	..	1 034	1 357	906	973	875	561	1 694	123
Tolls	..	..	235	458	1 000	2 714	509	0	383	2 249
Rentals of government buildings	..	..	149	145	189	132	191	69	139	42
INSESO: Medical goods and services	..	..	..	..	2 491	1 355	6 042	1 147	875	893
INSESO: Other goods and services	..	..	..	..	108	59	262	139	144	147
INSESO: Provincial medical fees	..	..	..	..	0	0	0	3 186	0	0
Fines, penalties and forfeits	..	..	0	0	269	258	199	462	451	461
INSESO: Sanctions, arrears and penalties	..	..	..	..	269	258	199	462	451	461
Miscellaneous and unidentified revenue	..	..	22 380	10 307	27 716	56 481	8 492	31 837	10 843	4 286
Total tax and non-tax revenue	..	..	2 354 613	2 127 636	2 629 588	2 105 235	1 157 882	1 265 740	1 471 741	1 269 702

.. Not available

Note: Year ending 31st December.

The data are on a cash basis.

Disaggregated figures for non-tax revenues collected by the Instituto Nacional de Seguridad Social de Guinea Ecuatorial (INSESO) were not available for the year 2019. Individual line items labelled "INSESO" in this table under 2019 were estimated by applying the revenue breakdown for INSESO revenues in 2018 to the known total INSESO revenus for 2019. This affects interest and dividends; sales of goods and services; fines, penalties and forfeits; and miscellaneous and unidentified revenues.

Source: Ministry of Finance, Economy and Planning; Instituto Nacional de Seguridad Social de Guinea Ecuatorial (INSESO).

StatLink https://doi.org/10.1787/888934284488

Table 6.15. **Eswatini**

Details of non-tax revenue / Recettes non fiscales détaillées

Million SZL

	1999	2000	2009	2010	2014	2015	2016	2017	2018	2019
Total non-tax revenue	**1 404**	**1 546**	**5 611**	**2 668**	**7 958**	**7 542**	**6 734**	**8 378**	**7 297**	**8 301**
Grants[1]	0	0	0	0	0	0	0	0	0	0
Property income	141	95	282	553	353	494	1 196	1 038	1 069	1 784
Rents and royalties	0	0	1	3	56	72	75	81	81	143
Land concession rents, postal revenue	0	0	0	0	0	0	0	0	0	0
Rents attributed to social security funds	0	0	1	3	56	72	75	81	81	143
Interest and dividends	117	91	279	548	283	391	878	896	919	1 546
Local interest collected by central government	39	21	123	538	0	60	7	-30	28	16
Central bank profit	0	0	145	0	214	245	287	244	0	430
External interest and interest on capital	74	69	1	0	11	0	2	4	3	2
Dividends	4	1	9	8	0	11	115	115	106	207
Interest and dividends collected by social security funds	0	0	1	1	58	75	467	564	783	891
Other property income	24	4	1	1	13	31	244	62	69	95
Quitrents	0	0	0	0	0	0	0	0	0	0
Local government property income	24	4	1	1	13	31	244	62	69	95
Sales of goods and services	38	40	116	115	71	73	216	154	325	137
Sundry fees	7	13	54	38	6	6	144	64	246	39
Passports, citizenship and resident permits	5	5	24	25	25	25	29	35	33	40
Rental of government real estate	3	3	7	7	10	11	12	13	13	13
Driver's licences, motor vehicle certification	1	1	5	8	8	11	15	14	15	16
Hospital and medical services	4	5	6	6	7	6	7	7	8	8
Hire of government plants and vehicles	0	0	13	21	0	0	0	0	0	0
Aviation fees	14	12	1	0	0	0	0	0	0	0
Sale of government furniture and vehicles	0	0	1	6	6	7	1	10	2	2
Sale of agricultural products and services	2	2	1	1	3	2	3	3	3	3
Public service transport fees	1	0	1	1	2	1	1	1	1	1
Sale of government publications	0	0	1	1	1	1	2	1	1	1
Prison industry sales	0	0	0	0	0	0	0	0	0	0
Local government sales of goods and services	0	0	2	1	2	2	3	5	5	14
Fines, penalties and forfeits	3	4	20	28	32	33	42	43	46	49
Traffic fines	2	2	10	15	15	13	14	15	15	16
Judicial fines and other penalties	1	1	9	10	15	18	22	24	24	25
Interest and penalties on late tax payments	0	0	1	1	2	2	5	5	4	5
PAYE penalties[2]	1	1	1	1	0	0	0	0	0	0
Fines, penalties and forfeits (local non-tax revenue)	0	0	0	0	0	0	0	0	3	2
Miscellaneous and unidentified revenue	1 222	1 407	5 192	1 972	7 502	6 942	5 280	7 143	5 856	6 332
SACU revenue	1 221	1 406	5 189	1 969	7 487	6 931	5 252	7 109	5 844	6 318
SACU penalties	0	0	2	2	14	9	12	18	9	7
Miscellaneous and unidentified revenue (local non-tax revenue)	0	0	2	2	1	3	16	16	3	7
Total tax and non-tax revenue	2 675	2 872	9 586	7 255	15 253	15 449	15 874	18 479	18 188	20 194

Note: Data are reported on a fiscal year basis beginning 1st April. For example, the data for 2019 represent April 2019 to March 2020.

The data are on a cash basis.

Revenues from motor vehicle licences, the change of ownership fees and the registration of new motor vehicles are considered as tax revenue under the OECD classification as set out in the Interpretative Guide in Annex A and are classified under Heading 5211 (Recurrent taxes paid by households: motor vehicles). The national classification of Eswatini classifies these revenues as non-tax revenues.

Revenues from business and sundry licences are considered as tax revenue under the OECD classification, as set out in the Interpretative Guide in Annex A and are classified under Heading 5211 (Recurrent taxes paid on use of goods and perform activities other than on motor vehicles). The national classification of Eswatini classifies these revenues as non-tax revenues. The revenues from the registrations of specific goods (e.g. firearms) are considered as tax revenue under the OECD classification, as set out in the Interpretative Guide in Annex A and are classified under Heading 5220 (Non-recurrent taxes on use of goods and perform activities). The national classification of Eswatini classifies these revenues as non-tax revenues. The revenues from the education loans' repayments do not represent an increase of net worth resulting from a transaction and therefore are not considered as revenues under the OECD classification, as set out in the Interpretative Guide in Annex B.

Revenues from the registrations of specific goods (e.g. firearms) are considered as tax revenue under the OECD classification, as set out in the Interpretative Guide in Annex A and are classified under Heading 5220 (Non-recurrent taxes on use of goods and perform activities). The national classification of Eswatini classifies these revenues as non-tax revenues. The revenues from the education loans' repayments do not represent an increase of net worth resulting from a transaction and therefore are not considered as revenues under the OECD classification, as set out in the Interpretative Guide in Annex B.

Revenues from the education loans' repayments do not represent an increase of net worth resulting from a transaction and therefore are not considered as revenues under the OECD classification, as set out in the Interpretative Guide in Annex B.

Grants: The data are not available up to 2011.

Revenue from PAYE Penalties, tax interests and penalties on taxes are considered as non-tax revenue under the OECD classification, as set out in the Interpretative Guide in Annex A. The national classification of Eswatini classifies it as tax revenues.

1. The data are not available up to 2011.
2. Revenue from PAYE Penalties, tax interests and penalties on taxes are considered as non-tax revenue under the OECD classification, as set out in the Interpretative Guide in Annex A. The national classification of Eswatini classifies it as tax revenues.

Source: Eswatini Revenue Authority; Local Government; Eswatini National Provident Fund and Public Service Pension Fund; Ministry of Economic Planning and Development; Central Government.

StatLink https://doi.org/10.1787/888934284507

Table 6.16. **Ghana**

Details of non-tax revenue / Recettes non fiscales détaillées

Million GHS

	1999	2000	2009	2010	2014	2015	2016	2017	2018	2019
Total non-tax revenue	**..**	**97**	**1 972**	**2 306**	**6 369**	**8 512**	**6 777**	**8 199**	**9 594**	**10 801**
Grants	..	57	1 101	1 080	814	2 689	1 141	1 535	1 135	986
Project grants	..	24	544	591	787	1 744	1 034	1 535	1 121	986
Programme grants	..	34	399	288	27	945	106	0	14	0
International debt relief	..	0	158	201	0	0	0	0	0	0
Property income	..	7	355	347	2 727	2 628	1 803	3 263	4 639	5 125
Rents and royalties	..	0	0	0	1 075	908	757	1 346	1 969	2 328
Mineral royalties (aside from oil)	..	..	..	..	517	518	578	749	744	1 057
Oil revenues	..	..	..	..	554	384	176	589	1 213	1 252
Lodgements to MDAs and MMDAs: surface rentals from oil/PHF interest	..	..	..	..	4	6	3	8	12	19
Lodgements to MDAs and MMDAs: fees from granting of new stability agreements	..	..	..	..	0	0	0	0	0	0
Revenue from oil companies (includes corporate tax)	..	..	..	..	0	0	0	0	0	0
Interest and dividends	..	7	355	347	1 653	1 720	1 046	1 916	2 670	2 797
Lodgements to MDAs and MMDAs: dividend, interest and profits from oil companies	..	0	0	0	1 435	995	491	1 586	2 531	2 691
Lodgements to MDAs and MMDAs: dividend, interest and profits aside from oil companies	..	7	355	347	218	726	556	331	139	106
Other property income	..	0	0	0	0	0	0	0	0	0
Sales of goods and services	..	32	515	879	2 827	3 195	3 833	3 401	3 719	4 576
Retentions by MDAs and MMDAs	..	23	409	685	2 497	2 531	3 368	2 849	3 165	3 953
Lodgements to MDAs and MMDAs: fees and charges	..	10	106	194	330	663	466	553	555	623
Lodgements to MDAs and MMDAs: gas receipts	..	0	0	0	0	2	0	0	0	0
Fines, penalties and forfeits	..	0	0	0	0	0	0	0	0	0
Miscellaneous and unidentified revenue	..	0	0	0	0	0	0	0	101	115
Yield from budget capping policy	..	..	..	..	..	..	..	..	101	115
Total tax and non-tax revenue	..	584	7 124	9 001	25 312	32 104	36 272	43 499	51 964	58 114

.. Not available

Note: Year ending 31st December.

The data are on a cash basis.

Figures exclude non-tax revenues collected by sub-national governments as the data are not available.

Revenues for MDAs (Municipalities, Departments and Agencies) and MMDAs (Metropolitan, Municipal and District Assemblies) contain a mixture of revenues collected at the local level, and revenues collected at a federal level. These are reported as revenues to the central government.

Yield from budget capping policy has been added to the classification in this edition. The Earmarked Funds and Capping Realignment Bill was passed into law in 2017.

Source: Ghana Statistical Service.

StatLink https://doi.org/10.1787/888934284520

Table 6.17. **Kenya**

Details of non-tax revenue / Recettes non fiscales détaillées

Million KES

	1999	2000	2009	2010	2014	2015	2016	2017	2018	2019
Total non-tax revenue	**..**	**..**	**65 325**	**33 643**	**76 497**	**113 760**	**119 549**	**156 955**	**164 490**	**146 138**
Grants	..	..	39 337	14 060	27 397	29 501	37 452	42 110	55 858	30 218
Grants from foreign governments - Capital	..	..	19 669	0	7 355	2 644	2 641	1 831	354	215
Grants from foreign governments - Current	..	..	0	0	0	0	0	0	2 342	2 074
Grants from foreign governments - Cash through exchequer	..	..	10 676	3 108	514	1 383	1 573	1 423	2 342	2 074
Grants from foreign governments - Direct payments treated as Appropriations in Aid (AIA)	..	..	8 992	6 107	6 841	16 098	16 275	12 840	17 658	15
Grants from International orgs - Capital	..	..	0	0	0	5 533	5 914	11 514	12 029	6 734
Grants from International orgs - Current	..	..	0	0	0	3 843	4 757	6 440	11 759	10 668
Grants from International orgs - Cash through Exchequer	..	..	0	4 845	5 205	0	6 293	8 062	9 374	8 437
Grants from International orgs - Direct payments-Treated as Appropriations in Aid (AIA)	..	..	0	0	7 482	0	0	0	0	0
Property income	..	..	9 616	9 921	11 876	16 216	22 309	34 049	43 670	49 308
Rents and royalties	..	..	1 134	1 184	1 694	695	743	665	1 606	1 604
Rent of land	..	..	1 063	1 108	1 588	8	25	38	753	638
Kenya Airports Authority (KAA) concession fees	..	..	71	77	106	113	114	127	131	134
Base titanium royalty	..	..	0	0	0	338	356	295	491	520
Mining royalties	..	..	0	0	0	136	143	118	95	117
Royalties from soda ash	..	..	0	0	0	100	105	87	135	195
Interest and dividends	..	..	8 483	8 736	5 865	10 781	18 225	28 053	34 137	39 704
Profits and dividends	..	..	6 919	8 354	5 865	9 002	15 919	26 022	32 023	37 526
Interests	..	..	1 564	382	0	1 779	2 306	2 032	2 114	2 178
Other property income	..	..	0	0	4 317	4 740	3 341	5 330	7 927	8 000
Surplus funds from regulatory authority	..	..	0	0	4 317	4 740	3 341	5 330	7 927	8 000
Sales of goods and services	..	..	2 773	2 302	28 990	45 303	47 042	46 601	47 730	55 382
Work permits	..	..	0	0	900	4 098	5 226	5 363	2	8 333
Road transit toll	..	..	463	457	495	562	674	737	766	840
Immigration visas and other consular fees	..	..	0	0	606	2 822	3 063	3 144	8 980	5 083
Fees under traffic act	..	..	1 659	1 188	108	0	0	0	1 326	1 647
Land administration fees	..	..	0	0	148	1 826	586	915	722	959
Motor driver's licences	..	..	650	656	0	0	0	1 270	0	0
Passport fees	..	..	0	0	125	570	845	867	1 116	2 461
Rent of government buildings and housing	..	..	0	0	54	135	213	332	157	690
Other fees for administrative services	..	..	0	0	128	556	542	556	902	1 870
Hire of security service fees	..	..	0	0	18	372	321	330	854	566
Registration of organisations, professionals and agreements	..	..	0	0	46	296	360	369	36	121
Registration of births, deaths and marriages	..	..	0	0	62	214	193	198	370	313
Other non-tax revenue collected by local government	..	..	..	..	26 300	33 850	35 020	32 520	32 500	32 500
Fines, penalties and forfeits	..	..	140	229	1 443	1 459	1 470	1 098	1 124	1 567
Miscellaneous and unidentified revenue	..	..	13 460	7 131	6 792	21 281	11 275	33 097	16 108	9 663
Contribution from government employees to social and welfare schemes within government	..	..	0	341	204	871	462	390	203	213
National Social Security Fund	..	..	5 355	6 790	6 588	9 210	9 486	9 491	9 988	9 160
Other Miscellaneous	..	..	8 105	0	0	11 200	1 327	23 216	5 917	290
Total tax and non-tax revenue	..	..	550 767	573 806	1 053 411	1 198 979	1 351 320	1 556 611	1 647 088	1 755 883

.. Not available

Note: Data are reported on a fiscal year basis beginning 1st July. For example, the data for 2019 represent July 2018 to June 2019.

The data are on a cash basis.

Detailed non-tax revenue data are not readily available for 2001, 2002, 2003, 2004, 2006, 2011 and 2012. Figures exclude non-tax revenues collected by sub-national governments as the data are not available.

The national classification of Kenya classifies revenues from the airport revenue, aviation revenue, petroleum development levy, FMV, road maintenance levy, sugar levy, petroleum regulatory levy, merchant superintendent shipping levy, railway development levy, revenue Stamps, KEBS and land rates as non-tax revenues. They are considered in this publication as tax revenues under the OECD classification, as set out in the Interpretative Guide in Annex A.

Source: Kenya Revenue Authority Statistical Service.

StatLink https://doi.org/10.1787/888934284545

Table 6.18. **Lesotho**

Details of non-tax revenue / Recettes non fiscales détaillées

Million LSL

	1999	2000	2009	2010	2014	2015	2016	2017	2018	2019
Total non-tax revenue	**..**	**..**	**6 576**	**5 786**	**9 312**	**9 113**	**7 609**	**8 900**	**8 813**	**9 043**
Grants	..	..	731	1 306	635	966	1 229	1 005	1 373	1 256
Property income	..	..	418	1 284	728	829	816	657	819	628
Rents and royalties	..	..	301	598	416	428	454	445	501	452
Water royalties	..	..	166	133	172	175	204	141	144	107
Mining and other royalties	..	..	135	465	244	252	251	304	357	345
Interest and dividends	..	..	117	686	312	401	362	213	319	176
Other property income	..	..	0	0	0	0	0	0	0	0
Sales of goods and services	..	..	509	568	915	919	1 045	1 084	1 082	917
Fines, penalties and forfeits	..	..	0	0	0	0	0	0	0	16
Miscellaneous and unidentified revenue	..	..	4 918	2 628	7 034	6 398	4 519	6 154	5 538	6 226
SACU revenue	..	..	4 918	2 628	7 034	6 398	4 519	6 154	5 538	6 226
Total tax and non-tax revenue	..	..	9 171	8 719	14 494	14 974	13 597	14 890	15 796	16 005
Total non-tax revenue excluding grants	..	..	5 845	4 480	8 677	8 147	6 380	7 895	7 439	7 787
Memo items:										
Excise taxes collected on behalf of the SACU Common Revenue Pool	..	..	99	110	108	102	128	191	212	215
Import duties collected on behalf of the SACU Common Revenue Pool	..	..	25	32	94	145	108	121	145	147

.. Not available

Note: Data are on a fiscal year basis beginning 1st April. For example, the data for 2019 represent April 2019 to March 2020.

Data are reported on a cash basis.

Source: Lesotho Revenue Authority.

StatLink https://doi.org/10.1787/888934284564

Table 6.19. **Madagascar**

Details of non-tax revenue / Recettes non fiscales détaillées

Million MGA

	1999	2000	2009	2010	2014	2015	2016	2017	2018	2019
Total des recettes non fiscales	**0**	**172 677**	**354 828**	**619 717**	**656 663**	**504 711**	**726 921**	**929 098**	**1 340 511**	**1 385 109**
Dons	0	153 554	272 643	351 388	592 127	423 925	611 340	806 948	1 207 985	1 240 807
Dons - programmes des gouvernements étrangers	..	0	0	0	206 018	39 869	226 095	292 600	410 118	356 627
Dons - projets des institutions internationales	..	153 554	256 408	336 704	386 109	384 056	385 245	514 348	797 867	884 180
Ressources PPTE	..	0	16 235	14 684	0	0	0	0	0	0
Revenus de la propriété	0	17 649	78 711	266 340	50 097	59 980	94 467	107 633	109 916	119 659
Loyers et redevances	..	5 649	46 785	241 311	16 061	14 064	12 024	8 634	14 663	12 931
Intérêts et dividendes	..	12 000	31 926	25 029	34 036	45 916	82 443	98 999	95 253	106 728
Autres revenus de la propriété	..	0	0	0	0	0	0	0	0	0
Ventes de biens et de services	0	1 474	1 779	1 989	12 228	5 225	20 389	4 886	3 778	4 757
Amendes, pénalités et confiscations	0	0	0	0	0	0	0	0	0	0
Recettes diverses et non identifiées	0	0	1 695	0	2 211	15 581	725	9 631	18 832	19 886
Total des recettes fiscales et non fiscales	523 080	775 877	2 140 018	2 600 566	3 358 580	3 650 753	4 507 907	5 416 139	6 639 267	7 273 981

.. Non disponible

Note : Année civile se terminant le 31 décembre.

Les données sont sur la base des encaissements.

Les chiffres n'incluent pas les recettes non fiscales collectées par les collectivités locales car elles ne sont pas disponibles.

Source : Ministère de l'Économie et des Finances de Madagascar.

StatLink https://doi.org/10.1787/888934284583

Table 6.20. **Malawi**

Details of non-tax revenue / Recettes non fiscales détaillées

Million MWK

	1999	2000	2009	2010	2014	2015	2016	2017	2018	2019
Total non-tax revenue	..	..	**89 761**	**105 601**	**112 961**	**124 112**	**159 138**	**202 474**	**126 362**	**145 819**
Grants	..	..	75 980	78 448	79 183	79 392	131 007	147 706	70 155	109 255
Grants from foreign governments - Current	..	..	14 766	18 782	25 055	20 769	12 323	8 962	0	0
Grants from foreign governments - Capital	..	..	24 347	25 844	41 046	47 519	49 542	73 505	44 300	0
Grants from international orgs - Current	..	..	36 866	33 822	13 083	10 711	67 302	65 239	25 855	30 705
Grants from international orgs - Capital	..	..	0	0	0	393	1 840	0	0	78 551
Property income	..	..	0	3 466	20 638	32 815	13 653	22 837	20 083	7 555
Rents and royalties	..	..	..	0	0	0	0	0	0	0
Interest and dividends	..	..	..	3 466	20 638	32 815	13 653	22 837	20 083	7 555
Parastatal dividends	..	..	..	3 466	20 638	32 815	13 653	22 837	20 083	7 555
Other property income	..	..	..	0	0	0	0	0	0	0
Sales of goods and services	..	..	8 633	13 724	10 667	11 397	14 478	20 607	34 639	27 064
Fertiliser sales revenue	..	..	3 236	736	0	0	0	0	0	0
Receipts from fertiliser option	..	..	0	0	0	0	0	0	0	0
Maize sales	..	..	0	0	0	0	0	0	0	0
Departmental receipts	..	..	5 396	12 988	10 667	11 397	14 478	20 607	34 639	27 064
Fines, penalties and forfeits	..	..	133	205	2 472	509	0	0	1 485	1 945
Penalties	..	..	133	205	2 472	509	..	..	1 485	1 945
Miscellaneous and unidentified revenue	..	..	5 015	9 758	0	0	0	11 325	0	0
Other current transfers not elsewhere classified	..	..	5 015	9 758	..	..	..	11 325	..	..
Total tax and non-tax revenue	..	..	214 024	258 346	522 419	609 438	763 359	998 258	1 007 257	1 132 530

.. Not available

Note: Data are on a fiscal year basis beginning 1st July. For example, the data for 2019 represent July 1, 2018 to June 30, 2019. 2018 and 2019 figures are projections.

Figures exclude revenues from business licenses and permits collected by city and district councils from business entities within their jurisdictions.

Source: Ministry of Finance, Economic Planning and Development of Malawi.

StatLink https://doi.org/10.1787/888934284602

Table 6.21. **Mali**

Details of non-tax revenue / Recettes non fiscales détaillées

Million XOF

	1999	2000	2009	2010	2014	2015	2016	2017	2018	2019
Total des recettes non fiscales	**60 940**	**122 795**	**341 060**	**256 632**	**227 378**	**197 471**	**175 908**	**311 733**	**224 545**	**314 056**
Dons	41 748	102 481	296 785	190 540	162 500	112 124	98 310	159 914	136 049	208 841
Dons - gouvernements étrangers	0	0	45 520	22 263	18 188	20 665	8 639	14 208	6 129	8 056
Dons - institutions internationales	41 748	102 481	243 150	160 368	127 529	79 066	71 942	127 477	110 927	183 184
Ressources PPTE	0	0	8 115	7 909	12 909	12 393	17 729	18 229	18 993	17 601
Ressources exceptionnelles: reconversion dette monétaire fonds de concours	0	0	0	0	3 874	0	0	0	0	0
Revenus de la propriété	5 680	9 669	23 104	34 564	35 055	46 966	33 747	115 029	48 426	60 664
Loyers et redevances	252	358	245	650	756	1 735	750	81 041	21 023	15 877
Concessions ordinaires	233	336	245	262	401	1 315	276	80 510	20 425	15 049
Redevances superficiaires	19	22	0	388	263	262	240	421	371	465
Taxe d'extraction	0	0	0	0	92	158	234	110	107	364
Autres loyers et redevances - extrabudgétaires	0	0	0	0	0	0	0	0	121	..
Intérêts et dividendes	5 428	9 311	22 191	32 873	34 118	44 810	32 544	33 252	25 157	43 745
Revenus des valeurs mobilières, des titres et des dividendes	5 406	9 296	20 995	30 500	30 745	41 261	29 761	8 059	7 201	24 624
Autres intérêts et dividendes (budget d'état)	22	15	0	0	0	0	0	21 563	15 726	17 093
Interêts des comptes bancaires (INPS)	0	0	1 196	2 373	3 373	3 549	2 783	3 630	2 230	2 029
Autres revenus de la propriété	0	0	669	1 041	181	420	453	736	2 246	1 041
Autres revenus de la propriété (CMSS)	..	..	0	0	48	140	142	87	47	..
Autres revenus de la propriété (INPS)	..	..	669	1 041	133	281	311	649	2 199	1 041
Ventes de biens et de services	4 002	3 924	7 561	13 208	12 091	22 849	23 991	19 947	21 868	21 418
Prestations, évacuations, importations, exportations - extrabudgétaires	0	0	0	0	0	0	0	0	3 351	..
Droits de chancellerie	410	886	2 215	2 152	2 225	4 310	3 033	3 914	4 255	9 033
Passeports et cartes d'identités,	377	473	2 391	2 609	3 487	2 680	1 494	1 352	3 251	5 345
Recettes sur rôles (Trésor - BN)	1 619	981	37	91	0	0	0	0	0	0
Frais d'administration, voitures	402	497	866	813	1 021	1 200	1 342	1 355	1 137	1 163
Ventes en douanes	10	15	62	117	12	26	66	18	19	87
Location des immeubles de l'état	1	393	0	0	0	0	29	0	0	0
Autres ventes de biens et de services (budget d'état)	1 183	679	419	6 460	3 701	12 598	14 571	8 206	6 584	2 917
Recettes de la Caisse Malienne de Sécurité Sociale (CMSS) - hors cotisations	0	0	726	699	999	905	1 672	1 146	779	..
Recettes de l'Institut National de Prévoyance Sociale (INPS) - hors cotisations	0	0	845	267	646	1 040	1 784	3 956	1 436	2 872
Location des immeubles de l'état - extrabudgétaires	..	..	0	0	0	0	0	0	517	..
Autres ventes de biens et de services - extrabudgétaires	..	..	0	0	0	0	0	0	540	..
Amendes, pénalités et confiscations	2 894	2 780	8 462	8 010	9 782	12 704	15 196	7 289	8 753	16 288
Pénalités sur impots directs	123	352	1 911	3 939	4 742	4 753	7 580	3 529	2 983	4 481
Pénalités sur impôts indirects	2 029	1 528	2 789	1 418	2 729	3 101	3 794	1 247	1 800	5 197
Amendes et confiscations	541	710	2 137	1 268	1 292	2 738	2 357	1 301	1 487	2 007
Transactions forestières, pêche et chasse	76	98	93	153	137	0	0	0	0	0
Frais et amendes judiciaires	125	98	344	249	258	397	386	302	296	..
Autres pénalités (budget d'état)	0	0	353	77	87	624	69	51	50	96
Pénalités et frais contentieux (INPS)	0	0	835	906	537	1 151	1 010	859	2 137	4 507
Recettes diverses et non identifiées	6 616	3 935	5 147	10 309	7 950	2 769	4 665	9 554	9 448	6 846
Compensations des moins values de recettes	0	0	0	0	0	0	0	0	0	0
Amendes arbitrées	287	268	353	66	112	41	80	94	60	89
Autres recettes diverses	6 329	3 667	4 794	10 243	7 838	2 728	4 585	9 460	8 099	6 756
Autres recettes diverses - extrabudgétaires	..	..	..	..	..	..	..	..	1 289	..
Total des recettes fiscales et non fiscales	304 111	362 157	1 033 638	1 004 877	1 216 339	1 372 331	1 547 057	1 803 523	1 488 463	2 021 283
Pour mémoire : Redevances Statistiques (taxe UEMOA)	1 326	1 394	0	0	0	0	0	0	0	0

.. Non disponible

Note : Année civile se terminant le 31 décembre.

Les données sont sur la base des encaissements.

Les chiffres n'incluent pas les recettes non fiscales collectées par les collectivités locales car elles ne sont pas disponibles.

Les recettes sur prestations sportives étaient sous la rubrique « Recettes diverses et non identifiées » dans les éditions précédentes, mais sont désormais classifiées sous la rubrique « Ventes de biens et de services ».

Les aliénations des immeubles et les subventions des entrepôts ne sont plus considérés des recettes publiques du Mali dans les Statistiques des recettes publiques en Afrique.

Source : Ministère de l'Économie et des Finances et la Direction Nationale du Trésor et de la Comptabilité Publique du Mali.

StatLink https://doi.org/10.1787/888934284621

Table 6.22. **Mauritania / Mauritanie**

Details of non-tax revenue / Recettes non fiscales détaillées

Million MRU

	1999	2000	2009	2010	2014	2015	2016	2017	2018	2019
Total des recettes non fiscales	**..**	**..**	**7 841**	**9 833**	**11 877**	**12 868**	**10 914**	**11 469**	**18 008**	**15 862**
Dons	..	..	3	830	0	1 988	1 600	1 096	201	2 211
Dons courants états étrangers	..	..	3	0	0	1 988	1 600	1 096	0	0
Dons courants organismes	..	..	0	830	0	0	0	0	201	2 211
Revenus de la propriété	..	..	6 906	8 164	10 823	9 551	7 936	9 343	15 148	11 783
Loyers et redevances	..	..	5 565	6 835	6 965	8 112	6 900	8 180	13 840	10 612
Accords de pêche	..	..	3 733	3 945	3 263	4 068	4 966	5 048	5 859	6 665
Droits d'accès pêche	..	..	259	208	236	318	850	1 524	1 643	869
Licences télécom et sanctions	..	..	93	3	544	1 906	451	464	452	347
Mine : permis d'exploitation et de recherche	..	..	482	1 562	797	635	613	620	615	902
Pétrole : bonus de signature	..	..	0	65	60	0	0	460	5 141	1 637
Pétrole : redevances et autres	..	..	989	1 035	2 037	1 150	11	24	85	123
Redevances et concessions domaniales	..	..	10	16	28	35	10	39	45	69
Intérêts et dividendes	..	..	1 341	1 329	3 858	1 439	1 035	1 161	1 308	1 171
Autres revenus de la propriété	..	..	0	0	0	0	0	3	0	0
Ventes de biens et de services	..	..	114	106	410	486	468	447	508	458
Visas	..	..	0	0	67	150	231	162	179	178
Passeport	..	..	0	0	134	102	86	149	167	93
Carte grise et permis de conduire	..	..	0	0	51	54	34	24	40	59
Frais administratifs	..	..	114	106	159	181	118	92	98	106
Frais universités, instituts et centres nationaux	..	..	0	0	0	0	0	20	24	21
Amendes, pénalités et confiscations	..	..	178	206	389	393	458	366	519	476
Amendes de pêche	..	..	105	75	69	57	57	130	80	139
Autres amendes	..	..	73	131	320	336	401	236	439	336
Recettes diverses et non identifiées	..	..	640	526	255	450	453	218	1 632	934
Total des recettes fiscales et non fiscales	..	..	20 664	25 008	42 041	41 938	42 836	46 597	58 325	56 466

.. Non disponible

Note : Année civile se terminant le 31 décembre.

Les données sont sur la base des encaissements

Les données de cette édition sont en monnaie MRU, devise officielle de la Mauritanie depuis le 1er janvier 2018. Elle remplace la monnaie MRO, devise utilisée dans les éditions précédentes.

Les chiffres n'incluent pas les recettes des droits de conservation foncière . Elles sont incluses dans les recettes fiscales comme le préconise la classification OCDE (voir le guide d'interprétation en Annexe A) mais considérées comme des recettes non fiscales en Mauritanie.

Source : Ministère des Finances de la Mauritanie

StatLink https://doi.org/10.1787/888934284640

Table 6.23. **Mauritius / Maurice**

Details of non-tax revenue / Recettes non fiscales détaillées

Million MUR

	1999	2000	2009	2010	2014	2015	2016	2017	2018	2019
Total non-tax revenue	**3 278**	**3 293**	**11 914**	**11 458**	**11 517**	**11 331**	**13 644**	**16 627**	**20 279**	**14 070**
Grants	135	161	2 783	1 991	940	1 202	345	2 920	2 635	1 998
Grants from foreign governments	..	..	1	2	569	183	122	1 915	2 248	1 580
Grants from international organizations	..	..	2 782	1 989	371	1 019	223	1 005	387	418
Property income	2 339	2 370	6 627	5 020	5 193	3 604	5 048	4 583	5 060	4 151
Rents and royalties	0	0	962	1 284	1 087	752	961	960	1 171	1 192
Interest and dividends	0	0	1 344	979	1 404	873	679	534	1 051	430
Interest	..	..	415	392	461	382	360	236	271	244
Dividends	..	..	929	587	943	492	319	298	780	186
Other property income	2 339	2 370	4 320	2 756	2 701	1 979	3 408	3 089	2 838	2 529
Other property income - Budgetary	1 838	1 692	2 406	1 549	1 437	1 392	2 289	1 810	1 039	1 138
Other property income - Extra-budgetary	33	58	504	349	170	33	22	63	235	235
Other property income - Social security funds	404	544	1 313	777	1 038	529	1 058	1 169	1 531	1 103
Other property income - Regional	0	0	10	11	11	5	5	13	12	19
Other property income - Local	64	76	87	71	46	20	34	34	20	34
Sales of goods and services	542	626	1 810	2 028	3 738	3 644	3 800	3 889	4 056	4 358
Work/occupational permits	0	0	66	95	205	194	203	205	266	277
Extra-budgetary fees, charges, and non-industrial sales	141	177	571	543	1 118	1 219	1 054	1 180	1 671	1 362
Fees, charges, and non-industrial sales by social security funds	16	20	0	51	140	78	156	159	0	271
Regional government sales of goods and services	0	0	4	5	7	4	4	9	11	7
Local government sales of goods and services	41	60	98	113	691	353	713	678	445	619
Other sales of goods and services	345	370	1 071	1 222	1 577	1 797	1 669	1 658	1 663	1 821
Fines, penalties and forfeits	46	65	219	272	332	292	247	305	284	359
Budgetary fines, penalties and forfeits	46	65	198	269	326	290	244	251	238	339
Extra-budgetary fines, penalties and forfeits	0	0	19	0	2	0	0	49	34	0
Regional government fines, penalties and forfeits	0	0	2	3	4	2	2	5	5	5
Local government fines, penalties and forfeits	0	0	0	0	0	0	0	0	8	15
Miscellaneous and unidentified revenue	216	70	477	2 147	1 314	2 588	4 205	4 931	8 244	3 204
Budgetary miscellaneous and unidentified revenue	113	10	46	1 803	139	157	167	250	242	229
Extra-budgetary miscellaneous and unidentified revenue	97	44	365	203	1 173	1 092	1 771	4 460	3 085	1 209
Miscellaneous and unidentified revenue for social security funds	4	4	0	3	0	0	0	0	0	0
Regional government miscellaneous and unidentified revenue	0	0	3	1	1	0	1	52	1	0
Local government miscellaneous and unidentified revenue	3	13	63	47	0	0	0	0	3	11
Transfers from special funds	0	0	0	0	1	1 339	2 266	171	4 014	1 755
Total tax and non-tax revenue	22 868	25 439	67 191	69 862	87 294	90 555	95 983	105 211	116 031	117 456

.. Not available

Note: Data are on a fiscal year basis beginning 1st July for years prior to 2010 (for example the data for 2009 represent July 2008 to June 2009) and are on a calendar year basis from 2010-15. Mauritius went back to a July-June fiscal year in 2015. Figures for 2016 correspond to the July-June 2015/16 fiscal year, while figures for 2015 correspond to the January-December calendar year. The calendar year 2015 is not used in national budget reporting by Mauritius, which means that official figures are not available for all revenue categories for this period.

Where data were missing for 2015, quarterly revenue figures at the aggregate level were used along with fiscal year revenue data to produce estimates. The data are on a cash basis.

Revenues reported as "Transfers from special funds" in fact represent funds raised from various sources, including tax revenues, non-tax revenues, and inter-governmental transfers which are not properly classified as revenues. Special Funds are special purpose vehicles set up by way of legislation for a specific purpose, i.e., to finance a dedicated programme or projects. Funds are transferred to the Fund from the Consolidated Fund through an appropriate expenditure item in the budget. Such Funds also generate their own revenue in terms of, for example, a levy imposed on petroleum products or contributions from international institutions and friendly countries. As such, once the dedicated programme or projects are completed, the available balance in the Special Funds are transferred to the Consolidated Fund and reported as revenues in budget documents for Mauritius.

Source: Mauritius Revenue Authority for the central government budgetary tax data from 2007 to 2014. Statistics Mauritius for extra-budgetary, local government, regional government and social security revenues from 1990 to 2019, as well as for budgetary central government tax revenues up to 2006; Ministry of Finance budget estimates for detailed revenue figures for the periods July 2005-June 2008, for 2016-19, and for the figures used to estimate calendar year 2015 revenues.

StatLink https://doi.org/10.1787/888934284659

Table 6.24. **Morocco / Maroc**

Details of non-tax revenue / Recettes non fiscales détaillées

Million MAR

	1999	2000	2009	2010	2014	2015	2016	2017	2018	2019
Total des recettes non fiscales	..	**9 278**	**27 634**	**27 970**	**34 913**	**38 673**	**35 225**	**36 921**	**40 466**	**49 088**
Dons	..	2	1	199	0	0	0	0	0	0
Revenus de la propriété	..	3 125	9 470	9 786	10 938	8 934	9 425	8 604	9 836	10 401
Loyers et redevances	..	1 507	3 813	3 868	5 387	5 192	4 237	4 583	4 738	4 865
Redevance gazoduc	..	298	1 695	1 442	2 438	1 765	999	1 016	1 538	1 011
Redevances et contributions pour licence de pêche en haute mer	..	94	399	329	538	520	593	739	235	773
Redevances pour l'occupation du domaine public	..	132	233	331	279	281	195	257	273	260
Autres redevances	..	7	54	63	3	6	10	8	6	10
Loyers et redevances reçues par les collectivités locales	..	977	1 432	1 703	2 128	2 620	2 440	2 563	2 686	2 809
Intérêts et dividendes	..	1 618	5 657	5 918	5 551	3 742	5 188	4 021	5 098	5 537
Dividendes des monopoles	..	1 008	5 422	5 584	4 970	3 236	4 675	3 526	4 650	5 197
Intérêts sur placements et avances	..	419	20	96	322	195	199	174	119	4
Interêts et dividendes reçus par collectivités locales	..	191	215	239	259	311	315	322	329	336
Autres revenus de la propriété	..	0	0	0	0	0	0	0	0	0
Ventes de biens et de services	..	4 573	11 352	10 286	14 417	16 009	14 746	16 890	17 990	20 791
Cartes d'identités, passeports et documents divers	..	453	483	567	220	498	718	759	950	1 111
Produits de certains établissements publics	..	1 544	4 949	2 990	4 551	5 462	3 149	4 432	4 425	7 487
Revenus des immeubles domaniaux (loyers, charges locatives, etc.)	..	137	226	250	217	265	312	302	335	327
Autres produits et divers	..	175	663	646	864	965	791	1 199	1 661	825
Ventes de biens et de services par collectivités locales	..	2 265	5 031	5 832	8 566	8 819	9 777	10 198	10 619	11 040
Amendes, pénalités et confiscations	..	398	2 495	2 802	2 690	2 994	3 179	2 973	3 963	5 872
Amendes et condamnations pécuniaires	..	17	30	21	56	61	68	63	66	63
Amendes transactionnelles	..	36	149	130	893	706	593	471	481	425
Autres (produits des confiscations, pénalités et amendes autres que fiscales)	..	6	1	1	1	0	0	0	0	0
Majorations et pénalités	..	339	2 315	2 650	1 740	2 226	2 518	2 439	3 416	5 385
Recettes diverses et non identifiées	..	1 180	4 315	4 897	6 868	10 736	7 875	8 454	8 678	12 024
Fonds de concours	..	147	3 191	3 597	2 564	3 453	2 187	2 250	1 944	1 973
Recettes en atténuation des dépenses de la dette	..	801	230	480	2 230	4 386	1 894	691	963	3 164
Reversements sur traitements et salaires	..	55	249	99	63	62	60	1 300	957	919
Créances sur le trésor prescrites	..	30	54	39	78	97	163	260	305	866
Autres (divers remboursement à l'Etat)	..	7	6	6	396	254	254	46	11	12
Recettes diverses et non identifiées des collectivités locales	..	139	587	677	1 536	2 484	3 316	3 907	4 498	5 089
Total des recettes fiscales et non fiscales	..	100 178	234 991	244 738	291 835	303 742	313 649	334 103	353 162	375 614

.. Non disponible

Note : Année civile se terminant le 31 décembre.

Les données sont sur la base des encaissements.

Majorations et pénalités (DGI) : Les recettes des majorations et pénalités relatives aux impôts sont considérées comme des recettes non fiscales. La classification nationale du Maroc les compte comme des recettes fiscales.

Source : Ministère de l'Économie et des Finances.

StatLink https://doi.org/10.1787/888934284678

Table 6.25. **Namibia / Namibie**

Details of non-tax revenue / Recettes non fiscales détaillées

Million NAD

	1999	2000	2009	2010	2014	2015	2016	2017	2018	2019
Total non-tax revenue	**..**	**..**	**10 461**	**7 948**	**21 342**	**20 781**	**17 447**	**23 812**	**21 336**	**22 799**
Grants	..	..	201	24	110	152	0	1	72	98
Property income	..	..	1 218	1 373	2 334	2 568	2 474	3 026	2 571	2 653
Rents and royalties	..	..	585	1 015	1 377	1 482	1 477	1 691	1 869	1 520
Diamond royalties	..	..	231	602	1 043	1 060	978	1 203	1 255	707
Other mineral royalties	..	..	261	280	201	309	391	343	347	546
Fishing quota levies	..	..	93	133	133	113	108	145	267	267
Interest and dividends	..	..	634	358	957	1 086	997	1 335	702	1 133
Other property income	..	..	0	0	0	0	0	0	0	0
Sales of goods and services	..	..	421	534	734	628	835	1 092	1 228	1 027
Fines, penalties and forfeits	..	..	35	43	47	78	67	95	90	99
Miscellaneous and unidentified revenue	..	..	8 585	5 975	18 117	17 355	14 071	19 598	17 375	18 922
SACU Revenue Pool Share	..	..	8 585	5 975	18 117	17 355	14 071	19 598	17 375	18 922
Total tax and non-tax revenue	..	..	24 282	23 682	50 419	52 754	51 490	59 306	56 504	59 046

.. Not available

Note: Data are on a cash basis.

Data are on a fiscal year basis beginning 1st April. For example, the data for 2019 represent April 2019 to March 2020.

Figures exclude tax revenues collected by sub-national governments as the data are not available.

Source: Ministry of Finance of Namibia.

StatLink https://doi.org/10.1787/888934284697

Table 6.26. **Niger**

Details of non-tax revenue / Recettes non fiscales détaillées

Million XOF

	1999	2000	2009	2010	2014	2015	2016	2017	2018	2019
Total des recettes non fiscales	..	**65 671**	**158 246**	**179 681**	**326 622**	**323 732**	**313 103**	**388 363**	**510 606**	**576 125**
Dons	..	59 240	126 900	130 144	222 124	232 611	270 255	342 117	428 900	514 000
Revenus de la propriété	..	4 751	23 866	28 436	42 838	40 249	31 921	28 929	47 496	30 975
Loyers et redevances	..	4 673	12 759	14 977	34 589	32 963	19 974	16 095	38 235	16 258
Bonus de signature	..	0	0	0	16 082	17 044	0	0	22 974	0
Redevance minière (RM)	..	4 519	11 660	14 381	13 195	11 323	13 105	8 850	7 214	6 877
Redevance superficaire pétrole	..	0	0	0	3 064	2 776	3 093	3 138	3 046	4 443
Publicité foncière	..	50	498	429	1 024	950	1 476	2 149	2 650	1 801
Redevance superficaire mine	..	0	0	0	396	449	1 001	1 117	1 463	2 191
Retenue pour logements	..	6	0	25	276	173	165	228	139	182
Concessions provisoires	..	0	544	86	212	164	740	190	288	286
Permis de coupe de bois	..	65	34	42	277	52	358	295	191	277
Bornage de terrains	..	4	17	9	32	20	23	23	190	124
Concessions définitives	..	29	6	5	31	12	12	103	82	76
Intérêts et dividendes	..	0	10 950	13 166	7 990	6 996	11 613	12 459	8 864	14 333
Dividendes	..	..	7 716	12 081	2 994	2 990	3 990	7 542	5 263	10 558
Bénéfices pétroliers	..	..	0	0	4 857	3 577	3 674	4 042	3 430	3 651
Intérêts créditeurs	..	..	3 234	1 084	140	430	3 949	876	170	124
Autres revenus de la propriété	..	78	157	293	259	290	334	375	398	384
Droits d'occupation du domaine public	..	78	157	293	259	290	334	375	398	384
Ventes de biens et de services	..	85	2 835	289	39 120	36 492	2 730	4 733	15 429	7 503
Vente de licence de téléphonie cellulaire	..	0	0	0	34 000	34 000	0	0	10 000	2 000
Commission sur transferts banque centrale (BCEAO)	..	0	1 571	42	3 691	1 090	799	3 093	3 905	3 826
Vente passeports/visa interpol	..	0	0	0	288	469	961	760	731	1 076
Vaccination internationale	..	0	0	0	201	239	275	217	179	154
Emission cartes grises/transport	..	0	0	0	141	143	121	180	3	51
Recettes des régies forestières	..	30	171	159	263	127	46	26	20	13
Ventes imprimés DGI/DGD	..	0	0	0	90	104	51	74	43	13
Droit de chancellerie	..	0	3	3	4	76	8	10	17	10
Location d'immeubles	..	9	248	63	22	9	27	21	29	22
Autres ventes de biens et services	..	46	843	21	419	235	442	352	503	337
Amendes, pénalités et confiscations	..	1 348	2 240	3 816	6 653	6 744	4 215	7 433	9 612	10 908
Amendes et pénalités de la DGI	..	1 188	933	2 296	4 289	4 035	2 281	5 167	7 727	8 162
Amendes et frais de police	..	0	433	482	916	1 230	820	895	909	1 553
Amendes et confiscations	..	159	229	214	478	842	628	602	561	471
Amendes, frais et pénalités (gendarmerie et police)	..	0	614	769	861	595	428	707	266	431
Amendes et saisies forêts et chasse	..	1	22	45	84	26	9	8	32	212
Amendes et frais de justice	..	0	7	8	18	9	42	42	85	52
Amendes et saisies sur contrôle des prix-poids-mesure	..	0	1	1	7	8	7	13	32	26
Recettes diverses et non identifiées	..	248	2 405	16 995	15 887	7 635	3 983	5 151	9 168	12 739
Autres recettes diverses - Trésor National	..	0	1 000	16 461	15 155	4 921	3 021	3 681	8 539	12 386
Autres recettes diverses	..	248	364	420	732	779	962	1 269	251	188
Reversements UEMOA et produits divers ARC	..	0	1 041	114	0	1 935	0	0	0	0
Commissariat à l'Organisation du Hadjj et de la Oumra (COHO)	..	0	0	0	0	0	0	201	378	166
Total des recettes fiscales et non fiscales	..	181 490	515 695	553 142	989 793	1 044 271	958 003	1 003 807	1 307 277	1 362 476
Pour mémoire :										
Prélèvement communautaire de la CEDEAO	..	448	2 650	5 302	4 433	4 893	3 961	0	0	7 651
Prélèvement communautaire UEMOA	..	866	0	0	0	0	4 518	0	0	6 540

Table 6.26. **Niger** *(cont.)*

Details of non-tax revenue / Recettes non fiscales détaillées

.. Non disponible

Note : Année civile se terminant le 31 décembre.

Les données sont sur la base des encaissements.

Les chiffres n'incluent pas les données des recettes non fiscales collectées par les collectivités locales car elles ne sont pas disponibles.

Les données des dons sont issues de la base de données de la publication FMI (2021), *Perspectives de l'économie mondiale (PEM) d'avril 2021*.

Les données pour la période 2000-04 doivent être interprétées avec prudence car les données non fiscales collectées par la Direction Générale du Trésor et de la Comptabilité Publique (DGTCP) ne sont pas disponibles pour cette période.

Selon la classification OCDE (voir le guided'interprétation en Annexe B), le produit de la vente d'immeuble bâtis n'est pas considéré comme une recette (fiscale ou non fiscale) car il ne représente pas une augmentation de la valeur nette résultant d'une transaction. La classification du Niger compte ces recettes comme des recettes non fiscales.

Le prélèvement communautaire de la CEDEAO (Communauté économique des États de l'Afrique de l'Ouest) et le prélèvement communautaire de solidarité de l'UEMOA (Union Économique et Monétaire Ouest Africaine) ne sont pas compris dans le total des recettes fiscales ou des recettes non fiscales comme le préconise la classification OCDE (voir le guide d'interprétation en Annexe A) et sont présentés ici à titre de rubrique « Pour mémoire ». La classification du Niger les compte comme des recettes.

1. Le prélèvement communautaire de la CEDEAO (Communauté économique des États de l'Afrique de l'Ouest) et le prélèvement communautaire de solidarité de l'UEMOA (Union Economique et Monétaire Ouest Africaine) ne sont pas compris dans le total des recettes fiscales ou des recettes non fiscales comme le préconise la classification OCDE (voir le guide d'interprétation en Annexe A) et est présenté ici à titre de rubrique « Pour mémoire ». La classification du Niger les compte comme des recettes.

Source : Direction Générale des Impôts

StatLink https://doi.org/10.1787/888934284716

Table 6.27. **Nigeria / Nigéria**

Details of non-tax revenue / Recettes non fiscales détaillées

Million NGN

	1999	2000	2009	2010	2014	2015	2016	2017	2018	2019
Total non-tax revenue	..	..	..	**4 273 105**	**4 346 522**	**2 716 478**	**2 156 625**	**2 872 115**	**3 760 180**	**4 640 750**
Grants	..	..	..	335	8 912	49 288	125 059	141 055	0	0
Property income	..	..	..	4 266 330	4 309 750	2 622 660	2 007 436	2 731 060	2 636 270	3 127 320
Rents and royalties	..	..	..	4 266 330	4 309 750	2 622 660	2 007 436	2 731 060	2 636 270	3 127 320
Revenue from oil	..	..	..	3 574 420	3 320 800	2 059 110	1 607 090	2 100 870	1 395 650	1 734 790
Revenue from royalties	..	..	..	691 910	988 950	563 550	400 346	628 690	1 235 200	1 387 220
Revenue from fees and licences	..	..	..	0	0	0	0	1 500	5 420	5 310
Interest and dividends	..	..	..	0	0	0	0	0	0	0
Other property income	..	..	..	0	0	0	0	0	0	0
Sales of goods and services	..	..	..	0	0	0	0	0	0	0
Fines, penalties and forfeits	..	..	..	0	0	0	0	0	0	0
Miscellaneous and unidentified revenue	..	..	..	6 440	27 860	44 530	24 130	0	1 123 910	1 513 430
Total tax and non-tax revenue	..	..	..	8 296 702	11 232 659	8 477 903	7 570 536	9 419 129	11 927 217	13 320 426

.. Not available

Note: Year ending 31st December.

The data are on a cash basis.

Statistics on grant revenues were not available for 2018 and 2019.

"Revenue from oil" refers to government share of revenues from revenue sharing agreements with oil and exploration companies.

"Revenue from fees and licenses" refers to government fees collected in exchange for granting Oil Prospecting Licenses (OPL) and Oil Mining Leases (OML).

"Revenue from royalties" includes royalties charged to oil and mineral exploration companies.

Miscellaneous and unidentified revenue includes some revenues from dividends and issued profits from state-owned enterprises.

Source: Federal Inland Revenue Service.

StatLink https://doi.org/10.1787/888934284735

Table 6.28. **Rwanda**

Details of non-tax revenue / Recettes non fiscales détaillées

Million RWF

	1999	2000	2009	2010	2014	2015	2016	2017	2018	2019
Total non-tax revenue	**67 156**	**79 888**	**363 942**	**415 465**	**514 565**	**529 400**	**520 541**	**556 992**	**650 724**	**627 711**
Grants	63 460	76 710	347 397	397 352	421 821	374 600	339 336	359 731	398 686	380 691
Property income	..	..	..	..	..	..	..	..	..	..
Rents and royalties	..	..	..	..	..	..	..	..	..	..
Interest and dividends	..	..	..	..	..	..	..	..	..	..
Other property income	..	..	..	..	..	..	..	..	..	..
Sales of goods and services	..	..	..	..	..	..	..	..	..	..
Fines, penalties and forfeits	..	..	..	..	..	..	..	..	..	..
Miscellaneous and unidentified revenue	3 696	3 178	16 545	18 113	92 745	154 800	181 205	197 261	252 038	247 020
Total tax and non-tax revenue	132 535	148 797	753 881	856 189	1 380 119	1 526 632	1 636 177	1 805 009	2 052 226	2 239 441

.. Not available

Note: Year ending 31st December.

The data are on a cash basis.

Figures exclude non-tax revenues collected by sub-national governments as the data are not available.

Figures exclude fines related to tax revenues as it is not possible to split these out from tax revenues. Revenues from fines related to taxes are now classified as non-tax revenues following a change in the OECD classification. Rwanda considers these revenues as tax revenues.

Miscellaneous and unidentified revenue: This category includes non-tax fines, administrative fees and revenue from public property and public assets for Rwanda. These data could not be disaggregated to allocate revenue to the relevant non-tax revenue categories.

Source: Rwanda Revenue Authority.

StatLink https://doi.org/10.1787/888934284754

Table 6.29. **Senegal / Sénégal**

Details of non-tax revenue / Recettes non fiscales détaillées

Million XOF

	1999	2000	2009	2010	2014	2015	2016	2017	2018	2019
Total des recettes non fiscales	**63 500**	**68 000**	**219 900**	**203 550**	**394 700**	**366 943**	**522 831**	**500 930**	**450 211**	..
Dons	61 600	64 000	182 800	161 850	253 500	232 034	244 348	264 000	256 420	224 569
Revenus de la propriété	0	0	34 700	39 600	81 300	84 990	83 413	84 230	97 691	..
Loyers et redevances	..	..	6 300	20 300	25 200	35 790	31 943	33 200	53 591	65 987
Intérêts et dividendes	..	..	28 400	19 300	56 100	49 200	51 470	51 030	44 100	..
Autres revenus de la propriété	..	..	0	0	0	0	0	0	0	..
Ventes de biens et de services	0	0	0	0	0	0	0	0	0	0
Amendes, pénalités et confiscations	0	0	0	0	49 000	28 220	0	0	0	13 000
Recettes diverses et non identifiées	1 900	4 000	2 400	2 100	10 900	21 700	195 070	152 700	96 100	..
Recettes exceptionnelles (Swapp et Sonatel)	0	0	0	0	0	0	139 770	0	24 000	..
Divers reversements	1 900	4 000	2 400	2 100	10 900	21 700	55 300	152 700	72 100	..
Total des recettes fiscales et non fiscales	574 748	627 295	1 358 398	1 471 349	1 981 565	2 090 075	2 443 175	2 488 028	2 573 716	..

.. Non disponible

Note : Année civile se terminant le 31 décembre.

Les données sont sur la base des encaissements.

Les chiffres n'incluent pas les données des recettes fiscales collectées par les collectivités locales car elles ne sont pas disponibles.

2019: Les données des dons sont issues du FMI.

Loyer et redevance, 2019: Y compris 22 au titre des redevances minières.

Amendes, pénalités et confiscations: Les recettes des amendes et les pénalités sur impôts et taxes sont considérées comme des recettes non fiscales. Cependant, il n'a pas été possible de séparer le versement des amendes et pénalités des recettes correspondant aux impôts auxquels ces amendes et pénalités se rattachent et sont donc exlues de cette rubrique. La classification nationale du Sénégal les compte comme des recettes fiscales. Les montants des années 2017 à 2019 concernent uniquement les recouvrements de la DGID.

Recettes diverses et non identifiées : Y compris transferts de capitaux non compris ailleurs.

Source : Ministère de l'Économie, des Finances et du Plan.

StatLink https://doi.org/10.1787/888934284773

Table 6.30. **Seychelles**

Details of non-tax revenue / Recettes non fiscales détaillées

Million SCR

	1999	2000	2009	2010	2014	2015	2016	2017	2018	2019
Total non-tax revenue	..	..	**1 067**	**725**	**1 424**	**1 237**	**1 488**	**1 247**	**1 511**	**1 408**
Grants	..	..	317	101	532	144	271	173	281	94
Property income	..	..	400	357	366	519	602	539	731	798
Rents and royalties	..	..	197	115	161	215	226	247	267	252
Fishing licence fees	..	..	180	93	0	0	0	0	0	0
Annual EU fishing licence fees to access Seychelles EEZ	..	..	0	0	47	43	36	37	42	1
EU fishing licence: vessel fee	..	..	0	0	21	37	33	29	35	79
Non EU fishing licence fees	..	..	0	0	40	60	64	72	72	1
Local fishing licence fees	..	..	0	0	0	1	1	0	2	54
SPF - Rental income	..	..	17	22	53	74	93	108	115	118
Interest and dividends	..	..	203	241	205	304	375	292	465	546
Income from interest and dividends (main budget)	..	..	148	206	151	228	304	207	377	442
FSA rental income (dividends)	..	..	0	0	18	11	14	23	29	33
SPF - Interest income	..	..	46	22	23	51	46	48	44	51
SPF - Investment/dividend income	..	..	9	12	13	14	12	14	14	21
Other property income	..	..	0	0	0	0	1	0	0	0
Sales of goods and services	..	..	181	191	448	462	565	489	466	465
Fines, penalties and forfeits	..	..	0	0	0	0	0	0	0	0
Miscellaneous and unidentified revenue	..	..	168	77	79	111	50	46	33	50
Total tax and non-tax revenue	..	..	4 384	4 321	6 650	6 701	7 596	7 960	8 975	9 013

.. Not available

Note: Year ending 31st December.

The data are on a cash basis.

Figures exclude non-tax revenues collected by sub-national governments as the data are not available.

For the first time, this edition includes revenues collected by the Seychelles Pension Fund (SPF). In addition to the revenues labelled "SPF" under "Rents and royalties" and "Interest and dividends", some, generally negligible, SPF revenues are counted under "Other property income", "Sales of goods and services", and "Miscellaneous and unidentified revenue". SPF revenues are not reported as government revenues in Seychelles government documents.

Heading "Rents and royalties": This category includes fishing licences fees considered as non-tax revenues in accordance with the OECD classification, as set out in the Interpretative Guide in Annex A. The Seychelles classifies these revenues as tax revenues.

Heading "Interest and dividends": For the first time, this edition reports the revenues of the Financial Services Authority Seychelles as general government revenue. Previous editions reported only the funds transferred from the FSA to the general government, which were classified as dividends. FSA revenues are not reported as government revenues in Seychelles government documents.

Source: Seychelles Revenue Commission; Seychelles Ministry of Finance, Economic Planning and Trade; Financial Services Authority Seychelles Annual Reports; and Seychelles Pension Fund Annual Reports.

StatLink https://doi.org/10.1787/888934284792

Table 6.31. **South Africa / Afrique du Sud**

Details of non-tax revenue / Recettes non fiscales détaillées

Million ZAR

	1999	2000	2009	2010	2014	2015	2016	2017	2018	2019
Total non-tax revenue	**4 277**	**4 135**	**12 893**	**16 192**	**19 922**	**17 934**	**20 234**	**21 886**	**27 705**	**29 398**
Grants	452	637	1 844	1 012	1 960	1 467	1 800	1 458	1 276	1 155
Property income	1 820	1 378	3 651	8 170	12 102	10 113	11 189	12 726	16 845	20 986
Rents and royalties	0	0	854	4 448	5 489	3 772	5 948	7 834	9 049	11 831
Interest and dividends	1 820	1 378	2 798	3 721	6 613	6 341	5 240	4 891	7 796	9 154
Interest	661	714	2 133	2 524	4 467	4 487	3 981	3 485	6 834	8 276
Dividends	1 159	664	665	1 197	2 146	1 853	1 259	1 406	963	878
Other property income	0	0	0	0	0	0	0	0	0	0
Sales of goods and services	1 894	2 006	2 314	2 335	1 663	2 159	2 592	2 629	2 321	2 715
Fines, penalties and forfeits	111	114	4 846	4 425	3 647	3 665	4 206	4 786	6 877	4 144
Interest on overdue tax: individuals	..	..	1 182	1 225	918	993	1 301	1 698	1 991	1 563
Interest on overdue tax: companies	..	..	1 966	1 744	1 554	1 707	2 239	2 622	3 135	2 214
Other fines, penalties and forfeits	111	114	1 698	1 457	1 174	965	667	466	1 752	367
Miscellaneous and unidentified revenue	0	0	238	251	550	531	448	287	386	399
Total tax and non-tax revenue	200 050	215 696	661 205	722 722	1 070 735	1 188 804	1 263 007	1 348 397	1 451 051	1 498 287
***Memo items:** SACU expenditure*	..	..	27 915	17 915	51 738	51 022	39 448	55 951	48 289	..

.. Not available

Note: Data are reported on a fiscal year basis beginning 1st April. For example, the data for 2019 represent April 2019 to March 2020. The data are on a cash basis.

Figures exclude non-tax revenues collected by sub-national governments as the data are not available.

The grants data represent total grants and donations received mainly from foreign governments and multilateral institutions. Moreover, this flow does not go through the Government Revenue fund, it is earmarked for specific projects implemented across government (by line departments). Unaudited estimates for grants are used for the fiscal year 2019/20.

Memo items: the Southern African Customs Union (SACU) expenditure records the difference between South Africa contributions to the SACU pool and the South Africa revenue share from the SACU pool that includes the balance of the "surplus/deficit" for that fiscal year and allocations to the SACU secretariat. The figures for 2013/14 figures differ from numbers published in South African tax statistics since some Fuel Levy imports were included in that year. 2017/18 and 2018/19 figures are unaudited and 2019/20 figures are not available.

Source: National Treasury of South Africa. Data for grants are from the financial statements of the Reconstruction and Development Fund Programme (RDP) Fund administered by the office of Accountant General.

StatLink https://doi.org/10.1787/888934284811

Table 6.32. **Togo**

Details of non-tax revenue / Recettes non fiscales détaillées

Million XOF

	1999	2000	2009	2010	2014	2015	2016	2017	2018	2019
Total des recettes non fiscales	..	**18 987**	**213 466**	**189 745**	**97 064**	**102 957**	**114 513**	**135 695**	**216 888**	**200 351**
Dons	..	4 292	64 886	80 357	45 762	57 238	75 601	88 527	105 895	122 423
Dons projets	..	4 292	47 610	62 257	45 762	47 539	64 333	40 208	72 712	60 355
Dons programmes	..	0	17 276	18 100	0	9 699	11 267	48 319	33 183	62 068
Revenus de la propriété	..	10 040	89 245	92 473	29 585	25 555	21 201	31 185	41 010	37 962
Loyers et redevances	..	5 548	67 240	42 400	8 468	3 837	3 640	4 125	3 426	6 843
Redevances minières	..	0	0	0	7 367	1 270	1 372	1 850	2 322	1 777
Redevances de réhabilitation de l'Aéroport International Gnassingbé Eyadéma (AIGE)	..	5 548	0	0	1 101	2 240	1 819	1 828	665	3 543
Redevance contour global	..	0	0	0	0	0	408	447	332	330
Autres recettes domaniales	..	0	67 240	42 400	0	327	42	0	106	1 194
Intérêts et dividendes	..	4 492	22 005	50 073	21 117	21 718	17 560	27 061	37 584	31 119
Dividendes	..	2 416	8 090	6 745	13 172	16 179	11 335	21 784	31 592	25 366
Intérêts de placement	..	771	794	985	7 507	4 307	307	1	1	5
Produits divers (commissions, transferts BCEAO et intérêts)	..	0	0	0	190	201	4 642	4 649	5 234	5 181
Autres produits financiers	..	1 304	13 120	42 344	248	1 032	1 276	627	758	567
Autres revenus de la propriété	..	0	0	0	0	0	0	0	0	0
Ventes de biens et de services	..	1 365	1 291	140	17 690	7 692	9 017	8 623	57 099	25 308
Loyers d'immeuble	..	0	0	0	428	201	1 626	267	386	228
Redevances téléphoniques	..	0	0	0	11 949	2 000	1 500	1 573	50 440	15 500
Recettes de services	..	1 365	1 291	140	4 261	4 752	5 286	6 047	6 064	9 349
Recettes consulaires	..	0	0	0	1 052	739	605	736	210	230
Amendes, pénalités et confiscations	..	1 222	784	495	2 131	1 359	953	1 318	1 148	1 679
Amendes et pénalités (recettes fiscales)	..	955	429	262	912	989	754	1 129	821	1 132
Amendes et penalités (recettes douanières)	..	267	355	232	1 219	369	199	189	326	547
Recettes diverses et non identifiées	..	2 069	57 260	16 280	1 895	11 114	7 741	6 042	11 737	12 978
Confiscations et ventes en douane	..	0	0	0	385	954	4 226	2 459	9 616	6 488
Ordre de recettes (gestion antérieure)	..	0	0	0	0	6	262	53	43	0
Ordre de recettes (gestion courante)	..	0	0	0	85	95	53	65	175	27
Divers reversements	..	785	0	0	1 271	9 754	2 985	3 207	1 114	6 368
Autres recettes non fiscales	..	1 284	57 260	16 280	154	305	216	259	789	96
Total des recettes fiscales et non fiscales	..	118 981	446 023	440 185	568 562	636 513	701 320	721 365	793 416	834 865

.. Non disponible

Note : Année civile se terminant le 31 décembre.

Les données sont sur la base des encaissements.

Les recettes non fiscales incluent les recettes des autres ministères ou directions, autres que le Ministère de l'Économie et des Finances.

Les chiffres n'incluent pas les autres recettes collectées par les collectivités locales pour leur propre compte, car elles ne sont pas disponibles. La classification nationale du Togo considère le Prélèvement pour apurement de la dette du secteur pétrolier (PADSP) comme une recette non fiscale. Cette recette est considérée comme une recette fiscale dans cette publication comme le préconise la classification OCDE (voir le guide d'interprétation en Annexe A).

Amendes et pénalités (recettes fiscales): Ces recettes sont classifiées comme des recettes non fiscales dans cette publication comme le préconise la classification OCDE (voir le guide d'interprétation en Annexe B). La classification nationale du Togo comptabilise ces recettes comme des recettes fiscales.

Confiscations et ventes en douane: Cette rubrique comprend les recettes provenant des confiscations et ventes en douane et les reversements du prélèvement communautaire de solidarité qui sont classifiés comme des recettes non fiscales dans cette publication comme le préconise la classification OCDE (voir le guide d'interprétation en Annexe B. La classification nationale du Togo considère ces recettes comme des recettes fiscales douanières. Avant 2014, ces recettes étaient comptabilisés dans la rubrique « Amendes et pénalités (recettes douanières) ».

Source : Office Togolais des Recettes.

StatLink https://doi.org/10.1787/888934284830

Table 6.33. **Tunisia / Tunisie**

Details of non-tax revenue / Recettes non fiscales détaillées

Million TND

	1999	2000	2009	2010	2014	2015	2016	2017	2018	2019
Total des recettes non fiscales	..	**725**	**1 896**	**1 799**	**1 903**	**1 749**	**1 539**	**2 770**	**3 254**	**3 828**
Dons	..	7	178	54	368	292	130	201	236	249
Revenus de la propriété	..	525	1 327	1 299	976	863	915	1 623	2 105	2 237
Loyers et redevances	..	185	444	435	357	350	388	1 251	1 353	1 043
Redevances pétrolières et du gaz	..	177	423	415	337	328	366	1 224	1 324	1 017
Loyers	..	8	21	19	20	22	23	27	29	26
Intérêts et dividendes	..	341	883	864	618	513	527	372	752	1 194
Intérêts	..	56	59	56	42	41	8	53	72	72
Transferts des entreprises publiques et bénéfices de la Banque Centrale	..	274	789	796	503	430	447	262	631	1 068
Remises sur crédit	..	3	2	2	3	3	4	4	4	3
Autres intérêts et dividendes non compris ailleurs	..	9	33	10	70	39	68	53	44	50
Autres revenus de la propriété	..	0	0	0	0	0	0	0	0	0
Ventes de biens et de services	..	22	33	40	24	28	32	42	72	53
Ventes de produits divers	..	21	31	38	22	26	30	40	70	50
Frais administratifs	..	1	2	2	2	2	2	2	2	2
Amendes, pénalités et confiscations	..	87	169	186	346	378	273	708	532	998
Recettes diverses et non identifiées	..	85	190	220	188	189	190	197	309	292
Total des recettes fiscales et non fiscales	..	7 922	17 596	18 942	26 901	27 362	28 135	32 580	37 078	43 278

.. Non disponible

Note : Année civile se terminant le 31 décembre.

Les données sont sur la base des encaissements.

Les chiffres n'incluent pas les données des recettes non fiscales collectées par les collectivités locales car elles ne sont pas disponibles.

Dons : Les dons affectés pour les Fonds spéciaux du Trésor et les Fonds de concours sont compris dans les données des dons des gouvernements et institutions étrangers.

Recettes diverses et non identifiées : Les recettes diverses et non identifiées incluent entre autres des recettes accidentelles à divers titres et des recettes non fiscales des Fonds spéciaux du Trésor et des Fonds de concours.

Source : Ministère des Finances.

StatLink https://doi.org/10.1787/888934284849

Table 6.34. **Uganda / Ouganda**

Details of non-tax revenue / Recettes non fiscales détaillées

Million UGX

	1999	2000	2009	2010	2014	2015	2016	2017	2018	2019
Total non-tax revenue	**408 888**	**568 523**	**928 312**	**921 459**	**827 086**	**1 109 069**	**1 400 151**	**1 239 490**	**1 191 569**	**1 695 619**
Grants	406 936	566 605	884 809	863 608	702 488	930 809	1 147 209	949 743	774 198	1 201 553
Budget support	161 736	255 205	530 854	467 338	191 442	258 151	339 676	259 263	154 513	594 860
Project grants	245 200	311 400	353 955	396 270	511 046	672 658	807 533	690 480	619 684	606 693
Property income	0	0	3 076	4 061	8 237	8 684	10 914	16 930	17 766	16 893
Rents and royalties	..	..	3 076	4 061	8 237	8 684	10 914	16 930	17 766	16 893
Mining royalties	..	..	3 076	4 061	8 237	8 684	10 914	16 930	17 766	16 893
Interest and dividends	..	..	0	0	0	0	0	0	0	0
Other property income	..	..	0	0	0	0	0	0	0	0
Sales of goods and services	1 951	1 919	40 426	53 790	116 361	169 575	242 029	272 818	399 605	477 173
Driver's permits[1]	1 951	1 919	9 483	12 373	14 147	15 921	18 245	33 561	37 335	39 425
Migration fees	..	..	18 483	23 317	49 993	90 913	123 251	121 892	140 196	139 778
Passport fees	..	..	3 448	4 614	10 413	12 800	21 660	21 065	25 950	37 338
Uganda Registration Services Bureau	..	..	0	0	20 490	23 470	24 417	32 549	21 461	56 259
Other administrative fees	..	..	9 012	13 486	21 317	26 472	54 456	63 750	174 663	204 373
Fines, penalties and forfeits	0	0	0	0	0	0	0	0	0	0
Miscellaneous and unidentified revenue[2]	0	0	0	0	0	0	0	0	0	0
Total tax and non-tax revenue	1 353 791	1 568 183	4 665 879	5 173 480	8 892 155	10 870 499	12 442 513	13 670 804	15 259 159	17 826 256

.. Not available

Note: Data are reported on a fiscal year basis beginning 1st July. For example, the data for 2019 represent July 2018 to June 2019.

The data are on a cash basis.

Figures exclude non-tax revenues collected by sub-national governments as the data are not available.

Heading "Driver's permits" is considered as non-tax revenue according to the OECD classification described in the Interpretative Guide. The national classification of Uganda classifies it as tax revenues.

Heading "Miscellaneous and unidentified revenue" includes non-tax fines, administrative fees and revenue from public property and public assets. These data could not be disaggregated to allocate revenue to the relevant non-tax revenue categories.

1. Revenue from drivers permits are considered as non-tax revenue according the OECD classification described in the Interpretative Guide. The national classification of Uganda classifies it as tax revenues.
2. This category includes non-tax fines, administrative fees and revenue from public property and public assets. These data could not be disaggregated to allocate revenue to the relevant non-tax revenue categories.

Source: Uganda Revenue Authority.

StatLink https://doi.org/10.1787/888934284868

Revenue Statistics in Africa 1990-2019/Statistiques des recettes publiques en Afrique 1990-2019

Annex A

The OECD classification of taxes and interpretative guide[1]

Table of contents

A.1. The OECD classification of taxes

1. 1000 Taxes on income, profits and capital gains
   - 1100 Taxes on income, profits and capital gains of individuals
     - 1110 On income and profits
     - 1120 On capital gains
   - 1200 Corporate taxes on income, profits and capital gains
     - 1210 On income and profits
     - 1220 On capital gains
   - 1300 Unallocable as between 1100 and 1200
2. 2000 Social security contributions
   - 2100 Employees
     - 2110 On a payroll basis
     - 2120 On an income tax basis
   - 2200 Employers
     - 2210 On a payroll basis
     - 2220 On an income tax basis
   - 2300 Self-employed or non-employed
     - 2310 On a payroll basis
     - 2320 On an income tax basis
   - 2400 Unallocable as between 2100, 2200 and 2300
     - 2410 On a payroll basis
     - 2420 On an income tax basis
3. 3000 Taxes on payroll and workforce
4. 4000 Taxes on property
   - 4100 Recurrent taxes on immovable property
     - 4110 Households
     - 4120 Other
   - 4200 Recurrent taxes on net wealth
     - 4210 Individual
     - 4220 Corporate
   - 4300 Estate, inheritance and gift taxes
     - 4310 Estate and inheritance taxes
     - 4320 Gift taxes
   - 4400 Taxes on financial and capital transactions
   - 4500 Other non-recurrent taxes on property
     - 4510 On net wealth
     - 4520 Other non-recurrent taxes
   - 4600 Other recurrent taxes on property

5. 5000 Taxes on goods and services

5100 Taxes on production, sale, transfer, leasing and delivery of goods and rendering of services

5110 General taxes

5111 Value added taxes

5112 Sales taxes

5113 Other general taxes on goods and services

5120 Taxes on specific goods and services

5121 Excises

5122 Paid by other than business or unidentifiable

5123 Paid by other than business or unidentifiable

5124 Paid by other than business or unidentifiable

5125 Taxes on investment goods

5126 Taxes on specific services

5127 Other taxes on international trade and transactions

5128 Other taxes on specific goods and services

5130 Unallocable as between 5110 and 5120

5200 Taxes on use of goods, or on permission to use goods or perform activities

5210 Recurrent taxes

5211 Paid by households in respect of motor vehicles

5212 Paid by others in respect of motor vehicles

5213 Other recurrent taxes

5220 Non recurrent taxes

5300 Unallocable as between 5100 and 5200

6. 6000 Other taxes

6100 Paid solely by business

6200 Paid by other than business or unidentifiable

A.2. Coverage

General criteria

1. In the OECD classification the term "taxes" is confined to compulsory unrequited payments to general government. Taxes are unrequited in the sense that benefits provided by government to taxpayers are not normally in proportion to their payments.

2. The term "tax" does not include fines, penalties and compulsory loans paid to government. Borderline cases between tax and non-tax revenues in relation to certain fees and charges are discussed in §11–14.

3. General government consists of the central administration, agencies whose operations are under its effective control, state and local governments and their administrations, certain social security schemes and autonomous governmental entities, excluding public enterprises. This definition of government follows that of the 2008 *System of National Accounts* (SNA).[2] In that publication, the general government sector and its sub-sectors are defined in Chapter 4, paragraphs 4.117 to 4.165.

4. Extra-budgetary units are part of the general government system. These are general government entities with individual budgets that are not fully covered by the main or general budget. These entities operate under the authority or control of a central, state, or local government. Extra-budgetary entities may have their own revenue sources, which may be supplemented by grants (transfers) from the general budget or from other sources. Even though their budgets may be subject to approval by the legislature, similar to that of budgetary accounts, they have discretion over the volume and composition of their spending. Such entities may be established to carry out specific government functions, such as road construction, or the nonmarket production of health or education services. Budgetary arrangements vary widely across countries, and various terms are used to describe these entities, but they are often referred to as "extra-budgetary funds" or "decentralised agencies."

5. Compulsory payments to supra-national bodies and their agencies are no longer included as taxes as from 1998, with some exceptions. However, custom duties collected by EU member states on behalf of the European Union are still identified as memorandum items and included in overall tax revenue amounts in the country tables of the country in which they are collected (See §99). In countries where the church forms part of general government church taxes are included, provided they meet the criteria set out in §1 above. As the data refer to receipts of general government, levies paid to non-government bodies, welfare agencies or social insurance schemes outside general government, trade unions or trade associations, even where such levies are compulsory, are excluded. Compulsory payments to general government earmarked for such bodies are, however, included, provided that the government is not simply acting in an agency capacity.[3] Profits from fiscal monopolies are distinguished from those of other public enterprises and are treated as taxes because they reflect the exercise of the taxing power of the state by the use of monopoly powers (see §65–67), as are profits received by the government from the purchase and sale of foreign exchange at different rates (see §74).

6. Taxes paid by governments (e.g., social security contributions and payroll taxes paid by governments in their capacity as an employer, consumption taxes on their purchases or taxes on their property) are not excluded from the data provided. However, where it is possible to identify the amounts of revenue involved,[4] they are shown in Chapter 4.2 of this Report.

7. The relationship between this classification and that of the System of National Accounts (SNA) is set out in Sections A.9 and A.11 below. Because of the differences between the two classifications, the data shown in national accounts are sometimes calculated or classified differently from the practice set out in this guide. These and other differences are mentioned where appropriate (e.g., in §30 below) but it is not possible to refer to all of them. There may also be some differences between this classification and that employed domestically by certain national administrations (e.g., see §12 below), so that OECD and national statistics data may not always be consistent: any such differences, however, are likely to be very slight in terms of amounts of revenues involved.

Social security contributions

8. Compulsory social security contributions, as defined in §39, and paid to general government, are treated here as tax revenues. Being compulsory payments to general government they clearly resemble taxes. They may, however, differ from other taxes in that the receipt of social security benefits depends, in most countries, upon appropriate contributions having been made, although the size of the benefits is not necessarily related to the amount of the contributions. Better comparability between countries is obtained by treating social security contributions as taxes, but they are listed under a separate heading so that they can be distinguished in any analysis.

9. The strict dividing line between tax revenues (compulsory unrequited payments to general government) and non-tax compulsory payments (NTCPs) (payments that are either requited or made to other institutions) is clearly defined. However, within the range of different compulsory payments to governments existing across countries, it is not always straightforward in practice to decide whether specific payments are either taxes or NTCPs. For example, compulsory pension savings that are controlled by general government and that accumulate on an individual account earning a market return or a rate that compensates for inflation would at first sight be categorised as NTCPs as opposed to taxes. However, even these payments might still be 'unrequited' and therefore classify as taxes instead of NTCPs (for example if these pension savings are not paid out when the taxpayer dies before reaching the pension age and the funds are then used to provide a minimum pension to all taxpayers that are insured). These issues result in the social security revenue figures reported for most countries being based on the premise that all types of compulsory payments to general government are judged to some extent to have a re-distributional element. It should be noted that this conclusion is based on a typically broad interpretation of the term 'unrequited' in the tax definition.

10. Social security contributions which are either voluntary or not payable to general government (see §1) are not treated as taxes, though in some countries, as indicated in the country footnotes, there are difficulties in completely eliminating voluntary contributions and certain compulsory payments to the private sector from the revenue figures. Imputed social security contributions are also not treated as taxes.

Fees, user charges and licence fees

11. Apart from vehicle licence fees, which are universally regarded as taxes, it is not easy to distinguish between those fees and user charges which are to be treated as taxes and those which are not, since, whilst a fee or charge is levied in connection with a specific service or activity, the strength of the link between the fee and the service provided may vary considerably, as may the relation between the amount of the fee and the cost of providing

the service. Where the recipient of a service pays a fee clearly related to the cost of providing the service, the levy may be regarded as requited and under the definition of §1 would not be considered as a tax. In the following cases, however, a levy could be considered as 'unrequited':

a. where the charge greatly exceeds the cost of providing the service;
b. where the payer of the levy is not the receiver of the benefit (e.g., a fee collected from slaughterhouses to finance a service which is provided to farmers);
c. where government is not providing a specific service in return for the levy which it receives even though a licence may be issued to the payer (e.g., where the government grants a hunting, fishing or shooting licence which is not accompanied by the right to use a specific area of government land);
d. where benefits are received only by those paying the levy but the benefits received by each individual are not necessarily in proportion to his payments (e.g., a milk marketing levy paid by dairy farmers and used to promote the consumption of milk).

12. In marginal cases, however, the application of the criteria set out in §1 can be particularly difficult. The solution adopted — given the desirability of international uniformity and the relatively small amounts of revenue usually involved — is to follow the predominant practice among tax administrations rather than to allow each country to adopt its own view as to whether such levies are regarded as taxes or as non-tax revenue.[5]

13. A list of the main fees and charges in question and their normal[6] treatment in this publication is as follows:

- *Non-tax revenues:* court fees; driving licence fees; harbour fees; passport fees; radio and television licence fees where public authorities provide the service.
- *Taxes within heading 5200:* permission to perform such activities as distributing films; hunting, fishing and shooting; providing entertainment or gambling facilities; selling alcohol or tobacco; permission to own dogs or to use or own motor vehicles or guns; severance taxes.

14. In practice it may not always be possible to isolate tax receipts from non-tax revenue receipts when they are recorded together. If it is estimated that the bulk of the receipts derive from non-tax revenues, the whole amount involved is treated as a non-tax revenue; otherwise, such government receipts are included and classified according to the rules provided in §32 below.

Royalties

15. The ownership of subsoil assets in the form of deposits of minerals or fossil fuels (coal, oil, or natural gas) depends upon the way in which property rights are defined by law and also on international agreements in the case of deposits below international waters. In some cases, either the ground below which the mineral deposits are located, the deposits themselves or both may belong to a local or central government unit.

16. In such cases, these general government units may grant leases to other institutional units that permit them to extract these deposits over a specified period of time in return for a payment or series of payments. These payments are often described as 'royalties' but they are essentially rent that accrues to owners of natural resources in return for putting these assets at the disposal of other units for specified periods of time. The rent may take the form of periodic payments of fixed amounts, irrespective of the rate of extraction, or, more commonly, they may be a function of the quantity, volume, or value of the asset extracted. Enterprises engaged in exploration on government land may make payments to general government units

in exchange for the right to undertake test drilling or otherwise investigate the existence and location of subsoil assets. Such payments are also recorded as rents even though no extraction may take place. These payments are therefore classified as non-tax revenues.

17. The same principles apply when other institutional units are granted leases that permit them to fell timber in natural forests on land owned by general government units. These payments are also classified as non-tax revenues.

18. These rents or royalties paid to general government should not be confused with taxes on income and profits, severance taxes, business licenses, or other taxes. If the payments are levied on the profits from the extraction activity, then they should be classified as taxes on incomes, profits and gains (1000). In addition, any severance payments that are imposed on the extraction of minerals and fossil fuels from reserves owned privately or by another government should be classified as taxes. Payments related to the gross value of production should be classified as other taxes on goods and services (5128). Payments for a license or permit to conduct extraction operations should be classified as taxes on use of goods and on permission to use goods or perform activities (5213).

Fines and penalties

19. In principle, fines and penalties charged on overdue taxes or penalties imposed for the attempted evasion of taxes should not be recorded as tax revenues. However it may not be possible to separate payments of fines or other penalties from the revenues from the taxes to which they relate. In this case the fines and penalties relating to a particular tax are recorded together with the revenues from that tax and fines and penalties paid with revenue from unidentifiable taxes are classified as other taxes in Category 6000. Fines not relating to tax offences (e.g., for parking offences), or not identifiable as relating to tax offences, are also not treated as tax revenues.

A.3. Basis of reporting

Accrual reporting

20. The data reported in this publication for recent years are predominantly recorded on an accrual basis, i.e. recorded at the time that the tax liability was created. Further information is provided in the footnotes to the country table in Chapter 4 of the Report.

21. However, data for earlier years are still predominantly recorded on a cash basis, i.e. at the time at which the payment was received by government. Thus, for example, taxes withheld by employers in one year but paid to the government in the following year and taxes due in one year but actually paid in the following year are both included in the receipts of the second year. Corrective transactions, such as refunds, repayments and drawbacks, are deducted from gross revenues of the period in which they are made.

22. Data on tax revenues are recorded without offsets for the administrative expenses connected with tax collection. Similarly, where the proceeds of tax are used to subsidise particular members of the community, the subsidy is not deducted from the yield of the tax, though the tax may be shown net of subsidies in the national records of some countries.

23. As regards fiscal monopolies (heading 5122), only the amount actually transferred to the government is included in government revenues. However, if any expenditures of fiscal monopolies are considered to be government expenditures (e.g., social expenditures undertaken by fiscal monopolies at the direction of the government) they are added back for the purpose of arriving at tax revenue figures (see §65 below).

The distinction between tax and expenditure provisions[7]

24. Because this publication is concerned only with the revenue side of government operations, no account being taken of the expenditure side, a distinction has to be made between tax and expenditure provisions. Normally there is no difficulty in making this distinction as expenditures are made outside the tax system and the tax accounts and under legislation separate from the tax legislation. In borderline cases, cash flow is used to distinguish between tax provisions and expenditure provisions. Insofar as a provision affects the flow of tax payments from the taxpayer to the government, it is regarded as a tax provision and is taken into account in the data shown in this publication. A provision which does not affect this flow is seen as an expenditure provision and is disregarded in the data recorded in this publication.

25. Tax allowances, exemptions and deductions against the tax base clearly affect the amount of tax paid to the government and are therefore considered as tax provisions. At the other extreme, those subsidies which cannot be offset against tax liability and which are clearly not connected with the assessment process, do not reduce tax revenues as recorded in this publication. Tax credits are amounts deductible from tax payable (as distinct from deductions from the tax base). Two types of tax credits are distinguished, those (referred to here as wastable tax credits) which are limited to the amount of the tax liability and therefore cannot give rise to a payment by the authorities to the taxpayer, and those (referred to as non-wastable tax credits) which are not so limited, so that the excess of the credit over the tax liability can be paid to the taxpayer.[8] A wastable tax credit, like a tax allowance, clearly affects the amount of tax paid to the government, and is therefore considered as a tax provision. The practice followed for non-wastable tax credits[9] is to distinguish between the 'tax expenditure component',[10] which is that portion of the credit that is used to reduce or eliminate a taxpayer's liability, and the 'transfer component', which is the portion that exceeds the taxpayer's liability and is paid to that taxpayer. Reported tax revenues should be reduced by the amount of the tax expenditure component but not by the amount of the transfer component. In addition, the amounts of the tax expenditure and transfer components should be reported as memorandum items in the country tables. Countries that are unable to distinguish between the tax expenditure and transfer components should indicate whether or not the tax revenues have been reduced by the total of these components, and provide any available estimates of the amounts of the two components. Further information is given in of the Report, which illustrates the effect of alternative treatments of non-wastable tax credits on tax to GDP.

Calendar and fiscal years

26. National authorities whose fiscal years do not correspond to the calendar year show data, where possible, on a calendar year basis to permit maximum comparability with the data of other countries. There remain a few countries where data refer to fiscal years. For these the GDP data used in the comparative tables also correspond to the fiscal years.

A.4. General classification criteria

The main classification criteria

27. The classification of receipts among the main headings (1000, 2000, 3000, 4000, 5000 and 6000) is generally governed by the base on which the tax is levied: 1000 income, profits and capital gains; 2000 and 3000 earnings, payroll or number of employees; 4000 property; 5000 goods and services; 6000 multiple bases, other bases or unidentifiable bases. Where a

tax is calculated on more than one base, the receipts are, where possible, split among the various headings (see §32 and §81). The headings 4000 and 5000 cover not only taxes where the tax base is the property, goods or services themselves but also certain related taxes. Thus, taxes on the transfer of property are included in 4400[11] and taxes on the use of goods or on permission to perform activities in 5200. In headings 4000 and 5000 a distinction is made in certain sub-headings between recurrent and non-recurrent taxes: recurrent taxes are defined as those levied at regular intervals (usually annually) and non-recurrent taxes are levied once and for all (see also §47 to §50, §53, §54 and §79 for particular applications of this distinction).

28. Earmarking of a tax for specific purposes does not affect the classification of tax receipts. However, as explained in §39 on the classification of social security contributions, the conferment of an entitlement to social benefits is crucial to the definition of the 2000 main heading.

29. The way that a tax is levied or collected (e.g., by use of stamps) does not affect classification.

Classification of taxpayers

30. In certain sub-headings distinctions are made between different categories of taxpayers. These distinctions vary from tax to tax:

a. *Between individuals and corporations in relation to income and net wealth taxes*

The basic distinction is that corporation income taxes, as distinct from individual income taxes, are levied on the corporation as an entity, not on the individuals who own it, and without regard to the personal circumstances of these individuals. The same distinction applies to net wealth taxes on corporations and those on individuals. Taxes paid on the profits of partnerships and the income of institutions, such as life insurance or pension funds, are classified according to the same rule. They are classified as corporate taxes (1200) if they are charged on the partnership or institution as an entity without regard to the personal circumstances of the owners. Otherwise, they are treated as individual taxes (1100). Usually, there is different legislation for the corporation taxes and for the individual taxes.[12] The distinction made here between individuals and corporations does not follow the sector classification between households, enterprises, and so on of the System of National Accounts for income and outlay accounts. The SNA classification requires certain unincorporated businesses[13] to be excluded from the household sector and included with non-financial enterprises and financial institutions. The tax on the profits of these businesses, however, cannot always be separated from the tax on the other income of their owners, or can be separated only on an arbitrary basis. No attempt at this separation is made here and the whole of the individual income tax is shown together without regard to the nature of the income chargeable.

b. *Between households and others in relation to taxes on immovable property*

Here the distinction is that adopted by the SNA for the production and consumption expenditure accounts. The distinction is between households as consumers (i.e. excluding non-incorporated business) on the one hand and producers on the other hand. However, taxes on dwellings occupied by households, whether paid by owner-occupiers, tenants or landlords, are classified under households. This follows the common distinction made between taxes on domestic property versus taxes on business property. Some countries are not, however, in a position to make this distinction.

c. *Between households and others in relation to motor vehicle licences*

Here the distinction is between households as consumers on the one hand and producers on the other, as in the production and consumption expenditure accounts of the SNA.

d. *Between business and others in relation to the residual taxes (6000)*

The distinction is the same as in c) above between producers on the one hand and households as consumers on the other hand. Taxes which are included under the heading 6000 because they involve more than one tax base or because the tax base does not fall within any of the previous categories but which are identifiable as levyable only on producers and not on households are included under 'business'. The rest of the taxes which are included under the heading 6000 are shown as 'other' or non-identified.

Surcharges

31. Receipts from surcharges in respect of particular taxes are usually classified with the receipts from the relevant tax whether or not the surcharge is temporary. If, however, the surcharge has a characteristic which would render it classifiable in a different heading of the OECD list, receipts from the surcharge are classified under that heading separately from the relevant tax.

Unidentifiable tax receipts and residual sub-headings

32. A number of cases arise where taxes cannot be identified as belonging entirely to a heading or sub-heading of the OECD classification and the following practices are applied in such cases:

a. The heading is known, but it is not known how receipts should be allocated between sub-headings: receipts are classified in the appropriate residual sub-heading (1300, 2400, 4520, 4600, 5130, 5300 or 6200).

b. It is known that the bulk of receipts from a group of taxes (usually local taxes) is derived from taxes within a particular heading or sub-heading, but some of the taxes in the group whose amount cannot be precisely ascertained may be classifiable in other headings or sub-headings: receipts are shown in the heading or sub-heading under which most of the receipts fall.

c. Either the heading nor sub-heading of a tax (usually local) can be identified: the tax is classified in 6200 unless it is known that it is a tax on business in which case it is classified in 6100.

A.5. Commentaries on items of the list

1000 — Taxes on income, profits and capital gains

33. This heading covers taxes levied on the net income or profits (i.e. gross income minus allowable tax reliefs) of individuals and enterprises. Also covered are taxes levied on the capital gains of individuals and enterprises, and gains from gambling.

34. Included in the heading are:

a. taxes levied predominantly on income or profits, though partially on other bases. Taxes on various bases which are not predominantly income or profits are classified according to the principles laid down in §32 and §81;

b. taxes on property, which are levied on a presumed or estimated income as part of an income tax (see also §47(a), (c) and (d));

c. compulsory payments to social security fund contributions that are levied on income but do not confer an entitlement to social benefits. When such contributions do confer an entitlement to social benefits, they are included in heading 2000 (see §39);

d. receipts from integrated scheduler income tax systems are classified as a whole in this heading, even though certain of the scheduler taxes may be based upon gross income and may not take into account the personal circumstances of the taxpayer.

35. The main subdivision of this heading is between levies on individuals (1100) and those on corporate enterprises (1200). Under each subdivision a distinction is made between taxes on income and profits (1110 and 1210), and taxes on capital gains (1120 and 1220). If certain receipts cannot be identified as appropriate to either 1100 or 1200, or if in practice this distinction cannot be made (e.g., because there are no reliable data on the recipients of payments from which withholding taxes are deducted) they are classified in 1300 as not-allocable.

Treatment of credits under imputation systems

36. Under imputation systems of corporate income tax, a company's shareholders are wholly or partly relieved of their liability to income tax on dividends paid by the company out of income or profits liable to corporate income tax. In countries with such systems,[14] part of the tax on the company's profits is available to provide relief against the shareholders' own tax liability. The relief to the shareholder takes the form of a tax credit, the amount of which may be less than, equal to, or more than the shareholder's overall tax liability. If the tax credit exceeds this tax liability the excess may be payable to the shareholder. As this type of tax credit is an integral part of the imputation system of corporate income tax, any payment to the shareholders is treated as a repayment of tax and not as expenditure (compare the treatment of other tax credits described in §25).

37. As the tax credit under imputation systems (even when exceeding tax liability) is to be regarded as a tax provision, the question arises whether it should be deducted from individual income tax receipts (1110) or corporate income tax receipts (1210). In this Report, the full amount of corporate income tax paid is shown under 1210 and no imputed tax is included under 1110. Thus, the full amount of the credit reduces the amount of 1110 whether the credit results in a reduction of personal income tax liability or whether an actual refund is made because the credit exceeds the income tax liability. (Where, however, such tax credits are deducted from corporation tax in respect of dividends paid to corporations the amounts are deducted from the receipts of 1210).

1120 and 1220 — Taxes on capital gains

38. These sub-headings comprise taxes imposed on capital gains, 1120 covering those levied on the gains of individuals and 1220 those levied on the gains of corporate enterprises, where receipts from such taxes can be separately identified. In many countries this is not the case and the receipts from such taxes are then classified with those from the income tax. Heading 1120 also includes taxes on gains from gambling.

2000 — Social security contributions

39. Classified here are all compulsory payments that confer an entitlement to receive a (contingent) future social benefit. Such payments are usually earmarked to finance social benefits and are often paid to institutions of general government that provide such benefits. However, such earmarking is not part of the definition of social security contributions

and is not required for a tax to be classified here. However, conferment of an entitlement is required for a tax to be classified under this heading. So, levies on income or payroll that are earmarked for social security funds but do not confer an entitlement to benefit are excluded from this heading and shown under personal income taxes (1100) or taxes on payroll and workforce (3000). Taxes on other bases, such as goods and services, which are earmarked for social security benefits are not shown here but are classified according to their respective bases because they generally confer no entitlement to social security benefits.

40. Contributions for the following types of social security benefits would, *inter alia*, be included: unemployment insurance benefits and supplements, accident, injury and sickness benefits, old-age, disability and survivors' pensions, family allowances, reimbursements for medical and hospital expenses or provision of hospital or medical services. Contributions may be levied on both employees and employers.

41. Contributions may be based on earnings or payroll ('on a payroll basis') or on net income after deductions and exemptions for personal circumstances ('on an income tax basis'), and the revenues from the two bases should be separately identified if possible. However, where contributions to a general social security scheme are on a payroll basis, but the contributions of particular groups (such as the self-employed) cannot be assessed on this basis and net income is used as a proxy for gross earnings, the receipts may still be classified as being on a payroll basis. In principle, this heading excludes voluntary contributions paid to social security schemes. When separately identifiable these are shown in the memorandum item on the financing of social security benefits. In practice, however, they cannot always be separately identified from compulsory contributions, in which case they are included in this heading.

42. Contributions to social insurance schemes which are not institutions of general government and to other types of insurance schemes, provident funds, pension funds, friendly societies or other saving schemes are not considered as social security contributions. Provident funds are arrangements under which the contributions of each employee and of the corresponding employer on his/her behalf are kept in a separate account earning interest and withdrawable under specific circumstances. Pension funds are separately organised schemes negotiated between employees and employers and carry provisions for different contributions and benefits, sometimes more directly tied to salary levels and length of service than under social security schemes. When contributions to these schemes are compulsory or quasi-compulsory (e.g., by virtue of agreement with professional and union organisations) they are shown in the memorandum item (refer to Chapter 4.2 of the Report).

43. Contributions by government employees and by governments in respect of their employees, to social security schemes classified within general government are included in this heading. Contributions to separate schemes for government employees, which can be regarded as replacing general social security schemes, are also regarded as taxes.[15] Where, however, a separate scheme is not seen as replacing a general scheme and has been negotiated between the government, in its role as an employer, and its employees, it is not regarded as social security and contributions to it are not regarded as taxes, even though the scheme may have been established by legislation.

44. This heading excludes 'imputed' contributions, which correspond to social benefits paid directly by employers to their employees or former employees or to their representatives (e.g., when employers are legally obliged to pay sickness benefits for a certain period).

45. Contributions are divided into those of employees (2100), employers (2200), and self-employed or non-employed (2300), and then further sub-divided according to the basis on which they are levied. Employees are defined for this purpose as all persons engaged in activities of business units, government bodies, private non-profit institutions, or other paid employment, except the proprietors and their unpaid family members in the case of unincorporated businesses. Members of the armed forces are included, irrespective of the duration and type of their service, if they contribute to social security schemes. The contributions of employers are defined as their payments on account of their employees to social security schemes. Where employees or employers are required to continue the payment of social security contributions when the employee becomes unemployed these contributions, data permitting, are shown in 2100 and 2200 respectively. Accordingly, the sub-heading 2300 is confined to contributions paid by the self-employed and by those outside of the labour force (e.g., disabled or retired individuals).

3000 — Taxes on payroll and workforce

46. These consist of taxes payable by enterprises assessed either as a proportion of the wages or salaries paid or as a fixed amount per person employed. They do not include compulsory social security contributions paid by employers or any taxes paid by employees themselves out of their wages or salaries

4000 — Taxes on property

47. This heading covers recurrent and non-recurrent taxes on the use, ownership or transfer of property. These include taxes on immovable property or net wealth, taxes on the change of ownership of property through inheritance or gift and taxes on financial and capital transactions. The following kinds of tax are excluded from this heading:

a. taxes on capital gains resulting from the sale of a property (1120 or 1220);

b. taxes on the use of goods or on permission to use goods or perform activities (5200); see §76;

c. taxes on immovable property levied on the basis of a presumed net income which take into account the personal circumstances of the taxpayer. They are classified as income taxes along with taxes on income and capital gains derived from property (1100);

d. taxes on the use of property for residence, where the tax is payable by either proprietor or tenant and the amount payable is a function of the user's personal circumstances (pay, dependants, and so on). They are classified as taxes on income (1100);

e. taxes on building in excess of permitted maximum density, taxes on the enlargement, construction or alteration of certain buildings beyond a permitted value and taxes on building construction. They are classified as taxes on permission to perform activities (5200);

f. taxes on the use of one's own property for special trading purposes like selling alcohol, tobacco, meat or for exploitation of land resources (e.g., United States severance taxes). They are classified as taxes on permission to perform activities (5200).

4100 — *Recurrent taxes on immovable property*

48. This sub-heading covers taxes levied regularly in respect of the use or ownership of immovable property.

- these taxes are levied on land and buildings;
- they can be in the form of a percentage of an assessed property value based on a national rental income, sales price, or capitalised yield; or in terms of other characteristics of real property, (for example size or location) from which a presumed rent or capital value can be derived.
- such taxes can be levied on proprietors, tenants, or both. They can also be paid by one level of government to another level of government in respect of property under the jurisdiction of the latter.
- debts are not taken into account in the assessment of these taxes, and they differ from taxes on net wealth in this respect.

49. Taxes on immovable property are further sub-divided into those paid by households (4110) and those paid by other entities (4120), according to the criteria set out in §30(*b*) above.

4200 — *Recurrent taxes on net wealth*

50. This sub-heading covers taxes levied regularly (in most cases annually) on net wealth, i.e. taxes on a wide range of movable and immovable property, net of debt. It is sub-divided into taxes paid by individuals (4210) and taxes paid by corporate enterprises (4220) according to the criteria set out in §30(*a*) above. If separate figures exist for receipts paid by institutions, the tax payments involved are added to those paid by corporations.

4300 — *Estate, inheritance and gift taxes*

51. This sub-heading is divided into taxes on estates and inheritances (4310) and taxes on gifts (4320).[16] Estate taxes are charged on the amount of the total estate whereas inheritance taxes are charged on the shares of the individual recipients; in addition the latter may take into account the relationship of the individual recipients to the deceased.

4400 — *Taxes on financial and capital transactions*

52. This sub-heading comprises, *inter alia*, taxes on the issue, transfer, purchase and sale of securities, taxes on cheques, and taxes levied on specific legal transactions such as validation of contracts and the sale of immovable property. The heading does not include:

a. taxes on the use of goods or property or permission to perform certain activities (5200);
b. fees paid to cover court charges, charges for birth, marriage or death certificates, which are normally regarded as non-tax revenues (see §11);
c. taxes on capital gains (1000);
d. recurrent taxes on immovable property (4100);
e. recurrent taxes on net wealth (4200);
f. once-and-for-all levies on property or wealth (4500).

4500 — *Other non-recurrent taxes on property*[16]

53. This sub-heading covers once-and-for-all, as distinct from recurrent, levies on property. It is divided into taxes on net wealth (4510) and other non-recurrent taxes on property (4520). Heading 4510 would include taxes levied to meet emergency expenditures, or for

redistribution purposes. Heading 4520 would cover taxes levied to take account of increases in land value due to permission given to develop or provision of additional local facilities by general government, any taxes on the revaluation of capital and once-and-for-all taxes on particular items of property.

4600 — *Other recurrent taxes on property*

54. These rarely exist in OECD member countries, but the heading would include taxes on goods such as cattle, jewellery, windows, and other external signs of wealth.

5000 — *Taxes on goods and services*

55. All taxes and duties levied on the production, extraction, sale, transfer, leasing or delivery of goods, and the rendering of services (5100), or in respect of the use of goods or permission to use goods or to perform activities (5200) are included here. The heading thus covers:

a. multi-stage cumulative taxes;

b. general sales taxes — whether levied at manufacture/production, wholesale or retail level;

c. value-added taxes;

d. excises;

e. taxes levied on the import and export of goods;

f. taxes levied in respect of the use of goods and taxes on permission to use goods, or perform certain activities;

g. taxes on the extraction, processing or production of minerals and other products.

56. Borderline cases between this heading and heading 4000 (taxes on property) and 6100 (other taxes on business) are referred to in §47, §52 and §78. Residual sub-headings (5300) and (5130) cover tax receipts which cannot be allocated between 5100 and 5200 and between 5110 and 5120, respectively; see §32.

5100 — *Taxes on the production, sale, transfer, leasing and delivery of goods and rendering of services*

57. This sub-heading consists of all taxes, levied on transactions in goods and services on the basis of their intrinsic characteristics (e.g., value, weight of tobacco, strength of alcohol, and so on) as distinct from taxes imposed on the use of goods, or permission to use goods or perform activities, which fall under 5200.

5110 — *General taxes on goods and services*

58. This sub-heading includes all taxes, other than import and export duties (5123 and 5124), levied on the production, leasing, transfer, delivery or sales of a wide range of goods and/or the rendering of a wide range of services, irrespective of whether they are domestically produced or imported and irrespective of the stage of production or distribution at which they are levied. It thus covers value-added taxes, sales taxes and multi-stage cumulative taxes. Receipts from border adjustments in respect of such taxes when goods are imported are added to gross receipts for this category, and repayments of such taxes when goods are exported are deducted. These taxes are subdivided into 5111 value-added taxes, 5112 sales taxes, 5113 turnover and other general taxes on goods and services.

59. Borderline cases arise between this heading and taxes on specific goods (5120) when taxes are levied on a large number of goods, for example, the United Kingdom purchase tax

(repealed in 1973) and the Japanese commodity tax (repealed in 1988). In conformity with national views, the former United Kingdom purchase tax is classified as a general tax (5112) and the former Japanese commodity tax as excises (5121).

5111 — *Value-added taxes*

60. All general consumption taxes charged on value-added are classified in this sub-heading, irrespective of the method of deduction and the stages at which the taxes are levied. In practice, all OECD countries with value-added taxes normally allow immediate deduction of taxes on purchases by all but the final consumer and impose tax at all stages. In some countries the heading may include certain taxes, such as those on financial and insurance activities, either because receipts from them cannot be identified separately from those from the value-added tax, or because they are regarded as an integral part of the value-added tax, even though similar taxes in other countries might be classified elsewhere (e.g., 5126 as taxes on services or 4400 as taxes on financial and capital transactions).

5112 — *Sales taxes*

61. All general taxes levied at one stage only, whether at manufacturing or production, wholesale or retail stage are classified here.

5113 — *Turnover and other general taxes on goods and services*

62. These are multi-stage cumulative taxes and taxes where elements of consumption taxes are combined with multistage taxes. These taxes are levied each time a transaction takes place without deduction for taxes paid on inputs. Multi-stage taxes can be combined with elements of value-added or sales taxes.

5120 — *Taxes on specific goods and services*

63. Excises, profits generated and transferred from fiscal monopolies, and customs and imports duties as well as taxes on exports, foreign exchange transactions, investment goods and betting stakes and special taxes on services, which do not form part of a general tax of 5110, are included in this category.

5121 — *Excises*

64. Excises are taxes levied as a product specific unit tax on a predefined limited range of goods. Excises are usually levied at differentiated rates on nonessential or luxury goods, alcoholic beverages, tobacco, and energy. Excises may be imposed at any stage of production or distribution and are usually assessed as a specific charge per unit based on characteristics by reference to the value, weight, strength, or quantity of the product. Included are special taxes on individual products such as sugar, sugar beets, matches, and chocolates; taxes levied at varying rates on a certain range of goods; and taxes levied on tobacco goods, alcoholic drinks, motor fuels, and hydrocarbon oils. If a tax collected principally on imported goods also applies, or would apply, under the same law to comparable domestically produced goods, then the revenue from this tax is classified as arising from excises rather than from import duties. This principle applies even if there is no comparable domestic production or no possibility of such production. Taxes on the use of utilities such as water, electricity, gas, and energy are regarded as excises rather than taxes on specific services (5126). Excises exclude those taxes that are levied as general taxes on goods and services (5110); profits of fiscal monopolies (5122); customs and other import duties (5123); or taxes on exports (5124).

5122 — *Profits of fiscal monopolies*

65. This sub-heading covers that part of the profits of fiscal monopolies which is transferred to general government or which is used to finance any expenditures considered to be government expenditures (see §23). Amounts are shown when they are transferred to general government or used to make expenditures considered to be government expenditures.

66. Fiscal monopolies reflect the exercise of the taxing power of government by the use of monopoly powers. Fiscal monopolies are non-financial public enterprises exercising a monopoly in most cases over the production or distribution of tobacco, alcoholic beverages, salt, matches, playing cards and petroleum or agricultural products (i.e. on the kind of products which are likely to be, alternatively or additionally, subject to the excises of 5121), to raise the government revenues which in other countries are gathered through taxes on dealings in such commodities by private business units. The government monopoly may be at the production stage or, as in the case of government-owned and controlled liquor stores, at the distribution stage.

67. Fiscal monopolies are distinguished from public utilities such as rail transport, electricity, post offices, and other communications, which may enjoy a monopoly or quasi-monopoly position but where the primary purpose is normally to provide basic services rather than to raise revenue for government. Transfers from such other public enterprises to the government are considered as non-tax revenues. The traditional concept of fiscal monopoly is not generally extended to include state lotteries, the profits of which are usually accordingly regarded as non-tax revenues. However, they can be included as tax revenues if the prime reason for their operation is to raise revenues to finance government expenditure. Fiscal monopoly profits are distinguished from export and import monopoly profits (5127) transferred from marketing boards or other enterprises dealing with international trade.

5123 — *Customs and other import duties*

68. Taxes, stamp duties and surcharges restricted by law to imported products are included here. Also included are levies on imported agricultural products which are imposed in member countries of the European Union and amounts paid by certain of these countries under the Monetary Compensation Accounts (MCA) system.[17] Starting from 1998, customs duties collected by European Union member states on behalf of the European Union are no longer reported under this heading in the country tables (in Chapter 4 of the Report). Excluded here are taxes collected on imports as part of a general tax on goods and services, or an excise applicable to both imported and domestically produced goods.

5124 — *Taxes on exports*

69. In the 1970s, export duties were levied in Australia, Canada and Portugal as a regular measure and they have been used in Finland for counter-cyclical purposes. Some member countries of the European Union pay, as part of the MCA system, a levy on exports (see note 16 to §68). Where these amounts are identifiable, they are shown in this heading. This heading does not include repayments of general consumption taxes or excises or customs duties on exported goods, which should be deducted from the gross receipts under 5110, 5121 or 5123, as appropriate.

5125 — *Taxes on investment goods*

70. This sub-heading covers taxes on investment goods, such as machinery. These taxes may be imposed for a number of years or temporarily for counter-cyclical purposes. Taxes

on industrial inputs which are also levied on consumers [e.g., the Swedish energy tax which is classified under (5121)] are not included here.

5126 — *Taxes on specific services*

71. All taxes assessed on the payment for specific services, such as taxes on insurance premiums, banking services, gambling and betting stakes (e.g., from horse races, football pools, lottery tickets), transport, entertainment, restaurant and advertising charges, fall into this category. Taxes levied on the gross income of companies providing the service (e.g., gross insurance premiums or gambling stakes received by the company) are also classified under this heading. Tax revenues from bank levies and payments to deposit insurance and financial stability schemes are provisionally included here for the 2012 edition. The detailed classification is set out in §108.

72. Excluded from this sub-heading are:

a. taxes on services forming part of a general tax on goods and services (5110);

b. taxes on electricity, gas and energy (5121 as excises);

c. taxes on individual gains from gambling (1120 as taxes on capital gains of individuals and non-corporate enterprises) and lump-sum taxes on the transfer of private lotteries or on the permission to set up lotteries (5200);[18]

d. taxes on cheques and on the issue, transfer or redemption of securities (4400 as taxes on financial and capital transactions).

5127 — *Other taxes on international trade and transactions*

73. This sub-heading covers revenue received by the government from the purchase and sale of foreign exchange at different rates. When the government exercises monopoly powers to extract a margin between the purchase and sales price of foreign exchange, other than to cover administrative costs, the revenue derived constitutes a compulsory levy exacted in indeterminate proportions from both purchaser and seller of foreign exchange. It is the common equivalent of an import duty and export duty levied in a single exchange rate system or of a tax on the sale or purchase of foreign exchange. Like the profits of fiscal monopolies and import or export monopolies transferred to government, it represents the exercise of monopoly powers for tax purposes and is included in tax revenues.

74. The sub-heading covers also the profits of export or import monopolies, which do not however exist in OECD countries, taxes on purchase or sale of foreign exchange, and any other taxes levied specifically on international trade or transactions.

5128 — *Other taxes on specific goods and services*

75. This item includes taxes on the extraction of minerals, fossil fuels and other exhaustible resources from deposits owned privately or by another government together with any other unidentifiable receipts from taxes on specific goods and services. Taxes on the extraction of exhaustible resources are usually a fixed amount per unit of quality or weight, but can be a percentage of value. The taxes are recorded when the resources are extracted. Payments from the extraction of exhaustible resources from deposits owned by the government unit receiving the payment are classified as rent.

5200 — *Taxes on use of goods or on permission to use goods or perform activities*

76. This sub-heading covers taxes which are levied in respect of the use of goods as distinct from taxes on the goods themselves. Unlike the latter taxes – reported under 5100 –, they are

not assessed on the value of the goods but usually as fixed amounts. Taxes on permission to use goods or to perform activities are also included here, as are pollution taxes not based upon the value of particular goods. It is sometimes difficult to distinguish between compulsory user charges and licence fees which are regarded as taxes and those which are excluded as non-tax revenues. The criteria which are employed are noted in §11–12.

77. Although the sub-heading refers to the 'use' of goods, registration of ownership rather than use may be what generates liability to tax, so that the taxes of this heading may apply to the ownership of animals or goods rather than their use (e.g., race horses, dogs and motor vehicles) and may apply even to unusable goods (e.g., unusable motor vehicles or guns).

78. Borderline cases arise with:

a. taxes on the permission to perform business activities which are levied on a combined income, payroll or turnover base and, accordingly, are classified following the rules in §81;

b. taxes on the ownership or use of property of headings 4100, 4200 and 4600. The heading 4100 is confined to taxes on the ownership or tenancy of immovable property and – unlike the taxes of 5200 – they are related to the value of the property. The net wealth taxes and taxes on chattels of 4200 and 4600 respectively are confined to the ownership rather than the use of assets, apply to groups of assets rather than particular goods and again are related to the value of the assets,

5210 — *Recurrent taxes on use of goods and on permission to use goods or perform activities*

79. The principal characteristic of taxes classified here is that they are levied at regular intervals and that they are usually fixed amounts. The most important item in terms of revenue receipts is vehicle licence taxes. This sub-heading also covers taxes on permission to hunt, shoot, fish or to sell certain products and taxes on the ownership of dogs and on the performance of certain services, provided that they meet the criteria set out in §11–12. The sub-divisions of 5210 are user taxes on motor vehicles paid by households (5211) and those paid by others (5212). Sub-heading 5213 covers dog licences and user charges for permission to perform activities such as selling meat or liquor when the levies are on a recurring basis. It also covers recurrent general licences for hunting, shooting and fishing where the right to carry out these activities is not granted as part of a normal commercial transaction (e.g., the granting of the licence is not accompanied by the right to use a specific area which is owned by government).

5220 — *Non-recurrent taxes on use of goods and on permission to use goods or perform activities*

80. This section covers non-recurrent taxes levied on the use of goods or on permission to use goods or perform activities and taxes levied each time goods are used. It includes taxes levied on the emission or discharge into the environment of noxious gases, liquids or other harmful substances.

- Payments for tradable emission permits issued by governments under cap and trade schemes should be recorded here at the time the emissions occur. No revenue should be recorded for permits that governments issue free of charge. The accrual basis of recording means that there can be a timing difference between the cash being received by government for the permits and the time the emission occurs. In the national accounts, this timing gives rise to a financial liability for government during the period.

- Payments made for the collection and disposal of waste or noxious substances by public authorities should be excluded as they constitute a sale of services to enterprises.

81. Other taxes falling under heading 5200 that are not levied recurrently are also included here. Thus, once-and-for-all payments for permission to sell liquor or tobacco or to set up betting shops are included provided they meet the criteria set out in §11–12.

6000 — Other taxes

82. Taxes levied on a base, or bases, other than those described under headings 1000, 3000, 4000 and 5000, or on bases of which cannot be considered to be related to any one of these headings, are included here. Where taxes are levied on a multiple base and it is possible to estimate the receipts related to each base the separate amounts are included under the appropriate headings. If separate amounts cannot be estimated and it is known that most of the receipts are derived from one base, the whole of the receipts are classified according to that base. Otherwise, they are classified here. Other revenues included here are presumptive taxes not included elsewhere in the classification system, taxes on individuals in the form of a poll tax or capitation tax, stamp taxes not related to financial and capital transactions nor falling exclusively on a single category of transaction, expenditure taxes where personal deductions or exemptions are applied and unidentifiable tax receipts. A subdivision is made between taxes levied wholly or predominantly on business (6100) and those levied on others (6200).

A.6. Conciliation with National Accounts

83. This section of the tables provides a re-conciliation between the OECD calculation of total tax revenues and the total of all taxes and social contributions paid to general government as recorded in the country's National Accounts. Where the country is a member of the European Union (EU), the comparison is between the OECD calculation of total tax revenues and the sum of tax revenues and social contributions recorded in the combination of the general government and the institutions of the EU sectors of the National Accounts.

A.7. Memorandum item on the financing of social security benefits

84. In view of the varying relationship between taxation and social security contributions and the cases referred to in §39 to §45, a memorandum item collects together all payments earmarked for social security-type benefits, other than voluntary payments to the private sector. Data are presented as follows (refer to Chapter 4.2 of the Report):

a. Taxes of 2000 series.

b. Taxes earmarked for social security benefits.

c. Voluntary contributions to the government.

d. Compulsory contributions to the private sector.

Guidance on the breakdown of (a) to (d) above is provided in §39 to §45.

A.8. Memorandum item on identifiable taxes paid by government

85. Identifiable taxes actually paid by government are presented in a memorandum item classified by the main headings of the OECD classification of taxes. In the vast majority of countries, only social security contributions and payroll taxes paid by government can

be identified. These are, however, usually the most important taxes paid by governments (refer to Chapter 4.2 of the Report).

A.9. Relation of OECD classification of taxes to national accounting systems

86. A system of national accounts (SNA) seeks to provide a coherent framework for recording and presenting the main flows relating respectively to production, consumption, accumulation and external transactions of a given economic area, usually a country or a major region within a country. Government revenues are an important part of the transactions recorded in SNA. The final version of the 2008 SNA was jointly published by five international organisations: the United Nations, the International Monetary Fund, the European Union, the Organisation for Economic Co-operation and Development, and the World Bank in August 2009. The *System* is a comprehensive, consistent and flexible set of macroeconomic accounts. It is designed for use in countries with market economies, whatever their stage of economic development, and also in countries in transition to market economies. The important parts of the SNA's conceptual framework and its definitions of the various sectors of the economy have been reflected in the OECD's classification of taxes.

87. There are, however, some differences between the OECD classification of taxes and SNA concepts that are listed below. They arise because the aim of the former is to provide the maximum disaggregation of statistical data on what are generally regarded as taxes by tax administrations.

a. OECD includes compulsory social security contributions paid to general government in total tax revenues. Imputed and voluntary contributions plus those paid to private funds are not treated as taxes (§8 and §10 above);
b. there are different points of view on whether or not some levies and fees are classified as taxes (§11 and §12 above);
c. OECD excludes imputed taxes or subsidies resulting from the operation of official multiple exchange rates or from the central bank paying a rate of interest on required reserves that is different from other market rates;
d. there are differences in the treatment of non-wastable tax credits

88. As noted in §1 and §2, headings 1000 to 6000 of the OECD list of taxes cover all unrequited payments to general government, other than compulsory loans and fines. Such unrequited payments including fines, but excluding compulsory loans can be obtained from adding together the following figures in the 2008 SNA

- value-added type taxes (D.211);
- taxes and duties on imports, excluding VAT (D.212);
- export taxes (D.213);
- taxes on products, excluding VAT, import and export taxes (D.214);
- other taxes on production (D.29);
- taxes on income (D.51);
- other current taxes (D.59);
- social contributions (D.61), excluding voluntary contributions;
- capital taxes (D.91).

A.10. The OECD classification of taxes and the International Monetary Fund (GFS) system

89. The coverage and valuation of tax revenues in the GFS system and the 2008 SNA are very similar. Therefore, the differences between the OECD classification and that of the 2008 SNA (see §87 above) also apply to the GFS. In addition the International Monetary Fund subdivides the OECD 5000 heading into section IV (Domestic Taxes on Goods and Services) and section V (Taxes on International Trade and Transactions). This reflects the fact that while the latter usually yield insignificant amounts of revenue in OECD countries, this is not the case in many non-OECD countries.

A.11. Comparison of the OECD classification of taxes with other international classifications

90. The table below describes an item by item comparison of the OECD classification of taxes and the classifications used in the following:

a. System of National Accounts (2008 SNA);

b. European System of Accounts (2010 ESA);

c. IMF *Government Finance Statistics Manual* (GFSM2014).

91. These comparisons represent those that would be expected to apply in the majority of cases. However in practice some flexibility should be used in their application. This is because in particular cases, countries can adopt varying approaches to the classification of revenues in National Accounts.

OECD Classification	2008 SNA	2010 ESA	GFSM2014
1000 Taxes on income, profits and capital gains			
1100 Individuals			
1110 Income and profits	D51-8.61a	D51A	1111
1120 Capital gains	D51-8.61c, d	D51C, D	1111
1200 Corporations			
1210 Income and profits	D51-8.61b	D51B	1112
1220 Capital gains	D51-8.61c	D51C	1112
1300 Unallocable as between 1100 and 1200			1113
2000 Social security contributions			
2100 Employees	D613-8.85	D613	1211
2200 Employers	D611-8.83	D611	1212
2300 Self-employed, non-employed	D613-8.85	D613	1213
2400 Unallocable as between 2100, 2200 and 2300			1214
3000 Taxes on payroll and workforce	D29-7.97a	D29C	112
4000 Taxes on property			
4100 Recurrent taxes on immovable property			
4110 Households	D59-8.63a	D59A	1131
4120 Other	D29-7.97b	D29A	1131
4200 Recurrent net wealth taxes			
4210 Individual	D59-8.63b	D59A	1132
4220 Corporations	D59-8.63b	D59A	1132
4300 Estate, inheritance and gift taxes			
4310 Estate and inheritance taxes	D91-10.207b	D91A	1133
4320 Gift taxes	D91-10.207b	D91A	1133
4400 Taxes on financial and capital transactions	D59-7.96d; D29-7.97e	D214B, C	114114; 1161
4500 Other non-recurrent taxes on property	D91-10.207a	D91B	1135
4600 Other recurrent taxes on property	D59-8.63c	D59A	1136

OECD Classification	2008 SNA	2010 ESA	GFSM2014
5000 Taxes on goods and services			
5100 Taxes on production, sale and transfer of goods and services			
5110 General taxes on goods and services			
5111 Value-added taxes	D211-7.89	D211; D29G	11411
5112 Sales taxes	D2122-7.94a; D214-7.96a	D21224; D214I	11412
5113 Other general taxes on goods and services	D214-7.96a	D214I	11413
5120 Taxes on specific goods and services			
5121 Excises	D2122-7.94b; D214-7.96b	D21223; D214A, B, D	1142
5122 Profits of fiscal monopolies	D214-7.96e	D214J	1143
5123 Customs and other import duties	D2121-7.93	D2121; D21221, 2	1151
5124 On exports	D213-7.95a	D214K	1152-4
5125 On investment goods			
5126 On specific services	D2122-7.94c; D214-7.96c	D21225; D214E, F, G, H; D29F	1144; 1156
5127 Other taxes on international trade and transactions	D2122-7.94d D29-7.95b D29-7.97g D59-8.64d	D21226; D29D; D59E	1153; 1155-6
5128 Other taxes on specific goods and services			1146
5130 Unallocable between 5110 and 5120			
5200 Taxes on use of goods and on permission to use goods or perform activities			
5210 Recurrent taxes on use of goods and on permission to use goods or perform activities			
5211 Motor vehicle taxes households	D59-8.64c	D59D	11451
5212 Motor vehicles taxes others	D29-7.97d	D214D; D29B	11451
5213 Other recurrent taxes on use of goods and on permission to use goods or perform activities	D29-7.97c, d, f D59-8.64c	D29B, E, F; D59D	11452
5220 Non-recurrent taxes on permission to use goods or perform activities			11452
5300 Unallocable as between 5100 and 5200			
6000 Other taxes			
6100 Payable solely by business			1161
6200 Payable by other than business, or unidentifiable	D59-8.64a, b	D59B, C	1162

A.12. Attribution of tax revenues by sub-sectors of general government

92. The OECD classification requires a breakdown of tax revenues by sub-sectors of government. The definition of each sub-sector and the criteria to be used to attribute tax revenues between these sub-sectors are set out below. They follow the guidance of the 2008 SNA and GFSM 2014.

Sub-sectors of general government to be identified

a) Central government

93. The central government sub-sector includes all governmental departments, offices, establishments and other bodies which are agencies or instruments of the central authority whose competence extends over the whole territory, with the exception of the administration of social security funds. Central government therefore has the authority to impose taxes on all resident and non-resident units engaged in economic activities within the country.

b) State, provincial or regional government

94. This sub-sector consists of intermediate units of government exercising a competence at a level below that of central government. It includes all such units operating independently of central government in a part of a country's territory encompassing a number of smaller

localities, with the exception of the administration of social security funds. In unitary countries, regional governments may be considered to have a separate existence where they have substantial autonomy to raise a significant proportion of their revenues from sources within their control and their officers are independent of external administrative control in the actual operation of the unit's activities.

95. At present, federal countries comprise the majority of cases where revenues attributed to intermediate units of government are identified separately. Spain is the only unitary country in this position. In the remaining unitary countries, regional revenues are included with those of local governments.

c) Local government

96. This sub-sector includes all other units of government exercising an independent competence in part of the territory of a country, with the exception of the administration of social security funds. It encompasses various urban and/or rural jurisdictions (e.g., local authorities, municipalities, cities, boroughs, districts).

d) Social security funds

97. Social security funds form a separate sub-sector of general government. The social security sub-sector is defined in the 2008 SNA by the following extracts from paragraphs 4.124 to 4.126 and 4.147:

> *"Social security schemes are social insurance schemes covering the community as a whole or large section of the community that are imposed and controlled by government units. The schemes cover a wide variety of programmes, providing benefits in cash or in kind for old age, invalidity or death, survivors, sickness and maternity, work injury, unemployment, family allowance, health care, etc. There is not necessarily a direct link between the amount of the contribution paid by an individual and the benefits he or she may receive." (Paragraph 4.124).*
>
> *"When social security schemes are separately organised from the other activities of government units and hold their assets and liabilities separately from the latter and engage in financial transactions on their own account they qualify as institutional units that are described as social security funds." (Paragraph 4.125).*
>
> *"The amounts raised, and paid out, in social security contributions and benefits may be deliberately varied in order to achieve objectives of government policy that have no direct connection with the concept of social security as a scheme to provide social benefits to members of the community. They may be raised or lowered in order to influence the level of aggregate demand in the economy, for example. Nevertheless, so long as they remain separately constituted funds, they must be treated as separate institutional units in the SNA. (Paragraph 4.126).*
>
> *"The social security funds sub-sector (of general government) consists of the social security funds operating at all levels of government. Such funds are social insurance schemes covering the community as a whole or large section of the community that are imposed by government units." (Paragraph 4.147).*

98. This definition of social security funds is followed in the OECD classification with the two following exceptions which are excluded

- Schemes imposed by government and operated by bodies outside the general government sector, as defined in §3 of this manual; and
- Schemes to which all contributions are voluntary.

Supra-national Authorities

99. This sub-sector covers the revenue-raising operations of supra-national authorities within a country. In practice, the only relevant supra-national authority in the OECD area is that of the institutions of the European Union (EU). As from 1998, supra-national authorities are no longer included in the *Revenue Statistics*, to achieve consistency with the SNA definition of general government which excludes them. For example, income taxes and social security contributions collected by European Institutions and paid by European civil servants who are resident of EU member countries should not be included. However the specific levies paid by the member states of the EU continue to be included in total tax revenues and they are shown under this heading.

Criteria to be used for the attribution of tax revenues

100. When a government collects taxes and pays them over in whole or in part to other governments, it is necessary to determine whether the revenues should be considered to be those of the collecting government which it distributes to others as grants, or those of the beneficiary governments which the collecting government receives and passes on only as their agent. The criteria to be used in the attribution of revenues are set out in §101 to §104 which replicate paragraphs 3.70 to 3.73 from the 2008 SNA.

101. In general, a tax is attributed to the government unit that

a. exercises the authority to impose the tax (either as a principal or through the delegated authority of the principal),

b. has final discretion to set and vary the rate of the tax

102. Where an amount is collected by one government for and on behalf of another government, and the latter government has the authority to impose the tax, and set and vary its rate, then the former is acting as an agent for the latter and the tax is reassigned. Any amount retained by the collecting government as a collection charge should be treated as a payment for a service. Any other amount retained by the collecting government, such as under a tax-sharing arrangement, should be treated as a current grant. If the collecting government was delegated the authority to set and vary the rate, then the amount collected should be treated as tax revenue of this government.

103. Where different governments jointly and equally set the rate of a tax and jointly and equally decide on the distribution of the proceeds, with no individual government having ultimate overriding authority, then the tax revenues are attributed to each government according to its respective share of the proceeds. If an arrangement allows one government unit to exercise ultimate overriding authority, then all of the tax revenue is attributed to that unit.

104. There may also be the circumstance where a tax is imposed under the constitutional or other authority of one government, but other governments individually set the tax rate in their jurisdictions. The proceeds of the tax generated in each respective government's jurisdiction are attributed as tax revenues of that government.

Levies paid by member states of the European Union

105. The levies paid by the member states of the EU take the form specific levies which include

a. custom duties and levies on agricultural goods (5123),

b. gross monetary compensation accounts (5123 if relating to imports and 5124 if relating to exports); and

c. Steel, coal, sugar and milk levies (5128).

106. The custom duties collected by member states on behalf of the EU are recorded

- on a gross of collection fee basis;
- using figures adjusted so that duties are shown on a 'final destination' as opposed to a 'country of first entry' basis where such adjustments can be made. These adjustments concern in particular duties collected at important (sea) ports. Although the EU duties are collected by the authorities of the country of first entry, when possible these duties should be excluded from the revenue of the collecting country and be included in the revenue of the country of final destination

107. This is the specific EU levy that most clearly conforms to the attribution criterion described in §99 above. Consequently as from 1998, these amounts are footnoted as a memorandum item to EU member state country tables and no longer shown under heading 5123. However the figures are included in the total tax revenue figures on the top line for all the relevant years shown in the tables.

A.13. Provisional classification of revenues from bank levies and payments to deposit insurance and financial stability schemes

108. The OECD have adopted the following interim approach to reporting revenue from bank levies plus deposit insurance and stability fees for the 2012 and subsequent editions of *OECD Revenue Statistics*. It is recommended that the amounts should be recorded under category 5126.

- Compulsory payments of stability fees, bank levies and deposit insurance should generally be treated as tax revenues where the payments are made to General Government and allocated to the governments' consolidated or general funds so that the Government is free to make immediate use of the money for the purposes that it chooses. This principle would apply regardless of whether the Government is promising to make payments to guarantee the banks' customer deposits in some future contingency.
- If the compulsory payments are made to general government and placed in funds that are earmarked to be entirely channelled back to the sector of the economy that comprises the companies that are subject to the payment, they would still generally be treated as tax revenues on the grounds that the funds would be available for the government and would reduce its budget deficit, the fee is unrequited for an individual entity and the amounts raised could be unrelated to any eventual pay out to depositors or expenditure on wider support for the financial sector.
- Payments to made to the smaller long-standing schemes for insuring 'retail' deposits, where the payment levels are consistent with the costs of insurance should be classified as fee for service.
- Any payments which involve governments realising the assets of a failed institution or receiving a priority claim on its assets in liquidation in order to fund payments of compensation to customers for their lost deposits would be treated as a fee for a service as opposed to tax revenues.
- Compulsory payments that are made to funds operated outside the government sector and non-state institutions backed by the deposit takers and all payments to voluntary schemes should not be treated as tax revenues.

Notes

1. References in this OECD Interpretative Guide to Sections or Parts of "this Report" refer to OECD (2020), Revenue Statistics 2020, OECD Publishing, Paris
2. All references to SNA are to the 2008 edition.
3. See section A.12 of this guide for a discussion of the concept of agency capacity.
4. It is usually possible to identify amounts of social security contributions and payroll taxes, but not other taxes paid by government.
5. If, however, a levy which is considered as non-tax revenue by most countries is regarded as a tax — or raises substantial revenue — in one or more countries, the amounts collected are footnoted at the end of the relevant country tables, even though the amounts are not included in total tax revenues.
6. Names, however, can frequently be misleading. For example, though a passport fee would normally be considered a non-tax revenue, if a supplementary levy on passports (as is the case in Portugal) were imposed in order to raise substantial amounts of revenue relative to the cost of providing the passport, the levy would be regarded as a tax under 5200.
7. A more detailed explanation of this distinction can be found in the special feature, 'Current issues in reporting tax revenues', in the 2001 edition of the *Revenue Statistics*.
8. Sometimes the terms 'non-refundable' and 'refundable' are used, but it may be considered illogical to talk of 'refundable' when nothing has been paid.
9. A different treatment, however, is accorded to non-wastable tax credits under imputation systems of corporate income tax (§36–38).
10. This is not strictly a true tax expenditure in the formal sense. Such tax expenditures require identification of a benchmark tax system for each country or, preferably, a common international benchmark. In practice it has not been possible to reach agreement on a common international benchmark.
11. Unless based on the profit made on a sale, in which case they would be classified as capital gains taxes under 1120 or 1220.
12. In some countries the same legislation applies to both individual and corporate enterprises for particular taxes on income. However, the receipts from such taxes are usually allocable between individuals and enterprises and can therefore be shown in the appropriate sub-heading.
13. For example, " sufficiently self-contained and independent that they behave in the same way as corporations.......(including) keeping a complete set of accounts" (2008 SNA, section 4.44).
14. In Canada — a country also referred to as having an imputation system — the (wastable) tax credit for the shareholder is in respect of domestic corporation tax deemed to have been paid whether or not a corporation tax liability has arisen. As there is no integral connection between the corporation tax liability and the credit given against income tax under such systems, these credits for dividends are treated, along with other tax credits, on the lines described in §25.
15. This may also apply where a scheme for government employees existed prior to the introduction of a general social security scheme.
16. In the 2008 SNA these are regarded as capital transfers and not as taxes (see section A.8).
17. This is the system by which the European Union adjusts for differences between the exchange rates used to determine prices under the Common Market Agricultural Policy and actual exchange rates. Payments under the system may relate to imports or exports and where these amounts are separately identifiable they are shown under the appropriate heading (5123 or 5124). In this Report, these amounts are shown gross (i.e. without deducting any subsidies paid out under the MCA system).
18. Transfers of profits of State lotteries are regarded as non-tax revenues (see also §67).

Annexe A

Classification des impôts de l'OCDE et Guide d'interprétation[1]

Table des matières

A.1. Classification des impôts de l'OCDE

1. 1000 Impôts sur le revenu, les bénéfices et les gains en capital
    - 1100 Impôts sur le revenu, les bénéfices et les gains en capital des personnes physiques
        - 1110 Sur le revenu et les bénéfices
        - 1120 Sur les gains en capital
    - 1200 Impôts sur le revenu, les bénéfices et les gains en capital des sociétés
        - 1210 Sur le revenu et les bénéfices
        - 1220 Sur les gains en capital
    - 1300 Non ventilables entres les rubriques 110 et 1200
2. 2000 Cotisations de sécurité sociale
    - 2100 A la charge des salariés
        - 2110 Sur la base du salaire
        - 2120 Sur la base de l'impôt sur le revenu
    - 2200 A la charge des employeurs
        - 2210 Sur la base du salaire
        - 2220 Sur la base de l'impôt sur le revenu
    - 2300 A la charge des travailleurs indépendants ou des personnes n'occupant pas d'emploi
        - 2310 Sur la base du salaire
        - 2320 Sur la base de l'impôt sur le revenu
    - 2400 Non ventilables entre les rubriques 2100, 2200 et 2300
        - 2410 Sur la base du salaire
        - 2420 Sur la base de l'impôt sur le revenu
3. 3000 Impôts sur les salaires et la main-d'œuvre
4. 4000 Impôts sur le patrimoine
    - 4100 Impôts périodiques sur la propriété immobilière
        - 4110 Ménages
        - 4120 Autres agents
    - 4200 Impôts périodiques sur l'actif net
        - 4210 Personnes physiques
        - 4220 Sociétés
    - 4300 Impôts sur les mutations par décès, les successions et les donations
        - 4310 Impôts sur les mutations par décès et les successions
        - 4320 Impôts sur les donations
    - 4400 Impôts sur les transactions mobilières et immobilières
    - 4500 Autres impôts non périodiques sur le patrimoine
        - 4510 Impôts sur l'actif net
        - 4520 Autres impôts non périodiques
    - 4600 Autres impôts périodiques sur le patrimoine

5. 5000 Impôts sur les biens et services

5100 Impôts sur la production, la vente, le transfert, la location et la livraison des biens et la prestation de services

5110 Impôts généraux

5111 Taxes sur la valeur ajoutée

5112 Impôts sur les ventes

5113 Impôts sur le chiffre d'affaires et autres impôts généraux sur les biens et services

5120 Impôts sur des biens et des services déterminés

5121 Accises

5122 Bénéfices des monopoles fiscaux

5123 Droits de douane et autres droits à l'importation

5124 Taxes à l'exportation

5125 Impôts sur les biens d'équipement

5126 Impôts sur des services déterminés

5127 Autres impôts sur les transactions et les échanges internationaux

5128 Autres impôts sur des biens et services déterminés

5130 Non ventilables entre les rubriques 5110 et 5120

5200 Impôts sur l'utilisation des biens ou l'autorisation d'utiliser des biens ou d'exercer des activités

5210 Impôts périodiques

5211 A la charge des ménages au titre de véhicules à moteur

5212 A la charge d'autres agents au titre de véhicules à moteur

5213 Autres impôts périodiques

5220 Impôts non périodiques

5300 Non ventilables entre les rubriques 5100 et 5200

6. 6000 Autres impôts

6100 A la charge exclusive des entreprises

6200 A la charge d'autre agents que les entreprises ou non identifiables

A.2. Champ couvert

Principes généraux

1. Dans la classification de l'OCDE, le terme « impôts » désigne uniquement les versements obligatoires effectués sans contrepartie au profit des administrations publiques. Les impôts n'ont pas de contrepartie en ce sens que, normalement, les prestations fournies par les administrations au contribuable ne sont pas proportionnelles à ses versements.

2. Le terme « impôts » ne couvre pas les amendes, les pénalités, ni les prêts obligatoires aux administrations. Les cas dans lesquels la délimitation entre recettes fiscales et non fiscales est délicate à tracer, pour certains droits et taxes d'utilisation, sont examinés dans les § 11 à 14.

3. Les administrations publiques comprennent l'administration centrale et les organismes dont les opérations sont sous son contrôle effectif, les administrations régionales et locales et leurs services, les organismes de sécurité sociale et les entités publiques autonomes, à l'exception des entreprises publiques. Cette définition des administrations est calquée sur celle du Système de comptabilité nationale 2008 (SCN)[2]. Dans cette publication, les administrations publiques et leurs sous-secteurs sont décrits dans le chapitre 4, paragraphes 4.117 à 4.165.

4. Les unités extrabudgétaires sont des composantes du système des administrations publiques. Il s'agit d'entités d'administration publique dotées de budgets distincts, qui ne sont pas intégralement financés par le budget central ou général. Ces organismes fonctionnent sous l'autorité ou le contrôle d'une administration centrale, d'un État fédéré ou d'une collectivité locale. Les entités extrabudgétaires peuvent disposer de leurs propres sources de recettes, qui peuvent être complétées par des dotations (transferts) provenant du budget général ou d'autres sources. Même si leurs budgets peuvent être soumis à l'approbation du corps législatif, comme les comptes budgétaires, elles disposent d'une certaine latitude quant au volume et à la composition de leurs dépenses. Ces entités peuvent être mises en place pour exercer des fonctions spécifiques des administrations publiques, telles que la construction de routes ou la production non marchande de services de santé ou d'éducation. Les dispositions budgétaires peuvent varier grandement suivant les pays, et différents termes sont utilisés pour décrire ces entités, mais elles sont souvent qualifiées de « fonds extrabudgétaires » ou d'« organismes autonomes ».

5. Les paiements obligatoires à des organismes supranationaux et aux organismes qui en dépendent ne sont plus compris depuis 1998 parmi les impôts sauf quelques exceptions. En effet, les droits de douane collectés par les États membres de l'Union européenne pour le compte de celle-ci sont toujours présentés à titre de rubrique « Pour mémoire » et compris dans le total des recettes fiscales (voir § 99). Dans les pays où les églises font partie des administrations publiques, les impôts sur les cultes sont inclus dans ces paiements, à condition qu'ils répondent aux critères énoncés au § 1 ci-dessus. Comme les données se réfèrent aux montants encaissés par les administrations publiques, les contributions versées à des organismes privés, aux organismes sociaux ou régimes de sécurité sociale extérieurs aux administrations publiques, aux syndicats ou aux associations professionnelles sont exclues, même si elles sont obligatoires. Sont toutefois inclus les versements obligatoires aux administrations publiques dont le montant est affecté à ces organismes, à condition que l'administration ne fasse pas simplement office d'agent collecteur[3]. On a distingué les bénéfices des monopoles fiscaux de ceux d'autres entreprises publiques et on les a considérés comme des impôts parce qu'ils reflètent l'exercice du pouvoir d'imposition de l'État par l'intermédiaire du monopole (voir § 65 à 67), comme le sont les bénéfices de l'État provenant de l'achat et de la vente de monnaies étrangères à des taux différents (voir § 74).

6. Les impôts payés par les administrations elles-mêmes (tels que les cotisations de sécurité sociale et les impôts sur les salaires payés par les administrations en tant qu'employeurs (2200 et 3000), les impôts sur la consommation qu'elles acquittent à l'occasion de leurs achats ou les impôts sur leur patrimoine) sont inclus dans les données présentées. Toutefois, lorsqu'il est possible de les isoler, les montants provenant de ces impôts[4] sont indiqués dans le chapitre 4.2 de cette publication.

7. Les rapports entre cette classification et celle du Système de comptabilité nationale (SCN) sont indiqués dans les sections A.9 et A.11. À cause des différences qui existent entre les deux classifications, les statistiques de la comptabilité nationale ne sont pas toujours établies ou classées suivant la pratique adoptée dans le présent guide. Ces différences et d'autres encore sont mentionnées dans les cas appropriés (voir par exemple § 30), mais il est impossible de toutes les signaler. Il peut y avoir aussi certaines différences entre cette classification et celle utilisée par certaines administrations nationales (voir par exemple § 12), aussi les statistiques nationales et celles de l'OCDE ne peuvent pas toujours être compatibles ; ces différences, cependant, sont vraisemblablement très insignifiantes dans les montants des recettes en cause.

Cotisations de sécurité sociale

8. Les cotisations obligatoires de sécurité sociale, définies au § 39, qui sont versées aux administrations publiques, font partie des recettes fiscales. Elles sont évidemment assimilables à des impôts puisqu'il s'agit de versements obligatoires à des administrations publiques. Mais elles peuvent différer toutefois des autres impôts du fait que le paiement des prestations de sécurité sociale dépend dans la plupart des pays du versement des cotisations appropriées, encore qu'il n'y ait pas forcément un lien entre l'importance des prestations et le montant des cotisations. La comparabilité entre les pays sera meilleure si on considère les cotisations de sécurité sociale comme des impôts ; elles figurent cependant sous une rubrique distincte de façon à permettre un traitement séparé pour n'importe quelle analyse.

9. La distinction stricte entre les recettes fiscales (qui sont des paiements obligatoires sans contrepartie aux administrations publiques) et les prélèvements obligatoires non fiscaux (PONF) (qui sont soit des paiements avec contrepartie aux administrations publiques, soit des paiements destinés à d'autres organismes) est clairement définie. Néanmoins, dans la palette des divers prélèvements obligatoires destinés aux administrations publiques qui existent dans les différents pays, il n'est pas toujours évident de déterminer en pratique si tel ou tel prélèvement est un impôt ou un PONF. Ainsi, l'épargne-retraite obligatoire qui est placée sous le contrôle des administrations publiques et qui s'accumule sur un compte individuel rémunéré à un taux correspondant au rendement du marché ou destiné à compenser l'inflation semble, à première vue, constituer une forme de PONF, et non d'impôt. Toutefois, ces paiements peuvent encore être considérés comme « sans contrepartie » et, par conséquent, être classés dans les impôts et non dans les PONF (par exemple si cette épargne-retraite n'est pas remboursée au cas où le contribuable décède avant d'atteindre l'âge de la retraite, et si les fonds en question sont utilisés ensuite pour verser une pension minimale à tous les contribuables qui sont assurés). En conséquence, les chiffres relatifs aux recettes de sécurité sociale indiqués pour la plupart des pays reposent sur l'hypothèse que l'on considère que tous les types de prélèvements obligatoires destinés aux administrations publiques comportent, dans une certaine mesure, un élément redistributif. Il convient de noter que cette conclusion découle d'une interprétation généralement large du terme « sans contrepartie » dans la définition de l'impôt.

10. Les cotisations de sécurité sociale qui sont facultatives ou qui ne sont pas versées à des administrations publiques (voir § 1) ne sont pas considérées comme des impôts, bien que dans certains pays (comme il est indiqué dans les notes correspondantes), il soit difficile d'éliminer complètement les cotisations facultatives et certains versements obligatoires au secteur privé des statistiques relatives aux recettes publiques. Les cotisations de sécurité sociale imputées ne sont pas considérées comme des impôts.

Droits, taxes d'utilisation et droits de licence

11. Si l'on excepte les droits perçus sur les permis de circulation des véhicules à moteur, qui sont universellement considérés comme des impôts, il n'est pas facile de distinguer les droits et taxes d'utilisation qui doivent être traitées comme des impôts de celles qui ne doivent pas l'être. Si, en effet, un droit ou une taxe est perçu au titre d'un service ou d'une activité déterminée, le lien entre ce prélèvement et la prestation fournie peut être plus ou moins important, de même que la relation entre le montant du prélèvement et le coût de la prestation. Lorsque le bénéficiaire d'une prestation acquitte un droit dont le montant est clairement lié au coût de la prestation fournie, on peut considérer que le prélèvement comporte une contrepartie, et d'après la définition donnée au § 1, il ne sera pas traité comme un impôt. Toutefois, dans les cas suivants, les prélèvements seraient 'sans contrepartie':

a. lorsque le prélèvement est très supérieur au coût de la prestation fournie ;
b. lorsque le redevable de la contribution n'est pas le bénéficiaire de la prestation correspondante (par exemple, un droit perçu sur l'abattage du bétail pour financer un service qui est fourni aux agriculteurs) ;
c. lorsque l'État ne fournit pas un service déterminé en contrepartie du droit qu'il perçoit, même si un permis est délivré à celui qui acquitte le droit (par exemple, lorsque l'État délivre des permis de chasse, de pêche ou de port d'armes qui ne sont pas assortis du droit d'utiliser une parcelle déterminée de terres appartenant à l'État) ;
d. lorsque les bénéficiaires de la prestation sont les personnes qui ont acquitté le droit, mais que la prestation dont chacun bénéficie n'est pas nécessairement en rapport avec le montant de ses propres versements (par exemple, le droit de commercialisation du lait acquitté par les fermiers qui sert à promouvoir la consommation de lait.

12. Dans des cas limites, cependant, l'application des critères énoncés au § 1 peut être particulièrement difficile. La solution adoptée, dans un souci d'uniformité entre les pays et eu égard aux montants relativement faibles des recettes en cause, consiste à s'en tenir à la pratique prépondérante des administrations fiscales plutôt que de laisser chaque pays décider si ces prélèvements sont des impôts ou des recettes non fiscales[5].

13. On trouvera ci-après la liste des principaux droits et taxes en question et leur traitement normal[6] dans la présente publication :

- *Recettes non fiscales* : frais de justice ; droits de délivrance de permis de conduire ; droits portuaires ; redevances de passeport ; redevances de radio et de télévision lorsque le service est assuré par les pouvoirs publics.
- *Impôts du sous-groupe 5200:* autorisation d'exercer certaines activités telles que : distribution de films ; chasse, pêche et utilisation d'armes à feu ; organisation de spectacles ou de jeux et paris ; vente de boissons alcoolisées ou de tabacs ; autorisation de posséder des chiens et d'utiliser ou posséder des véhicules à moteur ou des armes à feu ; taxes d'extraction.

14. Dans la pratique, il se peut qu'il ne soit pas toujours possible d'isoler les recettes fiscales des recettes non fiscales quand elles sont enregistrées ensemble. Si l'on estime qu'il s'agit surtout de recettes non fiscales, l'ensemble sera traité comme tel ; dans le cas contraire, les recettes seront comptabilisées et classées conformément aux règles énoncées au § 32.

Redevances

15. La propriété des gisements prenant la forme de minéraux ou de combustibles fossiles (charbon, pétrole ou gaz naturel) dépend de la façon dont les droits de propriété sont définis par la loi, et aussi par les conventions internationales quand les gisements sont situés sous les eaux internationales. Dans certains cas, soit le terrain sous lequel les gisements sont situés, soit les gisements eux-mêmes, soit les deux peuvent appartenir à une administration publique centrale ou locale.

16. Ces unités des administrations publiques peuvent alors consentir un bail à d'autres unités institutionnelles en les autorisant à exploiter ces gisements pendant une période déterminée, en contrepartie d'un paiement ou d'une série de paiements. Ces paiements sont souvent qualifiés de redevances (« royalties »), mais ils n'en constituent pas moins essentiellement des loyers, qui reviennent aux propriétaires des ressources naturelles considérées parce qu'ils mettent ces actifs à la disposition d'autres unités institutionnelles pour des durées déterminées. Ces loyers peuvent prendre la forme de versements périodiques d'un montant fixe, indépendant du rythme d'extraction ; plus vraisemblablement, ils peuvent être fonction de la quantité, du volume ou de la valeur des actifs extraits. Les entreprises engagées dans des activités de prospection sur des terrains publics peuvent effectuer des paiements aux unités de l'administration publique concernées, en contrepartie de l'autorisation de procéder à des forages d'essai ou de réaliser par d'autres moyens des recherches concernant l'existence et la localisation de gisements. Ces paiements sont également considérés comme des loyers, même en l'absence d'extraction. Ils sont donc classés dans les recettes non fiscales.

17. Les mêmes principes s'appliquent lorsque d'autres unités institutionnelles se voient consentir un bail leur permettant de couper du bois dans des forêts naturelles sur des terrains appartenant à des unités des administrations publiques. Ces paiements sont également classés dans les recettes non fiscales.

18. Ces loyers ou redevances versés aux administrations publiques ne doivent pas être confondus avec les impôts sur le revenu et les bénéfices, les taxes d'extraction, les taxes professionnelles ou d'autres impôts. Si ces paiements sont prélevés sur les bénéfices tirés des activités d'extraction, ils doivent être classés dans les impôts sur le revenu, les bénéfices et les gains en capital (1000). En outre, toute taxe d'extraction relative à des minéraux ou des combustibles fossiles extraits de réserves privées ou appartenant à d'autres administrations publiques doit être classée dans les impôts. Les paiements liés à la valeur brute de la production doivent être classés dans les autres impôts sur des biens et services déterminés (5128). Les paiements effectués en contrepartie d'une autorisation ou d'un permis d'extraction doivent être classés dans les impôts sur l'utilisation des biens ou l'autorisation d'utiliser des biens ou d'exercer des activités (5200).

Amendes et pénalités

19. En principe, les amendes et pénalités portant sur les impôts impayés ou les pénalités appliquées en cas de tentative d'évasion fiscale ne doivent pas être enregistrées comme des recettes fiscales. Cependant, il se peut qu'il ne soit pas possible de séparer le versement des amendes et pénalités des recettes correspondant aux impôts auxquels ces amendes et

pénalités se rattachent. Dans ce cas, les amendes et pénalités associés à un impôt particulier sont enregistrées avec les recettes correspondant à cet impôt alors que les amendes et pénalités liées à des recettes correspondant à des impôts non-identifiés sont classées comme autres impôts dans la catégorie 6000. Les amendes qui ne concernent pas des infractions fiscales (comme les infractions au stationnement), ou qui ne sont pas identifiables en tant que telles, ne sont pas non plus considérées comme des recettes fiscales.

A.3. Bases de comptabilisation

Droits constatés

20. Les données enregistrées dans cette publication pour les années récentes sont essentiellement indiquées en droits constatés, c'est-à-dire qu'elles sont enregistrées au moment du fait générateur de l'impôt. D'autres informations sont fournies dans les notes des tableaux par pays au chapitre 4 de ce rapport.

21. Toutefois, les données des années antérieures sont encore principalement comptabilisées sur la base des décaissements, c'est-à-dire au moment où l'administration reçoit le versement. Ainsi, les impôts retenus à la source par les employeurs au cours d'un exercice, mais versés à l'administration au cours de l'exercice suivant, et les impôts dus au titre d'une année mais effectivement versés l'année suivante, figurent les uns et les autres dans les recettes du second exercice. Les restitutions, remboursements et retraits résultant d'opérations rectificatives sont déduits des recettes brutes de la période au cours de laquelle ces opérations sont effectuées.

22. Les données relatives aux recettes fiscales sont comptabilisées, sans déduction compensatoire des dépenses administratives liées au recouvrement de l'impôt. De même, lorsque le produit d'un impôt sert à subventionner certains membres de la collectivité, la subvention n'est pas déduite du rendement de l'impôt, encore que certains pays fassent figurer dans leurs données l'impôt après déduction des subventions.

23. Pour les monopoles fiscaux (sous-groupe 5122), seul le montant effectivement transféré à l'État est inclus dans les recettes publiques. Toutefois, les dépenses des monopoles fiscaux qui sont considérées comme des dépenses publiques (par exemple, des dépenses de caractère social engagées par les monopoles fiscaux à l'instigation de l'État) sont ajoutées après coup pour calculer le montant des recettes fiscales (voir § 65).

La distinction entre dispositions fiscales et dépenses directes[7]

24. Étant donné que la présente publication ne vise que les recettes publiques en faisant abstraction des dépenses, il convient de distinguer entre les dispositions fiscales et les dépenses directes. Normalement, cette distinction ne soulève aucune difficulté, car les dépenses directes sont effectuées en dehors du système fiscal et des comptes fiscaux et en vertu de dispositions législatives distinctes. Dans les cas limites, on recourt, pour établir la distinction, au principe de la comptabilisation sur la base des paiements. Dans la mesure où une disposition affecte le montant des paiements du contribuable à l'État, elle est considérée comme une disposition fiscale dont il est tenu compte dans les données figurant dans cette publication. Une disposition qui n'affecte pas ce montant est considérée comme une dépense directe dont il n'est pas tenu compte dans les données reproduites dans cette publication.

25. Il est clair que les abattements fiscaux, exonérations et déductions de l'assiette de l'impôt modifient le montant de l'impôt acquitté à l'État ; il s'agit donc de dispositions fiscales. Inversement, les formes d'aides qui ne sont pas imputables sur l'impôt et n'ont

donc aucun lien avec le processus d'imposition, ne réduisent pas les recettes publiques qui sont consignées dans ce volume. Les crédits d'impôt sont des montants déductibles de l'impôt à acquitter (par opposition aux déductions, qui sont opérées sur l'assiette de l'impôt). On distingue deux catégories de crédits d'impôt : ceux (que l'on qualifiera ici de 'non récupérables') qui sont limités au montant de l'impôt à acquitter et ne peuvent donc donner lieu à un versement de l'administration au contribuable, et ceux (qualifiés ici de 'récupérables') qui n'ont pas cette limite, de sorte que l'excédent du crédit sur l'impôt peut être versé au contribuable[8]. Le crédit d'impôt non récupérable, comme un abattement fiscal, affecte évidemment le montant de l'impôt acquitté à l'État ; aussi est-il considéré comme une disposition fiscale. La solution adoptée pour les crédits d'impôts récupérables[9] consiste à distinguer l'élément de « dépense fiscale »[10], qui est la part du crédit utilisée pour réduire ou supprimer l'impôt dû par le contribuable, et l'« élément de transfert », qui correspond à la part excédant l'impôt dû par le contribuable et qui lui est reversée. Les recettes fiscales rapportées doivent être diminuées du montant de l'élément de dépense, mais non de l'élément de transfert. En outre, les montants de l'élément de dépense fiscale et de l'élément de transfert doivent être indiqués pour mémoire dans les tableaux par pays. Les pays qui ne sont pas en mesure de faire la distinction entre l'élément de dépense fiscale et l'élément de transfert doivent indiquer si leurs recettes fiscales ont été ou non diminuées du montant total de ces éléments, et fournir toutes les estimations dont ils disposent concernant les montants de ces deux éléments. Des informations complémentaires figurent dans le chapitre 1 de ce Rapport, qui fait apparaître les effets des différents traitements possibles des crédits d'impôts récupérables sur les ratios impôt rapportant les impôts au PIB.

Année civile et année fiscale (exercice budgétaire)

26. Les autorités nationales dont l'exercice budgétaire ne correspond pas à l'année civile fournissent, autant que possible, leurs données sur la base de l'année civile afin de faciliter au maximum la comparaison avec les données des autres pays. Les données d'un petit nombre de pays se réfèrent à l'exercice budgétaire. Pour ceux-ci, les statistiques de PIB utilisées dans les tableaux comparatifs portent aussi sur les exercices budgétaires.

A.4. Principes généraux de classification

Les fondements essentiels de la classification

27. Les recettes sont classées par groupes principaux (1000, 2000, 3000, 4000, 5000, 6000) suivant l'assiette de l'impôt : 1000 revenus, bénéfices et gains en capital ; 2000 et 3000 salaires et nombre d'employés ; 4000 patrimoine ; 5000 biens et services ; 6000 assiettes diverses, autres ou non identifiables. Lorsqu'un impôt est calculé en fonction de plusieurs assiettes, les recettes sont, chaque fois que c'est possible, réparties entre les divers groupes (voir § 32 et § 81). Les groupes 4000 et 5000 ne comprennent pas seulement les impôts ayant pour assiette le patrimoine, les biens ou les services eux-mêmes, mais aussi certains impôts connexes. Ainsi, les impôts sur les mutations du patrimoine sont classés dans le groupe 4400[11] et les impôts sur l'utilisation des biens, ou l'autorisation d'exercer une activité, dans le groupe 5200. Dans les groupes 4000 et 5000, une distinction est faite dans certains sous-groupes entre impôts périodiques et impôts non périodiques : on entend par impôts périodiques ceux qui sont perçus à intervalles réguliers (ordinairement tous les ans) et par impôts non périodiques ceux qui ne sont perçus qu'une seule fois (voir aussi les § 47 à 50, § 53, § 54, et § 79 pour une application particulière de cette distinction).

28. L'affectation spéciale de certaines recettes fiscales n'influe pas sur leur classification. Toutefois comme explicité au § 39 sur la classification des cotisations de sécurité sociale, l'octroi d'un droit aux prestations sociales est crucial dans la définition de la rubrique principale 2000.

29. La manière selon laquelle un impôt est perçu ou recouvré (par exemple, au moyen de timbres) n'affecte pas sa classification.

Classification des contribuables

30. Dans certains sous-groupes, des distinctions sont faites entre les différentes catégories de contribuables. Ces distinctions varient d'un impôt à l'autre :

a. *Ventilation des impôts sur le revenu et sur l'actif net entre personnes physiques et sociétés*

La distinction fondamentale entre les impôts sur le revenu des sociétés et les impôts sur le revenu des personnes physiques est que les premiers sont perçus sur la société en tant qu'entité et non sur les personnes physiques qui en sont propriétaires, donc sans tenir compte de la situation personnelle de celles-ci. La même distinction est applicable aux impôts sur l'actif net des sociétés et des personnes physiques. Les impôts perçus sur les bénéfices des sociétés de personnes et sur le revenu de certaines institutions comme les caisses d'assurance-vie ou de retraite, sont classés selon le même principe. Ils sont compris dans les impôts sur les sociétés (1200) lorsqu'ils sont perçus sur la société de personnes ou l'institution en tant qu'entité sans que la situation personnelle des propriétaires entre en ligne de compte ; dans les autres cas, ils sont considérés comme des impôts sur les personnes physiques (1100). Ordinairement, les impôts sur les sociétés et les impôts sur les personnes physiques sont régis par des dispositions législatives différentes[12]. La distinction qui est faite ici entre personnes physiques et sociétés ne reprend pas la classification par secteur (ménages, entreprises, etc.) adoptée dans les comptes de revenus et de dépenses du SCN. Cette dernière classification exclut du secteur des ménages certaines entreprises non constituées en sociétés[13] et les fait figurer parmi les entreprises non financières et les institutions financières. Toutefois, l'impôt sur les bénéfices de ces entreprises ne peut pas toujours être isolé de l'impôt sur les autres revenus des propriétaires de ces entreprises, ou ne peut l'être que d'une façon arbitraire. On n'a pas cherché ici à faire la distinction et l'impôt sur le revenu des personnes physiques figure globalement, quelle que soit la nature du revenu imposable.

b. *Ventilation des impôts sur les biens immobiliers entre ménages et autres agents*

En l'occurrence, la distinction est celle qui a été adoptée par le SCN dans les comptes de production et de consommation. On distingue, en effet, les ménages en tant que consommateurs d'une part (c'est-à-dire à l'exclusion des entreprises individuelles), et les producteurs d'autre part. Cependant, les impôts sur les logements occupés par les ménages, qu'ils soient à la charge des propriétaires qui les occupent, du locataire ou du propriétaire, sont classés comme étant à la charge des ménages. C'est la distinction faite habituellement entre les impôts sur les biens des personnes et les impôts sur les biens des entreprises. Toutefois, certains pays ne sont pas en mesure d'établir cette distinction.

c. *Ventilation des permis de circuler des véhicules à moteur entre taxes à la charge des ménages et à la charge d'autres agents*

On distingue ici les ménages en tant que consommateurs d'une part, et producteurs d'autre part, comme dans les comptes de production et de consommation du SCN.

d. Ventilation des autres impôts (6000) entre les entreprises et les autres agents

Il est fait la même distinction qu'au point (c) ci-dessus entre les producteurs, d'une part, et les ménages consommateurs d'autre part. Les impôts qui figurent dans le groupe 6000 parce qu'ils ne comportent pas une assiette unique ou parce que leur assiette ne relève d'aucune des catégories précédentes, mais qui ne sont manifestement perçus que sur les producteurs et non sur les ménages, sont classés comme étant 'à la charge des entreprises'. Les autres impôts du groupe 6000 figurent sous la rubrique 'à la charge d'autres agents' ou 'non identifiés'.

Surtaxes

31. Les recettes des surtaxes relatives à des impôts particuliers sont classées ordinairement avec les recettes de l'impôt correspondant, que la surtaxe ait ou non un caractère temporaire. Toutefois, si l'une des caractéristiques de la surtaxe permet de la classer sous une rubrique différente de la classification de l'OCDE, les recettes de cette surtaxe sont classées sous cette rubrique et non pas avec les recettes de l'impôt correspondant

Recettes fiscales non identifiables et sous-groupes résiduels

32. Il arrive parfois qu'on ne puisse déterminer si des impôts relèvent entièrement d'un groupe ou d'un sous-groupe de la classification de l'OCDE ; dans ces cas on applique les méthodes suivantes :

a. le groupe est connu, mais on ne sait pas comment répartir les recettes entre les sous-groupes ; les recettes sont alors classées dans le sous-groupe résiduel approprié (1300, 2400, 4520, 4600, 5130, 5300 ou 6200) ;

b. on sait que l'ensemble des recettes d'un groupe d'impôts (ordinairement des impôts locaux) provient d'impôts relevant d'un groupe ou sous-groupe particulier, mais certains impôts du groupe, dont le montant ne peut être déterminé avec précision, peuvent être classés dans d'autres groupes ou sous-groupes ; dans ce cas les recettes sont comptabilisées dans le groupe ou sous-groupe dont relève l'essentiel des recettes ;

c. il est impossible d'identifier le groupe ou le sous-groupe d'un impôt (ordinairement un impôt local) ; l'impôt est alors classé dans le groupe 6200, à moins qu'il ne s'agisse d'un impôt manifestement à la charge des entreprises, auquel cas il est classé dans le sous-groupe 6100.

A.5. Commentaires sur les postes de la liste

1000 — Impôts sur le revenu, les bénéfices et les gains en capital

33. Ce groupe couvre les impôts prélevés sur le revenu ou le bénéfice net (c'est-à-dire le revenu brut déduction faite des abattements autorisés) des personnes physiques et des entreprises. Sont aussi couverts les impôts prélevés sur les gains en capital des personnes physiques et des entreprises et sur les gains provenant de jeux.

34. Ce groupe comprend :

a. les impôts perçus principalement sur les revenus ou les bénéfices, bien qu'ils puissent l'être partiellement sur d'autres bases. Les impôts qui ont une autre assiette principale que le revenu ou les bénéfices sont classés selon les principes énoncés aux § 32 et § 81 ;

b. les impôts sur la propriété immobilière, qui sont perçus sur la base d'un revenu présumé ou estimé faisant partie de l'assiette de l'impôt sur le revenu (voir aussi § 47 (a), (c) et (d)) ;

c. les versements obligatoires aux caisses de sécurité sociale qui sont prélevés sur les revenus mais ne donnent pas droit à des prestations sociales. Lorsque ces contributions donnent droit à des prestations sociales, elles figurent à la rubrique 2000 (voir § 39) ;

d. les recettes provenant d'impôts cédulaires sur le revenu intégrés dans le régime général qui sont globalement classés dans ce groupe, bien que certains de ces impôts soient sur le revenu brut et ne tiennent pas toujours compte de la situation personnelle du contribuable.

35. Les impôts figurant dans ce groupe sont subdivisés en deux grands sous-groupes, les impôts sur le revenu des personnes physiques (1100) et les impôts sur le revenu des sociétés (1200), une ventilation étant faite dans chacun d'eux entre les impôts sur le revenu et les bénéfices (1110 et 1210) et les impôts sur les gains en capital (1120 et 1220). Si certaines recettes ne peuvent être identifiées comme relevant soit du sous-groupe 1100, soit du sous-groupe 1200, ou si cette distinction ne peut être faite dans la pratique (parce qu'il n'y a pas de données fiables sur les bénéficiaires des paiements sur lesquels la retenue à la source est faite), elles sont classées dans le sous-groupe 1300 (non ventilables).

Traitement des crédits d'impôt dans les systèmes d'imputation

36. Dans les régimes d'imputation de l'impôt sur les bénéfices des sociétés, les actionnaires bénéficient d'une compensation totale ou partielle d'imposition sur les dividendes que la société leur a versés et pour lesquels elle a acquitté l'impôt sur le revenu des sociétés. Dans les pays qui appliquent un tel régime, une fraction de l'impôt sur les bénéfices des sociétés sert à alléger l'impôt dû par l'actionnaire. Cet allégement prend la forme d'un crédit d'impôt, dont le montant peut être inférieur, égal ou supérieur au montant total de l'impôt dont il est redevable. Si le crédit d'impôt dépasse ce montant, l'excédent peut être versé à l'actionnaire. Comme ce type de crédit d'impôt fait partie intégrante des systèmes d'imputation de l'impôt sur le revenu des sociétés, tout paiement à l'actionnaire est considéré comme un remboursement d'impôt et non comme une dépense (se référer au traitement des autres crédits d'impôt exposé au § 25).

37. Puisque, dans les systèmes d'imputation, le crédit d'impôt (même lorsqu'il dépasse l'impôt dû) est censé être une disposition fiscale, on peut se demander s'il doit être déduit des recettes de l'impôt sur le revenu des personnes physiques (1110) ou de celles de l'impôt sur les bénéfices de sociétés (1210). Dans ce Rapport le montant intégral de l'impôt acquitté sur les bénéfices des sociétés figure sous le poste 1210 et aucun impôt imputé n'est inclus dans le poste 1110. Le montant total du crédit d'impôt réduit donc le montant des recettes du poste 1110, que ce crédit se traduise par une réduction de l'impôt dû sur le revenu des personnes physiques ou par un remboursement réel du fait que le crédit dépasse le montant de l'impôt. (Cependant, lorsque ces crédits sont déduits de l'impôt sur les sociétés au titre de dividendes versés à des sociétés, le montant est déduit des recettes du poste 1210).

1120 et 1220 — Impôts sur les gains en capital

38. Ces postes comprennent les impôts perçus sur les gains en capital, le sous-groupe 1120 comptabilisant les impôts prélevés sur les gains des personnes physiques et le sous-groupe 1220 ceux qui sont perçus sur les gains des entreprises constituées sous forme de sociétés,

lorsque ces recettes peuvent être ventilées. Ce n'est pas le cas dans de nombreux pays et les recettes de ces impôts sont alors classées avec celles de l'impôt sur le revenu. Les impôts sur les gains provenant de jeux sont aussi classés sous le poste 1120.

2000 — Cotisations de sécurité sociale

39. Figurent dans ce groupe tous les versements obligatoires qui donnent le droit de bénéficier d'une prestation sociale future (éventuelle). Ces versements sont généralement affectés au financement de prestations sociales et souvent effectués au profit d'institutions ou d'administrations publiques qui fournissent de telles prestations. Cependant, cette affectation n'entre pas dans la définition des cotisations de sécurité sociale et n'est pas nécessaire pour qu'un impôt soit classé dans cette rubrique. Cependant, il faut qu'un impôt confère un droit pour être classé dans cette rubrique. Par conséquent, les prélèvements sur les revenus ou la masse salariale qui sont affectés aux caisses de sécurité sociale mais ne donnent aucun droit à des prestations sont exclus de cette rubrique et figurent à celle des impôts sur le revenu des personnes physiques (1100) ou des impôts sur les salaires et la main-d'œuvre (3000). Les impôts assis sur d'autres bases, telles que les biens et services, qui sont affectés à des prestations de sécurité sociale, ne sont pas indiqués ici, mais sont classés en fonction de leurs bases respectives parce qu'en général ils ne donnent pas droit à des prestations de sécurité sociale.

40. Seraient entre autres incluses les cotisations au titre des catégories suivantes de prestations de sécurité sociale : les allocations d'assurance-chômage et les compléments, les allocations pour accidents, blessures et maladie, les pensions de retraite, d'invalidité et de survivant, les allocations familiales, les remboursements de dépenses médicales et d'hospitalisation ou la fourniture de services médicaux ou hospitaliers. Les cotisations peuvent être collectées à la fois auprès des employés et des employeurs.

41. Les cotisations peuvent être assises sur les gains ou la masse salariale (« sur la base du salaire ») ou sur le revenu net après déductions et exemptions en fonction de la situation personnelle (« sur la base de l'impôt sur le revenu ») et les recettes correspondant à ces deux bases doivent être identifiées séparément si possible. Cependant, lorsque les cotisations à un régime général de sécurité sociale sont assises sur la masse salariale, mais que les cotisations de groupes particuliers (tels que les travailleurs indépendants) ne peuvent être évaluées sur cette base et que le revenu net est utilisé comme valeur rapprochée des gains bruts, les recettes peuvent encore être considérées comme assises sur la masse salariale. En principe, cette rubrique exclut les cotisations facultatives à des régimes de sécurité sociale. Lorsqu'elles peuvent être identifiées séparément, elles figurent pour mémoire dans le tableau indiquant le financement des prestations de sécurité sociale. Toutefois, en pratique, elles ne peuvent pas toujours être distinguées des cotisations facultatives, et dans ce cas elles figurent à cette rubrique.

42. Les cotisations à des régimes d'assurance sociale qui ne relèvent pas des pouvoirs publics et à d'autres régimes d'assurance ou de prévoyance, aux caisses de retraite, sociétés de secours mutuel ou autres systèmes d'épargne, ne sont pas considérées comme des cotisations de sécurité sociale. Les caisses de prévoyance résultant d'arrangements aux termes desquels les cotisations de chaque salarié et celles que l'employeur verse en son nom sont comptabilisées séparément dans un compte productif d'intérêts d'où elles peuvent être retirées dans des conditions biens déterminées. Les caisses de retraite sont des régimes autonomes organisés par négociations entre salariés et employeurs, qui comportent diverses contributions et prestations, parfois liées plus directement au salaire et à la durée

d'activité que dans les régimes de sécurité sociale. Lorsque les cotisations à ces régimes sont obligatoires ou quasi obligatoires (par exemple en vertu d'un accord entre organisations professionnelles et syndicales), elles sont comptabilisées dans le poste pour mémoire (voir le chapitre 4.2 du rapport).

43. Les cotisations versées par les agents des administrations et par les administrations au titre de leurs agents à des régimes de sécurité sociale relevant des pouvoirs publics sont incluses dans ce groupe. Sont aussi assimilées à des impôts les cotisations à des régimes particuliers réservés aux agents des administrations qui sont censés remplacer un régime général de la sécurité sociale[14]. Par contre, lorsqu'un régime distinct n'est pas censé remplacer un régime général et résulte de négociations entre l'administration, agissant en qualité d'employeur, et ses agents, il n'est pas considéré comme un régime de sécurité sociale et les cotisations à ce titre ne sont pas assimilées à des impôts, même si le régime a été institué par des dispositions législatives.

44. Cette rubrique ne comprend pas les cotisations 'imputées', qui correspondent aux prestations sociales versées directement par les employeurs à leurs salariés, ou anciens salariés, ou à leurs représentants (par exemple, lorsque des employeurs sont légalement tenus de verser des prestations maladies pendant une certaine période).

45. Le groupe comprend les cotisations à la charge des salariés (2100), à la charge des employeurs (2200), et à la charge des travailleurs indépendants ou des personnes n'occupant pas d'emploi (2300). À cet effet, on entend par salariés toutes les personnes qui exercent une activité dans des entreprises, des administrations, des institutions privées sans but lucratif, ou qui occupent d'autres emplois rémunérés, à l'exception des propriétaires et des membres de leur famille non rémunérés dans le cas d'entreprises individuelles. Sont également compris les membres des forces armées, quelle que soit la durée et la nature de leurs services, s'ils cotisent à un régime de sécurité sociale. Par cotisations à la charge des employeurs, on entend les versements qu'ils effectuent au régime de sécurité sociale pour le compte de leurs salariés. Si, en cas de chômage, les salariés ou employeurs sont tenus de continuer à effectuer ces versements, ces derniers doivent figurer respectivement dans les sous-groupes 2100 et 2200. En conséquence, le sous-groupe 2300 est réservé aux cotisations versées par les travailleurs indépendants et par ceux qui n'appartiennent pas à la population active (comme les handicapés ou les retraités).

3000 — Impôts sur les salaires et la main-d'œuvre

46. Il s'agit d'impôts que doivent acquitter les entreprises, déterminés en proportion des salaires et des traitements payés, ou d'après un montant fixe par personne employée. Ils ne comprennent pas les cotisations obligatoires de sécurité sociale payées par les employeurs, ni les impôts payés par les salariés sur leurs traitements et leurs salaires.

4000 — Impôts sur le patrimoine

47. Ce groupe couvre les impôts périodiques et non périodiques sur l'utilisation, la propriété ou la mutation des biens. Sont comptabilisés ici les impôts sur la propriété immobilière et sur l'actif net, les impôts sur les mutations par décès, les successions et les donations, et les impôts sur les transactions mobilières et immobilières. Sont exclus de ce groupe :

a. les impôts sur les gains en capital provenant de la vente d'un bien (1120 ou 1220) ;
b. les impôts sur l'utilisation des biens ou l'autorisation d'utiliser des biens ou d'exercer des activités (5200) [voir § 76] ;

c. les impôts immobiliers perçus sur la base d'un revenu net présumé qui tiennent compte de la situation personnelle du contribuable. Ces impôts sont classés dans le groupe 1100 en tant qu'impôts sur le revenu, avec les impôts sur le revenu et les gains en capital provenant des biens immobiliers ;
d. les impôts sur l'utilisation de biens immobiliers aux fins d'habitation qui sont à la charge du propriétaire ou du locataire et dont le montant est fonction de la situation personnelle de l'utilisateur (salaire, personnes à charge, etc.). Ils sont classés dans le groupe 1100 en tant qu'impôts sur le revenu ;
e. les impôts sur les constructions dépassant la densité autorisée, les impôts sur l'extension, la construction ou la modification de certains immeubles au-delà d'une valeur autorisée et les impôts sur la construction d'immeubles. Ces impôts sont classés dans le poste 5200 en tant qu'impôts sur l'autorisation d'exercer certaines activités ;
f. les impôts sur l'utilisation de biens immobiliers par le propriétaire à des fins commerciales particulières, comme la vente de boissons alcoolisées, de tabac, de viande, ou pour l'exploitation de sols ou terrains (par exemple aux États-Unis, les taxes d'extraction). Ils sont classés dans le poste 5200 en tant qu'impôts sur l'autorisation d'exercer certaines activités.

4100 — Impôts périodiques sur la propriété immobilière

48. Ce sous-groupe comprend les impôts prélevés régulièrement au titre de l'utilisation ou de la propriété de biens immobiliers.

- ces impôts sont prélevés sur les terrains et les bâtiments ;
- ces impôts sont calculés en pourcentage de la valeur du bien évalué d'après un revenu locatif fictif, le prix de vente ou le rendement capitalisé, ou en fonction d'autres caractéristiques du bien, comme sa dimension ou son emplacement, d'où l'on peut déduire une valeur locative présumée ou la valeur du capital.
- ces impôts sont à la charge du propriétaire, du locataire ou des deux. Ils peuvent également être payés par une administration à une autre administration au titre d'un bien relevant de la compétence de cette dernière.
- il n'est pas tenu compte des dettes pour la détermination de l'assiette de ces impôts, contrairement aux impôts sur l'actif net.

49. Les impôts sur la propriété immobilière sont en outre subdivisés en impôts acquittés par les ménages (4110) et impôts acquittés par d'autres agents (4120), suivant les critères exposés au § 30(*b*) ci-dessus.

4200 — Impôts périodiques sur l'actif net

50. Ce sous-groupe comprend les impôts prélevés régulièrement (dans la plupart des cas annuellement) sur l'actif net, c'est-à-dire les impôts perçus sur un large éventail de biens mobiliers et immobiliers, endettement déduit. Il est subdivisé en impôts acquittés par des personnes physiques (4210), et en impôts acquittés par des sociétés (4220) selon les critères exposés plus haut au § 30(a). Si les recettes provenant des institutions sont comptabilisées à part, 66res doivent être ajoutées aux impôts des entreprises.

4300 — *Impôts sur les mutations par décès, les successions et les donations*

51. Ce sous-groupe comprend les impôts sur les mutations par décès et les successions (4310) et les impôts sur les donations (4320). Les impôts sur les mutations par décès sont calculés soit sur l'ensemble de la masse successorale, soit en fonction de la part de chacun des bénéficiaires (« part héréditaire ») ; en outre, ces derniers impôts peuvent tenir compte du degré de parenté entre chacun des bénéficiaires et le défunt.

4400 — *Impôts sur les transactions mobilières et immobilières*

52. Sont compris, entre autres, dans ce sous-groupe les impôts sur l'émission, le transfert, l'achat et la vente de valeurs mobilières, les impôts sur les chèques, ainsi que les droits perçus à l'occasion d'actes juridiques déterminés, comme la validation de contrats et la vente de biens immobiliers. Sont exclus :

a. les impôts sur l'utilisation de biens, mobiliers ou immobiliers, ou l'autorisation d'exercer certaines activités (5200) ;
b. les droits acquittés au titre de frais de justice, ou pour la délivrance de certificats de naissance, de mariage ou de décès, car ces droits sont considérés comme des recettes non fiscales (voir § 11) ;
c. les impôts sur les gains en capital (1000) ;
d. les impôts périodiques sur la propriété immobilière (4100) ;
e. les impôts périodiques sur l'actif net (4200) ;
f. les prélèvements sur le patrimoine ou sur l'actif net effectués une fois pour toutes (4500) ;

4500 — *Autres impôts non périodiques sur le patrimoine*[16]

53. Ce sous-groupe comprend les prélèvements sur le patrimoine effectués une fois pour toutes (par opposition aux prélèvements périodiques). Il est subdivisé en impôts sur l'actif net (4510) et en autres impôts non périodiques sur le patrimoine (4520). Le poste 4510 inclurait les impôts perçus pour couvrir des dépenses exceptionnelles ou à des fins de redistribution. Le poste 4520 comprendrait les impôts prélevés pour tenir compte d'une plus-value prise par les terrains du fait que les administrations publiques ont autorisé l'extension ou l'aménagement d'installations locales, ainsi que les impôts sur la réévaluation du capital ou les impôts perçus une seule fois sur certains biens déterminés.

4600 — *Autres impôts périodiques sur le patrimoine*

54. Ils sont rares dans des pays Membres de l'OCDE ; ce sous-groupe comprendrait les impôts sur des biens tels que le cheptel, les bijoux, les fenêtres et les signes extérieurs de richesse.

5000 — *Impôts sur les biens et services*

55. Ce poste couvre tous les impôts et droits perçus sur la production, l'extraction, la vente, le transfert, la location ou la livraison de biens et la prestation de services (5100), ou sur l'utilisation ou l'autorisation d'utiliser des biens ou d'exercer des activités (5200). Ce groupe comprend donc :

a. les taxes cumulatives en cascade ;
b. les taxes générales sur les ventes — perçues au stade de la production ou de la fabrication, du gros ou du détail ;

c. les taxes sur la valeur ajoutée ;
d. les accises ;
e. les taxes perçues à l'importation et à l'exportation de biens ;
f. les impôts perçus sur l'utilisation de biens et sur l'autorisation d'utiliser des biens ou d'exercer certaines activités ;
g. les impôts sur l'extraction, le traitement ou la production de minéraux et autres produits.

56. Les cas douteux de délimitation entre ce groupe et le groupe 4000 (impôts sur le patrimoine) et le sous-groupe 6100 (autres impôts à la charge des entreprises) sont examinés aux § 47, § 52 et § 78. Des postes résiduels (5300 et 5130) ont été prévus pour comptabiliser les recettes fiscales qui ne peuvent être ventilées respectivement entre les postes 5100 et 5200 et entre les postes 5110 et 5120 (voir § 32).

5100 — Impôts sur la production, la vente, le transfert, la location et la livraison de biens et la prestation de services

57. Ce sous-groupe comprend tous les impôts perçus sur les transactions afférentes à des biens ou services, en fonction de leurs caractéristiques propres (comme la valeur, le poids du tabac, le degré d'alcool, etc.), à la différence des impôts perçus au titre de l'utilisation ou de l'autorisation d'utiliser des biens ou d'exercer des activités, qui entrent dans le sous-groupe 5200.

5110 — Impôts généraux sur les biens et services

58. Ce sous-groupe comprend tous les impôts, autres que les droits à l'importation et à l'exportation (5123 et 5124), perçus sur la production, la location, le transfert, la livraison ou la vente d'une gamme de biens ou la prestation d'une gamme de services, qu'ils soient produits dans le pays ou importés, et quel que soit le stade de la production ou de la distribution aux quel ils sont perçus. Il couvre ainsi les taxes sur la valeur ajoutée, les taxes sur les ventes et les taxes de caractère cumulatif en cascade. On a ajouté aux recettes brutes de cette catégorie les recettes provenant de la compensation à la frontière de ces impôts lorsque les biens sont importés, et déduit les remboursements d'impôts effectués lorsque les marchandises sont exportées. Ces impôts sont ventilés en : taxes sur la valeur ajoutée (5111), impôts sur les ventes (5112), impôts sur le chiffre d'affaires et autres impôts généraux sur les biens et services (5113).

59. Certains cas se trouvent à la limite entre ce sous-groupe et celui des impôts sur des biens et services déterminés (5120) lorsque ces impôts sont perçus sur un grand nombre de biens, comme dans le cas de la « *purchase tax* » au Royaume-Uni (abrogée en 1973) et l'impôt japonais sur les biens marchands (abrogé en 1988). Conformément aux options nationales, la « *purchase tax* » britannique est classée impôt général (5112) et l'impôt japonais dans les accises (5121).

5111 — Taxes sur la valeur ajoutée

60. Sont classés dans ce sous-groupe tous les impôts généraux sur la consommation prélevée sur la valeur ajoutée, quels que soient le mode de déduction et les stades auxquels ils sont perçus. En pratique, tous les pays de l'OCDE où existe une taxe sur la valeur ajoutée autorisent normalement la déduction immédiate des taxes sur les achats par tous les redevables, à l'exception du consommateur final, et imposent la taxe à tous les stades. Dans certains pays, le poste peut inclure aussi certains impôts, comme les taxes sur les activités

financières et les assurances, soit parce que les recettes correspondantes ne peuvent être dissociées de celles de la taxe sur la valeur ajoutée, soit parce qu'elles sont considérées comme faisant partie intégrante de la taxe sur la valeur ajoutée, même si les taxes similaires qui existent dans d'autres pays peuvent être classées autrement (par exemple, sous le poste 5126 comme impôts sur les services ou sous le poste 4400 comme impôts sur les transactions mobilières et immobilières).

5112 — *Impôts sur les ventes*

61. Sont classés ici tous les impôts perçus à un stade unique, que ce soit celui de la fabrication, de la production, du gros ou du détail.

5113 — *Impôts sur le chiffre d'affaires et autres impôts généraux sur les biens et services*

62. Il s'agit des taxes cumulatives en cascade et des taxes qui combinent des éléments de taxe sur la consommation et des taxes en cascade. Ces impôts sont prélevés sur chaque transaction sans déduction des taxes acquittées en amont. Les taxes en cascade peuvent être combinées avec des éléments de taxe sur la valeur ajoutée ou d'impôts sur les ventes.

5120 — *Impôts sur des biens et des services déterminés*

63. Ce sous-groupe couvre les accises, les bénéfices engendrés et transférés par les monopoles fiscaux, et les droits de douane et à l'importation, ainsi que les taxes à l'exportation, les opérations de change, les biens d'équipement et les paris, et aussi les impôts spéciaux sur les services qui ne font pas partie d'un impôt général du sous-groupe 5110.

5121 — *Accises*

64. Les accises sont des impôts spécifiques perçus par unité produite sur une gamme limitée de biens prédéfinie. Les accises sont généralement prélevées à des taux différenciés sur des biens non essentiels ou de luxe, les boissons alcoolisées, les produits à base de tabac et l'énergie. Les accises peuvent être perçues à un stade quelconque de la production ou de la distribution et sont calculées généralement sur la base d'un prélèvement spécifique par unité correspondant aux caractéristiques du produit considéré, par référence à sa valeur, son poids, son degré ou son volume. Cette subdivision couvre ainsi les impôts spéciaux sur certains produits tels que le sucre, la betterave, les allumettes et le chocolat ; les impôts prélevés à des taux variables sur une gamme déterminée de produits ; ainsi que les impôts perçus sur les produits à base de tabac, les boissons alcoolisées, les combustibles et les hydrocarbures. Si un impôt frappant principalement des produits importés doit ou devrait également être perçu sur des produits nationaux comparables, suivant la même législation, les recettes de cet impôt doivent alors être classées dans la catégorie des accises et non dans celle des droits à l'importation. Ce principe vaut également même s'il n'existe pas, ou ne peut exister, de production nationale comparable. Les impôts prélevés sur la consommation de services d'utilité publique (eau, électricité, gaz et autres formes d'énergie) sont considérés comme des accises, et non comme des impôts sur des services déterminés (5126). Ne sont pas inclus dans les accises les prélèvements entrant dans les catégories des impôts généraux sur les biens et services (5110), des bénéfices des monopoles fiscaux (5122), des droits de douane et autres droits à l'importation (5123) ou des taxes à l'exportation (5124).

5122 — *Bénéfices des monopoles fiscaux*

65. Ce sous-groupe couvre la fraction des bénéfices des monopoles fiscaux qui est transférée aux administrations publiques ou qui sert à financer des dépenses considérées comme

dépenses publiques (voir § 23). Les montants sont comptabilisés lorsqu'ils sont transférés aux administrations publiques ou utilisés pour effectuer des dépenses considérées comme des dépenses publiques.

66. Les monopoles fiscaux reflètent l'exercice du pouvoir d'imposition de l'État par l'intermédiaire du monopole. Les monopoles fiscaux sont des entreprises publiques non financières, qui exercent dans la plupart des cas un monopole sur la production ou la distribution du tabac, des boissons alcoolisées, du sel, des allumettes, des cartes à jouer et des produits pétroliers ou agricoles (c'est-à-dire, sur le genre de produits qui peuvent être soumis, principalement ou accessoirement, aux accises du poste 5121), pour procurer des recettes publiques qui, dans d'autres pays, sont obtenues par le biais d'impôts frappant les transactions sur ces produits d'entreprises privées. Le monopole d'État peut être exercé au stade de la production, ou au stade de la distribution comme dans le cas des magasins de vente de boissons alcoolisées qui appartiennent à l'État et sont contrôlés par lui.

67. Les monopoles fiscaux sont différents des services publics, comme les chemins de fer, l'électricité, les postes et autres moyens de communication, qui peuvent avoir une position de monopole ou de quasi-monopole, mais dont l'objet principal est, normalement, de fournir des services essentiels et non pas de procurer des recettes à l'État. Les transferts à l'administration de ces autres entreprises publiques sont considérés comme des recettes non fiscales. La notion traditionnelle de monopole fiscal n'a généralement pas été élargie pour inclure les loteries nationales, dont les bénéfices sont habituellement considérés comme des recettes non fiscales. Cependant, ces bénéfices peuvent être considérés comme des recettes fiscales quand la raison principale de la mise en œuvre de ces loteries est l'augmentation des recettes pour financer les dépenses publiques. On distingue les bénéfices des monopoles fiscaux des bénéfices des monopoles d'exportation et d'importation (5127), qui sont transférés des offices de commercialisation ou d'autres entreprises s'occupant du commerce international.

5123 — *Droits de douane et autres droits à l'importation*

68. Figurent ici les taxes, droits de timbre et surtaxes qui, selon la loi sont perçus exclusivement sur des produits importés. Sont aussi inclus dans ce poste les droits perçus sur l'importation de denrées agricoles dans les pays Membres de l'Union Européenne et les montants acquittés par certains de ces pays en vertu du Système de Montants Compensatoires[15]. À partir de 1998 les droits de douane collectés par les États membres de l'Union européenne pour le compte de l'Union européenne ne sont plus reportés sous cette rubrique dans les tableaux par pays (chapitre 4 de ce rapport). Sont exclues ici les taxes perçues sur les importations au titre d'un impôt général sur les biens et les services ou d'une accise applicable aussi bien aux produits importés qu'aux produits fabriqués dans le pays.

5124 — *Taxes à l'exportation*

69. Pendant les années 70, les droits à l'exportation étaient perçus normalement en Australie, au Canada et au Portugal, et ils étaient utilisés en Finlande à des fins conjoncturelles. Certains pays Membres de l'Union Européenne acquittent, dans le cadre du système des montants compensatoires, une taxe sur les exportations (voir la note 16 du § 68). Lorsque ces montants sont identifiables, ils sont inclus dans ce poste. Ce dernier ne comprend pas les remboursements effectués au titre d'impôts généraux sur la consommation d'accises ou de droits de douane sur des biens exportés, qui doivent être déduits des recettes brutes comptabilisées, selon le cas, sous le poste 5110, 5121 ou 5123.

5125 — *Impôts sur les biens d'équipement*

70. Ce sous-groupe comprend les impôts perçus sur les biens d'équipement, comme les machines. Ils peuvent exister depuis un certain nombre d'années ou avoir un caractère temporaire et être prélevés à des fins conjoncturelles. Ne sont pas inclus les impôts sur les 'inputs' industriels qui frappent aussi les consommateurs (comme l'impôt suédois sur l'énergie qui est classé sous le poste 5121).

5126 — *Impôts sur des services déterminés*

71. Sous ce poste figurent tous les impôts calculés sur la rémunération de services spécifiques, comme les taxes sur les primes d'assurance, les taxes sur les services bancaires, sur les jeux et paris (par exemple : courses de chevaux, pronostics de football, billets de loterie nationale), les transports, les spectacles, les restaurants et la publicité. Les impôts prélevés sur le revenu brut des sociétés prestataires d'un service (exemple : primes d'assurance brutes, mises de jeux encaissées par les sociétés) sont classés sous ce poste. Les recettes fiscales provenant des prélèvements sur les banques et des contributions aux mécanismes de garantie des dépôts et de stabilité financière sont provisoirement classés ici pour l'édition 2012. La classification détaillée est présentée au § 108.

72. Ne figurent pas sous ce poste :

a. les impôts sur les services qui font partie d'un impôt général sur les biens et services et sont classés sous le poste 5110 ;

b. les taxes sur l'électricité, le gaz et l'énergie (classées sous le poste 5121 en tant qu'accises) ;

c. les taxes sur les gains personnels tirés de jeux et paris (qui sont classées sous le poste 1120, en tant qu'impôts sur les gains en capital des personnes physiques et entreprises individuelles) et les montants forfaitaires perçus sur le transfert de loteries privées ou sur l'autorisation de créer des loteries (5200)[16] ;

d. les impôts sur les chèques et sur l'émission, le transfert ou le remboursement de valeurs mobilières, (qui sont classés sous le poste 4400, en tant qu'impôts sur les transactions mobilières et immobilières).

5127 — *Autres impôts sur les transactions et les échanges internationaux*

73. Ce sous-groupe couvre les recettes perçues par l'État sur l'achat et la vente de monnaies étrangères à des taux différents. Lorsque l'État exerce le privilège exclusif dont il dispose pour s'assurer une marge entre le prix d'achat et le prix de vente de devises qui ne se réduit pas à la simple couverture des frais administratifs, ce bénéfice représente un prélèvement obligatoire imposé dans des proportions indéterminées à l'acheteur et au vendeur des monnaies étrangères. Il équivaut normalement au droit à l'importation et au droit à l'exportation perçus dans un système de taux de change unique, ou à une taxe sur la vente ou l'achat de monnaies étrangères. Comme les bénéfices des monopoles fiscaux et des monopoles d'importation ou d'exportation transférés à l'État, il représente l'exercice d'un monopole aux fins d'imposition et est inclus dans les recettes fiscales.

74. Ce sous-groupe comprend aussi les bénéfices des monopoles d'exportation ou d'importation, bien qu'il n'en existe pas dans les pays de l'OCDE, les impôts sur l'achat ou la vente de devises et tous les autres impôts perçus spécifiquement sur les opérations ou les échanges internationaux.

5128 — *Autres impôts sur des biens et services déterminés*

75. Cette rubrique comprend les impôts sur l'extraction de minéraux, combustibles fossiles et autres ressources non renouvelables provenant de gisements privés ou détenus par une autre administration, ainsi que toute autre recette non ventilable provenant des impôts sur des biens et services déterminés. Les impôts sur l'extraction de ressources non renouvelables correspondent généralement à un montant forfaitaire par unité de qualité ou de poids, mais peuvent être calculés ad valorem. Les impôts sont comptabilisés à la date d'extraction des ressources. Les versements tirés de l'extraction de ressources non renouvelables issues de gisements appartenant à l'administration publique qui perçoit ces versements sont classés en tant que loyers.

5200 — *Impôts sur l'utilisation des biens ou l'autorisation d'utiliser des biens ou d'exercer des activités*

76. Ce sous-groupe comprend les taxes prélevées en raison de l'utilisation de biens, indépendamment des impôts frappant les biens eux-mêmes. Contrairement à ceux-ci (5100), les impôts du sous-groupe 5200 ne sont pas calculés d'après la valeur des biens, mais ordinairement d'après un montant forfaitaire. Sont aussi couverts les impôts perçus au titre du droit d'utiliser des biens ou d'exercer des activités, comme les taxes sur la pollution qui ne reposent pas sur la valeur de biens déterminés. Il est parfois difficile de distinguer les taxes d'utilisation et droits de licence obligatoires, qui sont considérés comme des impôts, de ceux qui ne le sont pas parce qu'ils sont assimilés à des recettes non fiscales ; les critères appliqués sont ceux indiqués aux § 11 et 12.

77. Bien que le sous-groupe se réfère à l'utilisation des biens, le fait générateur de l'impôt peut être aussi bien l'enregistrement de la propriété, de sorte que les impôts relevant de ce sous-groupe peuvent viser la possession d'animaux ou de biens plutôt que leur utilisation (par exemple, les chevaux de course, les chiens, les véhicules à moteur) et même s'appliquer à des biens inutilisables (comme les véhicules à moteur ou les fusils inutilisables).

78. Les cas limites concernent :

a. les impôts sur l'autorisation d'exercer des activités commerciales, qui sont classés selon les règles exposées au § 81 lorsqu'ils ont une assiette mixte associant le revenu, les salaires versés ou le chiffre d'affaires ;

b. les impôts sur la propriété ou l'utilisation de la propriété de biens visés par les postes 4100, 4200 et 4600. Le poste 4100 ne vise que les impôts sur la propriété ou la location de biens immobiliers et, contrairement aux impôts du sous-groupe 5200, ils sont fonction de la valeur du bien. Les impôts sur l'actif net et les impôts sur les biens meubles des sous-groupes 4200 et 4600 visent la propriété et non pas l'utilisation des biens, couvrent un groupe d'actifs et non pas de biens particuliers et sont aussi fonction de la valeur du bien.

5210 — *Impôts périodiques sur l'utilisation de biens ou sur l'autorisation d'utiliser des biens ou d'exercer certaines activités*

79. Ces impôts ont pour principale caractéristique d'être perçus à intervalles réguliers et de représenter ordinairement des montants forfaitaires. Le poste le plus important, du point de vue du volume des recettes, est constitué par les permis de circulation des véhicules. Ce sous-groupe inclut aussi les taxes perçues lors de la délivrance de permis de chasse, de tir ou de pêche, ou l'autorisation de vendre certains produits, ainsi que les taxes sur la possession de chiens et sur la prestation de certains services à condition qu'elles

répondent aux critères définis aux § 11 et 12. Les subdivisions du poste 5210 comprennent les taxes d'utilisation de véhicules à moteur à la charge des ménages (5211) et à la charge d'autres agents (5212). Le poste 5213 couvre les plaques de chiens et les taxes perçues pour l'autorisation d'exercer certaines activités, comme la vente de viande et d'alcool, lorsque les prélèvements ont un caractère périodique. Il couvre aussi les permis généraux de chasse, de port d'armes et de pêche, lorsque le droit d'exercer ces activités n'est pas accordé au titre d'une opération commerciale normale (par exemple, la délivrance du permis ne comporte pas le droit d'utiliser une parcelle déterminée de terrain appartenant à l'État).

5220 — Impôts non périodiques sur l'utilisation de biens ou sur l'autorisation d'utiliser des biens ou d'exercer certaines activités

80. Cette rubrique recouvre les taxes non périodiques perçues sur l'utilisation de biens ou sur l'autorisation d'utiliser des biens ou d'exercer certaines activités et celles qui sont prélevées chaque fois que des biens sont utilisés.

- Les impôts prélevés sur l'émission ou le rejet dans l'environnement de gaz toxiques, liquides nocifs ou autres substances dangereuses figurent ici. Les paiements au titre des permis d'émission négociables délivrés par les administrations publiques dans le cadre des dispositifs de plafonnement et d'échange doivent également être comptabilisés sous cette rubrique au moment où les émissions sont produites. Les permis délivrés gratuitement par les administrations ne donnent lieu à aucun enregistrement comptable de recettes.
- La comptabilisation en droits constatés implique un éventuel délai entre la date à laquelle l'administration perçoit le règlement des permis et la date à laquelle les émissions sont produites. Dans les comptes nationaux, ce délai se traduit pour l'administration par un engagement financier sur la période.
- Il convient d'exclure les paiements effectués au titre de la collecte et de l'élimination de déchets ou de substances nocives par les autorités publiques, étant donné qu'il s'agit là de vente de services aux entreprises.

81. D'autres impôts non périodiques qui relèvent du poste 5200 sont aussi classés dans cette rubrique. Ainsi figurent les paiements uniques effectués au titre de l'autorisation de vendre des boissons alcoolisées ou des tabacs ou d'ouvrir des guichets de « paris mutuels », à condition qu'ils répondent aux critères définis aux § 11 et 12.

6000 — Autres impôts

82. Ce groupe couvre les impôts prélevés sur une ou plusieurs assiettes différentes de celles qui sont indiquées pour les groupes 1000, 3000, 4000 et 5000, ou sur des assiettes qui ne peuvent être considérées comme liées à l'une de celles afférentes à ces groupes. Lorsque des impôts sont perçus sur plusieurs assiettes différentes, et qu'il est possible d'évaluer les recettes liées à chaque assiette, les montants correspondants sont inclus dans le groupe approprié. S'il est impossible d'évaluer le montant correspondant à chaque assiette, et si l'on sait que l'essentiel des recettes provient des impôts perçus sur une assiette donnée, la totalité des recettes est classée en fonction de cette assiette. Sinon, les impôts sont classés dans le présent groupe. Sont également inclus dans ce groupe les impôts forfaitaires non inclus ailleurs dans le système de classification, les impôts prélevés sur les personnes physiques sous la forme de taxe civique ou d'impôt de capitation, les droits de timbre qui ne sont pas liés à des transactions mobilières ou immobilières et qui n'entrent pas exclusivement dans une catégorie de transactions, les impôts sur les dépenses dès lors qu'ils s'accompagnent

d'abattements et d'exonérations individuels, ainsi que les recettes fiscales non identifiables. Ce poste est divisé en impôts exclusivement ou principalement à la charge des entreprises (6100) et en impôts à la charge d'autres contribuables (6200).

A.6. Conciliation avec les comptes nationaux

83. Cette section des tableaux permet de concilier les calculs des recettes fiscales totales de l'OCDE et l'ensemble des impôts et cotisations sociales versés aux administrations publiques qui sont enregistrés dans les comptes nationaux par pays. Lorsque le pays en question est membre de l'Union européenne (UE) la comparaison est effectuée entre les calculs des recettes fiscales totales des pays de l'OCDE et la somme des recettes fiscales et cotisations de sécurité sociale perçues par les administrations publiques et les institutions des secteurs de l'Union européenne des comptes nationaux.

A.7. Poste pour mémoire relatif au financement des prestations de sécurité sociale

84. Le rapport entre les impôts et les cotisations de sécurité sociale étant variable, et en raison des problèmes évoqués aux § 39 à 45, on a réuni dans un poste pour mémoire l'ensemble des versements affectés à des prestations du type sécurité sociale, en dehors des versements facultatifs au secteur privé. Les données sont présentées de la façon suivante (voir le chapitre 4.2)

a. impôts du groupe 2000 ;
b. impôts affectés aux prestations de sécurité sociale ;
c. cotisations facultatives à l'administration ;
d. cotisations obligatoires au secteur privé.

Les § 39 à 45 ci-dessus contiennent des directives pour la ventilation entre ces quatre catégories

A.8. Poste pour mémoire relatif aux impôts identifiables payés par les administrations

85. Les impôts effectivement payés par les administrations elles-mêmes et que l'on peut identifier sont indiqués dans un poste pour mémoire et classés suivant les grandes rubriques de la classification des impôts de l'OCDE. Dans la très grande majorité des pays, seuls peuvent être identifiées en l'occurrence les cotisations de sécurité sociale et les impôts sur les salaires, mais il s'agit là en général des impôts les plus importants acquittés par les administrations (voir le chapitre 4.2 de cette publication).

A.9. Rapport de la classification des impôts de l'OCDE avec les systèmes nationaux de comptabilité nationale

86. Un système de comptabilité nationale (SCN) tend à fournir un cadre cohérent pour enregistrer et présenter les principaux flux relatifs à la production, à la consommation, à l'accumulation et aux transactions extérieures d'une zone économique donnée, d'ordinaire un pays ou une grande région d'un pays. Les recettes publiques sont une partie importante des transactions enregistrées dans le SCN. La version finale du SCN 2008 a été diffusée conjointement par cinq organisations internationales : les Nations Unies, le Fonds Monétaire International, l'Union européenne, l'Organisation de Coopération et de Développement Économiques et la Banque Mondiale, en août 2009. Le Système est un ensemble complet,

cohérent et souple de comptes macro-économiques. Il est élaboré pour être utilisé dans les pays à économie de marché quel que soit leur niveau de développement économique ainsi que dans les pays en transition vers l'économie de marché. De larges extraits du cadre théorique ainsi que les définitions des divers secteurs de l'économie du SCN figurent dans la classification des impôts de l'OCDE.

87. Il existe cependant un certain nombre de différences entre la classification des impôts de l'OCDE et les concepts du SCN qui sont indiqués ci-dessous. Ils proviennent du fait que l'objectif de cette classification est de permettre une ventilation aussi large que possible des données statistiques pour ce que les administrations fiscales conviennent de considérer de manière générale comme des impôts.

a. l'OCDE inclut les cotisations obligatoires de sécurité sociale payées aux administrations publiques dans les recettes fiscales totales. Les cotisations sociales facultatives et imputées ainsi que celles versées aux caisses privées ne sont pas considérées comme des impôts (§ 8 et 10 ci-dessus) ;
b. les avis diffèrent sur la question de savoir s'il y a lieu de classer certains prélèvements et redevances dans les impôts (§ 11 et 12 ci-dessus) ;
c. l'OCDE exclut les impôts imputés ou les subventions résultant d'opérations de taux de change officiels multiples et ceux résultant du fait que la banque centrale paye un taux d'intérêt sur les réserves obligatoires différent des autres taux du marché ;
d. il existe des différences dans le traitement des crédits d'impôt récupérables.

88. Comme on l'a noté aux § 1 et 2, les groupes 1000 à 6000 de la classification de l'OCDE comprennent tous les versements sans contrepartie aux administrations publiques, à l'exclusion des prêts obligatoires et des amendes. On peut obtenir le total de ces versements sans contrepartie, amendes incluses, mais prêts obligatoires exclus, en additionnant les postes suivants du SCN 2008 :

- impôts du type valeur ajoutée (D.211) ;
- droits et taxes sur les importations à l'exclusion de la TVA (D.212) ;
- droits sur les exportations (D.213) ;
- taxes sur les produits, à l'exclusion de la TVA, des droits sur les importations et les exportations (D.214) ;
- autres impôts sur la production (D.29) ;
- impôts sur le revenu (D.51) ;
- autres impôts périodiques (D.59) ;
- cotisations de sécurité sociale (D.61) à l'exclusion des cotisations facultatives ;
- impôts sur le capital (D.91).

A.10. La classification des impôts de l'OCDE et le système du Fonds monétaire international (SFP)

89. Le périmètre et l'évaluation des recettes fiscales dans le système de statistiques de finances publiques (SFP) et dans le système de comptabilité nationale de 2008 (SCN 2008) sont très proches. Par conséquent, les différences entre la classification de l'OCDE et celle du SCN 2008 (voir § 87 ci-dessus) sont également valables pour les SFP. En outre, le Fonds monétaire international subdivise le groupe 5000 de la classification de l'OCDE en une section iv (Taxes intérieures sur les biens et services) et une section v (Taxes sur

les transactions et les échanges internationaux). Cela tient à ce que le rendement de ces dernières taxes représente généralement des sommes infimes dans les pays de l'OCDE ce qui n'est pas le cas dans beaucoup de pays non membres.

A.11. Comparaison de la classification des impôts de l'OCDE et des autres classifications internationales des recettes publiques

90. Le tableau ci-dessous décrit point par point la comparaison entre la classification des impôts de l'OCDE et les classifications suivantes :

a. Système des comptes nationaux (SCN 2008) ;

b. Système européen des comptes (SEC 2010) ;

c. Manuel de statistiques des finances publiques du Fonds monétaire international (MSFP 2014).

91. Ces comparaisons correspondent à celles qui devraient s'appliquer dans la majorité des cas. Toutefois, en pratique il faut faire preuve d'une certaine souplesse dans leur application. En effet, dans certains cas, les pays peuvent adopter des méthodes diverses de classification des recettes dans les comptes nationaux.

OECD Classification	2008 SNA	2010 ESA	GFSM2014
1000 Taxes on income, profits and capital gains			
1100 Individuals			
1110 Income and profits	D51-8.61a	D51A	1111
1120 Capital gains	D51-8.61c, d	D51C, D	1111
1200 Corporations			
1210 Income and profits	D51-8.61b	D51B	1112
1220 Capital gains	D51-8.61c	D51C	1112
1300 Unallocable as between 1100 and 1200			1113
2000 Social security contributions			
2100 Employees	D613-8.85	D613	1211
2200 Employers	D611-8.83	D611	1212
2300 Self-employed, non-employed	D613-8.85	D613	1213
2400 Unallocable as between 2100, 2200 and 2300			1214
3000 Taxes on payroll and workforce	D29-7.97a	D29C	112
4000 Taxes on property			
4100 Recurrent taxes on immovable property			
4110 Households	D59-8.63a	D59A	1131
4120 Other	D29-7.97b	D29A	1131
4200 Recurrent net wealth taxes			
4210 Individual	D59-8.63b	D59A	1132
4220 Corporations	D59-8.63b	D59A	1132
4300 Estate, inheritance and gift taxes			
4310 Estate and inheritance taxes	D91-10.207b	D91A	1133
4320 Gift taxes	D91-10.207b	D91A	1133
4400 Taxes on financial and capital transactions	D59-7.96d; D29-7.97e	D214B, C	114114; 1161
4500 Other non-recurrent taxes on property	D91-10.207a	D91B	1135
4600 Other recurrent taxes on property	D59-8.63c	D59A	1136
5000 Taxes on goods and services			
5100 Taxes on production, sale and transfer of goods and services			
5110 General taxes on goods and services			
5111 Value-added taxes	D211-7.89	D211; D29G	11411
5112 Sales taxes	D2122-7.94a; D214-7.96a	D21224; D214I	11412
5113 Other general taxes on goods and services	D214-7.96a	D214I	11413

OECD Classification	2008 SNA	2010 ESA	GFSM2014
5120 Taxes on specific goods and services			
5121 Excises	D2122-7.94b; D214-7.96b	D21223; D214A, B, D	1142
5122 Profits of fiscal monopolies	D214-7.96e	D214J	1143
5123 Customs and other import duties	D2121-7.93	D2121; D21221, 2	1151
5124 On exports	D213-7.95a	D214K	1152-4
5125 On investment goods			
5126 On specific services	D2122-7.94c; D214-7.96c	D21225; D214E, F, G, H; D29F	1144; 1156
5127 Other taxes on international trade and transactions	D2122-7.94d; D29-7.95b D29-7.97g; D59-8.64d	D21226; D29D; D59E	1153; 1155-6
5128 Other taxes on specific goods and services			1146
5130 Unallocable between 5110 and 5120			
5200 Taxes on use of goods and on permission to use goods or perform activities			
5210 Recurrent taxes on use of goods and on permission to use goods or perform activities			
5211 Motor vehicle taxes households	D59-8.64c	D59D	11451
5212 Motor vehicles taxes others	D29-7.97d	D214D; D29B	11451
5213 Other recurrent taxes on use of goods and on permission to use goods or perform activities	D29-7.97c, d, f D59-8.64c	D29B, E, F; D59D	11452
5220 Non-recurrent taxes on permission to use goods or perform activities			11452
5300 Unallocable as between 5100 and 5200			
6000 Other taxes			
6100 Payable solely by business			1161
6200 Payable by other than business, or unidentifiable	D59-8.64a, b	D59B, C	1162

A.12. Répartition des recettes fiscales par sous-secteurs d'administration publique

92. La classification de l'OCDE appelle une ventilation des recettes fiscales par sous-secteurs d'administration. On trouvera ci-après la définition de chaque sous-secteur et les critères à utiliser pour répartir entre eux les recettes fiscales. Ces définitions et critères suivent les orientations qui figurent dans le SCN 2008 et le MSFP 2014.

Sous-secteurs des administrations publiques à identifier

a) Administration centrale

93. Le sous-secteur des administrations centrales groupe tous les ministères, bureaux, établissements et autres organismes qui sont des services ou des moyens d'action du pouvoir central et dont la compétence s'étend à la totalité du territoire, à l'exception de l'administration des caisses de sécurité sociale. L'administration centrale a donc le pouvoir de prélever des impôts sur toutes les unités résidentes et non résidentes exerçant des activités économiques à l'intérieur du pays.

b) Administration d'un État fédéré, d'une province ou d'une région

94. Ce sous-secteur comprend les unités administratives intermédiaires et inclut toutes les unités administratives dont la compétence s'exerce indépendamment de l'Administration centrale sur une partie du territoire englobant un certain nombre de petites localités, à l'exception des caisses de sécurité sociale. Dans les pays unitaires, les administrations régionales peuvent être considérées comme dotées d'une existence distincte lorsqu'elles

disposent d'une autonomie substantielle pour percevoir une part importante de leurs recettes de sources placées sous leur contrôle et lorsque leurs agents ne sont pas soumis à un contrôle administratif externe dans l'exercice des activités de l'unité.

95. Actuellement, les pays à structure fédérale représentent la majorité des cas dans lesquels les recettes attribuées aux unités administratives intermédiaires sont identifiées séparément. L'Espagne est le seul pays à structure unitaire qui se trouve dans cette situation. Dans les autres pays unitaires, les recettes des administrations régionales sont incluses dans celles des administrations locales.

c) Collectivités locales

96. Ce sous-secteur comprend toutes les autres unités administratives exerçant une compétence indépendante sur une partie du territoire d'un pays, à l'exception des administrations des caisses de sécurité sociale. Il englobe les diverses circonscriptions urbaines et/ou rurales (par exemple les collectivités locales, les municipalités, les villes, les bourgs ou les districts).

d) Caisses de sécurité sociale

97. Les caisses de sécurité sociale constituent un sous-secteur distinct des administrations publiques. Le sous-secteur de la sécurité sociale est défini dans le SCN de 2008 par les extraits suivants des paragraphes 4.124 à 4.126 et 4.147 :

> « *Les systèmes de sécurité sociale sont des systèmes d'assurance sociale qui couvrent l'ensemble de la collectivité ou d'importants sous-ensembles de la collectivité : ces systèmes sont imposés et contrôlés par les administrations publiques. Ces systèmes couvrent une grande variété de programmes qui consistent à fournir des prestations, en espèces ou en nature, au titre des circonstances suivantes : vieillesse, invalidité ou décès, survie, maladie et maternité, accident du travail, chômage, allocations familiales, soins de santé etc. Il n'existe pas nécessairement de lien direct entre le montant de la cotisation versée par un particulier et les prestations qu'il est susceptible de recevoir* » (paragraphe 4.124).

> « *Lorsque les systèmes de sécurité sociale ont une organisation distincte des autres activités des administrations publiques et détiennent des actifs et des engagements indépendamment de ces dernières et effectuent des opérations financières pour leur propre compte, ils peuvent être considérés comme des unités institutionnelles désignées sous le nom de caisses de sécurité sociale* » (paragraphe 4.125).

> « *Il est possible de faire varier de façon discrétionnaire les montants prélevés et versés sous forme de cotisations de sécurité sociale et de prestations afin d'atteindre des objectifs de politique publique qui n'ont pas de lien direct avec la notion de sécurité sociale en tant que système visant à fournir des prestations à des membres de la collectivité. Ainsi, ces cotisations ou prestations peuvent être augmentées ou diminuées afin d'influer sur le niveau de la demande globale au sein de l'économie. Néanmoins, tant que ces caisses restent indépendantes, elles doivent être traitées comme des unités institutionnelles distinctes dans le SCN* ». (paragraphe 4.126).

> « *Le sous-secteur des administrations de sécurité sociale comprend les administrations de sécurité sociale opérant à tous les niveaux des administrations publiques. Les administrations de sécurité sociale sont des systèmes couvrant l'ensemble de la collectivité ou d'importants sous-ensembles de la collectivité qui sont rendus obligatoires et contrôlés par des administrations publiques* » (paragraphe 4.147).

98. Cette définition des administrations de sécurité sociale est suivie dans la classification de l'OCDE à l'exception des régimes suivants :

- Les régimes imposés par l'administration et exploités par des organismes extérieurs au secteur des administrations publiques, tel qu'il est défini au § 3 de ce manuel et
- Les régimes qui perçoivent des cotisations facultatives.

Autorités supranationales

99. Ce sous-secteur s'applique aux activités de collecte de recettes publiques des autorités supranationales sur le territoire d'un pays. En pratique, le seul cas d'autorité supranationale de la zone de l'OCDE est celui des institutions de l'Union européenne (UE). Depuis 1998, les autorités supranationales ne figurent plus dans les Statistiques des recettes publiques dans un souci de cohérence avec la définition du SCN des administrations publiques qui les exclut. Par exemple, les impôts sur le revenu et des contributions de sécurité sociale rassemblées par des Institutions européennes et payé par les fonctionnaires européens qui sont résidents de pays membres de l'Union européenne ne devraient pas être inclus. Toutefois, les prélèvements spécifiques versés par les États membres à l'Union européenne continuent à être inclus dans les recettes fiscales totales et ils sont indiqués sous cette rubrique.

Critères à utiliser pour l'attribution des recettes fiscales

100. Lorsqu'une administration collecte l'impôt et le reverse, en totalité ou en partie, à d'autres administrations, il est nécessaire de déterminer si ces recettes doivent être considérées comme étant celles de l'administration qui les perçoit et les répartit entre d'autres administrations ou celles des administrations bénéficiaires auxquelles l'administration qui les a perçues les a transférées en simple qualité d'agent. Les critères à utiliser dans l'attribution des recettes sont indiqués aux § 101 à 104, qui reprennent les paragraphes 3.70 à 3.73 du SCN 2008.

101. En général, un impôt est attribué à l'Unité administrative qui :

a. exerce le pouvoir de percevoir l'impôt (soit en tant que détenteur de ce pouvoir soit par délégation de l'autorité qui le détient),

b. dispose du pouvoir discrétionnaire final de fixer et de faire varier le taux de l'impôt.

102. Lorsqu'une somme est collectée par une administration au profit d'une autre administration et en son nom, et que cette dernière a le pouvoir de percevoir l'impôt et de fixer et de faire varier son taux, la première intervient comme agent pour le compte de la dernière et l'impôt est réaffecté. Toute somme retenue par l'administration collectrice au titre des frais de recouvrement doit être considérée comme la rémunération d'un service rendu. Toute autre somme conservée par l'administration collectrice, notamment dans le cadre d'un accord de partage d'impôt, doit être considérée comme une subvention courante. Si l'administration collectrice s'est vu déléguer le pouvoir de fixer et de faire varier le taux, le montant recouvré doit être considéré comme une recette fiscale de cette administration.

103. Lorsque des administrations différentes fixent conjointement et sur un pied d'égalité la répartition du produit de cet impôt, aucune administration ne disposant d'un pouvoir prépondérant en dernier ressort, les recettes fiscales sont attribuées à chaque administration en fonction de sa part respective du produit de l'impôt. Si un accord permet à une unité administrative d'exercer un pouvoir prépondérant en dernier ressort, la totalité des recettes fiscales est attribuée à cette unité.

104. Dans certains cas aussi, un impôt est perçu dans le cadre des compétences d'une administration qui résulte de la constitution ou d'autres dispositions mais d'autres administrations fixent individuellement le taux d'imposition sur leurs territoires. Le produit de l'impôt généré sur les territoires respectifs de chaque administration est attribué à l'administration en question comme constituant ses recettes fiscales.

Versements effectués par les États membres de l'Union européenne

105. Les versements effectués par les États membres de l'Union européenne prennent la forme de prélèvements spécifiques qui comprennent :

a. les droits de douane et les prélèvements agricoles (5123),

b. les montants compensatoires monétaires bruts (5123 si relatifs aux importations et 5124 si relatifs aux exportations), et

c. les prélèvements de la CECA, les cotisations sucre et les taxes de coresponsabilité sur le lait (5128).

106. Les droits de douane collectés par les États membres pour le compte de l'Union européenne sont comptabilisés :

- sur une base qui ne tient pas compte des droits d'encaissement,
- en utilisant des chiffres corrigés de manière à exprimer les droits sur la base de la « destination finale » et non du « pays de première entrée » lorsque de telles corrections sont possibles. Ces corrections concernent en particulier les droits prélevés dans des ports (maritimes) importants. Bien que les droits de l'UE soient prélevés par les autorités du pays de première entrée, ces droits doivent être dans la mesure du possible déduits des recettes du pays qui les recouvre et inclus dans les recettes du pays de destination finale.

107. Ces droits de l'UE sont le plus clairement conformes au critère d'attribution décrit au § 99 ci-dessus. En conséquence, à partir de 1998, ces montants sont mentionnés dans une note de bas de page à titre de rubrique « Pour mémoire » dans les tableaux des États membres de l'UE (chapitre 4 du Rapport) et ne figurent plus sous la rubrique 5123. Toutefois, ces montants sont inclus dans les grands totaux des recettes fiscales à la ligne supérieure pour toutes les années indiquées dans les tableaux.

A.13. Classification provisoire des recettes provenant des prélèvements sur les banques et des contributions aux mécanismes de garantie des dépôts et de stabilité financière

108. L'OCDE a provisoirement adopté, depuis l'édition 2012 de ses *Statistiques des recettes publiques*, le principe suivant concernant l'enregistrement comptable des recettes issues des prélèvements sur les banques ainsi que des redevances acquittées au titre de la garantie des dépôts et de la stabilité financière. Il est recommandé que les montants concernés soient comptabilisés à la rubrique 5126.

- Les redevances de stabilité, les prélèvements sur les banques et les contributions à la garantie des dépôts, qu'il est obligatoire d'acquitter, doivent généralement être traitées comme des recettes fiscales lorsque les versements sont effectués au profit de l'administration publique et affectés au budget consolidé ou général des administrations de sorte que les pouvoirs publics soient libres d'utiliser les fonds sans délai aux fins qu'ils jugent opportunes. Ce principe s'appliquerait indépendamment du fait que l'administration promette ou non d'effectuer des versements pour garantir les dépôts des clients des établissements bancaires si la situation l'exigeait à l'avenir.

- Si les paiements obligatoires sont effectués au profit de l'administration publique et imputés à des budgets dont les ressources doivent être entièrement réaffectées au secteur de l'économie qui englobe les entreprises assujetties à ces paiements, ceux-ci seront toujours traités, en règle générale, comme des recettes fiscales étant donné que les fonds seraient disponibles pour l'administration et réduiraient son déficit budgétaire, que la redevance est sans contrepartie pour les entités individuelles et que les montants collectés pourraient être dissociés de tout versement en faveur des déposants ou de toute dépense visant à soutenir plus largement le secteur financier.
- Les contributions aux mécanismes traditionnels de moindre envergure destinés à garantir les dépôts de détail, contributions dont le montant est aligné sur le coût de la garantie, doivent être classées en tant que redevances pour services rendus.
- Tout versement au titre de la réalisation par une administration des actifs d'un établissement en faillite ou du recouvrement par cette administration d'une créance prioritaire sur les actifs de l'établissement en cours de liquidation, effectué en vue de financer l'indemnisation des clients ayant perdu leurs dépôts, serait traité comme une redevance par opposition aux recettes fiscales.

Les contributions obligatoires aux fonds administrés en-dehors du secteur public et aux organismes non étatiques bénéficiant du soutien des institutions collectrices de dépôts ainsi que toutes les contributions aux mécanismes facultatifs ne doivent pas être traitées comme des recettes fiscales.

Notes

1. « Les références dans cette annexe aux chapitres ou aux sections de « ce rapport » sont issues de OCDE (2020), Statistiques des recettes publiques 2020, Éditions OCDE, Paris. »
2. Toutes les références au SCN concernent l'édition de 2008.
3. Se reporter à la section A.12 de ce manuel pour l'examen de cette notion.
4. Il est en général possible d'identifier les montants des cotisations de sécurité sociale et les impôts sur les salaires, mais pas les autres impôts payés par les administrations.
5. En revanche, si un ou plusieurs pays considèrent comme un impôt un droit que la plupart des pays font entrer dans les recettes non fiscales ou qui procure des recettes substantielles, les montants ainsi perçus figureront dans une note de renvoi à la fin des tableaux par pays correspondants, même s'ils ne sont pas inclus dans le total des recettes fiscales.
6. Les appellations peuvent cependant être souvent trompeuses. Ainsi, une redevance de passeport sera normalement considérée comme une recette non fiscale, alors qu'un prélèvement additionnel sur les passeports (comme c'est le cas au Portugal), qui a pour but de procurer un montant substantiel de recettes eu égard au coût de délivrance du passeport, sera considéré comme un impôt du sous-groupe 5200.
7. On trouvera des précisions sur cette distinction dans l'étude spéciale intitulée « L'information sur les recettes fiscales : problèmes actuels », de l'édition de 2001 des *Statistiques des recettes publiques*.
8. On utilise parfois les expressions « non remboursable » et « remboursable » mais il peut paraître illogique de parler de « remboursement » lorsque rien n'a été versé.
9. Toutefois, dans les systèmes d'imputation de l'impôt sur les sociétés, les crédits d'impôts récupérables sont traités différemment (§ 36 à 38).
10. Il ne s'agit pas d'une véritable dépense fiscale au sens strict. De telles dépenses fiscales supposent que l'on identifie un système fiscal de référence pour chaque pays ou, de préférence, une norme internationale commune. En pratique, il n'a pas été possible de parvenir à un accord sur une norme internationale commune.
11. Sauf s'ils sont calculés sur le bénéfice résultant de la vente, auquel cas ils seraient classés parmi les impôts sur les gains en capital dans le sous-groupe 1120 ou 1220.

12. Dans certains pays, la même législation est applicable aux personnes physiques et aux entreprises dans le cas d'impôts sur le revenu particulier. Cependant, les recettes procurées par ces impôts peuvent, en général, être ventilées et figurent donc dans les deux sous-groupes appropriés.

13. Ainsi, « celles qui sont suffisamment autonomes et indépendantes pour que leur fonctionnement soit comparable à celui d'une société… (y compris) la tenue de comptes complets » (2008 SCN section 4.44).

14. Il peut en être ainsi lorsqu'un régime en faveur des administrations existait avant l'instauration d'un régime général de sécurité sociale.

15. Système selon lequel l'Union Européenne ajuste les effets des différences entre les taux de change utilisés pour fixer les prix des produits agricoles dans le cadre de la politique agricole commune, et le taux de change réel. Les paiements effectués selon ce système portent sur les importations ou les exportations; lorsqu'ils sont identifiables, ces montants figurent dans la rubrique appropriée (5123 ou 5124). Dans ce guide, sont inclus les montants bruts, c'est-à-dire sans déduction d'aucune prime payée dans le cadre du système des montants compensatoires.

16. Les transferts de bénéfices de loteries d'État sont considérés comme des recettes non fiscales (voir aussi § 67).

Revenue Statistics in Africa 1990-2019/Statistiques des recettes
publiques en Afrique 1990-2019

Annex B

Interpretative guide to non-tax revenue in Revenue Statistics in Africa

Table of contents

B.1. Coverage

The definition of non-tax revenues and the main subcategories identified in this publication generally correspond to the concepts laid out in the 2014 IMF Government Finance Statistics Manual (GFSM). Non-tax revenues refer to increases in government net worth resulting from transactions other than tax revenues. They exclude funds arising from the repayment of previous lending by governments or from borrowing, or proceeds derived from sales of fixed capital assets, stocks, land and intangible assets or private gifts.

Non-tax revenues are made up of the following elements.

B.2. Grants

The GFSM 2014 states "Grants are transfers receivable by government units from non-resident government units or international organisations without the receipt of any goods, services, or assets in return. Grants are normally receivable in cash, but may also take the form of the receipt of goods or services (in kind)". These transfers are un-refundable and unrequited. Grants encompass reparations and gifts given for particular projects or programmes. The term "grants" is not used to refer to transfers to or from non-governmental units and excludes inter-governmental transfers. The remission of funds collected by one government for another in an agency capacity should not be shown as receipt of a grant by the beneficiary government but as its direct receipt of revenue.

B.3. Property income

This category includes income to government arising from their ownership of property, enterprises, financial assets, or intangible assets when government units place them at the disposal of other units. Sales of non-financial assets such as the sales of lands are not recorded as revenue because disposal of such an asset does not increase the net worth. Similarly, repayments on loans and loan disbursements are not revenue. Property income may take the form of dividends, interest, land rents, royalties, or withdrawals from entrepreneurial income. The main components are:

- Interest and dividends: Interest is the revenue earned by the government unit from a financial asset by putting it at the disposal of another institutional unit. Dividends are the revenue earned by placing equity funds at the disposal of a corporation (resident or non-resident corporation). This category also consists of profits of state-owned enterprises except those classified as fiscal monopolies (see §62-§64 of the OECD Interpretative Guide to tax revenue in Annex A), export and import monopoly profits (see §70-§71 of the same document) or those providing public utilities such as rail transport, electricity, post offices and other communications. In this category are included revenue from public financial institutions such as the central banks' profits, profits transferred or distributed from the operation of monetary authority functions outside the central bank and the profits of state lotteries transferred to the government. Transfers from public utilities enterprises are recorded as non-tax revenue under "sales of goods and services" whereas profits for fiscal, export or import monopolies are classified as tax revenue.
- Rents or royalties: Rent is the revenue generated from natural resources, such as land, mining, or oil resources, when a government unit places these at the disposal of private or foreign entities. The rents received relate to a resource lease-giving agreement for the exploitation and extraction of a natural resource by the lessee in return for a payment.

Payments for exploration rights are also treated as rent. Rents should not be confused with other payments a government may receive related to the exploitation of subsoil and similar assets, such as severance taxes, business licenses, or other taxes (e.g. value added taxes, excises, taxes on exports, etc.). They should also not be taken to mean incomes from the rental of buildings and equipment, which are treated as sales of goods and services. Revenues from rents and royalties are in some cases difficult to establish and depend on the agreement between the government unit and the lessee. For example rents, royalties and taxes such as corporate income taxes and VAT are sometimes encompassed in a single payment to the general government. In such cases the revenue should be classified under the category to which the majority of revenue belongs (see §71 of Annex A for further explanation.)

- Other property income: This includes revenue earned by a government unit placing funds at a disposal of quasi-corporations.[1] Conceptually this source of revenue is equivalent to that of dividends from a corporation but by definition, quasi-corporations cannot distribute income in the form of dividends. This category of "other property income" also includes retained or reinvested earnings, i.e. the percentage of distributable revenue not paid out as dividends, but retained by the corporation or quasi-corporation on foreign investment; property income from investment income disbursements and unidentified property income.

B.4. Sales of goods and services

Revenue under the category "sales of goods and services" is generally reported on a gross basis, without deduction of costs. Since these costs can represent a significant proportion of revenues, they cannot be regarded in total as funds available for governments to finance their general activities. This contrasts with tax revenues, where the collection costs are usually a small proportion of revenue. This difference implies that it may not be meaningful to sum tax and non-tax revenues as part of a calculation of generally available funds.

The proceeds of sales of nonfinancial assets such as the sale of buildings or lands are not classified as revenues since their disposal does not increase the net worth.

Sales of goods and services consist of:

- Sales by market establishments.[2]
- Administrative fees for services (i.e. fees for drivers' licences, passports, visas, court fees, harbour fees, fees for birth, marriage or death certificates, patent registrations, radio and television licenses when public authorities provide general broadcasting services).
- Administrative fees that are sales of services associated with a regulatory function of government (such as fees for the inspection of premises before delivering a business licence) and considered to be proportional to the cost of producing the service are included in this category. If the fee in return for the service provided by the government unit is disproportionate, then the fee will be classified as a tax. Specific examples of fees that are considered taxes include fees for permission to perform activities such as hunting, fishing and shooting; and fees for business registration where this is a legal requirement for the business to operate.
- Sales by nonmarket establishments such as fees at government hospitals, tuition fees at government schools and admission fees to museums and parks.
- Leasing of buildings and equipment.

B.5. Fines, penalties and forfeits

The GFSM 2014 states "Fines and penalties are compulsory transfers imposed by courts of law or bodies for violations of laws or administrative rules. Out-of-court agreements are also included (...). Forfeits are amounts deposited with a general government unit pending a legal or administrative proceeding, and that will be transferred to the unit upon resolution". For example traffic fines are included here. Fines and penalties charged on overdue taxes or penalties imposed for the evasion of taxes should be recorded in this category and not as taxes. However if it is not possible to separate the amounts paid in taxes and fines, the whole amount should be classified under the tax to which the fine relates (see §14 of Annex A for further explanation).

B.6. Other social contributions

This category includes the actual and imputed contributions to social insurance schemes operated by governments as employers on behalf of their employees that do not create a future defined liability. This category also includes the sum of the total voluntary contributions.[3] Excluded from this category are any contributions to funds in which the contributions of each participant and of his employer on his behalf are kept in a separate account earning interest and withdrawable under specified circumstances or any contributions to a pension fund autonomous to the general government. This category is not included in this publication.

B.7. Miscellaneous and unidentified revenue

This category consists of unidentified non-tax revenues or those that do not fit into any of the other categories listed above. It includes revenue such as gifts and transfers from individuals, private non-profit institutions, nongovernmental foundations, corporations, or sources other than governments and international organisations. Major non-recurrent payments receivable in compensation for extensive damages or serious injuries not covered by insurance policies are also included, such as payments of compensation for damages caused by major explosions; oil spillages; or payments receivable for damage to property other than payments from an insurance settlement.

Notes

1. Quasi-corporations are unincorporated enterprises that exercise some functions of corporations, but have not been granted separate legal personality by statute.
2. A market establishment is an establishment that charges economically significant prices.
3. The IMF includes these contributions as part of their total of social security contributions.

Revenue Statistics in Africa 1990-2019/Statistiques des recettes publiques en Afrique 1990-2019

ANNEXE B

Guide d'interprétation des recettes non fiscales dans les Statistiques des recettes publiques en Afrique

Table des matières

B.1. Champ couvert

La définition des recettes non fiscales et des principales sous-catégories décrites dans la présente publication coïncident en grande partie avec les notions retenues dans le manuel des statistiques de finances publiques du FMI de 2014 (manuel SFP 2014). Les recettes non fiscales désignent des augmentations de la valeur nette résultant d'une transaction et qui ne sont pas des recettes fiscales. Elles excluent les fonds relatifs au remboursement de prêts consentis antérieurement par les administrations ou liés à des emprunts, ainsi que le produit de la cession d'actifs immobilisés, d'éléments de stocks, de terrains, d'actifs immatériels et les dons à titre privé.

Les recettes non fiscales se composent des éléments suivants.

B.2. Dons

Selon le manuel SFP 2014, les dons sont des transferts qu'une administration publique reçoit d'une autre administration publique étrangère ou d'une organisation internationale, sans recevoir de cette dernière un bien, un service ou un actif en contrepartie directe. Les dons sont habituellement reçus en espèces, mais peuvent aussi prendre la forme de biens ou de services (en nature). Ces transferts sont non remboursables et sans contrepartie. Les dons recouvrent les réparations et dons assignés à des projets ou programmes particuliers. Le terme de « dons » n'est pas employé pour désigner les transferts réalisés par des entités autres que des administrations publiques ou effectués en leur faveur et exclut les transferts entre administrations. Le versement de fonds collectés par une administration qui agit en qualité de mandataire ne devrait pas entrer dans la catégorie des dons perçus par l'administration bénéficiaire, mais bien s'ajouter aux recettes directement perçues par cette dernière.

B.3. Revenus de la propriété

Cette catégorie regroupe les recettes publiques découlant de la détention de biens fonciers, de parts de sociétés, d'actifs financiers ou d'actifs immatériels que certaines unités administratives ont mis à la disposition d'autres unités administratives. Les cessions d'actifs non financiers comme la vente de terrains ne sont pas enregistrées en tant que recettes parce que la cession de tels actifs n'a pas d'effet sur la valeur nette. De même, les remboursements de prêts et les prêts octroyés ne sont pas des recettes. Les revenus de la propriété peuvent prendre la forme de dividendes, d'intérêts, de revenus fonciers, de redevances, ou de prélèvements sur des revenus d'entreprises. Les principales composantes en sont les suivantes :

- Intérêts et dividendes : Les intérêts sont les revenus perçus par une unité administrative au titre d'un actif financier qu'elle met à la disposition d'une autre unité institutionnelle. Les dividendes sont les recettes perçues par une unité qui met des capitaux à la disposition d'une société (qu'elle soit ou non un résident du pays concerné). Cette catégorie recouvre également les bénéfices d'entreprises détenues par une administration, en excluant les monopoles fiscaux (voir paragraphes 62 à 64 du Guide d'interprétation de l'OCDE en Annexe A), les monopoles d'exportation et d'importation (voir paragraphes 70 et 71 du même document) ainsi que les entreprises qui fournissent des services publics comme les chemins de fer, l'électricité, les postes et autres moyens de communication. Sont regroupés dans cette catégorie les revenus provenant d'institutions financières publiques comme les bénéfices de la banque centrale, les bénéfices transférés ou distribués au titre de fonctions de l'autorité monétaire exercées en dehors de la banque centrale et les bénéfices liés aux loteries nationales qui sont transférés à l'administration. Les transferts émanant d'entreprises qui assurent des services publics sont comptabilisés dans la rubrique « ventes de biens et de services » alors que les bénéfices des monopoles fiscaux, d'exportation ou d'importation constituent des recettes fiscales.

- Loyers et redevances : Les loyers sont des revenus générés lorsqu'une unité administrative met à la disposition d'autres entités privées ou étrangères des ressources naturelles, comme des terrains ou des gisements de minéraux ou de pétrole. Les loyers perçus sont liés à des accords de concession relatifs à l'exploitation et à l'extraction d'une ressource naturelle par un concessionnaire en contrepartie d'un paiement. Les paiements en échange de droits de prospection doivent également être traités comme des loyers. Les loyers sont à distinguer des autres paiements qu'une administration publique peut recevoir pour l'exploitation d'actifs du sous-sol et d'autres actifs du même type, par exemple les paiements de taxes d'extraction, patentes ou autres impôts (taxes sur la valeur ajoutée, accises, taxes à l'exportation, etc.). Il ne faut pas non plus confondre loyers et revenus de la location de bâtiments et d'équipements, par exemple, qui sont classés dans les ventes de biens et de services. Les revenus liés aux loyers et redevances sont parfois difficiles à déterminer car ils dépendent de la nature de l'accord conclu entre l'unité administration et le concessionnaire. À titre d'exemple, un versement unique effectué en faveur des administrations publiques peut regrouper le paiement de loyers, de redevances et d'autres obligations fiscales comme l'impôt sur les bénéfices des sociétés ou la TVA. Dans un tel cas, le paiement est classé dans la catégorie qui correspond à la majeure partie du versement considéré (voir paragraphe 71 en Annexe A pour plus de précisions).
- Autres revenus de la propriété : Cette catégorie inclut les recettes perçues par une unité administrative qui met des capitaux à la disposition de quasi-sociétés[1]. Cette source de recettes est en substance équivalente à des dividendes versés par une société mais, par définition, les quasi-sociétés ne distribuent pas de bénéfices sous forme de dividendes. Cette catégorie englobe de plus les bénéfices non distribués ou réinvestis, à savoir la fraction du bénéfice distribuable qui n'a pas été versée sous forme de dividendes, mais conservée par la société ou quasi-société sur des investissements étrangers ; les revenus de la propriété provenant de versements de revenus d'investissements et revenus de la propriété non identifiés.

B.4. Ventes de biens et de services

Les recettes qui entrent dans cette catégorie sont enregistrées en valeur brute, sans déduction de coûts. Dans la mesure où les coûts peuvent représenter une part importante des recettes, le montant total des ventes biens et de services ne peut pas être considéré comme un montant dont l'administration dispose dans son intégralité pour financer ses activités générales. C'est une différence notable avec les recettes fiscales, auxquelles sont associés des coûts de recouvrement qui ne représentent le plus souvent qu'une faible part des recettes. De ce fait, le montant obtenu par addition des recettes fiscales et non fiscales ne fournit pas forcément une bonne évaluation des fonds généralement disponibles.

Le produit généré par la cession d'actifs non financiers tels que des bâtiments ou des terrains n'est pas enregistré en tant que recettes étant donné que la cession de tels actifs n'a pas d'effet sur la valeur nette.

Les ventes de biens et de services se composent des éléments suivants :

- les ventes des établissements marchands[2].

- les droits administratifs pour services fournis (droits sur les permis de conduire, sur les passeports, sur les visas ; droits de procédure ; droits portuaires ; droits pour l'établissement d'actes de naissance, de mariage, de décès ; frais de dépôt de brevet ; licences de radio et télévision lorsque les autorités publiques fournissent des services généraux de radiodiffusion).
- Les droits administratifs qui sont des ventes de biens et de services associés à une fonction régulatrice des administrations publiques (comme les droits perçus au titre d'une inspection d'installations menée en vue de la délivrance d'un permis d'exploitation) sont inclus lorsqu'ils sont considérés comme étant proportionnels au coût de production du service en question. Lorsque les droits perçus en contrepartie d'un service fourni par l'administration sont disproportionnés par rapport aux coûts, ils sont considérés comme des impôts. Parmi les droits ainsi classés dans la catégorie des recettes fiscales figurent notamment les droits perçus pour l'octroi de permis d'exercer des activités telles que la chasse, la pêche et l'utilisation d'armes à feu ; et les droits d'enregistrement d'une société dès lors que les entreprises sont tenues par la loi de procéder à un tel enregistrement pour pouvoir exercer leur activité.
- les ventes par les établissements non marchands, comme les droits prélevés par les hôpitaux publics, les droits de scolarité des écoles publiques et les droits d'entrée aux musées et parcs.
- la location de bâtiments et d'équipements.

B.5. Amendes, pénalités et confiscations

Le manuel des statistiques de finances publiques du FMI de 2014 définit les amendes et pénalités comme des transferts obligatoires imposés aux unités par des tribunaux ou des organismes pour infraction à la loi ou aux règlements administratifs. Les accords extra-judiciaires sont également inclus. Les confiscations sont les montants déposés auprès d'une unité d'administration publique pendant le déroulement d'une procédure judiciaire ou administrative puis transférés à cette unité au moment du règlement de celle-ci. À titre d'exemple, les amendes sanctionnant les contraventions au code de la route entrent dans cette catégorie. Les amendes et pénalités appliquées au titre d'arriérés d'impôts ou les pénalités pour fraude fiscale devraient également être comptabilisées ici et non comme des recettes fiscales. Toutefois, s'il est impossible de distinguer les montants qui correspondent respectivement à l'impôt et aux pénalités, la somme totale est rattachée aux recettes générées par l'impôt qui a motivé l'application des pénalités (voir paragraphe 14 en Annexe A pour plus de précisions).

B.6. Autres cotisations sociales

Cette catégorie englobe les cotisations sociales effectives et imputées aux régimes d'assurance sociale gérés par des administrations publiques en qualité d'employeurs pour le compte de leurs employés qui ne génèrent pas de passif défini dans des périodes futures. Cette catégorie inclut également la somme des contributions volontaires totales[3]. Toutefois, sont exclues les cotisations à des fonds dans lesquels les cotisations de chaque salarié et celles que l'employeur verse en son nom sont comptabilisées séparément dans un compte productif d'intérêts d'où elles peuvent être retirées dans des conditions biens déterminées, ainsi que les cotisations à des fonds de pension autonomes vis-à-vis des administrations publiques. Cette catégorie n'est pas incluse aux fins de la présente publication.

B.7. Recettes diverses et non identifiées

Cette catégorie regroupe toutes les recettes non fiscales qui ne peuvent être identifiées ou qui n'entrent dans aucune des catégories décrites précédemment. Elle englobe des dons et transferts provenant de personnes physiques, d'institutions privées sans but lucratif, de fondations non gouvernementales, de sociétés ou de sources autres que les administrations publiques et les organisations internationales. Les paiements non récurrents d'un montant élevé reçus par les administrations publiques en compensation de dommages importants non couverts par des polices d'assurance sont également inclus, ainsi que des paiements d'indemnités en compensation de dommages causés par des explosions de grande ampleur, le déversement d'hydrocarbures, ou des paiements exigibles en cas de dommages matériels autres que les paiements au titre d'une indemnisation par une assurance.

Notes

1. Les quasi-sociétés sont des entreprises non constituées en sociétés qui exercent certaines de leurs activités comme des sociétés, mais n'ont pas reçu de personnalité juridique distincte en vertu de la loi.
2. Un établissement marchand est une entité qui pratique des prix économiquement significatifs.
3. Le FMI comptabilise ces cotisations dans le total des cotisations de sécurité sociale.

www.ingramcontent.com/pod-product-compliance
Ingram Content Group UK Ltd.
Pitfield, Milton Keynes, MK11 3LW, UK
UKHW051456290926
15471UKWH00008B/1243

9 789264 964792